Pro Oracle Database 11g Administration

Darl Kuhn

Apress®

Pro Oracle Database 11g Administration

ISBN-13 (pbk): 978-1-4302-2970-4

ISBN-13 (electronic): 978-1-4302-2971-1

President and Publisher: Paul Manning
Lead Editor: Jonathan Gennick
Technical Reviewer: Bernard Lopuz
Editorial Board: Steve Anglin, Mark Beckner, Ewan Buckingham, Gary Cornell, Jonathan Gennick, Jonathan Hassell, Michelle Lowman, Matthew Moodie, Duncan Parkes, Jeffrey Pepper, Frank Pohlmann, Douglas Pundick, Ben Renow-Clarke, Dominic Shakeshaft, Matt Wade, Tom Welsh
Coordinating Editor: Anita Castro
Copy Editors: Mary Behr and Tiffany Taylor
Compositor: MacPS, LLC
Indexer: BIM Indexing & Proofreading Services
Artist: April Milne
Cover Designer: Anna Ishchenko

Distributed to the book trade worldwide by Springer Science+Business Media, LLC., 233 Spring Street, 6th Floor, New York, NY 10013. Phone 1-800-SPRINGER, fax (201) 348-4505, e-mail orders-ny@springer-sbm.com, or visit www.springeronline.com.

For information on translations, please e-mail rights@apress.com or visit www.apress.com.

Apress and friends of ED books may be purchased in bulk for academic, corporate, or promotional use. eBook versions and licenses are also available for most titles. For more information, reference our Special Bulk Sales–eBook Licensing web page at www.apress.com/info/bulksales.

To Heidi, Brandi, and Lisa.

Contents at a Glance

iv

Contents

About the Author

 **Darl Kuhn** is currently a senior DBA working for Oracle Corporation. He has coauthored four other books: *Oracle SQL Recipes* (Apress, 2009), *Linux Recipes for Oracle DBAs* (Apress, 2009), *RMAN Recipes for Oracle Database 11g* (Apress, 2008), and *Oracle RMAN Pocket Reference* (O'Reilly Media, 2001). He also teaches advanced database courses at Regis University. Darl does volunteer DBA and developer work for the Rocky Mountain Oracle Users Group. He has a graduate degree from Colorado State University and currently lives near Frog Rock, Colorado, with his wife, Heidi, and daughters, Brandi, and Lisa.

About the Technical Reviewer

 **Bernard Lopuz** is a senior technical support analyst at Oracle Corporation since 2001, and he is an Oracle Certified Professional (OCP). Before he became an Oracle DBA, he was a programmer developing Unisys Linc and Oracle applications as well as interactive voice response (IVR) applications such as telephone banking voice-processing applications. Bernard was coauthor of the *Linux Recipes for Oracle DBAs* (Apress, 2008) and technical reviewer of two other books, namely, *Oracle RMAN Recipes* (Apress, 2007) and *Pro Oracle SQL* (Apress, 2010). He has a bachelor's degree in computer engineering from the Mapúa Institute of Technology in Manila, Philippines. Bernard was born in Iligan, Philippines, and now resides in Ottawa, Canada, with his wife, Leizle, and daughters, Juliet and Carol. Aside from tinkering with computers, Bernard is a soccer and basketball fanatic.

Acknowledgments

Special thanks go to Jonathan Gennick for providing invaluable input on the content, style, tone, and organization of this book. A huge thanks goes to Bernard Lopuz for his numerous suggestions and additions. Bernard also authored Chapter 20 on Oracle Secure Backup. Thanks also to the project manager Anita Castro and the copy editor Mary Behr and Tiffany Taylor. It takes a team to create a book like this.

Thanks to the numerous DBAs and developers who I've learned database administration techniques from over the years: Heidi Kuhn, Scott Schulze, Bob Suehrstedt, Dave Jennings, Pete Mullineaux, Ken Toney, Jay Nielsen, Tim Gorman, Shawn Heisdorffer, Doug Davis, Abid Malik, Sujit Pattanaik, Janet Bacon, Sue Wagner, Barb Sannwald, Ulises Llull, Ken Roberts, Roger Murphy, Mehran Sowdaey, Dan Fink, Guido Handley, Margaret Carson, Nehru Kaja, Tim Colbert, Robin Askham, Jon Nordby, Lou Ferrante, John Liu, Glenn Balanoff, Sam Conn, Bill Padfield, Inder Ganesan, Shari Plantz-Masters, Denise Duncan, Brad Blake, Mike Nims, Mark James, Arup Nanda, Charles Kim, Sam Alapati, Ravi Narayanaswamy, Kevin Bayer, Abdul Ebadi, Kevin Hoyt, Trent Sherman, Sandra Montijo, Jim Secor, Maureen Frazzini, Sean Best, Stephan Haisley, Geoff Strebel, Frank Bommarito, Patrick Gates, Krish Hariharan, Buzzy Cheadle, Mark Blair, Mike Hutchinson, Karen Kappler, Ennio Murroni, Beth Loker, Mike Eason, Tom Wheltle, Debbie Earman, Greg Roberts, Gabor Gyurovszky, Chad Heckman, Scott Norris, Mihir Shah, Joey Canlas, Gary Smith, Michael Del Toro, Mark Lutze, Kevin Quinlivan, Dave Bourque, Kevin Powers, Roy Backstrom, David Carpenter, Terri Durbin, Dean Price, Kathy Albrecht, Marina Richards, Andy Brown, Greg Oehmen, Erin Fox, Larry Carpenter, Joe Meeks, Ashish Ray, Amit Khatri, and Gaurav Mehta.

Thanks also to supportive colleagues: Mike Tanaka, John Lilly, Dave Wood, Laurie Bourgeois, Steve Buckmelter, Casey Costley, John DiVirgilio, John Goggin, Brett Guy, Simon Ip, Pascal Ledru, Kevin O'Grady, Peter Schow, Jeff Shoup, Todd Wichers, Doug Cushing, Will Thornburg, Steve Roughton, Ambereen Pasha, Dinesh Neelay, Thom Chumley, Jim LoPresti, Jeff Sherard, Dona Smith, Tae Kim, Gary Schut, Erik Jasiak, Don Gritzmacher, Carson Vowles, Aaron Isom, Deni Staheli, Mohan Koneru, Kristi Jackson, Karolyn Vowles, Ashley Jackson, Amin Jiwani, Mark Molnar, Khagendra Muthe, Kye Bae, Khanh Truong, Darcy O'Connor, Brad Vowles, Arvin Kuhn, Darin Christensen, Terry Roam, Odean Bowler, and Jim Stark.

Introduction

Many companies from large to small use Oracle technology. At the heart of this technology is an Oracle database. Businesses use this technology to store and manage mission critical data. This information is the basis for making intelligent business decisions. Companies that effectively transform data into intelligence quickly gain a competitive edge in the market place.

Oracle DBAs play a pivotal role with implementing and leveraging Oracle database technology. DBAs add value by ensuring that databases are created in an efficient manner and optimal maintained. DBAs are often queried for architectural advice on features, implementation, data migrations, SQL coding, tuning, and so forth. DBAs fill the role of the go to person for anything related to Oracle.

The job of an Oracle database administrator is often complex and challenging. This book focuses on practical examples and techniques for ensuring a smoothly operating database environment. The content within is drawn from years of experience of working with Oracle technology. This book shows you from the ground up how a senior DBA manages a multifaceted database environment. I try to focus on demonstrating how to correctly implement features with scalability and maintainability in mind.

I hope you find the material in this book useful. The goal is to elevate you to a professional level database administrator. Being a DBA doesn't have to constantly painful. The key is to correctly implement the technology the first time, don't paint yourself into a corner with a badly implemented feature, and proactively manage your surroundings.

This book doesn't show you the most complex and sophisticated techniques used in the database administration. I try to keep my techniques as simple as possible, yet robust enough to manage any level of chaos and complexity. You should be able to take the concepts demonstrated in this book and build on them to help you manage any type of database environment.

Audience

This book is for DBAs who want real-world guidance on how to efficiently configure and maintain complex database environments. Whether you are a novice or an expert, this book contains practical examples of how to implement Oracle database technology. This book is for those who want advice from a real-world DBA on how Oracle database technology is effectively implemented and maintained.

Book Structure

The book is divided into several sections, with each covering a logical group of database administration topics as follows:

Chapters 1, 2, and 3 concentrate on creating a working environment. This includes installing the Oracle software, creating databases.

Chapters 4 and 5 deal with managing critical database files. Topics covered are tablespaces, datafiles, control files, and online redo log files.

Chapters 6, 7, 8, 9, and 10 discuss configuring users and database objects such as tables, constraints, indexes, views, synonyms, sequences, and so forth.

Chapters 11 and 12 detail how to create and maintain large database objects and partitioned tables and indexes.

Chapters 13, 14, and 15 show how DBAs use tools such as Data Pump, external tables, and materialized views to mange and distribute large amounts of data.

Chapters 16, 17, 18, 19, and 20 take a deep dive into backup and recovery concepts. Both user managed backups and RMAN backup and recovery are discussed in detail.

Chapters 21 and 22 focus on techniques used to automate database jobs and how to troubleshoot typical problems that DBAs encounter.

Conventions Used in This Book

The following typographical conventions are used in this book:

- $ is used to denote Linux/Unix commands that can be run by the operating system owner of the Oracle binaries (usually named oracle).
- # is used to denote Linux/Unix commands that should be run as the root operating system user.
- SQL> is used to denote one line SQL*Plus statements.
- Monospaced font is used for code examples, utility names, file names, URLs, and directory paths.
- *Italic* is used to highlight a new concept or word.
- UPPERCASE indicates names of database objects like views, tables, and corresponding column names.
- < > is used where you need to provide input, such as a filename or password.

Comments

I've tried to keep this book as error free as possible. However, mistakes happen or inadvertently get overlooked. If you find any type of error in this book, whether it be a typo or an erroneous command, please let me now about it. You can submit any issues by going to the main Apress web page at: http://www.apress.com. Search for this book and then use the errata page to submit corrections.

Contacting the Author

If you have any questions regarding the book, feel free to contact me directly at the following email address: darl.kuhn@gmail.com.

■ ■ ■

## CHAPTER 1

Installing the Oracle Binaries

Oracle installations can be large, complex, and cumbersome. This is one reason you usually ask an Oracle DBA to install the software. You want somebody who has previously performed installations and knows how to troubleshoot when problems arise. For this reason, installing the Oracle software (binaries) is a task that every DBA must be proficient with.

For whatever reason, many DBAs don't use techniques for automating installations. Either they're unaware of these methods or they perceive the automated methods to be unreliable. Therefore, most DBAs typically use the graphical mode of the Oracle Universal Installer (OUI). Although the graphical installer is a good tool, it doesn't lend itself well to repeatability and automation. Running the graphical installer is a manual process during which you're presented with options to choose from on multiple screens. Even if you know which options to choose, you still may inadvertently click an undesired choice.

The graphical installer can also be problematic when you're performing remote installations and the network bandwidth is insufficient. In these situations, you can find yourself waiting for dozens of minutes for a screen to repaint itself on your local screen. You need a different technique for efficient installations on remote servers.

This chapter focuses on techniques for installing Oracle in an efficient and repeatable manner. This includes silent installations, which rely on a response file. A *response file* is a text file in which you assign values to variables that govern the installation. DBAs often don't realize the power of repeatability and efficiency that can be achieved through using response files.

■ **Note** This chapter only covers installing the Oracle software. The task of creating a database is covered in Chapter 2.

Understanding the Optimal Flexible Architecture

Before you install Oracle and start creating databases, you must understand Oracle's Optimal Flexible Architecture (OFA) standard. This standard is widely employed for specifying consistent directory structures and file-naming conventions used when installing and creating Oracle databases.

■ **Note** One irony of this ubiquitous OFA "standard" is that almost every DBA in some manner customizes it to fit the unique requirements of their environment.

Because most shops implement a form of the OFA standard, it's critical to understand this structure. Figure 1–1 shows the directory structure and file names used with the OFA standard. Not all of the directories and files used in an Oracle environment appear in this figure (there's not enough room for them to fit on a page). However, all of the critical and most frequently used directories and files are displayed.

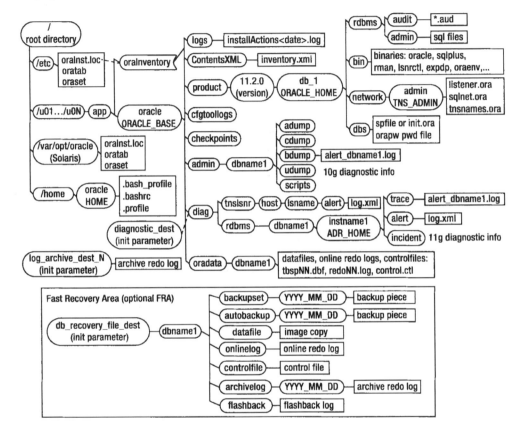

Figure 1–1. Oracle's Optimal Flexible Architecture standard

The OFA standard includes several directories that it's important for you to be familiar with:

Oracle inventory directory

Oracle base directory (ORACLE_BASE)

Oracle home directory (ORACLE_HOME)

Oracle network files directory (TNS_ADMIN)

Automatic Diagnostic Repository (ADR_HOME)

These directories are discussed in the following subsections.

Oracle Inventory Directory

The Oracle inventory directory stores the inventory of Oracle software installed on the server. This directory is required and is shared among all installations of Oracle software on a server. When you first install Oracle, the installer checks to see whether there is an existing OFA-compliant directory structure in the format of /u[01-09]/app. If such a directory exists, then the installer creates an Oracle inventory directory such as

/u01/app/oraInventory

If you have the ORACLE_BASE variable defined for the oracle operating system user, then the installer creates a directory as follows for the location of Oracle inventory:

ORACLE_BASE/../oraInventory

For example, if ORACLE_BASE is defined to be /ora01/app/oracle, then the installer defines the location of Oracle inventory to be

/ora01/app/oraInventory

If the installer doesn't find a recognizable OFA-compliant directory structure or an ORACLE_BASE variable, then the location of Oracle inventory is created under the HOME directory of the oracle user. For example, if the HOME directory is /home/oracle, then the location of Oracle inventory is

/home/oracle/oraInventory

Oracle Base Directory

The Oracle base directory is the topmost directory for Oracle software installations. You can install one or more versions of the Oracle software beneath this directory. The OFA standard for the Oracle base directory is as follows:

/<mount_point>/app/<software_owner>

The mount point used is typically named something like /u01, /ora01, /oracle, or /oracle01. You can name this mount point according to whatever your standard is for your environment. I prefer to use a mount point name like /ora01. It's short and, when I look at the mount points on a database server, I can immediately tell which mount points are used for the Oracle database. Also, a short mount-point name is easier to use when you're querying the data dictionary to report on the physical aspects of your database. Additionally, a shorter mount-point name makes for less typing when you're navigating through directories via operating system commands.

The software owner is typically named oracle. This is the operating system user that you use to install the Oracle software (binaries). A fully formed Oracle base directory path is something like

/ora01/app/oracle

Oracle Home Directory

The Oracle home directory defines the installation location of software for a particular product such as Oracle Database 11g, Oracle Database 10g, and so on. You must install different products or different releases of a product in separate Oracle homes. The recommended OFA-compliant Oracle home directory is as follows:

ORACLE_BASE/product/<version>/<install_name>

In the previous line of code, the version is something like 11.2.0.1 or 10.2.0.1. The install_name value is something like db_1, devdb1, test2, or prod1. Here is an example Oracle home name for an 11.2 database:

/ora01/app/oracle/product/11.2.0.1/db_1

■ Note Some DBAs dislike the db_1 string on the end of the ORACLE_HOME directory and see no need for it. The reason for the db_1 is that you may have two separate installations of binaries: a development installation and a test installation. If you don't require that configuration in your environment, feel free to drop the extra string on the end.

Oracle Network Files Directory

Some Oracle utilities use the value TNS_ADMIN to locate network configuration files. This directory is defined to be ORACLE_HOME/network/admin. This directory typically contains the tnsnames.ora and listener.ora Oracle Net files.

Automatic Diagnostic Repository

Starting with Oracle Database 11g, the ADR_HOME directory specifies the location of the diagnostic files related to Oracle. These files are crucial to troubleshooting problems with the Oracle database. This directory is defined to be ORACLE_BASE/diag/rdbms/dbname/instname, where dbname is your database name and instname is your instance name. In single-instance environments, the database name and instance name are the same, with the exception that the database name is in lowercase and the instance name is in uppercase. For example, in the next line, the database name is specified by o11r2, whereas the instance name is specified as O11R2:

/ora01/app/oracle/diag/rdbms/o11r2/O11R2

Now that you understand the OFA standard, you see how it's used when installing the Oracle binaries. For example, you need to specify directory values for the ORACLE_BASE and ORACLE_HOME directories when running the Oracle installer.

Installing Oracle

Suppose you're new on the job, and your manager asks you how long it will take to install a new set of Oracle Database 11g binaries on a server. You reply that it will take less than an hour. Your boss is incredulous and states that previous DBAs always estimated at least a day to install the Oracle binaries (software) on a new server. You reply, "Actually, it's not that complicated, but DBAs do tend to overestimate installations because it's hard to predict everything that might go wrong."

When you're handed a new server and are given the task of installing the Oracle binaries, this usually refers to the process of downloading and installing the software required before you can create an Oracle database. This process involves several steps:

Create the operating system dba group and the operating system oracle user.

Ensure that the operating system is configured adequately for an Oracle database.

Obtain the database installation software from Oracle.

Unzip the database installation software.

Configure the response file, and run the Oracle silent installer.

Troubleshoot any issues.

These steps are detailed in the following subsections.

■ Note Any version of the database that Oracle designates as a base release (10.1.0.2, 10.2.0.1, 11.1.0.6, and 11.2.0.1) can be freely downloaded from Oracle's technology network web site (http://otn.oracle.com). However, be aware that any subsequent patch downloads require a purchased license. In other words, downloading base software requires an Oracle Technology Network (OTN) logon (free), whereas downloading a patchset requires a My Oracle Support account (paid support account).

Step 1. Create the Operating System Group and User

If you work in a shop with a good system administrator (SA), then steps 1 and 2 usually are performed by the SA. If you don't have an SA, then you have to perform these steps yourself (this is often the case in small shops where you're required to perform many different job functions). You need root access to accomplish these steps.

As root, use the groupadd command to add operating system groups. In Linux/Unix environments, Oracle recommends that you create three operating system groups: oinstall, dba, and oper. The oinstall group has privileges to manipulate the installation files and perform installations and upgrades. Operating system users assigned to the dba group can connect to the database with sysdba database privileges. Operating system users assigned to the oper group can connect to the database with sysoper database privileges.

The idea behind the three separate groups is to be able to allow separate operating system users to perform various database tasks. For example, you may have one user who typically installs the Oracle software and is assigned the oinstall group, and other users who require sysdba or sysoper privileges who are assigned the dba and oper groups, respectively.

Having said that, many shops create just one operating system group, dba, and use that group to install software and perform all sysdba and sysoper functions. I typically only use one group (dba).

If you have root access, you can run the groupadd command as shown here:

```
# groupadd dba
```

If you don't have access to a root account, then you need to get your system administrator to run the previous commands. If you have a company requirement that a group be set up with the same group ID on different servers, then use the -g option. This example explicitly sets the group ID to 505:

```
# groupadd -g 505 dba
```

You can verify that the group was added successfully by inspecting the contents of the /etc/group file. Here is a typical entry created in the /etc/group file:

```
dba:x:501:
```

If for any reason you need to remove a group, use the groupdel command. If you need to modify a group, use the groupmod command.

Next, use the useradd command to add operating system users. This command requires root access. The following command creates an operating system account named oracle, with the primary group being dba and the oinstall group specified as a supplementary group:

```
# useradd -g dba -G oinstall oracle
```

If you don't have access to a root account, then you need your system administrator to run the useradd command. If you have a company requirement that a user be set up with the same user ID across multiple servers, then use the -u option. This example explicitly sets the user ID to 500:

```
# useradd -u 500 -g dba -G oinstall oracle
```

You can verify user account information by viewing the /etc/passwd file. Here is what you can expect to see after running the useradd command:

```
oracle:x:500:500::/home/oracle:/bin/bash
```

You can also use the id command to display the operating system user and group information:

```
$ id
uid=500(oracle) gid=500(dba) groups=500(dba)
```

On most Linux systems, the default value for the HOME variable is /home/oracle, and the default shell is the Bash shell. You can display the value of HOME and SHELL as follows:

```
$ echo $HOME
$ echo $SHELL
```

If you need to modify a user, use the usermod command. If you need to remove an operating system user, use the userdel command. You need root privileges to run the userdel command. This example removes the oracle user from the server:

```
# userdel oracle
```

Step 2. Ensure That the Operating System Is Adequately Configured

The tasks associated with this step vary somewhat for each database release and operating system. You must refer to the Oracle installation manual for the database release and operating system vendor to get the exact requirements. To perform this step, you're required to verify and configure operating system components such as the following:

Memory and swap space

System architecture (processor)

Free disk space (Oracle now takes almost 5GB of space to install)

Operating system version and kernel

Operating system software (required packages and patches)

Run the following command to confirm the size of memory on a Linux server:

```
$ grep MemTotal /proc/meminfo
```

To verify the amount of memory and swap space, run the following command:

```
$ free -t
```

To verify the amount of space in the /tmp directory, enter this command:

```
$ df -h /tmp
```

To display the amount of free disk space, execute this command:

```
$ df -h
```

To verify the operating system version, enter this command:

```
$ cat /proc/version
```

To verify kernel information, run the following command:

```
$ uname -r
```

To determine whether the required packages are installed, execute the following and provide the required package name:

```
$ rpm -q <package_name>
```

Again, database server requirements vary quite a bit by operating system and database version. You can download the specific installation manual from Oracle's web site at www.oracle.com/documentation.

■ Note The OUI displays any deficiencies in operating system software and hardware. Running the installer is covered in the "Step 5" section.

Step 3. Obtain the Oracle Installation Software

Usually, the easiest way to obtain the Oracle software is to download it from the Oracle software web site: www.oracle.com/technology/software. Navigate to the software download page, and download the Oracle database version that is appropriate for the type of operating system and hardware on which you want to install it (Linux, Solaris, Windows, and so on).

Step 4. Unzip the Files

Before you unzip the files, I recommend that you create a standard directory where you can place the Oracle installation media. You should do this for a couple of reasons:

When you come back to a box a week, month, or year later, you'll want to be able to easily find the installation media.

Standard directory structures help you organize and understand quickly what has or hasn't been installed on the box.

Create a standard set of directories to contain the files used to install the Oracle software. I like to store the installation media in a directory such as /ora01/orainst and then create a subdirectory there for each version of the Oracle software that is installed on the box:

```
$ mkdir -p /ora01/orainst/10.2.0.1
$ mkdir -p /ora01/orainst/10.2.0.4
```

```
$ mkdir -p /ora01/orainst/11.2.0.1
```

Now, move the installation files to the appropriate directory, and unzip them there:

```
$ mv linux_11gR2_database_1of2.zip  /ora01/orainst/11.2.0.1
$ mv linux_11gR2_database_2of2.zip  /ora01/orainst/11.2.0.1
```

Use the unzip command for unbundling zipped files. The Oracle Database 11g release 2 software is unzipped as shown:

```
$ unzip linux_11gR2_database_1of2.zip
$ unzip linux_11gR2_database_2of2.zip
```

On some installations of Oracle, you may find that the distribution file is provided as a compressed cpio file. You can uncompress and unbundle the file with one command as follows:

```
$ cat 10gr2_db_sol.cpio.gz | gunzip | cpio -idvm
```

Step 5. Configure the Response File, and Run the Installer

You can run the OUI in one of two modes: graphical or silent. Typically, DBAs use the graphical installer. However, I strongly prefer using the silent install option for the following reasons:

Silent installs don't require the availability of X Window System software.

You avoid performance issues with remote graphical installs that can be extremely slow when trying to paint screens locally.

Silent installs can be scripted and automated. This means every install can be performed with the same consistent standards regardless of which team member is performing the install (I even have the SA install the Oracle binaries this way).

The key to performing a silent install is to use a response file. After unzipping the Oracle software, find the sample response files that Oracle provides:

```
$ find . -name "*.rsp"
```

Depending on the version of Oracle and the operating system platform, the names and number of response files that you find may be quite different. The next two subsections show two scenarios: an Oracle Database 10g release 2 and an Oracle Database 11g release 2 silent install.

Oracle Database 10*g* Scenario

A variety of default response files ship with the Oracle installation software. These files vary somewhat depending on the database version and operating system. For example, here are the response files provided in an Oracle Database 10g release 2 (Solaris) environment:

```
$ find . -name "*.rsp"
./response/emca.rsp
./response/custom.rsp
./response/enterprise.rsp
./response/dbca.rsp
./response/netca.rsp
./response/standard.rsp
./install/response/se.rsp
./install/response/pe.rsp
./install/response/ee.rsp
./inst.rsp
```

Copy the enterprise.rsp file to the current working directory, and give it a different name (so that you always have the original to reference):

```
$ cp response/enterprise.rsp inst.rsp
```

Edit the inst.rsp file with an operating system utility such as vi, and provide values for the response file variables. Here are the minimal values you need to provide for a typical Oracle Database 10g installation:

```
RESPONSEFILE_VERSION=2.2.1.0.0
# install group, I use dba, many others use oinstall
UNIX_GROUP_NAME=dba
FROM_LOCATION="/ora01/orainst/10.2.0.1/stage/products.xml"
n_configurationOption=3
s_nameForDBAGrp=dba
s_nameForOPERGrp=dba
ORACLE_HOME=/ora01/app/oracle/product/10.2.0.4/db_1
ORACLE_HOME_NAME=OHOME10
```

■ Note Refer to the Oracle Universal Installer Guide available on Oracle's OTN web site for a complete description of all response-file variables.

I don't modify any other response-file values in this scenario. I leave them blank or leave them with the defaults already specified. Now, run the runInstaller utility in silent mode, providing a full directory path to the response file location:

```
$ ./runInstaller -ignoreSysPrereqs -force -silent \
-responseFile /ora01/orainst/10.2.0.1/inst.rsp
```

■ Note On Windows, the setup.exe command is equivalent to the Linux/Unix runInstaller command.

The installer displays quite a bit of output. If all system checks pass, it takes a few minutes to install the Oracle software. After it successfully completes, you should see this message:

```
The following configuration scripts /ora01/app/oracle/product/10.2.0.4/db_1/root.sh
need to be executed as root for configuring the system.
```

Log in as root, and run root.sh:

```
# /ora01/app/oracle/product/10.2.0.4/db_1/root.sh
```

I usually accept the defaults. After root.sh runs, you should have a good installation of the Oracle software and can create a database (database creation is covered in Chapter 2).

Oracle Database 11*g* Scenario

Here are the response files provided with an Oracle Database 11g release 2 on a Linux server:

```
$ find . -name "*.rsp"
./response/db_install.rsp
./response/dbca.rsp
./response/netca.rsp
```

Copy one of the response files so that you can modify it. This example copies the db_install.rsp file to the current working directory and names the file inst.rsp:

```
$ cp response/db_install.rsp inst.rsp
```

Keep in mind that the format of response files can differ quite a bit depending on the Oracle database version. For example, there are major differences from Oracle Database 11g release 1 to Oracle Database 11g release 2. When you install a new release, you have to inspect the response file and determine which parameters must be set. Here is a partial listing of an Oracle Database 11g release 2 response file (the first two lines of the following file should be on one line, but is placed on two lines in this book to fit on one page):

```
oracle.install.responseFileVersion=
/oracle/install/rspfmt_dbinstall_response_schema_v11_2_0
oracle.install.option=INSTALL_DB_SWONLY
ORACLE_HOSTNAME=ora03
UNIX_GROUP_NAME=dba
oracle.install.db.DBA_GROUP=dba
oracle.install.db.OPER_GROUP=dba
INVENTORY_LOCATION=/ora01/orainst/11.2.0.1/database/stage/products.xml
SELECTED_LANGUAGES=en
ORACLE_HOME=/oracle/app/oracle/product/11.2.0/db_1
ORACLE_BASE=/oracle/app/oracle
DECLINE_SECURITY_UPDATES=true
oracle.install.db.InstallEdition=EE
oracle.install.db.isCustomInstall=true
```

Be sure to modify the appropriate parameters for your environment. If you're unsure what to set the ORACLE_HOME and ORACLE_BASE values to, see the this chapter's first section, "Understanding the Optimal Flexible Architecture," which has a description of the OFA standard directories.

There are sometimes idiosyncrasies to these parameters that are specific to a release. For example, in Oracle Database 11g release 2, if you don't want to specify your My Oracle Support (MOS) login information, then you need to set the following:

```
DECLINE_SECURITY_UPDATES=true
```

If you don't set `DECLINE_SECURITY_UPDATES` to `TRUE`, then you're expected to provide your MOS login information. If you don't do so, the installation won't succeed.

After you've configured your response file, you can run the Oracle installer in silent mode. Notice that you have to put the entire directory path for the location of your response file:

```
$ ./runInstaller -ignoreSysPrereqs -force -silent -responseFile \
/ora01/orainst/11.2.0.1/database/inst.rsp
```

The previous command is entered on two lines. The first line is continued to the second line via the \ (backward slash) character.

If you encounter errors with the installation process, you can view the associated log file. Each time you attempt to run the installer, it creates a log file with a unique name that includes a timestamp. The log file is created in the oraInventory/logs directory. You can stream the output to your screen as the OUI writes to it:

```
$ tail -f <logfile name>
```

The log file is named something like:

```
installActions2009-04-25_11-42-51AM.log
```

If everything runs successfully, in the output, you're notified that you need to run the root.sh script as the root user:

```
#Root scripts to run
/oracle/app/oracle/product/11.2.0/db_1/root.sh
```

Run the root.sh script as the root operating system user. After you do that, you should be able to create an Oracle database (database creation is covered in Chapter 2).

■ **Note** On Linux/Unix platforms, the root.sh script contains commands that must be run as the root user. This script needs to modify the owner and permissions of some of the Oracle executables (such as the nmo executable). Some versions of root.sh prompt you as to whether you want to accept the default values. Usually, it's suitable to accept the default values.

Step 6. Troubleshoot Any Issues

If you encounter an error using a response file, 90 percent of the time it's due to an issue with how you set the variables in the response file. Inspect those variables carefully, and ensure that they're set correctly. Also, if you don't fully specify the command-line path to the response file, you receive errors such as this:

```
OUI-10203: The specified response file 'enterprise.rsp' is not found.
```

Here is another common error when the path or name of the response file is incorrectly specified:

```
OUI-10202:No response file is specified for this session.
```

Listed next is the error message you receive if you enter a wrong path to your products.xml file within the response file's FROM_LOCATION variable:

```
OUI-10133:Invalid staging area
```

Also, be sure you provide the correct command-line syntax when running a response file. If you incorrectly specify or misspell an option, you may receive a misleading error message such as DISPLAY not set. When using a response file, you don't need to have your DISPLAY variable set. This message is confusing because in this scenario, the error is caused by an incorrectly specified command-line option and has nothing to do with the DISPLAY variable. Check all options entered from the command line, and ensure that you haven't misspelled an option.

Another common issue occurs when you specify an ORACLE_HOME and the silent installation thinks the given home already exists:

```
Check complete: Failed <<<<
Problem: Oracle Database 11g Release 2 can only be installed in a new Oracle Home
Recommendation: Choose a new Oracle Home for installing this product.
```

Check your inventory.xml file (in the oraInventory/ContentsXML directory), and make sure there's not a conflict with an already-existing Oracle home name.

When you're troubleshooting issues with Oracle installations, remember that the installer uses two key files to keep track of what software has been installed and where: oraInst.loc and inventory.xml. Table 1-1 describes the files used by the Oracle installer.

Table 1-1. Useful Files for Troubleshooting Oracle Installation Issues

File name	Directory Location	Contents
oraInst.loc	The location of this file varies by operating system. On Linux, this file is in /etc; on Solaris, it's in /var/opt/oracle.	oraInventory directory location and installation operating system group
inst.loc	\\HKEY_LOCAL_MACHINE\\Software\Oracle (Windows registry)	Inventory information
inventory.xml	oraInventory/ContentsXML/inventory.xml	Oracle home names and corresponding directory location
.log files	oraInventory/logs	Installation log files, which are extremely useful for troubleshooting

Installing with a Copy of an Existing Installation

DBAs sometimes install Oracle software by using a utility such as tar to copy an existing installation of the Oracle binaries to a different server (or a different location on the same server). This approach is fast and simple (especially compared to downloading and running the Oracle installer). This technique allows DBAs to easily install the Oracle software on multiple servers and at the same time ensure that each installation is identical.

Installing Oracle with an existing copy of the binaries is a two-part process:

Copy the binaries using an operating system utility.

Attach the Oracle home.

These steps are detailed in the next two subsections.

■ **Tip** MOS note 300062.1 contains instructions on how to clone an existing Oracle installation.

Step 1. Copy the Binaries Using an Operating System Utility

You can use any operating system copy utility to perform this step. The Linux/Unix tar, scp, and rsync utilities are commonly used by DBAs to copy files. This example shows how to use the Linux/Unix tar utility to replicate an existing set of Oracle binaries to a different server. First, locate the target Oracle home binaries that you want to copy:

```
$ echo $ORACLE_HOME
/oracle/app/oracle/product/11.2.0/db_1
```

In this example, the tar utility copies every file and subdirectory in or below the db_1 directory:

```
$ cd $ORACLE_HOME
$ cd ..
$ tar -cvf orahome.tar db_1
```

Now, copy the orahome.tar file to the server where you want to install the Oracle software. In this example, the tar file is copied to the /oracle/app/oracle/product/11.2.0.1 directory on a different server. The tar file is extracted there and creates a db_1 directory as part of the extract:

```
$ cd /oracle/app/oracle/product/11.2.0.1
```

Make sure you have plenty of disk space available to extract the files. A typical Oracle installation can consume at least 3–4GB of space. Use the Linux/Unix df command to verify that you have enough space:

```
$ df -h | sort
```

Next, extract the files:

```
$ tar -xvf orahome.tar
```

When the tar command completes, there should be a db_1 directory beneath the /oracle/app/oracle/product/11.2.0.1 directory.

■ **Tip** Use the tar -tvf <tarfile_name> command to preview which directories and files are restored without actually restoring them.

Listed next is a powerful one-line combination of commands that allows you to bundle the Oracle files, copy them to a remote server, and have them extracted remotely:

```
$ tar -cvf - <locDir> | ssh <remoteNode> "cd <remoteDir>; tar -xvf -"
```

For example, the following command copies everything in the dev_1 directory to the remote ora03 server /home/oracle directory:

```
$ tar -cvf - dev_1 | ssh ora03 "cd /home/oracle; tar -xvf -"
```

ABSOLUTE PATHS VS. RELATIVE PATHS

Some older, non-GNU versions of tar use absolute paths when extracting files. The next line of code shows an example of specifying the absolute path when creating an archive file:

```
$ tar -cvf orahome.tar /home/oracle
```

Specifying an absolute path with non-GNU versions of tar can be dangerous. These older versions of tar restore the contents with the same directories and file names from which they were copied. This means any directories and file names that previously existed on disk are overwritten.

When using older versions of tar, it's much safer to use a relative pathname. The next example first changes to the /home directory and then creates an archive of the oracle directory (relative to the current working directory):

```
$ cd /home
$ tar -cvf orahome.tar oracle
```

The previous example uses the relative path name.

You don't have to worry about absolute vs. relative paths on most Linux systems. This is because these systems use the GNU version of tar. This version strips off the leading / and restores files relative to where your current working directory is located.

Use the man tar command if you're not sure whether you have a GNU version of the tar utility. You can also use the tar -tvf <tarfile name> command to preview which directories and files are restored to what locations.

Step 2. Attach the Oracle Home

One issue with using a copy of an existing installation to install the Oracle software is that if you later attempt to upgrade the software, the upgrade process will throw an error and abort. This is because a copied installation isn't registered in oraInventory. Before you upgrade a set of binaries installed via a copy, you must first register the Oracle home so that it appears in the inventory.xml file. This is called *attaching* an Oracle home.

To attach an Oracle home, you need to know the location of your oraInst.loc file on your server. On Linux servers, this file is usually located in the /etc directory. On Solaris, this file is usually located in the /var/opt/oracle directory.

After you've located your oraInst.loc file, navigate to the ORACLE_HOME/oui/bin directory (on the server where you installed the Oracle binaries from a copy):

```
$ cd $ORACLE_HOME/oui/bin
```

Now, attach the Oracle home by running the runInstaller utility as shown:

```
$ ./runInstaller -silent -attachHome -invPtrLoc /etc/oraInst.loc \
ORACLE_HOME="/oracle/app/oracle/product/11.2.0.1/db_1" ORACLE_HOME_NAME="ONEW"
```

You should see a message like this if successful:

```
The inventory pointer is located at /etc/oraInst.loc
The inventory is located at /oracle/app/oracle/oraInventory
'AttachHome' was successful.
```

You can also examine the contents of your oraInventory/ContentsXML/inventory.xml file. Here's a partial snippet of the line inserted into the inventory.xml file as a result of running the runInstaller utility with the attachHome option:

```
<HOME NAME="ONEW" LOC="/oracle/app/oracle/product/11.2.0.1/db_1" TYPE="O" IDX="3"/>
```

Upgrading Oracle Software

You can also upgrade a version of the Oracle software using the silent installation method. For example, let's see how you upgrade from Oracle Database 10g 10.2.0.1 to version 10.2.0.4.

■ Note Upgrading the Oracle software isn't the same as upgrading an Oracle database. This section only deals with using the silent install method for upgrading the Oracle software. Additional steps are involved with upgrading a database. Refer to MOS note 730365.1 for documentation on how to upgrade a database from one version to another.

First, download the upgrade version from the MOS web site, http://support.oracle.com (you need a valid support contract to do this). For this example, for Solaris, the file name is p6810189_10204_Solaris-64.zip. Copy the file to the database server on which you want to perform the Oracle upgrade. Place it in a directory such as /orahome/orainst/10.2.0.4. Now, unzip the file:

```
$ unzip p6810189_10204_Solaris-64.zip
```

The unzip command should take only a few minutes to unbundle the file. After it's finished, find the sample response file associated with this upgrade:

```
$ find . -name "*.rsp"
```

Here is the location of the response file for this example:

```
./Disk1/response/patchset.rsp
```

Change location to the Disk1 directory:

```
$ cd Disk1
```

Next, copy the response file from the response directory to the current working directory:

```
$ cp response/patchset.rsp inst.rsp
```

Open the response file with an operating system editor utility such as vi:

```
$ vi inst.rsp
```

Modify the parameters to match your environment. Here are the most notable parameters to modify for this particular Oracle Database 10g 10.2.0.4 upgrade:

```
UNIX_GROUP_NAME=dba
FROM_LOCATION=/ora01/orainst/10.2.0.4/Disk1/stage/products.xml
ORACLE_HOME=/ora01/app/oracle/product/10.2.0.4/db_1
ORACLE_HOME_NAME=OHOME10
```

In the previous list, the `ORACLE_HOME` and `ORACLE_HOME_NAME` variables must match the values of the set of binaries you're upgrading. If you're upgrading an existing Oracle installation, ensure that no databases are running that are using the binaries you're upgrading.

Now, run the runInstaller utility in silent mode as follows:

```
$ ./runInstaller -ignoreSysPrereqs -force -silent -responseFile \
/orahome/orainst/10.2.0.4/Disk1/inst.rsp
```

When you're performing an upgrade, there are two basic scenarios. Here is scenario A:

Shut down any databases using the Oracle home to be upgraded.

Upgrade the Oracle home binaries.

Start up the database, and run any required upgrade scripts.

Here are the steps for the scenario B approach to an upgrade:

Leave the existing Oracle home as it is—don't upgrade it.

Install a new Oracle home that is the same version as the old Oracle home.

Upgrade the new Oracle home to the desired version.

When you're ready, shut down the database using the old Oracle home, set the OS variables to point to the new upgraded Oracle home, start the database, and run any required upgrade scripts.

Which of the previous two scenarios is better? Scenario B has the advantage of leaving the old Oracle home as it is; therefore, if you need to switch back to the old Oracle home for any reason, you have those binaries available. Scenario B has the disadvantage of requiring extra disk space to contain two installations of Oracle home. This usually isn't an issue, because after the upgrade is complete, you can delete the old Oracle home when it's convenient.

Reinstalling After Failed Installation

You may run into the situation where you're attempting to install Oracle and for some reason the installation fails. You correct the issue and attempt to re-run the Oracle installer. However, you receive this message:

```
Check complete: Failed <<<<
Problem: Oracle Database 10g Release 2 can only be installed in a new Oracle Home
Recommendation: Choose a new Oracle Home for installing this product.
```

In this situation, Oracle thinks the software has already been installed for a couple of reasons:

Files in the ORACLE_HOME directory are specified in the response file.

An existing Oracle home and location in your oraInventory/ContentsXML/inventory.xml file match what you have specified in the response file.

Oracle doesn't allow you to install a new set of binaries over an existing Oracle home. If you're sure you don't need any of the files in the ORACLE_HOME directory, you can remove them (be very careful—ensure that you absolutely want to do this). This example navigates to ORACLE_HOME and then removes the dev_1 directory and its contents:

```
$ cd $ORACLE_HOME
$ cd ..
$ rm -rf dev_1
```

Also, even if there are no files in the ORACLE_HOME directory, the installer inspects the inventory.xml file for previous Oracle home names and locations. In the inventory.xml file, you must remove the entry that corresponds to the Oracle home location that matches the Oracle home you're trying to install to. To remove the entry, first locate your oraInst.loc file, which contains the directory of your oraInventory. Navigate to the oraInventory/ContentsXML directory. Make a copy of inventory.xml before you modify it:

```
$ cp inventory.xml inventory.xml.old
```

Edit the inventory.xml file with an operating system utility (such as vi), and remove the line that contains the Oracle home information of your previously failed installation. You can now attempt to execute the runInstaller utility again.

Applying Interim Patches

Sometimes you're required to apply a patch to resolve a database issue or eradicate a bug. You usually obtain patches from the MOS web site and install them with the opatch utility. Here are the basic steps for applying a patch:

Obtain the patch from MOS (requires a valid support contract).

Unzip the patch file.

Carefully read the README.txt file for special instructions.

Shut down any databases and processes using the Oracle home to which the patch is being applied.

Apply the patch.

Verify that the patch was installed successfully.

A brief example will help illustrate the process of applying a patch. In this example, patch number 7695070 is used to fix an issue with the time zone format in a 10.2.0.4 database on a Solaris box. First, download the p7695070_10204_Solaris-64.zip file from MOS (https://support.oracle.com). Next, unzip the file on the server where the patch is being applied:

```
$ unzip p7695070_10204_Solaris-64.zip
```

The README.txt instructs you to change the directory as follows:

```
$ cd 7695070
```

Make sure you follow the instructions included in the README.txt, such as shutting down any databases that use the Oracle home to which the patch is being applied:

```
$ sqlplus / as sysdba
SQL> shutdown immediate;
```

Next, apply the patch. Ensure that you perform this step as the owner of the Oracle software (usually the oracle operating system account). Also make sure your ORACLE_HOME variable is set to point to the Oracle home to which you're applying the patch. In this example, because the opatch utility isn't in a path included in the PATH directory, you specify the entire path:

```
$ $ORACLE_HOME/OPatch/opatch apply
```

Finally, verify that the patch was applied by listing the inventory of patches:

```
$ $ORACLE_HOME/OPatch/opatch lsinventory
```

Here is some sample output for this example:

```
Interim patches (1) :
Patch  7695070      : applied on Fri Apr 09 16:09:38 MDT 2010
   Created on 24 Jun 2009, 02:32:42 hrs US/Pacific
   Bugs fixed:
     7695070
```

▓ **Tip** For more information regarding the opatch utility, refer to MOS note 242993.1.

Installing Remotely with the Graphical Installer

In today's global environment, DBAs often find themselves tasked with installing Oracle software on remote Linux/Unix servers. In these situations, I strongly suggest that you use the silent installation mode with a response file (as mentioned earlier in this chapter). However, if you want to install Oracle on a remote server via the graphical installer, this section of the chapter describes the required steps.

▓ **Note** If you're in a Windows-based environment, use the Remote Desktop Connection or VNC to install software remotely.

One issue that arises is how to run the Oracle installer on a remote server and have the graphical output displayed to your local computer. Figure 1–2 shows the basic components and utilities required to remotely run the Oracle graphical installer.

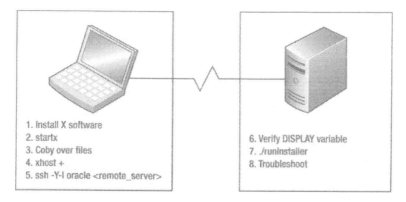

Figure 1–2. Components needed for a remote Oracle graphical installation

Listed next are the steps to set up your environment to display the graphical screens on your local computer while remotely running the Oracle installer:

Install software on the local computer that allows for X Window System emulation and secure networking.

Start an X session on the local computer, and issue the startx command.

Copy the Oracle installation files to the remote server.

Run the xhost command.

Log in to the remote computer from an X terminal.

Ensure that the DISPLAY variable is set correctly on the remote computer.

Execute the runInstaller utility on the remote server.

Troubleshoot.

These steps are explained in the following subsections.

Step 1. Install X Software and Networking Utilities on the Local PC

If you're installing Oracle on a remote server and you're using your home PC, then you first need to install software on your PC that allows you to run X Window System software and run commands such as ssh (secure shell) and scp (secure copy). Several free tools are available that provide this functionality. For example, one such tool is Cygwin. You can download it from http://x.cygwin.com. Be sure you install the packages that provide the X emulation and secure networking utilities such as ssh and scp.

Step 2. Start an X Session on the Local Computer

After you install on your local computer the software that allows you to run X Window System software, you can open an X terminal window and start the X server via the startx command:

```
$ startx
```

Here is a snippet of the output:

```
xauth:  creating new authority file /home/test/.serverauth.3012
waiting for X server to begin accepting connections .
```

When the X software has started, run a utility such as xeyes to determine whether X is working properly:

```
$ xeyes
```

Figure 1–3 shows what a local terminal session looks like using the Cygwin X terminal session tool.

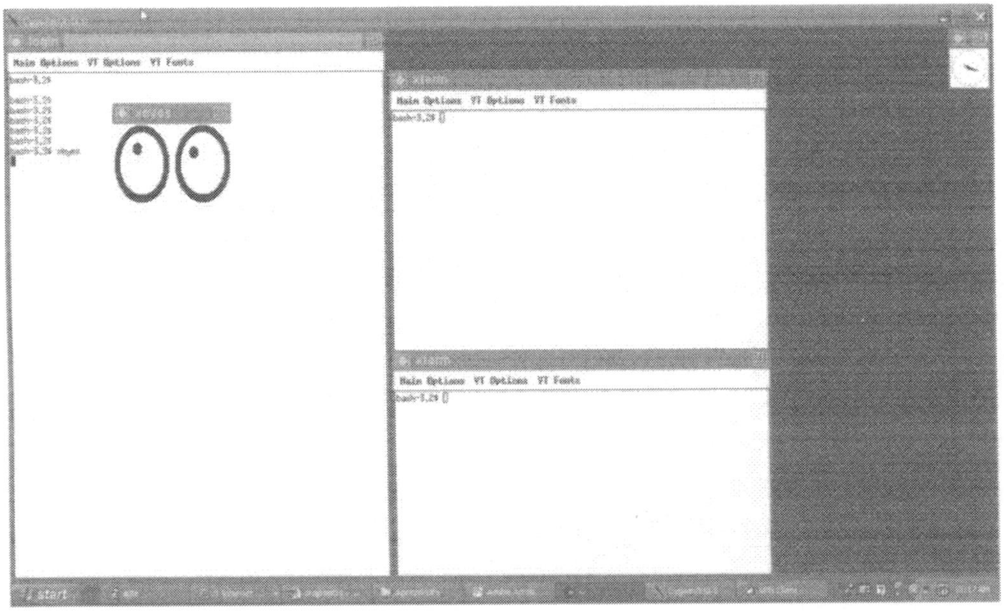

Figure 1–3. Running xeyes utility on local computer

If you can't get a utility such as xeyes to execute, stop at this step until you get it working. You must have correctly functioning X software before you can remotely install Oracle using the graphical installer.

Step 3. Copy the Oracle Installation Media to the Remote Server

From the X terminal, run the scp command to copy the Oracle installation media to the remote server. Here is the basic syntax for using scp:

```
$ scp <localfile> <username>@<remote_server>:<remote_directory>
```

The next line of code copies the Oracle installation media to a remote Oracle operating system user on a remote server in the home directory oracle:

```
$ scp linux_11gR2_database_1of2.zip oracle@shrek2:.
```

Step 4. Run the xhost Command

From the X screen, enable access to the remote host via the xhost command. This command must be run from your local computer:

```
$ xhost +
access control disabled, clients can connect from any host.
```

The prior command allows any client to connect to the local X server. If you want to enable remote access specifically for the remote computer on which you're installing the software, provide an IP address or hostname (of the remote server). In this example, the remote hostname is tst-z1.central.sun.com:

```
$ xhost +tst-z1.central.sun.com
tst-z1.central.sun.com being added to access control list
```

Step 5. Log In to the Remote Computer from X

From your local X terminal, use the ssh utility to log on to the remote server on which you want to install the Oracle software:

```
$ ssh -Y -l oracle <hostname>
```

Step 6. Ensure that the DISPLAY Variable Is Set Correctly on the Remote Computer

When you've logged on to the remote box, verify that your DISPLAY variable has been set:

```
$ echo $DISPLAY
```

You should see something similar to this:

```
localhost:10.0
```

If your DISPLAY variable isn't set, you must ensure that it's set to a value that reflects your local home computer location. From your local home computer, you can use the ping or arp utility to determine the IP address that identifies your local computer. Run the following command on your home computer:

```
C:\> ping <local_computer>
```

■ Tip If you don't know your local home computer name, on Windows you can look in the Control Panel, in the System window, on the Computer Name tab.

Now, from the remote server, execute the following command to set the DISPLAY variable to contain the IP address of the local computer:

```
$ export DISPLAY=129.151.31.147:0.0
```

Note that you must append the :0.0 to the end of the IP address. If you're using the C shell, use the setenv command to set the DISPLAY variable:

```
$ setenv DISPLAY 129.151.31.147:0.0
```

If you're unsure which shell you're using, use the echo command to display the SHELL variable:

```
$ echo $SHELL
```

Step 7. Execute the runInstaller Utility

Navigate to the directory where you copied and unzipped the Oracle software on the remote server. Locate the runInstaller utility, and run it as shown:

```
$ ./runInstaller
```

If everything goes well, you should see a screen like the one in Figure 1-4.

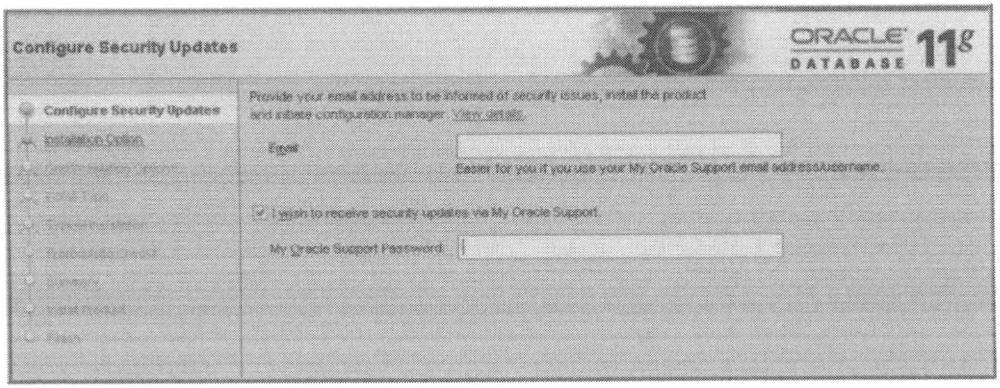

Figure 1-4. *Oracle Universal Installer 11g welcome screen*

From here, you can point and click your way through an Oracle installation of the software. Many DBAs are more comfortable installing the software through a graphical screen. This is a particularly good method if you aren't familiar with Oracle's installation process and want to be prompted for input and be presented with reasonable default values.

Step 8. Troubleshoot

Most issues with remote installations occur in steps 4, 5, and 6. Make sure you've properly enabled remote-client access to your local X server (running on your home computer) via the xhost command. The xhost command must be run on the local computer where you want the graphical display presented. Using the + (plus sign) with the remote hostname adds a host to the local access list. This enables the remote server to display an X window on the local host. If you type the xhost command by itself (with no parameters), it displays all remote hosts that can display X sessions on the local computer:

```
$ xhost
access control disabled, clients can connect from any host
```

Setting the DISPLAY operating system variable on the remote server is also crucial. This allows you to remotely log in to another host and display an X application back to your local computer. The DISPLAY variable must be set on the remote database server, and it must be set to contain information that points it to the local computer on which you want the graphical screen displayed.

Summary

This chapter detailed techniques for efficiently installing the Oracle binaries. These methods are especially useful if you work in environments where you are geographically separated from the database servers. The Oracle silent installation method is efficient because it doesn't require graphical software and uses a response file that helps enforce consistency from one installation to the next. When working in chaotic and constantly changing environments you should benefit from the installation tips and procedures described here.

Many DBAs feel more comfortable using Oracle's graphical installer for installing the database software. However, using the graphical installer can be troublesome where the server is in a remote location or embedded deeply within a secure network. A slow network or a security feature can greatly impede the graphical installation process. In this situations make sure you correctly configure the required X software and operating system variables (such as DISPLAY).

It's critical as a DBA to be an expert with Oracle installation procedures. If the Oracle installation software isn't correctly installed you won't be able to successfully create a database. Once you have properly installed Oracle, you can go on to the next step of starting the background processes and creating a database. The topics of starting Oracle and issuing a creating a database are discussed next in Chapter 2.

■ ■ ■

Implementing a Database

Chapter 1 detailed how to efficiently install the Oracle binaries. After you've installed the Oracle software, the next logical task is creating a database. There are two standard ways for creating Oracle databases:

- Use the Database Configuration Assistant (dbca) utility
- Run a CREATE DATABASE statement from SQL*Plus

Oracle's dbca utility has a graphical interface from which you can configure and create databases. This visual tool is easy to use and has a very intuitive interface. If you need to create a development database and get going quickly, then this tool is more than adequate. Having said that, I normally don't use the dbca utility to create databases. In Linux/Unix environments, the dbca tool depends on X software and an appropriate setting for the operating system DISPLAY variable. The dbca utility therefore requires some setup and can perform poorly if you're installing on remote servers when the network throughput is slow.

The dbca utility also allows you to create a database in silent mode without the graphical component. Using dbca in silent mode with a response file is an efficient way to create databases in a consistent and repeatable manner. This approach also works well when you're installing on remote servers where the network connection could be slow or you don't have the appropriate X software installed.

When you're creating databases on remote servers, it's usually easier and more efficient to use SQL*Plus. The SQL*Plus approach is simple and inherently scriptable. In addition, SQL*Plus works no matter how slow the network connection is, and it isn't dependent on a graphical component. Therefore, I almost always use the SQL*Plus technique to create databases.

This chapter starts by showing you how to quickly create a database using SQL*Plus and also how to make your database remotely available by enabling a listener process. Later, the chapter shows you how to use the dbca utility in silent mode with a response file to create a database.

Setting Operating System Variables

Before getting into creating a database, you need to know a bit about operating system variables, which are often called *environment variables*. Specifically, you need to know how to set these in support of your Oracle Database environment. You can take several different approaches. This chapter discusses three, beginning with a manual approach and ending with the approach that I personally prefer.

A Manually Intensive Approach

In Linux/Unix, when you're using the Bourne, Bash, or Korn shell, you can set operating system variables manually from the operating system command line using the export command:

```
$ export ORACLE_HOME=/ora01/app/oracle/product/11.2.0/db_1
$ export ORACLE_SID=O11R2
$ export LD_LIBRARY_PATH=/usr/lib:$ORACLE_HOME/lib
$ export PATH=$ORACLE_HOME/bin:$PATH
```

For the C or tcsh shell, use the setenv command to set variables:

```
$ setenv ORACLE_HOME <path>
$ setenv ORACLE_SID <sid>
$ setenv LD_LIBRARY_PATH <path>
$ setenv PATH <path>
```

Another way that DBAs set these variables is by placing the previous export or setenv commands into a startup file such as .bash_profile, .bashrc, or .profile. That way, the variables are automatically set upon login.

However, manually setting OS variables (either from the command line or from a startup file) isn't the optimal way of instantiating these variables. For example, if you have multiple databases with multiple Oracle homes on a box, manually setting these variables quickly becomes unwieldy and not very maintainable.

Oracle's Approach to Setting OS Variables

A much better method for setting OS variables uses a script that uses a file that contains the names of all Oracle databases on a server and their associated Oracle homes. This approach is flexible and maintainable. For example, if a database's Oracle home changes (for example, after an upgrade), you only have to modify one file on the server and not hunt down where the Oracle home variables may be hard-coded into scripts.

Oracle provides a mechanism for automatically setting the required OS variables. Oracle's approach relies on two files: oratab and oraenv.

Understanding oratab

You can think of the entries in the oratab file as a registry of what databases are installed on a box and their corresponding Oracle home directories.

The oratab file is automatically created for you when you install the Oracle software. On Linux boxes, oratab is usually placed in the /etc directory. On Solaris servers, the oratab file is placed in the /var/opt/oracle directory. If for some reason the oratab file isn't automatically created, you can manually create the directory and file.

The oratab file is used in Linux/Unix environments for the following:

- Automating the sourcing of required OS variables

- Automating the start and stop of Oracle databases on the server

The oratab file has three columns with the following format:

```
<database_sid>:<oracle_home_dir>:Y|N
```

The Y or N indicates whether you want Oracle to automatically restart on reboot of the box; Y indicates yes, and N indicates no. Automating the startup and shutdown of your database is covered in detail in Chapter 21, "Automating Jobs."

Comments in the oratab file start with a pound sign (#). Here's a typical oratab file entry:

```
# 11g prod databases
O11R2:/oracle/app/oracle/product/11.2.0/db_1:N
ORC11G:/oracle/app/oracle/product/11.2.0/db_1:N
```

Several Oracle-supplied utilities use the oratab file:

- oraenv uses oratab to set the operating system variables.

- dbstart uses it to automatically start the database on server reboots (if the third field in oratab is Y).

- dbstop uses it to automatically stop the database on server reboots (if the third field in oratab is Y).

The oraenv tool is discussed in the next section.

Using oraenv

If you don't properly set the required OS variables for an Oracle environment, then utilities such as SQL*Plus, Oracle Recovery Manager (RMAN), Data Pump, and so on won't work correctly. The oraenv utility automates the setting of required OS variables (such as ORACLE_HOME, ORACLE_SID, and PATH) on an Oracle database server. This utility is used in Bash, Korn, and Bourne shell environments (if you're in a C shell environment, there is a corresponding coraenv utility).

The oraenv utility is located in the ORACLE_HOME/bin directory. You can run it manually like this:

```
$ . oraenv
```

Note that the syntax to run this from the command line requires a space between the dot (.) and the oraenv tool. You're prompted for ORACLE_SID and ORACLE_HOME values:

```
ORACLE_SID = [oracle] ?
ORACLE_HOME = [/home/oracle] ?
```

You can also run the oraenv utility in a non-interactive way by setting OS variables before you run it. This is useful for scripting when you don't want to be prompted for input:

```
$ export ORACLE_SID=oracle
$ export ORAENV_ASK=NO
$ . oraenv
```

My Approach to Setting OS Variables

I don't use Oracle's oraenv file to set the OS variables (see the previous section for details of Oracle's approach). Instead, I use a script named oraset. The oraset script depends on the oratab file being in the correct directory and of the expected format:

```
<database_sid>:<oracle_home_dir>:Y|N
```

As mentioned in the previous section, the Oracle installer should create an oratab file for you in the correct directory. If it doesn't, then you can manually create and populate the file. In Linux, the oratab file is usually created in the /etc directory. On Solaris servers, the oratab file is located in /var/opt/oracle. Here is an example:

```
O11R2:/ora01/app/oracle/product/11.2.0/db_1:N
DEV1:/ora02/app/oracle/product/11.2.0/db_1:N
```

The names of the databases on the previous lines are O11R2 and DEV1. The path of each database's Oracle home directory is next on the line (separated from the database name by a colon [:]). The last column contains Y or N and indicates whether you want the databases to automatically be restarted when the system reboots.

Next, use a script that reads the oratab file and sets the operating system variables. Here is an example of an oraset script that reads the oratab file and presents a menu of choices (based on the database names in the oratab file):

```
#!/bin/bash
# Why:    Sets Oracle environment variables.
# Setup: 1. Put oraset file in /var/opt/oracle
#        2. Ensure /var/opt/oracle is in $PATH
# Usage: batch mode: . oraset <SID>
#        menu mode:  . oraset
#========================================================
OTAB=/var/opt/oracle/oratab
if [ -z $1 ]; then
  SIDLIST=$(grep -v '#' ${OTAB} | cut -f1 -d:)
  # PS3 indicates the prompt to be used for the Bash select command.
  PS3='SID? '
  select sid in ${SIDLIST}; do
    if [ -n $sid ]; then
      HOLD_SID=$sid
      break
    fi
  done
else
  if grep -v '#' ${OTAB} | grep -w "${1}:">/dev/null; then
    HOLD_SID=$1
  else
    echo "SID: $1 not found in $OTAB"
  fi
  shift
fi
#
export ORACLE_SID=$HOLD_SID
export ORACLE_HOME=$(grep -v '#' $OTAB|grep -w $ORACLE_SID:|cut -f2 -d:)
export ORACLE_BASE=${ORACLE_HOME%%/product*}
export TNS_ADMIN=$ORACLE_HOME/network/admin
export ADR_HOME=$ORACLE_BASE/diag/rdbms/$(echo $HOLD_SID|tr A-Z a-z)/$HOLD_SID
export PATH=$ORACLE_HOME/bin:/usr/ccs/bin:/opt/SENSsshc/bin/\
:/bin:/usr/bin:.:/var/opt/oracle
export LD_LIBRARY_PATH=/usr/lib:$ORACLE_HOME/lib
```

You can run the oraset script either from the command line or from a startup file (such as .profile, .bash_profile, or .bashrc). To run oraset from the command line, place the oraset file in a standard location like /var/opt/oracle and run as follows:

```
$ . /var/opt/oracle/oraset
```

Note that the syntax to run this from the command line requires a space between the dot (.) and the rest of the command. When you run oraset from the command line, you should be presented with a menu like this:

```
1) O11R2
2) DEV1
```

In this example, you can now enter 1 or 2 to set the OS variables required for whichever database you want to use. This allows you to interactively set up OS variables regardless of the number of database installations on the server.

You can also call the oraset file from an operating system startup file. Here is a sample entry in the .bashrc file:

```
. /var/opt/oracle/oraset
```

Now, every time you log on to the server, you're presented with a menu of choices that you can use to indicate the database for which you want the OS variables set.

Creating a Database

This section explains how to manually create an Oracle database with the SQL*Plus CREATE DATABASE statement. Listed next are the steps required to create a database:

1. Set the operating system variables.
2. Configure the initialization file.
3. Create the required directories.
4. Create the database.
5. Create a data dictionary.

Each of these steps is covered in the following subsections.

Step 1. Set the Operating System Variables

Before you run SQL*Plus (or any other Oracle utility), you must set several OS variables:

- ORACLE_HOME
- PATH
- ORACLE_SID
- LD_LIBRARY_PATH

The ORACLE_HOME variable defines the default directory location for the initialization file, which is ORACLE_HOME/dbs on Linux/Unix. On Windows, this directory is usually ORACLE_HOME\database. The ORACLE_HOME variable is also important because it defines the directory location of the Oracle binary files (such as sqlplus) that are in ORACLE_HOME/bin.

The PATH variable specifies which directories are looked in by default when you type a command from the operating system prompt. In almost all situations, you require ORACLE_HOME/bin (the location of the Oracle binaries) to be included in your PATH variable.

The ORACLE_SID variable defines the default name of the database you're attempting to create. ORACLE_SID is also used as the default name for the initialization file, which is init<ORACLE_SID>.ora.

The LD_LIBRARY_PATH variable is important because it specifies where to search for libraries on Linux/Unix boxes. The value of this variable is typically set to include ORACLE_HOME/lib.

Step 2: Configure the Initialization File

Oracle requires that you have an initialization file in place before you attempt to start the instance. The initialization file is used to configure features such as memory and to control file locations. You can use two types of initialization files:

- Server parameter binary file (spfile)

- init.ora text file

Oracle recommends that you use an spfile for reasons such as these:

- You can modify the contents of the spfile with the SQL ALTER SYSTEM statement.

- You can use remote-client SQL sessions to start the database without requiring a local (client) initialization file.

These are good reasons to use an spfile. However, some shops still use the traditional init.ora file. The init.ora file also has advantages:

- You can directly edit it with an operating system text editor.

- You can place comments in it that contain a history of modifications.

When I first create a database, I find it easier to use an init.ora file. This file can be easily converted later to an spfile if required (via the CREATE SPFILE FROM PFILE statement). Here are the contents of a typical Oracle Database 11g init.ora file:

```
db_name=O11R2
db_block_size=8192
memory_target=800M
memory_max_target=800M
processes=200
control_files=(/ora01/dbfile/O11R2/control01.ctl,/ora02/dbfile/O11R2/control02.ctl)
job_queue_processes=10
open_cursors=300
fast_start_mttr_target=500
undo_management=AUTO
undo_tablespace=UNDOTBS1
remote_login_passwordfile=EXCLUSIVE
```

Ensure that the initialization file is named correctly and located in the appropriate directory. When starting your instance, Oracle looks in the default location for a binary initialization file named spfile<ORACLE_SID>.ora. If there is no binary spfile, Oracle looks for a text file with the name init<ORACLE_SID>.ora. Oracle throws an error if it can't find an initialization file (either spfile or init.ora) in the default location. You can explicitly tell Oracle which directory and file to use by specifying the PFILE clause of the STARTUP statement, which allows you to specify a nondefault directory and name of a client (not server) initialization file.

On Linux/Unix systems, the initialization file (either a text init.ora or binary spfile) is by default located in the ORACLE_HOME/dbs directory. On Windows, the default directory is ORACLE_HOME\database.

Table 2–1 lists best practices when configuring an Oracle initialization file.

Table 2–1. Initialization File Best Practices

Best Practice	Reasoning
Oracle recommends that you use a binary server parameter file (spfile). However, I still use the old text init.ora files in some cases.	Use whichever type of initialization parameter file you're comfortable with. If you have a requirement to use an spfile, then by all means implement one.
In general, don't set initialization parameters if you're not sure of their intended purpose. When in doubt, use the default.	Setting initialization parameters can have far-reaching consequences in terms of database performance. Only modify parameters if you know what the resulting behavior will be.
For 11g, set the memory_target and memory_max_target initialization parameters.	Doing this allows Oracle to manage all memory components for you.
For 10g, set the sga_target and sga_target_max initialization parameters.	Doing this lets Oracle manage most memory components for you.
For 10g, set pga_aggregate_target and workarea_size_policy.	Doing this allows Oracle to manage the memory used for the sort space.
Starting with 10g, use the automatic UNDO feature. This is set using the undo_management and undo_tablespace parameters.	Doing this allows Oracle to manage most features of the UNDO tablespace.
Set open_cursors to a higher value than the default. I typically set it to 500. Active online transaction processing (OLTP) databases may need a much higher value.	The default value of 50 is almost never enough. Even a small one-user application can exceed the default value of 50 open cursors.
Name the control files with the pattern /<mount_point>/dbfile/<database_name>/controlON.ctl.	This deviates slightly from the Optimal Flexible Architecture (OFA) standard. I find this location easier to navigate to, as opposed to being located under ORACLE_BASE.
Use at least two control files, preferably in different locations using different disks.	If one control file becomes corrupt, it's always a good idea to have at least one other control file available.

Step 3: Create the Required Directories

Any directories referenced in the initialization file or CREATE DATABASE statement must be created on the server before you attempt to create a database. For example, in the previous section's initialization file, the control files are defined as

```
control_files=(/ora01/dbfile/011R2/control01.ctl,/ora02/dbfile/011R2/control02.ctl)
```

From the previous line, ensure that you've created the directories /ora01/dbfile/011R2 and /ora02/dbfile/011R2 (modify this according to your environment). In Linux/Unix, you can create directories and any parent directories required by using the mkdir command with the p switch:

```
$ mkdir -p /ora01/dbfile/011R2
$ mkdir -p /ora02/dbfile/011R2
```

Also ensure that you create any directories required for datafiles and online redo logs referenced in the CREATE DATABASE statement (see the section "Step 4: Create the Database"). For this example, here are the directories required:

```
$ mkdir -p /ora01/dbfile/011R2
$ mkdir -p /ora01/dbfile/011R2
$ mkdir -p /ora01/dbfile/011R2
$ mkdir -p /ora02/oraredo/011R2
$ mkdir -p /ora03/oarredo/011R2
```

If you create the previous directories as the root user, ensure that the oracle user and dba group are properly set to own the directories, subdirectories, and files. This example recursively changes the owner and group of the following directories:

```
# chown -R oracle:dba /ora01
# chown -R oracle:dba /ora02
# chown -R oracle:dba /ora03
```

If you're using Oracle Database 10g or lower, make sure any background dump directories that are listed in the initialization file are created:

```
$ mkdir -p /ora01/app/oracle/admin/DB10G/udump
$ mkdir -p /ora01/app/oracle/admin/DB10G/bdump
$ mkdir -p /ora01/app/oracle/admin/DB10G/adump
$ mkdir -p /ora01/app/oracle/admin/DB10G/cdump
```

Step 4: Create the Database

After you've established OS variables, created an initialization file, and created any required directories, you can create a database. This step explains how to use the CREATE DATABASE statement to create a database.

Before you can run the CREATE DATABASE statement, you must start the background processes and allocate memory via the STARTUP NOMOUNT statement:

```
$ sqlplus / as sysdba
SQL> startup nomount;
```

When you issue a STARTUP NOMOUNT statement, SQL*Plus attempts to read the initialization file in the ORACLE_HOME/dbs directory (see the earlier section "Step 2: Create the Initialization File"). The STARTUP

NOMOUNT statement instantiates the background processes and memory areas used by Oracle. At this point, you have an Oracle instance, but you have no database.

▪ **Note** An Oracle instance is defined to be the background processes and memory areas. The Oracle database is defined to be the physical files on disk.

Listed next is a typical Oracle CREATE DATABASE statement:

```
CREATE DATABASE O11R2
  maxlogfiles 16
  maxlogmembers 4
  maxdatafiles 1024
  maxinstances 1
  maxloghistory 680
  character set "UTF8"
DATAFILE '/ora01/dbfile/O11R2/system01.dbf'
  SIZE 500m
  EXTENT MANAGEMENT LOCAL
UNDO TABLESPACE undotbs1 DATAFILE '/ora02/dbfile/O11R2/undotbs01.dbf'
  SIZE 800m
SYSAUX DATAFILE '/ora03/dbfile/O11R2/sysaux01.dbf'
  SIZE 200m
DEFAULT TEMPORARY TABLESPACE temp TEMPFILE '/ora03/dbfile/O11R2/temp01.dbf'
  SIZE 800m
DEFAULT TABLESPACE users DATAFILE '/ora02/dbfile/O11R2/users01.dbf'
  SIZE 20m
LOGFILE GROUP 1
  ('/ora02/oraredo/O11R2/redo01a.rdo',
   '/ora03/oraredo/O11R2/redo01b.rdo')  SIZE 100m,
      GROUP 2
  ('/ora02/oraredo/O11R2/redo02a.rdo',
   '/ora03/oraredo/O11R2/redo02b.rdo' ) SIZE 100m,
      GROUP 3
  ('/ora02/oraredo/O11R2/redo03a.rdo',
   '/ora03/oraredo/O11R2/redo03b.rdo' ) SIZE 100m
USER sys    IDENTIFIED BY secretfoo
USER system IDENTIFIED BY secretfoobar;
```

In this example, the script is placed in a file named credb.sql and is run from the SQL*Plus prompt as the sys user:

```
SQL> @credb.sql
```

If it's successful, you should see the following message:

```
Database created.
```

If any errors are thrown while the CREATE DATABASE statement is running, check the alert log file. Typical errors occur when required directories don't exist, or the memory allocation isn't enough, or some operating system limit has been exceeded. If you're unsure of the location of your alert log, issue the following:

```
SQL> show parameter background_dump_dest
```

There are few key things to note about the prior CREATE DATABASE statement example. For example, notice that the SYSTEM datafile is defined as locally managed. This means any tablespace created in this database must be locally managed (as opposed to dictionary managed). Oracle throws an error if you attempt to create a dictionary-managed tablespace in this database. This is the desired behavior.

A dictionary-managed tablespace uses the Oracle data dictionary to manage extents and free space, whereas a locally managed tablespace uses a bitmap in each datafile to manage its extents and free space. Locally managed tablespaces have these advantages:

- No rollback information is generated.

- No coalescing is required.

- Contention for resources in the data dictionary is reduced.

- Recursive space management is reduced.

Also notice that the TEMP tablespace is defined to be the default temporary tablespace. This means any user created in the database automatically has the TEMP tablespace assigned to them as their default temporary tablespace. You can verify the default temporary tablespace with this query:

```
select *
from database_properties
where property_name = 'DEFAULT_TEMP_TABLESPACE';
```

Finally, notice that the USERS tablespace is defined to be the default permanent tablespace for any users created that don't have a default tablespace defined in a CREATE USER statement. You can run this query to determine the default temporary tablespace:

```
select *
from database_properties
where property_name = 'DEFAULT_PERMANENT_TABLESPACE';
```

Table 2–2 lists best practices to consider when you're creating an Oracle database.

Table 2–2. Best Practices for Creating an Oracle Database

Best Practice	Reasoning
Make the SYSTEM tablespace locally managed.	Doing this enforces that all tablespaces created in this database are locally managed.
Use the REUSE clause with caution. Normally, you should use it only when you're re-creating a database.	The REUSE clause instructs Oracle to overwrite existing files, regardless of whether they're in use. This is dangerous.
Create a default temporary tablespace with TEMP somewhere in the name.	Every user should be assigned a temporary tablespace of type TEMP, including the SYS user. If you don't specify a default temporary tablespace, the SYSTEM tablespace is used. You *never* want a user to be assigned a temporary tablespace of SYSTEM. If your database doesn't have a default temporary tablespace, use the ALTER DATABASE DEFAULT TEMPORARY TABLESPACE statement to assign one.

Best Practice	Reasoning
Create a default permanent tablespace named USERS.	This ensures that users are assigned a default permanent tablespace other than SYSTEM. If your database doesn't have a default permanent tablespace, use the ALTER DATABASE DEFAULT TABLESPACE statement to assign one.
Use the USER SYS and USER SYSTEM clauses to specify nondefault passwords.	Doing this creates the database with nondefault passwords for database accounts that are usually the first targets for hackers.
Create at least three redo log groups with two members each.	At least three redo log groups provides time for the archive process to write out archive redo logs between switches. Two members mirror the online redo log members, providing some fault tolerance.
Name the redo logs something like redoNA.rdo.	This deviates slightly from the OFA standard, but I've had files with the extension of .log accidentally deleted more than once (it shouldn't ever happen, but it has).
Make the database name somewhat intelligent, such as PAPRD, PADEV1, or PATST1.	This helps you determine what database you're operating in and whether it's a production, development, or test environment.
Use the ? variable when you're creating the data dictionary (see the section "Step 5: Create a Data Dictionary"). Don't hardcode the directory path.	SQL*Plus interprets the ? as the directory contained in the OS ORACLE_HOME variable. This prevents you from accidentally running scripts from the wrong version of ORACLE_HOME.

Note that the CREATE DATABASE statement used in this step deviates slightly from the OFA standard in terms of the directory structure. I prefer not to place the Oracle datafiles, online redo logs, and control files under ORACLE_BASE (as specified by the OFA standard). I instead directly place files under directories named /<mount_point>/<file_type>/<database_name>, because the path names are much shorter. The shorter path names make command-line navigation to directories easier, and the names fit more cleanly in the output of SQL SELECT statements. Figure 2–1 displays this deviation from the OFA standard.

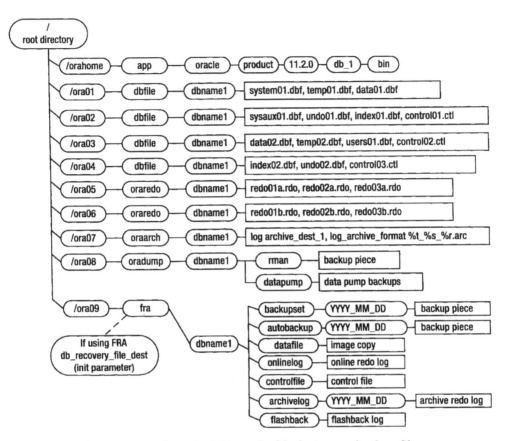

Figure 2-1. A slight deviation from the OFA standard for laying out database files

It's not my intention to have you use nonstandard OFA structures. Rather, do what makes sense for your environment and requirements. Apply reasonable standards that foster manageability, maintainability, and scalability.

Step 5. Create a Data Dictionary

After your database is successfully created, you can instantiate the data dictionary by running two scripts. These scripts are created when you install the Oracle binaries. You must run these scripts as the SYS schema:

```
SQL> show user
USER is "SYS"
```

Before I create the data dictionary, I like to spool an output file that I can inspect in the event of unexpected errors:

```
SQL> spool create_dd.lis
```

Now, create the data dictionary:

```
SQL> @?/rdbms/admin/catalog.sql
SQL> @?/rdbms/admin/catproc.sql
```

After you successfully create the data dictionary, as the SYSTEM schema, create the product user profile tables:

```
SQL> connect system/<password>
SQL> @?/sqlplus/admin/pupbld
```

These tables allow SQL*Plus to disable commands on a user-by-user basis. If the pupbld.sql script isn't run, then all non-sys users see the following warning when logging in to SQL*Plus:

```
Error accessing PRODUCT_USER_PROFILE
Warning: Product user profile information not loaded!
You may need to run PUPBLD.SQL as SYSTEM
```

These errors can be ignored. If you don't want to see them when logging into SQL*Plus, make sure you run the pupbld.sql script.

At this point, you should have a fully functional database. You next need to configure and implement your listener to enable remote connectivity, and optionally set up a password file. Those tasks are described in the next two sections.

Configuring and Implementing the Listener

After you've installed binaries and created a database, you need to make the database accessible to remote client connections. You do this by configuring and starting the Oracle listener. Appropriately named, the *listener* is the process that listens for connection requests from remote clients. If you don't have a listener started on the database server, then you can't connect from a remote client.

When you're setting up a new environment, configuring the listener is a two-step process:

1. Configure the listener.ora file.

2. Start the listener.

The listener.ora file is located by default in the ORACLE_HOME/network/admin directory. This is the same directory that the TNS_ADMIN operating system variable should be set to. Here is a sample listener.ora file that contains network-configuration information for one database:

```
LISTENER =
  (DESCRIPTION_LIST =
    (DESCRIPTION =
      (ADDRESS_LIST =
        (ADDRESS = (PROTOCOL = TCP)(HOST = ora03)(PORT = 1521))
      )
    )
  )

SID_LIST_LISTENER =
  (SID_LIST =
```

```
(SID_DESC =
  (GLOBAL_DBNAME = O11R2)
  (ORACLE_HOME = /oracle/app/oracle/product/11.2.0/db_1)
  (SID_NAME = O11R2)
  )
)
```

This code listing has two sections. The first defines the listener name and service; in this example, the listener name is LISTENER. The second section defines the list of SIDs for which the listener is listening for incoming connections (to the database). The format of the SID list name is SID_LIST_<name of listener>. The name of the listener must appear in the SID list name. The SID list name in this example is SID_LIST_LISTENER.

After you have a listener.ora file in place, you can start the listener background process with the lsnrctl utility:

```
$ lsnrctl start
```

You should see informational messages such as the following:

```
Listener Parameter File
/oracle/app/oracle/product/11.2.0/db_1/network/admin/listener.ora
Listener Log File
/oracle/app/oracle/diag/tnslsnr/ora03/listener/alert/log.xml
Listening Endpoints Summary...
(DESCRIPTION=(ADDRESS=(PROTOCOL=tcp)(HOST=ora03.regis.local)(PORT=1521)))
Services Summary...
Service "O11R2" has 1 instance(s).
  Instance "O11R2", status UNKNOWN, has 1 handler(s) for this service...
```

When the listener has been started, you can test remote connectivity from a SQL*Plus client as follows:

```
$ sqlplus user/pass@'server:port/db_name'
```

In the next line of code, the user and password are system/manager, connecting to the ora03 server, port 1521, to a database named O11R2:

```
$ sqlplus system/manager@'ora03:1521/O11R2'
```

This example demonstrates what is known as the *easy connect* naming method of connecting to a database. It's *easy* because it doesn't rely on any setup files or utilities. The only information you have to know is a username, password, server, port, and SID.

Another common connection method is *local naming*. This method relies on connection information in the TNS_ADMIN/tnsnames.ora file. In this example, the tnsnames.ora file is edited and the following Transparent Network Substrate (TNS, Oracle's network architecture) entry is added:

```
O11R2 =
  (DESCRIPTION =
    (ADDRESS = (PROTOCOL = TCP)(HOST = ora03)(PORT = 1521))
    (CONNECT_DATA = (SERVICE_NAME = O11R2)))
```

Now, from the operating system command line, you establish a connection by referencing the O11R2 TNS information that was placed in the tnsnames.ora file:

```
$ sqlplus system/manager@O11R2
```

This connection method is *local* because it relies on a local client copy of the tnsnames.ora file to determine the Oracle Net connection details. By default, SQL*Plus inspects the directory defined by the

OS variable TNS_ADMIN for a file named tnsnames.ora. If the tnsnames.ora file contains the alias specified in the SQL*Plus connection string (in this example, O11R2), the connection details are determined from the entry in the tnsnames.ora file.

The other connection-naming methods that Oracle uses are *external naming* and *directory naming*. Refer to the *Oracle Net Services Administrator's Guide* for further details (available on Oracle's OTN web site).

Creating a Password File

Creating a password file is optional. There are some good reasons for requiring a password file:

- You want to assign non-sys users to have sysdba or sysoper privileges.

- You want to connect remotely to your database via Oracle Net with sysdba or sysoper privileges.

- An Oracle feature or utility requires the use of a password file.

Perform the following steps to implement a password file:

1. Create the password file with the orapwd utility.

2. Set the initialization parameter REMOTE_LOGIN_PASSWORDFILE to EXCLUSIVE.

In a Linux/Unix environment, use the orapwd utility to create a password file as follows:

```
$ cd $ORACLE_HOME/dbs
$ orapwd file=orapw<ORACLE_SID> password=<sys password>
```

In a Linux/Unix environment, the password file is usually stored in ORACLE_HOME/dbs; and in Windows, it's typically placed in the ORACLE_HOME\database directory.

The format of the filename that you specify in the previous command may vary by OS. For example, on Windows, the format is PWD<ORACLE_SID>.ora. The following shows the syntax in a Windows environment:

```
c:\> cd %ORACLE_HOME%\database
c:\> orapwd file=PWD<ORACLE_SID>.ora password=<sys password>
```

To enable the use of the password file, set the initialization parameter REMOTE_LOGIN_PASSWORDFILE to EXCLUSIVE. Setting this value to EXCLUSIVE instructs Oracle to allow only one instance to connect to the database and also specifies that the password file can contain schemas other than sys. Table 2-3 details the meanings of the possible values for REMOTE_LOGIN_PASSWORDFILE.

Table 2-3. Values for remote_login_passwordfile

Value	Meaning
EXCLUSIVE	One instance can connect to the database. Users other than sys can be in the password file.
SHARED	Multiple databases can share a password file. sys is the only user allowed in the password file. Oracle returns an ORA-01999 if you attempt to grant sysdba privileges to a user when the value is set to SHARED.
NONE	Oracle ignores the password file. Only local privileged accounts can connect as sysdba.

You can add users to the password file via the GRANT SYSDBA statement. The following example grants sysdba privileges and adds the user heera to the password file:

```
SQL> grant sysdba to heera;
Grant succeeded.
```

Enabling a password file also allows you to connect to your database remotely with sysdba privileges via an Oracle Net connection:

```
$ sqlplus <username>/<password>@<database connection string> as sysdba
```

This allows you to do remote maintenance with sysdba privileges that would otherwise require you to physically log on to the database server.

■ Tip You can query the V$PWFILE_USERS view to display users granted sysdba and sysoper privileges.

The concept of a privileged user is also important to RMAN backup and recovery. Like SQL*Plus, RMAN uses OS authentication and password files to allow privileged users to connect to the database. Only a privileged account is allowed to back up, restore, and recover a database.

Starting and Stopping the Database

Before you can start and stop an Oracle instance, you must set the proper OS variables (previously covered in this chapter). You also need access to either a privileged OS account or a privileged database user account. Connecting as a privileged user allows you to perform administrative tasks such as starting, stopping, and creating databases. You can use either OS authentication or a password file to connect to your database as a privileged user.

Understanding Authentication

OS authentication means that if you can log on to an authorized operating system account, you're allowed to connect to your database without the requirement of an additional password. OS authentication is administered by assigning special privileges to OS accounts.

When you install the Oracle binaries in a Linux/Unix environment, you're required to specify at installation time the names of the OS groups (usually named dba and oper) that are assigned the database privileges of sysdba and sysoper. In a Windows environment, an OS group is automatically created (typically named ora_dba) and assigned to the OS user who installs the Oracle software.

The sysdba and sysoper privileges allow you to perform administrative tasks such as starting and stopping your database. As shown in Table 2–4, the sysoper privilege contains a subset of the sysdba privileges.

Table 2–4. Privileges of sysdba and sysoper

System Privilege	Authorized Operations
sysdba (all privileges of the sys schema)	Start up and shut down, alter database, create and drop database, toggle archivelog mode, recover database
sysoper	Start up and shut down, alter database, toggle archivelog mode, recover database

Any OS account assigned to the authorized OS groups can connect to the database without a password and perform administrative operations. In Linux/Unix, it's common to create an oracle OS account and assign its primary group to be dba. Here's an example of displaying the user and group ID information with the Linux/Unix id command and then connecting to the database using OS authentication:

```
$ id
uuid=100(oracle) gid=101(dba)
$ sqlplus / as sysdba
```

In Windows environments, you can verify which OS users belong to the ora_dba group as follows: select Start ➤ Control Panel ➤ Administrative Tools ➤ Computer Management ➤ Local Users and Groups ➤ Groups. You should see a group named something like ora_dba. You can click that group and view which OS users are assigned to it.

In addition, for OS authentication to work in Windows environments, you must have the following entry in your sqlnet.ora file:

```
SQLNET.AUTHENTICATION_SERVICES=(NTS)
```

The sqlnet.ora file is located in the ORACLE_HOME/network/admin directory.

Starting the Database

Starting and stopping your database is a task that you perform frequently. To start/stop your database, connect with a sysdba or sysoper privileged user account, and issue the startup and shutdown statements. The following example uses OS authentication to connect to the database:

```
$ sqlplus / as sysdba
```

After you're connected as a privileged account, you can start your database as follows:

```
SQL> startup;
```

▓ **Note** Stopping and restarting your database in quick succession is known colloquially in the DBA world as *bouncing* your database.

However, if the parameter file (pfile or spfile) isn't located in ORACLE_HOME/dbs for Linux/Unix or in ORACLE_HOME\database for Windows, then you have to include the pfile clause to reference an init.ora file as follows:

```
SQL> startup pfile=C:\temp\initORCL.ora
```

You should see messages from Oracle indicating that the system global area (SGA) has been allocated. The database is mounted and then opened:

```
ORACLE instance started.
Total System Global Area  289406976 bytes
Fixed Size                 11235813 bytes
Variable Size              31415926 bytes
Database Buffers          192937984 bytes
Redo Buffers                1235711 bytes
Database mounted.
Database opened.
```

From the prior output, the database startup operation goes through three distinct phases in opening an Oracle database:

1. Starting the instance

2. Mounting the database

3. Opening the database

You can step through these one at a time when you start your database. First, start the Oracle instance (background processes and memory structures):

```
SQL> startup nomount;
```

Next, mount the database. At this point, Oracle reads the control files:

```
SQL> alter database mount;
```

Finally, open the datafiles and online redo log files:

```
SQL> alter database open;
```

In most cases, you issue a STARTUP statement with no parameters to start your database. Table 2–5 describes the meanings of parameters that you can use with the database STARTUP statement.

Table 2–5. Parameters Available with the startup Command

Parameter	Meaning
FORCE	Shuts down the instance with ABORT before restarting it. Useful for troubleshooting startup issues. Not normally used.
RESTRICT	Only allows users with the RESTRICTED SESSION privilege to connect to the database.
PFILE	Specifies the client parameter file to be used when starting the instance.
QUIET	Suppresses the display of SGA information when starting the instance.
NOMOUNT	Starts background processes and allocates memory. Doesn't read control files.
MOUNT	Starts background processes, allocates memory, and reads the control files.
OPEN	Starts background processes, allocates memory, reads control files, and opens online redo logs and datafiles.
OPEN RECOVER	Attempts media recovery before opening the database.
OPEN READ ONLY	Opens the database in read-only mode.
UPGRADE	Used when upgrading a database.
DOWNGRADE	Used when downgrading a database.

Stopping the Database

Normally, you use the SHUTDOWN IMMEDIATE statement to stop a database. The IMMEDIATE parameter instructs Oracle to halt database activity and roll back any open transactions:

```
SQL> shutdown immediate;
Database closed.
Database dismounted.
ORACLE instance shut down.
```

For a detailed definition of the parameters available with the SHUTDOWN statement, refer to Table 2–6. In most cases, SHUTDOWN IMMEDIATE is an acceptable method of shutting down your database. If you issue the SHUTDOWN command with no parameters, it's equivalent to issuing SHUTDOWN NORMAL.

Table 2–6. Parameters Available with the SHUTDOWN Command

Parameter	Meaning
NORMAL	Wait for users to log out of active sessions before shutting down.
TRANSACTIONAL	Wait for transactions to finish, and then terminate the session.
TRANSACTIONAL LOCAL	Perform a transactional shutdown for local instance only.
IMMEDIATE	Terminate active sessions immediately. Open transactions are rolled back.
ABORT	Terminate the instance immediately. Transactions are terminated and aren't rolled back.

Starting and stopping your database is a fairly simple process. If the environment is set up correctly, you should be able to connect to your database and issue the appropriate STARTUP and SHUTDOWN statements.

■ Tip If you experience any issues with starting or stopping your database, look in the alert log for details. The alert log usually has a pertinent message regarding any problems.

You should rarely need to use the SHUTDOWN ABORT statement. Usually, SHUTDOWN IMMEDIATE is sufficient. Having said that, there's nothing wrong with using SHUTDOWN ABORT. If SHUTDOWN IMMEDIATE isn't working for any reason, then use SHUTDOWN ABORT.

On a few rare occasions, the SHUTDOWN ABORT statement doesn't work. In those situations, you can use ps -ef | grep smon to locate the Oracle system-monitor process, and then use the Linux/Unix kill command to terminate the instance. When you kill a required Oracle background process, this causes the instance to abort. Obviously, you should use an operating system kill command only as a last resort.

DATABASE VS. INSTANCE

Although DBAs often use the terms *database* and *instance* synonymously, these two terms refer to very different architectural components. In Oracle, the term *database* refers to the physical files that make up a database: the datafiles, online redo log files, and control files. The term *instance* refers to the background processes and memory structures.

For example, you can create an instance without having a database present. Before a database is physically created, you must start the instance with the STARTUP NOMOUNT statement. In this state, you have background processes and memory structures without any associated datafiles, online redo logs, or control files. The database files aren't created until you issue the CREATE DATABASE statement.

Another important point to remember is that an instance can only be associated with one database, whereas a database can be associated with many different instances (as with Oracle Real Application Clusters [RAC]). An instance can mount and open a database one time only. Each time you stop and start a database, a new instance is associated with it. Previously created background processes and memory structures are never associated with a database.

To demonstrate this concept, close a database with the ALTER DATABASE CLOSE statement:

```
SQL> alter database close;
```

If you attempt to restart the database, you receive an error:

```
SQL> alter database open;
ERROR at line 1:
ORA-16196: database has been previously opened and closed
```

This is because an instance can only ever mount and open one database. You must stop and start a new instance before you can mount and open the database.

Using a Response File to Create a Database

In some situations, you may want to use the Database Configuration Assistant (dbca) utility to create a database via a response file because using dbca in graphical mode isn't feasible. This may be due to slow networks or the unavailability of X software. To create a database using dbca in silent mode, perform the following steps:

1. Locate the dbca.rsp file.

2. Make a copy of the dbca.rsp file.

3. Modify the copy of the dbca.rsp file for your environment.

4. Run the dbca utility in silent mode.

First, navigate to the location in which you copied the Oracle database installation software, and use the find command to locate dbca.rsp:

```
$ find . -name dbca.rsp
./orainst/11.2.0.1/database/response/dbca.rsp
```

Copy the file so you're not modifying the original (so you always have a good original file):

```
$ cp dbca.rsp mydb.rsp
```

Now, edit the mydb.rsp file. You minimally need to modify the following parameters: GDBNAME, SID, SYSPASSWORD, SYSTEMPASSWORD, SYSMANPASSWORD, DBSNMPPASSWORD, DATAFILEDESTINATION, STORAGETYPE, CHARACTERSET, and NATIONALCHARACTERSET. Shown next is an example of modified values in the mydb.rsp file:

```
[CREATEDATABASE]
GDBNAME = "ORC11G"
SID = "ORC11G"
TEMPLATENAME = "General_Purpose.dbc"
SYSPASSWORD = "foo"
SYSTEMPASSWORD = "foo"
SYSMANPASSWORD = "foo"
DBSNMPPASSWORD = "foo"
DATAFILEDESTINATION ="/ora01/ORC11G"
STORAGETYPE="FS"
CHARACTERSET = "AL32UTF8"
NATIONALCHARACTERSET= "UTF8"
```

Next, run the dbca utility in silent mode using a response file:

```
$ dbca -silent -responseFile /ora01/orainst/11.2.0.1/database/response/mydb.rsp
```

You should see output such as

```
Copying database files
1% complete
...
Creating and starting Oracle instance
...
62% complete
Completing Database Creation
...
100% complete
Look at the log file
"/oracle/app/oracle/cfgtoollogs/dbca/ORC11G/ORC11G.log" for further details.
```

If you look in the log files, notice that the dbca utility uses the rman utility to restore the datafiles used for the database. Then, it creates the instance and performs post-installation steps. On a Linux server, you should also have an entry in the /etc/oratab file for your new database.

Many DBAs launch dbca and configure databases in GUI mode, but a few exploit the options available to them using the response file. With effective utilization of the response file, you can consistently automate the database-creation process. You can modify the response file to build databases on Automatic Storage Management (ASM) and even create RAC databases. In addition, you can control just about every aspect of the response file, similar to launching the dbca in graphical mode.

Dropping a Database

If you have an unused database that you need to drop, you can use the DROP DATABASE statement to accomplish this. Doing so removes all datafiles, control files, and online redo logs associated with the database.

Needless to say, use extreme caution when dropping a database. Before you drop a database, ensure that you're on the correct server and are connected to the correct database. On a Linux/Unix system, issue the following OS command from the operating system prompt:

```
$ uname -a
```

Next, connect to SQL*Plus, and be sure you're connected to the database you want to drop:

```
SQL> select name from v$database;
```

After you've verified that you're in the correct database environment, issue the following SQL commands from a SYSDBA privileged account:

```
SQ> shutdown immediate;
SQL> startup mount exclusive restrict;
SQL> drop database;
```

■ **Caution** Obviously, you should be careful when dropping a database. You *aren't* prompted when dropping the database and, as of this writing, there is no UNDROP ACCIDENTALLY DROPPED DATABASE command. Use *extreme* caution when dropping a database, because this operation removes datafiles, control files, and online redo log files.

The DROP DATABASE command is useful when you have a database that needs to be removed. It may be a test database or an old database that is no longer used. The DROP DATABASE command doesn't remove old archive redo log files. You must manually remove those files with an operating system command (such as rm in Linux/Unix or del at the Windows command prompt). You can also instruct RMAN to remove archive redo log files.

How Many Databases on One Server?

Sometimes, when you're creating new databases, this question arises: How many databases should you put on one server? One extreme is to have only one database running on each database server. This architecture is illustrated in Figure 2-2, which shows two different database servers, each with its own installation of the Oracle binaries. This type of setup is profitable for the hardware vendor but in many environments isn't an economical use of resources.

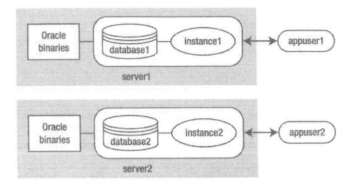

Figure 2–2. Architecture with one server per database

If you have enough memory, CPU, and disk resources, then you should consider creating multiple databases on one server. You can create a new installation of the Oracle binaries for each database or have multiple databases share one set of Oracle binaries. Figure 2–3 shows a configuration using one set of Oracle binaries that's shared by multiple databases on one server. Of course, if you have requirements for different versions of the Oracle binaries, you must have multiple Oracle homes to house those installations.

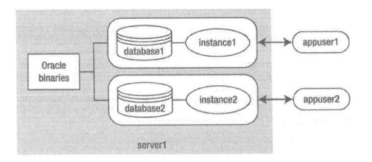

Figure 2–3. Multiple databases sharing one set of Oracle binaries on a server

If you don't have the CPU, memory, or disk resources to create multiple databases on one server, consider using one database to host multiple applications and users, as shown in Figure 2–4. In environments like this, be careful not to use public synonyms, because there may be collisions between applications. It's typical to create different schemas and tablespaces to be used by different applications in such environments.

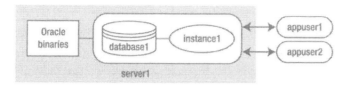

Figure 2–4. One database used by multiple applications and users

You must consider several architectural aspects when determining whether to use one database to host multiple applications and users:

- Do the applications generate vastly different amounts of redo, which may necessitate differently sized online redo logs?

- Are the queries used by applications dissimilar enough to require different amounts of undo, sorting space, and memory sizes?

- Does the type of application require a different database block size, such as 8KB for an OLTP database and 32KB for a data warehouse?

- Are there any security, availability, replication, and performance requirements that require an application to be isolated?

- Does an application require any features available only in the Enterprise Edition of Oracle?

- Does an application require the use of any special Oracle features such as Data Guard, partitioning, Streams, or RAC?

- What are the backup and recovery requirements for each application? Does one application require online backups and the other application not? Does one application require tape backups?

- Is any application dependent on an Oracle database version? Will there be different database upgrade schedules and requirements?

Table 2–7 describes the advantages and disadvantages of these architectural considerations regarding how to use Oracle databases and applications.

Table 2-7. Oracle Database Configuration Advantages and Disadvantages

Configuration	Advantages	Disadvantages
One database per server	Dedicated resources for the application using the database. Completely isolates applications from each other.	Most expensive. Requires more hardware.
Multiple databases and Oracle homes per server	Requires fewer servers.	Multiple databases competing for disk, memory, and CPU resources.
Multiple databases and one installation of Oracle binaries on the server	Requires fewer servers. Doesn't require multiple installations of the Oracle binaries.	Multiple databases competing for disk, memory, and CPU resources.
One database and one Oracle home serving multiple applications	Least expensive.	Multiple databases competing for disk, memory, and CPU resources. Multiple applications dependent on one database. One single point of failure.

Summary

After you've installed the Oracle binaries, you can create a database. Before creating a database, make sure you've correctly set the required operating system variables. You also need an initialization file and need to pre-create any necessary directories. You should carefully think about which initialization parameters should be set to a nondefault value. In general, I try to use as many default values as possible and only change an initialization parameter when there's a good reason.

This chapter focused on using SQL*Plus to create databases. This is an efficient and repeatable method for creating a database. When you're crafting a CREATE DATABASE statement, consider the size of the datafiles and online redo logs. You should also put some thought into how many groups of online redo logs you require and how many members per group.

I've worked in some environments where management dictated the requirement of one database per server. Usually that is overkill. A fast server with large memory areas and many CPUs should be capable of hosting several different databases. You have to determine what architecture meets your business requirements when deciding how many databases to place on one box.

After you've created a database, the next step is to configure the environment so you can efficiently navigate, operate, and monitor the database. These tasks are described in the next chapter.

■ ■ ■

## CHAPTER 3

Configuring an Efficient Environment

After you install the Oracle binaries and create a database, you should configure your environment to enable you to operate efficiently. Regardless of the functionality of graphical database administration tools, DBAs still need to perform many tasks from the operating system command line and manually execute SQL statements. A database administrator who takes advantage of the operating system and SQL has a clear advantage over a DBA who doesn't.

In any database environment (Oracle, MySQL, and so on), an effective DBA uses advanced operating system features to enable quick directory navigation, locating files, repeating commands, displaying system bottlenecks, and so forth. To achieve this efficiency, you must be knowledgeable of the operating system that houses the database.

In addition to being proficient with the operating system, you must also be skillful with the SQL interface into the database. Although you can glean much diagnostic information from graphical interfaces, SQL enables you to take a deeper dive into the internals to do advanced troubleshooting and derive database intelligence.

This chapter lays the foundation for efficient use of the OS and SQL to manage your databases. You can use the following operating system and database features to configure your environment for effectiveness:

- Operating system variables

- Shell aliases

- Shell functions

- Shell scripts

- SQL scripts

When you're in a stressful situation, it's paramount to have an environment that quickly enables you to know where you are and what accounts you're using, and to have tools that enable you to quickly identify problems. The techniques described in this chapter are like levers: they provide leverage to quickly do large amounts of work. These tools let you focus on the issues you may be facing instead of verifying your location or worrying about command syntax.

This chapter begins by detailing operating system techniques for enabling maximum efficiency. Later sections show how you can use these tools to automatically display environment details, navigate the file system, proactively monitor the database, and triage.

> ■ **Tip** Consistently use one operating system shell when working on your database servers. I recommend that you use the Bash shell; it contains all of the most useful features from the other shells (Korn and C), plus it has additional features that add to its ease of use.

Customizing Your Operating System Command Prompt

Typically, DBAs work with multiple servers and multiple databases. In these situations, you may have numerous terminals sessions open on your screen. You can run the following types of commands to identify your current working environment:

```
$ hostname -a
$ id
$ who am i
$ echo $ORACLE_SID
$ pwd
```

To avoid confusion about which server you're working on, it's often desirable to configure your command prompt to display information regarding its environment, such as the machine name and database SID. In this example, the command prompt name is customized to include the hostname, user, and Oracle SID:

```
$ PS1='[\h:\u:${ORACLE_SID}]$ '
```

The \h specifies the hostname. The \u specifies the current operating system user. $ORACLE_SID contains the current setting for your Oracle instance identifier. Here is what the command prompt now looks like for this example:

```
[ora03:oracle:devdb1]$
```

The command prompt contains three pieces of important information about the environment: server name, operating system user name, and database name. When you're navigating among multiple environments, setting the command prompt can be an invaluable tool for keeping track of where you are and what environment you're in.

If you want the operating system prompt automatically configured when you log in, then you need to set it in a startup file. In a Bash shell environment, you typically use the .bashrc file. This file is normally located in your HOME directory. Place the following line of code in .bashrc:

```
PS1='[\h:\u:${ORACLE_SID}]$ '
```

When you place this line of code in the startup file, then any time you log in to the server, your operating system prompt is set automatically for you. In other shells, such as the Korn shell, the .profile file is the startup file.

Depending on your personal preference, you may want to modify the command prompt for your particular needs. For example, many DBAs like the current working directory displayed in the command prompt. To display the current working directory information, add the \w variable:

```
$ PS1='[\h:\u:\w:${ORACLE_SID}]$ '
```

As you can imagine, a wide variety of options are available for the information shown in the command prompt. Here's another popular format:

```
$ PS1='[\u@${ORACLE_SID}@\h:\w]$ '
```

Table 3–1 lists many of the Bash shell variables you can use to customize the operating system command prompt.

Table 3–1. Bash Shell Backslash-Escaped Variables Used for Customizing the Command Prompt

Variable	Description
\a	ASCII bell character
\d	Date in "weekday month date" format
\h	Hostname
\e	ASCII escape character
\j	Number of jobs managed by the shell
\l	Base name of the shell's terminal device
\n	Newline
\r	Carriage return
\s	Name of the shell
\t	Time in 24-hour HH:MM:SS format
\T	Time in 12-hour HH:MM:SS format
\@	Time in 12-hour a.m./p.m. format
\A	Time in 24-hour HH:MM format
\u	Current shell
\v	Version of the Bash shell
\V	Release of the Bash shell
\w	Current working directory
\W	Base name of the current working directory
\!	History number of command
\$	If the effective UID is 0, then displays #; otherwise, displays $

The variables available for use with your command prompt vary somewhat by operating system and shell. For example, in a Korn shell environment, the hostname variable displays the server name in the operating system prompt:

```
$ export PS1="[`hostname`]$ "
```

Customizing Your SQL Prompt

DBAs often use SQL*Plus to perform daily administrative tasks. Often, you'll work on servers that contain multiple databases. Obviously, each database contains multiple user accounts. When connected to a database, you can run the following commands to verify your username and database connection:

```
SQL> show user;
SQL> select name from v$database;
```

A more efficient way to determine your username and SID is to set your SQL prompt to display that information. For example:

```
SQL> SET SQLPROMPT '&_USER.@&_CONNECT_IDENTIFIER.> '
```

An even more efficient way to configure your SQL prompt is to have it automatically run the SET SQLPROMPT command when you log in to SQL*Plus. Follow these steps to fully automate this:

1. Create a file named login.sql, and place in it the SET SQLPROMPT command.

2. Set your SQLPATH operating system variable to include the directory location of login.sql. In this example, the SQLPATH operating system variable is set in the .bashrc operating system file, which is executed each time a new shell is logged in to or started. Here is the entry:

```
export SQLPATH=$HOME/scripts
```

3. Create a file named login.sql in the HOME/scripts directory. Place the following line in the file:

```
SET SQLPROMPT '&_USER.@&_CONNECT_IDENTIFIER.> '
```

4. To see the result, you can either log out and log back in to your server, or source the .bashrc file directly:

```
$ . ./.bashrc
```

Now, log in to SQL. Here is an example of what the SQL*Plus prompt looks like:

```
SYS@devdb1>
```

If you connect to a different user, this should be reflected in the prompt:

```
SQL> conn system/foo
```

The SQL*Plus prompt now displays

```
SYSTEM@devdb1
```

Setting your SQL prompt is an easy way to remind yourself which environment and user you're currently connected as. This will help prevent you from accidentally running a SQL statement in the wrong environment. The last thing you want is to think you're in a development environment, and then discover that you've run a script to delete objects while connected in a production environment.

Table 3–2 contains a complete list of SQL*Plus variables that you can use to customize your prompt.

Table 3-2. Predefined SQL*Plus Variables

Variable	Description
_CONNECT_IDENTIFIER	Connection identifier, such as the Oracle SID
_DATE	Current date
_EDITOR	Editor used by the SQL EDIT command
_O_VERSION	Oracle version
_O_RELEASE	Oracle release
_PRIVILEGE	Privilege level of the current connected session
_SQLPLUS_RELEASE	SQL*Plus release number
_USER	Current connected user

Creating Shortcuts for Frequently Used Commands

In Linux/Unix environments, you can use two common methods to create shortcuts to other commands: create aliases for often-repeated commands, and use functions to create a shortcut for a group of commands. The following sections describe ways you can use these two techniques.

Using Aliases

You'll often need to navigate to various directories on a server. For example, one such location is the database background process-logging directory. To navigate to this directory, you have to type something similar to this:

```
$ cd /ora01/app/oracle/admin/O10R24/bdump
```

You can use the alias command to create a shortcut to accomplish the same task. An *alias* is a simple mechanism for creating a short piece of text that executes other shell commands. This example creates an alias named bdump that changes directories to a background location that is dependent on the value of the ORACLE_SID variable:

```
$ alias bdump='cd /ora01/app/oracle/admin/$ORACLE_SID/bdump'
```

Now you can type bdump, which does the same thing as changing your current working directory to the Oracle background dump directory.

To show all aliases that have been defined, use the alias command with no arguments:

```
$ alias
```

Listed next are some common examples of alias definitions you can use:

```
alias l.='ls -d .*'
```

```
alias ll='ls -l'
alias lsd='ls -altr | grep ^d'
alias bdump='cd /ora01/app/oracle/admin/$ORACLE_SID/bdump'
alias sqlp='sqlplus "/ as sysdba"'
alias shutdb='echo "shutdown immediate;" | sqlp'
alias startdb='echo "startup;" | sqlp'
```

If you want to remove an alias definition from your current environment, use the unalias command. The following example removes the alias for lsd:

```
$ unalias lsd
```

Using a Function

You can also use a function to create command shortcuts. The following line of code creates a simple function named bdump:

```
$ function bdump { cd /ora01/app/oracle/admin/$ORACLE_SID/bdump; }
```

You can now type bdump at the command line to change your working directory to the Oracle background dump directory.

Using functions is usually preferable over using aliases. Functions are more powerful than aliases because of features such as the ability to operate on parameters passed in on the command line, and allowing for complex coding.

To demonstrate the power of functions, consider a scenario in which you have different versions of databases installed on a server, and the background-dump destination differs depending on the version. With a function, you can build in the logic that checks to see which version of the database you're using and navigates accordingly:

```
function bdump {
echo $ORACLE_HOME | grep 11 >/dev/null
if [ $? -eq 0 ]; then
  lower_sid=$(echo $ORACLE_SID | tr '[:upper:]' '[:lower:]')
  cd $ORACLE_BASE/diag/rdbms/$lower_sid/$ORACLE_SID/trace
else
  cd $ORACLE_BASE/admin/$ORACLE_SID/bdump
fi
} # bdump
```

The previous lines of function code would be difficult to replicate using an alias. With functions, you can code as much logic as you need and pass in variables if required.

DBAs commonly establish functions by setting them in the HOME/.bashrc file. A better way to manage functions is to create a file that stores only function code, and call that file from the .bashrc file. It's also better to store special-purpose files in directories that you've created for these files. For example, create a directory named bin under HOME; in the bin directory, create a file named dba_fcns; and place in it your function code. Now, call the dba_fcns file from the .bashrc file. Here is an example of an entry in a .bashrc file:

. $HOME/bin/dba_fcns

Listed next is a small sample of some of the types of functions you can use:

```
#-----------------------------------------------------------#
# find largest files below this point
function flf {
  find . -ls | sort -nrk7 | head -10
}
#-----------------------------------------------------------#
# find largest directories consuming space below this point
function fld {
  du -S . | sort -nr | head -10
}
#-------------------------------------------
# view alert log
  function valert {
    echo $ORACLE_HOME | grep 11 >/dev/null
    if [ $? -eq 0 ]; then
      lower_sid=$(echo $ORACLE_SID | tr '[:upper:]' '[:lower:]')
      view $ORACLE_BASE/diag/rdbms/$lower_sid/$ORACLE_SID/trace/alert_$ORACLE_SID.log
    else
      view $ORACLE_BASE/admin/$ORACLE_SID/bdump/alert_$ORACLE_SID.log
    fi
  } # valert
#-----------------------------------------------------------#
```

If you ever wonder whether a shortcut is an alias or a function, use the type command to verify a command's origin. This example verifies that bdump is a function:

```
$ type bdump
```

Here is the output:

```
bdump is a function
bdump ()
{
    echo $ORACLE_HOME | grep 11;
    if [ $? -eq 0 ]; then
        lower_sid=$(echo $ORACLE_SID | tr '[:upper:]' '[:lower:]');
        cd $ORACLE_BASE/diag/rdbms/$lower_sid/$ORACLE_SID/trace;
    else
        cd $ORACLE_BASE/admin/$ORACLE_SID/bdump;
    fi
}
```

Rerunning Commands Quickly

When there are problems with a database server, you need to be able to quickly run commands from the operating system prompt. You may be having some sort of performance issue and want to run commands that navigate you to directories that contain log files, or you may want to display the top consuming processes from time to time. In these situations, you don't want to waste time having to retype command sequences.

One timesaving feature of the Bash shell is that it has several methods for editing and rerunning previously executed commands. The following list highlights several options available for manipulating previously typed commands:

- Scrolling with the up and down arrow keys

- Using Ctrl+P and Ctrl+N

- Listing the command history

- Searching in reverse

- Setting the command editor

Each of these techniques is described briefly in the following sections.

Scrolling with the Up and Down Arrow Keys

You can use the up arrow to scroll up through your recent command history. As you scroll through previously run commands, you can rerun a desired command by pressing the Enter or Return key.

If you want to edit a command, use the Backspace key to erase characters, or use the left arrow to navigate to the desired location in the command text. After you've scrolled up through command stack, use the down arrow to scroll back down through previously viewed commands.

▪ **Note** If you're familiar with Windows, scrolling through the command stack is similar to using the DOSKEY utility.

Pressing Ctrl+P and Ctrl+N

The Ctrl+P keystroke (pressing the Ctrl and P keys at the same time) displays your previously entered command. If you've pressed Ctrl+P several times, you can scroll back down the command stack by pressing Ctrl+N (pressing the Ctrl and N keys at the same time).

Listing the Command History

You can use the history command to display commands that the use previously entered:

```
$ history
```

Depending on how many commands have previously been executed, you may see a lengthy stack. You can limit the output to the last n number of commands by providing a number with the command. For example, the following lists the last five commands that were run:

```
$ history 5
```

Here is some sample output:

```
273  cd -
274  grep -i ora alert.log
275  ssh -Y -l oracle 65.217.177.98
276  pwd
277  history 5
```

To run a previously listed command in the output, use an exclamation point (!, sometimes called the *bang*) followed by the history number. In this example, to run the pwd command on line 276, use ! as follows:

```
$ !276
```

To run the last command you ran, use !!, as shown here:

```
$ !!
```

Searching in Reverse

Press Ctrl+R, and you're presented with the Bash shell reverse-search utility:

```
$ (reverse-i-search)`':
```

From the reverse-i-search prompt, as you type each letter, the tool automatically searches through previously run commands that have text similar to the string you entered. As soon as you're presented with the desired command match, you can rerun the command by pressing the Enter or Return key. To view all commands that match a string, press Ctrl+R repeatedly. To exit the reverse search, press Ctrl+C.

Setting the Command Editor

You can use the set -o command to make your command-line editor be either vi or emacs. This example sets the command-line editor to be vi:

```
$ set -o vi
```

Now, when you press Esc+K, you're placed in a mode where you can use vi commands to search through the stack of previously entered commands.

For example, if you want to scroll up the command stack, you can use the K key; and similarly, you can scroll down using the J key. When in this mode, you can use the slash (/) key and then type a string to be searched for in the entire command stack.

▓ **Tip** Before you attempt to use the command editor feature, be sure you're thoroughly familiar with either the vi or emacs editor.

A short example will illustrate the power of this feature. Say you know that you ran the ls -altr command about an hour ago. You want to run it again, but this time without the r (reverse-sort) option. To enter the command stack, press Esc+K:

```
$ Esc+K
```

You should now see the last command you executed. To search the command stack for the ls command, type /ls and then press Enter or Return:

```
$ /ls
```

The most recently executed ls command appears at the prompt:

```
$ ls -altr
```

To remove the r option, use the right arrow key to place the prompt over the r on the screen, and press X to remove the r from the end of the command. After you've edited the command, press the Enter or Return key to execute it.

Developing Standard Scripts

I've worked in shops where the database administration team developed hundreds of scripts and utilities to help manage an environment. One company had a small squad of DBAs whose job function was to maintain the environmental scripts. I think that's overkill. I tend to use a small set of focused scripts, where each script is usually less than 50 lines long. If you develop a script that another DBA can't understand or maintain, then it's probably too complicated.

■ **Note** All the scripts in this chapter are available for download from the Apress web site at www.apress.com. Go to the catalog page for this book. Look for the Source Code link under the book's cover image.

This section contains several short shell functions, shell scripts, and SQL scripts that can help you manage a database environment. This is by no means a complete list of scripts—rather, it provides a starting point you can build on. Each subsection heading is the name of a script.

■ **Note** Before you attempt to run a shell script, ensure that it's executable. Use the chmod command to achieve this: chmod 750 <script>

---

dba_setup

Usually, you'll set a common set of operating system variables and aliases in the same manner for every database server. When navigating among servers, you should set these variables and aliases in a consistent and repeatable manner. Doing so helps you (or your team) efficiently operate in every environment. For example, it's extremely useful to have the operating system prompt set in a consistent way when you work with dozens of different servers. This helps you quickly identify what box you're on, which OS user you're logged in as, and so on.

One technique is to store these standard settings in a script and then have that script executed automatically when you log in to a server. I usually create a script named dba_setup to set these operating system variables and aliases. You can place this script in a directory like HOME/bin and automatically execute the script via a startup script (covered later in this chapter in the "Organizing Scripts" section). Here are the contents of a typical dba_setup script:

```
# set prompt
PS1='[\h:\u:${ORACLE_SID}]$ '
#
export EDITOR=vi
export VISUAL=$EDITOR
export SQLPATH=$HOME/scripts
set -o vi
#
# list directories only
alias lsd="ls -p | grep /"
# show top cpu consuming processes
alias topc="ps -e -o pcpu,pid,user,tty,args | sort -n -k 1 -r | head"
# show top memory consuming processes
alias topm="ps -e -o pmem,pid,user,tty,args | sort -n -k 1 -r | head"
#
alias sqlp='sqlplus "/ as sysdba"'
alias shutdb='echo "shutdown immediate;" | sqlp'
alias startdb='echo "startup;" | sqlp'
```

dba_fcns

Use this script to store operating system functions that help you navigate and operate in your database environment. Functions tend to have more functionality than aliases. You can be quite creative with the number and complexity of functions you use. The idea is that you want a consistent and standard set of functions that you can call, no matter which database server you're logged onto.

For example, you may often need to navigate to the directory where the database alert log is located. If you work in environments that contain multiple versions of Oracle, the alert log location varies by database version. Contained in the next script is a function that determines whether you're in an Oracle Database 11g environment (or not) and navigates you to the appropriate location of the alert log. You can establish the functions by manually running the script like this:

```
$ . dba_fcns
```

Now you have a function named bdump that you can execute:

```
$ bdump
```

For this environment, the function changed my directory to this:

```
/oracle/app/oracle/diag/rdbms/o11r2/O11R2/trace
```

Place this script in a directory such as HOME/bin. Usually, you'll have this script automatically called when you log in to a server via a startup script (covered later, in the "Organizing Scripts" section). Here are some typical functions you can use:

```
#-------------------------------------------------------------#
# show environment variables in sorted list
  function envs {
    if test -z "$1"
      then /bin/env | /bin/sort
      else /bin/env | /bin/sort | /bin/grep -i $1
    fi
  } # envs
#-------------------------------------------------------------#
# login to sqlplus
  function sp {
    time sqlplus "/ as sysdba"
  } # sp
#-------------------------------------------------------------#
# find largest files below this point
function flf {
  find . -ls | sort -nrk7 | head -10
}
#-------------------------------------------------------------#
# find largest directories consuming space below this point
function fld {
  du -S . | sort -nr | head -10
}
#-------------------------------------------------------------#
# cd to bdump
  function bdump {
    echo $ORACLE_HOME | grep 11 >/dev/null
    if [ $? -eq 0 ]; then
      lower_sid=$(echo $ORACLE_SID | tr '[:upper:]' '[:lower:]')
      cd $ORACLE_BASE/diag/rdbms/$lower_sid/$ORACLE_SID/trace
    else
      cd $ORACLE_BASE/admin/$ORACLE_SID/bdump
    fi
  } # bdump
#-------------------------------------------------------------#
# view alert log
  function valert {
    echo $ORACLE_HOME | grep 11 >/dev/null
    if [ $? -eq 0 ]; then
      lower_sid=$(echo $ORACLE_SID | tr '[:upper:]' '[:lower:]')
      view $ORACLE_BASE/diag/rdbms/$lower_sid/$ORACLE_SID/trace/alert_$ORACLE_SID.log
    else
      view $ORACLE_BASE/admin/$ORACLE_SID/bdump/alert_$ORACLE_SID.log
    fi
  } # valert
#-------------------------------------------------------------#
```

tbsp_chk.bsh

This script checks to see if any tablespaces are surpassing a certain fullness threshold. Store this script in a directory like HOME/bin. Make sure you modify the script to contain the correct username, password, and e-mail address for your environment.

You also need to establish the required operating system variables such as ORACLE_SID and ORACLE_HOME. You can either hard-code those variables into the script or call a script that sources the variables for you. The next script calls a script named oraset that establishes the operating system variables. The details of this script are covered in Chapter 2. You don't have to use this script—the idea is to have a consistent and repeatable way of establishing operating system variables for your environment.

You can run this script from the command line. For example, I passed it the database name (O11R2) and wanted to see what tablespaces had less than 20% space left:

```
$ tbsp_chk.bsh O11R2 20
```

The output indicates that two tablespaces for this database have less than 20% space left:

```
space not okay
0 % free UNDOTBS1, 17 % free SYSAUX,
```

Here are the contents of the tbsp_chk.bsh script:

```
#!/bin/bash
#
if [ $# -ne 2 ]; then
  echo "Usage: $0 SID threshold"
  exit 1
fi
# either hard code OS variables or source them from a script.
# see Chapter 2 for details on the oraset script
# source oracle OS variables
. /var/opt/oracle/oraset $1
#
crit_var=$(
sqlplus -s <<EOF
system/foo
SET HEAD OFF TERM OFF FEED OFF VERIFY OFF
COL pct_free FORMAT 999
SELECT (f.bytes/a.bytes)*100 pct_free,'% free',a.tablespace_name||','
FROM
(SELECT NVL(SUM(bytes),0) bytes, x.tablespace_name
FROM dba_free_space y, dba_tablespaces x
WHERE x.tablespace_name = y.tablespace_name(+)
AND x.contents != 'TEMPORARY' AND x.status != 'READ ONLY'
AND x.tablespace_name  NOT LIKE 'UNDO%'
GROUP BY x.tablespace_name) f,
(SELECT SUM(bytes) bytes, tablespace_name
FROM dba_data_files
GROUP BY tablespace_name) a
WHERE a.tablespace_name = f.tablespace_name
AND  (f.bytes/a.bytes)*100 <= $2
ORDER BY 1;
EXIT;
EOF)
if [ "$crit_var" = "" ]; then
  echo "space okay"
else
  echo "space not okay"
  echo $crit_var
```

```
  echo $crit_var | mailx -s "tbsp getting full on $1" dkuhn@gmail.com
fi
exit 0
```

Usually, you run a script like this automatically on a periodic basis from a scheduling utility such as cron. Here is a typical cron entry that runs the script once an hour:

```
# Tablespace check
2 * * * * /orahome/bin/tbsp_chk.bsh INVPRD 10 1>/orahome/bin/log/tbsp_chk.log 2>&1
```

This cron entry runs the job and stores any informational output in the tbsp_chk.log file.

conn.bsh

You need to be alerted if there are issues with connecting to databases. This script checks to see if a connection can be established to the database. If a connection can't be established, an e-mail is sent. Place this script in a directory such as HOME/bin. Make sure you modify the script to contain the correct username, password, and e-mail address for your environment.

You also need to establish the required operating system variables such as ORACLE_SID and ORACLE_HOME. You can either hard-code those variables into the script or call a script that sources the variables for you. Like the previous script, this script calls a script named oraset that establishes the operating system variables. (See Chapter 2.)

The script requires that the ORACLE_SID be passed to it. For example:

```
$ conn.bsh INVPRD
```

If the script can establish a connection to the database, the following message is displayed:

```
success
db ok
```

Here are the contents of the conn.bsh script:

```
#!/bin/bash
if [ $# -ne 1 ]; then
  echo "Usage: $0 SID"
  exit 1
fi
# either hard code OS variables or source them from a script.
# see Chapter 2 for details on the oraset script
# source oracle OS variables
. /var/opt/oracle/oraset $1
#
echo "select 'success' from dual;" | sqlplus -s darl/foo@INVPRD | grep success
if [[ $? -ne 0 ]]; then
  echo "problem with $1" | mailx -s "db problem" dkuhn@sun.com
else
  echo "db ok"
fi
#
exit 0
```

This script is usually automated via a utility such as cron. Here's a typical cron entry:

```
# Check to connect to db.
45 * * * * /orahome/bin/conn.bsh INVPRD 1>/orahome/bin/log/conn.log 2>&1
```

This cron entry runs the script once per hour. Depending on your availability requirements, you may want to run a script like this on a more frequent basis.

filesp.bsh

Use the following script to check for an operating mount point that is filling up. Place the script in a directory such as HOME/bin. You need to modify the script so that the mntlist variable contains a list of mount points that exist on your database server. Because this script isn't running any Oracle utilities, there is no reason to set the Oracle-related operating system variables (as with the previous shell scripts):

```
#!/bin/bash
mntlist="/orahome /oraredo /oraarch /ora01 /oradump01 /"
for ml in $mntlist
do
echo $ml
usedSpc=$(df -h $ml | awk '{print $5}' | grep -v capacity | cut -d "%" -f1 -)
BOX=$(uname -a | awk '{print $2}')
#
case $usedSpc in
[0-9])
arcStat="relax, lots of disk space: $usedSpc"
;;
[1-7][0-9])
arcStat="disk space okay: $usedSpc"
;;
[8][0-9])
arcStat="space getting low: $usedSpc"
echo $arcStat | mailx -s "space on: $BOX" dkuhn@sun.com
;;
[9][0-9])
arcStat="warning, running out of space: $usedSpc"
echo $arcStat | mailx -s "space on: $BOX" dkuhn@sun.com
;;
[1][0][0])
arcStat="update resume, no space left: $usedSpc"
echo $arcStat | mailx -s "space on: $BOX" dkuhn@sun.com
;;
*)
arcStat="huh?: $usedSpc"
esac
#
BOX=$(uname -a | awk '{print $2}')
echo $arcStat
#
done
#
exit 0
```

You can run this script manually from the command line like this:

$ filesp.bsh

Here is the output for this database server:

```
/orahome
disk space okay: 56
/oraredo1
disk space okay: 17
/oraarch1
disk space okay: 37
/ora01
space getting low: 81
/oradump01
disk space okay: 29
/
disk space okay: 65
```

This is the type of script you should run on an automated basis from a scheduling utility such as cron. Here is a typical cron entry:

```
# Filesystem check
7 * * * * /orahome/bin/filesp.bsh 1>/orahome/bin/log/filesp.log 2>&1
```

login.sql

Use this script to customize aspects of your SQL*Plus environment. When logging in to SQL*Plus, in Linux/Unix, the login.sql script is automatically executed if it exists in a directory contained within the SQLPATH variable. If the SQLPATH variable hasn't been defined, then SQL*Plus looks for login.sql in the current working directory from which SQL*Plus was invoked. For example, here's how the SQLPATH variable is defined in my environment:

```
$ echo $SQLPATH
/home/oracle/scripts
```

Create the login.sql script in the /home/oracle/scripts directory. It contains the following lines:

```
-- set SQL prompt
SET SQLPROMPT '&_USER.@&_CONNECT_IDENTIFIER.> '
```

Now, when I log in to SQL*Plus, my prompt is automatically set:

```
$ sqlplus / as sysdba
SYS@O11R2>
```

top.sql

The following script lists the top CPU-consuming SQL processes. It's useful for identifying problem SQL statements. Place this script in a directory such as HOME/scripts:

```
select * from(
select
 sql_text
,buffer_gets
,disk_reads
,sorts
,cpu_time/1000000 cpu_sec
,executions
,rows_processed
```

```
from v$sqlstats
order by cpu_time DESC)
where rownum < 11;
```

Here's how you execute this script:

```
SQL> @top
```

Here is a small snippet of the output, showing a SQL statement that is consuming a large amount of database resources:

```
SQL_TEXT
--------------------------------------------------------------------------
insert into reg_queue (registration_urn,registration_data,client_ip_addr, relay_
BUFFER_GETS DISK_READS      SORTS   CPU_SEC EXECUTIONS ROWS_PROCESSED
----------- ---------- ---------- ---------- ---------- ---------------
    6079221       2482      28309 986.704467     697494         997467
```

lock.sql

This script displays sessions that have locks on tables that are preventing other sessions from completing work. The script shows details about the blocking and waiting sessions. You should place this script in a directory such as HOME/scripts. Here are the contents of lock.sql:

```
select s1.username blkg_user, s1.machine blkg_ws, s1.sid blkg_sid,
       s2.username wait_user, s2.machine wait_ws, s2.sid wait_sid,
       lo.object_id blkd_obj_id, do.owner, do.object_name
from v$lock l1, v$session s1, v$lock l2, v$session s2,
     v$locked_object lo, dba_objects do
where s1.sid = l1.sid
  and s2.sid = l2.sid
  and l1.id1 = l2.id1
  and s1.sid = lo.session_id
  and lo.object_id = do.object_id
  and l1.block = 1
  and l2.request > 0;
```

The lock.sql script is useful for determining what session has a lock on an object and also for showing the blocked session. You can run this script from SQL*Plus as follows:

```
SQL> @lock.sql
```

Here is a partial listing of the output (truncated so that it fits on one page):

```
BLKG_USER  BLKG_WS              BLKG_SID WAIT_USER  WAIT_WS
---------- -------------------- ---------- ---------- --------------------
MV         ora03.regis.local          88 INV_APP    ora03.regis.local
```

users.sql

This script displays information about when users were created and whether their account is locked. The script is useful when you're troubleshooting connectivity issues. Place it in a directory such as HOME/scripts. Here is a typical users.sql script to display user account information:

```
SELECT
  username
 ,account_status
 ,lock_date
 ,created
FROM dba_users
ORDER BY username;
```

You can execute this script from SQL*Plus as follows:

```
SQL> @users.sql
```

Here is some sample output:

```
USERNAME              ACCOUNT_STATUS                   LOCK_DATE CREATED
--------------------  -------------------------------  --------- ---------
CLUSTERUSER           OPEN                                       09-MAY-10
DIP                   EXPIRED & LOCKED                 09-MAY-10 09-MAY-10
DP122764              LOCKED                           07-JAN-10 09-JUL-10
```

Organizing Scripts

When you have a set of scripts and utilities, you should organize them such that they're consistently implemented for each database server. Follow these steps to implement the preceding DBA utilities for each database server in your environment:

1. Create operating system directories in which to store the scripts.

2. Copy your scripts and utilities to the directories created in step 1.

3. Configure your startup file to initialize the environment.

The previous steps are detailed in the following subsections.

Step 1: Create Directories

Create a standard set of directories on each database server to store your custom scripts. A directory beneath the HOME directory of the oracle user is usually a good location. I usually create the following three directories:

- HOME/bin. Standard location for shell scripts that are run in an automated fashion (such as from cron).

- HOME/bin/log. Standard location for log files generated from the scheduled shell scripts.

- HOME/scripts. Standard location to store SQL scripts.

You can use the mkdir command to create the previous directories as follows:

```
$ mkdir -p $HOME/bin/log
$ mkdir $HOME/scripts
```

It doesn't matter where you place the scripts or what you name the directories, as long as you have a standard location so that when you navigate from server to server, you always find the same files in the same locations. In other words, it doesn't matter what the standard is, as long as you have a standard.

Step 2: Copy Files to Directories

Place your utilities and scripts in the appropriate directories. Copy the following files to the HOME/bin directory:

```
dba_setup
dba_fcns
tbsp_chk.bsh
conn.bsh
filesp.bsh
```

Place the following SQL scripts in the HOME/scripts directory:

```
login.sql
top.sql
lock.sql
users.sql
```

Step 3: Configure the Startup File

Place the following code in the .bashrc file or the equivalent startup file for the shell you use (.profile for the Korn shell). Here's an example of how to configure the .bashrc file:

```
# Source global definitions
if [ -f /etc/bashrc ]; then
        . /etc/bashrc
fi
#
# source oracle OS variables
. /var/opt/oracle/oraset <default_database>
#
# User specific aliases and functions
. $HOME/bin/dba_setup
. $HOME/bin/dba_fcns
```

Now, each time you log in to an environment, you have full access to all the operating system variables, aliases, and functions established in the dba_setup and dba_fcns files. If you don't want to log off and back on, then run the file manually using the . (dot) command. This command executes the lines contained within a file. The following example runs the .bashrc file:

```
$ . $HOME/.bashrc
```

The . instructs the shell to *source* the script. Sourcing tells the shell process you're currently logged on to, to inherit any variables set with an export command in an executed script. If you don't use the . notation, then the variables set within the script are visible only in the context of the subshell that is spawned when the script is executed.

▓ **Note** In the Bash shell, the `source` command is equivalent to the . (dot) command.

Summary

This chapter describes how to configure an efficient environment. This is especially important for DBAs who manage multiple databases on multiple servers. Regular maintenance and troubleshooting activities require you to log on directly to the database server. To promote efficiency and sanity, you should develop a standard set of operating system tools and SQL scripts that help you maintain multiple environments. You can use standard features of the OS to assist with navigating, repeating commands, showing system bottlenecks, quickly finding critical files, and so on.

The techniques for configuring a standard OS are especially useful when you're working on multiple servers with multiple databases. When you have multiple terminal sessions running simultaneously, it's easy to lose your bearings and forget which session is associated with a particular server and database. With just a small amount of setup, you can ensure that your OS prompt always shows information such as the host and database. Likewise, you can always set your SQL prompt to show the username and database connection. These techniques help ensure that you don't accidentally run a command or script in the wrong environment.

After you have installed the Oracle binaries, created a database, configured your environment, you are ready to perform additional database administration tasks such as creating tablespaces for the applications. The topic of tablespace creation and maintenance is described in the next chapter.

CHAPTER 4

■ ■ ■

Tablespaces and Datafiles

As you saw in Chapter 2, when you create a database, typically five tablespaces are created when you execute the CREATE DATABASE statement:

- SYSTEM

- SYSAUX

- UNDO

- TEMP

- USERS

A *tablespace* is a logical container that allows you to manage groups of datafiles. A tablespace has one more datafiles associated with it. A datafile can be associated with only one tablespace. In other words, a datafile can't be shared between two tablespaces. A *datafile* is the physical file that is created on disk. The datafile stores data for database objects such as tables and indexes. Figure 4–1 shows the logical constructs used to manage space in a database.

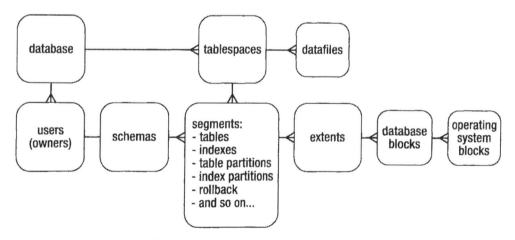

Figure 4–1. Relationships of logical storage objects and physical datafiles

The previously listed five tablespaces—SYSTEM, SYSAUX, UNDO, TEMP, and USERS—are the minimal set of storage containers you need to operate a database. As you open a database for use, you should quickly create additional tablespaces to store application data. This chapter discusses the purpose of the standard set of tablespaces, the need for additional tablespaces, and how to manage these critical database storage containers.

Understanding the First Five

The SYSTEM tablespace provides storage for the Oracle data-dictionary objects. This tablespace is where all objects owned by the SYS user are stored. The SYS user should be the only user that owns objects created in the SYSTEM tablespace.

Starting with Oracle Database 10g, the SYSAUX (system auxiliary) tablespace is created when you create the database. This is an auxiliary tablespace used as a data repository for Oracle database tools such as Enterprise Manager, Statspack, LogMiner, Logical Standby, and so on.

The UNDO tablespace stores the information required to roll back uncommitted data. This tablespace contains information about data as it existed before an insert, update, or delete statement (this is sometimes referred to as a *before image* copy of the data). This information is used to roll back uncommitted data in the event of a crash recovery and to provide read consistency for SQL statements.

Some Oracle SQL statements require a sort area, either in memory or on disk. For example, the results of a query may need to be sorted before being returned to the user. Oracle first uses memory to sort the query results; and when there isn't sufficient room in memory, the TEMP tablespace is used as a sorting area on disk. When you create a database, typically you create the TEMP tablespace and specify it to be the default temporary tablespace for any users you create.

The USERS tablespace is often used as a default permanent tablespace for table and index data for users. As shown in Chapter 2, you can create a default permanent tablespace for users when you create the database.

Understanding the Need for More

Although you could put every database user's data in the USERS tablespace, this usually isn't scalable or maintainable for any type of serious database application. Instead, it's more efficient to create additional tablespaces for application users. You typically create at least two tablespaces specific for each application using the database: one for the application table data and one for the application index data. For example, for the APP user, you can create tablespaces named APP_DATA and APP_INDEX for table and index data, respectively.

DBAs used to separate table and index data for performance reasons. The thinking was that separating table data from index data would reduce I/O contention. This is because each tablespace and associated datafiles could be placed on different disks with separate controllers.

With modern storage configurations that have multiple layers of abstraction between the application and the underlying physical storage devices, it's debatable whether you can realize any performance gains by creating multiple separate tablespaces. But there still are valid reasons for creating multiple tablespaces for table and index data:

- Backup and recovery requirements may be different for the tables and indexes.

- Indexes may have different storage requirements than the table data.

In addition to separate tablespaces for data and indexes, you sometimes create separate tablespaces for objects of different sizes. For example, if an application has very large tables, you can create an APP_DATA_LARGE tablespace that has a large extent size, and a separate APP_DATA_SMALL tablespace that has a smaller extent size.

Depending on your requirements, you should consider creating separate tablespaces for each application using the database. For example, for an inventory application, create INV_DATA and

INV_INDEX; and for an HR application, create HR_DATA and HR_INDEX. Here are some reasons to consider creating separate tablespaces for each application using the database:

- Applications may have different availability requirements. Separate tablespaces let you take tablespaces offline for one application while not affecting another application.

- Applications may have different backup and recovery requirements. Separate tablespaces let tablespaces be backed up and recovered independently.

- Applications may have different storage requirements. Separate tablespaces allow for different settings for extent sizes and segment management.

- You may have some data that is purely read only. Separate tablespaces let you put a tablespace that contains only read-only data into read-only mode.

This chapter focuses on the most common and critical tasks associated with creating and maintaining tablespaces and datafiles. The next section discusses creating tablespaces, and the chapter progresses to more advanced topics such as moving and renaming datafiles.

Creating Tablespaces

You use the CREATE TABLESPACE statement to create tablespaces. The Oracle SQL reference manual contains more than 12 pages of syntax and examples for creating tablespaces. In most scenarios, you need to use only a few of the features available, namely locally managed extent allocation, and automatic segment space management. The following code snippet demonstrates how to create a tablespace that utilizes the most common features:

```
create tablespace tools
  datafile '/ora01/dbfile/INVREP/tools01.dbf'
  size 100m
  extent management local
  uniform size 128k
  segment space management auto;
```

You need to modify this script for your environment. For example, the directory path, datafile size, and uniform extent size should be changed per environment requirements.

You create tablespaces as locally managed by using the EXTENT MANAGEMENT LOCAL clause. A locally managed tablespace uses a bitmap in the datafile to efficiently determine whether an extent is in use. The storage parameters NEXT, PCTINCREASE, MINEXTENTS, MAXEXTENTS, and DEFAULT aren't valid for extent options in locally managed tablespaces.

▪ Note A locally managed tablespace with uniform extents must be minimally sized for at least five database blocks per extent.

As you add data to objects in tablespaces, Oracle automatically allocates more extents to an associated tablespace datafile as needed to accommodate the growth. You can instruct Oracle to allocate a uniform size for each extent via the UNIFORM SIZE [size] clause. If you don't specify a size, then the default uniform extent size is 1MB.

The uniform extent size that you use varies depending on the storage requirements of your tables and indexes. I usually create several tablespaces for a given application. For example, you can create one tablespace for small objects that has a uniform extent size of 512KB, one tablespace for medium-sized objects that has a uniform extent size of 4MB, one tablespace for large objects with a uniform extent size of 16MB, and so on.

Alternatively, you can specify that Oracle determine the extent size via the AUTOALLOCATE clause. Oracle allocates extent sizes of 64KB, 1MB, 8MB, or 64MB. Using AUTOALLOCATE is appropriate when you think objects in one tablespace will be of varying sizes.

The SEGMENT SPACE MANAGEMENT AUTO clause instructs Oracle to manage the space within the block. When you use this clause, there is no need to specify parameters such as PCTUSED, FREELISTS, and FREELIST GROUPS. The alternative to AUTO space management is MANUAL. When you use MANUAL, you can adjust the previously mentioned parameters depending on the needs of your application. I recommend that you use AUTO and not MANUAL. Using AUTO vastly reduces that number of parameters you'd otherwise need to configure and manage.

When a datafile fills up, you can instruct Oracle to automatically increase the size of the datafile with the AUTOEXTEND feature. I recommend that you don't use this feature. Instead, you should monitor tablespace growth and add space as necessary. Manually adding space is preferable to having a runaway SQL process that accidentally grows a tablespace until it has consumed all space on a mount point. If you inadvertently fill up a mount point that contains a control file or the Oracle binaries, you can hang your database.

If you do use the AUTOEXTEND feature, I recommend that you always specify a corresponding MAXSIZE so that a runaway SQL process doesn't accidentally fill up a tablespace that in turn fills up a mount point.

Here's an example of creating an autoextending tablespace with a cap on its maximum size:

```
create tablespace tools
  datafile '/ora01/dbfile/INVREP/tools01.dbf'
  size 100m
  autoextend on maxsize 1000m
  extent management local
  uniform size 128k
  segment space management auto;
```

When you're using CREATE TABLESPACE scripts in different environments, it's useful to be able to parameterize portions of the script. For example, in development, you may size the datafiles at 100MB, whereas in production the datafiles may be 1000GB. Use ampersand & variables to make CREATE TABLESPACE scripts more portable among environments.

The next listing defines ampersand variables at the top of the script, and those variables determine the sizes of datafiles created for the tablespaces:

```
define tbsp_large=5G
define tbsp_med=500M
--
create tablespace reg_data
  datafile '/ora01/oradata/INVREP/reg_data01.dbf'
  size &&tbsp_large
  extent management local
  uniform size 128k
  segment space management auto;
--
create tablespace reg_index
  datafile '/ora01/oradata/INVREP/reg_index01.dbf'
  size &&tbsp_med
  extent management local
  uniform size 128k
  segment space management auto;
```

Using ampersand variables allows you to modify the script once and have the variables reused throughout the script. You can parameterize all aspects of the script, including datafile mount points and extent sizes.

You can also pass the values of the ampersand variables in to the CREATE TABLESPACE script from the SQL*Plus command line. This lets you avoid hard-coding a specific size in the script and instead provide the sizes at runtime. To accomplish this, first define at the top of the script the ampersand variables to accept the values being passed in:

```
define tbsp_large=&1
define tbsp_med=&2
--
create tablespace reg_data
  datafile '/ora01/oradata/INVREP/reg_data01.dbf'
  size &&tbsp_large
  extent management local
  uniform size 128k
  segment space management auto;
--
create tablespace reg_index
  datafile '/ora01/oradata/INVREP/reg_index01.dbf'
  size &&tbsp_med
  extent management local
  uniform size 128k
  segment space management auto;
```

Now you can pass variables in to the script from the SQL*Plus command line. The following example executes a script named cretbsp.sql and passes in two values that set the ampersand variables to 5G and 500M, respectively:

```
SQL> @cretbsp 5G 500M
```

Table 4–1 summarizes the best practices for creating and managing tablespaces.

Table 4–1. Best Practices for Managing Tablespaces

Best Practice	Reasoning
Create separate tablespaces for different applications using the same database.	If a tablespace needs to be taken offline, it affects only one application.
For an application, separate table data from index data in different tablespaces.	Table and index data may have different storage requirements.
Don't use the AUTOALLOCATE feature for datafiles. If you do use AUTOALLOCATE, specify a maximum size.	Specifying a maximum size prevents a runaway SQL statement from filling up a storage device.
Create tablespaces as locally managed. You shouldn't create a tablespace as dictionary managed.	This provides better performance and manageability.
For a tablespace's datafile naming convention, use a name that contains the tablespace name followed by a two-digit number that's unique within datafiles for that tablespace.	Doing this makes it easy to identify which datafiles are associated with which tablespaces.

Best Practice	Reasoning
Try to minimize the number of datafiles associated with a tablespace.	You have fewer datafiles to manage.
In tablespace CREATE scripts, use ampersand variables to define aspects such as storage characteristics.	This makes scripts more reusable among various environments.

Renaming a Tablespace

Sometimes you need to rename a tablespace. You may want to do this because a tablespace was initially erroneously named, or you may want the tablespace name to better conform to your database naming standards. Use the ALTER TABLESPACE statement to rename a tablespace. This example renames a tablespace from FOOBAR to USERS:

```
SQL> alter tablespace foobar rename to users;
```

When you rename a tablespace, Oracle updates the name of the tablespace in the data dictionary, control files, and data headers. Keep in mind that renaming a tablespace doesn't rename any associated datafiles. Renaming datafiles is covered later in this chapter.

■ Note You can't rename the SYSTEM tablespace or the SYSAUX tablespace.

Controlling the Generation of Redo

For some types of applications, you may know beforehand that you can easily re-create the data. An example might be a data-warehouse environment where you perform direct path inserts or use SQL*Loader to load data. In these scenarios, you can turn off the generation of redo for direct path loading. You use the NOLOGGING clause to do this:

```
create tablespace inv_mgmt_data
  datafile '/ora02/dbfile/O11R2/inv_mgmt_data01.dbf'' size 100m
  extent management local
  uniform size 128k
  segment space management auto
  nologging;
```

If you have an existing tablespace and want to alter its logging mode, use the ALTER TABLESPACE statement:

```
SQL> alter tablespace inv_mgmt_data nologging;
```

You can confirm the tablespace logging mode by querying the DBA_TABLESPACES view:

```
SQL> select tablespace_name, logging from dba_tablespaces;
```

The generation of redo logging can't be suppressed for regular INSERT, UPDATE, and DELETE statements. For regular Data Manipulation Language (DML) statements, the NOLOGGING clause is ignored. The NOLOGGING clause does apply, however, to the following types of DML:

- Direct path INSERT statements
- Direct path SQL*Loader

The NOLOGGING clause also applies to the following types of DDL statements:

- CREATE TABLE ... AS SELECT
- ALTER TABLE ... MOVE
- ALTER TABLE ... ADD/MERGE/SPLIT/MOVE/MODIFY PARTITION
- CREATE INDEX
- ALTER INDEX ... REBUILD
- CREATE MATERIALIZED VIEW
- ALTER MATERIALIZED VIEW ... MOVE
- CREATE MATERIALIZED VIEW LOG
- ALTER MATERIALIZED VIEW LOG ... MOVE

Be aware that if redo isn't logged for a table or index, and you have a media failure before the object is backed up, then you can't recover the data. You receive an ORA-01578 error indicating that there is logical corruption of the data.

■ Note You can also override the tablespace level of logging at the object level. For example, even if a tablespace specified as NOLOGGING, you can create a table with the LOGGING clause.

Changing a Tablespace's Write Mode

In environments such as data warehouses, you may need to load data into tables and then never modify the data again. To enforce that all objects in a tablespace can't be modified, you can alter the tablespace to be read-only. To do this, use the ALTER TABLESPACE statement:

```
SQL> alter tablespace inv_mgmt_rep read only;
```

One advantage of a read-only tablespace is that you only have to back it up once. You should be able to restore the datafiles from a read-only tablespace no matter how long ago the backup was made.
If you need to modify the tablespace out of read-only mode, you do so as follows:

```
SQL> alter tablespace inv_mgmt_rep read write;
```

Make sure you re-enable backups of a tablespace after you place it in read/write mode.

■ **Note** You can't make a tablespace that contains active rollback segments read-only. For this reason, the SYSTEM tablespace can't be made read-only, because it contains the SYSTEM rollback segment.

In Oracle Database 11g and above, you can modify individual tables to be read-only. For example:

```
SQL> alter table my_tab read only;
```

While in read-only mode, you can't issue any insert, update, or delete statements against the table. Making individual tables read/write can be advantageous when you're doing maintenance (such as a data migration) when you want to ensure that users don't update the data.

This example modifies a table back to read/write mode:

```
SQL> alter table my_tab read write;
```

Dropping a Tablespace

If you have a tablespace that is unused, it's best to drop it so it doesn't clutter your database, consume unnecessary resources, and potentially confuse DBAs who aren't familiar with the database. Before dropping a tablespace, it's a good practice to first take it offline:

```
SQL> alter tablespace inv_data offline;
```

You may want to wait to see if anybody screams that an application is broken because it can't write to a table or index in the tablespace to be dropped. When you're sure the tablespace isn't required, drop the tablespace and delete its datafiles:

```
SQL> drop tablespace inv_data including contents and datafiles;
```

■ **Tip** You can drop a tablespace whether it's online or offline. The exception to this is the SYSTEM tablespace, which can't be dropped. It's always a good idea to take a tablespace offline before you drop it. By doing so, you can better determine if an application is using any objects in the tablespace. If you attempt to query a table in an offline tablespace, you receive an "ORA-00376: file can't be read at this time" error.

Dropping a tablespace using INCLUDING CONTENTS AND DATAFILES permanently removes the tablespace and any of its datafiles. Make certain the tablespace doesn't contain any data you want to keep before you drop it.

If you attempt to drop a tablespace that contains a primary key that is referenced by a foreign key associated with a table in a different tablespace (than the one you're trying to drop), you receive this error:

```
ORA-02449: unique/primary keys in table referenced by foreign keys
```

Run this query first to determine whether any foreign-key constraints will be affected:

```
select  p.owner,
        p.table_name,
        p.constraint_name,
        f.table_name referencing_table,
        f.constraint_name foreign_key_name,
        f.status fk_status
from    dba_constraints P,
        dba_constraints F,
        dba_tables T
where   p.constraint_name = f.r_constraint_name
and     f.constraint_type = 'R'
and     p.table_name = t.table_name
and     t.tablespace_name = UPPER('&tablespace_name')
order by 1,2,3,4,5;
```

If there are referenced constraints, you need to first drop the constraints or use the CASCADE CONSTRAINTS clause of the DROP TABLESPACE statement. This statement uses CASCADE CONSTRAINTS to automatically drop any affected constraints:

```
SQL> drop tablespace inv_data including contents and datafiles cascade constraints;
```

This statement drops any referential-integrity constraints from tables outside the tablespace being dropped that reference tables within the dropped tablespace.

If you drop a tablespace that has required objects in a production system, the results can be catastrophic. You must perform some sort of recovery to get the tablespace and its objects back. Needless to say, be very careful when dropping a tablespace. Table 4–2 lists recommendations to consider when you do this.

Table 4–2. Best Practices for Dropping Tablespaces

Best Practice	Reasoning
Before dropping a tablespace, run a script similar to this to determine if any objects exist in the tablespace: `select owner, segment_name, segment_type` `from dba_segments` `where tablespace_name=upper('&&tbsp_name');`	Doing this ensures that no tables or indexes exist in the tablespace before you drop it.
Consider renaming tables in a tablespace before you drop the tablespace.	If any applications are using tables within the tablespace to be dropped, the application throws an error when a required table is renamed.
If there are no objects in the tablespace, resize the associated datafiles to a very small number like 10MB.	Reducing the size of the datafiles to a miniscule amount of space quickly shows whether any applications are trying to access objects that require space in a tablespace.
Make a backup of your database before dropping a tablespace.	This ensures that you have a way to recover objects that are discovered to be in use after you drop the tablespace.

Best Practice	Reasoning
Take the tablespace and datafiles offline before you drop the tablespace. Use the ALTER TABLESPACE statement to take the tablespace offline.	This helps determine if any applications or users are using objects in the tablespaces. They can't access the objects if the tablespace and datafiles are offline.
When you're sure a tablespace isn't in use, use the DROP TABLESPACE ... INCLUDING CONTENTS AND DATAFILES statement.	This removes the tablespace and physically removes any datafiles associated with the tablespace. Some DBAs don't like this approach, but you should be fine if you've taken the necessary precautions.

Using Oracle Managed Files

The Oracle Managed File (OMF) feature automates many aspects of tablespace management, such as file placement, naming, and sizing. You control OMF by setting the following initialization parameters:

- DB_CREATE_FILE_DEST

- DB_CREATE_ONLINE_LOG_DEST_N

- DB_RECOVERY_FILE_DEST

If you set these parameters before you create the database, Oracle uses them for the placement of the datafiles, control files, and online redo logs. You can also enable OMF after your database has been created. Oracle uses the values of the initialization parameters for the locations of any newly added datafiles and online redo-log files. Oracle also determines the name of the newly added file.

The advantage of using OMF is that creating tablespaces is simplified. For example, the CREATE TABLESPACE statement doesn't need to specify anything other than the tablespace name. First, enable the OMF feature by setting the DB_CREATE_FILE_DEST parameter:

```
SQL> alter system set db_create_file_dest='/ora01/OMF';
```

Now, issue the CREATE TABLESPACE statement:

```
SQL> create tablespace inv1;
```

This statement creates a tablespace named INV1 with a default datafile size of 100MB. You can override the default by specifying a size:

```
SQL> create tablespace inv2 datafile size 20m;
```

One limitation of OMF is that you're limited to one directory for the placement of datafiles. If you want to add datafiles to a different directory, you can alter the location dynamically:

```
SQL> alter system set db_create_file_dest='/ora02/OMF';
```

Although this procedure isn't a huge deal, I find it easier not to use OMF. Most of the environments I've worked in have many mount points assigned for database use. You don't want to have to modify an initialization parameter every time you need a datafile added to a directory that isn't in the current definition of DB_CREATE_FILE_DEST. It's easier to issue a CREATE TABLESPACE statement or ALTER TABLESPACE statement that has the file-location and storage parameters in the script. It isn't cumbersome to provide directory names and filenames to the tablespace-management statements.

Creating a Bigfile Tablespace

The bigfile feature allows you to create a tablespace with a potentially very large datafile assigned to it. The advantage of using the bigfile feature is that you can create very large files. With an 8KB block size, you can create a datafile as large as 32TB. With a 32KB blocksize, you can create a datafile up to 128TB.

Use the BIGFILE clause to create a bigfile tablespace:

```
create bigfile tablespace inv_big_data
  datafile '/ora02/dbfile/O11R2/inv_big_data01.dbf'
  size 10g
  extent management local
  uniform size 128k
  segment space management auto;
```

As long as you have plenty of space associated with the filesystem supporting the bigfile tablespace datafile, you can store massive amounts of data in a tablespace.

One potential disadvantage of using a bigfile tablespace is that if for any reason you run out of space on a filesystem that supports the datafile associated with the bigfile, you can't expand the size of the tablespace (unless you can add space to the filesystem). You can't add more datafiles to a bigfile tablespace if they're placed on separate mount points. A bigfile tablespace allows only one datafile to be associated with it.

You can make the bigfile tablespace the default type of tablespace for a database using the ALTER DATABASE SET DEFAULT BIGFILE TABLESPACE statement. However, I don't recommend doing that. You could potentially create a tablespace, not know it was a bigfile tablespace (because you forgot it was the default, or you're a new DBA on the project and didn't realize it), and create a tablespace on a mount point. Then, when you discovered that you needed more space, you wouldn't know that you couldn't add another datafile on a different mount point for this tablespace because it was bigfile constrained.

Displaying Tablespace Size

DBAs often use monitoring scripts to alert them when they need to increase the space allocated to a tablespace. The following script displays the percentage of free space left in a tablespace and datafile:

```
SET PAGESIZE 100 LINES 132 ECHO OFF VERIFY OFF FEEDB OFF SPACE 1 TRIMSP ON
COMPUTE SUM OF a_byt t_byt f_byt ON REPORT
BREAK ON REPORT ON tablespace_name ON pf
COL tablespace_name FOR A17    TRU HEAD 'Tablespace|Name'
COL file_name       FOR A40    TRU HEAD 'Filename'
COL a_byt                FOR 9,990.999 HEAD 'Allocated|GB'
COL t_byt                FOR 9,990.999 HEAD 'Current|Used GB'
COL f_byt                FOR 9,990.999 HEAD 'Current|Free GB'
COL pct_free             FOR 990.0     HEAD 'File %|Free'
COL pf                   FOR 990.0     HEAD 'Tbsp %|Free'
COL seq NOPRINT
DEFINE b_div=1073741824
--
SELECT 1 seq, b.tablespace_name, nvl(x.fs,0)/y.ap*100 pf, b.file_name file_name,
  b.bytes/&&b_div a_byt, NVL((b.bytes-SUM(f.bytes))/&&b_div,b.bytes/&&b_div) t_byt,
  NVL(SUM(f.bytes)/&&b_div,0) f_byt, NVL(SUM(f.bytes)/b.bytes*100,0) pct_free
FROM dba_free_space f, dba_data_files b
 ,(SELECT y.tablespace_name, SUM(y.bytes) fs
   FROM dba_free_space y GROUP BY y.tablespace_name) x
```

```
,(SELECT x.tablespace_name, SUM(x.bytes) ap
   FROM dba_data_files x GROUP BY x.tablespace_name) y
WHERE f.file_id(+) = b.file_id
AND   x.tablespace_name(+) = y.tablespace_name
and   y.tablespace_name =  b.tablespace_name
AND   f.tablespace_name(+) = b.tablespace_name
GROUP BY b.tablespace_name, nvl(x.fs,0)/y.ap*100, b.file_name, b.bytes
UNION
SELECT 2 seq, tablespace_name,
   j.bf/k.bb*100 pf, b.name file_name, b.bytes/&&b_div a_byt,
   a.bytes_used/&&b_div t_byt, a.bytes_free/&&b_div f_byt,
   a.bytes_free/b.bytes*100 pct_free
FROM v$temp_space_header a, v$tempfile b
  ,(SELECT SUM(bytes_free) bf FROM v$temp_space_header) j
  ,(SELECT SUM(bytes) bb FROM v$tempfile) k
WHERE a.file_id = b.file#
ORDER BY 1,2,4,3;
```

If you don't have any monitoring in place, you're alerted via the SQL statement that is attempting to perform an insert or update operation that requires more space but isn't able to allocate more. For example:

```
ORA-01653: unable to extend table INVENTORY by 128 in tablespace INV_IDX
```

After you determine that a tablespace needs more space, you need to either increase the size of a datafile or add a datafile to a tablespace. These topics are discussed in the next section.

Altering Tablespace Size

When you've determined which datafile you want to resize, first make sure you have enough disk space to increase the size of the datafile on the mount point on which the datafile exists:

```
$ df -h | sort
```

Use the ALTER DATABASE DATAFILE ... RESIZE command to increase the datafile's size. This example resizes the datafile to 5GB:

```
SQL> alter database datafile '/ora01/oradata/INVREP/reg_data01.dbf' resize 5g;
```

If you don't have space on an existing mount point to increase the size of a datafile, then you must add a datafile. To add a datafile to an existing tablespace, use the ALTER TABLESPACE ... ADD DATAFILE statement:

```
SQL> alter tablespace reg_data
        add datafile '/ora01/dbfile/INVREP/reg_data02.dbf' size 100m;
```

If you have bigfile tablespaces, then you can't use the ALTER DATABASE ... DATAFILE statement to change the size of a tablespace's datafile. To resize the single datafile associated with a bigfile tablespace, you must use the ALTER TABLESPACE clause:

```
SQL> alter tablespace bigstuff resize 1T;
```

Resizing datafiles can be a daily task when you're managing databases with heavy transaction loads. Increasing the size of an existing datafile allows you to add space to a tablespace without adding more datafiles. If there isn't enough disk space left on the storage device that contains an existing datafile, you can add a datafile in a different location to an existing tablespace.

If you want to add space to a temporary tablespace, first query the V$TEMPFILE view to verify the current size and location of temporary datafiles:

```
SQL> select name, bytes from v$tempfile;
```

Next, use the TEMPFILE option of the ALTER DATABASE statement:

```
SQL> alter database tempfile '/ora01/oradata/INVREP/temp01.dbf' resize 500m;
```

You can also add a file to a temporary tablespace via the ALTER TABLESPACE statement:

```
SQL> alter tablespace temp add tempfile '/ora01/oradata/INVREP/temp02.dbf' size 5000m;
```

Toggling Datafiles Offline and Online

Sometimes, when you're performing maintenance operations (such as renaming datafiles), you may need to first take a datafile offline. You can use either the ALTER TABLESPACE or the ALTER DATABASE DATAFILE statement to toggle datafiles offline and online.

Use the ALTER TABLESPACE ... OFFLINE NORMAL statement to take a tablespace and its associated datafiles offline. You don't need to specify NORMAL, because it's the default:

```
SQL> alter tablespace users offline;
```

When you place a tablespace offline in normal mode, Oracle checkpoints the datafiles associated with the tablespace. This ensures that all modified blocks in memory that are associated with the tablespace are flushed and written to the datafiles. You don't need to perform media recovery when you bring the tablespace and its associated datafiles back online.

You can't use the ALTER TABLESPACE statement to place tablespaces offline when the database is in mount mode. If you attempt to take a tablespace offline while the database is mounted (but not open), you receive the following error:

```
ORA-01190: database not open
```

■ **Note** When in mount mode, you must use the ALTER DATABASE DATAFILE statement to take a datafile offline.

When taking a tablespace offline, you can also specify ALTER TABLESPACE ... OFFLINE TEMPORARY. In this scenario, Oracle checkpoints all datafiles associated with the tablespace that are online. Oracle doesn't checkpoint offline datafiles associated with the tablespace.

You can specify ALTER TABLESPACE ... OFFLINE IMMEDIATE when taking a tablespace offline. Your database must be in archivelog mode in this situation. When using OFFLINE IMMEDIATE, Oracle doesn't checkpoint the datafiles. You must perform media recovery on the tablespace before bringing it back online.

■ **Note** You can't take the SYSTEM or UNDO tablespace offline while the database is open.

You can also use the ALTER DATABASE DATAFILE statement to take a datafile offline. If your database is open for use, then it must be in archivelog mode in order for you to take a datafile offline with the ALTER DATABASE DATAFILE statement. If you attempt to take a datafile offline using the ALTER DATABASE DATAFILE statement, and your database isn't in archivelog mode, you receive the following error:

```
SQL> alter database datafile 6 offline;
ORA-01145: offline immediate disallowed unless media recovery enabled
```

If your database isn't in archivelog mode, you must specify ALTER DATABASE DATAFILE ... OFFLINE FOR DROP when taking a datafile offline. You can specify the entire filename or provide the file number. In this example, datafile 6 is taken offline:

```
SQL> alter database datafile 6 offline for drop;
```

Now, if you attempt to online the offline datafile, you receive the following error:

```
SQL> alter database datafile 6 online;
ORA-0113: file 6 needs media recovery
```

When you use the OFFLINE FOR DROP clause, no checkpoint is taken on the datafile. This means you need to perform media recovery on the datafile before bringing it online. Performing media recovery applies any changes to the datafile that are recorded in the online redo logs that aren't in the datafiles themselves. Before you can bring online a datafile that was taken offline with the OFFLINE FOR DROP clause, you must perform media recovery on it. You can specify either the entire filename or the file number:

```
SQL> recover datafile 6;
```

If the redo information that Oracle needs is contained in the online redo logs, you should see this message:

```
Media recovery complete.
```

If your database isn't in archivelog mode, and if Oracle needs redo information not contained in the online redo logs to recover the datafile, then you can't recover the datafile and place it back online.

If your database is in archivelog mode, you can take it offline without the FOR DROP clause. In this scenario, Oracle ignores the FOR DROP clause. Even when your database is in archivelog mode, you need to perform media recovery on a datafile that has been taken offline with the ALTER DATABASE DATAFILE statement. Table 4–3 summarizes the options you must consider when taking a tablespace offline.

■ **Note** While the database is in mount mode (and not open), you can use the ALTER DATABASE DATAFILE command to take any datafile offline, including SYSTEM and UNDO.

Table 4–3. Options for Taking a Datafile Offline

Statement	Archivelog Mode Required?	Media Recovery Required When Toggling Online?	Works in Mount Mode?
ALTER TABLESPACE ... OFFLINE NORMAL	No	No	No
ALTER TABLESPACE ... OFFLINE TEMPORARY	No	Maybe: depends on whether any datafiles already have offline status	No
ALTER TABLESPACE ... OFFLINE IMMEDIATE	No	Yes	No
ALTER DATABASE DATAFILE ... OFFLINE	Yes	Yes	Yes
ALTER DATABASE DATAFILE ... OFFLINE FOR DROP	No	Yes	Yes

Renaming or Relocating a Datafile

You may occasionally need to rename a datafile. For example, you may need to move datafiles due to changes in the storage devices or move files that were somehow created in the wrong location.

Before you rename a datafile, you must take the datafile offline. (See the previous section.) Here are the steps for renaming a datafile:

1. Use the following query to determine the names of existing datafiles:

```
SQL> select name from v$datafile;
```

2. Take the datafile offline using either the ALTER TABLESPACE or ALTER DATABASE DATAFILE statement (see the previous section for details on how to do this). You can also shut down your database and then start it in mount mode; the datafiles can be moved while in this mode because they aren't open for use.

3. Physically move the datafile to the new location using either an OS command (like mv or cp) or the COPY_FILE procedure of the DBMS_FILE_TRANSFER built-in PL/SQL package.

4. Use either the ALTER TABLESPACE ... RENAME DATAFILE ... TO statement or the ALTER DATABASE RENAME FILE ... TO statement to update the control file with the new datafile name.

5. Alter the datafile online.

▓ **Note** If you need to rename datafiles associated with the SYSTEM or UNDO tablespace, you must shut down your database and start it in mount mode. When your database is in mount mode, you can rename datafiles associated with the SYSTEM or UNDO tablespace via the ALTER DATABASE RENAME FILE statement.

The following example demonstrates how to move the datafiles associated with a single tablespace. First, take the datafiles offline with the ALTER TABLESPACE statement:

```
SQL> alter tablespace users offline;
```

Now, from the operating system prompt, move two datafiles to a new location using the Linux/Unix mv command:

```
$ mv /ora02/dbfile/O11R2/users01.dbf /ora03/dbfile/O11R2/users01.dbf
$ mv /ora02/dbfile/O11R2/users02.dbf /ora03/dbfile/O11R2/users02.dbf
```

Update the control file with the ALTER TABLESPACE statement:

```
alter tablespace users
rename datafile
'/ora02/dbfile/O11R2/users01.dbf',
'/ora02/dbfile/O11R2/users02.dbf'
to
'/ora03/dbfile/O11R2/users01.dbf',
'/ora03/dbfile/O11R2/users02.dbf';
```

Finally, bring the datafiles within the tablespace back online:

```
SQL> alter tablespace users online;
```

If you want to rename datafiles from multiple tablespaces in one operation, you can use the ALTER DATABASE RENAME FILE statement (instead of the ALTER TABLESPACE...RENAME DATAFILE statement). The following example renames all datafiles in the database. Because the SYSTEM and UNDO tablespaces' datafiles are being moved, you must take the database offline first and then place it in mount mode:

```
SQL> conn / as sysdba
SQL> shutdown immediate;
SQL> startup mount;
```

Because the database is in mount mode, the datafiles aren't open for use, and thus there is no need to take the datafiles offline. Next, physically move the files via the Linux/Unix mv command:

```
$ mv /ora01/dbfile/O11R2/system01.dbf /ora02/dbfile/O11R2/system01.dbf
$ mv /ora01/dbfile/O11R2/sysaux01.dbf /ora02/dbfile/O11R2/sysaux01.dbf
$ mv /ora01/dbfile/O11R2/undotbs01.dbf /ora02/dbfile/O11R2/undotbs01.dbf
$ mv /ora01/dbfile/O11R2/users01.dbf /ora02/dbfile/O11R2/users01.dbf
$ mv /ora01/dbfile/O11R2/toos01.dbf /ora02/dbfile/O11R2/toos01.dbf
$ mv /ora01/dbfile/O11R2/users02.dbf /ora02/dbfile/O11R2/users02.dbf
```

■ **Note** You must move the files before you update the control file. The ALTER DATABASE RENAME FILE command expects the file to be in the renamed location. If the file isn't there, an error is thrown: "ORA-27037: unable to obtain file status."

Now you can update the control file to be aware of the new filename:

```
alter database rename file
'/ora01/dbfile/011R2/system01.dbf',
'/ora01/dbfile/011R2/sysaux01.dbf',
'/ora01/dbfile/011R2/undotbs01.dbf',
'/ora01/dbfile/011R2/users01.dbf',
'/ora01/dbfile/011R2/toos01.dbf',
'/ora01/dbfile/011R2/users02.dbf'
to
'/ora02/dbfile/011R2/system01.dbf',
'/ora02/dbfile/011R2/sysaux01.dbf',
'/ora02/dbfile/011R2/undotbs01.dbf',
'/ora02/dbfile/011R2/users01.dbf',
'/ora02/dbfile/011R2/toos01.dbf',
'/ora02/dbfile/011R2/users02.dbf';
```

You should be able to open your database:

```
SQL> alter database open;
```

Another way you can relocate all datafiles in a database is to re-create the control file with the CREATE CONTROLFILE statement. The steps for this operation are as follows:

1. Create trace file that contains a CREATE CONTROLFILE statement.

2. Locate the trace file that contains the CREATE CONTROLFILE statement.

3. Modify the trace file to display the new location of the datafiles.

4. Shut down the database.

5. Physically move the datafiles using an operating system command.

6. Start the database in nomount mode.

7. Run the CREATE CONTROLFILE command.

■ **Note** When you re-create a control file, be aware that any Oracle Recovery Manager (RMAN) information that was contained in the control file will be lost. If you're not using a recovery catalog, you can repopulate the control file with RMAN backup information using the RMAN CATALOG command.

The following example walks through the previous steps. First, you write a CREATE CONTROLFILE statement to a trace file via an ALTER DATABASE BACKUP CONTROLFILE TO TRACE statement:

```
SQL> alter database backup controlfile to trace noresetlogs;
```

This statement uses the NORESETLOGS clause. It instructs Oracle to write only one SQL statement to the trace file. If you don't specify NORESETLOGS, Oracle writes two SQL statements to the trace file: one to re-create the control file with the NORESETLOGS option, and one to re-create the control file with RESETLOGS. Normally, you know whether you want to reset the online redo logs as part of re-creating the control file. In this case, you know that you don't need to reset the online redo logs when you re-create the control file (because the online redo logs haven't been damaged and are still in the normal location for the database).

Now, locate the directory that contains the trace files for your database:

```
SQL> show parameter background_dump_dest
```

For this example, the directory is

```
/ora01/app/oracle/diag/rdbms/o11r2/O11R2/trace
```

Next, navigate to the trace directory on the operating system:

```
$ cd /ora01/app/oracle/diag/rdbms/o11r2/O11R2/trace
```

Look for the last trace file that was generated (or one that was generated at the same time you ran the ALTER DATABASE statement). In this example, the trace file is O11R2_ora_17017.trc.

Make a copy of the trace file, and open the copy with an operating system editor:

```
$ cp O11R2_ora_17017.trc mv.sql
```

Edit the mv.sql file. In this example, the trace file contains only one SQL statement (because I specified NORESTLOGS when creating the trace file). If you don't specify NORESETLOGS, the trace file contains two CREATE CONTROLFILE statements, and you must modify the trace file to remove the statement that contains the RESETLOGS as part of the statement.

Next, modify the names of the datafiles to the new locations where you want to move the datafiles. Here is a CREATE CONTROLFILE statement for this example:

```
CREATE CONTROLFILE REUSE DATABASE "O11R2" NORESETLOGS  ARCHIVELOG
    MAXLOGFILES 16
    MAXLOGMEMBERS 4
    MAXDATAFILES 1024
    MAXINSTANCES 1
    MAXLOGHISTORY 876
LOGFILE
  GROUP 1 (
    '/ora02/oraredo/O11R2/redo01a.rdo',
    '/ora03/oraredo/O11R2/redo01b.rdo'
  ) SIZE 100M BLOCKSIZE 512,
  GROUP 2 (
    '/ora02/oraredo/O11R2/redo02a.rdo',
    '/ora03/oraredo/O11R2/redo02b.rdo'
  ) SIZE 100M BLOCKSIZE 512,
  GROUP 3 (
     '/ora02/oraredo/O11R2/redo03a.rdo',
     '/ora03/oraredo/O11R2/redo03b.rdo'
  ) SIZE 100M BLOCKSIZE 512
DATAFILE
  '/ora02/dbfile/O11R2/system01.dbf',
  '/ora02/dbfile/O11R2/sysaux01.dbf',
  '/ora02/dbfile/O11R2/undotbs01.dbf',
```

```
    '/ora02/dbfile/011R2/users01.dbf',
    '/ora02/dbfile/011R2/toos01.dbf',
    '/ora02/dbfile/011R2/users02.dbf'
CHARACTER SET UTF8;
```

Now, shut down the database:

```
SQL> shutdown immediate;
```

Physically move the files from the operating system prompt. This example uses the Linux/Unix mv command to move the files:

```
$ mv /ora01/dbfile/011R2/system01.dbf /ora02/dbfile/011R2/system01.dbf
$ mv /ora01/dbfile/011R2/sysaux01.dbf /ora02/dbfile/011R2/sysaux01.dbf
$ mv /ora01/dbfile/011R2/undotbs01.dbf /ora02/dbfile/011R2/undotbs01.dbf
$ mv /ora01/dbfile/011R2/users01.dbf /ora02/dbfile/011R2/users01.dbf
$ mv /ora01/dbfile/011R2/toos01.dbf /ora02/dbfile/011R2/toos01.dbf
$ mv /ora01/dbfile/011R2/users02.dbf /ora02/dbfile/011R2/users02.dbf
```

Start up the database in nomount mode:

```
SQL> startup nomount;
```

And execute the file that contains the CREATE CONTROLFILE statement (in this example, mv.sql):

```
SQl > @mv.sql
```

If the statement is successful, you see the following message:

```
Control file created.
```

Finally, alter your database open:

```
SQL> alter database open;
```

USING ORADEBUG TO DISPLAY THE TRACE FILE'S NAME

When you're working with a trace file, another way of showing the file's name and location is to use the oradebug command. For example:

```
SQL> oradebug setmypid
SQL> alter database backup controlfile to trace noresetlogs;
SQL> oradebug tracefile_name
```

Here is the output after running the last statement:

```
/oracle/app/oracle/diag/rdbms/o11r2/011R2/trace/011R2_ora_9628.trc
```

This way, you can directly display the name of the trace file that you generated with the ALTER DATABASE BACKUP statement.

Summary

This chapter discussed managing tablespace and datafiles. Tablespaces are logical containers for a group of datafiles. Datafiles are the physical files on disk that contain data. You should plan carefully when creating tablespaces and the corresponding datafiles.

Tablespaces allow you to separate the data of one application from another. You can also separate tables from indexes. These allow you to customize storage characteristics of the tablespace for each application. Furthermore, tablespaces provide a way to better manage applications that have different availability and backup and recovery requirements. As a DBA, you must be proficient in managing tablespaces and datafiles. In any type of environment, you have to add, rename, relocate, and drop these storage containers.

Oracle requires three types of files for a database to operate: datafiles, control files, and online redo-log files. The next chapter in the book focuses on control file and online redo-log file management.

## CHAPTER 5

Managing Control Files and Online Redo Logs

An Oracle database consists of three types of mandatory files: datafiles, control files, and online redo logs. Chapter 4 focused on tablespaces and datafiles. This chapter focuses on managing control files and online redo logs. The first part of this chapter discusses typical control-file maintenance tasks such adding, moving, and removing control files. The latter part of the chapter focuses on how to manage online redo log files. You learn how to rename, resize, and relocate these critical files.

Managing Control Files

A *control file* is a small binary file that stores the following types of information:

- Database name
- Names and locations of datafiles
- Names and locations of online redo log files
- Current online redo log sequence number
- Checkpoint information
- Names and locations of Oracle Recovery Manager (RMAN) backup files (if using)

You can query much of the information stored in the control file from data-dictionary views. The following example displays the types of information stored in the control file by querying V$CONTROLFILE_RECORD_SECTION:

```
SQL> select distinct type from v$controlfile_record_section;
```

Here's a partial listing of the output:

```
TYPE
-----------------------------
FILENAME
TABLESPACE
RMAN CONFIGURATION
BACKUP CORRUPTION
PROXY COPY
FLASHBACK LOG
```

```
REMOVABLE RECOVERY FILES
DATAFILE
```

You can view database information stored in the control file via the V$DATABASE view:

```
SQL> select name, open_mode, created, current_scn from v$database;
```

Here is the output for this example:

```
NAME       OPEN_MODE            CREATED    CURRENT_SCN
---------  -------------------- ---------  -----------
ORC11G     READ WRITE           01-JAN-10    5077636
```

Every Oracle database must have at least one control file. When you start your database in nomount mode, the instance is aware of the location of the control files from the CONTROL_FILES parameter:

```
-- locations of control files are known to the instance
SQL> startup nomount;
```

At this point, the control files haven't been touched by any processes. When you alter your database into mount mode, the control files are read and opened for use:

```
-- control files opened
SQL> alter database mount;
```

If any of the control files listed in the CONTROL_FILES initialization parameter aren't available, then you can't mount your database.

When you successfully mount your database, the instance is aware of the locations of the datafiles and online redo logs, but hasn't yet opened them. After you alter your database into open mode, the datafiles and online redo logs are opened:

```
-- datafiles and online redo logs opened
SQL> alter database open;
```

The control file is created when the database is created. As you saw in Chapter 2, you should create at least two control files when you create your database (to avoid a single point of failure). If possible, you should have multiple control files stored on separate storage devices controlled by separate controllers.

Oracle writes to all control files specified by the CONTROL_FILES initialization parameter. If Oracle can't write to one of the control files, an error is thrown:

```
ORA-00210: cannot open the specified control file
```

If one of your control files becomes unavailable, shut down your database and resolve the issue before restarting. Fixing the problem may mean resolving a storage-device failure or modifying the CONTROL_FILES initialization parameter to remove the control-file entry for the control file that isn't available.

DISPLAYING THE CONTENTS OF A CONTROL FILE

You can use the ALTER SESSION statement to display the physical contents of the control file. For example:

```
SQL> oradebug setmypid
SQL> oradebug unlimit
SQL> alter session set events 'immediate trace name controlf level 9';
SQL> oradebug tracefile_name
```

The prior line displays the name of the trace file:

```
/oracle/app/oracle/diag/rdbms/o11r2/O11R2/trace/O11R2_ora_16946.trc
```

In Oracle Database 11*g*, the trace file is written to the $ADR_HOME/trace directory. In Oracle 10*g*, the directory is defined by the USER_DUMP_DEST initialization parameter. Here is a partial listing of the contents of the trace file:

```
***************************************************************************
DATABASE ENTRY
***************************************************************************
 (size = 316, compat size = 316, section max = 1, section in-use = 1,
  last-recid= 0, old-recno = 0, last-recno = 0)
 (extent = 1, blkno = 1, numrecs = 1)
 03/05/2010 14:14:11
 DB Name "O11R2"
 Database flags = 0x00404000 0x00001000
 Controlfile Creation Timestamp  03/05/2010 14:14:17
 Incmplt recovery scn: 0x0000.00000000
```

You can inspect the contents of the control file when troubleshooting or when you're trying to gain a better understanding of Oracle internals.

Viewing Control File Names and Locations

If your database is in a nomount state, a mounted state, or an open state, you can view the names and locations of the control files as follows:

```
SQL> show parameter control_files
```

You can also view control-file location and name information by querying the V$CONTROLFILE view. This query works while your database is mounted or open:

```
SQL> select name from v$controlfile;
```

If for some reason you can't start your database at all, and you need to know the names and locations of the control files, you can inspect the contents of the initialization file to see where they're located. If you're using an spfile, even though it's a binary file, you can still open it with a text editor. The safest approach is to make a copy of the spfile and then inspect its contents with an OS editor:

```
$ cp $ORACLE_HOME/dbs/spfileO11R2.ora $ORACLE_HOME/dbs/spfileO11R2.copy
$ vi $ORACLE_HOME/dbs/spfileO11R2.copy
```

If you're using a text-based initialization file, you can view the file directly with an OS editor or use the grep command:

```
$ grep -i control_files $ORACLE_HOME/dbs/initO11.ora
```

Adding a Control File

Adding a control file means copying an existing control file and making your database aware of the copy by modifying your CONTROL_FILES parameter. This task must be done while your database is shut down. This procedure only works when you have a good existing control file that can be copied. Adding a control file isn't the same thing as creating or restoring a control file.

If your database uses only one control file, and that control file becomes damaged, you need to either restore a control file from a backup (if available) and perform a recovery, or re-create the damaged control file. If you're using two or more control files, and one becomes damaged, you can use the remaining good control file(s) to quickly get your database into an operating state.

If a database is using only one control file, the basic procedure for adding a control file is as follows:

1. Alter the initialization file CONTROL_FILES parameter to include the new location and name of the control file.

2. Shut down your database.

3. Use an OS command to copy an existing control file to the new location and name.

4. Restart your database.

Depending on whether you use an spfile or an init.ora file, the previous steps varies slightly. The next two subsections detail these different scenarios.

Spfile Scenario

If your database is open, you can quickly determine whether you're using an spfile with the following SQL statement:

```
SQL> show parameter spfile
```

Here is some sample output:

```
NAME            TYPE     VALUE
--------------- -------- -------------------------------
spfile          string   /oracle/app/oracle/product/11. 2.0/db_1/dbs/spfileO11R2.ora
```

When you've determined that you're using an spfile, use the following steps to add a control file:

1. Determine the CONTROL_FILES parameter's current value:

```
SQL> show parameter control_files
```

The output shows that this database is using only one control file:

```
NAME                                TYPE        VALUE
----------------------------------- ----------- -----------------------------
control_files                       string      /ora01/dbfile/O11R2/control01.ctl
```

2. Alter your CONTROL_FILES parameter to include the new control file that you want to add, but limit the scope of the operation to the spfile (you can't modify this parameter in memory). Make sure you also include any control files listed in step 1:

```
SQL> alter system set control_files='/ora01/dbfile/O11R2/control01.ctl',
'/ora01/dbfile/O11R2/control02.ctl' scope=spfile;
```

3. Shut down your database:

```
SQL> shutdown immediate;
```

4. Copy an existing control file to the new location and name. In this example, a new control file named control02.ctl is created via the OS cp command:

```
$ cp /ora01/dbfile/O11R2/control01.ctl /ora01/dbfile/O11R2/control02.ctl
```

5. Start up your database:

```
SQL> startup;
```

You can verify that the new control file is being used by displaying the CONTROL_FILES parameter:

```
SQL> show parameter control_files
```

Here is the output for this example:

```
NAME                                 TYPE        VALUE
------------------------------------ ----------- ------------------------------
control_files                        string      /ora01/dbfile/O11R2/control01.ctl,
                                                 /ora01/dbfile/O11R2/control02.ctl
```

Init.ora Scenario

Run the following statement to verify that you're using an init.ora file. If you're not using an spfile, the VALUE column is blank:

```
SQL> show parameter spfile
NAME                                 TYPE        VALUE
------------------------------------ ----------- ------------------------------
spfile                               string
```

To add a control file when using a text init.ora file, perform the following steps:

1. Shut down your database:

```
SQL> shutdown immediate;
```

2. Edit your init.ora file with an OS utility (such as vi), and add the new control-file location and name to the CONTROL_FILES parameter. This example opens the init.ora file using vi, and adds control02.ctl to the CONTROL_FILES parameter:

```
$ vi $ORACLE_HOME/dbs/initO11R2.ora
```

Listed next is the CONTROL_FILES parameter after control02.ctl is added:

```
control_files='/ora01/dbfile/O11R2/control01.ctl',
'/ora01/dbfile/O11R2/control02.ctl'
```

3. From the OS, copy the existing control file to the location and name of the control file being added:

```
$ cp /ora01/dbfile/O11R2/control01.ctl /ora01/dbfile/O11R2/control02.ctl
```

4. Start up your database:

```
SQL> startup;
```

You can view the control files in use by displaying the CONTROL_FILES parameter:

```
SQL> show parameter control_files
```

For this example, here is the output:

```
NAME                                 TYPE          VALUE
------------------------------------ ------------ ------------------------------
control_files                        string        /ora01/dbfile/O11R2/control01.ctl,
                                                    /ora01/dbfile/O11R2/control02.ctl
```

■ **Note** See Chapter 4 for an example of re-creating a control file from a trace file.

Moving a Control File

You may occasionally need to move a control file from one location to another. For example, if new storage is added to the database server, you may want to move an existing control file to the newly available location.

The procedure for moving a control file is very similar to adding a control file. The only difference is that you rename the control file instead of copying it. This example shows how to move a control file when you're using an spfile:

1. Determine the CONTROL_FILES parameter's current value:

```
SQL> show parameter control_files
```

The output shows that this database is using only one control file:

```
NAME                                 TYPE          VALUE
------------------------------------ ------------ ------------------------------
control_files                        string        /ora01/dbfile/O11R2/control01.ctl
```

2. Alter your CONTROL_FILES parameter to reflect that you're moving a control file. In this example, the control file is currently in this location:

```
/ora01/dbfile/O11R2/control01.ctl
```

You're moving the control file to this location:

```
/ora02/dbfile/O11R2/control01.ctl
```

Alter the spfile to reflect the new location for the control file. You have to specify SCOPE=SPFILE because the CONTROL_FILES parameter can't be modified in memory:

```
SQL> alter system set
```

```
control_files='/ora02/dbfile/O11R2/control01.ctl' scope=spfile;
```

3. Shut down your database:

```
SQL> shutdown immediate;
```

4. At the OS prompt, move the control file to the new location. This example uses
    the OS mv command:

```
$ mv /ora01/dbfile/O11R2/control01.ctl /ora02/dbfile/O11R2/control01.ctl
```

5. Start up your database:

```
SQL> startup;
```

You can verify that the new control file is being used by displaying the CONTROL_FILES parameter:

```
SQL> show parameter control_files
```

Here is the output for this example:

```
NAME                                  TYPE        VALUE
------------------------------------- ----------- ---------------------------------
control_files                         string      /ora02/dbfile/O11R2/control01.ctl
```

Removing a Control File

You may run into a situation where you experience a media failure with a storage device that contains
one of your multiplexed control files:

```
ORA-00205: error in identifying control file, check alert log for more info
```

In this scenario, you still have at least one good control file. To remove a control file, follow these
steps.

1. Identify which control file has experienced media failure by inspecting the
    alert.log for information:

```
ORA-00202: control file: '/ora01/dbfile/O11R2/control02.ctl'
ORA-27037: unable to obtain file status
```

2. Remove the unavailable control file name from the CONTROL_FILES parameter. If
    you're using an init.ora file, modify the file directly with an OS editor (such as
    vi). If you're using an spfile, modify the CONTROL_FILES parameter with the
    ALTER SYSTEM statement. In this spfile example, the control02.ctl control file
    is removed from the CONTROL_FILES parameter:

```
SQL> alter system set control_files='/ora01/dbfile/O11R2/control01.ctl'
scope=spfile;
```

In this example, this database now has only one control file associated with it.
You should never run a production database with just one control file. See the
section "Adding a Control File" to add more control files to your database.

3. Stop and start your database:

```
SQL> shutdown immediate;
SQL> startup;
```

If SHUTDOWN IMMEDIATE doesn't work, use SHUTDOWN ABORT to shut down your database.

Managing Online Redo Logs

Online redo logs store a record of transactions that have occurred in your database. These logs provide a mechanism for you to recover your database in the event of a failure. You're required to have at least two *online redo-log groups* in your database. Each online redo log group must contain at least one *online redo-log member*. The member is the physical file that exists on disk. You can create multiple members in each redo log group, which is known as *multiplexing* your online redo log group.

■ **Tip** I highly recommend that you multiplex your online redo log groups with at least two members in each group and have each member on a separate physical device governed by a separate controller.

The *log writer* is the background process responsible for writing transaction information from the redo-log buffer to the online redo log files. The online redo-log group that the log writer is actively writing to is the *current online redo-log* group. The log writer writes simultaneously to all members of a redo-log group. The log writer needs to successfully write to only one member in order for the database to continue operating. Your database ceases operating if the log writer can't write successfully to at least one member of the current group.

When the current online redo-log group fills up, a *log switch* occurs, and the log writer starts writing to the next online redo-log group. The log writer writes to the online redo-log groups in a round-robin fashion. Because you have a finite number of online redo-log groups, eventually the contents of each online redo-log group are overwritten. If you want to save a history of the transaction information, you must place your database in *archivelog mode* (see Chapter 16 for details on how to enable archiving).

When your database is in archivelog mode, after every log switch, the archiver background process copies the contents of the online redo-log file to an *archived redo-log file*. In the event of a failure, the archived redo-log files allow you to restore the complete history of transactions that have occurred since your last database backup.

PURPOSE OF OPEN RESETLOGS

Sometimes you're required to open your database with the OPEN RESETLOGS clause (for more details, see Chapters 16 through 19 regarding backup and recovery). You may do this when re-creating a control file, performing a restore and recovery with a backup control file, or performing an incomplete recovery. When you open your database with the OPEN RESETLOGS clause, it either wipes out any existing online redo-log files or, if the files don't exist, re-creates them. You can query the MEMBER column of V$LOGFILE to see which files are involved with an OPEN RESETLOGS operation.

Why would you want to wipe out what's in the online redo logs? Take the example of an incomplete recovery, where the database is deliberately opened to a point in time in the past. In this situation, the system change number (SCN) information in the online redo logs contains transaction data that can never be recovered. Oracle forces you to open the database with OPEN RESETLOGS to purposely wipe out that information.

When you open your database with OPEN RESETLOGS, you create a new incarnation of your database and reset the log sequence number back to one. Oracle requires a new incarnation so as to avoid accidentally using any old archive redo logs (associated with a separate incarnation of the database) in the event that another restore and recovery is required.

Figure 5–1 displays a typical setup for the online redo-log files. This figure shows three online redo-log groups, with each group containing two members. The database is in archivelog mode. In the figure, group 2 has recently been filled with transactions, a log switch has occurred, and the log writer is now writing to group 3. The archiver process is copying the contents of group 2 to an archived redo-log file. When group 3 fills up, another log switch will occur, and the log writer will begin writing to group 1. At the same time, the archiver process will copy the contents of group 3 to archive log sequence 3 (and so forth).

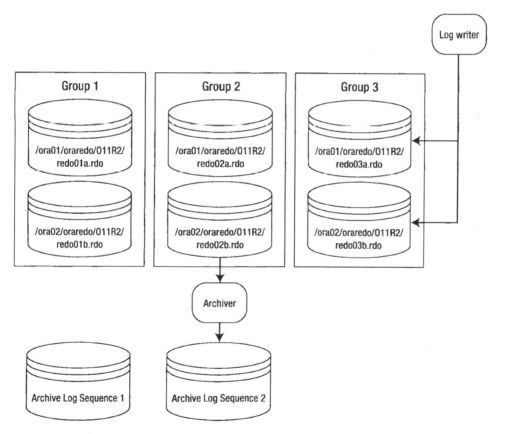

Figure 5–1. Online redo-log configuration

The online redo-log files aren't intended to be backed up. These files contain only the most recent redo-transaction information generated by the database. When you enable archiving, the archived redo-log files are the mechanism for protecting your database transaction history.

The contents of the current online redo-log files aren't archived until a log switch occurs. This means that if you lose all members of the current online redo-log file, you lose transactions. Listed next are several mechanisms you can implement to minimize the chance of failure with the online redo-log files:

- Multiplex groups to have multiple members.

- Never allow two members of the same group to share the same controller.

- Never put two members of the same group on the same physical disk.

- Ensure that OS file permissions are set appropriately.

- Use physical storage devices that are redundant (that is, RAID).

- Appropriately size the log files so that they switch and are archived at regular intervals.

- Set the ARCHIVE_LAG_TARGET initialization parameter to ensure that the online redo logs are switched at regular intervals.

■ **Note** The only tool provided by Oracle that can protect you and preserve all committed transactions in the event you lose all members of the current online redo-log group is Oracle Data Guard implemented in Maximum Protection Mode. For more details, see the *Data Guard Concepts and Administration* guide, available on Oracle's Oracle Technology Network (OTN) website.

The online redo-log files are never backed up by an RMAN backup or by a user-managed hot backup. If you did back up the online redo-log files, it would be meaningless to restore them. The online redo-log files contain the latest redo generated by the database. You wouldn't want to overwrite them from a backup with old redo information. For a database in archivelog mode, the online redo-log files contain the most recently generated transactions that are required to perform a complete recovery.

Displaying Online Redo-Log Information

Use the V$LOG and V$LOGFILE views to display information about online redo-log groups and corresponding members:

```
select a.group#,a.member,b.status,b.archived,bytes/1024/1024 mbytes
from v$logfile a, v$log b
where a.group# = b.group#
order by 1,2;
```

Here is some sample output:

```
GROUP# MEMBER                              STATUS     ARCHIVED  MBYTES
------ ----------------------------------- ---------- --------- ---------
     1 /ora01/oraredo/O11R2/redo01a.rdo    INACTIVE   YES            100
     1 /ora02/oraredo/O11R2/redo01b.rdo    INACTIVE   YES            100
     2 /ora01/oraredo/O11R2/redo02a.rdo    CURRENT    NO             100
     2 /ora02/oraredo/O11R2/redo02b.rdo    CURRENT    NO             100
```

When you're diagnosing online redo-log issues, the V$LOG and V$LOGFILE views are particularly helpful. You can query these views while the database is mounted or open. Table 5–1 briefly describes each view.

Table 5–1. Useful Views Related to Online Redo Logs

View	Description
V$LOG	Displays the online redo-log group information stored in the control file
V$LOGFILE	Displays online redo-log file member information

The STATUS column of the V$LOG view is particularly useful when you're working with online redo-logs groups. Table 5–2 describes each status and meaning for the V$LOG view.

Table 5–2. Status for Online Redo-Log Groups in the V$LOG View

Status	Meaning
CURRENT	The log group is currently being written to by the log writer.
ACTIVE	The log group is required for crash recovery and may or may not have been archived.
CLEARING	The log group is being cleared out by an ALTER DATABASE CLEAR LOGFILE command.
CLEARING_CURRENT	The current log group is being cleared of a closed thread.
INACTIVE	The log group isn't needed for crash recovery and may or may not have been archived.
UNUSED	The log group has never been written to; it was recently created.

The STATUS column of the V$LOGFILE view also contains useful information. This view contains information about each physical online redo-log file member of a log group. Table 5–3 provides descriptions of the status of each log-file member.

Table 5–3. Status for Online Redo-Log File Members in the V$LOGFILE View

Status	Meaning
INVALID	The log-file member is inaccessible or has been recently created.
DELETED	The log-file member is no longer in use.
STALE	The log-file member's contents aren't complete.
NULL	The log-file member is being used by the database.

It's important to differentiate between the STATUS column in V$LOG and the STATUS column in
V$LOGFILE. The STATUS column in V$LOG reflects the status of the log group. The STATUS column in
V$LOGFILE reports the status of the physical online redo-log file member. Refer to these tables when
diagnosing issues with your online redo logs.

Determining the Optimal Size of Online Redo-Log Groups

Try to size the online redo logs so they switch anywhere from two to six times per hour. The
V$LOG_HISTORY contains a history of how frequently the online redo logs have switched. Execute this
query to view the number of log switches per hour:

```
select count(*)
,to_char(first_time,'YYYY:MM:DD:HH24')
from v$log_history
group by to_char(first_time,'YYYY:MM:DD:HH24')
order by 2;
```

Here's a snippet of the output:

```
COUNT(*) TO_CHAR(FIRST
---------- -------------
        1 2010:03:23:20
        2 2010:03:23:22
       19 2010:03:23:23
       17 2010:03:24:00
       25 2010:03:24:01
       35 2010:03:24:02
       23 2010:03:24:03
        5 2010:03:24:04
       11 2010:03:24:05
        2 2010:03:24:06
```

From the previous output, you can see that a lot of redo generation occurred on March 24 from
about midnight to 3:00 a.m. This could be due to a nightly batch job or users in different time zones
updating data. For this database, the size of the online redo logs should be increased. You should try to
size the online redo logs to accommodate peak transaction loads on the database.

The V$LOG_HISTORY derives its data from the control file. Each time there is a log switch, an entry is
recorded in this view that details information, such as the time of the switch and the system change
number (SCN). As mentioned earlier, a general rule of thumb is that you should size your online redo-
log files so that they switch about two to six times per hour. You don't want them switching too often
because there is overhead with the log switch. Oracle initiates a checkpoint as part of a log switch.
During a checkpoint, the database-writer background process writes modified (also referred to as *dirty*)
blocks to disk, which is resource-intensive.

On the other hand, you don't want online redo-log files to never switch, because the current online
redo log contains transactions that you may need in the event of a recovery. If a disaster causes a media
failure in your current online redo log, you can lose those transactions that haven't been archived yet.

Use the ARCHIVE_LAG_TARGET initialization parameter to set a maximum amount of time (in seconds) between log switches. A typical setting for this parameter is 1800 seconds (30 minutes). A value of 0 (default) disables this feature. This parameter is commonly used in Oracle Data Guard environments to force log switches after the specified amount of time elapses.

You can also query the OPTIMAL_LOGFILE_SIZE column from the V$INSTANCE_RECOVERY view to determine if your online redo-log files have been sized correctly:

```
SQL> select optimal_logfile_size from v$instance_recovery;
```

Here is some sample output:

```
OPTIMAL_LOGFILE_SIZE
--------------------
349
```

This reports the redo-log file size (in megabytes) that is considered optimal based on the initialization parameter setting of FAST_START_MTTR_TARGET. Oracle recommends you configure all online redo logs to be at least the value of OPTIMAL_LOGFILE_SIZE. However, when sizing your online redo logs, you must take into consideration information about your environment (such as the frequency of the switches).

Determining the Optimal Number of Redo-Log Groups

Oracle requires at least two redo-log groups to function. But having just two groups sometimes isn't enough. To understand why two groups may not be enough, remember that every time a log switch occurs, it initiates a checkpoint. As part of a checkpoint, the database writer writes all modified (dirty) blocks from the system global area (SGA) to the datafiles on disk. Also recall that the online redo logs are written to in a round-robin fashion, and eventually the information in a given log is overwritten. Before the log writer can begin to overwrite information in an online redo log, all modified blocks in the SGA associated with the redo log must first be written to a datafile. If all modified blocks haven't been written to the datafiles, you see this message in the alert.log file:

```
Thread 1 cannot allocate new log, sequence <sequence number>
Checkpoint not complete
```

Another way to explain this issue is that Oracle needs to store in the online redo logs any information that would be required to perform a crash recovery. To help visualize this, see Figure 5–2.

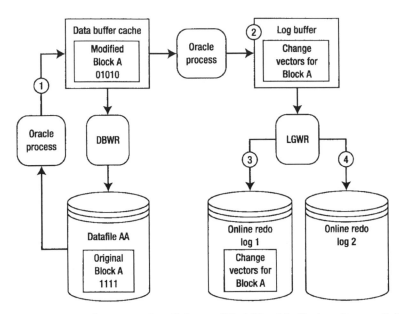

Figure 5–2. *Redo protected until the modified (dirty) buffer is written to disk.*

At time 1, Block A is read from Datafile AA into the buffer cache and modified. At time 2, the redo-change vector (how the block changed) information is written to the log buffer. At time 3, the log-writer process writes the Block A change-vector information to online redo log 1. At time 4, a log switch occurs, and online redo log 2 becomes the current online redo log.

Now, suppose that online redo log 2 fills up quickly and another log switch occurs, at which point the log writer attempts to write to online redo log 1. The log writer isn't allowed to overwrite information in online redo log 1 until the database writer writes Block A to Datafile AA. Until Block A is written to datafile AA, Oracle needs information in the online redo logs to recover this block in the event of a power failure or shutdown abort. Before Oracle overwrites information in the online redo logs, it ensures that blocks protected by redo have been written to disk. If these modified blocks haven't been written to disk, Oracle temporarily suspends processing until they have been written to disk. There are a few ways to resolve this issue:

- Add more redo-log groups.

- Lower the value of FAST_START_MTTR_TARGET. Doing so causes the database-writer process to write older modified blocks to disk in a smaller timeframe.

- Tune the database-writer process (modify DB_WRITER_PROCESSES).

If you notice that the Checkpoint not complete message is occurring often (say, several times a day), I recommend that you add one or more log groups to resolve the issue. Adding an extra redo log gives the database writer more time to write modified blocks in the database buffer cache to the datafiles before the associated redo with a block is overwritten. There is little downside to adding more redo-log groups. The main concern is that you could bump up against the MAXLOGFILES value that was used when you created the database. If you need to add more groups and have exceeded the value of MAXLOGFILES, then you must re-create your control file and specify a high value for this parameter.

If adding more redo-log groups doesn't resolve the issue, you should carefully consider lowering the value of FAST_START_MTTR_TARGET. When you lower this value, you can potentially see more I/O because the database-writer process is more actively writing modified blocks to datafiles. Ideally, it would be nice to verify the impact of modifying FAST_START_MTTR_TARGET in a test environment before making the change in production. You can modify this parameter while your instance is up; this means you can quickly modify it back to its original setting if there are unforeseen side effects.

Finally, consider increasing the value of the DB_WRITER_PROCESSES parameter. Carefully analyze the impact of modifying this parameter in a test environment before you apply it to production. This value requires that you stop and start your database; so, if there are adverse effects, it requires downtime to set this value back to the original setting.

Adding Online Redo-Log Groups

If you determine that you need to add an online redo-log group, use the ADD LOGFILE GROUP statement. In this example, the database already contains four online redo-log groups that are sized at 500M each. An additional log group is added that has two members and is sized at 500MB:

```
alter database add logfile group 5
('/ora01/oraredo/O11R2/redo05a.rdo',
 '/ora02/oraredo/O11R2/redo05b.rdo') SIZE 500M;
```

In this scenario, I highly recommend that the log group you add be the same size and have the same number of members as the existing online redo logs. If the newly added group doesn't have the same physical characteristics as the existing groups, it's harder to accurately determine performance issues with the online redo-log groups.

For example, if you have two log groups sized at 20MB, and you add a new log group sized at 200MB, this is very likely to produce the Checkpoint not complete issue described in the previous section. This is because flushing all modified blocks from the SGA that are protected by the redo in a 200MB log file can potentially take much longer than flushing modified blocks from the SGA that are protected by a 20MB redo-log file.

Resizing Online Redo-Log Groups

You may need to change the size of your online redo logs (see also the section "Determining the Optimal Size of Online Redo-Log Groups" earlier in this chapter). You can't directly modify the size of an existing online redo log (as you can a datafile). To resize an online redo log, you have to first add online redo-log groups that contain the size you want, and then drop the online redo logs that are the old size.

Say you want to resize the online redo logs to be 200MB each. First, you add the new groups that are 200MB using the ADD LOGFILE GROUP statement. The following example adds log group 4 with two members sized at 200MB:

```
alter database add logfile group 4
('/ora02/oraredo/O11R2/redo04a.rdo',
 '/ora03/oraredo/O11R2/redo04b.rdo') SIZE 200M;
```

■ Note You can specify the size of the log file in bytes, kilobytes, or megabytes.

After you've added the log files with the new size, you can drop the old online redo logs. A log group must have an INACTIVE status before you can drop it. You can check the status of the log group, as shown here:

```
SQL> select group#, status, archived, thread#, sequence# from v$log;
```

You can drop an inactive log group with the ALTER DATABASE DROP LOGFILE GROUP statement:

```
SQL> alter database drop logfile group <group #>;
```

If you attempt to drop the current online log group, Oracle returns an ORA-01623 error stating that you can't drop the current group. Use the ALTER SYSTEM SWITCH LOGFILE statement to switch the logs and make the next group the current group:

```
SQL> alter system switch logfile;
```

After a log switch, the log group that was previously the current group retains an active status as long as it contains redo that Oracle requires to perform crash recovery. If you attempt to drop a log group with an active status, Oracle throws an ORA-01624 error stating that the log group is required for crash recovery. Issue an ALTER SYSTEM CHECKPOINT command to make the log group inactive:

```
SQL> alter system checkpoint;
```

Additionally, you can't drop an online redo-log group if doing so leaves your database with only one log group. If you attempt to do this, Oracle throws an ORA-01567 error and informs you that dropping the log group isn't permitted because it would leave you with less than two log groups for your database (Oracle requires at least two log groups to function).

Dropping an online redo-log group doesn't remove the log files from the OS. You have to use an OS command to do this (such as the rm Linux/Unix command). Before you remove a file from the OS, ensure that it isn't in use and that you don't remove a live online redo-log file. For every database on the server, issue this query to view which online redo-log files are in use:

```
SQL> select member from v$logfile;
```

Before you physically remove a log file, first switch the online redo logs enough times so that all online redo-log groups have recently been switched; doing so causes the OS to write to the file and thus give it a new timestamp. For example, if you have three groups, ensure that you perform at least three log switches:

```
SQL> alter system switch logfile;
SQL> /
SQL> /
```

Now, verify at the OS prompt that the logfile you intend to remove doesn't have a new timestamp:

```
$ ls -altr
```

When you're absolutely sure the file isn't in use, you can remove it. The danger in removing a file is that if it happens to be an in-use online redo log and the only member of a group, you can cause serious damage to your database. Make sure you have a good backup of your database and that the file you're removing isn't used by any databases on the server.

Adding Online Redo-Log Files to a Group

You may occasionally need to add a log file to an existing group. For example, if you have an online redo-log group that contains only one member, you should consider adding a log file (to provide a higher level of protection against a single log-file member failure). Use the ALTER DATABASE ADD LOGFILE MEMBER statement to add a member file to an existing online redo-log group. You need to specify the new member file location, name, and group to which you want to add the file:

```
SQL> alter database add logfile member '/ora02/oraredo/O11R2/redo04c.rdo'
to group 4;
```

Ensure that you follow standards with regard to the location and names of any newly added redo-log files.

Removing Online Redo-Log Files from a Group

Occasionally, you may need to remove an online redo-log file. For example, your database may have experienced a failure with one member of a multiplexed group, and you want to remove the apostate member. First, make sure the log file you want to drop isn't in the current group:

```
SELECT a.group#, a.member, b.status, b.archived, SUM(b.bytes)/1024/1024 mbytes
FROM v$logfile a, v$log b
WHERE a.group# = b.group#
GROUP BY a.group#, a.member, b.status, b.archived
ORDER BY 1, 2
```

If you attempt to drop a log file that is in the group with the CURRENT status, you receive the following error:

```
ORA-01609: log 4 is the current log for thread 1 - cannot drop members
```

If you're attempting to drop a member from the current online redo-log group, then force a switch as follows:

```
SQL> alter system switch logfile;
```

Use the ALTER DATABASE DROP LOGFILE MEMBER statement to remove a member file from an existing online redo-log group. You don't need to specify the group number because you're removing a specific file:

```
SQL> alter database drop logfile member '/ora02/oraredo/O11R2/redo04a.rdo';
```

You also can't drop the last remaining log file of a group. A group must contain at least one log file. If you attempt to drop the last remaining log file in a group, you receive the following error:

```
ORA-00361: cannot remove last log member
```

Moving or Renaming Redo-Log Files

Sometimes, you need to move or rename online redo-log files. For example, you may have added some new mount points to the system, and you want to move the online redo logs to the new storage. You can use two methods to accomplish this task:

- Add the new log files in the new location, and drop the old log files.

- Physically rename the files from the OS.

If you can't afford any downtime, consider adding new log files in the new location and then dropping the old log files. See the section, "Adding Online Redo-Log Groups," for details on how to add a log group. Also see the section "Resizing Online Redo-Log Groups" for details on how to drop a log group.

You can also physically move the files from the OS. You can do this with the database open or closed. If your database is open, ensure that the files you move aren't part of the current online redo-log group (because those are actively written to by the log-writer background process). It's dangerous to try to do this task while your database is open because on an active system, the online redo logs may be switching at a rapid rate, which creates the possibility that you attempt to move a file at the same time it's switched to be the current online redo log.

The next example shows how to move the online redo-log files with the database shut down. Here are the steps:

1. Shut down your database:

```
SQL> shutdown immediate;
```

2. From the OS prompt, move the files. This example uses the mv command to accomplish this task:

```
$ mv /ora02/oraredo/011R2/redo01a.rdo /ora03/oraredo/011R2/redo01a.rdo
$ mv /ora02/oraredo/011R2/redo02a.rdo /ora03/oraredo/011R2/redo02a.rdo
$ mv /ora02/oraredo/011R2/redo03a.rdo /ora03/oraredo/011R2/redo03a.rdo
```

3. Start up your database in mount mode:

```
SQL> startup mount;
```

4. Update the control file with the new file locations and names:

```
SQL> alter database rename file '/ora02/oraredo/011R2/redo01a.rdo'
to '/ora03/oraredo/011R2/redo01a.rdo';
SQL> alter database rename file '/ora02/oraredo/011R2/redo02a.rdo'
to '/ora03/oraredo/011R2/redo02a.rdo';
SQL> alter database rename file '/ora02/oraredo/011R2/redo03a.rdo'
to '/ora03/oraredo/011R2/redo03a.rdo';
```

5. Open your database:

```
SQL> alter database open;
```

You can verify that your online redo logs are in the new locations by querying the V$LOGFILE view. I also recommend that you switch your online redo logs several times and then verify from the OS that the files have recent time stamps. Also check the alert.log file for any pertinent errors.

Summary

This chapter described how to configure and manage control files and online redo-log files. Control files and online redo logs are critical database files; a normally operating database can't function without them.

Control files are small binary files that contain information about the structure of the database. Any control files specified in the initialization file must be available for you to mount the database. If a control file becomes unavailable, then your database will cease operating until you resolve the issue. I highly recommend that you configure your database with at least three control files. If one control file becomes unavailable, you can replace it with a copy of a good existing control file. It's critical that you know how to configure, add, and remove these files.

Online redo logs are crucial files that record the database's transaction history. If you have multiple instances connected to one database, then each instance generates its own redo thread. Each database must be created with two or more online redo-log groups. You can operate a database with each group having just one online redo-log member. However, I highly recommend that you create your online redo-log groups with two members in each group. If an online redo log has at least one member that can be written to, your database will continue to function. If all members of an online redo-log group are unavailable, then your database will cease to operate. As a DBA, you must be extremely proficient with creating, adding, moving, and dropping these critical database files.

The chapters up to this point in the book have covered tasks such as installing the Oracle software, creating databases, and managing tablespaces, datafiles, control files, and online redo log files. The next several chapters concentrate on how to configure a database for application use, including topics such as creating users and database objects.

CHAPTER 6

■ ■ ■

Users and Basic Security

After you've installed the binaries, created a database, and created tablespaces, one of your next tasks is to create users and configure the security of the newly created accounts. A *user* is an account through which you can log in to the database and establish a connection. A *schema* is a collection of database objects (such as tables, indexes, and so on). A schema is owned by a user and has the same name as the user. The terms *user* and *schema* are often used synonymously by DBAs and developers. Distinguishing between the two terms isn't usually important, but there are some subtle differences.

Understanding Schemas vs. Users

When you log in to an Oracle database, you connect using a username and password. In this example, the user is INV_MGMT and the password is f00bar:

```
SQL> connect inv_mgmt/f00bar
```

When you connect as a user, by default you can manipulate objects in the schema owned by the user with which you connected to the database. For example, when you attempt to describe a table, Oracle by default accesses the current user's schema. Therefore, there is no reason to preface the table name with the currently connected user (owner). Suppose the currently connected user is INV_MGMT. Consider the following DESCRIBE command:

```
SQL> describe inventory;
```

The prior statement is identical in function to the following statement:

```
SQL> desc inv_mgmt.inventory;
```

You can alter your current user's session to point at a different schema via the ALTER SESSION statement:

```
SQL> alter session set current_schema = hr;
```

This statement doesn't grant the current user (in this example, INV_MGMT) any extra privileges. It does instruct Oracle to use the schema qualifier HR for any subsequent SQL statements that reference database objects. If the appropriate privileges have been granted, the INV_MGMT user can access the HR user's objects without having to prefix the schema name to the object name.

Managing Default Users

When you create a database, Oracle creates several default database users. The specific users that are created vary by database version. If you've just created your database, you can view the default user accounts as follows:

```
SQL> select username from dba_users order by 1;
```

Here is an example listing of some default database user accounts:

```
USERNAME
------------------------------
APPQOSSYS
DBSNMP
DIP
ORACLE_OCM
OUTLN
SYS
SYSTEM
```

To begin securing your database, you should minimally change the password for every default account and then lock any accounts that you're not using. After creating a database, I usually lock every default account and change their passwords to expired; I unlock default users only as they're needed. The following script generates the SQL statements that lock all users and set their passwords to expired:

```
select
  'alter user ' || username || ' password expire account lock;'
from dba_users;
```

A locked user can only be accessed by altering the user to an unlocked state. For example:

```
SQL> alter user outln account unlock;
```

A user with an expired password is prompted for a new password when first connecting to the database as that user. When connecting to a user, Oracle checks to see if the current password is expired, and if so prompts you as follows:

```
ORA-28001: the password has expired
Changing password for <user>
New password:
```

After entering the new password, you're prompted to enter it again:

```
Retype new password:
Password changed
Connected.
```

■ **Note** You can lock the SYS account, but this has no effect on your ability to connect as the SYS user using OS authentication or when using a password file.

If you've inherited a database from another DBA, then sometimes it's useful to determine whether another DBA created a user or if a user is a default account created by Oracle. As mentioned earlier, usually several user accounts are created for you when you create a database. The number of accounts varies somewhat by version and options installed. Run this query to display users that have been created by another DBA versus those created by Oracle (such as those created by default when the database is created):

```
select
 distinct u.username
,case when d.user_name is null then 'DBA created account'
 else 'Oracle created account'
 end
from dba_users     u
    ,default_pwd$ d
where u.username=d.user_name(+);
```

■ **Note** The `DEFAULT_PWD$` view is available starting with Oracle Database 11g. For more details about guidelines regarding checking for default passwords, see My Oracle Support note 227010.1.

When you're determining if a password is secure, it's useful to check to see whether the password for a user has ever been changed. If the password for a user has never been changed, this may be viewed as a security risk. This example performs such a check:

```
select
 name
,to_char(ctime,'dd-mon-yy hh24:mi:ss')
,to_char(ptime,'dd-mon-yy hh24:mi:ss')
,length(password)
from user$
where password is not null
and password not in ('GLOBAL','EXTERNAL')
and ctime=ptime;
```

In this script, the `CTIME` column contains the timestamp of when the user was created. The `PTIME` column contains the timestamp of when the password was changed. If the `CTIME` and `PTIME` are identical, then this indicates that the password has never been changed.

You should also check your database to determine whether any accounts are using default passwords. If you're using an Oracle Database 11g or higher, you can check the `DBA_USERS_WITH_DEFPWD` view to determine whether any Oracle-created user accounts are still set to the default password:

```
SQL> select * from dba_users_with_defpwd;
```

If you aren't using Oracle Database 11g, then you have to manually check the passwords or use a script. Listed next is a simple shell script that attempts to connect to the database using default passwords:

```
#!/bin/bash
if [ $# -ne 1 ]; then
  echo "Usage: $0 SID"
  exit 1
fi
# source oracle OS variables via oraset script.
# See chapter 2 for more details on setting OS variables.
. /var/opt/oracle/oraset $1
#
userlist="system sys dbsnmp dip oracle_ocm outln"
```

```
for u1 in $userlist
do
#
case $u1 in
system)
pwd=manager
cdb=$1
;;
sys)
pwd="change_on_install"
cdb="$1 as sysdba"
;;
*)
pwd=$u1
cdb=$1
esac
#
echo "select 'default' from dual;" | \
  sqlplus -s $u1/$pwd@$cdb | grep default >/dev/null
if [[ $? -eq 0 ]]; then
  echo "ALERT: $u1/$pwd@$cdb default password"
  echo "def pwd $u1 on $cdb" | mailx -s "$u1 pwd default" dkuhn@sun.com
else
  echo "cannot connect to $u1 with default password."
fi
done
exit 0
```

If this script detects a default password, an e-mail is sent to the appropriate (or unlucky, depending on how you look at it) DBA. The previous script is just a simple example; the point being that you need some sort of mechanism for detecting default passwords. You can create your own script or modify the previous script to suit your requirements.

SYS VS. SYSTEM

Oracle novices sometimes ask, "What's the difference between the SYS and SYSTEM schemas?" The SYS schema is the superuser of the database, owns all internal data-dictionary objects, and is used for tasks such as creating a database, starting or stopping the instance, backup and recovery, and adding or moving data files. These types of tasks typically require the SYSDBA or SYSOPER role. Security for these roles is often controlled through access to the OS account owner of the Oracle software. Additionally, security for these roles can be administered via a password file, which allows remote client/server access.

In contrast, the SYSTEM schema isn't very special. It's just a schema that has been granted the DBA role. Many shops lock the SYSTEM schema after database creation and never use it because it's often the first schema a hacker will try to access when attempting to break into a database.

Rather than risking an easily guessable entry point to the database, you can create a separate schema (named something other than SYSTEM) that has the DBA role granted to it. This DBA schema is used for administrative tasks such as creating users, changing passwords, granting database privileges, and so on. Having a separate DBA schema(s) for administrators provides more options for security and auditing.

Creating Users

When you're creating a user, you need to consider the following factors:

- User name
- Authentication method
- Basic privileges
- Default permanent tablespace
- Default temporary tablespace

These aspects of creating a user are discussed in the next few subsections.

Choosing a User Name and Authentication Method

Pick a user name that gives you an idea what application will be using the user. For example, if you have an inventory-management application, a good choice for a user name is INV_MGMT. Choosing a meaningful username helps identify the purpose of a user. This can be helpful especially if a system isn't documented appropriately.

Authentication is the method used to confirm that the user is authorized to use the account. Oracle supports three types of authentication:

- Password
- External service, such as the OS
- Global user via enterprise directory service (Oracle Internet Directory)

The most common method of authenticating a user is with a password. The external authentication method allows you to authenticate using smart cards, Kerberos, or the OS. This section shows examples of password verification and external authentication. Refer to the *Oracle Database Security Guide* and the *Oracle Database Advanced Security Administrator's Guide* (available at http://otn.oracle.com) for more information about external and global authentication methods.

When you're creating users as a DBA, your account must have the CREATE USER system privilege. You use the CREATE USER SQL statement to create users. This example creates a user named HEERA with the password CHAYA and assigns the default permanent tablespace USERS and the default temporary tablespace TEMP:

```
create user heera identified by chaya
default tablespace users
temporary tablespace temp;
```

This creates a bare-bones schema that has no privileges to do anything in the database. To make the user useful, you must minimally grant it the CREATE SESSION system privilege:

```
SQL> grant create session to heera;
```

If the new schema needs to be able to create tables, you need to grant it additional privileges like CREATE TABLE:

```
SQL> grant create table to heera;
```

The new schema also must have quota privileges granted for any tablespace in which it needs to create objects:

```
SQL> alter user heera quota unlimited on users;
```

■ **Note** A common technique is to grant the predefined roles of CONNECT and RESOURCE to newly created schemas. These roles contain system privileges such as CREATE SESSION and CREATE TABLE (and several others, which vary by release). I recommend against doing this, because Oracle has stated that those roles may not be available in future releases.

You can also create a user that is authenticated by an external service, such as the OS. In this scenario, you assume that if a user has been authenticated by the OS logon, that level of security is also good enough to allow access to the database. External authentication has some interesting advantages:

- Users with access to the server don't have to maintain a password to the database.

- Scripts that log on to the database don't have to use hard-coded passwords if executed by OS-authenticated users.

- Another database user can't hack into the externally identified user by trying to guess the username and password connection string. The only way to log on to an externally authenticated user is from an external authentication source (such as the OS).

- A DBA doesn't have to maintain a password for the database user.

When using external OS authentication, Oracle prefixes the value contained in OS_AUTHENT_PREFIX to the OS user connecting to the database. The default value for this parameter is OPS$. Oracle strongly recommends that you set the OS_AUTHENT_PREFIX parameter to a null string. For example:

```
SQL> alter system set os_authent_prefix='' scope=spfile;
```

You have to stop and start your database for this modification to take effect. After you've set the OS_AUTHENT_PREFIX variable, you can create an externally authenticated user. For example, say you have an OS user named jsmith and you want anybody with access to this OS user to be able to log in to the database without supplying a password. Use the CREATE EXTERNALLY statement to do this:

```
SQL> create user jsmith identified externally;
```

Now, when jsmith logs on to the database server, this user can connect to SQL*Plus as follows:

```
$ sqlplus /
```

No username or password is required because the user has already been authenticated by the OS.

Assigning Default Permanent and Temporary Tablespaces

When maintaining a database, you should verify the default and temporary tablespace settings to ensure that they meet your database standards. You can view user information by selecting from the DBA_USERS view:

```
select
 username
,password
,default_tablespace
,temporary_tablespace
from dba_users;
```

Here is some sample output:

```
USERNAME              PASSWORD              DEFAULT_TABLESP TEMPORARY_TABLE
--------------------  --------------------  --------------- ---------------
JSMITH                EXTERNAL              USERS           TEMP
DBSNMP                                      SYSAUX          TEMP
ORACLE_OCM                                  USERS           TEMP
APPQOSSYS                                   SYSAUX          TEMP
APPUSR                                      USERS           TEMP
```

None of your users, other than the SYS user, should have a default permanent tablespace of SYSTEM. You don't want any users other than SYS creating objects in the SYSTEM tablespace. The SYSTEM tablespace should be reserved for the SYS user's objects. If other users' objects existed in the SYSTEM tablespace, you'd run the risk of filling up that tablespace and compromising the availability of your database.

All of your users should be assigned a temporary tablespace that has been created as type temporary. Usually, this tablespace is named TEMP (see Chapter 4 for more details).

You never want any users with a temporary tablespace of SYSTEM. If a user has a temporary tablespace of SYSTEM, then any sort area for which they require temporary disk storage acquires extents in the SYSTEM tablespace. This can lead to the SYSTEM tablespace filling up. You don't want the SYSTEM tablespace ever filling up, because that can lead to a nonfunctioning database if the SYS schema can't acquire more space as its objects grow. To check for users that have a temporary tablespace of SYSTEM, run this script:

```
SQL> select username from dba_users where temporary_tablespace='SYSTEM';
```

Typically, I use a script name creuser.sql when creating a user. The script uses variables that define the user names, passwords, default tablespace name, and so on. For each environment (development, test, QA, beta, production) in which the script is executed, you can change the ampersand variables as required for each environment. For example, you can use a different password for each separate environment.

Here's an example creuser.sql script:

```
DEFINE cre_user=inv_mgmt
DEFINE cre_user_pwd=inv_mgmt_pwd
DEFINE def_tbsp=inv_data
DEFINE idx_tbsp=inv_index
DEFINE smk_ttbl=zzzzzzz
--
CREATE USER &&cre_user IDENTIFIED BY &&cre_user_pwd
DEFAULT TABLESPACE &&def_tbsp;
--
GRANT CREATE SESSION TO &&cre_user;
GRANT CREATE TABLE   TO &&cre_user;
--
ALTER USER &&cre_user QUOTA UNLIMITED ON &&def_tbsp;
ALTER USER &&cre_user QUOTA UNLIMITED ON &&idx_tbsp;
--
-- Smoke test
```

```
CONN &&cre_user/&&cre_user_pwd
CREATE TABLE &&smk_ttbl(test_id NUMBER) TABLESPACE &&def_tbsp;
CREATE INDEX &&smk_ttbl._idx1 ON &&smk_ttbl(test_id) TABLESPACE &&idx_tbsp;
INSERT INTO &&smk_ttbl VALUES(1);
DROP TABLE &&smk_ttbl;
```

SMOKE TEST

Smoke test is a term used in occupations such as plumbing, electronics, and software development. It refers to the first check done after initial assembly or after repairs in order to provide some level of assurance that the system works properly.

In plumbing, a smoke test forces smoke through the drainage pipes. The forced smoke helps to quickly identify cracks or leaks in the system. In electronics, a smoke test occurs when power is first connected to a circuit. This sometimes produces smoke if the wiring is faulty.

In software development, a smoke test is a simple test of the system to ensure that it has some level of workability. Many managers have reportedly been seen to have smoke coming out their ears when the smoke test fails.

Modifying Passwords

Use the ALTER USER command to modify an existing user's password. This example changes the HEERA user's password to FOOBAR:

```
SQL> alter user HEERA identified by FOOBAR;
```

You can change the password of another account only if you have the ALTER USER privilege granted to your user. This privilege is granted to the DBA role. After you change a password for a user, any subsequent connection to the database by that user must use the password changed by the ALTER USER statement.

In Oracle Database 11g or higher, when you modify a password, it's case-sensitive. If you're using Oracle Database 10g or lower, the password isn't case-sensitive.

SQL*PLUS PASSWORD COMMAND

You can change the password for a user with the SQL*Plus PASSWORD command. (Like all SQL*Plus commands, it can be abbreviated.) You're prompted for a new password:

```
SQL> passw heera
Changing password for heera
New password:
Retype new password:
Password changed
```

This method has the advantage of changing a password for a user without displaying the new password on the screen.

Enforcing Password Security

There are a couple schools of thought about enforcing password security:

- Use easily remembered passwords so you don't have them written down or recorded in a file somewhere. Because the passwords aren't sophisticated, they aren't very secure.

- Enforce a level of sophistication for passwords. Such passwords aren't easily remembered and thus must be recorded somewhere, which isn't secure.

You may choose to enforce a degree of password sophistication because you think it's the most secure option. Or you may be required to enforce password security by your corporate security team (and thus have no choice in the matter). This section isn't about debating which of the prior methods is preferable. Should you choose to impose a degree of sophistication (strength) for a password, this section describes how to enforce the rules.

You can enforce a minimum standard of password complexity by assigning a password-verification function to a user's profile. Oracle supplies a default password-verification function that you create by running the following script as the SYS schema:

```
SQL> @?/rdbms/admin/utlpwdmg
Function created.
Profile altered.
Function created.
```

For Oracle Database 11g, set the PASSWORD_VERIFY_FUNCTION of the DEFAULT profile to VERIFY_FUNCTION_11G:

```
SQL> alter profile default limit PASSWORD_VERIFY_FUNCTION verify_function_11G;
```

For Oracle Database 10g, set the PASSWORD_VERIFY_FUNCTION of the DEFAULT profile to VERIFY_FUNCTION:

```
SQL> alter profile default limit PASSWORD_VERIFY_FUNCTION verify_function;
```

If for any reason you need to back out of the new security modifications, run this statement to disable the password function:

```
SQL> alter profile default limit PASSWORD_VERIFY_FUNCTION null;
```

When enabled, the password-verification function ensures that users are correctly creating or modifying their passwords. The utlpwdmg.sql script creates a function that checks a password to ensure that it meets basic security standards such as minimum password length, password not the same as username, and so on. You can verify that the new security function is in effect by attempting to change the password of a user that has been assigned the DEFAULT profile. This example tries to change the password to less than the minimum length:

```
SQL> password
Changing password for HEERA
Old password:
New password:
Retype new password:
ERROR:
ORA-28003: password verification for the specified password failed
ORA-20001: Password length less than 8
Password unchanged
```

▪ **Note** For Oracle Database 11*g*, the minimum password length is eight characters. For Oracle Database 10*g*, the minimum length is four characters.

As mentioned earlier, starting with Oracle Database 11*g*, password case-sensitivity is enforced. You can disable this feature by setting the SEC_CASE_SENSITIVE_LOGON initialization parameter to FALSE:

```
SQL> alter system set sec_case_sensitive_logon = FALSE;
```

However, doing so isn't recommended. For most security requirements, you should have passwords that are case-sensitive.

Also keep in mind that it's possible to modify the code used to create the password-verification function. For example, you can open and modify the script used to create this function:

```
$ vi $ORACLE_HOME/rdbms/admin/utlpwdmg.sql
```

If you feel that the Oracle-supplied verification function is too strong or overly restrictive, you can create your own function and assign it to the appropriate database profiles.

Logging On as a Different User

This section details how to log on to a different user without having the clear-text form of the user's password. You may wish to do this in a couple of situations:

- You're copying a user from one environment (such as production) to a different environment (such as test), and you want to retain the original password.

- You're working in a production environment, and you need to be able to connect as the user who owns objects to execute CREATE TABLE statements, issue grants, and so on. In a production environment, you may not know the user's password because of poor maintenance procedures.

You need access to a DBA-privileged account to be able to log on as a different user without knowing the password. Here are the steps to do this:

1. As a DBA, temporarily store a user's encrypted password.

2. Change the user's password.

3. Connect to the user with the new password, and run Data Definition Language (DDL) statements.

4. Connect as a DBA, and change the password back to the original.

Be very careful before changing a user's password as describe in the previous steps. First, the application can't connect to the database while the password has been changed to a temporary setting. If the application repeatedly fails to successfully connect, this may lock the account when you exceed the FAILED_LOGIN_ATTEMPTS limit of a user's profile (the default is 10 failed attempts before the user is locked).

Furthermore, if you've modified the values of PASSWORD_REUSE_MAX (the number of days before a password can be reused) and PASSWORD_REUSE_TIME (the number of times a password must change before a password can be reused), then you can't reset the password back to its original value.

Listed next is an example that shows how to temporarily change a user's password and then set the password back to its original value. First, select the statement required to restore a user's password to what it's currently set to. In this example, the username is APPUSR:

```
select 'alter user appusr identified by values ' ||
'''' || password || '''' || ';'
from user$ where name='APPUSR';
```

Here is the output for this example:

```
SQL> alter user appusr identified by values 'A0493EBF86198724';
```

Now, modify the user's password to a known value (in this example, foo):

```
SQL> alter user appusr identified by foo;
```

Connect to the APPUSR user:

```
SQL> conn appusr/foo
```

After you're finished using the APPUSR user, change its password back to the original value:

```
SQL> alter user appusr identified by values 'A0493EBF86198724';
```

Again, be very cautious when performing this procedure, because you don't want to put yourself in a situation where a password-profile setting won't allow you to reset the password:

```
ORA-28007: the password cannot be reused
```

If you get this error, one option is to set the password to a brand-new value. However, doing so may have an undesirable impact on the application. If developers have hard-coded the password into response files, the application can't log on without changing the hard-coded password to the new password.

Your other option is to temporarily change the user's profile to allow the password to be reused. First, check to see what the current profile is for the user:

```
SQL> select username, profile from dba_users where username = UPPER('&&username');
```

Here is some sample output:

```
USERNAME                        PROFILE
------------------------------- ------------------------------
APPUSR                          SECURE
```

Now, create a profile that specifically allows a password to be reused without any restrictions:

```
CREATE PROFILE temp_prof LIMIT
PASSWORD_REUSE_MAX unlimited
PASSWORD_REUSE_TIME unlimited;
```

Next, assign the user the profile that doesn't limit the reuse of passwords:

```
SQL> alter user appusr profile temp_prof;
```

You should be able to modify the password as shown previously:

```
SQL> alter user appusr identified by values 'A0493EBF86198724';
```

If successful, you see this message:

```
User altered.
```

121

Make sure you set the profile back to the original value for the user:

```
SQL> alter user appusr profile secure;
```

Finally, drop the temporary profile so it isn't accidentally used in the future:

```
SQL> drop profile temp_prof;
```

Modifying Users

Sometimes you need to modify existing users for the following types of reasons:

- To change a user's password
- To lock or unlock a user
- To change the default permanent and/or temporary tablespace
- To change a profile or role
- To change system or object privileges
- To modify quotas on tablespaces

Use the ALTER USER statement to modify users. Listed next are several SQL statements that modify a user. This example changes a user's password using the IDENTIFIED BY clause:

```
SQL> alter user inv_mgmt identified by i2jy22a;
```

If you don't set a default permanent tablespace and temporary tablespace when you initially create the user, you can modify then after creation as shown here:

```
SQL> alter user inv_mgmt default tablespace users temporary tablespace temp;
```

This example locks a user account:

```
SQL> alter user inv_mgmt account lock;
```

And this example alters the user's quota on the USERS tablespace:

```
SQL> alter user inv_mgmt quota 500m on users;
```

Dropping Users

Before you drop a user, I recommend that you first lock the user. Locking the user prevents anybody from connecting to a locked database account. This allows you to determine better whether someone is using the account before it's dropped. Here's an example of locking a user:

```
SQL> alter user heera account lock;
```

Any user or application attempting to connect to this user now receives the following error:

```
ORA-28000: the account is locked
```

To view the users and lock dates in your database, issue this query:

```
SQL> select username, lock_date from dba_users;
```

To unlock an account, issue this command:

```
SQL> alter user heera account unlock;
```

Locking users is a very handy technique for securing your database and discovering which users are active.

Be aware that by locking a user, you aren't locking access to a user's objects. For example, if a USER_A has select, insert, update, and delete privileges on tables owned by USER_B, if you lock the USER_B account, USER_A can still issue Data Manipulation Language (DML) statements against the objects owned by USER_B. To determine whether the objects are being used, see the auditing section of Chapter 22.

■ **Tip** If a user's objects don't consume inordinate amounts of disk space, then before you drop the user, it's prudent to make a quick backup. See Chapter 13 for details on using Data Pump to back up a single user.

After you're sure that a user and its objects aren't needed, use the DROP USER statement to remove a database account. This example drops the user HEERA:

```
SQL> drop user heera;
```

The prior command won't work if the user owns any database objects. Use the CASCADE clause to remove a user and have its objects dropped:

```
SQL> drop user heera cascade;
```

■ **Note** The DROP USER statement may take an inordinate amount of time to execute if the user being dropped owns a vast number of database objects. In these situations, you may want to consider dropping the user's objects before dropping the user.

When you drop a user, any tables that it owns are also dropped. Additionally, all indexes, triggers, and referential-integrity constraints are removed. If referential integrity constraints exist in other schemas that depend on any dropped primary-key and unique-key constraints, the referential constraints in other schemas are also dropped. Oracle invalidates but doesn't drop any views, synonyms, procedures, functions, and packages that are dependent on the dropped user's objects.

Enforcing Password Security and Resource Limits

When you're creating users, sometimes requirements call for passwords to adhere to a set of security rules. For example, the password must be of a certain length and contain numeric characters. Also, when you set up database users, you may want to ensure that a certain user isn't capable of consuming inordinate amounts of CPU resources.

You can use a database profile to meet these types of requirements. An Oracle *profile* is a database object that serves two purposes:

- Enforcing password security settings

- Limiting system resources that a user consumes

These topics are discussed in the next two subsections.

Implementing Password Security

When you create a user, if no profile is specified, the DEFAULT profile is assigned to the newly created user. To view the current settings for a profile, issue the following SQL:

```
SQL> select profile, resource_name, resource_type, limit from dba_profiles;
```

Here is a partial listing of the output:

```
PROFILE      RESOURCE_NAME             RESOURCE_T LIMIT
----------   ------------------------  ---------- --------------------
DEFAULT      CONNECT_TIME              KERNEL     UNLIMITED
DEFAULT      PRIVATE_SGA               KERNEL     UNLIMITED
DEFAULT      FAILED_LOGIN_ATTEMPTS     PASSWORD   10
DEFAULT      PASSWORD_LIFE_TIME        PASSWORD   180
DEFAULT      PASSWORD_REUSE_TIME       PASSWORD   UNLIMITED
DEFAULT      PASSWORD_REUSE_MAX        PASSWORD   10
DEFAULT      PASSWORD_VERIFY_FUNCTION  PASSWORD   NULL
```

A profile's password restrictions are in effect as soon as the profile is assigned to a user. For example, from the previous output, if you've assigned the DEFAULT profile to a user, that user is allowed only 10 consecutive failed login attempts before the user account is automatically locked by Oracle. See Table 6–1 for a description of the password profile security settings.

■ **Tip** See My Oracle Support note 454635.1 for details on Oracle Database 11*g* DEFAULT profile changes.

You can alter the DEFAULT profile to customize it for your environment. For example, say you want to enforce a cap on the maximum number of days a password can be used. The next line of code sets the PASSWORD_LIFE_TIME of the DEFAULT profile to 300 days:

```
SQL> alter profile default limit password_life_time 300;
```

Table 6–1. Password Security Settings

Password Setting	Description	11*g* default	10*g* default
FAILED_LOGIN_ATTEMPTS	Number of failed login attempts before the schema is locked	10 attempts	10 attempts
PASSWORD_GRACE_TIME	Number of days after a password expires that the owner can log in with an old password	7 days	Unlimited
PASSWORD_LIFE_TIME	Number of days a password is valid	180 days	Unlimited
PASSWORD_LOCK_TIME	Number of days an account is locked after FAILED_LOGIN_ATTEMPTS has been reached	1 day	Unlimited
PASSWORD_REUSE_MAX	Number of days before a password can be reused	Unlimited	Unlimited
PASSWORD_REUSE_TIME	Number of times a password must change before a password can be reused	Unlimited	Unlimited
PASSWORD_VERIFY_FUNCTION	Database function used to verify the password	Null	Null

The PASSWORD_REUSE_TIME and PASSWORD_REUSE_MAX settings must be used in conjunction. If you specify an integer for one parameter (doesn't matter which one) and then UNLIMITED for the other parameter, the current password can never be reused.

If you want to specify that the DEFAULT profile password must be changed 10 times within 100 days before it can be reused, use a line of code similar to this:

```
SQL> alter profile default limit password_reuse_time 100 password_reuse_max 10;
```

Although using the DEFAULT profile is sufficient for many environments, you may need tighter security management. I recommend that you create custom security profiles and assign them to users as required. For example, create a profile specifically for application users:

```
CREATE PROFILE SECURE_APP LIMIT
PASSWORD_LIFE_TIME 200
PASSWORD_GRACE_TIME 10
PASSWORD_REUSE_TIME 1
PASSWORD_REUSE_MAX 1
FAILED_LOGIN_ATTEMPTS 3
PASSWORD_LOCK_TIME 1
PASSWORD_VERIFY_FUNCTION verify_function_11G;
```

After you create the profile, you can assign it to users as appropriate. The following SQL generates a SQL script named alt_prof_dyn.sql that you can use to assign users to the newly created profile:

```
set head off;
spo alt_prof_dyn.sql
select 'alter user ' || username || ' profile secure_app;'
from dba_users where username like '%APP%';
spo off;
```

Be careful when assigning profiles to application accounts that use the database. If you want to enforce that a password must change at a regular frequency, be sure you understand the impact on production systems. Passwords tend to get hard-coded into response files and code. Enforcing password changes in these environments can wreak havoc as you try to chase down all the places where the password is referenced. If you don't want to enforce the periodic changing of the password, you can set PASSWORD_LIFE_TIME to a high value such as 10000 (days).

Limiting Database Resource Usage

As mentioned earlier, the password-profile settings take effect as soon as you assign the profile to a user. Unlike password settings, kernel resource profile restrictions don't take effect until you set the RESOURCE_LIMIT initialization parameter to TRUE for your database. For example:

```
SQL> alter system set resource_limit=true scope=both;
```

To view the current setting of the RESOURCE_LIMIT parameter:

```
SQL> select name, value from v$parameter where name='resource_limit';
```

When you create a user, if you don't specify a profile, then the DEFAULT profile is assigned to the user. You can modify the DEFAULT profile with the ALTER PROFILE statement. The next example modifies the DEFAULT profile to limit CPU_PER_SESSION to 240000 (in hundredths of seconds):

```
SQL> alter profile default limit cpu_per_session 240000;
```

This limits any user with the DEFAULT profile to 2400 seconds of CPU use. You can set various limits in a profile. Table 6–2 describes the database resource settings you can limit via a profile.

Table 6–2. Database Resource Profile Settings

Profile Resource	Meaning
COMPOSITE_LIMIT	Limit based on a weighted-sum algorithm for these resources: CPU_PER_SESSION, CONNECT_TIME, LOGICAL_READS_PER_SESSION, and PRIVATE_SGA
CONNECT_TIME	Connect time in minutes
CPU_PER_CALL	CPU time limit per call in hundredths of seconds
CPU_PER_SESSION	CPU time limit per session in hundredths of seconds
IDLE_TIME	Idle time in minutes
LOGICAL_READS_PER_CALL	Blocks read per call
LOGICAL_READS_PER_SESSION	Blocks read per session
PRIVATE_SGA	Amount of space consumed in the shared pool
SESSIONS_PER_USER	Number of concurrent sessions

You can also create custom profiles and assign them to users via the CREATE PROFILE statement. You can then assign that profile to any existing database users. The following SQL statement creates a profile that limits resources, such as the amount of CPU an individual session can consume:

```
create profile user_profile_limit
limit
sessions_per_user 20
cpu_per_session 240000
logical_reads_per_session 1000000
connect_time 480
idle_time 120;
```

After you create a profile, you can assign it to a user. In the next example, user HEERA is assigned USER_PROFILE_LIMIT:

```
SQL> alter user heera profile user_profile_limit;
```

■ Note Oracle recommends that you use Database Resource Manager to manage database resource limits. However, I find database profiles (implemented via SQL) to be an effective and easy mechanism for limiting resources.

As part of the CREATE USER statement, you can specify a profile other than DEFAULT:

```
SQL> create user heera identified by foo profile user_profile_limit;
```

When should you use database profiles? You should always take advantage of the password-security settings of the DEFAULT profile. You can easily modify the default settings of this profile as required by your business rules.

A profile's kernel resource limits are useful when you have power users who need to connect directly to the database and run queries. For example, you can use the kernel resource settings to limit the amount of CPU time a user consumes, which is handy when a user writes a bad query that inadvertently consumes excessive database resources.

Managing Privileges

A database user must be granted privileges before the user can perform any task in the database. In Oracle, you assign privileges either by granting a specific privilege to a user or by granting the privilege to a role and then granting the role that contains the privilege to a user. There are two types of privileges: system privileges and object privileges. The following sections discuss these privileges in detail.

Assigning Database System Privileges

Database system privileges allow you to do tasks such as connecting to the database and creating and modifying objects. There are hundreds of different system privileges. You can view system privileges by querying the DBA_SYS_PRIVS view:

```
SQL> select distinct privilege from dba_sys_privs;
```

You can grant privileges to other users or roles. To be able to grant privileges, a user needs the GRANT ANY PRIVILEGE privilege or must have been granted a system privilege with ADMIN OPTION.

Use the GRANT statement to assign a system privileges to a user. For example, minimally a user needs CREATE SESSION to be able to connect to the database. You grant this system privilege as shown:

```
SQL> grant create session to inv_mgmt;
```

Usually, a user needs to do more than just connect to the database. For example, a user may need to create tables and other types of database objects. This example grants a user the CREATE TABLE and CREATE DATABASE LINK system privileges:

```
SQL> grant create table, create database link to inv_mgmt;
```

If you need to take away privileges, use the REVOKE statement:

```
SQL> revoke create table from inv_mgmt;
```

Oracle has a feature that allows you to grant a system privilege and also give that user the ability to administer a privilege. You do this with the WITH ADMIN OPTION clause:

```
SQL> grant create table to inv_mgmt with admin option;
```

I rarely use WITH ADMIN OPTION when granting privileges. Usually, a user with the DBA role is used to grant privileges, and that privilege isn't generally meted out to non-DBA users in the database. This is because it would be hard to keep track of who assigned what system privileges, for what reason, and when. In a production environment, this would be untenable.

You can also grant system privileges to the PUBLIC user group (I don't recommend doing this). For example, you could grant CREATE SESSION to all users that ever need to connect to the database, as follows:

```
SQL> grant create session to public;
```

Now every user that is created can automatically connect to the database. Granting system privileges to the PUBLIC user group is almost always a bad idea. As a DBA, one of your main priorities is to ensure that the data in the database is safe and secure. Granting privileges to the PUBLIC role is a sure way of not being able to manage who is authorized to perform specific actions within the database.

Assigning Database Object Privileges

Database object privileges allow you to access and manipulate other users' objects. The types of database objects on which you can grant privileges include tables, views, materialized views, sequences, packages, functions, procedures, user-defined types, and directories. To be able to grant object privileges, one of the following must be true:

- You own the object.

- You've been granted the object privilege with GRANT OPTION.

- You have the GRANT ANY OBJECT PRIVILEGE system privilege.

This example grants object privileges (as the object owner) to the INV_MGMT_APP user:

```
SQL> grant insert, update, delete, select on registrations to inv_mgmt_app;
```

The GRANT ALL statement is equivalent to granting INSERT, UPDATE, DELETE, and SELECT to an object. The next statement is equivalent to the prior statement:

```
SQL> grant all on registrations to inv_mgmt_app;
```

You can also grant INSERT and UPDATE privileges to tables at the column level. The next example grants INSERT privileges to specific columns in the INVENTORY table:

```
SQL> grant insert (inv_id, inv_name, inv_desc) on inventory to inv_mgmt_app;
```

If you want a user that is being granted object privileges to be able to subsequently grant those same object privileges to other users, then use the WITH GRANT OPTION clause:

```
SQL> grant insert on registrations to grouping_app with grant option;
```

Now the GROUPING_APP user can grant insert privileges on the REGISTRATIONS table to other users.

I rarely use the WITH GRANT OPTION when granting object privileges. This option allows other users to propagate object privileges to other users. This makes it hard to keep track of who assigned what object privileges, for what reason, when, and so on. In a production environment, this would be untenable. When you're managing a production environment, when problems arise, you need to know what changed and when and for what reason.

You can also grant object privileges to the PUBLIC user group (I don't recommend doing this). For example, you could grant select privileges on a table to PUBLIC:

```
SQL> grant select on registrations to public;
```

Now every user can select from the REGISTRATIONS table. Granting object privileges to the PUBLIC role is almost always a bad idea. As a DBA, one of your main priorities is to ensure that the data in the database is safe and secure. Granting object privileges to the PUBLIC role is a sure way of not being able to manage who can access what data in the database.

If you need to take away object privileges, then use the REVOKE statement. This example revokes DML privileges from the INV_MGMT_APP user:

```
SQL> revoke insert, update, delete, select on registrations from inv_mgmt_app;
```

Grouping and Assigning Privileges

A *role* is a database object that allows you to logically group system and/or object privileges together so you can assign those privileges in one operation to a user. Roles help you manage aspects of database security in that they provide a central object that has privileges assigned to it. You can subsequently assign the role to multiple users or other roles.

To create a role, connect to the database as a user that has the CREATE ROLE system privilege. Next, create a role and assign to it the system or object privileges that you want to group together. This example uses the CREATE ROLE statement to create the JR_DBA role:

```
SQL> create role jr_dba;
```

The next several lines of SQL grant system privileges to the newly created role:

```
SQL> grant select any table to jr_dba;
SQL> grant create any table to jr_dba;
SQL> grant create any view to jr_dba;
SQL> grant create synonym to jr_dba;
SQL> grant create database link to jr_dba;
```

Next, grant the role to any schema you want to possess those privileges:

```
SQL> grant jr_dba to lellison;
SQL> grant jr_dba to mhurd;
```

The users LELLISON and MHURD can now perform tasks such as creating synonyms, views, and so on. To view users assigned to roles, query the DBA_ROLE_PRIVS view:

```
SQL> select grantee, granted_role from dba_role_privs order by 1;
```

To view roles granted to your currently connected user, query from the USER_ROLE_PRIVS view:

```
SQL> select * from user_role_privs;
```

To revoke a privilege from a role, use the REVOKE command:

```
SQL> revoke create database link from jr_dba;
```

Similarly, use the REVOKE command to remove a role from a user:

```
SQL> revoke jr_dba from lellison;
```

■ Note Unlike other database objects, roles don't have owners. A role is defined by the privileges assigned to it.

PL/SQL AND ROLES

If you work with PL/SQL, sometimes you get this error when attempting to compile a procedure or a function:

```
PL/SQL: ORA-00942: table or view does not exist
```

What's confusing is that you can describe the table:

```
SQL> desc app_table;
```

Why doesn't PL/SQL seem to be able to recognize the table? It's because PL/SQL requires that the owner of the package, procedure, or function be explicitly granted privileges to any objects referenced in the code. The owner of the PL/SQL code can't have obtained the grants through a role.

When confronted with this issue, try this as the owner of the PL/SQL code:

```
SQL> set role none;
```

Now, try to run a SQL statement that accesses the table in question:

```
SQL> select count(*) from app_table;
```

If you can no longer access the table, then you've been granted access through a role. To resolve the issue, explicitly grant access to any tables to the owner of the PL/SQL code (as the owner of the table):

```
SQL> connect owner/pass
SQL> grant select on app_table to proc_owner;
```

You should be able to connect as the owner of the PL/SQL code and successfully compile your code.

Summary

After you create a database, one of your first tasks is to secure any default user accounts. One valid approach is to lock all the default accounts and open them only as they're required. Other approaches include changing and/or expiring the password. After the default users' accounts have been secured, you're responsible for creating users that need access to the database. This often includes application users, accounts for DBAs, and developers.

You should consider using a secure profile for any users you create. Additionally, think about password security when creating users. Oracle provides a password function that enforces a certain level of password sophistication. I recommend that you use a combination of profiles and a password function as a first step in creating a secure database.

As the databases ages, you need to maintain the user accounts. Usually, the requirements for database accounts change over time. You're responsible for ensuring that the correct system and object privileges are maintained for each account. With any legacy system, you'll eventually need to lock and drop users. Dropping unused accounts helps ensure that your environment is more secure and maintainable.

The next logical step after creating users is to create database objects. Chapter 7 deals with concepts related to table creation.

CHAPTER 7

■■■

Tables and Constraints

The previous chapters in this book cover topics that prepare you for the next logical step of creating database objects. For example, you need to install the Oracle binaries and create a database, tablespaces, and users before you start creating tables. Usually, the first objects created for an application are the tables, constraints, and indexes. This chapter focuses on the management of tables and constraints. The management of indexes is covered in Chapter 8.

A *table* is the basic storage container for data in a database. You create and modify the table structure via Data Definition Language (DDL) statements such as CREATE TABLE and ALTER TABLE. You access and manipulate table data via Data Manipulation Language (DML) statements (INSERT, UPDATE, DELETE, MERGE, and SELECT).

A *constraint* is a mechanism for enforcing that data adheres to business rules. For example, you may have a business requirement that all customer IDs be unique within a table. In this scenario, you can use a primary-key constraint to guarantee that all customer IDs inserted or updated in a CUSTOMER table are unique. Constraints inspect data as it's inserted, updated, and deleted to ensure that no business rules are violated.

This chapter deals with common techniques for creating and maintaining tables and constraints. Almost always, when you create a table, the table needs one or more constraints defined; therefore, it makes sense to cover constraint management along with tables. The first part of the chapter focuses on common table-creation and -maintenance tasks. The latter part of this chapter details constraint management.

Understanding Table Types

The Oracle database supports a vast and robust variety of table types. These various types are described in Table 7-1.

Table 7–1. Oracle Table Type Descriptions

Table Type	Description	Typical Use
Heap-organized	The default table type and the most commonly used.	Table type to use unless you have a specific reason to use a different type.
Temporary	Session private data, stored for the duration of a session or transaction. Space is allocated in temporary segments.	Program needs a temporary table structure to store and sort data. Table isn't required after program ends.
Index-organized (IOT)	Data stored in a B-tree index structure sorted by primary key.	Table is queried mainly on primary key columns. Provides fast random access.
Partitioned	A logical table that consists of separate physical segments.	Type used with large tables with millions of rows.
Clustered	A group of tables that share the same data blocks.	Type used to reduce I/O for tables that are often joined on the same columns.
External	Tables that use data stored in operating system files outside of the database.	Type lets you efficiently access data in a file outside of the database (like a CSV file).
Nested	A table with a column with a data type that is another table.	Rarely used.
Object	A table with a column with a data type that is an object type.	Rarely used.

This chapter focuses on the table types that are most often used, in particular heap-organized, index-organized, and temporary tables. Partitioned tables are used extensively in data warehouse environments and are covered separately in Chapter 12. For details on table types not covered in this chapter, see the Oracle SQL Reference Guide, which is available for download from http://otn.oracle.com.

The number of table features expands with each new version of Oracle. Consider this: the Oracle SQL Reference Guide presents nearly 80 pages of syntax associated with the CREATE TABLE statement. On top of that, the ALTER TABLE statement takes up another 80 plus pages of details related to table maintenance. For most situations, you typically need to use only a fraction of the table options available.

Creating a Table

Listed next are the general factors you should consider when creating a table:

- Type of table (heap-organized, temporary, index-organized, partitioned, and so on)
- Naming conventions
- Column data types and sizes
- Constraints (primary key, foreign keys, and so on)
- Index requirements (see Chapter 8 for details)
- Initial storage requirements
- Special features such as virtual columns, read-only, parallel, compression, no logging, and so on
- Growth requirements
- Tablespace(s) for the table and its indexes

Before you run a CREATE TABLE statement, you need to give some thought to each item in the previous list. To that end, DBAs often use data-modeling tools to help manage the creation of DDL scripts that are used to create database objects. Data-modeling tools allow you to visually define tables and relationships and the underlying database features.

Creating a Heap-Organized Table

You use the CREATE TABLE statement to create tables. When creating a table, at minimum you must specify the table name, column name(s), and data types associated with the columns. The Oracle default table type is heap-organized. The term *heap* means that the data isn't stored in a specific order in the table (instead, it's a heap of data). Here's a simple example of creating a heap-organized table with four columns:

```
create table d_sources(
d_source_id number not null,
source_type varchar2(32),
create_dtt date default sysdate not null,
update_dtt timestamp(5)
);
```

If you don't specify a tablespace, then the table is created in the default permanent tablespace of the user that creates the table. Allowing the table to be created in the default permanent tablespace is fine for a few small test tables. For anything more sophisticated, you should explicitly specify the tablespace in which you want tables created.

Usually, when you create a table, you should also specify constraints, such as the primary key. The following code shows the most common features you use when creating a table. This DDL defines primary keys, foreign keys, tablespace information, and comments:

```
create table operating_systems(
    operating_system_id    number(19, 0)      not null,
    version                varchar2(50),
    os_name                varchar2(256),
    release                varchar2(50),
    vendor                 varchar2(50),
    create_dtt             date               default sysdate not null,
    update_dtt             date,
    constraint operating_systems_pk primary key (operating_system_id)
    using index tablespace inv_mgmt_index
)
tablespace inv_mgmt_data
;
--
create unique index operating_system_uk1 on operating_systems
 (os_name, version, release, vendor)
tablespace inv_mgmt_index
;
--
create table computer_systems(
computer_system_id  number(38, 0) not null,
agent_uuid          varchar2(256),
operating_system_id number(19, 0) not null,
hardware_model      varchar2(50),
create_dtt          date default sysdate not null,
update_dtt          date,
constraint computer_systems_pk primary key (computer_system_id)
using index tablespace inv_mgmt_index
) tablespace inv_mgmt_data;
--
comment on column computer_systems.computer_system_id is
'Surrogate key generated via an Oracle sequence.';
--
create unique index computer_system_uk1 on computer_systems(agent_uuid)
tablespace inv_mgmt_index;
--
alter table computer_systems add constraint computer_systems_fk1
foreign key (operating_system_id)
references operating_systems(operating_system_id);
```

When creating a table, I usually don't specify table-level physical space properties. If you don't specify table-level space properties, then the table inherits its space properties from the tablespace in which it's created. This simplifies administration and maintenance. If you have tables that require different physical space properties, then you can create separate tablespaces to hold tables with differing needs. For example, you might create a DATA_LARGE tablespace with extent sizes of 16MB and a DATA_SMALL tablespace with extents sizes of 128KB, and choose where a table is created based on its storage requirements. See Chapter 4 for details regarding the creation of tablespaces.

Table 7–2 lists some guidelines to consider when creating tables. These aren't hard and fast rules; adapt them as needed for your environment. Some of these guidelines may seem like obvious suggestions. However, after inheriting many databases over the years, I've seen each of these recommendations violated in some way that makes database maintenance difficult and unwieldy.

Table 7-2. Guidelines to Consider When Creating Tables

Recommendation	Reasoning
Use standards when naming tables, columns, constraints, triggers, indexes, and so on.	Helps document the application and simplifies maintenance.
If a column always contains numeric data, make it a number data type.	Enforces a business rule and allows for the greatest flexibility, performance, and consistent results when using Oracle SQL math functions (which may behave differently for an "01" character versus a 1 number).
If you have a business rule that defines the length and precision of a number field, then enforce it: for example, NUMBER(7,2). If you don't have a business rule, make it NUMBER(38).	Enforces a business rule and keeps the data cleaner.
For character data that is of variable length, use VARCHAR2 (and not VARCHAR).	Follows Oracle's recommendation of using VARCHAR2 for character data (instead of VARCHAR). The Oracle documentation states that in the future, VARCHAR will be redefined as a separate data type.
If you have a business rule that specifies the maximum length of a column, then use that length, as opposed to making all columns VARCHAR2(4000).	Enforces a business rule and keeps the data cleaner.
Use DATE and TIMESTAMP data types appropriately.	Enforces a business rule, ensures that the data is of the appropriate format, and allows for the greatest flexibility when using SQL date functions.
Specify a separate tablespace for the table and indexes. Let the table and indexes inherit storage attributes from the tablespaces.	Simplifies administration and maintenance.
Most tables should be created with a primary key.	Enforces a business rule and allows you to uniquely identify each row.
Create a numeric surrogate key to be the primary key for each table. Populate the surrogate key from a sequence.	Makes joins easier and more efficient.
Create primary-key constraints out of line.	Allows you more flexibility when creating the primary key, especially if you have a situation where the primary key consists of multiple columns.

Recommendation	Reasoning
Create a unique key for the logical user: a recognizable combination of columns that makes a row unique.	Enforces a business rule and keeps the data cleaner.
Create comments for the tables and columns.	Helps document the application and eases maintenance.
Avoid large object (LOB data types if possible.	Prevents maintenance issues associated with LOB columns, like unexpected growth, performance issues when copying, and so on.
If a column always should always have a value, then enforce it with a NOT NULL constraint.	Enforces a business rule and keeps the data cleaner.
Create audit-type columns such as CREATE_DTT and UPDATE_DTT that are automatically populated with default values and/or triggers.	Helps with maintenance and figuring out when data was inserted and/or updated. Other types of audit columns to consider include the users who inserted and updated the row.
Use check constraints where appropriate.	Enforces a business rule and keeps the data cleaner.
Define foreign keys where appropriate.	Enforces a business rule and keeps the data cleaner.

Implementing Virtual Columns

With Oracle Database 11g and higher, you can create a *virtual column* as part of your table definition. A virtual column is based on one or more existing columns from the same table and/or a combination of constants, SQL functions, and user-defined PL/SQL functions. Virtual columns aren't stored on disk; they're evaluated at runtime when the SQL query executes. Virtual columns can be indexed and can have stored statistics.

Prior to Oracle Database 11g, you could simulate a virtual column via a SELECT statement or in a view definition. For example, this next SQL SELECT statement generates a virtual value when the query is executed:

```
select inv_id, inv_count,
  case when inv_count <= 100 then 'GETTING LOW'
       when inv_count > 100 then 'OKAY'
  end
from inv;
```

Why use a virtual column? The advantages of doing so are as follows:

- You can create an index on a virtual column. Internally, Oracle creates a function-based index.

- You can store statistics in a virtual column that can be used by the cost-based optimizer (CBO).

- Virtual columns can be referenced in WHERE clauses.

- Virtual columns are permanently defined in the database. There is one central definition of such a column

Here's an example of creating a table with a virtual column:

```
create table inv(
 inv_id number
,inv_count number
,inv_status generated always as (
  case when inv_count <= 100 then 'GETTING LOW'
       when inv_count > 100 then 'OKAY'
  end)
);
```

In the prior code listing, specifying GENERATED ALWAYS is optional. For example, the next listing is equivalent to the previous one:

```
create table inv(
 inv_id number
,inv_count number
,inv_status as (
  case when inv_count <= 100 then 'GETTING LOW'
       when inv_count > 100 then 'OKAY'
  end)
);
```

I prefer to add GENERATED ALWAYS because it reinforces in my mind that the column is always virtual. The GENERATED ALWAYS helps document inline what you've done. This helps with maintenance for other DBAs who come along long after you.

To view values generated by virtual columns, first insert some data into the table:

```
SQL> insert into inv (inv_id, inv_count) values (1,100);
```

Next, select from the table to view the generated value:

```
SQL> select * from inv;
```

Here is some sample output:

```
    INV_ID  INV_COUNT INV_STATUS
---------- ---------- -----------
         1        100 GETTING LOW
```

■ **Note** If you insert data into the table, nothing is stored in a column GENERATED ALWAYS AS. The virtual value is generated when you select from the table.

You can also alter a table to contain a virtual column:

```
alter table inv add(
inv_comm generated always as(inv_count * 0.1) virtual
);
```

And you can change the definition of an existing virtual column:

```
alter table inv modify inv_status generated always as(
case when inv_count <= 50 then 'NEED MORE'
     when inv_count >50 and inv_count <=200 then 'GETTING LOW'
     when inv_count > 200 then 'OKAY'
end);
```

You can access virtual columns in SQL queries (DML or DDL). For example, suppose you want to update a permanent column based on the value in a virtual column:

```
SQL> update inv set inv_count=100 where inv_status='OKAY';
```

A virtual column itself can't be updated via the SET clause of an UPDATE statement. However, you can reference a virtual column in the WHERE clause of an UPDATE or DELETE statement.

You can optionally specify the data type of a virtual column. If you omit the data type, Oracle derives the data type from the expression you use to define the virtual column.

Several caveats are associated with virtual columns:

- You can only define a virtual column on a regular heap-organized table. You can't define a virtual column on an index-organized table, an external table, a temporary table, object tables, or cluster tables.

- Virtual columns can't reference other virtual columns.

- Virtual columns can only reference columns from the table in which the virtual column is defined.

- The output of a virtual column must be a scalar value (a single value, not a set of values).

To view the definition of a virtual column, use the DBMS_METADATA package to view the DDL associated with the table. If you're selecting from SQL*Plus, you need to set the LONG variable to a value large enough to show all data returned:

```
SQL> set long 10000;
SQL> select dbms_metadata.get_ddl('TABLE','INV') from dual;
```

Here is a partial snippet of the output:

```
  CREATE TABLE "INV_MGMT"."INV"
   (    "INV_ID" NUMBER,
        "INV_COUNT" NUMBER,
        "INV_STATUS" VARCHAR2(11) GENERATED ALWAYS AS (CASE  WHEN "INV_COUNT"<=50 THEN
'NEED MORE' WHEN ("INV_COUNT">50 AND "INV_COUNT"<=200) THEN 'GETTING LOW' WHEN "
INV_COUNT">200 THEN 'OKAY' END) VIRTUAL VISIBLE ...
```

Making Read-Only Tables

Starting with Oracle Database 11g, you can place individual tables in read-only mode. Doing so prevents any INSERT, UPDATE, or DELETE statements from running against a table. In versions prior to Oracle Database 11g, the only way to make a table read-only was to either place the entire database into read-only mode or place a tablespace in read-only mode (making all tables in the tablespace read-only).

There are several reasons why you may require the read-only feature at the table level:

- The data in the table is historical and should never be updated in normal circumstances.

- You're performing some maintenance on the table and want to ensure that it doesn't change while it's being updated.

- You want to drop the table, but before you do, you want to place it in read-only mode to better determine if any users are attempting to update the table.

Use the ALTER TABLE statement to place a table in read-only mode:

```
SQL> alter table inv read only;
```

You can verify the status of a read-only table by issuing the following query:

```
SQL> select table_name, read_only from user_tables where read_only='YES';
```

To modify a read-only table to read-write, issue the following SQL:

```
SQL> alter table inv read write;
```

■ Note The read-only table feature requires that the database initialization COMPATIBLE parameter be set to 11.1.0 or higher.

Understanding Deferred Segment Creation

Starting with Oracle Database 11g Release 2, when you create a table, the creation of the associated segment is deferred until the first row is inserted into the table. This feature has some interesting implications. For example, if you have thousands of objects that you're initially creating for an application (such as when you first install it), no space is consumed by any of the tables (or associated indexes) until data is inserted into the application tables. This means the initial DDL runs more quickly when you create a table, but the first INSERT statement runs slightly slower.

To illustrate the concept of deferred segments, first create a table:

```
SQL> create table inv(inv_id number, inv_desc varchar2(30));
```

You can verify that the table has been created by inspecting USER_TABLES:

```
select
 table_name
,segment_created
from user_tables
where table_name='INV';
```

Here's some sample output:

```
TABLE_NAME                     SEG
------------------------------ ---
INV                            NO
```

Next, query USER_SEGMENTS to verify that a segment hasn't yet been allocated for this table:

```
select
 segment_name
,segment_type
,bytes
from user_segments
where segment_name='INV'
and segment_type='TABLE';
```

Here's the corresponding output for this example:

```
no rows selected
```

Now, insert a row into a table:

```
SQL> insert into inv values(1,'BOOK');
```

Rerun the query, selecting from USER_SEGMENTS, and notice that a segment has been created:

```
SEGMENT_NAME      SEGMENT_TYPE           BYTES
---------------   -----------------   ----------
INV               TABLE                  65536
```

If you're used to working with older versions of Oracle, the deferred-segment-creation feature can cause confusion. For example, if you have space-related monitoring reports that query DBA_SEGMENTS or DBA_EXTENTS, be aware that these views aren't populated that for a table or any indexes associated with the table until the first row is inserted into the table.

■ **Note** You can disable the deferred-segment-creation feature by setting the database-initialization parameter DEFERRED_SEGMENT_CREATION to FALSE. The default for this parameter is TRUE.

Allowing for Parallel SQL Execution

If you work with large tables, you may want to consider creating your tables as PARALLEL. This instructs Oracle to set the degree of parallelism to be used for any subsequent INSERT, UPDATE, DELETE, MERGE, and query statements. This example creates a table with a PARALLEL clause of 2:

```
create table inv_apr_10
parallel 2
as select * from inv
where create_dtt >= '01-apr-10' and create_dtt < '01-may-10';
```

You can specify PARALLEL, NOPARALLEL, or PARALLEL N. If you don't specify N, Oracle sets the degree of parallelism based on the PARALLEL_THREADS_PER_CPU initialization parameter.

■ **Tip** Keep in mind that PARALLEL_THREADS_PER_CPU can vary considerably from a development environment to a production environment. Your development box may contain only 2 CPUS, whereas a production server may have 32 CPUs. Therefore, if you don't specify the degree of parallelism, the behavior of parallel operations can vary widely depending on the environment.

Compressing Table Data

Oracle has had table compression for quite some time. Prior to Oracle Database 11g, the compression available was only suitable for data-warehouse environments, mainly because the table-level compression was CPU intensive and degraded the performance of DML statements. This type of compression usually wasn't suitable for online transaction processing (OLTP) environments.

■ **Note** OLTP table compression is a feature of the Oracle Advanced Compression option. The Oracle Advanced Compression option requires an additional license from Oracle.

Starting with Oracle Database 11g, you can do this:

```
create table inv(
 inv_id number
,inv_name varchar2(64)
) compress for oltp;
```

The COMPRESS FOR OLTP clause enables compression for all DML operations (in prior versions of Oracle, the compress feature was limited to direct-path INSERT operations). The OLTP compression doesn't immediately compress data as it's inserted and updated in a table. Rather, the compression occurs in a batch mode when the block reaches a certain internally defined threshold. When the threshold is reached, all of the uncompressed rows are compressed at the same time. The threshold at which compression occurs is determined by an internal algorithm.

■ **Note** Oracle also has a hybrid columnar compression feature that is available with the Oracle Exadata product. See Oracle's technology website (http://otn.oracle.com) for more details.

You can verify the compression for a table via the following SELECT statement:

```
select
 table_name
,compression
,compress_for
from user_tables where table_name='INV';
```

Here is some sample output:

```
TABLE_NAME                      COMPRESS COMPRESS_FOR
------------------------------- -------- ------------
INV                             ENABLED  OLTP
```

Avoiding Redo Creation

When you're creating a table, you have the option of specifying the NOLOGGING clause. The NOLOGGING feature can greatly reduce the amount of redo generation for certain types of operations. Sometimes, when you're working with large amounts of data, it's desirable for performance reasons to reduce the redo generation when you initially create and insert data into a table.

The downside to eliminating redo generation is that you can't recover the data created via NOLOGGING in the event a failure occurs after the data is loaded (and before you can back up the table). If you can tolerate some risk of data loss, then use NOLOGGING but back up the table soon after the data is loaded. If your data is critical, then don't use NOLOGGING. If your data can be easily re-created, then NOLOGGING is desirable when you're trying to improve performance of large data loads.

One perception is that NOLOGGING eliminates redo generation for the table for all DML operations. That isn't correct. The NOLOGGING feature never affects redo generation for normal DML statements (regular INSERT, UPDATE, and DELETE).

The NOLOGGING feature can significantly reduce redo generation for the following types of operations:

- SQL*Loader direct path load
- Direct path INSERT /*+ append */
- CREATE TABLE AS SELECT
- ALTER TABLE MOVE
- Creating or rebuilding an index

You need to be aware of some quirks (features) when using NOLOGGING. If your database is in FORCE LOGGING mode, then redo is generated for all operations, regardless of whether you specify NOLOGGING. When you're loading a table, if the table has a referential foreign-key constraint defined, then redo is generated regardless of whether you specify NOLOGGING.

You can specify NOLOGGING at one of the following levels:

- Statement
- CREATE TABLE or ALTER TABLE
- CREATE TABLESPACE or ALTER TABLESPACE

I prefer to specify the NOLOGGING clause at the statement or table level. In these scenarios, it's obvious to the DBA executing the statement or DDL that NOLOGGING is used. If you specify NOLOGGING at the tablespace level, then each DBA that creates objects within that tablespace must be aware of this tablespace-level setting. In teams with multiple DBAs, it's easy for one DBA to be unaware that another DBA has created a tablespace with NOLOGGING.

This example first creates a table with the NOLOGGING option:

```
create table inv(inv_id number)
tablespace users
nologging;
```

Next, do a direct-path insert via selecting from a table with historical data:

```
SQL> insert /*+ append */ into inv select inv_id from inv_mar_2010;
SQL> commit;
```

What happens if you have a media failure after you've populated a table in NOLOGGING mode (and before you've made a backup of the table)? After a restore and recovery operation, it will appear that the table has been restored:

```
SQL> desc inv
Name                                      Null?    Type
----------------------------------------- -------- ----------------------------
INV_ID                                              NUMBER
```

However, try to execute a query that scans every block in the table:

```
SOL> select * from inv;
```

An error is thrown, indicating that there is logical corruption in the datafile:

```
ORA-01578: ORACLE data block corrupted (file # 4, block # 11057)
ORA-01110: data file 4: '/ora02/dbfile/O11R2/users01.dbf'
ORA-26040: Data block was loaded using the NOLOGGING option
```

If you specify a logging clause at the statement level, it overrides any table or tablespace setting. If you specify a logging clause at the table level, it sets the default mode for any statements that don't specify a logging clause, and overrides the logging setting at the tablespace. If you specify a logging clause at the tablespace level, it sets the default logging for any CREATE TABLE statements that don't specify a logging clause.

You verify the logging mode of the database as follows:

```
SQL> select name, log_mode, force_logging from v$database;
```

The next statement verifies the logging mode of a tablespace:

```
SQL> select tablespace_name, logging from dba_tablespaces;
```

And this example verifies the logging mode of a table:

```
SQL> select owner, table_name, logging from dba_tables where logging = 'NO';
```

How do you tell whether Oracle logged redo for an operation? One way is to measure the amount of redo generated for an operation with logging enabled versus operating in NOLOGGING mode. If you have a development environment that you can test in, you can monitor how often the redo logs switch while the operation is taking place. Another simple test is to time how long the operation takes with and without logging. The operation performed in NOLOGGING mode should be faster (because a minimal amount of redo is being generated).

Creating a Table from a Query

Sometimes it's convenient to create a table based on the definition of an existing table. For example, say you want to create a quick backup of a table before you modify the table's structure or data. Use the CREATE TABLE AS SELECT statement (sometimes referred to colloquially as CTAS) to achieve this. For example:

```
create table cwp_user_profile_101910
as select * from cwp_user_profile;
```

The previous statement creates an identical table complete with data. If you don't want the data included, you just want the structure of the table replicated, then provide a WHERE clause that always evaluates to false (in this example, 1 will never equal 2):

```
create table cwp_user_profile_test
as select * from cwp_user_profile
where 1=2;
```

You can also specify that no redo be logged when a CTAS table is created. For large data sets, this can reduce the amount of time required to create the table:

```
create table cwp_user_profile_101910
nologging
as select * from cwp_user_profile;
```

Be aware that using the CTAS technique with the NOLOGGING clause creates the table as NOLOGGING and doesn't generate the redo required to recover the data that populates the table as the result of the SELECT statement. Also, if the tablespace is defined to be NOLOGGING (in which the CTAS table is being created), then no redo is generated. In these scenarios, you can't restore and recover your table in the event a failure occurs before you're able to back up the table. If your data is critical, then don't use the NOLOGGING clause.

You can also specify parallelism and storage parameters. Depending on the number of CPUs, you may see some performance gains:

```
create table cwp_user_profile_101910
nologging
tablespace staging_data
parallel 2
as select * from cwp_user_profile_tab;
```

▮ Note The CTAS technique doesn't create any indexes or triggers. You have to create indexes and triggers separately if you need those objects from the original table.

Modifying a Table

Altering a table is a common task. New requirements often mean that you need to rename, add, drop or change column data types. In development environments, changing a table is often a trivial task: you often don't have large quantities of data or hundreds of users simultaneously accessing a table. However, for active production systems, you need to understand the ramifications of trying to change tables that are currently being accessed and/or are already populated with data.

Obtaining the Needed Lock

When you modify a table, you must have an exclusive lock on the table. One issue is that if a DML transaction has a lock on the table, you can't alter the table. In this situation, you receive this error:

```
ORA-00054: resource busy and acquire with NOWAIT specified or timeout expired
```

The prior error message is somewhat confusing in that it leads you to believe that you can resolve the issue by acquiring a lock with NOWAIT. However, this is a generic message that is generated when the DDL you're issuing can't obtain an exclusive lock on the table. In this situation, you have a few options:

- After issuing the DDL command and receiving the ORA-00054 error, rapidly press the / (forward slash) key repeatedly in hopes of modifying the table between transactions.

- Shut down the database and start it in restricted mode, modify the table, and then open the database for normal use.

- In Oracle Database 11g and higher, set the DDL_LOCK_TIMEOUT parameter.

The last item in the previous list instructs Oracle to repeatedly attempt to run a DDL statement until it obtains the required lock on the table. You can set the DDL_LOCK_TIMEOUT parameter at the system or session level. This next example instructs Oracle to repeatedly retry to obtain a lock for 100 seconds:

```
SQL> alter session set ddl_lock_timeout=100;
```

The default value for the system-level DDL_LOCK_TIMEOUT initialization parameter is 0. If you want to modify the default behavior for every session in the system, issue an ALTER SYSTEM SET statement. The following command sets the default timeout value to 10 seconds for the system:

```
SQL> alter system set ddl_lock_timeout=10 scope=both;
```

Renaming a Table

There are a couple of reasons for renaming a table:

- To make the table conform to standards

- To better determine whether the table is being used before you drop it

This example renames a table from INV_MGMT to INV_MGMT_OLD:

```
SQL> rename inv_mgmt to inv_mgmt_old;
```

If successful, you should see this message:

```
Table renamed.
```

Adding a Column

Use the ALTER TABLE ... ADD statement to add a column to a table. This example adds a column to the INV table:

```
SQL> alter table inv add(inv_count number);
```

If successful, you should see this message:

```
Table altered.
```

Altering a Column

Occasionally, you need to alter a column to adjust its size or change its data type. Use the ALTER TABLE ... MODIFY statement to adjust the size of a column. This example changes the size of a column to 256 characters:

```
SQL> alter table inv modify inv_desc varchar2(256);
```

If you decrease the size of a column, first ensure that no values exist that are greater than the decreased size value:

```
SQL> select max(length(<column_name>)) from <table_name>;
```

When you change a column to NOT NULL, then there must be a valid value for each column. First, verify that there are no NULL values:

```
SQL> select <column_name> from <table_name> where <column_name> is null;
```

If any rows have a NULL value for the column you're modifying to NOT NULL, then you must first update the column to contain a value. Here is an example of modifying a column to NOT NULL:

```
SQL> alter table inv modify(inv_desc not null);
```

You can also alter the column to have a default value. The default value is used any time a record is inserted into the table but no value is provided for a column:

```
SQL> alter table inv modify(inv_desc default 'No Desc');
```

If you want to remove the default value of a column, then set it to be NULL:

```
SQL> alter table inv modify(inv_desc default NULL);
```

Sometimes you need to change a table's data type: for example, a column that was originally incorrectly defined as a VARCHAR2 needs to be changed to a NUMBER. Before you change a column's data type, first verify that all values for an existing column contain only valid numeric values. Here's a simple PL/SQL script to do this:

```
create or replace function isnum(v_in varchar2)
  return varchar is
  val_err exception;
  pragma exception_init(val_err, -6502); -- char to num conv. error
  scrub_num number;
begin
  scrub_num := to_number(v_in);
  return 'Y';
  exception when val_err then
  return 'N';
end;
/
```

You can use the ISNUM function to detect whether data in a column is numeric. The function defines a PL/SQL pragma exception for the ORA-06502 character-to-number conversion error. When this error is encountered, the exception handler captures it and returns an N. If the value passed in to the ISNUM function is a number, then a Y is returned. If the value can't be converted to a number, then an N is returned. After you've defined the function, you can run it as follows:

```
SQL> select hold_col from stage where isnum(hold_col)='N';
```

Similarly, when you modify a character column to a DATE or TIMESTAMP data type, it's prudent to first check to see whether the data can be successfully converted. Here's a function that does that:

```
create or replace function isdate(p_in varchar2, f_in varchar2)
return varchar is
scrub_dt date;
begin
scrub_dt := to_date(p_in, f_in);
return 'Y';
exception when others then
return 'N';
end;
/
```

When you call the ISDATE function, you need to pass it a valid date-format mask:

```
SQL> select hold_col from stage where isdate(hold_col,'YYYYMMDD')='N';
```

Renaming a Column

There are a couple of reasons to rename a column:

- Sometimes requirements change, and you want to modify the column name to better reflect what the column is used for.

- If you're planning to drop a column, it doesn't hurt to rename the column first to better determine whether any users or applications are accessing the column.

Use the ALTER TABLE ... RENAME statement to rename a column:

```
SQL> alter table inv rename column inv_count to inv_amt;
```

Dropping a Column

Tables sometimes end up having columns that are never used. This may be because the initial requirements changed or were inaccurate. If you have a table that contains an unused column, you should consider dropping it. If you leave an unused column in a table, you may run into issues with future DBAs not knowing what the column is used for, and the column can potentially consume space unnecessarily.

Before you drop a column, I recommend that you first rename it. Doing so gives you an opportunity to discover whether any users or applications are using the column. After you're confident the column isn't being used, first make a backup of the table using Data Pump export, and then drop the column. The previous strategies provide you with options if you drop a column and then subsequently realize that it's needed.

To drop a column, use the ALTER TABLE ... DROP statement:

```
SQL> alter table inv drop (inv_name);
```

Be aware that the DROP operation may take some time if the table from which you're removing the column contains a large amount of data. This time lag may result in transactions being delayed while the table is being modified (because the ALTER TABLE statement locks the table). In scenarios like this, you may want to first mark the column as unused and then later drop it when you have a maintenance window:

```
SQL> alter table inv set unused (inv_name);
```

When you mark a column as unused, it no longer shows up in the table description. The SET UNUSED clause doesn't incur the overhead associated with dropping the column. This technique allows you to quickly stop the column from being seen or used by SQL queries or applications. Any query that attempts to access an unused column receives the following error:

```
ORA-00904: ... invalid identifier
```

You can later drop any unused columns when you've scheduled some downtime for the application. Use the DROP UNUSED clause to remove any columns marked as UNUSED.

```
SQL> alter table inv drop unused columns;
```

Displaying Table DDL

Sometimes DBAs do a poor job of documenting what DDL is used when creating or modifying a table. Normally, you should maintain the database DDL code in a source-control repository or in some sort of modeling tool. If your shop doesn't have the DDL source code, then there are a few ways that you can manually reproduce DDL:

- Query the data dictionary
- Use the exp and imp utilities
- Use Data Pump
- Use the DBMS_METADATA package

Back in the olden days, say version 7 and earlier, DBAs often wrote SQL that queries the data dictionary to attempt to extract the DDL required to re-create objects. Although this method was better than nothing, it was often prone to errors because the SQL didn't account for every object-creation feature.

The exp and imp utilities are useful for generating DDL. The basic idea is that you export the object in question and then use the imp utility with the SCRIPT or SHOW option to display the DDL. This is a good method, but you often have to manually edit the output of the imp utility to produce the desired DDL.

The Data Pump utility is an excellent method for generating the DDL used to create database objects. Using Data Pump to generate DDL is covered in detail in Chapter 13.

The GET_DDL function of the DBMS_METADATA package is usually the quickest way to display the DDL required to create an object. This example shows how to generate the DDL for a table named INV:

```
SQL> set long 10000
SQL> select dbms_metadata.get_ddl('TABLE','INV') from dual;
```

Here is some sample output:

```
DBMS_METADATA.GET_DDL('TABLE','INV')
--------------------------------------------------------------------------------

  CREATE TABLE "DARL"."INV"
   (    "INV_ID" NUMBER,
        "INV_DESC" VARCHAR2(30),
        "INV_COUNT" NUMBER
   ) SEGMENT CREATION DEFERRED
  PCTFREE 10 PCTUSED 40 INITRANS 1 MAXTRANS 255 NOCOMPRESS LOGGING
  TABLESPACE "USERS"
```

The following SQL statement displays all the DDL for the tables in a schema:

```
select
dbms_metadata.get_ddl('TABLE',table_name)
from user_tables;
```

If you want to display the DDL for a table owned by another user, add the SCHEMA parameter to the GET_DDL procedure.

```
select
dbms_metadata.get_ddl(object_type=>'TABLE', name=>'INVENTORY', schema=>'INV_APP')
from dual;
```

■ **Note** You can display the DDL for almost any database object type, such as INDEX, FUNCTION, ROLE, PACKAGE, MATERIALIZED VIEW, PROFILE, CONSTRAINT, SEQUENCE, SYNONYM, and so on.

Dropping a Table

If you want to remove an object such as a table from a user, use the DROP TABLE statement. This example drops a table named INVENTORY:

```
SQL> drop table inventory;
```

You should see the following confirmation:

```
Table dropped.
```

If you attempt to drop a parent table that has a primary key or unique keys referenced as a foreign key in a child table, you see an error such as

```
ORA-02449: unique/primary keys in table referenced by foreign keys
```

You need to either drop the referenced foreign-key constraint(s) or use the CASCADE CONSTRAINTS option when dropping the parent table:

```
SQL> drop table inventory cascade constraints;
```

You must be the owner of the table or have the DROP ANY TABLE system privilege to drop a table. If you have the DROP ANY TABLE privilege, you can drop a table in a different schema by prepending the schema name to the table name:

```
SQL> drop table inv_mgmt.inventory;
```

If you don't prepend the table name with a user name, Oracle assumes you're dropping a table in your current user.

■ **Tip** If you're using Oracle Database 10g or higher, keep in mind that you can undrop an accidentally dropped table.

Undropping a Table

Suppose you accidentally drop a table, and you want to restore it. First, verify that the table you want to restore is in the recycle bin:

```
SQL> show recyclebin;
```

Here is some sample output:

ORIGINAL NAME	RECYCLEBIN NAME	OBJECT TYPE	DROP TIME
PURCHASES	BIN$YzqKOhN3Fh/gQHdAPLFgMA==$0	TABLE	2009-02-18:17:23:15

Next, use the FLASHBACK TABLE...TO BEFORE DROP statement to recover the dropped table:

```
SQL> flashback table purchases to before drop;
```

■ **Note** You can't FLASHBACK TABLE...TO BEFORE DROP for a table created in the SYSTEM tablespace.

In Oracle Database 10g and higher, when you issue a DROP TABLE statement, the table is renamed (to a name that starts with BIN$) and placed in the recycle bin. The recycle bin is a mechanism that allows you to view some of the metadata associated with a dropped object. You can view complete metadata regarding renamed objects by querying DBA_SEGMENTS:

```
select
  owner
,segment_name
,segment_type
,tablespace_name
from dba_segments
where segment_name like 'BIN$%';
```

Here is some sample output:

OWNER	SEGMENT_NAME	SEGMENT_TYPE	TABLESPACE_NAME
INV	BIN$kptXkzzMdFrgQAB/AQBsFw==$0	TABLE	USERS
INV	BIN$kptXkzzNdFrgQAB/AQBsFw==$0	TABLE	USERS

The FLASHBACK TABLE statement simply renames the table back to its original name. By default, the RECYCLEBIN feature is enabled in Oracle Database 10g and higher. You can change the default by setting the RECYCLEBIN initialization parameter to OFF.

I recommend that you not disable the RECYCLEBIN feature. It's safer to leave this feature enabled and purge the RECYCLEBIN to remove objects that you want permanently deleted. This means the space associated with a dropped table isn't released until you purge your RECYCLEBIN. If you want to purge the entire contents of the currently connected user's recycle bin, use the PURGE RECYCLEBIN statement:

```
SQL> purge recyclebin;
```

If you want to purge the recycle bin for all users in the database, then do the following as a DBA privileged user:

```
SQL> purge dba_recyclebin;
```

If you want to bypass the RECYCLEBIN feature and permanently drop a table, use the PURGE option of the DROP TABLE statement:

```
SQL> drop table dept purge;
```

You can't use the FLASHBACK TABLE statement to retrieve a table dropped with the PURGE option. All space used by the table is released, and any associated indexes and triggers are also dropped.

Removing Data from a Table

You can use either the DELETE statement or the TRUNCATE statement to remove records from a table. You need to be aware of some important differences between these two approaches. Table 7-3 summarizes the attributes of the DELETE and TRUNCATE statements.

Table 7-3. Features of DELETE and TRUNCATE

	DELETE	TRUNCATE
Choice of COMMIT or ROLLBACK	YES	NO
Generates undo	YES	NO
Resets the high-water mark to zero	NO	YES
Affected by referenced and enabled foreign-key constraints	NO	YES
Performs well with large amounts of data	NO	YES

Using DELETE

One big difference is that the DELETE statement can be either committed or rolled back. Committing a DELETE statement makes the changes permanent:

```
SQL> delete from inv;
SQL> commit;
```

If you issue a ROLLBACK statement instead of COMMIT, the table contains data as it was before the DELETE was issued.

Using TRUNCATE

TRUNCATE is a DDL statement. This means Oracle automatically commits the statement (and the current transaction) after it runs, so there is no way to roll back a TRUNCATE statement. If you need the option of choosing to roll back (instead of committing) when removing data, then you should use the DELETE statement. However, the DELETE statement has the disadvantage that it generates a great deal of undo and redo information. Thus for large tables, a TRUNCATE statement is usually the most efficient way to remove data.

This example uses a TRUNCATE statement to remove all data from the COMPUTER_SYSTEMS table:

```
SQL> truncate table computer_systems;
```

By default, Oracle deallocates all space used for the table except the space defined by the MINEXTENTS table-storage parameter. If you don't want the TRUNCATE statement to deallocate the extents, use the REUSE STORAGE parameter:

```
SQL> truncate table computer_systems reuse storage;
```

The TRUNCATE statement sets the high-water mark of a table back to zero. When you use a DELETE statement to remove data from a table, the high-water mark doesn't change. One advantage of using a TRUNCATE statement and resetting the high-water mark is that full-table scans only search for rows in blocks below the high-water mark. This can have significant performance implications.

You can't truncate a table that has a primary key defined that is referenced by an enabled foreign-key constraint in a child table—even if the child table contains zero rows. Oracle prevents you from doing this because in a multiuser system, there is a possibility that another session can populate the child table with rows in between the time you truncate the child table and the time you subsequently truncate the parent table. In this scenario, you must temporarily disable the referenced foreign-key constraints, issue the TRUNCATE statement, and then re-enable the constraints.

Because a TRUNCATE statement is DDL, you can't truncate two separate tables as one transaction. Compare this TRUNCATE behavior to that of DELETE. Oracle does allow you to use the DELETE statement to remove rows from a parent table while the constraints are enabled that reference a child table. This is because DELETE generates undo, is read-consistent, and can be rolled back.

▓ **Note** Another way to remove data from a table is to drop and re-create the table. However, this means you also have to re-create any indexes, constraints, grants, and triggers that belong to the table. Additionally, when you drop a table, it's temporarily unavailable until you re-create it and reissue any required grants. Usually, dropping and re-creating a table is acceptable only in a development or test environment.

Viewing and Adjusting the High-Water Mark

Oracle defines the *high-water mark* of a table as the boundary between used and unused space in a segment. When you create a table, Oracle allocates a number of extents to the table defined by the MINEXTENTS table-storage parameter. Each extent contains a number of blocks. Before data is inserted into the table, none of the blocks have been used, and the high-water mark is zero.

As data is inserted into a table, the high-water mark boundary is raised as extents are allocated. A DELETE statement doesn't reset the high-water mark.

You need to be aware of a couple of performance-related issues regarding the high-water mark:

- SQL query full-table scans

- Direct-path load-space usage

Oracle sometimes needs to scan every block of a table (under the high-water mark) when performing a query. This is known as a *full-table scan*. If a significant amount of data has been deleted from a table, a full-table scan can take a long time to complete, even for a table with zero rows.

Also, when doing direct-path loads, Oracle inserts data above the high-water mark line. Potentially, you can end up with a large amount of unused space in a table that is regularly deleted from and also is loaded via a direct-path mechanism.

You can use a couple of methods to detect space below the high-water mark:

- Autotrace tool
- DBMS_SPACE package

The autotrace tool provides a simple method for detecting high-water-mark issues. Autotrace is advantageous because it's easy to use and the output is easy to interpret.

You can use the DBMS_SPACE package to determine the high-water mark of objects created in tablespaces that use auto-space segment management. The DBMS_SPACE package allows you to programmatically check for high-water mark problems. The downside to this approach is that the output is somewhat cryptic and sometimes difficult to derive concrete answers from.

Tracing to Detect Space Below the High-Water Mark

You can run this simple test to detect whether you have an issue with unused space below the high-water mark:

1. SQL> set autotrace trace statistics
2. Run the query that performs the full-table scan.
3. Compare the number of rows processed to the number of logical I/Os (memory and disk accesses).

If the number of rows processed is low but the number of logical I/Os is high, you may have an issue with the number of free blocks below the high-water mark. Here's a simple example to illustrate this technique:

```
SQL> set autotrace trace statistics
```

The next query generates a full-table scan on the INV table:

```
SQL> select * from inv;
```

Here's a partial snippet of the output from AUTOTRACE:

```
no rows selected

Statistics
----------------------------------------------------------
       1405  consistent gets
          0  physical reads
```

The number of rows returned is zero, yet the consistent gets (memory accesses) is 1405. This indicates that there is free space beneath the high-water mark.

Next, truncate the table and run the query again:

```
SQL> truncate table inv;
SQL> select * from inv;
```

Here's a partial listing from the output of AUTOTRACE:

```
no rows selected

Statistics
----------------------------------------------------------
          3   consistent gets
          0   physical reads
```

Notice that the number of memory accesses has been reduced to 3.

Using DBMS_SPACE to Detect Space Below the High-Water Mark

You can use the DBMS_SPACE package to detect free blocks beneath the high-water mark. Here's an anonymous block of PL/SQL that you can call from SQL*Plus:

```
set serverout on size 1000000
declare
   p_fs1_bytes number;
   p_fs2_bytes number;
   p_fs3_bytes number;
   p_fs4_bytes number;
   p_fs1_blocks number;
   p_fs2_blocks number;
   p_fs3_blocks number;
   p_fs4_blocks number;
   p_full_bytes number;
   p_full_blocks number;
   p_unformatted_bytes number;
   p_unformatted_blocks number;
begin
   dbms_space.space_usage(
       segment_owner      => user,
       segment_name       => 'INV',
       segment_type       => 'TABLE',
       fs1_bytes          => p_fs1_bytes,
       fs1_blocks         => p_fs1_blocks,
       fs2_bytes          => p_fs2_bytes,
       fs2_blocks         => p_fs2_blocks,
       fs3_bytes          => p_fs3_bytes,
       fs3_blocks         => p_fs3_blocks,
       fs4_bytes          => p_fs4_bytes,
       fs4_blocks         => p_fs4_blocks,
       full_bytes         => p_full_bytes,
       full_blocks        => p_full_blocks,
       unformatted_blocks => p_unformatted_blocks,
       unformatted_bytes  => p_unformatted_bytes
   );
   dbms_output.put_line('FS1: blocks = '||p_fs1_blocks);
   dbms_output.put_line('FS2: blocks = '||p_fs2_blocks);
   dbms_output.put_line('FS3: blocks = '||p_fs3_blocks);
   dbms_output.put_line('FS4: blocks = '||p_fs4_blocks);
   dbms_output.put_line('Full blocks = '||p_full_blocks);
end;
/
```

In this scenario, you want to check the INV table for free space below the high-water mark. Here's the output of the previous PL/SQL:

```
FS1: blocks = 0
FS2: blocks = 0
FS3: blocks = 0
FS4: blocks = 1394
Full blocks = 0
```

In the prior output, the FS1 parameter shows that 0 blocks have 0% to 25% free space. The FS2 parameter shows that 0 blocks have 25% to 50% free space. The FS3 parameter shows that 0 blocks have 50% to 75% free space. The FS4 parameter shows there are 1394 blocks that with 75% to 100% free space. Finally, there are 0 full blocks. Because there are no full blocks and a large number of blocks are mostly empty, this is an indication that free space exists below the high-water mark.

How can you reduce a table's high-water mark? You can use several techniques to reset the high-water mark back to zero:

- Use a TRUNCATE statement

- Use ALTER TABLE ... SHRINK SPACE

- Use ALTER TABLE ... MOVE

Using the TRUNCATE statement was discussed earlier in this chapter. Shrinking a table and moving a table are discussed in the following subsections.

Shrinking a Table

To readjust the high-water mark, you must enable row movement for the table and then use the ALTER TABLE...SHRINK SPACE statement. The tablespace in which the table is created must have been built with automatic segment-space management enabled. You can determine the tablespace space-segment management type via this query:

```
SQL> select tablespace_name, segment_space_management from dba_tablespaces;
```

The SEGMENT_SPACE_MANAGEMENT value must be AUTO for the tablespace in which the table is created. Next, you need to enable row movement for the table to be shrunk. This example enables row movement for the INV table:

```
SQL> alter table inv enable row movement;
```

Now you can shrink the space used by the table:

```
SQL> alter table inv shrink space;
```

You can also shrink the space associated with any index segments via the CASCADE clause:

```
SQL> alter table inv shrink space cascade;
```

If for some reason you don't want to move the high-water mark when you shrink the table, then use the COMPACT clause:

```
SQL> alter table inv shrink space compact;
```

Moving a Table

Moving a table means either rebuilding the table in its current tablespace or building it in a different tablespace. You may want to move a table because its current tablespace has disk-space storage issues or you want to lower the table's high-water mark.

Use the ALTER TABLE ... MOVE statement to move a table from one tablespace to another. This example moves the PARTIES table to the MTS tablespace:

```
SQL> alter table parties move tablespace mts;
```

You can verify that the table has been moved by querying USER_TABLES:

```
SQL> select table_name, tablespace_name from user_tables where table_name='PARTIES';
TABLE_NAME           TABLESPACE_NAME
-------------------- --------------------
PARTIES              MTS
```

■ **Note** The ALTER TABLE ... MOVE statement doesn't allow DML to execute while it's running.

You can also specify NOLOGGING when you move a table:

```
SQL> alter table parties move tablespace mts nologging;
```

Moving a table with NOLOGGING eliminates most of the redo that would normally be generated when the table is relocated. The downside to using NOLOGGING is that if a failure occurs immediately after the table is moved (and hence you don't have a backup of the table after it's moved), then you can't restore the contents of the table. If the data in the table is critical, then don't use NOLOGGING when moving it.

When you move a table, all of its indexes are rendered unusable. This is because a table's index includes the ROWID as part of the structure. The table ROWID contains information about the physical location. Because the ROWID of a table changes when the table moves from one tablespace to another (because the table rows are now physically located in different datafiles), any indexes on the table contain incorrect information. To rebuild the index, use the ALTER INDEX ... REBUILD command.

ORACLE ROWID

Every row in every table has an address. The address of a row is determined from a combination of the following:

- Datafile number
- Block number
- Location of the row within the block
- Object number

You can display the address of a row in a table by querying the ROWID pseudo-column. For example:

```
SQL> select rowid, emp_id from emp;
```

Here's some sample output:

```
ROWID              EMP_ID
------------------ ----------
AAAFWXAAFAAAA1WAAA          1
```

The ROWID pseudo-column value isn't physically stored in the database. Oracle calculates its value when you query it. The ROWID contents are displayed as base 64 values that can contain the characters A–Z, a–z, 0–9, +, and /. You can translate the ROWID value into meaningful information via the DMBS_ROWID package. For example, to display the relative file number in which a row is stored, issue this statement:

```
SQL> select dbms_rowid.rowid_relative_fno(rowid), emp_id from emp;
```

Here's some sample output:

```
DBMS_ROWID.ROWID_RELATIVE_FNO(ROWID)     EMP_ID
------------------------------------ ----------
                                   5          1
```

You can use the ROWID value in the SELECT and WHERE clauses of a SQL statement. In most cases, the ROWID uniquely identifies a row. However, it's possible to have rows in different tables that are stored in the same cluster and so contain rows with the same ROWID.

Creating a Temporary Table

Use the CREATE GLOBAL TEMPORARY TABLE statement to create a table that stores data only provisionally. You can specify that the temporary table retain the data for a session or until a transaction commits. Use ON COMMIT PRESERVE ROWS to specify that the data be deleted at the end of the user's session. In this example, the rows will be retained until the user either explicitly deletes the data or terminates the session:

```
create global temporary table today_regs
on commit preserve rows
as select * from f_registrations
where create_dtt > sysdate - 1;
```

Specify ON COMMIT DELETE ROWS to indicate that the data should be deleted at the end of the transaction. The following example creates a temporary table named TEMP_OUTPUT and specifies that records should be deleted at the end of each committed transaction:

```
create global temporary table temp_output(
 temp_row varchar2(30))
on commit delete rows;
```

■ Note If you don't specify a commit method for a global temporary table, then the default is ON COMMIT DELETE ROWS.

159

You can create a temporary table and grant other users access to it. However, a session can only view the data that it inserts into a table. In other words, if two sessions are using the same temporary table, a session can't select any data inserted into the temporary table by a different session.

A global temporary table is useful for applications that need to briefly store data in a table structure. After you create a temporary table, it exists until you drop it. In other words, the definition of the temporary table is permanent; it's the data that is short-lived (in this sense, the phrase *temporary table* can be misleading).

You can view whether a table is temporary by querying the TEMPORARY column of DBA/ALL/USER_TABLES:

```
SQL> select table_name, temporary from user_tables;
```

Temporary tables are designated with a Y in the TEMPORARY column. Regular tables contain an N in the TEMPORARY column.

When you create records in a temporary table, space is allocated in your default temporary tablespace. You can verify this by running the following SQL:

```
SQL> select username, contents, segtype from v$sort_usage;
```

If you're working with a large number of rows and need better performance for selectively retrieving rows, you may want to consider creating an index on the appropriate columns in your temporary table:

```
SQL> create index temp_index on temp_output(temp_row);
```

Use the DROP TABLE command to drop a temporary table:

```
SQL> drop table temp_output;
```

TEMPORARY TABLE REDO

No redo data is generated for changes to blocks of a global temporary table. However, rollback (undo) data is generated for a transaction against a temporary table. Because the rollback data generates redo, some redo data is associated with a transaction for a temporary table. You can verify this by turning on statistics tracing and viewing the redo size as you insert records into a temporary table:

```
SQL> set autotrace on
```

Next, insert a few records into the temporary table:

```
SQL> insert into temp_output values(1);
```

Here's a partial snippet of the output (only showing the redo size):

```
140 redo size
```

The redo load is less for temporary tables than normal tables because the redo generated is only associated with the rollback (undo) data for a temporary table transaction.

Creating an Index-Organized Table

Index-organized tables (IOTs) are efficient objects when the table data is typically accessed through querying on the primary key. Use the ORGANIZATION INDEX clause to create an IOT:

```
create table prod_sku
(prod_sku_id number,
sku varchar2(256),
create_dtt timestamp(5),
constraint prod_sku_pk primary key(prod_sku_id)
)
organization index
including sku
pctthreshold 30
tablespace inv_mgmt_data
overflow
tablespace mts;
```

An IOT stores the entire contents of the table's row in a B-tree index structure. IOTs provide fast access for queries that have exact matches and/or range searches on the primary key.

All columns specified up to and including the column specified in the INCLUDING clause are stored in the same block as the PROD_SKU_ID primary-key column. In other words, the INCLUDING clause specifies the last column to keep in the table segment. Columns listed after the column specified in the INCLUDING clause are stored in the overflow data segment. In the previous example, the CREATE_DTT column is stored in the overflow segment.

PCTTHRESHOLD specifies the percentage of space reserved in the index block for the IOT row. This value can be from 1 to 50, and defaults to 50 if no value is specified. There must be enough space in the index block to store the primary key.

The OVERFLOW clause details which tablespace should be used to store overflow data segments. Notice that DBA/ALL/USER_TABLES includes an entry for the table name used when creating an IOT. Additionally, DBA/ALL/USER_INDEXES contains a record with the name of the primary-key constraint specified. The INDEX_TYPE column contains a value of IOT - TOP for IOTs:

```
SQL> select index_name,table_name,index type from user_indexes;
```

Managing Constraints

The next several sections in this chapter deal with constraints. Constraints provide a mechanism to ensure that data conforms to certain business rules. You must be aware of what types of constraints are available and when it's appropriate to use them. Oracle provides several types of constraints:

- Primary key

- Unique key

- Foreign key

- Check

- NOT NULL

Implementing and managing these constraints are discussed in the next several subsections.

Creating Primary-Key Constraints

When you implement a database, most tables you create require a primary-key constraint to guarantee that every record in the table can be uniquely identified. There are multiple techniques for adding a primary-key constraint to a table. The first example creates the primary key inline with the column definition:

```
create table dept(
 dept_id number primary key
,dept_desc varchar2(30));
```

If you select the CONSTRAINT_NAME from USER_CONSTRAINTS, notice that Oracle generates a cryptic name for the constraint (something like SYS_C003682). Use the following syntax to explicitly give a name to a primary-key constraint:

```
create table dept(
dept_id number constraint dept_pk primary key using index tablespace users,
dept_desc varchar2(30));
```

■ Note When you create a primary-key constraint, Oracle also creates a unique index with the same name as the constraint.

You can also specify the primary-key constraint definition after the columns have been defined. The advantage of doing this is that you can define the constraint on multiple columns. The next example creates the primary key when the table is created, but not inline with the column definition:

```
create table dept(
dept_id number,
dept_desc varchar2(30),
constraint dept_pk primary key (dept_id)
using index tablespace prod_index);
```

If the table has already been created and you want to add a primary-key constraint, use the ALTER TABLE statement. This example places a primary-key constraint on the DEPT_ID column of the DEPT table:

```
alter table dept
add constraint dept_pk primary key (dept_id)
using index tablespace users;
```

When a primary-key constraint is enabled, Oracle automatically creates a unique index associated with the primary-key constraint. Some DBAs prefer to first create a non-unique index on the primary-key column and then define the primary-key constraint:

```
SQL> create index dept_pk on dept(dept_id);
SQL> alter table dept add constraint dept_pk primary key (dept_id);
```

The advantage of this approach is that you can drop or disable the primary-key constraint independently of the index. When you're working with large data sets, you may want that sort of flexibility. If you don't create the index before creating the primary-key constraint, then whenever you drop or disable the primary-key constraint, the index is automatically dropped.

Confused about which method to use to create a primary key? All of the methods are valid and have their merits. Table 7–4 summarizes the primary-key and unique-key constraint creation methods. I've used all these methods to create primary-key constraints. Usually, I use the ALTER TABLE statement that adds the constraint after the table has been created.

Table 7–4. *Primary-Key and Unique-Key Constraint Creation Methods*

Constraint Creation Method	Advantages	Disadvantages
Inline, no name	Very simple	Oracle-generated name makes troubleshooting harder; less control over storage attributes; only applied to a single column
Inline, with name	Simple; user-defined name makes troubleshooting easier	Requires more thought than inline without name
Inline, with name and tablespace definition	User-defined name and tablespace; makes troubleshooting easier	Less simple
After column definition (out of line)	User-defined name and tablespace; can operate on multiple columns	Less simple
ALTER TABLE add just constraint	Lets you manage constraints in separate statements (and files) from table creation scripts; can operate on multiple columns	More complicated
CREATE INDEX, ALTER TABLE add constraint	Separates the index and constraint so you can drop/disable constraints without affecting the index; can operate on multiple columns	Most complicated, more to maintain, more moving parts

Enforcing Unique Key Values

In addition to creating a primary-key constraint, you should also create unique constraints on any combination of columns that should always be unique within a table. For example, for the primary key for a table, it's common to use a numeric key (sometimes called a *surrogate key*) that is populated via a sequence. In addition to the surrogate primary key, sometimes users have column(s) that the business uses to uniquely identify a record (also called a *logical key*). Using both a surrogate key and logical key

- Lets you efficiently join parent and child tables on a single numeric column
- Allows updates to logical-key columns without changing the surrogate key

A unique key guarantees uniqueness on the defined column(s) within a table. There are some subtle differences between primary-key and unique-key constraints. For example, you can define only one primary key per table, but there can be several unique keys. Also, a primary key doesn't allow a NULL value in any of its columns, whereas a unique key allows NULL values.

As with the primary-key constraint, you can use several methods to create a unique column constraint. This method uses the UNIQUE keyword inline with the column:

```
create table dept(
 dept_id number
,dept_desc varchar2(30) unique);
```

If you want to explicitly name the constraint, use the CONSTRAINT keyword:

```
create table dept(
 dept_id number
,dept_desc varchar2(30) constraint dept_desc_uk1 unique);
```

As with primary keys, Oracle automatically creates an index associated with the unique-key constraint. You can specify the tablespace information inline to be used for the associated unique index:

```
create table dept(
 dept_id number
,dept_desc varchar2(30) constraint dept_desc_uk1
   unique using index tablespace prod_index);
```

You can also alter a table to include a unique constraint:

```
SQL> alter table dept add constraint dept_desc_uk1 unique (dept_desc);
```

And you can create an index on the columns of interest before you define a unique-key constraint:

```
SQL> create index dept_desc_uk1 on dept(dept_desc);
SQL> alter table dept add constraint dept_desc_uk1 unique(dept_desc);
```

This can be helpful when you're working with large data sets and you want to be able to disable or drop the unique constraint without dropping the associated index.

▨ Note See Table 7–4 for a description of the advantages and disadvantages of the various unique-key and primary-key constraint creation methods.

Creating Foreign-key Constraints

Foreign-key constraints are used to ensure that a column value is contained within a defined list of values. Using a foreign-key constraint is an efficient way of enforcing that data must be a predefined value before an insert or update is allowed. This technique works well for the following scenarios:

- The list of values contains many entries.
- Other information about the lookup value needs to be stored.
- It's easy to select, insert, update, or delete values via SQL.

For example, suppose the EMP table is created with a DEPT_ID column. To ensure that each employee is assigned a valid department, you can create a foreign-key constraint that enforces the rule that each DEPT_ID in the EMP table must exist in the DEPT table.

▪ Tip If the condition you want to check for is a small list that doesn't change very often, consider using a check constraint instead of a foreign-key constraint. For example, if you have a column that will always be defined to contain either a 0 or a 1, a check constraint is an efficient solution.

You can use several methods to create a foreign-key constraint. The following example creates a foreign-key constraint on the DEPT_ID column in the EMP table:

```
create table emp(
emp_id number,
name varchar2(30),
dept_id constraint emp_dept_fk references dept(dept_id));
```

Notice that the DEPT_ID data type isn't explicitly defined. It derives the data type from the referenced DEPT_ID column of the DEPT table. You can also explicitly specify the data type when you define a column (regardless of the foreign-key definition):

```
create table emp(
emp_id number,
name varchar2(30),
dept_id number constraint emp_dept_fk references dept(dept_id));
```

You can also specify the foreign-key definition out of line from the column definition in the CREATE TABLE statement:

```
create table emp(
emp_id number,
name varchar2(30),
dept_id number,
constraint emp_dept_fk foreign key (dept_id) references dept(dept_id)
);
```

And you can alter an existing table to add a foreign-key constraint:

```
alter table emp
add constraint emp_dept_fk foreign key (dept_id)
references dept(dept_id);
```

▪ Note Unlike with primary-key and unique-key constraints, Oracle doesn't automatically add an index to the foreign-key column(s). You must explicitly create indexes on foreign-key columns.

Checking for Specific Data Conditions

A check constraint works well for lookups when you have a short list of fairly static values, such as a column that can be either Y or N. In this situation, the list of values most likely won't change, and no other information needs to be stored other than Y or N, so a check constraint is the appropriate solution. If you have a long list of values that needs to be periodically updated, then a table and a foreign-key constraint are a better solution.

Also, a check constraint works well for a business rule that must always be enforced and can be written with a simple SQL expression. If you have sophisticated business logic that must be validated, then the application code is more appropriate.

You can define a check constraint when you create a table. The following defines that the ST_FLG column must be either 0 or 1:

```
create table emp(
emp_id number,
emp_name varchar2(30),
st_flg number(1) CHECK (st_flg in (0,1))
);
```

A slightly better method is to give the check constraint a name:

```
create table emp(
emp_id number,
emp_name varchar2(30),
st_flg number(1) constraint st_flg_chk CHECK (st_flg in (0,1))
);
```

A more descriptive way to name the constraint is to embed information in the constraint name that describes the condition that was violated. For example:

```
CREATE table emp(
emp_id number,
emp_name varchar2(30),
st_flg number(1) constraint "st_flg must be 0 or 1" check (st_flg in (0,1))
);
```

You can also alter an existing column to include a constraint. The column must not contain any values that violate the constraint being enabled:

```
SQL> alter table emp add constraint "st_flg must be 0 or 1" check (st_flg in (0,1));
```

▪ **Note** The check constraint must evaluate to a true or unknown (NULL) value in the row being inserted or updated. You can't use subqueries or sequences in a check constraint. Also, you can't reference the SQL functions UID, USER, SYSDATE, and USERENV, or the pseudo-columns LEVEL or ROWNUM.

Enforcing Not Null Conditions

Another common condition to check for is whether a column is null; you use the NOT NULL constraint to do this. The NOT NULL constraint can be defined in several ways. The simplest technique is shown here:

```
create table emp(
emp_id number,
emp_name varchar2(30) not null);
```

A slightly better approach is to give the NOT NULL constraint a name that makes sense to you:

```
create table emp(
emp_id number,
emp_name varchar2(30) constraint emp_name_nn not null);
```

Use the ALTER TABLE command if you need to modify a column for an existing table. For the following command to work, there must not be any NULL values in the column being defined as NOT NULL:

```
SQL> alter table emp modify(emp_name not null);
```

■ **Note** If there are currently NULL values in a column that is being defined as NOT NULL, you must first update the table so that the column has a value in every row.

Disabling Constraints

One nice feature of Oracle is that you can disable and enable constraints without dropping and re-creating them. This means you avoid having to know the DDL statements that would be required to re-create the dropped constraints.

Occasionally, you need to disable constraints. For example, you may be trying to truncate a table but receive the following error message:

```
ORA-02266: unique/primary keys in table referenced by enabled foreign keys
```

Oracle doesn't allow a truncate operation on a parent table with a primary key that is referenced by an enabled foreign key in a child table. If you need to truncate a parent table, you first have to disable all of the enabled foreign-key constraints that reference the parent table's primary key. Run this query to determine the names of the constraints that need to be disabled:

```
select
b.table_name primary_key_table
,a.table_name fk_child_table
,a.constraint_name fk_child_table_constraint
from dba_constraints a
,dba_constraints b
where a.r_constraint_name = b.constraint_name
and a.r_owner = b.owner
and a.constraint_type = 'R'
and b.owner = upper('&table_owner')
and b.table_name = upper('&table_name');
```

For this example, there is only one foreign-key dependency:

```
PRIMARY_KEY_TABLE FK_CHILD_TABLE FK_CHILD_TABLE_CONST
-------------------- -------------------- --------------------
D_DATES F_SALES F_SALES_FK1
```

Use the ALTER TABLE statement to disable constraints on a table. In this case, there is only one foreign key to disable:

```
SQL> alter table f_sales disable constraint f_sales_fk1;
```

You can now truncate the parent table:

```
SQL> truncate table d_dates;
```

Don't forget to re-enable the foreign-key constraints after the truncate operation has completed, like this:

```
SQL> alter table f_sales enable constraint f_sales_fk1;
```

You can disable a primary key and all dependent foreign-key constraints with the CASCADE option of the DISABLE clause. For example, the next line of code disables all foreign-key constraints related to the D_DATES_PK primary-key constraint:

```
SQL> alter table d_dates disable constraint d_dates_pk cascade;
```

This statement doesn't cascade through all levels of dependencies; it only disables the foreign-key constraints directly dependent on D_DATES_PK. Also keep in mind that there is no ENABLE...CASCADE statement. To re-enable the constraints, you have to query the data dictionary to determine which constraints have been disabled and then re-enable them individually.

Sometimes you run into situations when loading data where it's convenient to disable all the foreign keys before loading data (perhaps from a schema-level import using the imp utility). In these situations, the imp utility imports the tables in alphabetical order and doesn't ensure that child tables are imported before parent tables. You may also want to run several import jobs in parallel to take advantage of parallel hardware. In such scenarios, you can disable the foreign keys, perform the import, and then re-enable the foreign keys.

Here's a script that uses SQL to generate SQL to disable all foreign-key constraints for a user:

```
set lines 132 trimsp on head off feed off verify off echo off pagesize 0
spo dis_dyn.sql
select 'alter table ' || a.table_name
|| ' disable constraint ' || a.constraint_name || ';'
from dba_constraints a
,dba_constraints b
where a.r_constraint_name = b.constraint_name
and a.r_owner = b.owner
and a.constraint_type = 'R'
and b.owner = upper('&table_owner');
spo off;
```

This script generates a file named dis_dyn.sql that contains the SQL statements to disable all the foreign-key constraints for a user.

Enabling Constraints

This section contains a few scripts to help you enable constraints that you've disabled. Listed next is a script that creates a file with the SQL statements required to re-enable any foreign-key constraints for tables owned by a specified user:

```
set lines 132 trimsp on head off feed off verify off echo off pagesize 0
spo enable_dyn.sql
select 'alter table ' || a.table_name
|| ' enable constraint ' || a.constraint_name || ';'
from dba_constraints a
,dba_constraints b
where a.r_constraint_name = b.constraint_name
and a.r_owner = b.owner
and a.constraint_type = 'R'
and b.owner = upper('&table_owner');
spo off;
```

When enabling constraints, by default Oracle checks to ensure that the data doesn't violate the constraint definition. If you're fairly certain that the data integrity is fine and that you don't need to incur the performance hit by revalidating the constraint, you can use the NOVALIDATE clause when re-enabling the constraints. Here's an example:

```
select 'alter table ' || a.table_name
|| ' modify constraint ' || a.constraint_name || ' enable novalidate;'
from dba_constraints a
,dba_constraints b
where a.r_constraint_name = b.constraint_name
and a.r_owner = b.owner
and a.constraint_type = 'R'
and b.owner = upper('&table_owner');
```

The NOVALIDATE clause instructs Oracle not to validate the constraints being enabled, but it does enforce that any new DML activities adhere to the constraint definition.

In multiuser systems, the possibility exists that another session has inserted data into the child table while the foreign-key constraint was disabled. If that happens, you see the following error when you attempt to re-enable the foreign key:

```
ORA-02298: cannot validate (<owner>.<constraint>) - parent keys not found
```

In this scenario, you can use the ENABLE NOVALIDATE clause:

```
SQL> alter table f_sales enable novalidate constraint f_sales_fk1;
```

To clean up the rows that violate the constraint, first ensure that you have an EXCEPTIONS table created in your user. If you don't have an EXCEPTIONS table, use this script to create one:

```
SQL> @?/rdbms/admin/utlexcpt.sql
```

Next, populate the EXCEPTIONS table with the rows that violate the constraint, using the EXCEPTIONS INTO clause:

```
SQL> alter table f_sales modify constraint f_sales_fk1 validate
exceptions into exceptions;
```

This statement still throws the ORA-02298 error as long as there are rows that violate the constraint. The statement also inserts records into the EXCEPTIONS table for any bad rows. You can now use the ROW_ID column of the EXCEPTIONS table to remove any records that violate the constraint.

Here you see that one row needs to be removed from the F_SALES table:

```
SQL> select * from exceptions;
ROW_ID OWNER TABLE_NAME CONSTRAINT
------------------ ---------- --------------- ---------------
AAAFVmAAFAAAAihAAA INV_MMGT F_SALES F_SALES_FK1
```

To remove the offending record, issue a DELETE statement:

```
SQL> delete from f_sales where rowid = 'AAAFVmAAFAAAAihAAA';
```

If the EXCEPTIONS table contains many records, you can run a query such as the following to delete by OWNER and TABLE_NAME:

```
delete from f_sales where rowid in
(select row_id
from exceptions
where owner=upper('&owner') and table_name = upper('&table_name'));
```

You may also run into situations where you need to disable primary-key or unique-key constraints. For example, you may want to perform a large data load, and for performance reasons want to disable the primary-key and unique-key constraints. You don't want to incur the overhead of having every row checked as it's inserted.

The same general techniques used for disabling foreign keys are applicable for disabling primary or unique keys. Run this query to display the primary-key and unique-key constraints for a user:

```
select
a.table_name
,a.constraint_name
,a.constraint_type
from dba_constraints a
where a.owner = upper('&table_owner')
and a.constraint_type in ('P','U')
order by a.table_name;
```

Here's some sample output:

```
TABLE_NAME CONSTRAINT_NAME C
-------------------------------- ------------------------------ -
DEPT SYS_C006507 P
D_DATES D_DATES_UK1 U
D_DATES D_DATES_PK P
```

When the table name and constraint name are identified, use the ALTER TABLE statement to disable the constraint:

```
SQL> alter table d_dates disable constraint d_dates_pk;
```

■ Note Oracle doesn't let you disable a primary-key or unique-key constraint that is referenced in an enabled foreign-key constraint. You first have to disable the foreign-key constraint.

Summary

This chapter focused on basic activities related to creating and maintaining tables. Tables are the containers that store the data within the database. Key table-management tasks include modifying, moving, deleting from, shrinking, and dropping. You must also be familiar with how to implement and use special table types such as temporary, index-organized, and read-only.

Oracle also provides various constraints to help you manage the data within tables. Constraints form the bedrock of data integrity. In most cases, each table should include a primary-key constraint that ensures that every row is uniquely identifiable. Additionally, any parent/child relationships should be enforced with foreign-key constraints. You can use unique constraints to implement business rules that require a column or combination of columns to be unique. Check and NOT NULL constraints ensure that columns contain business-specified data requirements.

After you create tables, the next logical activity is to create indexes where appropriate. Indexes are optional database objects that help improve performance. Index-creation and -maintenance tasks are covered in the next chapter.

CHAPTER 8

■■■

Indexes

An *index* is an optional database object that is primarily used to increase performance. These objects are defined on a table and one or more columns. A database index functions similarly to an index in the back of a book. A book index associates the information of interest with a page number. When you're locating information in a book, it's usually much faster to inspect the index first, determine the page number, and then turn to the desired page. If there were no index, you would have to inspect every page of the book to find information.

An Oracle index is similar to a book index in that it stores information about a database row and a corresponding row identifier (ROWID). When looking for a row of data in a table, Oracle first determines whether an index is available to expedite the row retrieval. If there is no available index, then Oracle reads each row in the table (this is known as a *full table scan*) to determine if the table contains the desired information.

Deciding When to Create an Index

The thought process behind creating an index is roughly as follows:

1. A poorly performing SQL statement is identified.

2. Somebody (DBA or developer) examines the SQL statement and determines which tables and columns are being accessed, by inspecting the SELECT, FROM, and WHERE clauses.

3. Somebody does some testing and recommends that an index be created based on a table and one or more columns.

At this point, the DBA usually examines the results of the testing and makes recommendations about how to implement the index (such as the type of index, features to consider, storage, and so on). The process for getting an index into a production environment is something like this:

1. The DBA makes a script that contains the CREATE INDEX statement.

2. The DBA applies the index in development and test environments.

3. After the quality-assurance folks certify that performance has indeed improved and that there have been no bad side effects, the DBA applies the index in the production environment.

Because indexes increase performance, why not create indexes on all tables and all columns? Indexes aren't magical silver bullets that solve all performance issues. Indexes aren't free; they consume disk space and database processing resources. Creating an index can actually have a detrimental performance impact if the index is infrequently or never used. Additionally it's possible that although an index increases the performance of one statement, it hurts the performance of other statements. You must be sure that the statements that are improved warrant the penalty being applied to other statements.

You should only add an index when you're certain it will improve performance. And after an index is implemented, you should monitor it to ensure that the Oracle optimizer is using it to speed up queries.

What to Think About

Oracle provides a wide assortment of indexing features and options. As a DBA or a developer, you need to be aware of the various features and how to utilize them. If you choose the wrong type of index or use a feature incorrectly, there may be serious detrimental performance implications. Listed next are aspects to consider before you create an index:

- Type of index

- Table column(s) to include

- Whether to use a single column or a combination of columns

- Special features such as the PARALLEL clause, NOLOGGING, compression, invisible indexes, and so on

- Uniqueness

- Naming conventions

- Tablespace placement

- Initial sizing requirements and growth

- Impact on performance of SELECT statements (improvement)

- Impact on performance of INSERT, UPDATE, and DELETE statements

- Global or local index, if the underlying table is partitioned

When you create an index you should give some thought to every aspect mentioned in the previous list. One of the first decisions you need to make is the type of index and the columns to include. Oracle provides a robust variety of index types. For most scenarios, you can use the default B-tree (balanced tree) index type. Other commonly used types are bitmap and function-based indexes. Table 8–1 describes the types of indexes available with Oracle.

Table 8–1. Oracle Index Type Descriptions

Index Type	Usage
B-tree	Default, balanced tree index, good for high-cardinality columns.
B-tree cluster	Used with clustered tables.
Hash cluster	Used with hash clusters.
Function	Good for columns that have SQL functions applied to them.
Global partitioned	Global index across all partitions in a partitioned table.
Local partitioned	Local index based on individual partitions in a partitioned table.
Reverse key	Useful to balance I/O in an index that has many sequential inserts.
Key compressed	Useful for concatenated indexes where the leading column is often repeated. Compresses leaf block entries.
Bitmap	Useful in data-warehouse environments with low-cardinality columns. These indexes aren't appropriate for online transaction processing (OLTP) databases where rows are heavily updated.
Bitmap join	Useful in data-warehouse environments for queries that join fact and dimension tables.
Domain	Specific for an application or cartridge.

This chapter focuses on the most commonly used indexes and features: B-tree, bitmap, reverse-key, and function-based indexes, and useful options. Partitioned indexes are covered in Chapter 12. If you need more information about index types or features not covered in this chapter or book, see Oracle's SQL Reference guide at http://otn.oracle.com.

Index-Management Guidelines

Misusing indexes can have serious negative performance effects. Indexes created of the wrong type or on the wrong columns do nothing but consume space and processing resources. As a DBA, you must have a strategy to ensure that indexes enhance performance and don't negatively impact applications.

Table 8–2 encapsulates many of the index-management concepts covered in this chapter. These recommendations aren't written in stone: adapt and modify them as needed for your environment.

Table 8–2. Index-Creation and -Maintenance Guidelines

Guideline	Reasoning
Add indexes judiciously. Test first to determine quantifiable performance gains.	Indexes consume disk space and processing resources. Don't add indexes unnecessarily.
Use the correct type of index.	Correct index usage maximizes performance. See Table 8–1 for more details.
Use a separate tablespace(s) for indexes (separate from tablespaces used for tables).	Table and index data may have different storage and/or backup and recovery requirements. Using separate tablespaces lets you manage indexes separately from tables.
When creating primary-key constraints or unique-key constraints, specify the tablespace for the index.	Doing this separates the table and index data, which may have different storage and/or backup and recovery requirements.
Let the index inherit its storage properties from the tablespace.	This makes it easier to manage and maintain index storage.
Use consistent naming standards.	This makes maintenance and troubleshooting easier.
Don't rebuild indexes unless you have a solid reason to do so.	Rebuilding indexes is generally unnecessary unless an index is corrupt or you want to move an index to different tablespace.
Monitor your indexes, and drop indexes that aren't used.	Doing this frees up physical space and improves the performance of Data Manipulation Language (DML) statements.
Before dropping an index, consider marking it as unusable or invisible.	This allows you to better determine if there are any performance issues before you drop the index. These options let you rebuild or re-enable the index without requiring the Data Definition Language (DDL) creation statement.
Create indexes on foreign-key columns.	Foreign-key columns are usually included in the WHERE clause when joining tables and thus improve performance of SQL SELECT statements. This can also improve performance when you're deleting a parent row and Oracle needs to look for any records in a child table.

Refer to these guidelines as you create and manage indexes in your databases. These recommendations are intended to help you correctly use index technology.

Creating Indexes

When you think about creating tables, you must think about the corresponding index architecture. Creating the appropriate indexes and using the correct index features usually results in dramatic performance improvements. Likewise, creating indexes on the wrong columns or using the features in the wrong situations can cause dramatic performance degradation.

As a DBA, you need to be aware of the types of indexes available with Oracle and when to use them. Creating indexes and implementing specific features are discussed in the next several subsections. The B-tree index is the most used and default index type and therefore is first in line.

Creating B-tree Indexes

The default index type in Oracle is a B-tree (balanced tree) index. To create a B-tree index on an existing table, use the CREATE INDEX statement. This example creates an index on the D_SOURCES table, specifying D_SOURCE_ID as the column:

```
SQL> create index d_sources_idx1 on d_sources(d_source_id);
```

By default, Oracle tries to create an index in your default tablespace. Sometimes that may be the desired behavior. But often, for manageability reasons, you want to create the index in a specific tablespace. Use the following syntax to instruct Oracle to build an index in a specific tablespace:

```
SQL> create index d_sources_idx1 on d_sources(d_source_id) tablespace dim_index;
```

░ **Tip** If you don't specify any physical storage properties for an index, the index inherits its properties from the tablespace in which it's created. This is usually an acceptable method for managing index storage.

Figure 8–1 shows the balanced, tree-like structure of a B-tree index created on a first-name column. This type of index has a hierarchical tree structure. When Oracle accesses the index, it starts with the top node called the root (or header) block. It uses this block to determine which second-level block (often referred to as a branch block) to read next. The second-level block points to several third-level leaf nodes that contain a ROWID and the name value. In this structure, it will take three I/O operations to find the ROWID. Once the ROWID is determined, Oracle will use it to read the table block that contains the ROWID.

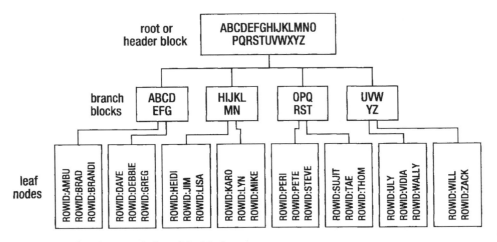

Figure 8-1. Oracle B-tree heirarchical index structure

The index definition is associated with a table and column(s). The index structure stores a mapping of a row's ROWID and the column data on which the index is built. A ROWID usually uniquely identifies a row within a database and contains information to physically locate a row (datafile, block, and row position within block).

Creating Concatenated Indexes

Oracle allows you to create an index that contains more than one column. Multicolumn indexes are known as *concatenated indexes*. These indexes are especially effective when you often use multiple columns in the WHERE clause when accessing a table.

For the examples in this section, the underlying table is created as follows:

```
create table inv(
 inv_name varchar2(30)
,cust_name varchar2(30));
```

Now, suppose you have this scenario, where two columns from the same table are used in the WHERE clause:

```
SQL> select cust_name from inv where inv_name='Mouse' and cust_name='Bob';
```

Because both INV_NAME and CUST_NAME are often used in WHERE clauses for retrieving data, it may be efficient to create a concatenated index on the two columns:

```
SQL> create index inv_idx3 on inv(inv_name, cust_name);
```

Often, it's not clear whether a concatenated index is more efficient than a single-column index. For the previous SQL statement, you may wonder whether it's more efficient to create two single-column index on INV_NAME and CUST_NAME, such as

```
SQL> create index idx1 on inv(inv_name);
SQL> create index idx2 on inv(cust_name);
```

However, if you're consistently selecting the columns that appear in the WHERE clause, then the optimizer will most likely use the concatenated index and not use the single-column indexes. Using a concatenated index in these situations is usually much more efficient. You can verify that the optimizer chooses the concatenated index by generating an explain plan. For example:

```
SQL> set autotrace trace exlain;
SQL> select cust_name from inv where inv_name='Mouse' and cust_name='Bob';
```

Here's some sample output indicating that the optimizer uses the concatenated index on INV_IDX3 to retrieve data:

```
---------------------------------------------------------------------------
| Id  | Operation         | Name     | Rows | Bytes | Cost (%CPU)| Time     |
---------------------------------------------------------------------------
|   0 | SELECT STATEMENT  |          |    1 |    34 |    1   (0)| 00:00:01 |
|*  1 |  INDEX RANGE SCAN | INV_IDX3 |    1 |    34 |    1   (0)| 00:00:01 |
---------------------------------------------------------------------------
```

In older versions of Oracle (circa v8), the optimizer would use a concatenated index only if the leading edge column(s) appeared in the WHERE clause. In modern versions, the optimizer uses a concatenated index even if the leading edge column(s) aren't present in the WHERE clause. This ability to use an index without reference to leading edge columns is known as the *skip-scan* feature.

A concatenated index that is used for skip-scanning is more efficient than a full-table scan. However, you should try to create concatenated indexes that use the leading column. If you're consistently using only a lagging edge column of a concatenated index, then consider creating a single-column index on the lagging column.

Implementing Function-Based Indexes

Function-based indexes are created with functions or expressions in their definitions. Sometimes, function-based indexes are required when queries use SQL functions. For example, consider the following query that uses a SQL UPPER function:

```
SQL> select emp_name from emp where UPPER(emp_name) = 'DAVE';
```

In this scenario, there may be a normal B-tree index on the EMP_NAME column, but Oracle won't use a regular index that exists on a column when a function is applied to it.

In this situation, you can create a function-based index to improve performance of queries that use a SQL function in the WHERE clause. This example creates a function-based index on UPPER(EMP_NAME):

```
SQL> create index user_upper_idx on emp(upper(emp_name));
```

Function-based indexes allow index lookups on columns referenced by functions in the WHERE clause of a SQL query. The index can be as simple as the preceding example, or it can be based on complex logic stored in a PL/SQL function.

▦ Note Any user-created SQL functions must be declared deterministic before they can be used in a function-based index. *Deterministic* means that for a given set of inputs, the function always returns the same results. You must use the keyword DETERMINISTIC when creating a user-defined function that you want to use in a function-based index.

If you want to see the definition of a function-based index, select from the `DBA/ALL/USER_IND_EXPRESSIONS` view to display the SQL associated with the index. If you're using SQL*Plus, be sure to issue a `SET LONG` command first. For example:

```
SQL> SET LONG 500
SQL> select index_name, column_expression from user_ind_expressions;
```

The `SET LONG` command in this example tells SQL*Plus to display up to 500 characters from the COLUMN_EXPRESSION column, which is of type `LONG`.

Creating Unique Indexes

When you create a B-tree index, you can also specify that the index be unique. Doing so ensures that non-`NULL` values are unique when you insert or update columns in a table.

Suppose you've identified a column (or combination of columns) in the table (outside of the primary key) that is used heavily in the `WHERE` clause. In addition, this column (or combination of columns) has the requirement that it be unique within a table. This is a good scenario in which to use a unique index. Use the `UNIQUE` clause to create a unique index:

```
SQL> create unique index inv_uidx1 on inv(sku_id);
```

▮ **Note** The unique index doesn't enforce uniqueness for `NULL` values inserted into the table. In other words, you can insert the value `NULL` into the indexed column for multiple rows.

You must be aware of some interesting nuances regarding unique indexes, primary-key constraints, and unique-key constraints. For a detailed discussion of primary-key constraints and unique-key constraints, see Chapter 7. When you create a primary-key constraint or a unique-key constraint, Oracle automatically creates a unique index and a corresponding constraint that is visible in `DBA/ALL/USER_CONSTRAINTS`.

When you only create a unique index explicitly (as in the example in this section), Oracle creates a unique index but doesn't add an entry for a constraint in `DBA/ALL/USER_CONSTRAINTS`. Why does this matter? Consider this scenario:

```
SQL> create unique index inv_uidx1 on inv(sku_id);
SQL> insert into inv(sku_id) values (1);
SQL> insert into inv(sku_id) values (1);
```

Here's the corresponding error message that is thrown:

```
ERROR at line 1:
ORA-00001: unique constraint (INV_MGMT.INV_UIDX1) violated
```

If you're asked to troubleshoot this issue, the first place you look is in `DBA_CONSTRAINTS` for a constraint named INV_UIDX1. However, there is no information:

```
select
  constraint_name
from dba_constraints
where constraint_name='INV_UIDX1';
no rows selected
```

The "no rows selected" message can be confusing: the error message thrown when you insert into the table indicates that a unique constraint has been violated, yet there is no information in the constraint-related data-dictionary views. In this situation, you have to look at DBA_INDEXES to view the details of the unique index that has been created.

If you want to have information related to the constraint in the DBA/ALL/USER_CONSTRAINTS views, you can explicitly associate a constraint after the index has been created:

```
SQL> alter table inv add constraint inv_uidx1 unique(sku_id);
```

In this situation, you can enable and disable the constraint independent of the index. However, because the index was created as unique, the index still enforces uniqueness regardless of whether the constraint has been disabled.

When should you explicitly create a unique index versus creating a constraint and having Oracle automatically create the index? There are no hard and fast rules. I prefer to create a unique-key constraint and let Oracle automatically create the unique index, because then I get information in both the DBA/ALL/USER_CONSTRAINTS views and the DBA/ALL/USER_INDEXES views.

But Oracle's documentation recommends that if you have a scenario where you're strictly using a unique constraint to improve query performance, it's preferable to create only the unique index. This is fine. If you take this approach, just be aware that you may not find any information in the constraint-related data-dictionary views.

Using Bitmap Indexes

Bitmap indexes are recommended for columns with a relatively low number of distinct values (low cardinality). You shouldn't use bitmap indexes on OLTP databases with high INSERT/UPDATE/DELETE activities, due to of locking issues. This is the case because the structure of the bitmap index results in potentially many rows being locked during DML operations, which results in locking problems for high-transaction OLTP systems.

Bitmap indexes are commonly used in data-warehouse environments. A typical star schema structure consists of a large fact table and many small dimension (lookup) tables. In these scenarios, it's common to create bitmap indexes on fact table foreign-key columns. The fact tables are typically loaded on a daily basis and (usually) aren't updated or deleted from.

Listed next is a simple example that demonstrates the creation and structure of a bitmap index. First you create a LOCATIONS table:

```
create table locations(
 location_id number
,region       varchar2(10)
);
```

Now, insert seven rows into the table:

```
insert into locations values(1,'NORTH');
insert into locations values(2,'EAST');
insert into locations values(3,'NORTH');
insert into locations values(4,'WEST');
insert into locations values(5,'EAST');
insert into locations values(6,'NORTH');
insert into locations values(7,'NORTH');
```

You use the BITMAP keyword to create a bitmap index. The next line of code creates a bitmap index on the REGION column of the LOCATIONS table:

```
SQL> create bitmap index reg_idx1 on locations(region);
```

A bitmap index stores the ROWID of a row and a corresponding bitmap. You can think of the bitmap as a combination of ones and zeros. A 1 indicates the presence of a value, and a 0 indicates that the value doesn't exist. Table 8–3 shows the resulting structure of the bitmap index.

Table 8–3. Structure of the REG_IDX1 Bitmap Index

Value/Row	Row 1	Row 2	Row 3	Row 4	Row 5	Row 6	Row 7
EAST	0	1	0	0	1	0	0
NORTH	1	0	1	0	0	1	1
WEST	0	0	0	1	0	0	0

For each value of REGION (EAST, NORTH, and WEST), an array of values is stored that indicates which rows contain a value for a particular REGION. For example, the EAST location has bit settings in row 2 and row 5 (meaning that the EAST location is present for those two rows).

Bitmap indexes are effective at retrieving rows when multiple AND and OR conditions appear in the WHERE clause. For example, to perform the task "find all rows with a region of EAST or WEST," a Boolean algebra OR operation is performed on the EAST and WEST bitmaps to quickly return the rows 2, 4, and 5. Table 8–4 shows the OR operation on the EAST and WEST bitmap as the last row.

Table 8–4. Results of an OR Operation

Value/Row	Row 1	Row 2	Row 3	Row 4	Row 5	Row 6	Row 7
EAST	0	1	0	0	1	0	0
NORTH	1	0	1	0	0	1	1
WEST	0	0	0	1	0	0	0
Boolean OR on EAST and WEST	0	1	0	1	1	0	0

▪ **Note** Bitmap indexes and bitmap join indexes are available only with the Oracle Enterprise Edition of the database.

Creating Bitmap Join Indexes

Bitmap join indexes store the results of a join between two tables in an index. Bitmap indexes are beneficial because they avoid joining tables to retrieve results. The syntax for a bitmap join index differs from a regular bitmap index in that it contains FROM and WHERE clauses. Here's the basic syntax for creating a bitmap join index:

```
create bitmap index <index_name>
on <fact_table> (<dimension_table.dimension_column>)
from <fact_table>, <dimension_table>
where <fact_table>.<foreign_key_column> = <dimension_table>.<primary_key_column>;
```

Bitmap join indexes are appropriate in situations where you're joining two tables using the foreign-key column(s) in one table that relate to primary-key column(s) in another table. For example, suppose you typically retrieve the CUSTOMER_NAME from the D_CUSTOMERS table while joining to a large F_SHIPMENTS fact table. This next example creates a bitmap join index between the F_SHIPMENTS and D_CUSTOMERS tables:

```
create bitmap index f_shipments_bm_idx1
on f_shipments(d_customers.cust_name)
from f_shipments, d_customers
where f_shipments.d_cust_id = d_customers.d_cust_id;
```

Now, consider a query such as this:

```
select
  d.cust_name
from f_shipments f, d_customers d
where f.d_cust_id = d.d_cust_id
and d.cust_name = 'Sun';
```

The optimizer can choose to use the bitmap join index and thus avoid the expense of having to join the tables.

Implementing Reverse-Key Indexes

Reverse-key indexes are similar to B-tree indexes except that the bytes of the index key are reversed when an index entry is created. For example, if the index values are 201, 202, and 203, the reverse-key index values are 102, 202, and 302:

```
Index value          Reverse key value
-------------        --------------------
201                  102
202                  202
203                  302
```

Reverse-key indexes can perform better in scenarios where you need a way to evenly distribute index data that would otherwise have similar values clustered together. Thus, when using a reverse-key index, you avoid having I/O concentrated in one physical disk location within the index during large inserts of sequential values.

Use the REVERSE clause to create a reverse-key index:

```
SQL> create index inv_idx1 on inv(inv_id) reverse;
```

You can verify that an index is reverse-key by running the following query:

```
SQL> select index_name, index_type from user_indexes;
```

Here's some sample output showing that the INV_IDX1 index is reverse-key:

```
INDEX_NAME                       INDEX_TYPE
-----------------------------    ---------------------------
INV_IDX1                         NORMAL/REV
USERS_IDX1                       NORMAL
```

■ **Note** You can't specify REVERSE for a bitmap index or an index-organized table.

Creating Key-Compressed Indexes

Index compression is useful for indexes that contain multiple columns where the leading index column value is often repeated. Compressed indexes in these situations have the following advantages:

- Reduced storage
- More rows stored in leaf blocks, which can result in less I/O when accessing a compressed index

Suppose you have a table defined as follows:

```
create table users(
 last_name  varchar2(30)
,first_name varchar2(30)
,address_id number);
```

You want to create a concatenated index on the LAST_NAME and FIRST_NAME columns. You know from examining the data that there is duplication in the LAST_NAME column. Use the COMPRESS N clause to create a compressed index:

```
SQL> create index users_idx1 on users(last_name, first_name) compress 2;
```

The prior line of code instructs Oracle to create a compressed index on two columns. You can verify that an index is compressed as follows:

```
select
 index_name
,compression
from
user_indexes where index_name like 'USERS%';
```

Here's some sample output indicating that compression is enabled for the index:

```
INDEX_NAME                       COMPRESS
-----------------------------    --------
USERS_IDX1                       ENABLED
```

■ **Note** You can't create a key-compressed index on a bitmap index.

Parallelizing Index Creation

In large database environments where you're attempting to create an index on a table that is populated with many rows, you may be able to reduce the time it takes to create the index by using the PARALLEL clause:

```
create index inv_idx1 on inv(inv_id)
parallel 2
tablespace inv_mgmt_data;
```

If you don't specify a degree of parallelism, Oracle selects a degree based on the number of CPUs on the box times the value of PARALLEL_THREADS_PER_CPU.

Avoiding Redo Generation When Creating an Index

You can optionally create an index with the NOLOGGING clause. Doing so has these implications:

- The redo isn't generated that would be required to recover the index in the event of a media failure.

- Subsequent direct-path operations also won't generate the redo required to recover the index information in the event of a media failure.

Here's an example of creating an index with the NOLOGGING clause:

```
create index inv_idx1 on inv(inv_id, inv_id2)
nologging
tablespace inv_mgmt_index;
```

The main advantage of NOLOGGING is that when you create the index, a minimal amount of redo information is generated, which can have significant performance implications for a large index. The disadvantage is that if you experience a media failure soon after the index is created (or have records inserted via a direct-path operation), and you must do a restore from a backup that was created prior to the index, you may see this error when the index is accessed:

```
ORA-01578: ORACLE data block corrupted (file # 4, block # 11407)
ORA-01110: data file 4: '/ora01/dbfile/O11R2/inv_mgmt_index01.dbf'
ORA-26040: Data block was loaded using the NOLOGGING option
```

This error indicates that the index is logically corrupt. In this scenario you must re-create or rebuild the index before it's usable. In most scenarios, it's acceptable to use the NOLOGGING clause when creating an index, because the index can be re-created or rebuilt without affecting the table on which the index is based.

You can run this query to view whether an index has been created with NOLOGGING:

```
SQL> select index_name, logging from user_indexes;
```

Implementing Invisible Indexes

In Oracle Database 11g and higher, you have the option of making an index invisible to the optimizer. Oracle still maintains invisible indexes but doesn't make them available for use by the optimizer. If you want the optimizer to use an invisible index, you can do so with a SQL hint.

Invisible indexes have a couple of interesting uses:

- Altering an index to invisible before dropping it allows you to quickly recover if you later determine that the index is required.

- You can add an invisible index to a third-party application without affecting existing code or support agreements.

These two scenarios are discussed in the following subsections.

Making an Existing Index Invisible

Suppose you've identified an index that isn't being used and are considering dropping it. In earlier releases of Oracle, you could mark the index as UNUSABLE and then later drop indexes that you were certain weren't being used. If you later determined that you needed an unusable index, the only way to re-enable the index was to rebuild it. For large indexes, this could take a long time and a lot of database resources.

Making an index invisible has the advantage that it only tells the optimizer to not use the index. The invisible index is still maintained as the underlying table has records inserted, updated, or deleted. If you decide that you later need the index, there is no need to rebuild it.

Use the INVISIBLE clause to make an index invisible:

```
SQL> alter index inv_idx1 invisible;
```

Next, monitor SQL queries and applications for degraded performance. After you're confident there will be no bad performance effects, you can drop the index:

```
SQL> drop index inv_idx1;
```

You can verify the visibility of an index via this query:

```
SQL> select index_name, status, visibility from user_indexes;
```

Here's some sample output:

```
INDEX_NAME                      STATUS    VISIBILITY
------------------------------- --------- ----------
INV_IDX1                        VALID     INVISIBLE
COMPUTER_SYSTEM_UK1             VALID     VISIBLE
```

Use the VISIBLE clause to make an invisible index visible to the optimizer again:

```
SQL> alter index inv_idx1 visible;
```

Guaranteeing Application Behavior Is Unchanged When You Add an Index

You can also use an invisible index is when you're working with third-party applications. Often, third-party vendors don't support customers adding their own indexes to an application. However, there may be a scenario in which you're certain you can increase a query's performance without impacting other queries in the application. You can create the index as invisible and then explicitly instruct a query to use the index via a hint:

```
SQL> create index inv_idx1 on inv(inv_id) invisible;
```

Next, ensure that the OPTIMIZER_USE_INVISIBLE_INDEXES initialization parameter is set to true. This instructs the optimizer to consider invisible indexes:

```
SQL> alter system set optimizer_use_invisible_indexes=true;
```

Now, use a hint to tell the optimizer that the index exists:

```
SQL> select /*+ index (inv INV_IDX1) */ inv_id from inv where inv_id=1;
```

You can verify that the index is being used by setting AUTOTRACE on and running the SELECT statement:

```
SQL> set autotrace trace explain;
SQL> select /*+ index (inv INV_IDX1) */ inv_id from inv where inv_id=1;
```

Here's some sample output indicating that the optimizer chose to use the invisible index:

```
--------------------------------------------------------------------------------
| Id  | Operation          | Name     | Rows  | Bytes | Cost (%CPU)| Time     |
--------------------------------------------------------------------------------
|   0 | SELECT STATEMENT   |          |     1 |    13 |     1   (0)| 00:00:01 |
|*  1 |  INDEX RANGE SCAN| INV_IDX1 |     1 |    13 |     1   (0)| 00:00:01 |
--------------------------------------------------------------------------------
```

Keep in mind that an invisible index only means the optimizer can't see the index. Just like any other index, an invisible index consumes space and resources during DML statements.

Using Index-Naming Standards

When you're creating and managing indexes, it's highly desirable to develop some standards regarding naming. Index-naming standards are desirable for the following reasons:

- Diagnosing issues is simplified when error messages contain information that indicates the table, index type, and so on.

- Reports that display index information are more easily grouped and therefore more readable and easier in which to see patterns and issues.

I usually don't care what the naming standards are as long as standards exist and are followed. Here are some sample index-naming guidelines:

- Primary-key index names should contain the table name and a suffix such as _PK.

- Unique-key index names should contain the table name and a suffix such as _UKN, where N is a number.

- Indexes on foreign-key columns should contain the foreign-key table and a suffix such as _FKN, where N is a number.

- Function-based index names should contain the table name and a suffix such as FCN, where N is a number.

Some shops use prefixes when naming indexes. All of these various naming standards are valid. The key is to use the standard consistently.

Specifying Index Tablespaces

When creating an index, if you don't specify a tablespace, by default the index is created in the default tablespace for the user. That approach is acceptable for development databases where you may not be concerned about managing indexes separately from tables. Or perhaps you're not concerned about the storage characteristics of the index because there's only a small amount of data.

For production databases, you should consider the following with regard to index storage:

- Creating indexes in a tablespace separate from table data

- Creating several tablespaces specifically for use with indexes, depending on their storage requirements

These topics are discussed in detail in the following subsections.

Placing Indexes in Tablespaces Separate from Tables

DBAs debate the merits of separating tables and indexes into different tablespaces. If you have the luxury of setting up a storage system from scratch and can set up mount points that have their own sets of disks and controllers, you may see some I/O benefits by separating tables and indexes into different tablespaces.

Nowadays, storage administrators often give you a large slice of storage in a SAN, and there's no way to guarantee that data and indexes will be stored physically on separate disks (and controllers). Thus you typically don't gain any performance benefits by separating tables and indexes into different tablespaces. Nevertheless, there are still valid reasons to separate index tablespaces from table tablespaces:

- You may want to implement different physical storage characteristics (such as extent size) for tables and indexes, and you prefer to allow the table and index to inherit their storage attributes from the tablespace.

- You prefer to have the option of being able to back up, restore, and recover table and index tablespaces separately.

- When running maintenance reports, you find it easier to manage tables and indexes when the reports have sections separated by tablespace.

If any of these reasons are valid for your environment, it's probably worth the extra effort to employ different tablespaces for tables and indexes. Here's a simple example of building a table and an index in separate tablespaces:

```
SQL> create table inv(inv_id number, inv_dtt date) tablespace inv_mgmt_data;
SQL> create index inv_idx1 on inv(inv_dtt) tablespace inv_mgmt_index;
```

I almost always use ampersand variables in scenarios like this. To do so, at the top of the script, define the names of the tablespaces to be used, and then refer to the ampersand variables within the script. This technique has the advantage of making scripts more portable from one environment (development, test, production, and so on) to another where the tablespaces may be differently named. For example:

```
define tab_tbsp_small=INV_MGMT_DATA
define ind_tbsp_small=INV_MGMT_INDEX
--
create table inv(inv_id number, inv_dtt date) tablespace &&tab_tbsp_small;
create index inv_idx1 on inv(inv_dtt) tablespace &&ind_tbsp_small;
```

Placing Indexes in Tablespaces Based on Extent Size

If you know how large an index may initially be or what its growth requirements are, consider placing the index in a tablespace that is appropriate in terms of the size of the tablespace and the size of the extents. I usually create at least two index tablespaces per application. Here's an example:

```
create tablespace inv_idx_small
  datafile '/ora01/dbfile/O11R2/inv_idx_small01.dbf'
  size 100m
  extent management local
  uniform size 128k
  segment space management auto;
--
create tablespace inv_idx_med
  datafile '/ora01/dbfile/O11R2/inv_idx_med01.dbf'
  size 1000m
  extent management local
  uniform size 4m
  segment space management auto;
```

Indexes that have small space and growth requirements are placed in the INV_IDX_SMALL tablespace, and indexes that have medium storage requirements would be created in INV_IDX_MED. If you discover that an index is growing at an unpredicted rate, consider dropping the index and re-creating it in a different tablespace or rebuilding the index in a more appropriate tablespace.

Maintaining Indexes

As applications age, you invariably have to perform some maintenance activities on existing indexes. You may need to rename an index to conform to newly implemented standards, or you may need to rebuild a large index to move it to a different tablespace that better suits the index's storage requirements. The following list shows common tasks associated with index maintenance:

- Renaming an index
- Displaying the DDL for an index
- Rebuilding an index
- Setting indexes to be unusable
- Dropping an index

Each of these items is discussed in the following subsections.

Renaming an Index

Sometimes you need to rename an index. The index may have been erroneously misnamed when it was created, or perhaps you want a name that better conforms to naming standards. Use the `ALTER INDEX ... RENAME TO` statement to rename an index:

```
SQL> alter index user1_index rename to emp_idx1;
```

You can verify that the index was renamed by querying the data dictionary:

```
select
  table_name
 ,index_name
 ,index_type
 ,tablespace_name
 ,status
from user_indexes
order by table_name, index_name;
```

Displaying Code to Re-create an Index

You may be performing routine maintenance activities, such as moving an index to a different tablespace, and before you do so, you want to verify the current storage settings. You can use the `DBMS_METADATA` package to display the DDL required to re-create an index. If you're using SQL*Plus, set the `LONG` variable to a value large enough to display all of the output. Here's an example:

```
SQL> set long 10000
SQL> select dbms_metadata.get_ddl('INDEX','INV_IDX1') from dual;
```

Here's a partial listing of the output:

```
CREATE INDEX "DARL"."INV_IDX1" ON "DARL"."INV" ("INV_ID", "INV_ID2")
PCTFREE 10 INITRANS 2 MAXTRANS 255 NOLOGGING COMPUTE STATISTICS
```

To show all index DDL for a user, run this query:

```
SQL> select dbms_metadata.get_ddl('INDEX',index_name) from user_indexes;
```

You can also display the DDL for a particular user. You must provide as input to the `GET_DDL` function the object type, object name, and schema. For example:

```
select
dbms_metadata.get_ddl(object_type=>'INDEX', name=>'INV_IDX1', schema=>'INV')
from dual;
```

Rebuilding an Index

There are a few good reasons to rebuild an index:

- The index has become corrupt (see the previous section on Avoiding Redo Generation When Creating an Index for the scenario in which you encounter logical corruption).

- You want to modify storage characteristics, such as changing the tablespace.

- An index that was previously marked as unusable now needs to be rebuilt to make it usable again.

Use the REBUILD clause to rebuild an index. This example rebuilds an index named INV_IDX1:

```
SQL> alter index inv_idx1 rebuild;
```

Oracle attempts to acquire a lock on the table and rebuild the index online. If there are any active transactions that haven't committed, then Oracle won't be able to obtain a lock, and the following error will be thrown:

```
ORA-00054: resource busy and acquire with NOWAIT specified or timeout expired
```

In this scenario, you can either wait until the there is little activity in the database or try setting the DDL_LOCK_TIMEOUT parameter:

```
SQL> alter session set ddl_lock_timeout=15;
```

The DDL_LOCK_TIMEOUT initialization parameter is available in Oracle Database 11g or higher. It instructs Oracle to repeatedly attempt to obtain a lock for the specified amount of time.

If no tablespace is specified, Oracle rebuilds the index in the tablespace in which the index currently exists. Specify a tablespace if you want the index rebuilt in a different tablespace:

```
SQL> alter index inv_idx1 rebuild tablespace inv_index;
```

If you're working with a large index, you may want to consider using features such as NOLOGGING and/or PARALLEL. This next example rebuilds an index in parallel while generating a minimal amount of redo:

```
SQL> alter index inv_idx rebuild parallel nologging;
```

◼ Note See the sections in this chapter on Avoiding Redo Generation When Creating an Index and Parallelizing Index Creation for details on using these features with indexes.

REBUILDING FOR PERFORMANCE REASONS

In the olden days (version 7 or so), in the name of performance, DBAs religiously rebuilt indexes on a regular basis. Just about every DBA had a script similar to the one listed next that uses SQL to generate the SQL required to rebuild indexes for a schema:

```
SPO ind_build_dyn.sql
SET HEAD OFF PAGESIZE 0 FEEDBACK OFF;
SELECT 'ALTER INDEX ' || index_name || ' REBUILD;'
FROM user_indexes;
SPO OFF;
SET FEEDBACK ON;
```

However, it's debatable whether rebuilding an index with the newer versions of Oracle achieves any performance gain. Usually, the only valid reason to rebuild an index is if the index has become corrupt or unusable, or you want to modify storage characteristics (such as the tablespace).

Making Indexes Unusable

If you've identified an index that is no longer being used, you can mark it as UNUSABLE. From that point forward, Oracle won't maintain the index, nor will the optimizer consider the index for use in SELECT statements. The advantage of marking the index as UNUSABLE (rather than dropping it) is that if you later determine that the index is being used, you can alter to a USABLE state and rebuild the index without needing the DDL on hand to re-create the index.

Here's an example of marking an index as UNUSABLE:

```
SQL> alter index inv_idx1 unusable;
```

You can verify that it's unusable via this query:

```
SQL> select index_name, status from user_indexes;
```

The index has an UNUSABLE status:

```
INDEX_NAME                    STATUS
----------------------------- --------
INV_IDX1                      UNUSABLE
```

If you determine that the index is needed (before you drop it), then it must be rebuilt to become usable again:

```
SQL> alter index inv_idx1 rebuild;
```

Another common scenario for marking indexes as UNUSABLE is if you're performing a large data load. When you want to maximize table-loading performance, you can mark the indexes as UNUSABLE before performing the load. After you've loaded the table, you must rebuild the indexes to make them usable again.

▦ **Note** The alternative to setting an index as UNUSABLE is to drop and re-create the index. This approach requires the CREATE INDEX DDL.

Monitoring Index Usage

You may have inherited a database, and as part of getting to know the database and application, you want to determine which indexes are being used (or not). The idea is that you can identify indexes that aren't being used and drop them, thus eliminating the extra overhead and storage required.

Use the ALTER INDEX...MONITORING USAGE statement to enable basic index monitoring. The following example enables index monitoring on an index named F_DOWN_DOM_FK9:

```
SQL> alter index F_DOWN_DOM_FK9 monitoring usage;
```

The first time the index is accessed, Oracle records this; you can view whether an index has been accessed via the V$OBJECT_USAGE view. To report which indexes are being monitored and have ever been used, run this query:

```
SQL> select * from v$object_usage;
```

Most likely, you won't monitor only one index. Rather, you'll want to monitor all indexes for a user. In this situation, use SQL to generate SQL to create a script you can run to turn on monitoring for all indexes. Here's such a script:

```
select
  'alter index ' || index_name || ' monitoring usage;'
from user_indexes;
```

The V$OBJECT_USAGE view only shows information for the currently connected user. If you inspect the TEXT column of DBA_VIEWS, notice the following line:

```
where io.owner# = userenv('SCHEMAID')
```

If you're logged in as a DBA privileged user and want to view the status of all indexes that have monitoring enabled (regardless of the user), execute this query:

```
select io.name, t.name,
       decode(bitand(i.flags, 65536), 0, 'NO', 'YES'),
       decode(bitand(ou.flags, 1), 0, 'NO', 'YES'),
       ou.start_monitoring,
       ou.end_monitoring
from sys.obj$ io
    ,sys.obj$ t
    ,sys.ind$ i
    ,sys.object_usage ou
where i.obj# = ou.obj#
and io.obj# = ou.obj#
and t.obj# = i.bo#;
```

The prior query removes the line from the query that restricts the currently logged-in user. This provides you with a convenient way to view all monitored indexes.

Dropping an Index

If you've determined that an index isn't being used, then it's a good idea to drop it. Unused indexes take up space and can potentially slow down DML statements (because the index must be maintained as part of those DML operations). Use the DROP INDEX statement to drop an index:

```
SQL> drop index inv_idx1;
```

Dropping an index is a permanent DDL operation; there is no way to undo an index drop other than to rebuild the index. Before you drop an index, it doesn't hurt to quickly capture the DDL required to rebuild the index. Doing so will allow you to re-create the index in the event you subsequently discover that you did need it after all.

Summary

Indexes are critical objects separate from tables; they vastly increase the performance of a database application. Your index architecture should be well planned, implemented, and maintained. Carefully choose which tables and columns are indexed. Although indexes dramatically increase the speed of queries, indexes can slow down DML statement because the index has to be maintained as the table data changes. Indexes also consume disk space and thus should be created only when required.

Oracle's B-tree index is the default index type and is sufficient for most applications. However, you should be aware of other index types and their uses. Specific features such as bitmap and function-based indexes should be implemented where applicable. You (the DBA) are expected to be an expert on index types and when to use them. Competent implementation of these features provides large performance benefits.

Indexes should be monitored to determine whether they're being used. When you detect unused indexes, consider making them invisible or marking them as unused. After you're certain an index isn't being accessed, drop it. Doing so eliminates the overhead associated with maintaining the index and frees up storage.

After you build a database and users and configure the database with tables and indexes, the next step is to create additional objects needed by the application and users. In addition to tables and indexes, other typical objects include views, synonyms, and sequences. Building these database objects is detailed in the next chapter.

Views, Synonyms, and Sequences

This chapter focuses on views, synonyms, and sequences. Views are used extensively in reporting applications and also to present subsets of data to applications. Synonyms provide a means to transparently allow users to display and use other users' objects. Sequences are often used to generate unique numbers that are used to populate primary-key and foreign-key values.

Note Although views, synonyms, and sequences may not seem as important as tables and indexes, the truth of the matter is that they're almost equally important to understand. An application with any level of sophistication will use what's discussed in this chapter.

Implementing Views

You can think of a view as a SQL statement stored in the database. Conceptually, when you select from a view, Oracle looks up the view definition in the data dictionary, executes the query the view is based on, and returns the results. Or, to put it another way, views are logical tables built on other tables and/or views. Views have the following functions:

- Create an efficient method of storing a SQL query for reuse.

- Provide an interface layer between an application and physical tables.

- Hide the complexity of a SQL query from an application.

- Report to a user about only a subset of columns and/or rows.

Creating a View

You can create views on tables, materialized views, or other views. For reference, the view-creation example in this section depends on the following base table:

```
create table sales(
sales_id number primary key
,amnt    number
,state   varchar2(2)
);
```

To create a view, your user account must have the CREATE VIEW system privilege. If you want to create a view in another user's schema, then you must have the CREATE ANY VIEW privilege.

Use the CREATE VIEW statement to create a view. The following code creates a view (or replaces it if the view already exists) that selects a subset of columns and rows from the SALES table:

```
create or replace view sales_rockies as
select
 sales_id
,amnt
,state
from sales
where state in ('CO','UT','WY','ID','AZ');
```

Now you can treat the SALES_ROCKIES view as if it were a table. The schema that has access to the view can perform any SELECT, INSERT, UPDATE, or DELETE operation for which it has object grants, and the Data Manipulation Language (DML) operation will result in the underlying table data being changed. For example, if a schema separate from the owner of the base table has INSERT privileges on the SALES table, then you can use the view in the INSERT statement:

```
insert into sales_rockies(
 sales_id, amnt, state)
values
(1,100,'CO');
```

Notice that you can insert a value into the view that results in a row in the underlying table that isn't selectable by the view:

```
insert into sales_rockies(
 sales_id, amnt, state)
values (2,123,'CA');
```

```
SQL> select * from sales_rockies;
```

```
  SALES_ID       AMNT ST
---------- ---------- --
         1        100 CO
```

If you only want the view to allow DML statements that result in data modifications that are selectable by the view statement, then use WITH CHECK OPTION (see the next section).

Checking Updates

If you want to allow only the underlying table data within the scope of the view to be changed, specify WITH CHECK OPTION:

```
create or replace view sales_rockies as
select
 sales_id
,amnt
,state
from sales
where state in ('CO','UT','WY','ID','AZ')
with check option;
```

Using `WITH CHECK OPTION` means that you can only insert or update rows that would be returned by the view query. For example, this `UPDATE` statement works because the statement isn't changing the underlying data in a way would result in the row not being returned by the view query:

```
SQL> update sales_rockies set state='ID' where sales_id=1;
```

However, this next update statement fails because it attempts to update the STATE column to a state that isn't selectable by the query on which the view is based:

```
SQL> update sales_rockies set state='CA' where sales_id=1;
```

In this example, the following error is thrown:

```
ERROR at line 1:
ORA-01402: view WITH CHECK OPTION where-clause violation
```

Creating Read-Only Views

If you don't want a user to be able to perform `INSERT`, `UPDATE`, or `DELETE` operations on a view, then don't grant those object privileges on the underlying table(s) to that user. You should also create a view with the `WITH READ ONLY` clause for any views for which you don't want the underlying tables to be modified (keep in mind that by default, the view is updatable, and the underlying objects can be modified if the object grants exist). This example creates a view with the `WITH READ ONLY` clause:

```
create or replace view sales_rockies as
select
 sales_id
,amnt
,state
from sales
where state in ('CO','UT','WY','ID','AZ')
with read only;
```

If you use views for reporting, and you never intend for the views to be used as a mechanism to update a table, then you should always create the views with the `WITH READ ONLY` clause. Doing so prevent accidental modifications to the underlying tables through a view that was never intended to be used for changing data.

Updatable Join Views

If you have multiple tables defined in the `FROM` clause of the SQL query on which the view is based, it's still possible to update the underlying tables. This is known as an *updatable join view*.

For reference purposes, here are the `CREATE TABLE` statements for the two tables used in the examples in this section:

```
create table emp(
 emp_id number primary key
,emp_name varchar2(15)
,dept_id number);
--
create table dept(
 dept_id number primary key
,dept_name varchar2(15),
 constraint emp_dept_fk
 foreign key(dept_id) references dept(dept_id));
```

For this example, here's some seed data for the two tables:

```
insert into dept values(1,'HR');
insert into dept values(2,'IT');
insert into dept values(3,'SALES');
insert into emp values(10,'John',2);
insert into emp values(20,'Bob',1);
insert into emp values(30,'Craig',2);
insert into emp values(40,'Joe',3);
insert into emp values(50,'Jane',1);
insert into emp values(60,'Mark',2);
```

Here's an example of an updatable join view based on the two prior base tables:

```
create or replace view emp_dept_v
as
select
 a.emp_id
,a.emp_name
,b.dept_name
,b.dept_id
from emp a, dept b
where a.dept_id = b.dept_id;
```

There are some restrictions regarding the columns on which DML operations are permitted. For example, columns in the underlying tables can be updated only if the following conditions are true:

- The DML statement must modify only one underlying table.

- The view must be created without the READ ONLY clause.

- The column being updated belongs to the key-preserved table in the join view (there is only one key-preserved table in a join view).

An underlying table in a view is *key-preserved* if the table's primary key can also be used to uniquely identify rows returned by the view. An example with data will help illustrate whether an underlying table is key-preserved. In this example, the primary key of the EMP table is the EMP_ID column. And the primary key of the DEPT table is the DEPT_ID column. Here's some sample data returned by the view listed previously listed in this section:

EMP_ID	EMP_NAME	DEPT_NAME	DEPT_ID
10	John	IT	2
20	Bob	HR	1
30	Craig	IT	2
40	Joe	SALES	3
50	Jane	HR	1
60	Mark	IT	2

As you can see from the output of the view, the EMP_ID column is always unique. Therefore, the EMP table is key-preserved (and its columns can be updated). On the other hand, the view's output shows that it's possible for the DEPT_ID column to be not unique. Therefore, the DEPT table isn't key-preserved (its columns can't be updated).

When you update the view, any modifications that result in columns that map to the underlying EMP table should be allowed because the EMP table is key-preserved in this view. For example, this UPDATE statement is successful:

```
SQL> update emp_dept_v set emp_name = 'Jon' where emp_name = 'John';
```

However, statements that result in updating the DEPT table's columns aren't allowed. The next statement attempts to update a column in the view that maps to the DEPT table:

```
SQL> update emp_dept_v set dept_name = 'HR West' where dept_name = 'HR';
```

Here's the resulting error message that's thrown:

```
ORA-01779: cannot modify a column which maps to a non key-preserved table
```

To summarize, a join view can select from many tables, but only one of the tables in the join view is key preserved. The primary-key and foreign-key relationships of the tables in the query determine which table is key-preserved, and not the data returned by the view.

Creating an INSTEAD OF Trigger

An INSTEAD OF trigger on a view instructs Oracle to execute PL/SQL code instead of using the DML statement. The INSTEAD OF trigger allows you to modify the underlying base tables in ways that you can't with regular join views.

I'm not a huge fan of INSTEAD OF triggers. In my opinion, if you're considering using them, you should rethink how you're issuing DML statements to modify base tables. Maybe you should allow the application to issue INSERT, UPDATE, and DELETE statements directly against the base tables instead of trying to build PL/SQL INSTEAD OF triggers on a view.

Think about how you'll maintain and troubleshoot issues with INSTEAD OF triggers. Will it be difficult for the next DBA to figure out how the base tables are being modified? Will it be easy for the next DBA or developer to make modifications to the INSTEAD OF triggers? When an INSTEAD OF trigger throws an error, will it be obvious what code is throwing the error and how to resolve the problem?

Having said that, if you determine that you require an INSTEAD OF trigger on a view, use the INSTEAD OF clause to create it, and embed it in it the required PL/SQL. This example creates an INSTEAD OF trigger on the EMP_DEPT_V view (created in the previous section):

```
create or replace trigger emp_dept_v_updt
instead of update on emp_dept_v
for each row
begin
  update emp set emp_name=UPPER(:new.emp_name)
  where emp_id=:old.emp_id;
end;
/
```

Now, when an update is issued against EMP_DEPT_V, instead of the DML being executed, Oracle intercepts the statement and runs the INSTEAD OF PL/SQL code. For example:

```
SQL> update emp_dept_v set emp_name='Jonathan' where emp_id = 10;
```

```
1 row updated.
```

Now you can verify that the trigger correctly updated the table by selecting the data:

```
SQL> select * from emp_dept_v;

    EMP_ID EMP_NAME         DEPT_NAME           DEPT_ID
---------- ---------------- ---------------- ----------
        10 JONATHAN         IT                        2
        20 Bob              HR                        1
        30 Craig            IT                        2
        40 Joe              SALES                     3
        50 Jane             HR                        1
        60 Mark             IT                        2
```

This code is a simple example, but it illustrates that you can have PL/SQL execute instead of the DML that was run on the view. Again, be careful when using INSTEAD OF triggers; be sure you're confident that you can efficiently diagnose and resolve any related issues that may arise.

Modifying a View Definition

If you need to modify the SQL query on which a view is based, then either drop and re-create the view or use the CREATE OR REPLACE syntax as in the previous examples. For instance, to add the REGION column to the SALES_ROCKIES view, run the following to replace the existing view:

```
create or replace view sales_rockies as
select sales_id, amnt, state, region
from sales
where state in ('CO','UT','WY','ID','AZ')
with read only;
```

The advantage of using the CREATE OR REPLACE method is that you don't have to reestablish access to the view for users with previously granted permissions.

The alternative to CREATE OR REPLACE is to drop and re-create the view with the new definition. If you drop and re-create the view, you must re-grant privileges to any users or roles that were previously granted access to the dropped and re-created object. For this reason, I almost never use the drop and re-create method when altering the structure of a view.

■ **Note** The ALTER VIEW command is used to modify a view's constraint attributes. You can also use the ALTER VIEW command to recompile a view.

Displaying the SQL Used to Create a View

Sometimes, when you're troubleshooting issues with the information a view returns, you need to see the SQL query on which the view is based. Use the following script to display the text associated with a particular view for a user:

```
select
  view_name
 ,text
from dba_views
where owner = upper('&owner')
and view_name like upper('&view_name');
```

You can also query ALL_VIEWS for the text of any view you have access to:

```
select
  text
from all_views
where owner='INV'
and view_name='INV_VIEW';
```

If you want to display the view text that exists within your schema, use USER_VIEWS:

```
select
 text
from user_views where view_name=upper('&view_name');
```

The TEXT column of DBA_VIEWS is of data type LONG. The default length displayed by a LONG data type in SQL*Plus is 80 characters. If you don't issue a SET LONG to a length greater than the number of characters in the TEXT column, only part of the view listing will be shown. You can determine the view length by querying the TEXT_LENGTH column of DBA/ALL/USER_VIEWS.

You can also use the DBMS_METADATA package's GET_DDL function to display a view's code. The data type returned from GET_DDL is a CLOB; therefore, if you run it from SQL*Plus, make sure you first set your LONG variable to a sufficient size to display all of the text. For example, here's how to set LONG to 5000 characters:

```
SQL> set long 5000
```

You need to provide the GET_DDL function with the object type, name, and schema, respectively. You can display the view code by invoking DBMS_METADATA.GET_DDL with a SELECT statement, as follows:

```
SQL> select dbms_metadata.get_ddl('VIEW','USER_VIEW','INV') from dual;
```

If you want to display the Data Definition Language (DDL) for all views for the currently connected user, run this SQL:

```
SQL> select dbms_metadata.get_ddl('VIEW', view_name) from user_views;
```

ORACLE INTERNAL VIEW DEFINITIONS

You may occasionally need the definition of an Oracle internal view. For example, you may be troubleshooting an issue and need to know more details about how Oracle is retrieving information from the data dictionary. Select from the V$FIXED_VIEW_DEFINITION view for definitions of the V$ views. This example selects the text of the V$BH view:

```
SQL> select view_definition from v$fixed_view_definition where view_name='V$BH';
```

Here's the corresponding output:

```
select file#, block#, class#, status, xnc, forced_reads,
forced_writes, lock_element, addr, lock_element_name,
lock_element_class, dirty, temp, ping, stale, direct,
new, objd, ts#  from gv$bh where inst_id = USERENV('Instance')
```

Displaying these definitions can also give you a better understanding of the intricacies of Oracle internals.

Renaming a View

There are a couple of good reasons to rename a view. You may want to change the name so that it better conforms to standard, or you may want to rename a view before dropping it so that you can better determine whether it's in use.

Use the RENAME statement to change the name of a view. This example renames the INV view to INV_OLD:

```
SQL> rename inv to inv_old;
```

You should see this message:

```
Table renamed.
```

Dropping a View

Before you drop a view, consider renaming it. If you're certain that a view isn't being used anymore, then it makes sense to keep your schema as clean as possible and drop any unused objects. Use the DROP VIEW statement to drop a view:

```
SQL> drop view inv_v;
```

Keep in mind that when you drop a view, any dependent views, materialized views, and/or synonyms become invalid.

Managing Synonyms

Synonyms provide a mechanism to create an alternate name for an object. For example, say USER1 is the currently connected user, and USER1 has select access to USER2's EMP table. Without a synonym, USER1 must select from USER2's EMP table as follows:

```
SQL> select * from user2.emp;
```

With a synonym, USER1 can do the following:

```
SQL> create synonym emp for user2.emp;
SQL> select * from emp;
```

You can create synonyms for the following types of database objects:

- Tables
- Views or object views
- Other synonyms
- Remote objects via a database link
- PL/SQL packages, procedures, and functions
- Materialized views
- Sequences
- Java class schema object
- User-defined object types

Creating a synonym that points to another object eliminates the need to specify the schema owner or name of the object. This lets you create a layer of abstraction between an object and the user, often referred to as *object transparency*. Synonyms allow you to transparently manage objects separately from the users who access the objects. You can also seamlessly relocate objects to different schemas or even different databases. The application code that references the sequences doesn't need to change—only the definition of the synonym.

░ Tip You can use synonyms to set up multiple application environments within one database. Each environment has its own synonyms that point to a different user's objects, allowing you to run the same code against several different schemas within one database. For example, you may do this because you can't afford to build a separate box or database for development, testing, quality assurance, production, and so on.

Creating a Synonym

Use the CREATE SYNONYM command to create an alias for another database object. The following example creates a synonym for a table named INV that's owned by the INV_MGMT user:

```
SQL> create or replace synonym inv for inv_mgmt.inv;
```

After you've created the INV synonym, you can operate on the INV_MGMT.INV table directly. If select access has been granted to the INV_MGMT.INV table, you can now select by referencing the synonym INV:

```
SQL> select * from inv;
```

The creation of the synonym doesn't create the privilege to access an object. Such privileges must be granted separately, usually before you create the synonym.

By default, when you create a synonym, it's a private synonym. This means it's owned by the user who created the synonym, and other users can't access the synonym unless they're granted the appropriate object privileges.

Creating Public Synonyms

You can also define a synonym to be public (see the prior section for a discussion of private synonyms), which means any user in the database has access to the synonym. Sometimes, an inexperienced DBA does the following:

```
SQL> grant all on books to public;
SQL> create public synonym books for inv_mgmt.books;
```

Now, any user who can connect to the database can perform any INSERT, UPDATE, DELETE, or SELECT operation on the BOOKS table that exists in the INV_MGMT schema. You may be tempted to do this so you don't have to bother setting up individual grants and synonyms for each schema that needs access. This is almost always a bad idea. There are a few issues with using public synonyms:

- Troubleshooting can be problematic if you're not aware of globally defined (public) synonyms.

- Applications that share one database can have collisions on object names if multiple applications use public synonyms that aren't unique within the database.

- Security should be administered as needed, not on a wholesale basis.

I usually try to avoid using public synonyms. However, there may be scenarios that warrant their use. For example, when Oracle creates the data dictionary, public synonyms are used to simplify the administration of access to internal database objects. To display any public synonyms in your database, run this query:

```
select owner, synonym_name
from dba_synonyms
where owner='PUBLIC';
```

Dynamically Generating Synonyms

Sometimes it's useful to dynamically generate synonyms for all tables or views for a schema that needs private synonyms. The following script uses SQL*Plus commands to format and capture the output of a SQL script that generates synonyms for all tables within a schema:

```
CONNECT &&master_user/&&master_pwd.@&&tns_alias
--
SET LINESIZE 132 PAGESIZE 0 ECHO OFF FEEDBACK OFF
SET VERIFY OFF HEAD OFF TERM OFF TRIMSPOOL ON
--
SPO gen_syns_dyn.sql
--
select 'create or replace synonym ' || table_name ||
       ' for ' || '&&master_user..' ||
  table_name || ';'
from user_tables;
--
SPO OFF;
--
SET ECHO ON FEEDBACK ON VERIFY ON HEAD ON TERM ON;
```

Look at the &&master_user variable with the two dots appended to it in the SELECT statement: what is the purpose of double-dot syntax? A single dot at the end of an ampersand variable instructs SQL*Plus to concatenate anything after the single dot to the ampersand variable. When you place two dots together, that tells SQL*Plus to concatenate a single dot to the string contained in the ampersand variable.

Displaying Synonym Metadata

The DBA/ALL/USER_SYNONYMS views contain information about synonyms in the database. Use the following SQL to view synonym metadata for the currently connected user:

```
select
  synonym_name, table_owner, table_name, db_link
from user_synonyms
order by 1;
```

202

The `ALL_SYNONYMS` view displays all private synonyms, all public synonyms, and any private synonyms owned by different users for which your currently connected user has select access to the underlying base table. You can display information for all private and public synonyms in your database by querying the `DBA_SYNONYMS` view.

The TABLE_NAME column in the `DBA/ALL/USER_SYNONYMS` views is a bit of a misnomer because TABLE_NAME can reference many types of database objects, such as another synonym, view, package, function, procedure, materialized view, and so on. Similarly, TABLE_OWNER refers to the owner of the object (and that object may not necessarily be a table).

When you're diagnosing data-integrity issues, sometimes you first want to identify what table or object is being accessed. You can select from what appears to be a table, but in reality it may be a synonym that points to a view that selects from a synonym which in turn points to a table in a different database.

The following query is often a starting point for figuring out whether an object is a synonym, a view, or a table:

```
select
 owner
,object_name
,object_type
,status
from dba_objects
where object_name like upper('&object_name%');
```

Notice that using the percent-sign wildcard character in this query allows you to enter the object's partial name. Therefore, the query has the potential to return information regarding any object that partially matches the text string you enter.

You can also use the `GET_DDL` function of the `DBMS_METADATA` package to display synonym metadata. If you want to display the DDL for all synonyms for the currently connected user, run this SQL:

```
SQL> select dbms_metadata.get_ddl('SYNONYM', synonym_name) from user_synonyms;
```

You can also display the DDL for a particular user. You must provide as input to the `GET_DDL` function the object type, object name, and schema:

```
select
dbms_metadata.get_ddl(object_type=>'SYNONYM', name=>'VDB', schema=>'INV')
from dual;
```

Renaming a Synonym

You may want to rename a synonym so it conforms to naming standards or so you can determine whether it's being used. Use the `RENAME` statement to change the name of a synonym:

```
SQL> rename inv_s to inv_st;
```

Notice that the output displays this:

```
Table renamed.
```

This message is somewhat misleading. It indicates a table has been renamed, when in this scenario it was a synonym.

Dropping a Synonym

Use the DROP SYNONYM statement to drop a private synonym:

```
SQL> drop synonym inv;
```

If it's a public synonym, then you need to specify PUBLIC when you drop it:

```
SQL> drop public synonym inv_pub;
```

Managing Sequences

A *sequence* is a database object that users can access to select unique integers. Sequences are typically used to generate integers for populating primary-key and foreign-key columns. You increment a sequence by accessing it via a SELECT, INSERT, or UPDATE statement. Oracle guarantees that a sequence number is unique when selected; no two user sessions can select the same sequence number.

There is no way to guarantee that occasional gaps won't occur in the numbers generated by a sequence. Usually, some number of sequence values are cached in memory, and in the event of an instance failure (power failure, shutdown abort), any unused values still in memory are lost. Even if you don't cache the sequence, nothing stops a user from acquiring a sequence as part of a transaction and then rolling back that transaction. But for most applications, it's acceptable to have a mostly gap-free unique integer generator. Just be aware that gaps can exist.

Creating a Sequence

For many applications, creating a sequence can be as simple as this:

```
SQL> create sequence inv_seq;
```

If you don't specify a starting number and a maximum number for a sequence, by default the starting number is 1, the increment is 1, and the maximum value is 10^{27}. This example specifies a starting value of 1000 and a maximum value of 1000000:

```
SQL> create sequence inv2 start with 10000 maxvalue 1000000;
```

Table 9–1 lists the various options available when you're creating a sequence.

Table 9–1. Sequence-Creation Options

Option	Description
INCREMENT BY	Specifies the interval between sequence numbers.
START WITH	Specifies the first sequence number generated.
MAXVALUE	Specifies the maximum value of the sequence.
NOMAXVALUE	Sets the maximum value of a sequence to a really big number (10^{28} -1).
MINVALUE	Specifies the minimum value of sequence.
NOMINVALUE	Sets the minimum value to 1 for an ascending sequence; sets the value to – (10^{28}–1) for a descending sequence.
CYCLE	Specifies that when the sequence hits a maximum or minimum value, it should start generating numbers from the minimum value for an ascending sequence and from the maximum value for a descending sequence.
NOCYCLE	Tells the sequence to stop generating numbers after a maximum or minimum value is reached.
CACHE	Specifies how many sequence numbers to preallocate and keep in memory. If CACHE and NOCACHE aren't specified, the default is CACHE 20.
NOCACHE	Specifies that sequence numbers aren't to be cached.
ORDER	Guarantees that the numbers are generated in the order of request.
NOORDER	Used if you don't need to guarantee that sequence numbers are generated in the order of request. This is usually acceptable and is the default.

Using Sequence Pseudo-columns

After a sequence is created, you can use two pseudo-columns to access the sequence's value:

- NEXTVAL
- CURRVAL

You can reference these pseudo-columns in any SELECT, INSERT, or UPDATE statements. To retrieve a value from the INV_SEQ sequence, access the NEXTVAL value as shown:

```
SQL> select inv_seq.nextval from dual;
```

Now that a sequence number has been retrieved for this session, you can use it multiple times by accessing the CURRVAL value:

```
SQL> select inv_seq.currval from dual;
```

The following example uses a sequence to populate the primary-key value of a parent table, and then uses the same sequence to populate the corresponding foreign-key values in a child table. The sequence can be accessed directly in the INSERT statement. The first time you access the sequence, use the NEXTVAL pseudo-column.

```
SQL> insert into inv(inv_id, inv_desc) values (inv_seq.nextval, 'Book');
```

If you want to reuse the same sequence value, you can reference it via the CURRVAL pseudo-column. Next, a record is inserted into a child table that uses the same value for the foreign-key column as its parent primary-key value:

```
insert into inv_lines
    (inv_line_id,inv_id,inv_item_desc)
      values
    (1, inv_seq.currval, 'Tome1');
--
insert into inv_lines
    (inv_line_id,inv_id,inv_item_desc)
      values
    (2, inv_seq.currval, 'Tome2');
```

Autoincrementing Columns

I occasionally get this request from a developer: "I used to work with another database, and it had a really cool feature that would allow you to create a table and as part of the table definition specify that a column should always be populated with an automatically incrementing number." I usually reply something like, "Oracle has no such feature. If you have an issue with this, please send an email to Larry at...." Or I inform the developer that they can either use the sequence number directly in an INSERT statement (as shown in the prior section) or select the sequence value into a variable and then reference the variable as needed.

If you really need an autoincrementing column, you can simulate this functionality by using triggers. For example, say you create a table and sequence as follows:

```
SQL> create table inv(inv_id number, inv_desc varchar2(30));
SQL> create sequence inv_seq;
```

Next, create a trigger on the INV table that automatically populates the INV_ID column from the sequence:

```
create or replace trigger inv_bu_tr
before insert on inv
for each row
begin
  select inv_seq.nextval into :new.inv_id from dual;
end;
/
```

Now, insert a couple of records into the INV table:

```
SQL> insert into inv (inv_desc) values( 'Book');
SQL> insert into inv (inv_desc) values( 'Pen');
```

Select from the table to verify that the INV_ID column is indeed populated automatically by the sequence:

```
SQL> select * from inv;
    INV_ID INV_DESC
---------- ----------------------------
         1 Book
         2 Pen
```

I usually don't like using this technique. Yes, it makes it easier for the developers, in that they don't have to worry about populating the key columns. However, it's more work for the DBA to generate the code required to maintain the columns to be automatically populated. Because I'm the DBA, and I like to keep the database code that I maintain as simple as possible, I usually tell the developers that we aren't using this autoincrementing column approach and that we'll instead use the technique of directly calling the sequence in the DML statements (as shown in the prior section).

GAP-FREE SEQUENCES

People sometimes worry unduly about ensuring that not a single sequence value is lost as rows are inserted into a table. In a few cases, I've seen applications fail due to gaps in sequence values. I have two thoughts on these issues:

- If you're worried about gaps, you aren't thinking correctly about the problem you're solving.

- If your application fails due to gaps, you're doing it wrong.

My words are strong, I know; but few if any applications need gap-free sequences. If you really and truly need gap-free sequences, then using Oracle sequence objects is the wrong approach. You must implement your own sequence generator. You'll need to go through agonizing contortions to ensure that no gaps exist. Those contortions will impair your code's performance. And in the end, you'll probably fail.

Using Multiple Sequences that Generate Unique Values

I once had a developer ask if it was possible to create multiple sequences for an application and guarantee that each sequence would generate numbers unique across all sequences. If you have this type of requirement, you can handle it a few different ways:

- If you're feeling grumpy, tell the developer that it's not possible and that the standard is to use one sequence per application (this is usually the approach I take).

- Set sequences to start and increment at different points.

- Use ranges of sequence numbers.

If you're not feeling grumpy, you can set up a small, finite number of sequences that always generate unique values by specifying an odd or even starting number and then incrementing the sequence by two. For example, you can set up two odd and two even sequence generators, something like this:

```
SQL> create sequence inv_seq_odd start with 1 increment by 2;
SQL> create sequence inv_seq_even start with 2 increment by 2;
SQL> create sequence inv_seq_odd_dwn start with -1 increment by -2;
SQL> create sequence inv_seq_even_dwn start with -2 increment by -2;
```

The numbers generated by these four sequences should never intersect. However, this approach is limited to being able to use only four sequences.

If you need more than four unique sequences, you can use ranges of numbers. For example:

```
SQL> create sequence inv_seq_low start with 1 increment by 1 maxvalue 10000000;
SQL> create sequence inv_seq_ml  start with 10000001 increment by 1 maxvalue 20000000;
SQL> create sequence inv_seq_mh  start with 20000001 increment by 1 maxvalue 30000000;
SQL> create sequence inv_seq_high start with 30000001 increment by 1 maxvalue 40000000;
```

With this technique, you can set up numerous different ranges of numbers to be used by each sequence. The downside is that you're limited by the number of unique values that can be generated by each sequence.

Using One Sequence or Many

Say you have an application with 20 tables. One question that comes up is whether you should use 20 different sequences to populate the primary-key and/or foreign-key columns for each table, or use just 1 sequence.

I recommend using just one sequence. One sequence is easier to manage than multiple sequences, it's less DDL code to manage, and it means fewer places to investigate when there are issues.

Sometimes developers raise issues such as

- Performance issues with only one sequence

- Sequence numbers that get too high

If you cache the sequence values, usually there are no performance issues with accessing sequences. The maximum number for a sequence is $10^{28}-1$, so if the sequence is incrementing by 1, you'll never reach the maximum value (at least, not in this lifetime).

However, in some scenarios where you're generating surrogate keys for the primary and child tables, it's convenient to use more than one sequence. In these situations, multiple sequences per application may be warranted. When you use this approach, you must remember to add a sequence when tables are added and potentially drop sequences as tables are removed. It isn't a big deal, but it means a little more maintenance for the DBA; and the developers must ensure that they use the correct sequence for each table.

Viewing Sequence Metadata

If you have DBA privileges, you can query the DBA_SEQUENCES view to display information about all sequences in the database. To view sequences that your schema owns, query the USER_SEQUENCES view:

```
select
  sequence_name
  ,min_value
  ,max_value
  ,increment_by
from user_sequences;
```

To view the DDL code required to recreate a sequence, access the DBMS_METADATA view. If you're using SQL*Plus to execute DBMS_METADATA, first ensure that you set the LONG variable:

```
SQL> set long 5000
```

This example extracts the DDL for INV_SEQ:

```
SQL> select dbms_metadata.get_ddl('SEQUENCE','INV_SEQ') from dual;
```

Here's a snippet of the output:

```
CREATE SEQUENCE   "INV_MGMT"."INV_SEQ"
MINVALUE 1 MAXVALUE 999999999999999999999
999999 INCREMENT BY 1 START WITH 1 CACHE 20 NOORDER   NOCYCLE
```

If you want to display the DDL for all sequences for the currently connected user, run this SQL:

```
SQL> select dbms_metadata.get_ddl('SEQUENCE',sequence_name) from user_sequences;
```

You can also generate the DDL for a sequence owned by a particular user by providing the SCHEMA parameter:

```
select
dbms_metadata.get_ddl(object_type=>'SEQUENCE', name=>'INV_SEQ', schema=>'INV_APP')
from dual;
```

Renaming a Sequence

Occasionally you may need to rename a sequence. For example, a sequence may have been created with an erroneous name, or you want to rename the sequence before dropping it from the database. Use the RENAME statement to do this. This example renames INV_SEQ to INV_SEQ_OLD:

```
SQL> rename inv_seq to inv_seq_old;
```

You should see the following message:

```
Table renamed.
```

In this case, the message indicates that the sequence has been renamed.

Dropping a Sequence

To drop a sequence, use the DROP SEQUENCE statement:

```
SQL> drop sequence inv;
```

To reset a sequence number, you can drop the sequence and re-create it with the desired starting point. The following code drops a sequence and then re-creates it to start at the number 1:

```
SQL> drop sequence cia_seq;
SQL> create sequence cia_seq start with 1;
```

■ **Tip** See the next section on resetting a sequence for an alternative approach to dropping and re-creating a sequence.

Resetting a Sequence

In a couple of scenarios, you may be required to change the current value of a sequence number:

- Scenario 1: Your task is to create a development environment from a copy of production. You create the copy of production with a Data Pump export. During the export process, some sequences are exported before the tables are exported. Because the application using the database doesn't stop transacting during the export, it increments the sequence by several thousand numbers beyond what the exported sequence contains. When you do the import and begin selecting from the sequence, you realize that the current value of the imported sequence is too low and contains numbers that are already in use in the tables. To work around this, you need to increment your sequence(s) one time with a large value beyond that currently used by keys in the tables.

- Scenario 2: You have a test database and periodically need to truncate tables and reset the sequence back to zero.

These two scenarios are detailed in the following subsections.

Setting the Current Value of a Sequence to a Higher or Lower Value

Oracle's documentation states, "to restart a sequence at a different number, you must drop and re-create it." That's not entirely accurate (as this section shows). In most cases, you should avoid dropping a sequence because you must re-grant permissions on the object to users that currently have select permissions on the sequence. This can lead to temporary downtime for your application while you track down users that need to be re-granted select permission.

The technique in this section demonstrates how to set the current value to a higher or lower value using the ALTER SEQUENCE statement. The basic procedure is as follows:

1. Alter INCREMENT BY to a large number.

2. Select from the sequence to increment it by the large positive or negative value.

3. Set INCREMENT BY back to its original value (usually 1).

This example sets the next value of a sequence number to 1000 integers higher than the current value:

```
SQL> alter sequence myseq increment by 1000;
SQL> select myseq.nextval from dual;
SQL> alter sequence myseq increment by 1;
```

You can also use this technique to set the sequence number to a much lower number than the current value. The difference is that the INCREMENT BY setting is a large negative number. For example, this sets the sequence back 1000 integers:

```
SQL> alter sequence myseq increment by -1000;
SQL> select myseq.nextval from dual;
SQL> alter sequence myseq increment by 1;
```

Resetting a Sequence Back to a Lower Value

Sometimes you need to reset a sequence back to a starting point. For example, you may have a test database in which you occasionally truncate all the table data and reset the sequence the application uses back to 1. Oracle doesn't provide a way to reset a sequence. You have two options in this situation:

- Drop the sequence and re-create it at the desired starting number.

- As a one-time operation, alter the sequence to increment by a large negative number, increment it once by that number, and then set the increment value back to a positive 1.

To quickly reset a sequence, you can drop and re-create it:

```
SQL> drop sequence myseq;
SQL> create sequence myseq;
```

The default starting number for a sequence is 1:

```
SQL> select myseq.nextval from dual;

   NEXTVAL
----------
         1
```

Or you can re-create the sequence with a starting value. For example, this creates a sequence starting with the number 1000:

```
SQL> create sequence myseq start with 1000;
```

One side effect of dropping and re-creating a sequence is that if other schemas access the sequence, you must re-grant them select access to the sequence. This is because when you drop an object, any grants that were associated with that object are also dropped. Dropping and re-creating a sequence like this can have an adverse impact on your application if you haven't done a good job of determining which users need access to the dropped and re-created sequence.

An alternative approach to dropping and re-creating the sequence is to alter the sequence's INCREMENT BY value to one integer below where you want to reset it, and then alter the sequence's INCREMENT BY value to 1. Doing so effectively resets the sequence without having to drop and re-create it and removes the need to re-grant select access to the sequence. This technique is shown in the next several lines of SQL code:

```
UNDEFINE seq_name
UNDEFINE reset_to
PROMPT "sequence name" ACCEPT '&&seq_name'
PROMPT "reset to value" ACCEPT &&reset_to
COL seq_id NEW_VALUE hold_seq_id
COL min_id NEW_VALUE hold_min_id
--
SELECT &&reset_to - &&seq_name..nextval - 1 seq_id
FROM dual;
--
SELECT &&hold_seq_id - 1 min_id FROM dual;
--
ALTER SEQUENCE &&seq_name INCREMENT BY &hold_seq_id MINVALUE &hold_min_id;
--
SELECT &&seq_name..nextval FROM dual;
--
```

```
ALTER SEQUENCE &&seq_name INCREMENT BY 1;
```

To ensure that the sequence has been set to the value you want, select the NEXTVAL from it:

```
SQL> select &&seq_name..nextval from dual;
```

This approach can be quite useful when you're moving applications through various development, test, and production environments. It allows you to reset the sequence without having to reissue object grants.

Summary

Views, synonyms, and sequences are used extensively in Oracle database applications. These objects (along with tables and indexes) provide the technology for creating sophisticated applications.

Views provide a way to create and store complex multi-table join queries that can then be used by databases users and applications. Views can be used to update the underlying base tables or can be created read-only for reporting requirements.

Synonyms (along with appropriate privileges) provide a mechanism to transparently allow a user to access objects that are owned by a separate schema. The user accessing a synonym only needs to know the synonym name, regardless of the underlying object type and owner. This lets the application designer seamlessly separate the owner of the objects from the users that access the objects.

Sequences generate unique integers that are often used by applications to populate primary-key and foreign-key columns. Oracle guarantees that when a sequence is accessed, it will always return a unique value to the selecting user.

After installing the Oracle binaries and creating a database and tablespaces, usually you create an application that consists of the owning user and corresponding tables, constraints, indexes, views, synonyms, and sequences. Metadata regarding these objects is stored internally in the data dictionary. The data dictionary is used extensively for monitoring, troubleshooting, and diagnosing issues. You must be thoroughly fluent with retrieving information from the data dictionary. Retrieving and analyzing data-dictionary information is the topic of the next chapter.

CHAPTER 10

■ ■ ■

Data Dictionary Basics

The previous chapters in this book focus on topics such as managing users, basic security, tables, indexes, and constraints. This chapter focuses on extracting information from the data dictionary regarding those topics. Each of the sections in this chapter contains one or more SQL queries that demonstrate how to extract information from the data dictionary regarding a specific type of database object.

The Oracle data dictionary houses information about all aspects of the database. It stores critical information about the physical characteristics of the database, users, objects, and dynamic performance metrics. A senior-level DBA must posses an expert knowledge of the data-dictionary views. This chapter focuses on how you can use the information in the data dictionary.

This chapter is a turning point in the book. It divides the book between basic DBA tasks and more advanced topics. You must have a solid understanding of the data dictionary and how to proactively extract information and reactively resolve issues. The first few sections of this chapter detail the data-dictionary architecture. Sections after that contain techniques and queries that you can use to retrieve information about the database.

Data-Dictionary Architecture

If you ever inherit a database and are asked to maintain and manage it, typically you'll inspect the contents of the data dictionary to determine the physical structure of the database and see what events are currently transacting. Toward this end, Oracle provides to two general categories of data-dictionary views:

- Static USER/ALL/DBA views

- Dynamic V$ and GV$ views

The USER/ALL/DBA views contain metadata (information) describing the physical makeup of the database. For example, when you create a table, the description of that table is considered metadata and is stored in the database. Whenever you change the definition of an object, Oracle updates the data dictionary correspondingly. You typically use these views to view the structure of the database and information about users and corresponding objects.

The V$ and GV$ views provide real-time statistics about events currently transacting in the database. You use these views to determine which users are connected to the database, what SQL is executing, whether system bottlenecks exist, and so forth.

Static Views

Oracle describes a subset of the data-dictionary views as *static.* These views are based on physical tables maintained internally by Oracle. Oracle's documentation states that these views are static in the sense that the data they contain doesn't change at a rapid rate (at least, not rapid when compared to the dynamic V$ and GV$ views). These views are stored in the SYSTEM tablespace.

The term *static* can sometimes be a misnomer. For example, the DBA_SEGMENTS and DBA_EXTENTS views change dynamically as the amount of data in your database grows and shrinks. Regardless, Oracle has made the distinction between static and dynamic, and it's important to understand this architectural nuance when querying the data dictionary. There are three types or levels of static views:

- USER
- ALL
- DBA

The USER views contain information available to the current user. For example, the USER_TABLES view contains information about tables owned by the current user. No special privileges are required to select from the USER-level views.

At the next level are the ALL static views. The ALL views show you all object information the current user has access to. For example, the ALL_TABLES view displays all database tables on which the current user can perform any type of Data Manipulation Language (DML) operation. No special privileges are required to query from the ALL-level views.

Next are the DBA static views. The DBA views contain metadata describing all objects in the database (regardless of ownership or access privilege). To access the DBA views, you must have a DBA role or SELECT_CATALOG_ROLE granted to the current user.

The static views are based on internal Oracle tables such as USER$, TAB$, and IND$. If you have access to the SYS schema, you can view underlying tables directly via SQL. For most situations, you only need to access the static views that are based on the underlying internal tables.

The data-dictionary tables (like USER$, TAB$, and IND$) are created during the execution of the CREATE DATABASE command. As part of creating a database, the sql.bsq file is executed, which builds these internal data-dictionary tables. The sql.bsq file is usually located in the ORACLE_HOME/rdbms/admin directory; you can view it via an operating system editing utility (such as vi in Unix or Notepad in Windows).

The static views are created when you run the catalog.sql script (usually, you run this script after the CREATE DATABASE operation succeeds). The catalog.sql script is located in the ORACLE_HOME/rdbms/admin directory. Figure 10–1 shows the process of creating the static data-dictionary views.

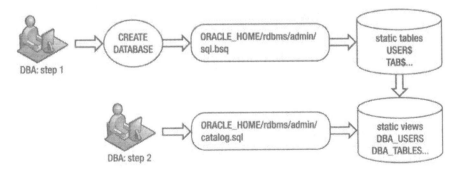

Figure 10–1. *Creating the static data-dictionary views*

Static views such as DBA_USERS, DBA_TABLES, and DBA_INDEXES are built on the static tables (such as USER$, TAB$ and IND$). You can view the creation scripts of these static views by querying the TEXT column of DBA_VIEWS. For example, this query selects the TEXT column of DBA_VIEWS:

```
SQL> set long 5000
SQL> select text from dba_views where view_name='DBA_VIEWS';
```

Here's the output:

```
select u.name, o.name, v.textlength, v.text, t.typetextlength, t.typetext,
       t.oidtextlength, t.oidtext, t.typeowner, t.typename,
       decode(bitand(v.property, 134217728), 134217728,
              (select sv.name from superobj$ h, "_CURRENT_EDITION_OBJ" sv
              where h.subobj# = o.obj# and h.superobj# = sv.obj#), null),
       decode(bitand(v.property, 32), 32, 'Y', 'N'),
       decode(bitand(v.property, 16384), 16384, 'Y', 'N')
from sys."_CURRENT_EDITION_OBJ" o, sys.view$ v, sys.user$ u, sys.typed_view$ t
where o.obj# = v.obj#
  and o.obj# = t.obj#(+)
  and o.owner# = u.user#
```

▨ **Note** If you manually create a database (not using the database-creation assistant), you must be connected as the SYS schema when you run the catalog.sql and catproc.sql scripts. The SYS schema is the owner of all objects in the data dictionary.

Dynamic Performance Views

The dynamic performance data-dictionary views are often referred to as the V$ and GV$ views. These views are constantly updated by Oracle and reflect the current condition of the instance and database. Dynamic views are critical for diagnosing real-time performance issues.

The V$ and GV$ views are indirectly based on the underlying X$ tables, which are internal memory structures that are instantiated when you start your Oracle instance. Some of the V$ views are available the moment the Oracle instance is started. For example, V$PARAMETER contains meaningful data after the STARTUP NOMOUNT command has been issued, and doesn't require the database to be mounted or open. Other dynamic views depend on information in the control file and therefore contain meaningful information only after the database has been mounted (like V$CONTROLFILE). Some V$ views provide kernel-processing information (like V$BH) and thus have useful results only after the database has been opened.

At the top layer, the V$ views are actually synonyms that point to underlying SYS.V_$ views. At the next layer down, the SYS.V_$ objects are views created on top of another layer of SYS.V$ views. The SYS.V$ views in turn are based on the SYS.GV$ views. At the bottom layer, the SYS.GV$ views are based on the X$ memory structures.

The top-level V$ synonyms and SYS.V_$ views are created when you run the catalog.sql script, which you usually run after the database is initially created. Figure 10–2 shows the process for creating the V$ dynamic performance views.

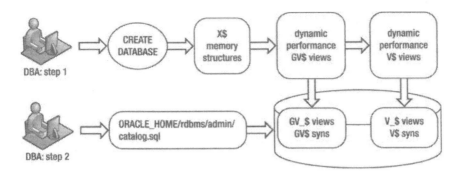

Figure 10–2. Creating the dynamic V$ performance data-dictionary views

Accessing the V$ views through the top-most synonyms is usually adequate for dynamic-performance information needs. On rare occasions, you'll want to query internal information that may not be available through the V$ views. In these situations, it's critical to understand the X$ underpinnings.

If you work with Oracle Real Application Clusters, you should be familiar with the GV$ global views. These views provide global dynamic-performance information regarding all instances in a cluster (whereas the V$ views are instance-specific). The GV$ views contain an INST_ID column for identifying specific instances in a clustered environment.

You can display the V$ and GV$ view definitions by querying the VIEW_DEFINITION column of the V$FIXED_VIEW_DEFINITION view. For example, this query displays the definition of the V$CONTROL_FILE:

```
select
view_definition
from v$fixed_view_definition
where view_name='V$CONTROLFILE';
```

Here's the output:

```
VIEW_DEFINITION
--------------------------------------------------------------------------------
select  STATUS , NAME, IS_RECOVERY_DEST_FILE, BLOCK_SIZE, FILE_SIZE_BLKS  from G
V$CONTROLFILE where inst_id = USERENV('Instance')
```

Derivable Documentation

Sometimes if you're troubleshooting an issue and are under pressure, you need to quickly extract information from the data dictionary to help resolve the problem. However, you may not know the exact name of a data-dictionary view or its associated columns. If you're like me, it's impossible to keep all the data-dictionary view names and column names in your head. Additionally, I work with databases from versions 8 through 11g, and it's difficult to keep track of which particular view may be available with a given release of Oracle.

Sometimes books and posters provide this information; but if you can't find exactly what you're looking for, you can use the documentation contained in the data dictionary itself. You can query from three views in particular:

- DBA_OBJECTS
- DICTIONARY
- DICT_COLUMNS

If you know roughly the name of the view from which you want to select information, you can first query from DBA_OBJECTS. For example, if you're troubleshooting an issue regarding materialized views, and you can't remember the exact names of the data-dictionary views associated with materialized views, you can do this:

```
select
 object_name
from dba_objects
where object_name like '%MV%'
and owner='SYS';
```

Sometimes that's enough to get you in the ballpark. But often you need more information about each view. This is where the DICTIONARY and DICT_COLUMNS views can be invaluable. The DICTIONARY view stores the name of the data-dictionary views. It has two columns:

```
SQL> desc dictionary
```

Name	Null?	Type
TABLE_NAME		VARCHAR2(30)
COMMENTS		VARCHAR2(4000)

For example, say you're troubleshooting an issue with materialized views, and you want to determine the name of data-dictionary views related to the materialized-view feature. You can run a query such as this:

```
select
 table_name
,comments
from dictionary where table_name like '%MV%';
```

Here's a short snippet of the output:

```
TABLE_NAME               COMMENTS
------------------------ ----------------------------------------------------------
DBA_MVIEW_LOGS           All materialized view logs in the database
DBA_MVIEWS               All materialized views in the database
DBA_MVIEW_ANALYSIS       Description of the materialized views accessible to dba
DBA_MVIEW_COMMENTS       Comments on all materialized views in the database
```

In this manner, you can quickly determine which view you need to access. If you want further information about the view, you can describe it. For example:

```
SQL> desc dba_mviews
```

If that doesn't provide you with enough information regarding the column names, you can query the DICT_COLUMNS view. This view provides comments about the columns of a data-dictionary view. For example:

```
select
 column_name
,comments
from dict_columns
where table_name='DBA_MVIEWS';
```

Here's a fraction of the output:

```
COLUMN_NAME              COMMENTS
```

```
-------------------------  ----------------------------------------------
OWNER                      Owner of the materialized view
MVIEW_NAME                 Name of the materialized view
CONTAINER_NAME             Name of the materialized view container table
QUERY                      The defining query that the materialized view instantiates
```

This way, you can generate and view documentation regarding most data-dictionary objects. This technique allows you to quickly identify appropriate views and which columns may help you in a troubleshooting situation.

Logical and Physical Database Structures

When a database is created, it contains multiple logical space containers called *tablespaces*. Each tablespace consists of one or more physical datafiles. Each datafile consists of many operating-system blocks. Each database contains many users. Each user has a schema that is the logical container for objects such as tables and indexes. Each table or index consists of a segment. If a table or index is partitioned, there are many partition segments for each partitioned table or partitioned index.

Each segment contains one or more extents. As a segment needs space, it allocates additional extents. An extent consists of a set of database blocks. A typical database block size for an online transaction processing (OLTP) database is 8KB. Each database block contains one or more operating-system blocks. Figure 10–3 describes the relationships between logical and physical structures in an Oracle database.

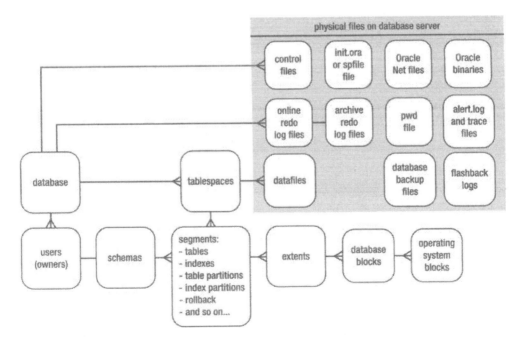

Figure 10–3. Oracle database logical and physical structure relationships

Table 10–1 describes some of the views used to report on database physical-space management. This isn't an exhaustive list; rather, this table contains the most commonly used views for monitoring database space.

Table 10–1. Overview of Database Space-Management Views

Data-Dictionary View	Purpose
V$DATABASE	Information about the database in the control file
DBA/ALL/USER_USERS	User account information
DBA/USER_TABLESPACES	Tablespace descriptions
DBA_DATA_FILES	Database datafile descriptions
DBA/USER_FREE_SPACE	Free extents in tablespaces
V$DATAFILE	Datafile information from the control file
V$DATAFILE_HEADER	Datafile information derived from the datafile header
DBA/ALL/USER_TABLES	Table attribute descriptions
DBA/ALL/USER_INDEXES	Index attribute descriptions
DBA/USER_SEGMENTS	Storage data for segments
DBA/ALL/USER_PART_TABLES	Partitioned table data
DBA/ALL/USER_PART_INDEXES	Partitioned index data
DBA/ALL/USER_TAB_PARTITIONS	Storage information for partitioned tables
DBA/ALL/USER_IND_PARTITIONS	Storage information for partitioned indexes
DBA/USER_EXTENTS	Extent information of each segment
V$CONTROLFILE	Names and size of control files
V$LOG	Online redo-log file information in the control file
V$LOG_HISTORY	Online redo-log file history information in control file
V$ARCHIVED_LOG	Archive log-file information in the control file

This chapter doesn't contain an exhaustive set of SQL scripts for querying data-dictionary objects. Rather, it covers basic techniques for querying the data dictionary about topics covered up to this point in the book (for example, users, tables, indexes, and so on). You should be able to build on the concepts in this chapter to fulfill any requirement you have for viewing data-dictionary metadata.

Displaying User Information

You may find yourself in an environment that contains hundreds of databases located on dozens of different servers. In such a scenario, you want to ensure that you don't run the wrong commands in the incorrect database. When performing DBA tasks, it's prudent to verify that you're connected as the appropriate account and to the correct database.

Currently Connected User

You can run the following types of SQL commands to verify the currently connected user and database information:

```
SQL> show user;
SQL> select * from user_users;
SQL> select name from v$database;
SQL> select instance_name, host_name from v$instance;
```

As shown in Chapter 3, an efficient way of staying aware of your environment is to set your SQL*Plus prompt automatically via the login.sql script to display user and instance information. This example manually sets the SQL prompt:

```
SQL> set sqlprompt '&_USER.@&_CONNECT_IDENTIFIER.> '
```

Here's what the SQL prompt now looks like:

```
SYS@O11R2>
```

You can also use the SYS_CONTEXT built-in SQL function to display a wide variety of details about your currently connected session. The general syntax for this function is as follows:

```
SYS_CONTEXT('<namespace>','<parameter>',[length])
```

This example displays the user, authentication method, host, and instance:

```
select
 sys_context('USERENV','CURRENT_USER') usr
,sys_context('USERENV','AUTHENTICATION_METHOD') auth_mth
,sys_context('USERENV','HOST') host
,sys_context('USERENV','INSTANCE_NAME') inst
from dual;
```

USERENV is a built-in Oracle namespace. More than 50 parameters are available when you use the USERENV namespace with the SYS_CONTEXT function. Table 10–2 describes some of the more useful parameters. Refer to the Oracle SQL Reference guide for a complete list of parameters available.

Table 10–2. Useful USERENV Parameters Available with SYS_CONTEXT

Parameter Name	Description
AUTHENTICATED_IDENTITY	Identity used in authentication
AUTHENTICATION_METHOD	Method of authentication
CURRENT_USER	Username for the currently active session
DB_NAME	Name specified by the DB_NAME initialization parameter
DB_UNIQUE_NAME	Name specified by the DB_UNIQUE_NAME initialization parameter
HOST	Hostname for the machine where the client initiated the database connection
INSTANCE_NAME	Instance name
IP_ADDRESS	IP address of the machine where the client initiated the database connection
ISDBA	TRUE if the user authenticated with DBA privileges through the operating system or password file
NLS_DATE_FORMAT	Date format for the session
OS_USER	Operating-system user from the machine where the client initiated the database connection
SERVER_HOST	Hostname of the machine where the database instance is running
SERVICE_NAME	Service name for the connection
SID	Session identifier
TERMINAL	Operating-system identifier for the client terminal

Users Currently Logged In

When you're debugging performance or connectivity issues, it's useful to view which users are connected to the database and the number of connections per user. If you want to view dynamic information such as users currently logged on to your database, as a user assigned the SELECT_CATALOG_ROLE, execute the following query:

```
select
  count(*)
 ,username
from v$session
group by username;
```

In Oracle Database 11g, the V$SESSION view has nearly 100 columns. Other columns that are commonly queried are OSUSER, SQL_ID, PROCESS, MACHINE, PORT, TERMINAL, and PROGRAM. See the *Oracle Database Reference* guide (available on Oracle's OTN website) for a complete list of columns and their descriptions.

Currently Executing SQL

If you want to view SQL statements that currently connected users are running, issue this query:

```
select
 a.sid
,a.username
,b.sql_text
from v$session a
     ,v$sqltext_with_newlines b
where a.sql_id = b.sql_id
order by
 a.username
,a.sid
,b.piece;
```

If you're using an Oracle Database 9i or earlier, the previous query won't work because the SQL_ID column isn't available. Here's a query that works for older versions of Oracle:

```
select
 a.sid
,a.username
,b.sql_text
from v$session a
     ,v$sqltext_with_newlines b
where a.sql_address     = b.address
and   a.sql_hash_value = b.hash_value
order by
 a.username
,a.sid
,b.piece;
```

■ **Tip** V$SQLTEXT_WITH_NEWLINES is identical to V$SQLTEXT with the exception that V$SQLTEXT_WITH_NEWLINES doesn't replace tabs and newlines with spaces.

User Accounts in the Database

If you want to view information about all user accounts that have been created (and not dropped) in the database, use the DBA_USERS view. The following displays information such as when each account was created, default and temporary tablespaces, and status:

```
set lines 132
col username form a15
col default_tablespace form a18
col temporary_tablespace form a20
col account_status form a16
--
select
  username
 ,default_tablespace
 ,temporary_tablespace
 ,account_status
 ,created
 ,lock_date
from dba_users
order by 1;
```

This query is useful for troubleshooting user-account issues such as determining whether an account is locked. The previous query uses SQL*Plus formatting statements to make the output readable. If you're not using SQL*Plus, you need to remove the formatting commands (everything preceding the two dashes --).

ALL_USERS AND SECURITY

Any schema with the CREATE SESSION system privilege can select schema information from the ALL_USERS view. For example:

```
select
  username
 ,created
from all_users
order by username;
```

This ability to select from ALL_USERS can be a security concern because it allows any user with minimal privileges (like CREATE SESSION) to view all user accounts in the database. Viewing all user information allows a malicious person to start guessing passwords for existing users. If you're a DBA, be sure you change the default passwords to well-known accounts and encourage users to use passwords that aren't easily guessable.

Viewing Table Information

DBAs often query the data dictionary for information about tables. Questions often arise regarding what users have access to what tables. Or when you're investigating physical space and performance issues, you may want to show how much storage a table consumes and how many rows are in each table. These types of topics are discussed in the next several sections.

Viewing Accessible Tables

Sometimes, when you're troubleshooting table-accessibility issues, the first thing to check is which tables you have access to. You can query the USER_TABLES view to display tables owned by the currently connected user:

```
select
 a.table_name
,b.created
,b.last_ddl_time
,a.last_analyzed
from user_tables  a, user_objects b
where a.table_name = b.object_name;
```

To view all tables to which your currently connected user has access—for example, via GRANT statements issued by other owners—use the ALL_TABLES view:

```
select
 table_name
,tablespace_name
from all_tables;
```

Querying the USER_TABLES view is a quick way to determine which tables exist in your current account, whereas the ALL_TABLES view contains every table to which you have any type of DML (SELECT, INSERT, UPDATE, and/or DELETE) access. If you have access to the DBA_TABLES view, you can also query the tables a user has access to via the following query:

```
select
 table_name
from dba_tables
where owner = upper('&owner');
```

When you're troubleshooting, you can check columns like CREATED and LAST_DDL_TIME, which tell when the structure of a table was last modified. Use the following query to view this information:

```
select
 a.table_name
,b.created
,b.last_ddl_time
,a.last_analyzed
from dba_tables  a
    ,dba_objects b
where a.table_name = b.object_name
and   a.owner      = upper('&owner');
```

Displaying Object Disk-Space Usage

When you're diagnosing database space issues, it's handy to view how much space a user's tables and indexes are consuming. The next query is useful when you want to view the space consumption of objects for a user:

```
UNDEFINE owner
COL summer FORM 999,999.999
SET LINES 132 TRIMSPOOL ON PAGES 100
SPO space.txt
```

```
SELECT
 segment_name
,partition_name
,tablespace_name
,segment_type
,SUM(bytes)/1024/1024 summer
FROM dba_extents
WHERE owner = UPPER('&&owner')
GROUP BY segment_name,partition_name,tablespace_name,segment_type
ORDER BY segment_name,partition_name;
SPO OFF;
```

This script prompts you for an object owner. If the table has partitions, the space per partition is displayed. You need access to DBA-level views to run the script. You can modify the script to point at the ALL or USER-level views to report on objects for the currently connected user account. This query also uses SQL*Plus-specific commands, such as setting the line size and column formatting, which are necessary to make the output readable.

Displaying Table Row Counts

When you're investigating performance or space issues, it's useful to display each table's row count. Run the following SQL code as a DBA-privileged schema. Notice that this script contains SQL*Plus-specific commands such as UNDEFINE and SPOOL. The script prompts you each time for a username:

```
UNDEFINE user
SPOOL tabcount_&&user..sql
SET LINESIZE 132 PAGESIZE 0 TRIMSPO Off VERIFY OFF FEED OFF TERM OFF
SELECT
   'SELECT RPAD(' || '''' || table_name || '''' ||',30)'
   || ',' || ' COUNT(*) FROM &&user..' || table_name || ';'
FROM dba_tables
WHERE owner = UPPER('&&user')
ORDER BY 1;
SPO OFF;
SET TERM ON
@@tabcount_&&user..sql
SET VERIFY ON FEED ON
```

This code generates a file named tabcount_<user>.sql that contains the SQL statements that select row counts from all tables in the specified schema. If the username you provide to the script is INVUSER, then you can run the generated script as follows.

```
SQL> @tabcount_invuser.sql
```

Keep in mind that if the table row counts are high, then this script can take a long time to run (several minutes).

Developers and DBAs often use SQL to generate SQL statements. This is a useful technique when you need to apply the same SQL process (repetitively) to many different objects, such as all tables in a schema..If you don't have access to DBA-level views, you can query the USER_TABLES view. For example:

```
SPO tabcount.sql
SET LINESIZE 132 PAGESIZE 0 TRIMSPO OFF VERIFY OFF FEED OFF TERM OFF
SELECT
   'SELECT RPAD(' || '''' || table_name || '''' ||',30)'
   || ',' || ' COUNT(*) FROM ' || table_name || ';'
```

```
FROM user_tables
ORDER BY 1;
SPO OFF;
SET TERM ON
@@tabcount.sql
SET VERIFY ON FEED ON
```

If you have accurate statistics, you can query the NUM_ROWS column of the DBA/ALL/USER_TABLES view. This column normally has a close row count if statistics are generated on a regular basis. The following query selects NUM_ROWS from the USER_TABLES view:

```
select
 table_name
,num_rows
from user_tables;
```

MANUALLY GENERATING STATISTICS

If you want to generate statistics for a table, use the DBMS_STATS package. This example generates statistics for a user and a table:

```
SQL> exec dbms_stats.gather_table_stats(ownname=>'INV',-
          tabname=>'F_SALES',-
          cascade=>true,estimate_percent=>20,degree=>4);
```

You can generate statistics for all objects for a user with the following code:

```
SQL> exec dbms_stats.gather_schema_stats(ownname => 'INV',-
          estimate_percent => DBMS_STATS.AUTO_SAMPLE_SIZE,-
          degree => DBMS_STATS.AUTO_DEGREE,-
          cascade => true);
```

The prior code instructs Oracle to estimate the percentage of the table to be sampled with the ESTIMATE_PERCENT parameter using DBMS_STATS.AUTO_SAMPLE_SIZE. Oracle also chooses the appropriate degree of parallelism with the DEGREE parameter setting of DBMS_STATS.AUTO_DEGREE. The CASCADE parameter instructs Oracle to generate statistics for indexes.

If you have partitioned tables and want to show row counts by partition, use the next few lines of SQL and PL/SQL code:

```
UNDEFINE user
SET SERVEROUT ON SIZE 1000000 VERIFY OFF
SPO part_count_&&user..txt
DECLARE
  counter  NUMBER;
  sql_stmt VARCHAR2(1000);
  CURSOR c1 IS
  SELECT table_name, partition_name
  FROM dba_tab_partitions
  WHERE table_owner = UPPER('&&user');
BEGIN
  FOR r1 IN c1 LOOP
    sql_stmt := 'SELECT COUNT(*) FROM &&user..' || r1.table_name
```

```
        ||' PARTITION ( '||r1.partition_name ||' )';
    EXECUTE IMMEDIATE sql_stmt INTO counter;
    DBMS_OUTPUT.PUT_LINE(RPAD(r1.table_name
      ||'('||r1.partition_name||')',30) ||' '||TO_CHAR(counter));
  END LOOP;
END;
/
SPO OFF
```

Displaying Index Information

DBAs often view index metadata. Sometimes you need to verify that an environment has all the correct indexes, or you may need to investigate a performance problem. This section contains several queries that are typically used to retrieve index information from the data dictionary.

Displaying Indexes for a Table

When you're dealing with performance issues, one of the first items to check is which columns are indexed on a table. First, ensure that the object you're dealing with is a table (and not a synonym or a view). Run the following query to check whether an object is a table or not:

```
select
  object_name
 ,object_type
from user_objects
where object_name=upper('&object_name');
```

This query prompts you for a SQL*Plus ampersand variable (OBJECT_NAME). If you're not using SQL*Plus, you may have to modify the query to explicitly query for a particular object.

When you've verified that the object is a table, query the USER_INDEXES view to display indexes for a particular table in your user. The USER_INDEXES view contains the index name information, and the USER_IND_COLUMNS view contains the columns that are indexed. If the index is built on more than one column, the COLUMN_POSITION column provides the order in which the columns appear in the index. For example:

```
select
 a.index_name
,a.column_name
,b.status
,b.index_type
,a.column_position
from user_ind_columns a
    ,user_indexes     b
where a.table_name = upper('&table_name')
and   a.index_name = b.index_name
order by a.index_name, a.column_position;
```

This query prompts you for a SQL*Plus ampersand variable (TABLE_NAME). If you're not using SQL*Plus, you may have to modify the query and name the table of interest. The indexes and the corresponding columns are displayed for the table you enter.

If you use function-based indexes, sometimes it's handy to display the expression used to create those indexes. The function expression is contained in the COLUMN_EXPRESSION column of the

DBA/ALL/USER_IND_EXPRESSIONS view. The following script displays that expression, along with the index and table names:

```
select
 table_name
,index_name
,column_expression
from user_ind_expressions
order by table_name;
```

Showing Foreign-Key Columns Not Indexed

After you've built an application, you should verify that all the foreign-key columns are indexed. The following query indicates for a schema which table columns have foreign-key constraints defined for them but don't have a corresponding index:

```
select
  a.constraint_name cons_name
 ,a.table_name   tab_name
 ,b.column_name cons_column
 ,nvl(c.column_name,'***No Index***') ind_column
from user_constraints   a
     join
     user_cons_columns b on a.constraint_name = b.constraint_name
     left outer join
     user_ind_columns  c on b.column_name = c.column_name
                        and b.table_name  = c.table_name
where constraint_type = 'R'
order by 2,1;
```

For older DBAs who aren't familiar with the ANSI SQL standard, here's a similar query that uses the Oracle-specific (+) syntax to denote an outer join:

```
select
  a.constraint_name cons_name
 ,a.table_name   tab_name
 ,b.column_name cons_column
 ,nvl(c.column_name,'***No Index***') ind_column
from user_constraints   a
     ,user_cons_columns b
     ,user_ind_columns  c
where constraint_type = 'R'
and a.constraint_name = b.constraint_name
and b.column_name     = c.column_name(+)
and b.table_name      = c.table_name(+)
order by 2,1;
```

Any column that has a foreign-key constraint but no corresponding index is noted in the last column of the output with the text ***No Index***. Here's some sample output:

CONS_NAME	TAB_NAME	CONS_COLUMN	IND_COLUMN
FK_DEPOSITS	DEPOSITS	BATCH_NO	***No Index***

The USER_CONSTRAINTS view contains definitions of all constraints in a user's schema. This is joined to USER_CONS_COLUMNS, which contains information about the columns accessible to the user that are used in constraints. You place a LEFT OUTER JOIN clause between USER_CONS_COLUMNS and USER_IND_COLUMNS because there may be a case where the view on the left side of the join has rows without corresponding rows on the right. You then apply the condition that any constraints reported by this query are of type R (a referential or foreign-key constraint).

Displaying Constraint Information

Constraints play a critical role in ensuring that data conforms to well-defined business rules. You need to be well versed with techniques for displaying the various types of constraints that can exist in a database. The following sections detail some techniques on how to query the data dictionary for constraint information.

Displaying Table Constraints

You occasionally need to view constraint information. For example, a user or developer may report that a constraint violation occurs when they try to insert or update data in a table (and they want you to figure out what's wrong with the database). You can query the DBA_CONSTRAINTS view to display constraint information for an owner and table name. The following script prompts you for two SQL*Plus ampersand variables (OWNER and TABLE_NAME); if you aren't using SQL*Plus, then you may need to modify the script with the appropriate values before you run the script:

```
select
  table_name
 ,(case constraint_type
    when 'P' then 'Primary Key'
    when 'R' then 'Foreign Key'
    when 'C' then 'Check'
    when 'U' then 'Unique'
    when 'O' then 'Read Only View'
    when 'V' then 'Check view'
    when 'H' then 'Hash expression'
    when 'F' then 'REF column'
    when 'S' then 'Supplemental logging'
  end) cons_type
 ,constraint_name cons_name
 ,search_condition check_cons
 ,status
from dba_constraints
where owner      like upper('&owner')
and    table_name like upper('&table_name')
order by cons_type;
```

The DBA/ALL/USER_CONSTRAINTS views document the constraints defined for tables in your database. Integrity constraints allow you to define rules about your data that are verified by the database engine before the data can be successfully added or modified. This ensures that your data has a high degree of quality.

The CONSTRAINT_TYPE column of the DBA/ALL/USER_CONSTRAINTS views is a one-character code. Currently, there are nine different types of constraints. Table 10–3 describes the integrity constraints available.

Table 10–3. Integrity Constraint Descriptions

Constraint Code	Meaning
C	Checks for a condition
P	Primary key
U	Unique key
R	Referential integrity (foreign key)
V	With check option on a view
O	With read-only on a view
H	Hash expression
F	Constraint with a REF column
S	Supplemental logging

■ **Note** The check-constraint types H, F, and S are available only in Oracle Database 11*g* or higher.

Showing Primary-Key and Foreign-Key Relationships

Sometimes, when you're diagnosing constraint issues, it's useful to show what primary-key constraint is associated with a foreign-key constraint. For example, perhaps you're attempting to insert into a child table and an error is thrown indicating that the parent key doesn't exist, and you want to display more information about the parent key constraint.

The following script queries the DBA_CONSTRAINTS view to determine the parent primary-key constraints that are related to child foreign-key constraints. You need to provide as input to the script the owner of the table and the child table for which you wish to display primary-key constraints:

```
select
 a.constraint_type cons_type
,a.table_name      child_table
,a.constraint_name child_cons
,b.table_name      parent_table
,b.constraint_name parent_cons
,b.constraint_type cons_type
from dba_constraints a
    ,dba_constraints b
where a.owner      = upper('&owner')
and a.table_name = upper('&table_name')
and a.constraint_type = 'R'
```

```
and a.r_owner = b.owner
and a.r_constraint_name = b.constraint_name;
```

The preceding script prompts you for two SQL*Plus ampersand variables (OWNER and TABLE_NAME); if you aren't using SQL*Plus, then you may need to modify the script with the appropriate values before you run the script.

The following output shows that there are two foreign-key constraints. It also shows the parent table primary-key constraints:

```
C CHILD_TABLE       CHILD_CONS            PARENT_TABLE     PARENT_CONS          C
- ---------------   --------------------  ---------------  --------------------  -
R REG_COMPANIES     REG_COMPANIES_FK2     D_COMPANIES      D_COMPANIES_PK       P
R REG_COMPANIES     REG_COMPANIES_FK1     CLUSTER_BUCKETS  CLUSTER_BUCKETS_PK   P
```

When the CONSTRAINT_TYPE column (of DBA/ALL/USER_CONSTRAINTS) contains an R value, this indicates that the row describes a referential-integrity constraint, which means the child-table constraint references a primary-key constraint. You use the technique of joining to the same table twice to retrieve the primary-key constraint information. The child-constraint columns (R_OWNER and R_CONSTRAINT_NAME) match with another row in the DBA_CONSTRAINTS view that contains the primary-key information.

You can also do the reverse of the prior query in this section; for a primary-key constraint, you want to find the foreign-key columns (if any) that correlate to it. The next script takes the primary-key record and looks to see if it has any child records that have a constraint type of R. When you run this script, you're prompted for the primary-key table owner and name:

```
select
   b.table_name          primary_key_table
  ,a.table_name          fk_child_table
  ,a.constraint_name     fk_child_table_constraint
from dba_constraints a
    ,dba_constraints b
where a.r_constraint_name = b.constraint_name
and    a.r_owner          = b.owner
and    a.constraint_type  = 'R'
and    b.owner            = upper('&table_owner')
and    b.table_name       = upper('&table_name');
```

Here's some sample output:

```
PRIMARY_KEY_TABLE     FK_CHILD_TABLE        FK_CHILD_TABLE_CONSTRAINT
-----------------     --------------------  ------------------------------
CLUSTER_BUCKETS       CB_AD_ASSOC           CB_AD_ASSOC_FK1
CLUSTER_BUCKETS       CLUSTER_CONTACTS      CLUSTER_CONTACTS_FK1
CLUSTER_BUCKETS       CLUSTER_NOTES         CLUSTER_NOTES_FK1
CLUSTER_BUCKETS       DOMAIN_NAMES          DOMAIN_NAMES_FK1
CLUSTER_BUCKETS       REG_COMPANIES         REG_COMPANIES_FK1
CLUSTER_BUCKETS       CB_MS_ASSOC           CB_MS_ASSOC_FK2
```

The output indicates that the CLUSTER_BUCKETS table has several foreign-key constraints that refer to it.

Viewing Basic Security Information

Basic database security is often administered through roles, object grants, and system-privilege grants. When there are data-accessibility issues, you must be proficient in retrieving information about these fundamental security constructs. The next few sections describe some techniques and queries for viewing role and grant assignments.

Displaying Granted Roles

You may find yourself investigating table-access issues and want to display the roles that a user has been granted. Use this query to view which roles are granted to the currently connected user:

```
select
 username
,granted_role
from user_role_privs;
```

The next query displays the roles that have been granted to a specific user (you're prompted for GRANTEE):

```
select
  grantee
 ,granted_role
from dba_role_privs
where grantee = upper('&grantee')
order by grantee;
```

The USER_ROLE_PRIVS and DBA_ROLE_PRIVS views describe roles granted to users. To display roles granted to roles, query the ROLE_ROLE_PRIVS view:

```
select
 role
,granted_role
from role_role_privs;
```

When you create a database, several predefined roles are created for you, including DBA and SELECT_CATALOG_ROLE. To view all the roles in your database (both predefined and user-created), select the ROLE column from DBA_ROLES:

```
select
 role
from dba_roles;
```

Here's some sample output of role names in a typical database:

```
CONNECT
RESOURCE
DBA
SELECT_CATALOG_ROLE
EXECUTE_CATALOG_ROLE
DELETE_CATALOG_ROLE
EXP_FULL_DATABASE
IMP_FULL_DATABASE
```

Displaying System Privileges

Database system privileges allow you to perform tasks such as connecting to the database and creating and modifying objects. For example, some commonly granted privileges are CREATE TABLE and CREATE VIEW. Query the DBA_SYS_PRIVS view to display which system privileges have been granted to users. Listed next is a simple script that prompts for the GRANTEE:

```
select
  grantee
 ,privilege
 ,admin_option
from dba_sys_privs
where grantee = UPPER('&grantee')
order by privilege;
```

To view system privileges granted to the currently connected user, run this query:

```
select
 username
,privilege
,admin_option
from user_sys_privs;
```

The USERNAME column shows whether the privilege has been granted to the currently connected user or if the privilege has been granted to PUBLIC.

The ROLE_SYS_PRIVS view displays what system privileges have been assigned to a role. When querying this view, you see only roles that have been granted to the currently connected schema. Here's an example query that lists privileges granted to a specified role:

```
select
 role
,privilege
from role_sys_privs
where role = upper('&role');
```

The prior SQL displays only database system privileges that have been directly granted to a user. To view any system privileges that have been granted through a role to a user, you have to also query a view such as ROLE_SYS_PRIVS. The following query displays system privileges granted either directly to the currently connected user or through any roles granted to the user:

```
select
 privilege
,'DIRECT GRANT'
from user_sys_privs
union
select
privilege
,'ROLE GRANT'
from role_sys_privs;
```

Two roles—CONNECT and RESOURCE—are commonly assigned to newly created accounts. However, Oracle recommends that you not assign these roles to users because they may not be available in future releases. Instead, Oracle advises that you create your own roles and assign privileges as required. Run the following query to view privileges assigned to these roles:

```
select
 grantee
```

```
,privilege
from dba_sys_privs
where grantee IN ('CONNECT','RESOURCE')
order by grantee;
```

Here's the output:

```
ROLE                      PRIVILEGE
------------------------  ------------------------
CONNECT                   CREATE SESSION
RESOURCE                  CREATE CLUSTER
RESOURCE                  CREATE INDEXTYPE
RESOURCE                  CREATE OPERATOR
RESOURCE                  CREATE PROCEDURE
RESOURCE                  CREATE SEQUENCE
RESOURCE                  CREATE TABLE
RESOURCE                  CREATE TRIGGER
RESOURCE                  CREATE TYPE
```

You can use a vast array of data-dictionary views to determine what users and roles have been assigned which system and object privileges. This section has touched on only a few examples. See Table 10–4 for a description of the various privilege-related data-dictionary views and their purposes.

Table 10–4. Privilege-Related Data-Dictionary Views

View	Description
DBA_ROLES	All roles in the database
DBA_ROLE_PRIVS	Roles granted to users and roles
DBA_SYS_PRIVS	All system privileges granted to users and roles
DBA_TAB_PRIVS	All object privileges granted to users and roles
DBA_COL_PRIVS	All column object grants
ROLE_ROLE_PRIVS	Roles granted to other roles; only for roles to which the user has access
ROLE_SYS_PRIVS	Privileges granted to other roles; only for roles to which the user has access
ROLE_TAB_PRIVS	Table privileges granted to roles; only for roles to which the user has access
ALL_TAB_PRIVS	Object grants for which the user is the object owner, grantor, or grantee; also object grants for which PUBLIC is the grantee
ALL_TAB_PRIVS_MADE	Object grants where the user is the object owner or grantor
ALL_TAB_PRIVS_RECD	Object grants where the user is the grantee or where PUBLIC is the grantee
ALL_COL_PRIVS	Column object grants where the user is the object owner, grantor, or grantee; also column grants where PUBLIC is the grantee
ALL_COL_PRIVS_MADE	Column object grants where the user is the object owner or grantor
ALL_COL_PRIVS_RECD	Column object grants where the user is the grantee or PUBLIC is the grantee

View	Description
USER_ROLE_PRIVS	Roles granted to the user
USER_SYS_PRIVS	System privileges granted to the user
USER_TAB_PRIVS	Object grants for which the user is the object owner, grantor, or grantee
USER_TAB_PRIVS_MADE	Object grants where the user is the object owner
USER_TAB_PRIVS_RECD	Object grants where the user is the grantee
USER_COL_PRIVS	Column object grants where the user is the object owner, grantor, or grantee
USER_COL_PRIVS_MADE	Column object grants where user is the object owner
USER_COL_PRIVS_RECD	Column object grants where the user is the grantee

Displaying Object Privileges

Object *privileges* are grants that allow you to perform DML operations (INSERT, UPDATE, and DELETE) on another user's tables. Before you can perform DML operations on another user's objects, you must be granted the appropriate privileges. Object privileges are managed through the GRANT and REVOKE statements.

Sometimes, when you're troubleshooting table-access issues, you need to view what DML privileges have been granted. The following query selects from the USER_TAB_PRIVS_RECD view to display the table privileges that have been granted to the currently connected user:

```
select
  owner
 ,table_name
 ,grantor
 ,privilege
from user_tab_privs_recd;
```

To view privileges that the current user has granted to other users, select from the USER_TAB_PRIVS_MADE view:

```
select
  grantee
 ,table_name
 ,grantor
 ,privilege
from user_tab_privs_made;
```

Run the following query to view table privileges that have been granted to your current user:

```
select grantee, table_name, privilege
from user_tab_privs
where grantee = sys_context('USERENV','CURRENT_USER')
order by table_name, privilege;
```

In the previous lines of code, the SYS_CONTEXT function is used to extract the current username from the session. Without qualifying the GRANTEE with your current username, the query also displays object privileges you've granted and privileges that have been granted by other users to your objects. The query can alternatively prompt you for your current username. For example:

```
select grantee, table_name, privilege
from user_tab_privs
where grantee = UPPER('&your_user_name')
order by table_name, privilege;
```

This next query selects from USER_TAB_PRIVS and ROLE_TAB_PRIVS to check for any object privileges that have been granted directly to the user or granted through a role that has been granted to the user:

```
select
  grantee
 ,owner
 ,table_name
 ,grantor
 ,privilege
from user_tab_privs
union
select
  role
 ,owner
 ,table_name
 ,'ROLE'
 ,privilege
from role_tab_privs
order by 2, 3;
```

The ROLE_TAB_PRIVS view shows table privileges that have been granted to a role to which the current user has access.

Displaying Object Dependencies

Say you need to drop a table, but before you drop it you want to display any objects that are dependent on the table. For example, you may have a table that has synonyms, views, materialized views, functions, procedures, and triggers that rely on it. Before making the changes you want to review what other objects are dependent on the object you're modifying. You can use the DBA_DEPENDENCIES view to display object dependencies. The following query prompts you for a username and an object name:

```
select '+' || lpad(' ',level+2) || type || ' ' || owner || '.' || name  dep_tree
from dba_dependencies
connect by prior owner = referenced_owner and prior name = referenced_name
and prior type = referenced_type
start with referenced_owner = upper('&object_owner')
and referenced_name = upper('&object_name')
and owner is not null;
```

In the output, each object listed has a dependency on the object you entered. Lines are indented to show the dependency of an object on the object in the preceding line:

```
DEP_TREE
---------------------------------------------------------------
+    TRIGGER STAR2.D_COMPANIES_BU_TR1
+    MATERIALIZED VIEW CIA.CB_RAD_COUNTS
+    SYNONYM STAR1.D_COMPANIES
+     SYNONYM CIA.D_COMPANIES
+      MATERIALIZED VIEW CIA.CB_RAD_COUNTS
```

In this example, the object being analyzed is a table named D_COMPANIES. Several synonyms, materialized views, and one trigger are dependent on this table. For example, the materialized view CB_RAD_COUNTS owned by CIA is dependent on the synonym D_COMPANIES owned by CIA, which in turn is dependent on the D_COMPANIES synonym owned by STAR1.

The DBA_DEPENDENCIES view contains a hierarchical relationship between the OWNER, NAME, and TYPE columns and their referenced column names of REFERENCED_OWNER, REFERENCED_NAME, and REFERENCED_TYPE. Oracle provides a number of constructs to perform hierarchical queries. For example, START WITH and CONNECT BY allow you to identify a starting point in a tree and walk either up or down the hierarchical relationship.

The previous SQL query in this section operates on only one object. If you want to inspect every object in a schema, you can use SQL to generate SQL to create scripts that display all dependencies for a schema's objects. The next section of code does that. For formatting and output, it uses some constructs specific to SQL*Plus, such as setting the page sizes and line size and spooling the output:

```
UNDEFINE owner
SET LINESIZE 132 PAGESIZE 0 VERIFY OFF FEEDBACK OFF TIMING OFF
SPO dep_dyn_&&owner..sql
SELECT 'SPO dep_dyn_&&owner..txt' FROM DUAL;
--
SELECT
'PROMPT ' || '_____'|| CHR(10) ||
'PROMPT ' || object_type || ': ' || object_name || CHR(10) ||
'SELECT ' || '''' '|| '+' || '''' || ' ' || '' || '' || LPAD('' || '''' || ' '
|| '''' || ',level+3)' || CHR(10) || ' ' || type || ' ' || '''' || ' ' || '''' ||
' ' || owner || ' ' || '''' || '.' || '''' || ' ' || name' || CHR(10) ||
' FROM dba_dependencies ' || CHR(10) ||
' CONNECT BY PRIOR owner = referenced_owner AND prior name = referenced_name '
|| CHR(10) ||
' AND prior type = referenced_type ' || CHR(10) ||
' START WITH referenced_owner = ' || '''' || UPPER('&&owner') || '''' || CHR(10) ||
' AND referenced_name = ' || '''' || object_name || '''' || CHR(10) ||
' AND owner IS NOT NULL;'
FROM dba_objects
WHERE owner = UPPER('&&owner')
AND object_type NOT IN ('INDEX','INDEX PARTITION','TABLE PARTITION');
--
SELECT 'SPO OFF' FROM dual;
SPO OFF
SET VERIFY ON LINESIZE 80 FEEDBACK ON
```

You should now have a script named dep_dyn_<owner>.sql created in the same directory from which you ran the script. This script contains all the SQL required to display dependencies on objects in the owner you entered. Run the script to display object dependencies. In this example, the owner is CIA:

```
SQL> @dep_dyn_cia.sql
```

When the script runs, it spools a file with the format dep_dyn_<owner>.txt. You can open that text file with an operating-system editor to view its contents. Here's a sample of the output from this example:

```
TABLE: DOMAIN_NAMES
+    FUNCTION STAR2.GET_DERIVED_COMPANY
+    TRIGGER STAR2.DOMAIN_NAMES_BU_TR1
+    SYNONYM CIA_APP.DOMAIN_NAMES
```

This output shows that the table DOMAIN_NAMES has three objects that are dependent on it: a function, a trigger, and a synonym.

UTLDTREE

Oracle provides a script that builds objects that you can use to display a dependency tree. To install UTLDTREE, run this script in the schema in which you want to analyze dependencies:

```
SQL> @?/rdbms/admin/utldtree
```

Now, you can build a dependency tree by executing the DEPTREE_FILL procedure. This procedure accepts three arguments, object type, owner, and object name:

```
SQL> exec deptree_fill('table','inv_mgmt','inv');
```

To display the dependency tree, issue this SQL statement:

```
SQL> select * from ideptree;
```

Be aware that when you run the UTLDTREE script, it drops and creates objects in the currently connected user account. Therefore, you should use this utility only in a test or development environment.

Displaying Differences in Schemas

Say you have a test database and a production database, and you want to determine whether there are any object differences between the test database schema and the production database schema. You don't have access to an expensive graphical tool that can show differences between schemas. What SQL techniques can you use to show the object differences between two schemas?

A basic technique for showing the differences between two schemas is as follows:

1. If the schemas are in two different databases, create database links to point at the two different environments.

2. Use the MINUS set operator to query the data dictionary views to display differences.

Here's an example that demonstrates how to display schema differences. In this example, you're connected to a central database that has Oracle Net access to two remote databases. You want to view the differences in schemas in the two remote databases. First, you create database links that point to the two different environments. This example uses SQL*Plus variables to define the two different schemas and passwords used to create the database links:

```
define user1=ccim_dev
define user1_pwd=ccim_pwd
define user2=ccim_prod
define user2_pwd=abc123
define conn1=@db1
define conn2=@db2
create database link db1 connect to &&user1 identified by &&user1_pwd
using 'sb-db5:1521/sb6';
create database link db2 connect to &&user2 identified by &&user2_pwd
using 'db-prod1:1521/scaprd';
```

The CREATE DATABASE LINK statements use the easy-connect naming method to determine the location of the remote database. The USING clause specifies the database-connection information using this syntax:

```
'<remote_server>:<port>/<service_name>'
```

After the database links are created, you run SQL statements that display metadata differences from the data-dictionary views. The next two statements use the MINUS set operator to determine whether there any differences between table names:

```
prompt ...Tables in db1 NOT IN db2
select table_name
from user_tables&&conn1
minus
select table_name
from user_tables&&conn2;

prompt ...Tables in db2 NOT IN db1
select table_name
from user_tables&&conn2
minus
select table_name
from user_tables&&conn1;
```

If you want to compare a local schema with a remote schema, then you need only one database link. In this situation, you must also define one of the connection variables to be blank:

```
define conn2=''
```

Now you can connect as a local user in your database and compare a remote schema to a local schema.

If you want to compare objects in two schemas in the same database, then you have to modify the scripts to include an OWNER and use the DBA or ALL data-dictionary view (instead of USER).

Listed next is a more complex example of comparing two schemas' objects. The following script compares several data-dictionary views for differences in metadata:

```
spo diff.txt

prompt Default or temp tablespace in db1 NOT IN db2
select default_tablespace, temporary_tablespace
from user_users&&conn1
minus
select default_tablespace, temporary_tablespace
from user_users&&conn2;
```

```
prompt Default or temp tablespace in db2 NOT IN db1
select default_tablespace, temporary_tablespace
from user_users&&conn2
minus
select default_tablespace, temporary_tablespace
from user_users&&conn1;

prompt Tablespace quotas in db1 NOT IN db2
select tablespace_name, max_bytes
from user_ts_quotas&&conn1
minus
select tablespace_name, max_bytes
from user_ts_quotas&&conn2;

prompt Tablespace quotas in db2 NOT IN db1
select tablespace_name, max_bytes
from user_ts_quotas&&conn2
minus
select tablespace_name, max_bytes
from user_ts_quotas&&conn1;

prompt Objects in db1 NOT IN db2
select object_name, object_type
from user_objects&&conn1
minus
select object_name, object_type
from user_objects&&conn2 order by 2;

prompt Objects in db2 NOT IN db1
select object_name, object_type
from user_objects&&conn2
minus
select object_name, object_type
from user_objects&&conn1 order by 2;

prompt Tables in db1 NOT IN db2
select table_name
from user_tables&&conn1
minus
select table_name
from user_tables&&conn2;

prompt Tables in db2 NOT IN db1
select table_name
from user_tables&&conn2
minus
select table_name
from user_tables&&conn1;

prompt Indexes in db2 NOT IN db1
select table_name, index_name, index_type, uniqueness
from user_indexes&&conn2
minus
select table_name, index_name, index_type, uniqueness
```

```
from user_indexes&&conn1 order by 1, 2;

prompt Table columns db1 NOT IN db2
select table_name, column_name
from user_tab_columns&&conn1
minus
select table_name, column_name
from user_tab_columns&&conn2 order by 1,2;

prompt Table columns in db2 NOT IN db1
select table_name, column_name
from user_tab_columns&&conn2
minus
select table_name, column_name
from user_tab_columns&&conn1 order by 1,2;

spo off;
```

This script is just a sample of what you can do with data-dictionary views to report on metadata differences between schemas. The script doesn't include every possible type of check. Rather, it includes enough to give you an example of how to find the most common types of differences that developers and DBAs look for. A full version of this script is available in the source code section of the Apress website (www.apress.com).

If you have access to a tool such as Enterprise Manager Change Management Pack, then you can use it to display differences between two schemas. A quick Google search shows dozens of tools available for comparing schemas. The purpose of the examples in this section isn't to compete with these tools, but to show that you can quickly create a set of SQL statements that display schema differences. You can easily augment and enhance these statements as required for your environment.

Summary

Sometimes you're handed an old database that has been running for years, and it's up to you to manage and maintain it. In some scenarios, you aren't given any documentation regarding the users and objects in the database. Even if you're provided with documentation, it may not be accurate or up to date. In this case, the data dictionary quickly becomes your source of documentation. You can use it to extract user information, the physical structure of the database, security information, objects and owners, currently connected users, and so forth.

Oracle provides static and dynamic views in the data dictionary. The static views contain information about the objects in the database. You can use these views to determine which tables are consuming the most space, contain the most rows, have the most extents allocated, and so on. The dynamic-performance views provide a real-time window into events currently transacting in the database. These views provide information about currently connected users, SQL executing, where resources are being consumed, and so on. DBAs use these views extensively to monitor and troubleshoot performance issues.

The book now turns its attention toward specialized Oracle features such as large objects, partitioning, Data Pump, and external tables. These topics are covered in the next several chapters.

■ ■ ■

Large Objects

Organizations often deal with substantial files that need to be stored and viewed by business users. *Large objects* (LOBs) generally refer to a data type that is suited for storing large and unstructured data such as text, log, image, video, sound, and spatial data. Oracle supports the following types of LOBs:

- LONG and LONG RAW
- Character large object (CLOB)
- National character large object (NCLOB)
- Binary large object (BLOB)
- Binary file (BFILE)

Prior to Oracle 8, the LONG and LONG RAW data types were your only options for storing large amounts of data in a column. You should no longer use these data types. The only reason I mention LONG and LONG RAW is because many legacy applications (Oracle's data dictionary, for example) still use them, and therefore you should be aware of their existence. You should otherwise use a CLOB or an NCLOB instead of LONG, and a BLOB instead of LONG RAW.

Describing Current LOB Types

Starting with Oracle version 8, the ability to store large files in the database vastly improved with the CLOB, NCLOB, BLOB, and BFILE data types. These additional LOB data types let you store much more data with greater functionality. Table 11–1 describes the types of Oracle LOBs available and their descriptions.

A CLOB is capable of storing large amounts of character data such as XML, text, or log files. An NCLOB is treated the same as a CLOB but can contain characters in the multibyte national character set for a database.

BLOBs store large amounts of binary data that typically isn't human readable. Typical uses for a BLOB are images, audio, and video data.

CLOBs, NCLOBs, and BLOBs are referred to as *internal LOBs*. This is because these data types are stored inside the Oracle database in datafiles. Internal LOBs participate in transactions and are covered by Oracle's database security, as well as its backup and recovery features.

BFILEs are referred to as *external LOBs*. BFILE columns store a pointer to a file on the operating system that is outside of the database. When it's not feasible to store a large binary file in the database, then use a BFILE.

Sometimes the question arises, "Should you use a BLOB or a BFILE?" BLOBs participate in database transactions and can be backed up, restored, and recovered by Oracle. BFILEs don't participate in database transactions, are read-only, and aren't covered by any Oracle security, backup and recovery, replication, or disaster-recovery mechanisms. BFILEs are more appropriate for large binary files that are read-only and don't change while an application is running. For example, you may have large binary video files that are referenced by a database application. In this scenario, the business determines that you don't need to create and maintain a 500TB database when all the application really needs is a pointer (stored in the database) to the locations of the large files on disk.

Table 11-1. Oracle Large Object Data Types

Data Type	Description	Maximum Size
LONG	Don't create tables with LONG data types This data type is supported for backward compatibility. Use a CLOB or an NCLOB instead.	2GB
LONG RAW	Don't create tables with LONG RAW columns. This data type is supported for backward compatibility. Use a BLOB instead.	2GB
CLOB	Character large object for storing character documents such as big text files, log files, XML files, and so on.	(4GB − 1)* blocksize
NCLOB	National character large object. Stores data in national character set format. Supports characters with varying width.	(4GB − 1) * blocksize
BLOB	Binary large object for storing unstructured bitstream data (images, video, and so on).	(4GB − 1) * blocksize
BFILE	Binary file large object stored on the filesystem outside of the database. BFILEs are read-only.	$2^{64} - 1$ bytes (operating system may impose a size limit that is less than this)

Illustrating LOB Locators, Indexes, and Chunks

Internal LOBs (CLOB, NCLOB, and BLOB) store data in pieces called *chunks*. A chunk is the smallest unit of allocation for a LOB and is made up of one or more database blocks. A LOB *locator* is stored in a row that contains a LOB column. The LOB locator points to a LOB *index*. The LOB index stores information regarding the LOB chunks. When a table is queried, the database uses the LOB locator and associated LOB index to locate the appropriate LOB chunks. Figure 11-1 shows the relationship between a table, a row, a LOB locator, and its associated index and chunks.

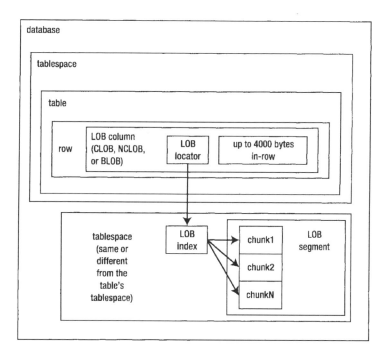

Figure 11–1. Relationship of table, row, LOB locator, LOB index, and LOB segment

The LOB locator for a BFILE stores the directory path and file name on the operating system. Figure 11–2 shows a BFILE LOB locator that references a file on the operating system.

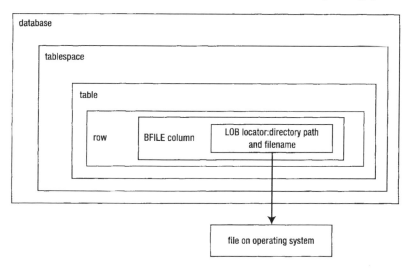

Figure 11–2. The BFILE LOB locator contains information to locate a file on the operating system.

> ■ **Note** The DBMS_LOB package performs operations on LOBs through the LOB locator.

Distinguishing Between BasicFiles and SecureFiles

Several significant improvements were made to LOBs in Oracle Database 11g. Oracle now distinguishes between two different types of underlying LOB architectures:

- BasicFile
- SecureFile

SecureFile is a new LOB architecture introduced in Oracle Database 11g. The SecureFile architecture has many new enhancements that improve the manageability and performance of LOBs. If you're using Oracle Database 11g or higher, then you should create your LOB columns with the SECUREFILE clause. Be aware that the SecureFile feature itself doesn't require an additional license. However, some of the SecureFile advanced features do require additional licenses (encryption, deduplication, and compression).

If you're not using Oracle Database 11g, then your only option is to use the BasicFile architecture. This is the default type of LOB created, and it's been available since Oracle version 8.

BasicFile

BasicFile is the name Oracle gives to the LOB architecture available prior to Oracle Database 11g. It's still important to understand the BasicFile LOBs because many shops use Oracle versions that don't support SecureFiles. You don't need to do anything special to enable the use of BasicFile LOBs; this is the default LOB architecture that is implemented when you create a table with LOB columns.

SecureFile

If you're using Oracle Database 11g or higher, then you have the option of using the SecureFile LOB architecture. It includes the following enhancements (over BasicFile LOBs):

- Encryption (requires Oracle Advanced Security Option)
- Compression (requires Oracle Advanced Compression Option)
- Deduplication (requires Oracle Advanced Compression Option)

SecureFile encryption lets you transparently encrypt LOB data (just like other data types). The compression feature allows for significant space savings. The deduplication feature eliminates duplicate LOBs that otherwise would be stored multiple times.

Prerequisites for SecureFiles

You need to do a small amount of planning before using SecureFiles. Specifically, use of SecureFiles requires the following:

- A SecureFile LOB must be stored in a tablespace using the automated segment space management feature (ASSM).

- The DB_SECUREFILE initialization setting must be either PERMITTED or ALWAYS.

A SecureFile LOB must be created within a tablespace using ASSM. To create an ASSM-enabled tablespace, specify the SEGMENT SPACE MANAGEMENT AUTO clause. For example:

```
create tablespace inv_mgmt_data
  datafile '/ora01/dbfile/O11R2/inv_mgmt_data01.dbf'
  size 1000m
  extent management local
  uniform size 1m
  segment space management auto;
```

If you have existing tablespaces, you can verify the use of ASSM by querying the DBA_TABLESPACES view. The SEGMENT_SPACE_MANAGEMENT column should have a value of AUTO for any tablespaces that you want to use with SecureFiles:

```
select
 tablespace_name
,segment_space_management
from dba_tablespaces;
```

Here's a snippet of the output indicating that the USER1 tablespace is using ASSM:

```
TABLESPACE_NAME                  SEGMEN
-----------------------------    ------
USER1                            AUTO
```

Also, SecureFiles require that the DB_SECUREFILE initialization setting is either PERMITTED or ALWAYS. The default value is PERMITTED. You can verify the value as follows:

```
SQL> show parameter db_securefile
NAME                                  TYPE         VALUE
------------------------------------  -----------  -----------------------------
db_securefile                         string       PERMITTED
```

You can use either ALTER SYSTEM or ALTER SESSION to modify the value of DB_SECUREFILE. Table 11–2 describes the valid values for DB_SECUREFILE.

Table 11–2. Description of DB_SECUREFILE Settings

DB_SECUREFILE **Setting**	**Description**
NEVER	The LOB is created as a BasicFile regardless of whether the SECUREFILE option is specified.
PERMITTED	SecureFile LOBs can be created.
ALWAYS	The LOB is created as a SecureFile type unless the underlying tablespace isn't using ASSM.
IGNORE	The SECUREFILE option is ignored, along with any SecureFile settings.

Creating a Table with a LOB Column

By default, when you create a LOB, it's a BasicFile LOB. The next subsection covers BasicFiles and is followed by a subsection on creating a SecureFile LOB. If you're using Oracle Database 11g and higher, I recommend that you always create a LOB as a SecureFile LOB. As discussed previously, SecureFiles allow you to use features such as compression and encryption.

Creating a BasicFile LOB Column

To create a LOB column, you have to specify a LOB data type. Listed next is a basic example of creating a table with a CLOB data type:

```
create table patchmain(
 patch_id number
,patch_desc clob);
```

When you create a table with a LOB column, you must be aware of some technical underpinnings. Review the following bulleted list and be sure you understand each point:

- LOBs by default are created as BasicFiles.

- Oracle creates a LOB segment and a LOB index for each LOB column.

- The LOB segment has a name of this format: SYS_LOB<string>.

- The LOB index has a name of this format: SYS_IL<string>.

- The <string> is the same for each LOB segment and its associated index.

- The LOB segment and index are created in the same tablespace as the table unless you specify a different tablespace.

- By default, nearly 4000 bytes of a LOB are stored in the table row (inline).

- With Oracle Database 11g release 2 and higher, a LOB segment and a LOB index aren't created until a record is inserted into the table (the so-called *deferred segment creation* feature). This means DBA/ALL/USER_SEGMENTS and DBA/ALL/USER_EXTENTS have no information in them until a row is inserted into the table.

Oracle creates a LOB segment and a LOB index for each LOB column. The LOB segment stores the data. The LOB index keeps track of where the chunks of LOB data are physically stored and in what order the LOB chunks should be accessed.

You can query the DBA/ALL/USER_LOBS view to display the LOB segment and LOB index names:

```
select
 table_name
,segment_name
,index_name
,securefile
,in_row
from user_lobs;
```

Here's the output for this example:

```
TABLE_NAME    SEGMENT_NAME                    INDEX_NAME                SECUREFILE  IN_ROW
-----------   -----------------------------   ----------------------    ----------  ------
PATCHMAIN     SYS_LOB0000024169C00002$$ SYS_IL0000024169C00002$$  NO          YES
```

You can also query DBA/USER/ALL_SEGMENTS to view information regarding LOB segments. As mentioned earlier, if you create a table in Oracle Database 11g release 2 and higher, an initial segment isn't created until you insert a row into the table (deferred segment creation). This can be confusing because you may expect a row to be present in DBA/ALL/USER_SEGMENTS immediately after you create the table:

```
select
 segment_name
,segment_type
,segment_subtype
,bytes/1024/1024 meg_bytes
from user_segments
where segment_name IN ('&&table_just_created',
                       '&&lob_segment_just_created',
                       '&&lob_index_just_created');
```

The prior query prompts for the segment names. The output shows no rows:

```
no rows selected
```

Next, insert a record into the table that contains the LOB column:

```
SQL> insert into patchmain values(1,'clob text');
```

Rerunning the query against USER_SEGMENTS shows that three segments have been created—one for the table, one for the LOB segment, and one for the LOB index:

```
SEGMENT_NAME                    SEGMENT_TYPE    SEGMENT_SU  MEG_BYTES
-----------------------------   ------------    ----------  ----------
PATCHMAIN                       TABLE           ASSM             .0625
SYS_IL0000024169C00002$$        LOBINDEX        ASSM             .0625
SYS_LOB0000024169C00002$$       LOBSEGMENT      ASSM             .0625
```

Creating a LOB in a Specific Tablespace

By default, the LOB segment is stored in the same tablespace as its table. You can specify a separate tablespace for a LOB segment by using the LOB...STORE AS clause of the CREATE TABLE statement. The next table-creation script creates the table in a tablespace, and creates separate tablespaces for the CLOB and BLOB columns:

```
create table patchmain
(patch_id   number
,patch_desc clob
,patch      blob
) tablespace users
 lob (patch_desc) store as (tablespace clob_data)
,lob (patch)      store as (tablespace blob_data);
```

You need to modify this query so that the tablespace names match your environment (or you can explicitly create CLOB_DATA and BLOB_DATA tablespaces). The following query verifies that three tablespaces are utilized for this table:

```
select table_name, tablespace_name, 'N/A' column_name
from user_tables
where table_name='PATCHMAIN'
union
select table_name, tablespace_name, column_name
from user_lobs
where table_name='PATCHMAIN';
```

Here's the output:

```
TABLE_NAME            TABLESPACE_NAME        COLUMN_NAME
--------------------  ---------------------  --------------------
PATCHMAIN             BLOB_DATA              PATCH
PATCHMAIN             CLOB_DATA              PATCH_DESC
PATCHMAIN             USERS                  N/A
```

I recommend that you always create a LOB with its storage specified in a separate tablespace from the table data. This is because LOBs have different growth patterns and require different storage characteristics (than the table data).

Creating a SecureFile LOB Column

If you don't specify the SECUREFILE clause when creating a table with a LOB column, then by default the LOB is created as a BasicFile LOB. This next example shows how to create a SecureFile LOB and place it in a tablespace separate from the table. As mentioned earlier, the tablespace that contains the Securefile LOB must be an ASSM-managed tablespace:

```
create table patchmain(
 patch_id    number
,patch_desc clob)
lob(patch_desc) store as securefile (tablespace lob_data);
```

■ **Tip** Oracle allows you to create a table with the STORE AS SECUREFILE clause in a non-ASSM tablespace. However, if you attempt to insert data into this table, the following error is displayed: "ORA-43853: SECUREFILE lobs can't be used in non-ASSM tablespace."

Before viewing the data dictionary, you can insert a record into the table to ensure that segment information is available (due to the deferred-segment-allocation feature in Oracle Database 11g release 2 and higher). For example:

```
SQL> insert into patchmain values(1,'clob text');
```

You can now verify a LOB's architecture by querying the USER_SEGMENTS view:

```
select
 segment_name
,segment_type
,segment_subtype
from user_segments;
```

Here's some sample output indicating that a LOB segment is a SecureFile:

```
SEGMENT_NAME              SEGMENT_TYPE          SEGMENT_SU
------------------------- --------------------- ----------
PATCHMAIN                 TABLE                 MSSM
SYS_IL0000023963C00002$$  LOBINDEX              ASSM
SYS_LOB0000023963C00002$$ LOBSEGMENT            SECUREFILE
```

You can also query the USER_LOBS view to verify the SecureFile LOB architecture:

```
select
 table_name
,segment_name
,index_name
,securefile
,in_row
from user_lobs;
```

Here's the output:

```
TABLE_NAME   SEGMENT_NAME                INDEX_NAME                 SEC IN_
------------ --------------------------- -------------------------- --- ---
PATCHMAIN    SYS_LOB0000023963C00002$$   SYS_IL0000023963C00002$$   YES YES
```

■ **Note** With SecureFiles, you no longer need to specify the following options: CHUNK, PCTVERSION, FREEPOOLS, FREELIST, and FREELIST GROUPS.

Creating a Partitioned LOB

You can create a partitioned table that has a LOB column. Doing so lets you spread a LOB across multiple tablespaces. Such partitioning helps with balancing I/O, maintenance, and backup and recovery operations.

You can partition LOBs by RANGE, LIST, or HASH. The next example creates a LIST-partitioned table in which LOB column data is stored in tablespaces separate from the table data:

```
CREATE TABLE patchmain(
 patch_id   NUMBER
,region     VARCHAR2(16)
,patch_desc CLOB)
LOB(patch_desc) STORE AS (TABLESPACE patch1)
PARTITION BY LIST (REGION) (
PARTITION p1 VALUES ('EAST')
LOB(patch_desc) STORE AS SECUREFILE
(TABLESPACE patch1 COMPRESS HIGH)
TABLESPACE inv_data1
,
PARTITION p2 VALUES ('WEST')
LOB(patch_desc) STORE AS SECUREFILE
(TABLESPACE patch2 DEDUPLICATE NOCOMPRESS)
TABLESPACE inv_data2
,
```

```
PARTITION p3 VALUES (DEFAULT)
LOB(patch_desc) STORE AS SECUREFILE
(TABLESPACE patch3 COMPRESS LOW)
TABLESPACE inv_data3
);
```

Notice that each LOB partition is created with its own storage options (the SecureFile features are covered a bit later in this chapter). You can view the details about the LOB partitions as shown:

```
select
 table_name
,column_name
,partition_name
,tablespace_name
,compression
,deduplication
from user_lob_partitions;
```

Here's some sample output:

```
TABLE_NAME    COLUMN_NAME    PARTITION_ TABLESPACE_NAME COMPRE DEDUPLICATION
------------  -------------- ---------- --------------- ------ -------------
PATCHMAIN     PATCH_DESC     P1         PATCH1          HIGH   NO
PATCHMAIN     PATCH_DESC     P2         PATCH2          NO     LOB
PATCHMAIN     PATCH_DESC     P3         PATCH3          LOW    NO
```

■ **Tip** You can also view DBA/ALL_USER_PART_LOBS for information about partitioned LOBs.

You can change the storage characteristics of a partitioned LOB column after it's been created. To do so, use the ALTER TABLE ... MODIFY PARTITION statement. This example alters a LOB partition to have a high degree of compression:

```
alter table patchmain modify partition p1
lob (patch_desc) (compress high);
```

The next example modifies a partitioned LOB so it doesn't keep duplicate values (via the DEDUPLICATE clause):

```
alter table patchmain modify partition p2
lob (patch_desc) (deduplicate lob);
```

■ **Note** Partitioning is an extra-cost option that is available only with the Oracle Enterprise Edition.

Maintaining LOB Columns

The following sections describe some common maintenance tasks that are performed on LOB columns or that involve LOB columns. You learn to move columns between tablespaces, to add new LOB columns to a table, and so forth.

Moving a LOB Column

As mentioned previously, if you create a table with a LOB column and don't specify a tablespace, then by default the LOB is created in the same tablespace as its table. This happens sometimes in environments where the DBAs don't plan ahead very well; only after the LOB column has consumed large amounts of disk space does the DBA wonder why the table has grown so big.

You can use the ALTER TABLE...MOVE...STORE AS statement to move a LOB column to a separate tablespace (from the table's tablespace). Here's the basic syntax:

```
alter table <table_name> move lob(<lob_name>) store as (tablespace <new_tablespace);
```

The next example moves the LOB column to the INV_CLOB tablespace:

```
alter table patchmain
move lob(patch_desc)
store as basicfile (tablespace inv_clob);
```

You can verify that the LOB was moved by querying USER_LOBS:

```
SQL> select table_name, column_name, tablespace_name from user_lobs;
```

If the LOB column is populated with large amounts of data, you almost always want to store the LOB in a tablespace separate from the rest of the table data. In these scenarios, the LOB data has different growth and storage requirements and is best maintained in its own tablespace.

Adding a LOB Column

If you have an existing table to which you want to add a LOB column, use the ALTER TABLE...ADD statement. The next statement adds the INV_IMAGE column to a table:

```
SQL> alter table inv add(inv_image blob);
```

This statement is fine for quickly adding a LOB column to a development environment. For anything else, you should specify the storage characteristics. For example, this specifies that a SecureFile LOB is created in the LOB_DATA tablespace:

```
alter table inv add(inv_image blob)
lob(inv_image) store as securefile(tablespace lob_data);
```

Removing a LOB Column

You may have a scenario where your business requirements change and you no longer need a column. Before you remove a column, consider renaming it so that you can better identify whether any applications or users are still accessing it:

```
SQL> alter table patchmain rename column patch_desc to patch_desc_old;
```

After you determine that nobody is using the column, use the ALTER TABLE...DROP statement to drop it:

```
SQL> alter table patchmain drop(patch_desc_old);
```

You can also remove a LOB column by dropping and re-creating a table (without the LOB column). This of course permanently removes any data as well.

Also keep in mind that in Oracle Database 10g or higher, if your recycle bin is enabled, then when you don't drop a table with the PURGE clause, space is still consumed by the dropped table. If you want to remove the space associated with the table, use the PURGE clause or purge the recycle bin after dropping the table.

Caching LOBs

By default, when reading and writing LOB columns, Oracle doesn't cache LOBs in memory. You can change the default behavior by setting the cache-related storage options. This example specifies that Oracle should cache a LOB column in memory:

```
create table patchmain(
 patch_id number
,patch_desc clob)
lob(patch_desc) store as (tablespace lob_data cache);
```

You can verify the LOB caching with this query:

```
SQL> select table_name, column_name, cache from user_lobs;
```

Here's some sample output:

```
TABLE_NAME           COLUMN_NAME           CACHE
-------------------- --------------------- ----------
PATCHMAIN            PATCH_DESC            YES
```

Table 11-3 describes the memory cache settings related to LOBs. If you have LOBs that are frequently read and written to, consider using the CACHE option. If your LOB column is read frequently but rarely written to, then the CACHE READS setting is more appropriate. If the LOB column is infrequently read or written to, then the NOCACHE setting is suitable.

Table 11-3. Cache Descriptions Regarding LOB Columns

Cache Setting	Meaning
CACHE	Oracle should place LOB data in the buffer cache for faster access.
CACHE READS	Oracle should place LOB data in the buffer cache for reads but not for writes.
NOCACHE	LOB data shouldn't be placed in the buffer cache. This is the default for both SecureFile and BasicFile LOBs.

Storing LOBs In and Out of Line

By default, up to approximately 4000 characters of a LOB column are stored in line with the table row. If the LOB is over 4000 characters, then Oracle automatically stores the LOB outside of the row data. The main advantage of storing a LOB in row is that small LOBs (less than 4000 characters) require less I/O, because Oracle doesn't have to search out of row for the LOB data.

However, storing LOB data in row isn't always desirable. The disadvantage of storing LOBs in row is that the table row sizes are potentially longer. This can impact the performance of full-table scans, range scans, and updates to columns other than the LOB column. In these situations, you may want to disable storage in the row. For example, you explicitly instruct Oracle to store the LOB outside of the row with the DISABLE STORAGE IN ROW clause:

```
create table patchmain(
 patch_id number
,patch_desc clob
,log_file   blob)
lob(patch_desc, log_file)
store as (
tablespace lob_data
disable storage in row);
```

If you want to store up to 4000 characters of a LOB in the table row, use the ENABLE STORAGE IN ROW clause when creating the table:

```
create table patchmain(
 patch_id number
,patch_desc clob
,log_file   blob)
lob(patch_desc, log_file)
store as (
tablespace lob_data
enable storage in row);
```

▨ **Note** The LOB locator is always stored in line with the row.

You can't modify the LOB storage in a row after the table has been created. The only ways to alter storage in row is to either move the LOB column or drop and re-create the table. This example alters the storage in row by moving the LOB column:

```
alter table patchmain
move lob(patch_desc)
store as (enable storage in row);
```

You can verify the in-row storage via the IN_ROW column of USER_LOBS:

```
select
 table_name
,column_name
,tablespace_name
```

```
,in_row
from user_lobs;
```

A value of YES indicates that the LOB is stored in row:

```
TABLE_NAME       COLUMN_NAME      TABLESPACE_NAME IN_ROW
---------------  ---------------  --------------- ------
PATCHMAIN        LOG_FILE         LOB_DATA        NO
PATCHMAIN        PATCH_DESC       LOB_DATA        YES
```

Using SecureFile Features

As mentioned previously in this chapter, the SecureFile LOB architecture allows you to compress LOB columns, eliminate duplicates, and transparently encrypt LOB data. These features provide high performance and manageability of LOB data and are available in Oracle Database 11g and higher. The next few subsections cover features specific to SecureFiles.

Compressing LOBs

If you're using SecureFile LOBs, then you can specify a degree of compression. The benefit is that the LOBs consume much less space in the database. The downside is that reading and writing the LOBs may take longer. See Table 11–4 for a description of the compression values.

This example creates a CLOB column with a low degree of compression:

```
CREATE TABLE patchmain(
 patch_id   NUMBER
,patch_desc CLOB)
LOB(patch_desc) STORE AS SECUREFILE
(COMPRESS LOW)
TABLESPACE inv_clob;
```

Table 11–4. Degrees of Compression Available with SecureFile LOBs

Compression Type	Description
HIGH	Highest degree of compression. Incurs higher latency when reading and writing the LOB.
MEDIUM	Medium level of compression. Default value if compression is specified but with no degree.
LOW	Lowest level of compression. Provides the lowest latency when reading and writing the LOB.
COMPRESS clause isn't specified.	No compression is used if you don't specify the COMPRESS clause.

If a LOB has been created as a SecureFile, you can alter its compression level. For example, this changes the compression to HIGH:

```
ALTER TABLE patchmain
MODIFY LOB(patch_desc)
(COMPRESS HIGH);
```

If you create a LOB with compression but decide that you don't want to use the feature, you can alter the LOB to have no compression via the NOCOMPRESS clause:

```
ALTER TABLE patchmain
MODIFY LOB(patch_desc)
(NOCOMPRESS);
```

■ Tip Try to enable compression, deduplication, and encryption through a CREATE TABLE statement. If you use an ALTER TABLE statement, the table is locked while the LOB is modified.

Deduplicating LOBs

If you have an application where identical LOBs are associated with two or more rows, you should consider using the SecureFile deduplication feature. When enabled, this instructs Oracle to check when a new LOB is inserted into a table and see whether that LOB is already stored in another row (for the same LOB column). If it's already stored, then Oracle stores a pointer to the existing identical LOB. This can potentially mean huge space savings for your application.

■ Note Deduplication requires the Oracle Advanced Compression option. See the *Oracle Database Licensing Information* guide (available on OTN) for more information.

This example creates a LOB column using the deduplication feature:

```
CREATE TABLE patchmain(
 patch_id   NUMBER
,patch_desc CLOB)
LOB(patch_desc) STORE AS SECUREFILE
(DEDUPLICATE)
 TABLESPACE inv_clob;
```

To verify that the deduplication feature is in effect, run this query:

```
select
 table_name
,column_name
,deduplication
from user_lobs;
```

Here's some sample output:

```
TABLE_NAME       COLUMN_NAME      DEDUPLICATION
---------------  ---------------  ---------------
PATCHMAIN        PATCH_DESC       LOB
```

If an existing table has a SecureFile LOB, then you can alter the column to enable deduplication:

```
alter table patchmain
modify lob(patch_desc) (deduplicate);
```

Here's another example that modifies a partitioned LOB to enable deduplication:

```
alter table patchmain modify partition p2
lob (patch_desc) (deduplicate lob);
```

If you decide that you don't want deduplication enabled, use the KEEP_DUPLICATES clause:

```
alter table patchmain
modify lob(patch_desc) (keep_duplicates);
```

Encrypting LOBs

You can transparently encrypt a SecureFile LOB column (just like any other column). Before you use encryption features, you must set up an encryption *wallet*. If you don't know how to setup a wallet, I've included a sidebar at the end of this subsection that describes this task. Also, see the *Oracle Advanced Security* guide (available on OTN) for more details.

■ **Note** The SecureFile encryption feature requires a license for the Oracle Advanced Security Option. See the *Oracle Database Licensing Information* guide (available on OTN) for more information.

The ENCRYPT clause enables SecureFile encryption using Oracle Transparent Data Encryption (TDE). The following example enables encryption for the PATCH_DESC LOB column:

```
CREATE TABLE patchmain(
 patch_id number
,patch_desc clob)
LOB(patch_desc) STORE AS SECUREFILE (encrypt)
tablespace inv_clob;
```

When you describe the table, the LOB column now shows that encryption is in effect:

```
SQL> desc patchmain;
Name                                       Null?    Type
------------------------------------------ -------- ----------------------------
 PATCH_ID                                           NUMBER
 PATCH_DESC                                         CLOB ENCRYPT
```

Here's a slightly different example that specifies the ENCRYPT keyword in line with the LOB column:

```
CREATE TABLE patchmain(
 patch_id    number
,patch_desc clob encrypt)
LOB (patch_desc) STORE AS SECUREFILE;
```

You can verify the encryption details by querying the DBA_ENCRYPTED_COLUMNS view:

```
select
 table_name
,column_name
,encryption_alg
from dba_encrypted_columns;
```

Here's the output for this example:

```
TABLE_NAME           COLUMN_NAME          ENCRYPTION_ALG
-------------------- -------------------- --------------------
PATCHMAIN            PATCH_DESC           AES 192 bits key
```

If you've already created the table, you can alter a column to enable encryption:

```
alter table patchmain modify
(patch_desc clob encrypt);
```

You can also specify an encryption algorithm. For example:

```
alter table patchmain modify
(patch_desc clob encrypt using '3DES168');
```

You can disable encryption for a SecureFile LOB column via the DECRYPT clause:

```
alter table patchmain modify
(patch_desc clob decrypt);
```

CREATING AN ENCRYPTION WALLET

Before you can use the Oracle TDE feature, you have to create and open a wallet. Here are the steps:

1. Create an operating system directory in which to store the wallet.

2. Specify the location of the wallet in the sqlnet.ora file:

```
ENCRYPTION_WALLET_LOCATION=
(SOURCE=
 (METHOD=FILE)
 (METHOD_DATA=
  (DIRECTORY=/opt/oracle/orawall)
))
```

3. Create the wallet:

```
SQL> alter system set encryption key authenticated by "foobar";
```

The wallet must be open for TDE to work. If the wallet is closed, you can't access encrypted columns. If you stop and restart your database, you must reopen the wallet before you can access encrypted columns.

```
SQL> alter system set encryption wallet open authenticated by "foobar";
```

In the prior statement, you must use the same password that you used when you created the wallet:

Migrating BasicFiles to SecureFiles

You can migrate BasicFile LOB data to SecureFiles via one of the following methods:

- Create a new table, load the data from the old table, and rename the tables.
- Move the table.
- Redefine the table online.

Each of these techniques is described in the following subsections.

Creating a New Table

Here's a brief example of creating a new table and loading data from the old table. In this example, PATCHMAIN_NEW is the new table being created with a SecureFile LOB.

```
create table patchmain_new(
 patch_id number
,patch_desc clob)
lob(patch_desc) store as securefile (tablespace lob_data);
```

Next, load the newly created table with data from the old table:

```
SQL> insert into patchmain_new select * from patchmain;
```

Now, rename the tables:

```
SQL> rename patchmain to patchmain_old;
SQL> rename patchmain_new to patchmain;
```

When using this technique, be sure any grants that were pointing at the old table are reissued for the new table.

Moving a Table to a SecureFile Architecture

You can also use the ALTER TABLE...MOVE statement to redefine the storage of a LOB as a SecureFile. For example:

```
alter table patchmain
move lob(patch_desc)
store as securefile (tablespace inv_clob);
```

You can verify that the column is now a SecureFile via this query:

```
SQL> select table_name, column_name, securefile from user_lobs;
```

The SECUREFILE column now has a value of YES:

```
TABLE_NAME      COLUMN_NAME      SEC
--------------- ---------------- ---
PATCHMAIN       PATCH_DESC       YES
```

Online Redefinition

You can also redefine a table while it's online via the DBMS_REDEFINITION package. Use the following steps to do an online redefinition:

1. Ensure that the table has a primary key. If the table doesn't have a primary key, then create one:

```
alter table patchmain
add constraint patchmain_pk
primary key (patch_id);
```

2. Create a new table that defines the LOB column(s) as SecureFile:

```
create table patchmain_new(
 patch_id number
,patch_desc clob)
lob(patch_desc)
store as securefile (tablespace lob_data);
```

3. Map the columns of the new table to the original table:

```
declare
  l_col_map varchar2(2000);
begin
  l_col_map := 'patch_id patch_id, patch_desc patch_desc';
  dbms_redefinition.start_redef_table(
    'DARL','PATCHMAIN','PATCHMAIN_NEW',l_col_map
  );
end;
/
```

4. Copy the data (this can take a long time if there are many rows):

```
set serverout on size 1000000
declare
  l_err_cnt integer :=0;
begin
  dbms_redefinition.copy_table_dependents(
    'DARL','PATCHMAIN','PATCHMAIN_NEW',1,TRUE, TRUE, TRUE, FALSE, l_err_cnt
  );
  dbms_output.put_line('Num Errors: ' || l_err_cnt);
end;
/
```

5. Finish the redefinition:

```
begin
  dbms_redefinition.finish_redef_table('DARL','PATCHMAIN','PATCHMAIN_NEW');
end;
/
```

You can confirm that the table has been redefined via this query:

```
SQL> select table_name, column_name, securefile from user_lobs;
```

Here's the output for this example:

```
TABLE_NAME            COLUMN_NAME           SECUREFILE
--------------------  --------------------  --------------------
PATCHMAIN_NEW         PATCH_DESC            NO
PATCHMAIN             PATCH_DESC            YES
```

Viewing LOB Metadata

You can use any of the DBA/ALL/USER_LOBS views to display information about LOBs in your database:

```
select
 table_name
,column_name
,index_name
,tablespace_name
from all_lobs
order by table_name;
```

Table 11–5 describes the columns available with DBA/ALL_LOBS:

Table 11–5. ALL_LOBS Column Descriptions

Column	Description
OWNER	Owner of the object that contains the LOB.
TABLE_NAME	Table name that contains the LOB.
COLUMN_NAME	Column name of the LOB.
SEGMENT_NAME	Segment name of the LOB.
TABLESPACE_NAME	Tablespace name that contains the LOB.
INDEX_NAME	Index name of the LOB.
CHUNK	Size in bytes of the LOB chunk.
PCTVERSION	Maximum percentage of LOB space used for versioning.
RETENTION	Maximum time duration for versioning of LOB space.
FREEPOOLS	Number of free pools for the LOB.
CACHE	YES indicates that the LOB data is placed in the buffer cache. NO indicates that the LOB data isn't placed in the buffer cache. CACHEREADS indicates that the LOB is brought into the cache for read operations only.
LOGGING	Whether changes to the LOB are logged in the redo stream.

Column	Description
ENCRYPT	Whether the LOB is encrypted.
COMPRESSION	Degree of compression,
DEDUPLICATION	Whether deduplication is used for the LOB.
IN_ROW	Whether some of the LOB is stored in line with the row.
FORMAT	Whether the LOB storage format depends on the endianness of the platform.
PARTITIONED	Whether the LOB is in a partitioned table.
SECUREFILE	Whether the LOB architecture is SecureFile.
SEGMENT_CREATED	Whether the LOB segment has been created.

Also keep in mind that a LOB segment has a corresponding index segment. Thus you can query both the segment and the index in the DBA/ALL/USER_SEGMENTS views for LOB information:

```
select
 segment_name
,segment_type
,tablespace_name
from user_segments
where segment_name like 'SYS_LOB%'
or    segment_name like 'SYS_IL%';
```

Loading LOBs

Loading LOB data isn't typically the DBA's job, but you should be familiar with techniques used to populate LOB columns. Developers may come to you for help with troubleshooting, performance, or space-related issues.

Loading a CLOB

First, create an Oracle database directory object that points to the operating system directory in which the CLOB file is stored. This directory object is used when loading the CLOB. In this example, the Oracle directory object is named LOAD_LOB and the operating system directory is /home/oracle/scripts:

```
SQL> create or replace directory load_lob as '/home/oracle/scripts';
```

For reference, listed next is the DDL used to create the table in which the CLOB file is loaded:

```
create table patchmain(
 patch_id number primary key
,patch_desc clob
,patch_file blob)
lob(patch_desc, patch_file)
store as securefile (compress low) tablespace lob_data;
```

This example also uses a sequence named PATCH_SEQ. Here's the sequence-creation script:

```
SQL> create sequence patch_seq;
```

The following bit of code uses the DBMS_LOB package to load a text file (named patch.txt) into a CLOB column. In this example, the table name is PATCHMAIN and the CLOB column is PATCH_DESC:

```
declare
  src_clb bfile; -- point to source CLOB on file system
  dst_clb clob;  -- destination CLOB in table
  src_doc_name varchar2(300) := 'patch.txt';
  src_offset integer := 1; -- where to start in the source CLOB
  dst_offset integer := 1;  -- where to start in the target CLOB
  lang_ctx integer := dbms_lob.default_lang_ctx;
  warning_msg number; -- returns warning value if bad chars
begin
  src_clb := bfilename('LOAD_LOB',src_doc_name); -- assign pointer to file
  --
  insert into patchmain(patch_id, patch_desc) -- create LOB placeholder
  values(patch_seq.nextval, empty_clob())
  returning patch_desc into dst_clb;
  --
  dbms_lob.open(src_clb, dbms_lob.lob_readonly); -- open file
  --
  -- load the file into the LOB
  dbms_lob.loadclobfromfile(
  dest_lob => dst_clb,
  src_bfile => src_clb,
  amount => dbms_lob.lobmaxsize,
  dest_offset => dst_offset,
  src_offset => src_offset,
  bfile_csid => dbms_lob.default_csid,
  lang_context => lang_ctx,
  warning => warning_msg
  );
  dbms_lob.close(src_clb); -- close file
  --
  dbms_output.put_line('Wrote CLOB: ' || src_doc_name);
end;
/
```

You can place this code in a file and execute it from the SQL command prompt. In this example, the file that contains the code is named clob.sql:

```
SQL> set serverout on size 1000000
SQL> @clob.sql
```

Here's the expected output:

```
Wrote CLOB: patch.txt
PL/SQL procedure successfully completed.
```

Loading a BLOB

Loading a BLOB is similar to loading a CLOB. This example uses the same directory object, table, and sequence from the previous example, which loaded a CLOB. Loading a BLOB is simpler than loading a CLOB because you don't have to specify character-set information.

This example loads a file named patch.zip into the PATCH_FILE BLOB column:

```
declare
  src_blb bfile; -- point to source BLOB on file system
  dst_blb blob;  -- destination BLOB in table
  src_doc_name varchar2(300) := 'patch.zip';
  src_offset integer := 1; -- where to start in the source BLOB
  dst_offset integer := 1;  -- where to start in the target BLOB
begin
  src_blb := bfilename('LOAD_LOB',src_doc_name); -- assign pointer to file
  --
  insert into patchmain(patch_id, patch_file)
  values(patch_seq.nextval, empty_blob())
  returning patch_file into dst_blb; -- create LOB placeholder column first
  dbms_lob.open(src_blb, dbms_lob.lob_readonly);
  --
  dbms_lob.loadblobfromfile(
  dest_lob => dst_blb,
  src_bfile => src_blb,
  amount => dbms_lob.lobmaxsize,
  dest_offset => dst_offset,
  src_offset => src_offset
  );
  dbms_lob.close(src_blb);
  dbms_output.put_line('Wrote BLOB: ' || src_doc_name);
end;
/
```

You can place this code in a file and run it from the SQL command prompt. In this example, the file that contains the code is named blob.sql:

```
SQL> set serverout on size 1000000
SQL> @blob.sql
```

Here's the expected output:

```
Wrote BLOB: patch.zip
PL/SQL procedure successfully completed.
```

Measuring LOB Space Consumed

As mentioned previously in this chapter, a LOB consists of an in-row lob locator, a LOB index, and a LOB segment that consists of one or more chunks. The space used by the LOB index is usually negligible compared to the space used by the LOB segment. You can view the space consumed by a segment by querying the BYTES column of DBA/ALL/USER_SEGMENTS (just like any other segment in the database). Here's a sample query:

```
select
 segment_name
```

```
,segment_type
,segment_subtype
,bytes/1024/1024 meg_bytes
from user_segments;
```

You can modify the query to specifically report on only LOBs by joining to the USER_LOBS view:

```
select
 a.table_name
,a.column_name
,a.segment_name
,a.index_name
,b.bytes/1024/1024 meg_bytes
from user_lobs a
     ,user_segments b
where a.segment_name = b.segment_name;
```

You can use the DBMS_SPACE.SPACE_USAGE package and procedure to report on the blocks being used by a LOB. This package only works on objects that have been created in an ASSM-managed tablespace. There are two different forms of the SPACE_USAGE procedure: one form reports on BasicFile LOBs, and the other form reports on SecureFile LOBs.

BasicFile Space Used

Here's an example of how to call DBMS_SPACE.SPACE_USAGE for a BasicFile LOB:

```
declare
    p_fs1_bytes number;
    p_fs2_bytes number;
    p_fs3_bytes number;
    p_fs4_bytes number;
    p_fs1_blocks number;
    p_fs2_blocks number;
    p_fs3_blocks number;
    p_fs4_blocks number;
    p_full_bytes number;
    p_full_blocks number;
    p_unformatted_bytes number;
    p_unformatted_blocks number;
begin
    dbms_space.space_usage(
        segment_owner    => user,
        segment_name     => 'SYS_LOB0000024082C00002$$',
        segment_type     => 'LOB',
        fs1_bytes        => p_fs1_bytes,
        fs1_blocks       => p_fs1_blocks,
        fs2_bytes        => p_fs2_bytes,
        fs2_blocks       => p_fs2_blocks,
        fs3_bytes        => p_fs3_bytes,
        fs3_blocks       => p_fs3_blocks,
        fs4_bytes        => p_fs4_bytes,
        fs4_blocks       => p_fs4_blocks,
        full_bytes       => p_full_bytes,
        full_blocks      => p_full_blocks,
```

```
        unformatted_blocks => p_unformatted_blocks,
        unformatted_bytes  => p_unformatted_bytes
    );
    dbms_output.put_line('Full bytes  = '||p_full_bytes);
    dbms_output.put_line('Full blocks = '||p_full_blocks);
    dbms_output.put_line('UF bytes    = '||p_unformatted_bytes);
    dbms_output.put_line('UF blocks   = '||p_unformatted_blocks);
end;
/
```

In this PL/SQL, you need to modify the code so that it reports on the LOB segment in your environment.

SecureFile Space Used

Here's an example of how to call DBMS_SPACE.SPACE_USAGE for a SecureFile LOB:

```
DECLARE
    l_segment_owner         varchar2(40);
    l_table_name            varchar2(40);
    l_segment_name          varchar2(40);
    l_segment_size_blocks   number;
    l_segment_size_bytes    number;
    l_used_blocks           number;
    l_used_bytes            number;
    l_expired_blocks        number;
    l_expired_bytes         number;
    l_unexpired_blocks      number;
    l_unexpired_bytes       number;
    --
    CURSOR c1 IS
    SELECT owner, table_name, segment_name
    FROM dba_lobs
    WHERE table_name = 'PATCHMAIN2';
BEGIN
    FOR r1 IN c1 LOOP
        l_segment_owner := r1.owner;
        l_table_name := r1.table_name;
        l_segment_name := r1.segment_name;
        --
        dbms_output.put_line('----------------------------');
        dbms_output.put_line('Table Name        : ' || l_table_name);
        dbms_output.put_line('Segment Name      : ' || l_segment_name);
        --
        dbms_space.space_usage(
            segment_owner         => l_segment_owner,
            segment_name          => l_segment_name,
            segment_type          => 'LOB',
            partition_name        => NULL,
            segment_size_blocks   => l_segment_size_blocks,
            segment_size_bytes    => l_segment_size_bytes,
            used_blocks           => l_used_blocks,
            used_bytes            => l_used_bytes,
```

```
        expired_blocks            => l_expired_blocks,
        expired_bytes             => l_expired_bytes,
        unexpired_blocks          => l_unexpired_blocks,
        unexpired_bytes           => l_unexpired_bytes
    );
    --
    dbms_output.put_line('segment_size_blocks: '|| l_segment_size_blocks);
    dbms_output.put_line('segment_size_bytes : '|| l_segment_size_bytes);
    dbms_output.put_line('used_blocks         : '|| l_used_blocks);
    dbms_output.put_line('used_bytes          : '|| l_used_bytes);
    dbms_output.put_line('expired_blocks      : '|| l_expired_blocks);
    dbms_output.put_line('expired_bytes       : '|| l_expired_bytes);
    dbms_output.put_line('unexpired_blocks    : '|| l_unexpired_blocks);
    dbms_output.put_line('unexpired_bytes     : '|| l_unexpired_bytes);
  END LOOP;
END;
/
```

Again, in this PL/SQL, you need to modify the code so that it reports on the table with the LOB segment in your environment.

Summary

Oracle lets you store large objects in databases via various LOB data types. LOBs facilitate the storage, management, and retrieval of video clips, images, movies, word-processing documents, large text files, and so on. Oracle can store these files in the database and thus provide backup and recovery and security protection (just as it does for any other data type). Oracle's CLOB data type is used to store large character text files that exceed 4000 characters (the maximum length of a VARCHAR2 column). BLOBs are used to store binary files such as images (JPEG or MPEG), movie files, sound files, and so on. If it's not feasible to store the file in the database, you can use a BFILE LOB.

Oracle provides two underlying architectures for LOBS: BasicFile and SecureFile. BasicFile is the LOB architecture that has been available since Oracle version 8. The SecureFile feature was introduced in Oracle Database 11g. SecureFile has many advanced options such as compression, deduplication, and encryption (these specific features require an extra license from Oracle).

LOBs provide a way to manage very large files. Oracle has another feature, partitioning, which allows you to manage very large tables and indexes. Partitioning is covered in detail in the next chapter.

CHAPTER 12

∎∎∎

Partitioning: Divide and Conquer

If you work with large tables and indexes, at some point you'll experience performance degradation as the row counts grow into the hundreds of millions. Even efficiently written SQL statements executing against appropriately indexed tables eventually slow down as table and index sizes grow into the gigabytes, terabytes, or even higher. For such situations, you have to devise a strategy that allows your database to scale with increasing data volumes.

Oracle provides two key scalability features—parallelism and partitioning—that enable good performance even with massively large databases. *Parallelism* allows Oracle to start more than one thread of execution to take advantage of multiple hardware resources. *Partitioning* allows subsets of a table or index to be managed independently (Oracle's "divide and conquer" approach). The focus of this chapter is partitioning strategies.

Partitioning lets you create a logical table or index that consists of separate segments that can each be accessed and worked on by separate threads of execution. Each partition of a table or index has the same logical structure, such as the column definitions, but can reside in separate containers. In other words, you can store each partition in its own tablespace and associated datafiles. This allows you to manage one large logical object as a group of smaller, more maintainable pieces.

This chapter uses various terms related to partitioning. Table 12-1 describes the meanings of terms you should be familiar with.

Table 12-1. Oracle Partitioning Terminology

Term	Meaning
Partitioning	Transparently implementing one logical table or index as many separate, smaller segments.
Partition key	One or more columns that unambiguously determine which partition a row is stored in.
Partition bound	Boundary between partitions.
Single-level partitioning	Partitioning using a single method.
Composite partitioning	Partitioning using a combination of methods.
Subpartition	Partition within a partition.
Partition independence	Ability to access partitions separately to perform maintenance operations without impacting the availability of other partitions.

Term	Meaning
Partition pruning	Elimination of unnecessary partitions. Oracle detects which partitions need to be accessed by a SQL statement and removes (prunes) any partitions that aren't needed.
Partition-wise join	Join executed in partition-sized pieces to improve performance by executing many smaller tasks in parallel rather than one, large task in sequence.
Local partitioned index	Index that uses the same partition key as its table.
Global partitioned index	Index that doesn't use the same partition key as its table.
Global nonpartitioned indexed	Regular index created on a partitioned table. The index itself isn't partitioned.

If you work with mainly small online transaction processing (OLTP) databases, you probably don't need to create partitioned tables and indexes. However, if you work with large OLTP databases or in data-warehouse environments, you can most likely benefit from partitioning. Partitioning is a key to designing and building scalable and highly available database systems.

What Tables Should Be Partitioned?

Following are some rules of thumb for determining whether to partition a table. In general, you should consider partitioning for

- Tables that are over 2GB in size.

- Tables that have more than 10 million rows, when SQL operations are getting slower as more data is added.

- Tables you know will grow large. It's better to create a table as partitioned rather than rebuild it as partitioned after performance begins to suffer as the table grows.

- Tables that have rows that can be divided in a way that facilitates parallel operations like loading, retrieval, or backup and recovery.

- Tables for which you want to archive the oldest partition on a periodic basis, and tables from which you want to drop the oldest partition regularly as data becomes stale.

One rule is that any table over 2GB in size is a potential candidate for partitioning. Run this query to show the top space-consuming objects in your database:

```
select * from (
select
 owner
,segment_name
,segment_type
,partition_name
,sum(extents) num_ext
```

```
,sum(bytes)/1024/1024 meg_tot
from dba_segments
group by owner, segment_name, segment_type, partition_name
order by sum(extents) desc)
where rownum <= 10;
```

Here's a snippet of the output from the query:

```
OWNER    SEGMENT_NAME          SEGMENT_TYPE     PARTITION_NAME  NUM_EXT  MEG_TOT
-------  --------------------  ---------------- --------------- -------- --------
REP_MV   REG_QUEUE_REP_ARCH    TABLE                             29,218   29,218
REP_MV   REG_QUEUE_REP         TABLE                             15,257   15,257
STAR2    F_INSTALLATIONS       TABLE PARTITION  INST_P_6          4,092    4,092
```

This output shows that a few large tables in this database may benefit from partitioning. For this database, if there are performance issues with these large objects, then partitioning may help.

If you're running the previous query from SQL*Plus, you need to apply some formatting to the columns to reasonably display the output within the limited width of your terminal:

```
set lines 132
col owner form a10
col segment_name form a20
col partition_name form a15
```

In addition to looking at the size of objects, if you can divide your data so that it facilitates operations such as loading data, querying, backups, archiving, and deleting, you should consider using partitioning. For example, if you work with a large table that contains data that is often accessed by a particular time range—such as by day, week, month, or year—it makes sense to consider partitioning.

A large table size combined with a good business reason means you should consider partitioning. Keep in mind that there is more setup work and maintenance when you partition a table. However, as mentioned earlier, it's much easier to partition a table during setup than it is to convert it after it's grown to an unwieldy size.

Note Partitioning is an extra-cost option that is available only with the Oracle Enterprise Edition. You have to decide based on your business requirements whether partitioning is worth the cost.

Creating Partitioned Tables

Oracle provides a robust set of methods for dividing tables and indexes into smaller subsets. For example, you can divide a table's data by date ranges, such as by month or year. Table 12-2 gives an overview of the partitioning strategies available.

Table 12–2. Partitioning Strategies

Partition Type	Description
Range	Allows partitioning based on ranges of dates, numbers, or characters.
List	Useful when the partitions fit nicely into a list of values, like state or region codes.
Hash	Allows even distribution of rows when there is no obvious partitioning key.
Composite	Allows combinations of other partitioning strategies.
Interval	Extends range partitioning by automatically allocating new partitions when new partition key values exceed the existing high range.
Reference	Useful for partitioning a child table based on a parent table column.
Virtual	Allows partitioning on a virtual column.
System	Allows the application inserting the data to determine which partition should be used.

The following subsections show examples of each partitioning strategy. In addition, you learn how to place partitions into separate tablespaces; to take advantage of all the benefits of partitioning, you need to understand how to assign a partition to its own tablespace.

Partitioning by Range

Range partitioning is frequently used. This strategy instructs Oracle to place rows in partitions based on ranges of values such as dates or numbers. As data is inserted into a range-partitioned table, Oracle determines which partition to place a row in based on the lower and upper bound of each range partition.

The range-based partition key is defined by the PARTITION BY RANGE clause in the CREATE TABLE statement. This determines which column is used to determine which partition a row belongs in. You'll see some examples shortly.

Each range partition requires a VALUES LESS THAN clause that identifies the non-inclusive value of the upper bound of the range. The first partition defined for a range has no lower bound. Any value less than the first partition's VALUES LESS THAN clause are inserted into the first partition. For partitions other than the first partition, the lower bound of a range is determined by the upper bound of the previous partition.

Optionally, you can create a range-partitioned table's highest partition with the MAXVALUE clause. Any row inserted that doesn't have a partition key that falls in any lower ranges is inserted into this topmost MAXVALUE partition.

Using a NUMBER for the Partition Key Column

Let's look at an example to illustrate the previous concepts. Suppose you're working in a data-warehouse environment where you typically have a fact table that stores information about an event (such as registrations, sales, downloads, and so forth). In this scenario the fact table contains a number column that represents a date. For example, the value 20110101 represents January 1, 2011. You want to partition the fact table based on this number column. This SQL statement creates a table with three partitions based on a range of numbers:

```
create table f_regs
(reg_count number
,d_date_id number
)
partition by range (d_date_id)(
partition p_2010 values less than (20110101),
partition p_2011 values less than (20120101),
partition p_max  values less than (maxvalue)
);
```

When creating a range-partitioned table, you don't have to specify a MAXVALUE partition. However, if you don't specify a partition with the MAXVALUE clause, and you attempt to insert a row that doesn't fall in any other defined ranges, you receive an error such as

```
ORA-14400: inserted partition key does not map to any partition
```

When you see that error, you have to add a partition that accommodates the partition-key value being inserted or add a partition with the MAXVALUE clause.

▥ Tip If you're using Oracle Database 11g or higher, consider using an interval partitioning strategy in which partitions are automatically added by Oracle when the high range value is exceeded. This topic is covered a bit later in the section "Creating Partitions on Demand."

You can view information about the partitioned table you just created by running the following query:

```
select
 table_name
,partitioning_type
,def_tablespace_name
from user_part_tables
where table_name='F_REGS';
```

Here's a snippet of the output:

```
TABLE_NAME           PARTITION DEF_TABLESPACE_NAME
-------------------- --------- -------------------------
F_REGS               RANGE     USERS
```

To view information about the partitions in the table, issue a query like this:

```
select
 table_name
,partition_name
,high_value
from user_tab_partitions
where table_name = 'F_REGS'
order by
 table_name
,partition_name;
```

Here's some sample output:

```
TABLE_NAME      PARTITION_NAME  HIGH_VALUE
--------------- --------------- -------------------------------
F_REGS          P_2010          20110101
F_REGS          P_2011          20120101
F_REGS          P_MAX           MAXVALUE
```

In this example, the D_DATE_ID column is the partitioning-key column. The VALUES LESS THAN clauses create the partition boundaries, which define the partition into which a row is inserted. The MAXVALUE parameter creates a partition in which to store rows that don't fit into the other defined partitions (including NULL values).

DETECTING WHEN ADDITIONAL HIGH RANGE IS REQUIRED

When you partition by range without specifying a MAXVALUE partition, you may not accurately predict when a new high partition will need to be added. In addition, the HIGH_VALUE column in the data dictionary is of the data type LONG, which means you can't apply the MAX function to return the current high value.

Listed next is a simple shell script that attempts to insert a record that contains a future date to determine if there is an accepting partition. If the record is inserted successfully, then the script rolls back the transaction. If the record fails to insert, an error is generated, and the script mails you an email:

```
#!/bin/bash
if [ $# -ne 1 ]; then
  echo "Usage: $0 SID"
  exit 1
fi
# See Chapter 2 for an example of sourcing OS variables.
# source oracle OS variables
. /var/opt/oracle/oraset $1
#
sqlplus -s <<EOF
darl/foo
WHENEVER SQLERROR EXIT FAILURE
COL date_id NEW_VALUE hold_date_id
SELECT to_char(sysdate+30,'yyyymmdd') date_id FROM dual;
--
INSERT INTO inv.f_regs (reg_count, d_date_id)
VALUES (0, '&hold_date_id');
ROLLBACK;
```

```
EOF
#
if [ $? -ne 0 ]; then
  mailx -s "Partition range issue: f_regs" dkuhn@oracle.com <<EOF
  check f_regs high range.
EOF
else
  echo "f_regs ok"
fi
#
exit 0
```

Ensure that you don't inadvertently add data to a production table with a script like this. You have to modify this script carefully to match your table and high-range partition-key column.

Using a TIMESTAMP for the Partition Key Column

You may have noticed that the example in the previous section created the column D_DATE_ID as a NUMBER data type instead of a DATE data type for the F_REGS table. One technique sometimes employed in data-warehouse environments uses an intelligent surrogate key for the primary key of the D_DATES dimension. It's intelligent because the key number represents a date. This lets you partition the fact table (F_REGS) on a range of numbers that always represent a date. Sometimes data-warehouse architects find this type of partitioning easier to work with than DATE- or TIMESTAMP-based fields.

To illustrate the previous point, the following example creates the F_REGS table with a TIMESTAMP data type for the D_DATE_DTT column:

```
create table f_regs
(reg_count  number
,d_date_dtt timestamp
)
partition by range (d_date_dtt)(
 partition p_2010 values less than (to_date('01-jan-2011','dd-mon-yyyy')),
 partition p_2011 values less than (to_date('01-jan-2012','dd-mon-yyyy')),
 partition p_max  values less than (maxvalue)
);
```

As shown in this code, I recommend that you use the TO_DATE function with a format mask to be sure there is no ambiguity about how the date should be interpreted. This technique is every bit as valid as using a NUMBER field for the partition key. Just keep in mind that whoever designs the data-warehouse tables may have a strong opinion about which technique to use.

One slight variation on this example leaves out the TO_DATE function. You must then ensure that the date string you use matches a date format recognized by Oracle. For example:

```
create table f_regs
(reg_count  number
,d_date_dtt timestamp
)
partition by range (d_date_dtt)(
 partition p_2010 values less than ('01-jan-11'),
 partition p_2011 values less than ('01-jan-12'),
 partition p_max  values less than (maxvalue)
);
```

If Oracle can't interpret a date correctly, an error is thrown:

```
ORA-01858: a non-numeric character was found where a numeric was expected
```

I recommend that you always use TO_DATE to explicitly instruct Oracle how to interpret the date. Doing so also provides a minimal level of documentation for anybody supporting the database.

Placing Partitions into Tablespaces

When you're working with large partitioned tables, I recommend that you place each partition in its own tablespace. Doing so allows you to manage the storage of each partition separate from the other partitions. This also lets you back up and recover the table partitions separately, because each partition is located in its own tablespace.

To understand the benefits of using a separate tablespace for each partition, first consider a nonpartitioned table scenario. This example creates a table and places the table into the P1_TBSP tablespace:

```
create table f_sales(
 sales_id  number
,amt       number
,d_date_id number)
tablespace p1_tbsp;
```

Now, as data is inserted into the F_SALES table, all the data is stored in the datafiles associated with the tablespace P1_TBSP. Figure 12–1 illustrates this point. There is no way for the data being inserted into a nonpartitioned table to be spread out across many tablespaces.

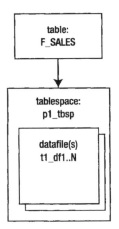

Figure 12–1. A nonpartitioned table

Compare the previous nonpartitioned architecture to that of a partitioned table. This example creates a partitioned table but doesn't specify tablespaces for the partitions:

```
create table f_sales (
 sales_id  number
,amt       number
,d_date_id number)
```

```
tablespace p1_tbsp
partition by range(d_date_id)(
 partition y11 values less than (20120101)
,partition y12 values less than (20130101)
,partition y13 values less than (20140101)
);
```

Figure 12–2 illustrates this approach. Notice that in this case, all partitions are stored in the same tablespace.

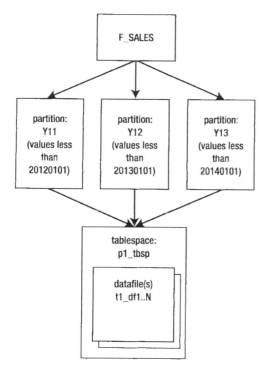

Figure 12–2. A partitioned table with only one tablespace

This approach has some advantages (over a nonpartitioned table) in that you can perform partition-maintenance operations (drop, split, merge, truncate, and so on) on one partition without affecting others (thus ensuring partition independence). However, this approach doesn't quite take advantage of all that partitioning has to offer.

The next example places each partition in a separate tablespace:

```
create table f_sales (
 sales_id  number
,amt       number
,d_date_id number)
tablespace p1_tbsp
partition by range(d_date_id)(
 partition y11 values less than (20120101)
```

```
    tablespace p1_tbsp
,partition y12 values less than (20130101)
    tablespace p2_tbsp
,partition y13 values less than (20140101)
    tablespace p3_tbsp
);
```

Now the data for each partition is physically stored in its own tablespace and corresponding datafiles (see Figure 12–3).

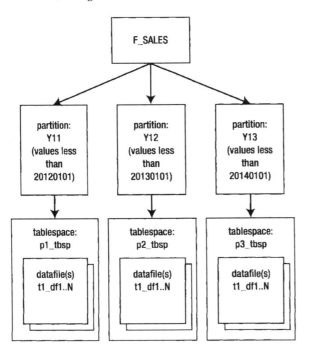

Figure 12–3. Partitions stored in separate tablespaces

An advantage of placing partitions in separate tablespaces is that you can back up and recover partitions independently (by backing up individual tablespaces). Also, if you have a partition that isn't being modified, you can change its tablespace to read-only and instruct utilities like Oracle Recovery Manager (RMAN) to skip backing up such tablespaces, thus increasing backup performance. Additionally, creating each partition in its own tablespace makes it easier to move data from OLTP databases to decision support system (DSS) databases, and it lets you place specific tablespaces and corresponding datafiles on separate storage devices to improve scalability and performance.

Also keep in mind that when you specify a tablespace for a partition, you can also specify any other storage settings (per tablespace). The next example explicitly sets the PCTFREE, PCTUSED, and NOLOGGING storage clauses for the tablespaces:

```
create table f_sales (
 sales_id   number
,amt        number
,d_date_id number)
tablespace p1_tbsp
partition by range(d_date_id)(
 partition y11 values less than (20120101)
    tablespace p1_tbsp pctfree 5 pctused 90 nologging
,partition y12 values less than (20130101)
    tablespace p2_tbsp pctfree 5 pctused 90 nologging
,partition y13 values less than (20140101)
    tablespace p3_tbsp pctfree 5 pctused 90 nologging
);
```

Partitioning by List

List partitioning works well for partitioning unordered and unrelated sets of data. For example, say you have a large table and want to partition it by state codes. To do so, use the PARTITION BY LIST clause of the CREATE TABLE statement. This example uses state codes to create three list-based partitions:

```
create table f_sales
 (reg_sales   number
 ,d_date_id   number
 ,state_code varchar2(20)
)
partition by list (state_code)
 ( partition reg_west values ('AZ','CA','CO','MT','OR','ID','UT','NV')
  ,partition reg_mid  values ('IA','KS','MI','MN','MO','NE','OH','ND')
  ,partition reg_rest values (default)
);
```

The partition key for a list-partitioned table can be only one column. Use the DEFAULT list to specify a partition for rows that don't match values in the list. If you don't specify a DEFAULT list, then an error is generated when a row is inserted with a value that doesn't map to the defined partitions. Run this SQL statement to view list values for each partition:

```
select
 table_name
,partition_name
,high_value
from user_tab_partitions
where table_name = 'F_SALES'
order by 1;
```

Here's the output for this example:

```
TABLE_NAME PARTITION_ HIGH_VALUE
---------- ---------- --------------------------------------------------
F_SALES    REG_MID    'IA', 'KS', 'MI', 'MN', 'MO', 'NE', 'OH', 'ND'
F_SALES    REG_REST   default
F_SALES    REG_WEST   'AZ', 'CA', 'CO', 'MT', 'OR', 'ID', 'UT', 'NV'
```

The HIGH_VALUE column displays the list values defined for each partition. This column is of data type LONG. If you're using SQL*Plus, you may need to set the LONG variable to a value higher than the default (80 bytes), to display the entire contents of the column:

```
SQL> set long 1000
```

Partitioning by Hash

Sometimes a large table doesn't contain an obvious column by which to partition the table, whether by range or by list. For example, suppose you have a table to store census data. Each person entered into the table has a government-assigned unique number (such as a Social Security Number in the US). In this scenario, you have a somewhat random primary key that doesn't follow a distinct pattern. This table is a candidate for partitioning by hash because it doesn't fit well into a range- or list-partitioning scheme.

Hash partitioning maps rows to partitions based on an internal algorithm that spreads data evenly across all defined partitions. You don't have any control over the hashing algorithm or how Oracle distributes the data. You specify how many partitions you'd like, and Oracle divides the data evenly based on the hash-key column.

To create hash-based partitions, use the PARTITION BY HASH clause of the CREATE TABLE statement. This example creates a table that is divided into three partitions; each partition is created in its own tablespace:

```
create table browns(
 brown_id number
,bear_name varchar2(30))
partition by hash(brown_id)
partitions 3
store in(tbsp1, tbsp2, tbsp3);
```

Of course, you have to modify details like the tablespace names to match those in your environment. Alternatively, you can eliminate the STORE IN clause, and Oracle places all partitions in your default tablespace. If you want to name both the tablespaces and partitions, you can specify them as follows:

```
create table browns(
 brown_id number
,bear_name varchar2(30))
partition by hash(brown_id)
(partition p1 tablespace tbsp1
,partition p2 tablespace tbsp2
,partition p3 tablespace tbsp3);
```

Hash partitioning has some interesting performance implications. All rows that share the same value for the hash key are inserted into the same partition. This means inserts are particularly efficient, because the hashing algorithm ensures that the data is distributed uniformly across partitions. Also, if you typically select for a specific key value, Oracle has to access only one partition to retrieve those rows. However, if you search by ranges of values, Oracle will most likely have to search every partition to determine which rows to retrieve. Thus range searches can perform poorly in hash-partitioned tables.

Blending Different Partitioning Methods

Oracle allows you to partition a table using multiple strategies (*composite partitioning*). Suppose you have a table that you want to partition on a number range, but you also want to subdivide each partition by a list of regions. The following example does just that:

```
create table f_sales(
  sales_amnt number
 ,reg_code   varchar2(3)
 ,d_date_id  number
)
partition by range(d_date_id)
subpartition by list(reg_code)
(partition p2010 values less than (20110101)
  (subpartition p1_north values ('ID','OR')
  ,subpartition p1_south values ('AZ','NM')
  ),
 partition p2011 values less than (20120101)
  (subpartition p2_north values ('ID','OR')
  ,subpartition p2_south values ('AZ','NM')
  )
);
```

You can view subpartition information by running the following query:

```
select
 table_name
,partitioning_type
,subpartitioning_type
from user_part_tables
where table_name = 'F_SALES';
```

Here's some sample output:

```
TABLE_NAME           PARTITION SUBPART
-------------------- --------- -------
F_SALES              RANGE     LIST
```

Run the next query to view information about the subpartitions:

```
select
 table_name
,partition_name
,subpartition_name
from user_tab_subpartitions
where table_name = 'F_SALES'
order by
 table_name
,partition_name;
```

Here's a snippet of the output:

```
TABLE_NAME            PARTITION_NAME        SUBPARTITION_NAME
--------------------  --------------------  --------------------
F_SALES               P2010                 P1_SOUTH
F_SALES               P2010                 P1_NORTH
F_SALES               P2011                 P2_SOUTH
F_SALES               P2011                 P2_NORTH
```

Prior to Oracle Database 11g, composite partitioning can be implemented as range-hash (available since version 8i) and range-list (available since version 9i). Starting with Oracle Database 11g, here are the composite partitioning strategies available:

- *Range-hash (8i):* Appropriate for ranges that can be subdivided by a somewhat random key, like ORDER_DATE and CUSTOMER_ID.

- *Range-list (9i):* Useful when a range can be further partitioned by a list, such as SHIP_DATE and STATE_CODE.

- *Range-range:* Appropriate when you have two distinct partition range values, like ORDER_DATE and SHIP_DATE.

- *List-range:* Useful when a list can be further subdivided by a range, like REGION and ORDER_DATE.

- *List-hash:* Useful for further partitioning a list by a somewhat random key, such as STATE_CODE and CUSTOMER_ID.

- *List-list:* Appropriate when a list can be further delineated by another list, such as COUNTRY_CODE and STATE_CODE.

As you can see, composite partitioning gives you a great deal of flexibility in the way you partition your data.

Creating Partitions on Demand

As of Oracle Database 11g, you can instruct Oracle to automatically add partitions to range-partitioned tables. The feature is known as *interval partitioning*. Oracle dynamically creates a new partition when data inserted exceeds the maximum bound of the range-partitioned table. The newly added partition is based on an interval that you specify (hence the name *interval partitioning*).

Suppose you have a range-partitioned table and want Oracle to automatically add a partition when values are inserted above the highest value defined for the highest range. You can use the INTERVAL clause of the CREATE TABLE statement to instruct Oracle to automatically add a partition to the high end of a range-partitioned table.

The following example creates a table that initially has one partition with a high-value range of 01-JAN-2012:

```
create table f_sales(
 sales_amt number
,d_date    date
)
partition by range (d_date)
interval(numtoyminterval(1, 'YEAR'))
store in (p1_tbsp, p2_tbsp, p3_tbsp)
(partition p1 values less than (to_date('01-jan-2012','dd-mon-yyyy'))
tablespace p1_tbsp);
```

The first partition is created in P1_TBSP. As Oracle adds partitions, it assigns a new partition to the tablespaces defined in the STORE IN clause (it's supposed to store them in a round-robin fashion, but isn't always consistent).

■ **Note** With interval partitioning, you can specify only a single key column from the table, and it must be either a DATE or a NUMBER data type.

The interval in this example is one year, specified by the INTERVAL(NUMTOYMINTERVAL(1, 'YEAR')) clause. If a record is inserted into the table with a D_DATE value greater than or equal to 01-JAN-2012, Oracle automatically adds a new partition to the high end of the table. You can check the details of the partition by running this SQL statement:

```
select
  table_name
 ,partition_name
 ,partition_position
 ,tablespace_name
 ,high_value
from user_tab_partitions
where table_name = 'F_SALES'
order by
 table_name
,partition_position;
```

Here's some sample output (the column headings have been shortened and the HIGH_VALUE column has been cut short so the output fits on the page):

```
TABLE_NAME PARTITION_ Part. Pos TABLESPACE HIGH_VALUE
---------- ---------- --------- ---------- ------------------------------
F_SALES    P1                 1 P1_TBSP    TO_DATE(' 2012-01-01 00:00:00'
```

Now, insert data above the high value for the highest partition:

```
SQL> insert into f_sales values(1,sysdate+1000);
```

Here's what the output from selecting from USER_TAB_PARTITIONS now shows:

```
TABLE_NAME PARTITION_ Part. Pos TABLESPACE HIGH_VALUE
---------- ---------- --------- ---------- ------------------------------
F_SALES    P1                 1 P1_TBSP    TO_DATE(' 2012-01-01 00:00:00'
F_SALES    SYS_P476           2 P3_TBSP    TO_DATE(' 2014-01-01 00:00:00'
```

A partition named SYS_P476 was automatically created with a high value of 2014-01-01. If you don't like the name that Oracle gives the partition, you can rename it:

```
SQL> alter table f_sales rename partition sys_p476 to p2;
```

Notice what happens when a value is inserted that falls into a year interval between the two partitions:

```
SQL> insert into f_sales values(1,sysdate+500);
```

Querying the USER_TAB_PARTITIONS table shows that another partition has been created because the value inserted falls into a year interval that isn't included in the existing partitions:

```
TABLE_NAME PARTITION_ Part. Pos TABLESPACE HIGH_VALUE
---------- ---------- --------- ---------- ----------------------------
F_SALES    P1                 1 P1_TBSP    TO_DATE(' 2012-01-01 00:00:00'
F_SALES    SYS_P477           2 P2_TBSP    TO_DATE(' 2013-01-01 00:00:00'
F_SALES    P2                 3 P3_TBSP    TO_DATE(' 2014-01-01 00:00:00'
```

You can also have Oracle add partitions by other increments of time, such as a week. For example:

```
create table f_sales(
 sales_amt number
,d_date    date
)
partition by range (d_date)
interval(numtodsinterval(7,'day'))
store in (p1_tbsp, p2_tbsp, p3_tbsp)
(partition p1 values less than (to_date('01-oct-2010', 'dd-mon-yyyy'))
tablespace p1_tbsp);
```

As data is inserted into weeks in the future, new weekly partitions will be created automatically. In this way, Oracle automatically manages the addition of partitions to the table.

Partitioning to Match a Parent Table

If you're using Oracle Database 11g or higher, you can use the PARTITION BY REFERENCE clause to specify that a child table should be partitioned in the same way as its parent. This allows a child table to inherit the partitioning strategy of its parent table. Any parent table partition-maintenance operations are also applied to the child record tables.

■ **Note** Before the advent of the partitioning-by-reference feature, you had to physically duplicate and maintain the parent table column in the child table. Doing so not only requires more disk space but also is a source of error when you're maintaining the partitions.

For example, say you have a parent ORDERS table and a child ORDER_ITEMS table that are related by primary-key and foreign-key constraints on the ORDER_ID column. The parent ORDERS table is partitioned on the ORDER_DATE column. Even though the child ORDER_ITEMS table doesn't contain the ORDER_DATE column, you wonder whether you can partition it so that the records are distributed the same way as in the parent ORDERS table. This example creates a parent table with a primary-key constraint on ORDER_ID and range partitions on ORDER_DATE:

```
create table orders(
 order_id   number
,order_date date
,constraint order_pk primary key(order_id)
)
partition by range(order_date)
(partition p10  values less than (to_date('01-jan-2010','dd-mon-yyyy'))
```

```
,partition p11  values less than (to_date('01-jan-2011','dd-mon-yyyy'))
,partition pmax values less than (maxvalue)
);
```

Next, you create the child ORDER_ITEMS table. It's partitioned by naming the foreign-key constraint as the referenced object:

```
create table order_items(
 line_id  number
,order_id number not null
,sku      number
,quantity number
,constraint order_items_pk  primary key(line_id, order_id)
,constraint order_items_fk1 foreign key (order_id) references orders
)
partition by reference (order_items_fk1);
```

Notice that the foreign-key column ORDER_ID must be defined as NOT NULL. The foreign-key column must be enabled and enforced.

You can inspect the partition-key columns via the following query:

```
select
 name
,column_name
,column_position
from user_part_key_columns
where name in ('ORDERS','ORDER_ITEMS');
```

Here's the output for this example:

```
NAME                 COLUMN_NAME           COLUMN_POSITION
-------------------- --------------------- ---------------
ORDERS               ORDER_DATE                          1
ORDER_ITEMS          ORDER_ID                            1
```

Notice that the child table is partitioned by the ORDER_ID column. This ensures that the child record is partitioned in the same manner as the parent record (because the child record is related to the parent record via the ORDER_ID key column).

When you create the referenced partition child table, if you don't explicitly name the child table partitions, by default Oracle creates partitions for the child table with the same partition names as its parent table. This example explicitly names the child table referenced partitions:

```
create table order_items(
 line_id  number
,order_id number not null
,sku      number
,quantity number
,constraint order_items_pk  primary key(line_id, order_id)
,constraint order_items_fk1 foreign key (order_id) references orders
)
partition by reference (order_items_fk1)
(partition c10
,partition c11
,partition cmax
);
```

You can't specify the partition bounds of a referenced table. Partitions of a referenced table are created in the same tablespace as the parent partition unless you specify tablespaces for the child partitions.

Partitioning on a Virtual Column

If you're using Oracle Database 11g or higher, you can partition on a virtual column (see Chapter 7 for a discussion of virtual columns). Here's a sample script that creates a table named EMP with the virtual column COMMISSION and a corresponding range partition for the virtual column:

```
create table emp (
 emp_id    number
,salary    number
,comm_pct number
,commission generated always as (salary*comm_pct)
)
partition by range(commission)
(partition p1 values less than (1000)
,partition p2 values less than (2000)
,partition p3 values less than (maxvalue));
```

This strategy allows you to partition on a column that isn't stored in the table but is computed dynamically. Virtual-column partitioning is appropriate when there is a business requirement to partition on a column that isn't physically stored in a table. The expression behind a virtual column can be a complex calculation, can return a subset of a column string, can combine column values, and so on. The possibilities are endless.

For example, you may have a 10-character string column in which the first 2 digits represent a region and last 8 digits represent a specific location (this is a bad design, but it happens). In this case, it may make sense from a business perspective to partition on the first two digits of this column (by region).

Giving an Application Control over Partitioning

You may have a rare scenario in which you want the application inserting records into a table to explicitly control which partition it inserts data into. If you're using Oracle Database 11g or higher, you can use the PARTITION BY SYSTEM clause to allow an INSERT statement to specify into which partition to insert data. This next example creates a system-partitioned table with three partitions:

```
create table apps
(app_id number
,app_amnt number)
partition by system
(partition p1
,partition p2
,partition p3);
```

When inserting data into this table, you must specify a partition. The next line of code inserts a record into partition P1:

```
SQL> insert into apps partition(p1) values(1,100);
```

When you're updating or deleting, if you don't specify a partition, Oracle scans all partitions of a system-partitioned table to find the relevant rows. Therefore, you should specify a partition when updating and deleting to avoid poor performance.

A system-partitioned table is helpful in unusual situations in which you need to explicitly control which partition a record is inserted into. This allows your application code to manage the distribution of records among the partitions. I recommend that you use this feature only when you can't use one of Oracle's other partitioning mechanisms to meet your business requirement.

Maintaining Partitions

When using partitions, you'll eventually have to perform some sort of maintenance operation. For example, you may be required to add, drop, truncate, split, and merge partitions. The various partition maintenance tasks are described in this section, starting with a description of the data-dictionary objects that relate to partitioning.

Viewing Partition Metadata

When you're maintaining partitions, it's helpful to view metadata information about the partitioned objects. Oracle provides many data-dictionary views that contain information about partitioned tables and indexes. Table 12–3 describes each of the views.

Keep in mind the DBA-level views contain data for all partitioned objects in the database, the ALL level shows partitioning information to which the currently connect user has access, and the USER-level views contain information for the partitioned objects owned by the currently connected user.

Table 12–3. Data-Dictionary Views Containing Partitioning Information

View	Contains
DBA/ALL/USER_PART_TABLES	Displays partitioned table information
DBA/ALL/USER_TAB_PARTITIONS	Contains information regarding individual table partitions
DBA/ALL/USER_TAB_SUBPARTITIONS	Shows subpartition-level table information regarding storage and statistics
DBA/ALL/USER_PART_KEY_COLUMNS	Displays partition-key columns
DBA/ALL/USER_SUBPART_KEY_COLUMNS	Contains subpartition-key columns
DBA/ALL/USER_PART_COL_STATISTICS	Shows column-level statistics
DBA/ALL/USER_SUBPART_COL_STATISTICS	Displays subpartition-level statistics
DBA/ALL/USER_PART_HISTOGRAMS	Contains histogram information for partitions
DBA/ALL/USER_SUBPART_HISTOGRAMS	Shows histogram information for subpartitions
DBA/ALL/USER_PART_INDEXES	Displays partitioned index information
DBA/ALL/USER_IND_PARTITIONS	Contains information regarding individual index partitions
DBA/ALL/USER_IND_SUBPARTITIONS	Shows subpartition-level index information
DBA/ALL/USER_SUBPARTITION_TEMPLATES	Displays subpartition template information

Two views you'll use quite often are DBA_PART_TABLES and the DBA_TAB_PARTITIONS. The DBA_PART_TABLES view contains table-level partitioning information such as partitioning method and default storage settings. The DBA_TAB_PARTITIONS view contains information about the individual table partitions, such as the partition name and storage settings for individual partitions.

Moving a Partition

Suppose you create a partitioned table as shown:

```
create table f_sales
 (reg_sales  number
 ,sales_amt  number
 ,d_date_id  number
 ,state_code varchar2(20)
)
partition by list (state_code)
 ( partition reg_west values ('AZ','CA','CO','MT','OR','ID','UT','NV')
  ,partition reg_mid  values ('IA','KS','MI','MN','MO','NE','OH','ND')
  ,partition reg_rest values (default)
);
```

Also for this partitioned table, you decide to create a local index on the STATE_CODE column:

```
SQL> create index f_sales_idx1 on f_sales(state_code) local;
```

You create a global index on the REG_SALES column:

```
SQL> create index f_sales_gidx1 on f_sales(reg_sales);
```

And you create a global partitioned index on the SALES_AMT column:

```
create index f_sales_gidx2 on f_sales(sales_amt)
global partition by range(sales_amt)
(partition pg1 values less than (25)
,partition pg2 values less than (50)
,partition pg3 values less than (maxvalue));
```

Later, you decide that you want to move a partition to a specific tablespace. In this scenario, you can use the ALTER TABLE...MOVE PARTITION statement to relocate a table partition. This example moves the REG_WEST partition to a new tablespace:

```
SQL> alter table f_sales move partition reg_west tablespace p1_tbsp;
```

It's a fairly simple operation to move a partition to a different tablespace. Whenever you do this, make sure you check on the status of any indexes associated with the table. When you move a table partition to a different tablespace, any associated indexes are invalidated; therefore, you must rebuild any local indexes associated with a table partition that has been moved. You can verify the status of global and local index partitions by querying the data dictionary. Here's a sample query:

```
select
 b.table_name
,a.index_name
,a.partition_name
,a.status
,b.locality
from user_ind_partitions a
    ,user_part_indexes   b
```

```
where a.index_name=b.index_name
and table_name = 'F_SALES';
```

Here's the output for this example. One global index and one partition of a local index need to be rebuilt:

```
TABLE_NAME           INDEX_NAME       PARTITION_ STATUS     LOCALITY
-------------------- ---------------- ---------- ---------- --------------------
F_SALES              F_SALES_IDX1     REG_MID    USABLE     LOCAL
F_SALES              F_SALES_IDX1     REG_REST   USABLE     LOCAL
F_SALES              F_SALES_IDX1     REG_WEST   UNUSABLE   LOCAL
F_SALES              F_SALES_GIDX2    PG1        UNUSABLE   GLOBAL
F_SALES              F_SALES_GIDX2    PG2        UNUSABLE   GLOBAL
F_SALES              F_SALES_GIDX2    PG3        UNUSABLE   GLOBAL
```

Notice that the entire global index is rendered unusable, and only one partition of the local index (the partition that was moved) is unusable. Keep in mind that any maintenance operation on a table invalidates every partition of any associated global partitioned indexes or global nonpartitioned indexes. To check for global nonpartitioned indexes, you need to look in the USER_INDEXES view. Here's a query for this example:

```
select
 index_name
,status
from user_indexes
where table_name ='F_SALES';
```

Here's some sample output:

```
INDEX_NAME       STATUS
---------------- ----------
F_SALES_IDX1     N/A
F_SALES_GIDX1    UNUSABLE
F_SALES_GIDX2    N/A
```

You need to rebuild any indexes or partitions in an unusable state. This example rebuilds the unusable partition of the local index:

```
SQL> alter index f_sales_idx1 rebuild partition reg_west tablespace p1_tbsp;
```

When you move a table partition to a different tablespace, this causes the ROWID of each record in the table partition to change. Because a regular index stores the table ROWID as part of its structure, the index partition is invalidated if the table partition moves. In this scenario, you must rebuild the index. When you rebuild the index partition, you have the option of moving it to a different tablespace.

Automatically Moving Updated Rows

By default, Oracle doesn't let you update a row by setting the partition key to a value outside of its current partition. For example, this statement updates the partition-key column (D_DATE_ID) to a value that would result in the row needing to exist in a different partition:

```
SQL> update f_regs set d_date_id = 20100901 where d_date_id = 20090201;
```

You receive the following error:

```
ORA-14402: updating partition key column would cause a partition change
```

In this scenario, use the ENABLE ROW MOVEMENT clause of the ALTER TABLE statement to allow updates to the partition key that would change the partition in which a value belongs. For this example, the F_REGS table is first modified to enable row movement:

```
SQL> alter table f_regs enable row movement;
```

You should now be able to update the partition key to a value that moves the row to a different segment. You can verify that row movement has been enabled by querying the ROW_MOVEMENT column of the USER_TABLES view:

```
SQL> select row_movement from user_tables where table_name='F_REGS';
```

You should see the value ENABLED:

```
ROW_MOVE
--------
ENABLED
```

To disable row movement, use the DISABLE ROW MOVEMENT clause:

```
SQL> alter table f_regs disable row movement;
```

Partitioning an Existing Table

You may have a nonpartitioned table that has grown quite large, and want to partition it. There are several methods for converting a nonpartitioned table to a partitioned table. Table 12–4 lists the pros and cons of various techniques.

Table 12–4. Methods of Converting a Nonpartitioned Table

Conversion Method	Advantages	Disadvantages
CREATE <new_part_tab> AS SELECT * FROM <old_tab>	Simple; can use NOLOGGING and PARALLEL options. Direct path load.	Requires space for both old and new tables.
INSERT /*+ APPEND */ INTO <new_part_tab> SELECT * FROM <old_tab>	Fast, simple. Direct path load.	Requires space for both old and new tables.
Data Pump EXPDP old table; IMPDP new table (or EXP IMP if using older version of Oracle)	Fast; less space required. Takes care of grants, privileges, and so on. Loading can be done per partition with filtering conditions.	More complicated because you need to use a utility.
Create partitioned <new_part_tab>; exchange partitions with <old_tab>	Potentially less downtime.	Many steps; complicated.
Use the DBMS_REDEFINITION package (newer versions of Oracle)	Converts existing table inline.	Many steps; complicated.
Create CSV file or external table; load <new_part_tab> with SQL*Loader	Loading can be done partition by partition.	Many steps; complicated.

One of the easiest ways from Table 12–4 to partition an existing table is to create a new table—one that *is* partitioned—and load it with data from the old table. Listed next are the required steps:

1. If this is a table in an active production database, you should schedule some downtime for the table to ensure that no active transactions are occurring while the table is being migrated.

2. Create a new partitioned table from the old with CREATE TABLE <new table>...AS SELECT * FROM <old table>.

3. Drop or rename the old table.

4. Rename the table created in step 1 to the name of the dropped table.

For example, let's assume that the F_REGS table used so far in this chapter was created as an unpartitioned table. The following statement creates a new table that *is* partitioned, taking data from the old table that isn't:

```
create table f_regs_new
partition by range (d_date_id)
(partition p2008 values less than(20090101),
 partition p2009 values less than(20100101),
 partition pmax values less than(maxvalue)
)
nologging
as select * from f_regs;
```

Now you can drop (or rename) the old nonpartitioned table and rename the new partitioned table to the old table name. Be sure you don't need the old table before you drop it with the PURGE option (because this permanently drops the table):

```
SQL> drop table f_regs purge;
SQL> rename f_regs_new to f_regs;
```

Finally, build any constraints, grants, indexes, and statistics for the new table. You should now have a partitioned table that replaces the old, nonpartitioned table.

For the last step, if the original table contains many constraints, grants, and indexes, you may want to use Data Pump expd or exp to export the original table without data. Then, after the new table is created, use Data Pump impdp or imp to create the constraints, grants, indexes, and statistics on the new table.

Adding a Partition

Sometimes it's hard to predict how many partitions you should initially make for a table. A typical example is a range-partitioned table that's created without a MAXVALUE-created partition. You make a partitioned table that contains enough partitions for two years into the future, and then you forget about the table. Some time in the future, application users report that this message is being thrown:

```
ORA-14406: updated partition key is beyond highest legal partition key
```

■ Tip Consider using interval partitioning, which enables Oracle to automatically add range partitions when the upper bound is exceeded.

For a range-partitioned table, if the table's highest bound isn't defined with a MAXVALUE, you can use the ALTER TABLE...ADD PARTITION statement to add a partition to the high end of the table. If you're not sure what the current upper bound is, query the data dictionary:

```
select
 table_name
,partition_name
,high_value
from user_tab_partitions
where table_name = UPPER('&&tab_name')
order by table_name, partition_name;
```

This example adds a partition to the high end of a range-partitioned table:

```
alter table f_regs
add partition p2011
values less than (20120101)
pctfree 5 pctused 95
tablespace p11_tbsp;
```

If you have a range-partitioned table with the high range bounded by MAXVALUE, you can't add a partition. In this situation, you have to split an existing partition (see the section "Splitting a Partition" in this chapter).

For a list-partitioned table, you can add a new partition only if there isn't a DEFAULT partition defined. The next example adds a partition to a list-partitioned table:

```
SQL> alter table f_sales add partition reg_east values('GA');
```

If you have a hash-partitioned table, use the ADD PARTITION clause as follows to add a partition:

```
alter table browns
add partition hash_5
tablespace p_tbsp
update indexes;
```

■ **Note** When you're adding to a hash partitioned table, if you don't specify the UPDATE INDEXES clause, any global indexes must be rebuilt. In addition, you must rebuild any local indexes for the newly added partition.

In general, after adding a partition to a table, always check the partitioned indexes to be sure they all still have a VALID status:

```
select
 b.table_name
,a.index_name
,a.partition_name
,a.status
,b.locality
from user_ind_partitions a
    ,user_part_indexes   b
where a.index_name=b.index_name
and table_name = upper('&&part_table');
```

Also check the status of any global nonpartitioned indexes:

```
select
 index_name
,status
from user_indexes
where table_name = upper('&&part_table');
```

Consider using the UPDATE INDEXES clause of the ALTER TABLE statement to automatically rebuild indexes when you're performing maintenance operations. In some cases, Oracle may not allow you to use the UPDATE INDEXES clause, in which case you have to manually rebuild any unusable indexes. I highly recommend that you always test a maintenance operation in a nonproduction database to determine any unforeseen side effects.

Exchanging a Partition with an Existing Table

Exchanging a partition is a common technique for loading new data into large partitioned tables. This feature allows you to take a stand-alone table and swap it with an existing partition (in an already-partitioned table). Doing that lets you transparently add fully loaded new partitions without affecting the availability or performance of operations against the other partitions in the table.

The following simple example illustrates the process. Say you have a range-partitioned table created as follows:

```
create table f_sales
(sales_amt number
,d_date_id number)
partition by range (d_date_id)
(partition p_2009 values less than (20100101),
 partition p_2010 values less than (20110101),
 partition p_2011 values less than (20120101)
);
```

You also create a bitmap index on the D_DATE_ID column:

```
create bitmap index d_date_id_fk1 on
f_sales(d_date_id)
local;
```

Now, add a new partition to the table that will store new data:

```
alter table f_sales
add partition p_2012
values less than(20130101);
```

Next, create a staging table, and insert data that falls in the range of values for the newly added partition:

```
create table workpart(
  sales_amt number
 ,d_date_id number);
insert into workpart values(100,20120201);
insert into workpart values(120,20120507);
```

Create a bitmap index on the WORKPART table that matches the structure of the bitmap index on F_SALES:

```
create bitmap index
d_date_id_fk2
on workpart(d_date_id);
```

Now, exchange the WORKPART table with the P_2012 partition:

```
alter table f_sales
exchange partition p_2012
with table workpart
including indexes
without validation;
```

A quick query of the F_SALES table verifies that the partition was exchanged successfully:

```
SQL> select * from f_sales partition(p_2012);
```

Here's the output:

```
SALES_AMT  D_DATE_ID
---------- ----------
       100   20120201
       120   20120507
```

This query displays that the indexes are all still usable:

```
SQL> select index_name, partition_name, status from user_ind_partitions;
```

You can also verify that a local index segment was created for the new partition:

```
select segment_name,segment_type,partition_name
from user_segments
where segment_name IN('F_SALES','D_DATE_ID_FK1');
```

Here's the output:

```
SEGMENT_NAME          SEGMENT_TYPE        PARTITION_
--------------------- ------------------- ----------
D_DATE_ID_FK1         INDEX PARTITION     P_2009
D_DATE_ID_FK1         INDEX PARTITION     P_2010
D_DATE_ID_FK1         INDEX PARTITION     P_2011
D_DATE_ID_FK1         INDEX PARTITION     P_2012
F_SALES               TABLE PARTITION     P_2009
F_SALES               TABLE PARTITION     P_2010
F_SALES               TABLE PARTITION     P_2011
F_SALES               TABLE PARTITION     P_2012
```

The ability to exchange partitions is an extremely powerful feature. It allows you to take a partition of an existing table and make it a stand-alone table, and at the same time make a stand-alone table (which can be fully populated before the partition exchange operation) part of a partitioned table. When you exchange a partition, Oracle updates the entries in the data dictionary to perform the exchange.

When you exchange a partition with the WITHOUT VALIDATION clause, you instruct Oracle not to validate that the rows in the incoming partition (or subpartition) are valid entries for the defined range. This has the advantage of making the exchange a very quick operation because Oracle is only updating pointers in the data dictionary to perform the exchange operation. You need to make sure your data is accurate if you use WITHOUT VALIDATION.

If a primary key is defined for the partitioned table, the table being exchanged must have the same primary-key structure defined. If there is a primary key, the WITHOUT VALIDATION clause doesn't stop Oracle from enforcing unique constraints.

Renaming a Partition

Sometimes you need to rename a table partition or index partition. For example, you may want to rename a partition before you drop it (to ensure that it's not being used). Also, you may want to rename objects so they conform to standards. In these scenarios, use the appropriate ALTER TABLE or ALTER INDEX statement.

This example uses the ALTER TABLE statement to rename a table partition:

```
SQL> alter table f_regs rename partition reg_p_1 to reg_part_1;
```

The next line of code uses the ALTER INDEX statement to rename an index partition:

```
SQL> alter index f_reg_dates_fk1 rename partition reg_p_1 to reg_part_1;
```

You can query the data dictionary to verify the information regarding renamed objects. This query shows partitioned table names:

```
select
 table_name
,partition_name
,tablespace_name
from user_tab_partitions;
```

Similarly, this query displays partitioned index information:

```
select
 index_name
,partition_name
,status
,high_value
,tablespace_name
from user_ind_partitions;
```

Splitting a Partition

Suppose you've identified a partition that has too many rows, and you want to split it into two partitions. Use the ALTER TABLE...SPLIT PARTITION statement to split an existing partition. The following example splits a partition in a range-partitioned table:

```
alter table f_regs split partition p2010 at (20100601)
into (partition p2010_a, partition p2010)
update indexes;
```

If you don't specify UPDATE INDEXES, you need to rebuild any local indexes associated with the split partition as well as any global indexes. You can verify the status of partitioned indexes with the following SQL:

```
SQL> select index_name, partition_name, status from user_ind_partitions;
```

The next example splits a list partition. First, here's the CREATE TABLE statement, which shows you how the list partitions were originally defined:

```
create table f_sales
 (reg_sales  number
 ,d_date_id  number
 ,state_code varchar2(20)
)
partition by list (state_code)
 ( partition reg_west values ('AZ','CA','CO','MT','OR','ID','UT','NV')
  ,partition reg_mid  values ('IA','KS','MI','MN','MO','NE','OH','ND')
  ,partition reg_rest values (default)
);
```

Next, the REG_MID partition is split:

```
alter table f_sales split partition reg_mid values ('IA','KS','MI','MN') into
(partition reg_mid_a,
 partition reg_mid_b);
```

The REG_MID_A partition now contains the values IA, KS, MI, and MN, and REG_MID_B is assigned the remaining values MO, NE, OH, and ND.

The split-partition operation allows you to create two new partitions from a single partition. Each new partition has its own segment, physical attributes, and extents. The segment associated with the original partition is deleted.

Merging Partitions

When you create a partition, sometimes it's hard to predict how many rows the partition will eventually contain. You may have two partitions that don't contain enough data to warrant separate partitions. In such a situation, use the ALTER TABLE...MERGE PARTITIONS statement to combine partitions.

This example merges the REG_P_1 partition into the REG_P_2 partition:

```
SQL> alter table f_regs merge partitions reg_p_1, reg_p_2 into partition reg_p_2;
```

In this example, the partitions are organized by a range of dates. The merged partition is defined to accept rows with the highest range of the two merged partitions. Any local indexes are also merged into the new single partition.

Be aware that merging partitions invalidates any local indexes associated with the merged partitions. Additionally, all partitions of any global indexes that exist on the table are marked as unusable. You can verify the status of the partitioned indexes by querying the data dictionary:

```
select
 index_name
,partition_name
,tablespace_name
,high_value,status
from user_ind_partitions
order by 1,2;
```

Here's some sample output showing what a global index and a local index look like after a partition merge:

INDEX_NAME	PARTITION_NAME	TABLESPACE_NAME	HIGH_VALUE	STATUS
F_GLO_IDX1	SYS_P680	IDX1		UNUSABLE
F_GLO_IDX1	SYS_P681	IDX1		UNUSABLE
F_GLO_IDX1	SYS_P682	IDX1		UNUSABLE

| F_LOC_FK1 | REG_P_2 | USERS | 20110101 | UNUSABLE |
| F_LOC_FK1 | REG_P_3 | TBSP3 | 20120101 | USABLE |

When you merge partitions, you can use the UPDATE INDEXES clause of the ALTER TABLE statement to instruct Oracle to automatically rebuild any associated indexes:

```
alter table f_regs merge partitions reg_p_1, reg_p_2 into partition reg_p_2
tablespace tbsp2
update indexes;
```

Keep in mind that the merge operation takes longer when you use the UPDATE INDEXES clause. If you want to minimize the length of the merge operation, don't use this clause. Instead, manually rebuild local indexes associated with a merged partition:

```
SQL> alter table f_regs modify partition reg_p_2 rebuild unusable local indexes;
```

You can rebuild each partition of a global index with the ALTER INDEX...REBUILD PARTITION statement:

```
SQL> alter index f_glo_idx1 rebuild partition sys_p680;
SQL> alter index f_glo_idx1 rebuild partition sys_p681;
SQL> alter index f_glo_idx1 rebuild partition sys_p682;
```

You can merge two or more partitions with the ALTER TABLE...MERGE PARTITIONS statement. The name of the partition into which you're merging can be the name of one of the partitions you're merging or a completely new name.

Before you merge two (or more) partitions, make certain the merged partition has enough space in its tablespace to accommodate all the merged rows. If there isn't enough space, you receive an error that the tablespace can't extend to the necessary size.

Dropping a Partition

You occasionally need to drop a partition. A common scenario is when you have old data that isn't used anymore, meaning the partition can be dropped.

First, identify the name of the partition you want to drop. Run the following query to list partitions for a particular table for the currently connected user:

```
select segment_name, segment_type, partition_name
from user_segments
where segment_name = upper('&table_name');
```

Next, use the ALTER TABLE...DROP PARTITION statement to remove a partition from a table. This example drops the P_2008 partition from the F_SALES table:

```
SQL> alter table f_sales drop partition p_2008;
```

You should see the following message:

```
Table altered.
```

If you want to drop a subpartition, use the DROP SUBPARTITION clause:

```
SQL> alter table f_sales drop subpartition p2_south;
```

You can query USER_TAB_SUBPARTITIONS to verify that the subpartition has been dropped.

■ **Note** Oracle doesn't let you drop all subpartitions of a composite-partitioned table. There must be at least one subpartition per partition.

When you drop a partition, there is no undrop operation. Therefore, before you do this, be sure you're in the correct environment and really do need to drop the partition. If you need to preserve the data in a partition to be dropped, merge the partition to another partition instead of dropping it.

You can't drop a partition from a hash-partitioned table. For hash-partitioned tables, you must coalesce partitions to remove one. And you can't explicitly drop a partition from a reference-partitioned table. When a parent table partition is dropped, it's also dropped from corresponding child reference-partitioned tables.

Generating Statistics for a Partition

After you load a large amount of data into a partition, you should generate statistics to reflect the newly inserted data. Use the EXECUTE statement to run the DBMS_STATS package to generate statistics for a particular partition. In this example, the owner is STAR, the table is F_SALES, and the partition being analyzed is P_2012:

```
exec dbms_stats.gather_table_stats(ownname=>'STAR',-
tabname=>'F_SALES',-
partname=>'P_2012');
```

If you're working with a large partition, you probably want to specify the percentage sampling size and degree of parallelism, and also generate statistics for any indexes:

```
exec dbms_stats.gather_table_stats(ownname=>'STAR',-
tabname=>'F_SALES',-
partname=>'P_2012',-
estimate_percent=>dbms_stats.auto_sample_size,-
degree=>dbms_stats.auto_degree,-
cascade=>true);
```

For a partitioned table, you can generate statistics on either a single partition or the entire table. I recommend that you generate statistics whenever a significant amount of data changes in the partition. You need to understand your tables and data well enough to determine whether generating new statistics is required.

Removing Rows from a Partition

You can use several techniques to remove rows from a partition. If the data in the particular partition is no longer needed, consider dropping the partition. If you want to remove the data and leave the partition intact, then you can either truncate or delete from it. Truncating a partition permanently and quickly removes the data. If you need the option of rolling back the removal of records, then you should delete (instead of truncate). Both truncating and deleting are described next.

First, identify the name of the partition from which you want to remove records:

```
select segment_name, segment_type, partition_name
from user_segments
where partition_name is not null;
```

Use the ALTER TABLE...TRUNCATE PARTITION statement to remove all records from a partition. This example truncates the P_2008 partition of the F_SALES table:

```
SQL> alter table f_sales truncate partition p_2008;
```

You should see the following message:

```
Table truncated.
```

In this scenario, that message doesn't mean the entire table was truncated—it only confirms that the specified partition was truncated.

Truncating a partition is an efficient way to quickly remove large amounts of data. When you truncate a partition, however, there is no rollback mechanism. The truncate operation permanently deletes the data from the partition.

If you need the option of rolling back a transaction, use the DELETE statement:

```
SQL> delete from f_sales partition(p_2008);
```

The downside to this approach is that if you have millions of records, the DELETE operation can take a long time to run. Also, for a large number of records, DELETE generates a great deal of rollback information. This can cause performance issues for other SQL statements contending for resources.

Manipulating Data within a Partition

If you need to select or manipulate data within one partition, specify the partition name as part the SQL statement. For example, you can select the rows from a specific partition as shown:

```
SQL> select * from f_sales partition (y11);
```

If you want to select from two (or more) partitions, then use the UNION clause:

```
select * from f_sales partition (y11)
union
select * from f_sales partition (y12);
```

If you're a developer and you don't have access to the data dictionary to view which partitions are available, you can use the following SELECT...PARTITION FOR <partition_key_value> syntax (available in Oracle Database 11g and higher). With this new syntax, you provide a partition-key value, and Oracle determines what partition that key value belongs in and returns the rows from the corresponding partition. For example:

```
SQL> select * from f_sales partition for (20101120);
```

You can also update and delete partition rows. This example updates a column in a partition:

```
SQL> update f_sales partition(Y11) set sales_amt=200;
```

You can use the PARTITION FOR <partition_key_value> syntax for update, delete, and truncate operations. For example:

```
SQL> update f_sales partition for (20101120) set sales_amt=200;
```

▓ Note See the previous section on removing rows for examples of deleting and truncating a partition.

Partitioning Indexes

In today's large database environments, indexes can also grow to unwieldy sizes. Partitioning indexes provides the same benefits as partitioning tables: improved performance, scalability, and maintainability.

You can create an index that uses its table-partitioning strategy (local), or you can create a partitioned index that uses a different partitioning method than its table (global). Both of these techniques are described in the following subsections.

Partitioning an Index to Follow Its Table

When you create an index on a partitioned table, you have the option of making it type LOCAL. A local partitioned index is partitioned in the same manner as the partitioned table. Each table partition has a corresponding index that contains ROWID values and index-key values for just that table partition. In other words, the ROWID values in a local partitioned index only point to rows in the corresponding table partition.

The following example illustrates the concept of a locally partitioned index. First, create a table that has only two partitions:

```
create table f_sales (
 sales_id   number
,sales_amt number
,d_date_id number)
tablespace p1_tbsp
partition by range(d_date_id)(
 partition y11 values less than (20120101)
    tablespace p1_tbsp
,partition y12 values less than (20130101)
    tablespace p2_tbsp
);
```

Next, use the LOCAL clause of the CREATE INDEX statement to create a local index on the partitioned table. This example creates a local index on the D_DATE_ID column of the F_SALES table:

```
SQL> create index f_sales_fk1 on f_sales(d_date_id) local;
```

Run the following query to view information about partitioned indexes:

```
select
 index_name
,table_name
,partitioning_type
from user_part_indexes
where table_name = 'F_SALES';
```

Here's some sample output:

```
INDEX_NAME                      TABLE_NAME PARTITION
------------------------------- ---------- ---------
F_SALES_FK1                     F_SALES    RANGE
```

Now, query the USER_IND_PARTITIONS table to view information about the locally partitioned index:

```
select
```

```
 index_name
,partition_name
,tablespace_name
from user_ind_partitions
where index_name = 'F_SALES_FK1';
```

Notice that an index partition has been created for each partition of the table, and that the index is created in the same tablespace as the table partition:

```
INDEX_NAME                        PARTITION_ TABLESPACE_NAME
------------------------------ ---------- ---------------
F_SALES_FK1                       Y11        P1_TBSP
F_SALES_FK1                       Y12        P2_TBSP
```

Figure 12–4 conceptually shows how a locally managed index is constructed.

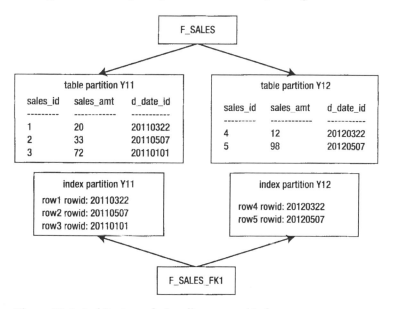

Figure 12–4. Architecture of a locally managed index

If you want the local index partitions to be created in a tablespace (or tablespaces) separate from the table partitions, specify those when creating the index:

```
create index f_sales_fk1 on f_sales(d_date_id) local
(partition y11 tablespace idx1
,partition y12 tablespace idx2);
```

Querying USER_IND_PARTITIONS now shows that the index partitions have been created in tablespaces separate from the table partitions:

```
INDEX_NAME                        PARTITION_ TABLESPACE_NAME
------------------------------ ---------- ---------------
F_SALES_FK1                       Y11        IDX1
F_SALES_FK1                       Y12        IDX2
```

If you specify the partition information when building a local-partitioned index, the number of partitions must match the number of partitions in the table on which the partitioned index is built.

Oracle automatically keeps local index partitions in sync with the table partitions. You can't explicitly add a partition to or drop a partition from a local index. When you add or drop a table partition, Oracle automatically performs the corresponding work for the local index. Oracle manages the local index partitions regardless of how the local indexes have been assigned to tablespaces.

Local indexes are common in data-warehouse and decision-support systems. If you query frequently by using the partitioned column(s), a local index is appropriate. This approach lets Oracle use the appropriate index and table partition to quickly retrieve the data.

There are two types of local indexes: local *prefixed* and local *nonprefixed*. A local-prefixed index is one in which the leftmost column of the index matches the table partition key. The previous example in this section is a local-prefixed index because its leftmost column (D_DATE_ID) is also the partition key for the table.

A nonprefixed-local index is one in which the leftmost column doesn't match the partition key used to partition the corresponding table. For example, this is a local-nonprefixed index:

```
SQL> create index f_sales_idx1 on f_sales(sales_amt) local;
```

The index is partitioned with the SALES_AMT column, which isn't the partition key of the table, and is therefore a nonprefixed index. You can verify whether an index is considered prefixed by querying the ALIGNMENT column from USER_PART_INDEXES:

```
select
 index_name
,table_name
,alignment
,locality
from user_part_indexes
where table_name = 'F_SALES';
```

Here's some sample output:

```
INDEX_NAME           TABLE_NAME           ALIGNMENT     LOCALI
-------------------- -------------------- ------------- ------
F_SALES_FK1          F_SALES              PREFIXED      LOCAL
F_SALES_IDX1         F_SALES              NON_PREFIXED  LOCAL
```

You may wonder why the distinction exists between prefixed and nonprefixed. A local-nonprefixed index means the index doesn't include the partition key as a leading edge of its index definition. This can have performance implications, in that a range scan accessing a nonprefixed index may need to search every index partition. If there are a large number of partitions, this can result in poor performance.

You can choose to create all local indexes as prefixed by including the partition-key column in the leading edge of the index. For example, you can create the F_SALES_IDX2 index as prefixed as follows:

```
SQL> create index f_sales_idx2 on f_sales(d_date_id, sales_amt) local;
```

Is a prefixed index better than a nonprefixed index? It depends on how you query your tables. You have to generate explain plans for the queries you use and examine whether a prefixed index is able to better take advantage of partition *pruning* (eliminating partitions to search in) than a nonprefixed index. Also keep in mind that a multicolumn prefixed local index consumes more space and resources than a nonprefixed local index.

Partitioning an Index Differently than Its Table

An index that is partitioned differently than its base table is known as a *global index*. An entry in a global index can point to any of the partitions of its base table. You can create a global index on any type of partitioned table.

You can create either a range-partitioned global index or a hash-based global index. Use the keyword GLOBAL to specify that the index is built with a partitioning strategy separate from its corresponding table. You must always specify a MAXVALUE when creating a range-partitioned global index. The following example creates a range-based global index:

```
create index f_sales_gidx1 on f_sales(sales_amt)
global partition by range(sales_amt)
(partition pg1 values less than (25)
,partition pg2 values less than (50)
,partition pg3 values less than (maxvalue));
```

Figure 12–5 shows that with a global index, the partitioning strategy of the index doesn't correspond to the partitioning strategy of the table.

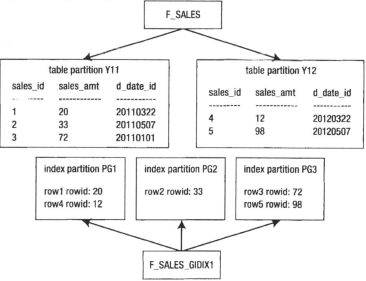

Figure 12–5. Architecture of a global index

The other type of global partitioned index is hash-based. This example creates a hash-partitioned global index:

```
create index f_sales_gidx2 on f_sales(sales_id)
global partition by hash(sales_id) partitions 3;
```

In general, global indexes are more difficult to maintain than local indexes. I recommend that you try to avoid using global indexes, and use local indexes whenever possible.

There is no automatic maintenance of global indexes (as there is with local indexes). With global indexes, you're responsible for adding and dropping index partitions. Also, many maintenance operations on the underlying partitioned table require that the global index partitions be rebuilt. The following operations on a heap-organized table render a global index unusable:

- ADD (HASH)
- COALESCE (HASH)
- DROP
- EXCHANGE
- MERGE
- MOVE
- SPLIT
- TRUNCATE

Consider using the UPDATE INDEXES clause when you perform maintenance operations. Doing so keeps the global index available during the operation and eliminates the need for rebuilding. The downside of using UPDATE INDEXES is that the maintenance operation takes longer due to the indexes being maintained during the action.

Global indexes are useful for queries that retrieve a small set of rows via an index. In these situations, Oracle can eliminate (prune) any unnecessary index partitions and efficiently retrieve the data. For example, global range-partitioned indexes are useful in OLTP environments where you need efficient access to individual records.

Partition Pruning

Partition pruning can greatly improve the performance of queries executing against partitioned tables. If a SQL query specifically accesses a table on a partition key, Oracle only searches the partitions that contain data the query needs (and doesn't access any partitions that don't contain data that the query requires—pruning them, so to speak).

For example, say a partitioned table is defined as follows:

```
create table f_sales (
 sales_id   number
,sales_amt number
,d_date_id number)
tablespace p1_tbsp
partition by range(d_date_id)(
 partition y10 values less than (20110101)
   tablespace p1_tbsp
,partition y11 values less than (20120101)
   tablespace p2_tbsp
,partition y12 values less than (20130101)
   tablespace p3_tbsp
);
```

Additionally, you create a local index on the partition-key column:

```
SQL> create index f_sales_fk1 on f_sales(d_date_id) local;
```

For this example, insert some sample data:

```
SQL> insert into f_sales values(1,100,20090202);
SQL> insert into f_sales values(2,200,20110202);
SQL> insert into f_sales values(3,300,20120202);
```

To illustrate the process of partition pruning, enable the autotrace facility:

```
SQL> set autotrace trace explain;
```

Now, execute a SQL statement that accesses a row based on the partition key:

```
select
 sales_amt
from f_sales
where d_date_id = '20110202';
```

Autotrace displays the explain plan. Some of the columns have been removed in order to fit the output on the page neatly:

```
---------------------------------------------------------------------------------
| Id  | Operation                           | Name       | Rows | Pstart| Pstop|
---------------------------------------------------------------------------------
|   0 | SELECT STATEMENT                    |            |   1  |       |      |
|   1 |  PARTITION RANGE SINGLE             |            |   1  |    2  |   2  |
|   2 |   TABLE ACCESS BY LOCAL INDEX ROWID | F_SALES    |   1  |    2  |   2  |
|*  3 |    INDEX RANGE SCAN                 | F_SALES_FK1|   1  |    2  |   2  |
---------------------------------------------------------------------------------
```

In this output, Pstart shows that the starting partition accessed is number 2. Pstop shows that the last partition accessed is number 2. In this example, partition 2 is the only partition used to retrieve data; the other partitions in the table aren't accessed at all by the query.

If a query is executed that doesn't use the partition key, then all partitions are accessed. For example:

```
SQL> select * from f_sales;
```

Here's the corresponding explain plan:

```
---------------------------------------------------------------------
| Id  | Operation            | Name     | Rows| Pstart| Pstop|
---------------------------------------------------------------------
|   0 | SELECT STATEMENT     |          |   3 |       |      |
|   1 |  PARTITION RANGE ALL |          |   3 |    1  |   3  |
|   2 |   TABLE ACCESS FULL  | F_SALES  |   3 |    1  |   3  |
---------------------------------------------------------------------
```

Notice in this output that the starting partition is number 1 and the stopping partition is number 3. This means partitions 1 through 3 are accessed by this query with no pruning of partitions.

This example is simple but demonstrates the concept of partition pruning. When you access the table by the partition key, you can drastically reduce the number of rows Oracle needs to inspect and process. This has huge performance benefits for queries that are able to prune partitions.

Summary

Oracle provides a partitioning feature that is critical for implementing large tables and indexes. Partitioning is vital for building highly scalable and maintainable applications. This feature works on the concept of logically creating an object (table or index) but implementing the object as several separate objects. A partitioned object allows you to build, load, maintain, and query on a partition-by-partition basis. Maintenance operations such as deleting, archiving, updating, and inserting data are manageable because you're working on only a small subset of the large logical table.

If you work in data-warehouse environments or with large databases, you must be highly knowledgeable of partitioning concepts. As a DBA, you're required to create and maintain partitioned objects. You have to make recommendations about table-partitioning strategies and where to use local and global indexes. These decisions have a huge impact on the usability and performance of the system.

After this chapter, the book focuses on utilities used to copy and move users, objects, and data from one environment to another. Oracle's Data Pump and External Table feature are covered in the next two chapters.

CHAPTER 13

■ ■ ■

Data Pump

Data Pump was introduced in Oracle Database 10g. It replaces the older exp/imp utilities. Data Pump enables you to quickly move data and/or metadata from one environment to another. You can use Data Pump in a variety of ways:

- Point-in-time logical backups of the entire database or subsets of data

- Replicating entire databases or subsets of data for testing or development

- Quickly generating Data Definition Language (DDL) required to re-create objects

Sometimes DBAs hold on to the old exp/imp utilities because they're familiar with the syntax and these utilities get the job done quickly. Even if those legacy utilities are easy to use, you should consider using Data Pump going forward. Data Pump contains substantial functionality over the old exp/imp utilities:

- Performance with large data sets, allowing you to efficiently export and import gigabytes of data

- Interactive command-line utility, which gives you the ability to disconnect and then later re-attach to active Data Pump jobs

- Ability to export and import large amounts of data from a remote database directly into a local database without creating a dump file

- Ability to make on-the-fly changes to schemas, tablespaces, datafiles, and storage settings from export to import

- Sophisticated filtering of objects and data

- Security controlled via database-directory objects

- Advanced features such as compression and encryption

This chapter begins with a discussion on the Data Pump architecture. Subsequent topics include basic export and import tasks, moving data across networks, filtering data, and running Data Pump in legacy mode.

Data Pump Architecture

Data Pump consists of the following components:

- expdp (Data Pump export utility)

- impdp (Data Pump import utility)

- DBMS_DATAPUMP PL/SQL package (Data Pump API)

- DBMS_METADATA PL/SQL package (Data Pump Metadata API)

The expdp and impdp utilities use the DBMS_DATAPUMP and DBMS_METADATA built-in PL/SQL packages when exporting and importing data and metadata. The DBMS_DATAPUMP package moves entire databases or subsets of data between database environments. The DBMS_METADATA package exports and imports information about database objects.

⬛ **Note** You can call the DBMS_DATAPUMP and DBMS_METADATA packages independently (outside of expdp and impdp) from SQL*Plus. I rarely call these packages directly from SQL*Plus; but you may have a specific scenario where it's desirable to interact directly with them. See the *Oracle Database PL/SQL Packages and Types Reference* guide (available on OTN) for more details.

When you start a Data Pump export or import job, a master operating-system process is initiated on the database server. This master process name has the format ora_dmNN_<SID>. On Linux/Unix systems, you can view this process from the operating-system prompt using the ps command:

```
$ ps -ef | grep ora_dm
  oracle 14950   717   0 10:59:06 ?           0:10 ora_dm00_STAGE
```

Depending on the degree of parallelism and the work specified, a number of worker processes are also started. The master process coordinates the work between master and worker processes. The worker process names have the format ora_dwNN_<SID>.

Also, when a user starts an export or import job, a database status table is created (owned by the user who starts the job). This table exists for the duration of the Data Pump job. The name of the status table is dependent on what type of job you're running. The table is named with the format SYS_<OPERATION>_<JOB_MODE>_NN, where OPERATION is either EXPORT or IMPORT. JOB_MODE can be FULL, SCHEMA, TABLE, TABLESPACE, and so on.

For example, if you're exporting a schema, a table is created in your account with the name SYS_EXPORT_SCHEMA_NN, where NN is a number that makes the table name unique in the user's schema. This status table contains information such as the objects exported/imported, start time, elapsed time, rows, error count, and so on. The status table has over 80 columns.

The status table is dropped by Data Pump upon successful completion of an export or import job. If you use the KILL_JOB interactive command, the master table is also dropped. If you stop a job with the STOP_JOB interactive command, the table isn't removed and is used in the event you restart the job.

If your job terminates abnormally, the master table is retained. You can delete the status table if you don't plan to restart the job.

When Data Pump runs, it uses a database-directory object to determine where to write and read dump files and log files. Usually, you specify which directory object you want Data Pump to use. If you don't specify a directory object, a default is used.

A Data Pump export creates an export file and a log file. The export file contains the objects being exported. The log file contains a record of the job activities.

Figure 13–1 shows the architectural components related to a Data Pump export job. Here's how you initiate the job from the command line:

```
$ expdp user/pwd dumpfile=exp.dmp logfile=exp.log directory=dp_dir
```

In this example, a database-directory object named DP_DIR is defined to reference the /oradump operating-system directory. The output files are defined via the command line to be exp.dmp and exp.log.

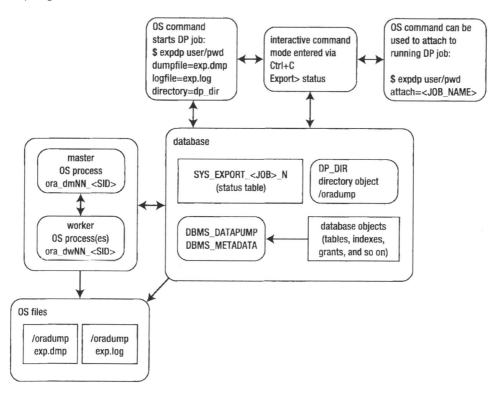

Figure 13–1. Data Pump export job components

Figure 13–2 displays the architectural components of a Data Pump import job. Here's how you initiate the job from the command line:

```
$ impdp user/pwd dumpfile=exp.dmp logfile=imp.log directory=dp_dir
```

In this example, the Data Pump import reads from a dump file named exp.dmp, which is located in the operating-system directory referenced by the database-directory object named DP_DIR. The import job reads the dump file and populates database objects.

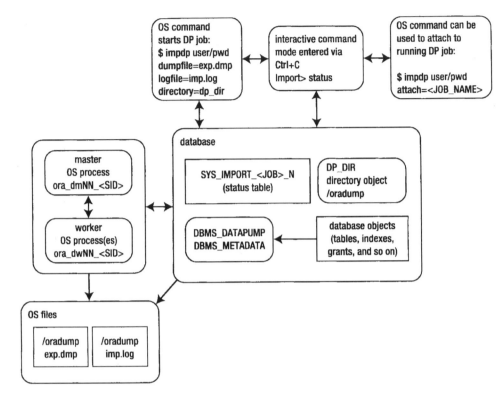

Figure 13-2. *Data Pump import job components*

For each Data Pump job, you must ensure that you have access to a directory object. The basics of exporting and importing are described in the next few sections.

Exporting Data

A small amount of setup is required when you run a Data Pump export job. Here are the steps:

1. Create a database-directory object that points to an operating-system directory that you want to write/read Data Pump files to/from.

2. Grant read, write on the directory to the database user running the export.

3. From the operating-system prompt, run the expdp utility.

Creating a Database Directory

Before you run a Data Pump job, you must create a database-directory object that corresponds to a physical location on disk that specifies where the dump files and log files are created. Use the CREATE

DIRECTORY command to accomplish this. This example creates a directory named dp_dir and specifies that it is to map to the /oradump physical location on disk:

```
SQL> create directory dp_dir as '/oradump';
```

To view the details of the newly created directory, issue this query:

```
SQL> select owner, directory_name, directory_path from dba_directories;
```

By default, when you install Oracle, one default directory object is created named DATA_PUMP_DIR. If you don't specify the DIRECTORY parameter when exporting or importing, Oracle by default attempts to use the default database-directory object. The default directory associated with DATA_PUMP_DIR can vary depending on the version of Oracle. On some systems, it may be ORACLE_HOME/rdbms/log; on other systems, it may point to ORACLE_BASE/admin/ORACLE_SID/dpdump. You have to inspect DBA_DIRECTORIES to verify the default location for your system.

Granting Access to the Directory

You need to grant permissions on the database-directory object to a user that wants to use Data Pump. Use the GRANT statement to allocate the appropriate privileges. If you want a user to be able to read from and write to the directory, you must grant security access as follows:

```
SQL> grant read, write on directory dp_dir to darl;
```

All directory objects are owned by the SYS user. If you're using a user account that has the DBA role granted to it, then you have the read and write privileges on the directory object. I usually perform Data Pump jobs with a user that has DBA granted to it (so I don't need to bother with granting access).

Taking an Export

When the directory object and grants are in place, you can use Data Pump to export information from a database. DBAs typically use exports for point-in-time backups of data and metadata. You can use these exports to either restore database objects or move data to different database environments. Suppose you recently created a table and populated it with data:

```
SQL> create table inv(inv_id number);
SQL> insert into inv values (123);
```

Now, you want to export the table. This example uses the previously created directory named DP_DIR. Data Pump uses the directory path specified by the directory object as the location on disk to write the dump file and log file:

```
$ expdp darl/foo directory=dp_dir tables=inv dumpfile=exp.dmp logfile=exp.log
```

The expdp job creates a file named exp.dmp in the /oradump directory that contains the information required to re-create the INV table and populate it with data as of the time the export was taken. In addition, a log file named exp.log is created in the /oradump directory that contains all the logging information associated with this export job.

If you don't specify a dump-file name, Data Pump creates a file named expdat.dmp. If a file named expdat.dmp already exists in the directory, then Data Pump throws an error. If you don't specify a log-file name, then Data Pump creates one named export.log. If a file already exists (named export.log), then Data Pump overwrites it.

Importing Data

One of the key reasons to export data is so that you can re-create database objects in other environments. Data Pump import uses an export dump file as its input and re-creates database objects contained in the export file. The procedure for importing is similar to exporting:

1. Create a database-directory object that points to an operating-system directory that you want to write/read Data Pump files to/from.

2. Grant read, write on the directory to the database user running the export or import.

3. From the operating system prompt, run the impdp command.

Suppose you accidentally drop the INV table that was previously created:

```
SQL> drop table inv purge;
```

You now want to re-create the INV table from the previous export. This example uses the same directory object that was created previously:

```
$ impdp darl/foo directory=dp_dir dumpfile=exp.dmp logfile=inv.log
```

You should now have the INV table re-created and populated with data as it was at the time of the export.

SECURITY ISSUES WITH THE OLD EXP UTILITY

The idea behind creating directory objects and then granting specific I/O access to the physical storage location is that you can more securely administer which users have the capability to generate read and write activities when normally they wouldn't have permissions. With the legacy exp utility, any user that has access to the tool by default has access to write or read a file to which the owner (usually oracle) of the Oracle binaries has access. It's conceivable that a malicious non-oracle operating-system user can attempt to run the exp utility to purposely overwrite a critical database file. For example, the following command can be run by any non-oracle operating-system user with execute access to the exp utility:

```
$ exp heera/foo file=/oradata04/SCRKDV12/users01.dbf
```

The exp process runs as the oracle operating-system user and therefore has read and write operating-system privileges on any oracle owned datafiles. In this exp example, if the users01.dbf file is a live database datafile, it's overwritten and rendered worthless. This can cause catastrophic damage to your database.

To prevent such catastrophes, with Oracle Data Pump, you first have to create a database object directory that maps to a specific directory and then additionally assign read and write privileges to that directory per user. This solves the security issues that exist with the old exp utility.

Interactive Command Mode

Data Pump provides an interactive command mode that allows you to monitor the status of a Data Pump job and modify on-the-fly a number of job characteristics. The interactive command mode is most useful for long-running Data Pump operations. In this mode, you can also stop, re-start, or terminate a currently running job. Each of these activities is discussed in the following subsections.

Entering Interactive Command Mode

There are two ways to get to the interactive command-mode prompt:

- Press Ctrl+C in a Data Pump job that you started via expdp or impdp.
- Use the ATTACH parameter to attach to a currently running job

When you run a Data Pump job from the command line, you're placed in the command-line mode. You should see output displayed to your terminal as a job progresses. If you want to exit command-line mode, press Ctrl+C. This places you in the interactive command-interface mode. For an export job, the prompt is

Export>

Type in the HELP command to view the export interactive commands available (see Table 13–1 for a description):

Export> help

Type EXIT to leave interactive command mode:

Export> exit

You should now be at the operating-system prompt.

Table 13–1. Export Interactive Commands

Command	Description
ADD_FILE	Adds files to the export dump set.
CONTINUE_CLIENT	Continues with interactive client mode.
EXIT_CLIENT	Exits the client session and returns to the operating-system prompt. Leaves the current job running.
FILESIZE	Defines file size for any subsequently created dump files.
HELP	Displays interactive export commands.
KILL_JOB	Terminates the current job.
PARALLEL	Increases or decreases the degree of parallelism.
START_JOB	Restarts the attached job.
STATUS	Displays the status of the currently attached job.
STOP_JOB [=IMMEDIATE]	Stops a job from processing (you can later restart it). Using the IMMEDIATE parameter quickly stops the job, but there may be some incomplete tasks.

You can press Ctrl+C for either an export or import job. For an import job, the interactive command-mode prompt is

Import>

To view all commands available, type HELP:

Import> help

The interactive command-mode import commands are summarized in table 13–2.

Table 13–2. Import Interactive Commands

Command	Description
CONTINUE_CLIENT	Continues with interactive logging mode.
EXIT_CLIENT	Exits the client session and returns to the operating-system prompt. Leaves the current job running.
HELP	Displays the available interactive commands.
KILL_JOB	Terminates the job it's currently connected to in the client.
PARALLEL	Increases or decreases the degree of parallelism.
START_JOB	Restarts a previously stopped job. START_JOB=SKIP_CURRENT restarts the job and skips any operations that were active when the job was stopped.
STATUS	Specifies the frequency at which the job status is monitored. Default mode is 0; the client reports job status changes whenever available in this mode.
STOP_JOB [=IMMEDIATE]	Stops a job from processing (you can later restart it). Using the IMMEDIATE parameter quickly stops the job, but there may be some incomplete tasks.

Type EXIT to leave the Data Pump status utility:

Import> exit

You should now be at the operating-system prompt.

Attaching to a Running Job

One powerful feature of Data Pump is that you can attach to a currently running job and view its progress and status. If you have DBA privileges, you can even attach to a job if you aren't the owner. You can attach to either an import or an export job via the ATTACH parameter.

Before you attach to a job, you must first determine the Data Pump job name (and owner name if you're not the owner of the job). Run the following SQL query to display currently running jobs:

```
SQL> select owner_name, operation, job_name, state from dba_datapump_jobs;
```

Here's some sample output:

```
OWNER_NAME        OPERATION         JOB_NAME              STATE
--------------    --------------    --------------------  ---------------
DARL              IMPORT            SYS_IMPORT_SCHEMA_02   EXECUTING
DARL              IMPORT            SYS_IMPORT_SCHEMA_01   NOT RUNNING
```

In this example, you're the owner of the job, so you use the ATTACH parameter without prepending the owner name to it. This is an import job, so you use the impdp command to attach to the job name SYS_IMPORT_SCHEMA_02:

```
$ impdp darl/engdev attach=sys_import_schema_02
```

If you aren't the owner of the job, you attach to the job by specifying the owner name and the job name:

```
$ impdp system/foobar attach=darl.sys_import_schema_02
```

You should now see the Data Pump command-line prompt:

```
Import>
```

Type STATUS to view the status of the currently attached job:

```
Import> status
```

Stopping and Restarting a Job

If you have a currently running Data Pump job that you want to temporarily stop, you can do so by first attaching to the interactive command mode. You may want to stop a job to resolve space issues or performance issues and then, after resolving the issues, restart the job. This example attaches to an import job:

```
$ impdp darl/foo attach=sys_import_table_01
```

Now, stop the job using the STOP_JOB parameter:

```
Import> stop_job
```

You should see this output:

```
Are you sure you wish to stop this job ([yes]/no):
```

Type YES to proceed with stopping the job. You can also specify that the job be stopped immediately:

```
Import> stop_job=immediate
```

When you stop a job with the IMMEDIATE option, there may be some incomplete tasks associated with the job. To restart a job, attach to interactive command mode and issue the START_JOB command:

```
Import> start_job
```

If you want to resume logging job output to your terminal, issue the CONTINUE_CLIENT command:

```
Import> continue_client
```

Terminating a Data Pump Job

You can instruct Data Pump to permanently kill an export or import job. First, attach to the job in interactive command mode, and then issue the KILL_JOB command:

```
Import> kill_job
```

You should be prompted with the following:

```
Are you sure you wish to stop this job ([yes]/no):
```

Type YES to permanently kill the job. Data Pump unceremoniously kills the job and drops the associated status table from the user running the export or import.

Tips for Getting Started

This section describes some common Data Pump features that I regularly use. These techniques can assist you in minimizing command-line errors and help verify what was exported or what objects and metadata are imported.

Use a Parameter File

Instead of typing commands on the command line, in many situations it's preferable to store the commands in a file and then reference the file when executing Data Pump export or import. Using parameter files makes tasks more repeatable and less prone to errors. You can place the commands in a file once and then reference that file multiple times.

Additionally, some of the Data Pump commands (like FLASHBACK_TIME) require the use of quotation marks; in these situations, it's sometimes hard to predict how the operating system will interpret the quotation marks. Whenever a command requires quotation marks, it's highly preferable to use a parameter file.

To use a parameter file, first create an operating text file that contains the commands you want to use to control the behavior of your job. This example uses the Linux/Unix vi command to create a text file named imp.par:

```
$ vi imp.par
```

Now, place the following commands in the imp.par file:

```
userid=darl/foo
directory=dp
dumpfile=invp.dmp
logfile=invp.log
tables=f_sales
```

Next, reference the parameter file via the PARFILE command-line option:

```
$ impdp parfile=pfile.ctl
```

Data Pump import processes the parameters in the file as if they were typed on the command line. If you find yourself repeatedly typing the same commands, then consider using a parameter file to increase your efficiency.

Estimating the Size of Export Jobs

If you're about to export a large amount of data, you can estimate the size of the file that Data Pump creates before you run the export. You may want to do this because you're concerned about the amount of space an export job needs.

To estimate the size, use the ESTIMATE_ONLY parameter. This example estimates the size of the export file for an entire database:

```
$ expdp dbauser/foo estimate_only=y full=y logfile=n
```

Here's a snippet of the output:

```
Estimate in progress using BLOCKS method...
Processing object type DATABASE_EXPORT/SCHEMA/TABLE/TABLE_DATA
.  estimated "REP_MV"."REG_QUEUE_REP"                   9.606 GB
.  estimated "REP_MV"."CWP_USER_PROFILE"                2.589 GB
.  estimated "REP_MV"."PRODUCT_INSTANCES_MV"     1.620 GB
.  estimated "REP_MV"."ROLES_MV"                                1.550 GB
.  estimated "STAR2"."F_DOWNLOADS":"DOWN_P_5"      1.450 GB
.  estimated "STAR2"."F_DOWNLOADS":"DOWN_P_11"     1.414 GB
```

Similarly, you can specify a schema name to get an estimate of the size required to export a user:

```
$ expdp dbauser/foo estimate_only=y schemas=star2 logfile=n
```

Here's an example of estimating the size required for two tables:

```
$ expdp dbauser/foo estimate_only=y tables=star2.f_downloads,star2.f_installations \
logfile=n
```

Listing the Contents of Dump Files

Data Pump has a very robust method of creating a file that contains all the SQL that's executed when an import job runs. Data Pump uses the DBMS_METADATA package to create the DDL that you can use to re-create objects in the Data Pump dump file.

Use the SQLFILE option of Data Pump import to list the contents of a Data Pump export file. This example creates a file named expfull.sql that contains the SQL statements that the import process calls (the file is placed in the directory defined by the DPUMP_DIR2 directory object):

```
$ impdp hr/hr DIRECTORY=dpump_dir1 DUMPFILE=expfull.dmp \
SQLFILE=dpump_dir2:expfull.sql
```

In the previous command, if you don't specify a separate directory (like dpump_dir2 in this example), then the SQL file is written to the location specified in the DIRECTORY option.

■ Tip You must run the previous command as a user with DBA privileges or the schema that performed the Data Pump export. Otherwise, you get an empty SQL file without the expected SQL statements in it.

When you use the SQLFILE option with an import, the impdp process doesn't import any data. It only creates a file that contains the SQL commands that would be run by the import process. It's sometimes handy to generate a SQL file for the following reasons:

- To preview and verify the SQL statements before running the import

- To manually run the SQL to pre-create database objects

- To create a DDL file that you can later inspect to see if there are differences in users from exports at different points in time

USING EXP/IMP TO RE-CREATE DDL

With the old exp/imp utilities, you can list the contents of the dump file in two different ways. First, you can use the INDEXFILE parameter with the imp utility. The following example uses imp to generate a file named tabind.sql from a file created by the exp utility:

```
$ imp dbauser/foo file=expdat.dmp indexfile=tabind.sql full=y
```

The previous command doesn't import anything. It only creates a file named tabind.sql containing commented-out SQL statements with table- and index-creation statements for any objects contained in the expdat.dmp file.

One issue with creating a SQL file with the INDEXFILE command is that it can be tedious to sort through the output file and un-comment-out the commented lines. The other issue is that the output file only contains SQL statements to create tables and indexes (and you may want to see the DDL for other database objects).

Another technique you can use to capture the DDL of an export file is the imp utility's SHOW parameter:

```
$ imp dbauser/foo file=expdat.dmp show=y log=contents.sql
```

The contents.sql file has all the SQL you need to re-create the objects in the dump file. However, you still need to modify the output file to take out non-SQL statements or unwanted text.

If you're using Oracle Database 10*g* or higher, use Data Pump's SQLFILE parameter to create the DDL for database objects. The SQLFILE parameter provides much cleaner and immediately usable DDL files (than the imp legacy utility).

Transferring Data

One major way you can use Data Pump is to copy data from one database to another. Often, the source and destination databases may be located in data centers thousands of miles apart. Data Pump offers several powerful features for efficiently copying data:

- Network link

- Copying datafiles (transportable tablespaces)

- External tables (see Chapter 14)

Using a network link allows you to take an export and import it into the destination database without having to create a dump file. This is a very efficient way of moving data.

Oracle also provides the transportable tablespace feature, which lets you copy the datafiles from a source database to the destination and then use Data Pump to transfer the associated metadata. These two techniques are described in this section.

▪ Note See Chapter 14 for a discussion of using external tables to transfer data.

Exporting and Importing Directly Across the Network

Sometimes you need to create a testing database and load it with production data. In scenarios like this, the production box is usually located remotely from the development box. Data Pump provides you the ability to take an export and directly import it into your target database without creating any intermediate dump files. This is a fast and efficient way to create new environments from existing environments.

An example will help illustrate how this works. For this example, the production database users are STAR2, CIA_APP, and CIA_SEL. You want to move these users into a testing database and name them STAR_JUL, CIA_APP_JUL, and CIA_SEL_JUL.

This task requires the following high-level steps:

1. Create users in the destination database to be imported into. Here's a sample script that creates the users in the testing database:

```
define star_user=star_jul
define star_user_pwd=star_jul_pwd
define cia_app_user=cia_jul_dec
define cia_app_user_pwd=cia_app_jul_pwd
define cia_sel_user=cia_sel_jul
define cia_sel_user_pwd=cia_sel_jul_pwd
--
create user &&star_user identified by &&star_user_pwd;
grant connect,resource to &&star_user;
alter user &&star_user default tablespace dim_data;
--
create user &&cia_app_user identified by &&cia_app_user_pwd;
grant connect,resource to &&cia_app_user;
alter user &&cia_app_user default tablespace cia_data;
--
create user &&cia_sel_user identified by &&cia_app_user_pwd;
grant connect,resource to &&cia_app_user;
alter user &&cia_sel_user default tablespace cia_data;
```

2. Create a database link in your testing database that points to your production database. The remote user referenced in the CREATE DATABASE LINK statement has the DBA role granted to it in the production database. Here's a sample CREATE DATABASE LINK script:

```
create database link dk
connect to darl identified by foobar
using 'dwdb1:1522/dwrep1';
```

3. Create a directory that points to the location where you want your log file to go:

```
SQL> create or replace directory engdev as '/orahome/oracle/ddl/engdev';
```

4. Run the import command on the testing box. This command references the remote database via the NETWORK_LINK parameter. This command also instructs Data Pump to map the production database user names to the newly created users in the testing database.

```
$ impdp darl/engdev directory=engdev network_link=dk \
schemas='STAR2,CIA_APP,CIA_SEL' \
remap_schema=STAR2:STAR_JUL,CIA_APP:CIA_APP_JUL,CIA_SEL:CIA_SEL_JUL \
parallel=4
```

This technique allows you to move large amounts of data between disparate databases without having to create or copy any dump files or datafiles. This is a very powerful Data Pump feature that lets you quickly and efficiently transfer data.

If you don't have Oracle Net connectivity between the two databases, then the steps to accomplish the same task are as follows:

1. Export the production database.

2. Copy the dump file to the testing database.

3. Import the dump file into the testing database.

Copying Datafile(s)

Oracle provides a mechanism for copying datafiles from one database to another in conjunction with using Data Pump to transport the associated metadata. This is known as the *transportable tablespace* feature. The amount of time this takes depends on how long it takes you to copy the datafiles to the destination server. This technique is appropriate for moving data in decision-support systems and data-warehousing environments.

Follow these steps to transport tablespaces:

1. Ensure that the tablespace is self-contained. These are some common violations of the self-contained rule:

   • An index in one tablespace can't point to a table in another tablespace that isn't in the set of tablespaces being transported.

   • A foreign-key constraint is defined on a table in one tablespace that references a primary-key constraint on a table in a tablespace that isn't in the set of tablespaces being transported.

Run the following check to see if the set of tablespaces being transported violates any of the self-contained rules:

```
SQL> exec dbms_tts.transport_set_check('INV_DATA,INV_INDEX', TRUE);
```

Now, see if Oracle detected any violations:

```
SQL> select * from transport_set_violations;
```

If you don't have any violations, you should see:

```
no rows selected
```

2. Make the tablespaces being transported read-only:

```
SQL> alter tablespace inv_data read only;
SQL> alter tablespace inv_index read only;
```

3. Use Data Pump to export the metadata for the tablespaces being transported:

```
$ expdp darl/foo directory=dp dumpfile=trans.dmp \
transport_tablespaces=INV_DATA,INV_INDEX
```

4. Copy the Data Pump export dump file to the destination server.

5. Copy the datafile(s) to the destination database. Place the files in the directory where you want them in the destination database server. The filename and directory path must match the import command used in the next step.

6. Import the metadata into the destination database. Use the following parameter file to import the metadata for the datafiles being transported:

```
userid=darl/foo
directory=dp
dumpfile=trans.dmp
transport_datafiles=/ora01/dbfile/O11R2/inv_data01.dbf,
/ora01/dbfile/O11R2/inv_index01.dbf
```

If everything goes well, you should see some output indicating success:

```
Processing object type TRANSPORTABLE_EXPORT/CONSTRAINT/REF_CONSTRAINT
Processing object type TRANSPORTABLE_EXPORT/POST_INSTANCE/PLUGTS_BLK
Job "DARL"."SYS_IMPORT_TRANSPORTABLE_01" successfully completed at 11:24:01
```

If the datafiles that are being transported have a different block size than the destination database, then you must modify your initialization file (or use an ALTER SYSTEM command) and add a buffer pool that contains the block size of the source database. For example, to add a 16KB buffer cache, place this in the initialization file:

```
db_16k_cache_size=200M
```

The transportable tablespace mechanism allows you to quickly move datafiles between databases, even if the databases use different block sizes or have different endian formats. This section doesn't discuss all the details involved with transportable tablespaces; the focus in this chapter is showing how to use Data Pump to transport data. For complete details on transportable tablespaces, refer to the *Oracle Database Administrator's Guide* available on OTN.

▓ Note To generate transportable tablespaces, you must use Oracle Enterprise Edition. You can use other editions of Oracle to import transportable tablespaces.

Exporting and Importing Tablespaces and Datafiles

Data Pump contains some flexible features for exporting and importing tablespaces and datafiles. This section shows Data Pump techniques that you can use when working with these important database objects.

Exporting Tablespace Metadata

Sometimes you want to replicate environments—say, a production environment into a testing environment. One of the first tasks is to replicate the tablespaces. You can use Data Pump to pull out just the DDL required to re-create the tablespaces for an environment:

```
$ expdp darl/foo directory=dp dumpfile=phredstg.dmp content=metadata_only full=y \
include=tablespace
```

The FULL parameter instructs Data Pump to export everything in the database. When you also specify INCLUDE, Data Pump exports only those objects. In this scenario, the dump file only has information in it regarding tablespaces.

Now you can use the SQLFILE parameter to view the DDL associated with the tablespaces that were exported:

```
$ impdp darl/foo directory=dp dumpfile=phredstg.dmp sqlfile=tbsp.sql
```

Recall that when you use the SQLFILE parameter, nothing is imported. The previous command only creates a file named tbsp.sql that contains SQL statements. You can modify the DDL and run it in the destination database environment; or, if nothing needs to change, you can directly use the dump file by importing it into the destination database.

Specifying Different Datafile Paths and Names

When you're exporting and then importing, sometimes you import tablespaces into a database where the directory structures are different from the original database. On the import step, the REMAP_DATAFILE allows you to seamlessly change the underlying names of datafiles. Here's a parameter file that contains the remapping statements:

```
userid=darl/foo
directory=dp
dumpfile=phredstg.dmp
full=y
include=tablespace:"like 'TBSP%'"
remap_datafile="'/ora01/dbfile/O11R2/tbsp101.dbf':'/ora02/O11R2/tb1.dbf'"
remap_datafile="'/ora01/dbfile/O11R2/tbsp201.dbf':'/ora02/O11R2/tb2.dbf'"
remap_datafile="'/ora01/dbfile/O11R2/tbsp301.dbf':'/ora02/O11R2/tb3.dbf'"
```

When Data Pump creates the tablespaces, for any paths that match the first part of the string (to the left of the colon [:]), the string is replaced with the text to the right of the colon.

Changing Segment and Storage Attributes

When importing, you can alter the storage attributes of a table by using the TRANSFORM parameter. The general syntax for this parameter is

```
TRANSFORM=transform_name:value[:object_type]
```

When you use SEGMENT_ATTRIBUTES:n for the transformation name, you can remove the following segment attributes during an import:

- Physical attributes
- Storage attributes

- Tablespaces

- Logging

Here's an example that removes the segment attributes:

```
$ impdp darl/foo directory=dp dumpfile=inv.dmp transform=segment_attributes:n
```

You can remove just the storage clause by using STORAGE:n:

```
$ impdp darl/foo directory=dp dumpfile=inv.dmp transform=storage:n
```

Importing into a Different Tablespace from the Original

Sometimes you're exporting out of one database and want to import objects into another database, but you want to change the tablespaces for the tables and indexes—in other words, create the objects in the destination database but in tablespaces different than the source database configuration.

This example remaps the user as well as the tablespaces. The original user and tablespaces are HEERA and TBSP1. This command imports the TICKET table into the CHAYA user and the V_DATA tablespace:

```
$ impdp darl/foo directory=dp dumpfile=rm.dmp remap_schema=HEERA:CHAYA \
remap_tablespace=TBSP1:V_DATA tables=heera.ticket
```

The REMAP_TABLESPACE feature doesn't re-create tablespaces. It only instructs Data Pump to place objects in different tablespaces (from where they were originally exported). When importing, if the tablespace that you're placing the object in doesn't exist, Data Pump throws an error.

Changing the Size of Datafiles

You can change the size of the datafiles when importing by using the TRANSFORM parameter with the PCTSPACE option. For example, if you want the tablespaces to be created at 20 percent of the original size, specify the following:

```
userid=darl/foo
directory=dp
dumpfile=phredstg.dmp
full=y
include=tablespace:"like 'TBSP%'"
transform=pctspace:20
```

The tablespaces are created with datafiles 20 percent of their original size. The extent allocation sizes are also 20 percent of their original definition. This feature is useful when used to export production data and then import it into a smaller database. In these scenarios, you may be filtering out some of the production data via the SAMPLE parameter or QUERY parameters (discussed in the next section).

Filtering Data and Objects

Data Pump has a vast array of mechanisms to filter data and metadata. You can influence what is excluded or included in a Data Pump export or import in the following ways:

- Use the QUERY parameter to export or import subsets of data.

- Use the SAMPLE parameter to export a percentage of the rows in a table.

- Use the CONTENT parameter to exclude or include data and metadata.

- Use the EXCLUDE parameter to specifically name items to be excluded.

- Use the INCLUDE parameter to name the items to be included (thereby excluding other non-dependent items not included in the list).

- Use parameters like SCHEMA to specify that you only want a subset of the database's objects (those that belong to the specified user or users).

Examples of each of these techniques are described in the following subsections.

 Note You can't use EXCLUDE and INCLUDE at the same time. These parameters are mutually exclusive.

Specifying a Query

You can use the QUERY parameter to instruct Data Pump to write to a dump file only rows that meet a certain criterion. You may want to do this if you're re-creating a test environment and only need subsets of the data. Keep in mind that this technique is unaware of any foreign-key constraints that may be in place, so you can't blindly restrict the data sets without considering parent/child relationships.

It has this general syntax for including a query:

```
QUERY = [schema.][table_name:] query_clause
```

The query clause can be any valid SQL clause. The query must be enclosed by either double quotes or single quotes. I recommend using double quotes because you may need single quotes embedded in the query to handle VARCHAR data. Also, you should use a parameter file so that there is no confusion about how the operating system interprets the quotation marks.

This example uses a parameter file and limits the rows exported for two tables. Here's the parameter file used when exporting:

```
userid=darl/foo
directory=dp
dumpfile=inv.dmp
tables=inv,reg
query=inv:"WHERE inv_desc='Book'"
query=reg:"WHERE reg_id <=20"
```

Say you place the previous lines of code in a file named inv.par. The export job references the parameter file as shown:

```
$ expdp parfile=inv.par
```

The resulting dump file only contains rows filtered by the QUERY parameters. Again, be mindful of any parent/child relationships, and ensure that what gets exported won't violate any constraints on the import.

You can also specify a query when importing data. Here's a parameter file that limits the rows imported into the INV table based on the INV_ID column:

```
userid=darl/foo
directory=dp
dumpfile=inv.dmp
tables=inv,reg
query=inv:"WHERE inv_id > 10"
```

The previous text is placed in a file named inv2.par and is referenced during the import as follows:

```
$ impdp parfile=inv2.par
```

Only the rows in the INV table that are filtered via the query are imported.

Exporting a Percentage of the Data

When exporting, the SAMPLE parameter instructs Data Pump to retrieve a certain percentage of rows based on a number you provide. Data Pump doesn't keep track of parent/child relationships when exporting. Therefore, this approach doesn't work well when you have tables linked via foreign-key constraints and you're trying to randomly select a percentage of rows.

Here's the general syntax for this parameter:

```
SAMPLE=[[schema_name.]table_name:]sample_percent
```

For example, if you want to export 10 percent of the data in a table, do so as follows:

```
$ expdp darl/foo directory=dp tables=inv sample=10 dumpfile=inv.dmp
```

This next example exports two tables, but only 30 percent of the REG table's data:

```
$ expdp darl/foo directory=dp tables=inv,reg sample=reg:30 dumpfile=inv.dmp
```

■ **Note** The SAMPLE parameter is only valid for exports.

Excluding Objects from the Export File

For export, the EXLUDE parameter instructs Data Pump to not export specified objects (whereas the INCLUDE parameter instructs Data Pump to only include specific objects in the export file). The EXCLUDE parameter has this general syntax:

```
EXCLUDE=object_type[:name_clause] [, ...]
```

The OBJECT_TYPE refers to a database object like TABLE or INDEX. To see which object types can be filtered, view the OBJECT_PATH column of DATABASE_EXPORT_OBJECTS, SCHEMA_EXPORT_OBJECTS, or TABLE_EXPORT_OBJECTS. For example, if you want to view what schema-level objects can be filtered, run this query:

```
SELECT
 object_path
FROM schema_export_objects
WHERE object_path NOT LIKE '%/%';
```

Here's a small snippet of the output:

```
OBJECT_PATH
------------------
STATISTICS
SYNONYM
SYSTEM_GRANT
TABLE
TABLESPACE_QUOTA
TRIGGER
```

The EXCLUDE parameter instructs Data Pump export to filter out specific objects from the export. For example, say you're exporting a table but want to exclude the indexes and grants:

```
$ expdp darl/foo directory=dp dumpfile=inv.dmp tables=inv exclude=index,grant
```

You can filter at a more granular level by using NAME_CLAUSE. The NAME_CLAUSE option of EXCLUDE allows you to specify a SQL filter. To exclude indexes that have names that start with the string "INV", you use the following:

```
exclude=index:"LIKE 'INV%'"
```

The previous line requires that you use quotation marks; in these scenarios, I recommend that you use a parameter file. This is because when you filter by the name of the object, it uses quotation marks. Sometimes it's hard to predict how the operating system will interpret quotation marks on the command line. Here's a parameter file that contains an EXCLUDE clause:

```
userid=darl/foo
directory=dp
dumpfile=inv.dmp
tables=inv
exclude=index:"LIKE 'INV%'"
```

A few aspects of the EXCLUDE clause may seem counterintuitive. For example, consider the following export parameter file:

```
userid=darl/foo
directory=dp
dumpfile=sch.dmp
exclude=schema:"='HEERA'"
```

If you attempt to exclude a user in this manner, an error is thrown. This is because the default mode of export is SCHEMA level, and Data Pump can't exclude and include a schema at the same time. If you want to exclude a user from an export file, specify the FULL mode and exclude the user:

```
userid=darl/foo
directory=dp
dumpfile=sch.dmp
exclude=schema:"='HEERA'"
full=y
```

Excluding Statistics

If you want to exclude statistics from your export job, you can do so using the EXCLUDE parameter. Here's an example:

```
$ expdp darl/foo directory=dp dumpfile=invp.dmp tables=f_sales exclude=statistics
```

By default, when you export a table object, any statistics are also exported. You can prevent statistics from being imported via the EXCLUDE parameter:

```
$ impdp darl/foo directory=dp dumpfile=invp.dmp tables=f_sales exclude=statistics
```

When importing, if you attempt to exclude statistics from a dump file that didn't originally include the statistics, then you receive this error:

```
ORA-39168: Object path STATISTICS was not found.
```

You also receive this error if the objects in the exported dump file never had statistics generated for them.

Including Only Specific Objects in an Export File

Use the INCLUDE parameter to include only certain database objects in the export file. The following example only exports the procedures and functions that a user owns:

```
$ expdp darl/foo dumpfile=proc.dmp directory=datapump include=procedure,function
```

The proc.dmp file that is created only contains the DDL required to re-create any procedures and functions the user owns.

When using INCLUDE, you can also specify that only specific PL/SQL objects should be exported:

```
$ expdp darl/foo directory=datapump dumpfile=ss.dmp \
include=function:\"=\'IS_DATE\'\"
```

When you're only exporting specific PL/SQL objects, because of the issues with having to escape quote marks on the operating-system command line, I recommend using a parameter file. When you use a parameter file, you don't have escape the quote marks. The following shows the contents of a parameter file that exports specific objects:

```
directory=datapump
dumpfile=pl.dmp
include=function:"='ISDATE'",procedure:"='DEPTREE_FILL'"
```

If you specify an object that doesn't exist, Data Pump throws an error but continues with the export operation:

```
ORA-39168: Object path FUNCTION was not found.
```

Exporting Table, Index, Constraint, and Trigger DDL

Suppose you want to export the DDL associated with tables, indexes, constraints, and triggers in your database. To do this, use the FULL export mode and only include tables:

```
$ expdp darl/foo directory=dp dumpfile=phredstg.dmp content=metadata_only full=y \
include=table
```

When you export an object, Data Pump also exports any dependent objects. So, when you export a table, you also get indexes, constraints, and triggers associated with the table.

Excluding Objects from Import

In general, you can use the same techniques used to filter objects in exports to exclude objects from being imported. Use the EXCLUDE parameter to exclude objects from being imported. For example, to exclude triggers and procedures from being imported:

```
$ impdp darl/foo dumpfile=d.dmp directory=dp exclude=TRIGGER,PROCEDURE
```

You can further refine what is excluded by adding a SQL clause. For example, say you want to not import triggers that begin with the letter *B*. Here's what the parameter file looks like:

```
userid=darl/foo
directory=dp
dumpfile=h.dmp
schemas=HEERA
exclude=trigger:"like 'B%'"
```

Including Objects in Import

You can use the INCLUDE parameter to reduce what is imported. Suppose you have a schema from which you want to import tables that begin with the letter *A*. Here's the parameter file:

```
userid=darl/foo
directory=dp
dumpfile=h.dmp
schemas=HEERA
include=table:"like 'A%'"
```

If you place the previous text in a file name h.par, then the parameter file can be invoked as follows:

```
$ impdp parfile=h.par
```

In this example, the HEERA schema must already exist. Only tables that start with the letter *A* are imported.

Common Data Pump Tasks

This section contains common features you can use with Data Pump. Many of these features are standard parts of Data Pump, such as creating a consistent export or taking action when imported objects already exist in the database. Other features, such as compression and encryption, require the Enterprise Edition of Oracle and/or an extra license. I'll point out these requirements (if relevant) for the Data Pump element being described.

Creating a Consistent Export

A *consistent* export means that all data in the export file is consistent as of a time or an system change number (SCN). When you're exporting an active database with many parent-child tables, then you should ensure that you get a consistent snapshot of the data. You create a consistent export by using either the FLASHBACK_SCN or FLASHBACK_TIME parameter.

This example uses the FLASHBACK_SCN parameter to take an export. To determine the current value of the SCN of your dataset, issue this query:

```
SQL> select current_scn from v$database;
```

Here's some typical output:

```
CURRENT_SCN
----------------
 8400741902387
```

Next, export using the FLASHBACK_SCN parameter:

```
$ expdp darl/foo directory=dp flashback_scn=8400741902387
```

The previous export command ensures that all data exported is consistent with any committed transactions in the database as of SCN 8400741902387.

When you use the FLASHBACK_SCN parameter, Data Pump ensures that the data in the export file is consistent as of the specified SCN. This means any transactions committed after the specified SCN aren't included in the export file.

▓ **Note** If you use the NETWORK_LINK parameter in conjunction with FLASHBACK_SCN, then the export is taken with the SCN consistent with the database referenced in the database link.

You can also use FLASHBACK_TIME to specify that the export file should be created with consistent committed transactions as of a specified time. When using FLASHBACK_TIME, Oracle determines the SCN that most closely matches the time specified and uses that to produce an export consistent with that SCN. The syntax for using FLASHBACK_TIME is as follows:

```
FLASHBACK_TIME="TO_TIMESTAMP{<value>}"
```

For some operating systems, double quotes directly on the command line must be escaped by a backslash character (\), because the operating system treats the double quotes as special characters. Due to issues regarding how operating systems treat quote marks, it's much more straightforward to use a parameter file. Here are the contents of a parameter file that uses FLASHBACK_TIME:

```
directory=datapump
content=metadata_only
dumpfile=exp.dmp
flashback_time="to_timestamp('26-oct-2009 07:03:00','dd-mon-yyyy hh24:mi:ss')"
```

Depending on your operating system, the command-line version of the previous example must be specified as follows:

```
flashback_time=\"to_timestamp\(\'26-oct-2009 07:03:00\',
```

```
\'dd-mon-yyyy hh24:mi:ss\'\)\"
```

This line of code should be specified on one line. It's wrapped on two lines in this book to fit on the page.

You can't specify both FLASHBACK_SCN and FLASHBACK_TIME when taking an export; these two parameters are mutually exclusive. If you attempt to use both parameters at the same time, Data Pump throws the following error message and halts the export job:

```
ORA-39050: parameter FLASHBACK_TIME is incompatible with parameter FLASHBACK_SCN
```

■ **Note** The FLASHBACK_SCN and FLASHBACK_TIME parameters are only applicable to the Oracle flashback query functionality. These parameters aren't applicable to flashback database or flashback drop.

Importing When Objects Already Exist

When export and importing data, often you import into a schema that already has the objects created (tables, indexes, and so on). In this situation, you should import the data but instruct Data Pump to not try to create already-existing objects.

You can achieve this with the TABLE_EXISTS_ACTION and CONTENT parameters. The next example instructs Data Pump to append data in any tables that already exist via the TABLE_EXISTS_ACTION=APPEND option. Also used is the CONTENT=DATA_ONLY option, which instructs Data Pump to not run any DDL to create objects (only load data):

```
$ impdp darl/foo directory=dk dumpfile=inv.dmp table_exists_action=append \
content=data_only
```

Existing objects aren't modified in any way, and any new data that exists in the dump file is inserted into any tables.

You may wonder what happens if you just use the TABLE_EXISTS_ACTION option and don't combine it with the CONTENT:

```
$ impdp darl/foo directory=dk dumpfile=inv.dmp table_exists_action=append
```

The only difference is that Data Pump attempts to run DDL commands to create objects if they exist. It doesn't stop the job from running, but you see an error message in the output indicating that the object already exists. Here's a snippet of the output for the previous command:

```
ORA-39152: Table "INV_MGMT"."INV" exists. Data will be appended to existing table
but all dependent metadata will be skipped due to table_exists_action of append
```

The default for the TABLE_EXISTS_ACTION parameter is SKIP, unless you also specify the parameter of CONTENT=DATA_ONLY. If you use CONTENT=DATA_ONLY, then the default for TABLE_EXISTS_ACTION is APPEND.

The TABLE_EXISTS_ACTION parameter takes the following options:

- SKIP (default if not combined with CONTENT=DATA_ONLY)

- APPEND (default if combined with CONTENT=DATA_ONLY)

- REPLACE

- TRUNCATE

The SKIP option tells Data Pump to not process the object if it exists. The APPEND option instructs Data Pump to not delete existing data, but rather to add data to the table without modifying any existing data. The REPLACE option instructs Data Pump to drop and re-create objects; this parameter isn't valid when the CONTENT parameter is used with the DATA_ONLY option. The TRUNCATE parameter instructs Data Pump to delete rows from tables via a TRUNCATE statement.

The CONTENT parameter takes the following parameter options:

- ALL (default)

- DATA_ONLY

- METADATA_ONLY

The ALL option instructs Data Pump to load both data and metadata contained in the dump file; this is the default behavior. The DATA_ONLY option instructs Data Pump to load only table data into existing tables; no database objects are created. The METADATA_ONLY option only creates objects; no data is loaded.

▓ Note With the old imp utility, you can instruct the import process to ignore existing objects via the ignore=y option.

Renaming a Table

Starting with Oracle Database 11g, you have the option of renaming a table during import operations. There are many reasons you may want to rename a table when importing it. For example, you may have a table in the target schema that has the same name as the table you want to import. You can rename a table when importing by using the REMAP_TABLE parameter. This example imports the table from the HEERA user INV table to the HEERA user INVEN table:

```
$ impdp darl/foo directory=dk dumpfile=inv.dmp tables=heera.inv \
remap_table=heera.inv:inven
```

Here's the general syntax for renaming a table:

```
REMAP_TABLE=[schema.]old_tablename[.partition]:new_tablename
```

or

```
REMAP_TABLE=[schema.]old_tablename[:partition]:new_tablename
```

Notice that this syntax doesn't allow you to rename a table into a different schema. If you're not careful, you may attempt to do the following (thinking that you're moving a table and renaming it in one operation):

```
$ impdp darl/foo directory=dk dumpfile=inv.dmp tables=heera.inv \
remap_table=heera.inv:scott.inven
```

You end up with a table in the HEERA schema named SCOTT.INVEN. That can be confusing. If you want to import a table into a different schema and rename it at the same time, use REMAP_SCHEMA with the REMAP_TABLE parameters:

```
$ impdp darl/foo directory=dk dumpfile=inv.dmp remap_schema=heera:darl \
tables=heera.inv remap_table=heera.inv:invent
```

■ **Note** The process of renaming a table wasn't entirely bug-free in Oracle Database 11*g* release 1. It's been corrected in Oracle Database 11*g* release 2. See My Oracle Support Note 886762.1 for more details.

Remapping Data

Starting with Oracle Database 11g, when either exporting or importing, you can apply a PL/SQL function to alter a column value. For example, you may have an auditor who needs to look at the data, and one requirement is that you apply a simple obfuscation function to sensitive columns. The data doesn't need to be encrypted, it just needs to be changed enough that the auditor can't readily determine the value of the LAST_NAME column in the CUSTOMERS table.

This example first creates a simple package that is used to obfuscate the data:

```
create or replace package obfus is
  function obf(clear_string varchar2) return varchar2;
  function unobf(obs_string varchar2) return varchar2;
end obfus;
/
--
create or replace package body obfus is
  fromstr varchar2(62) := '0123456789ABCDEFGHIJKLMNOPQRSTUVWXYZ' ||
             'abcdefghijklmnopqrstuvwxyz';
  tostr varchar2(62)   := 'defghijklmnopqrstuvwxyzabc3456789012' ||
             'KLMNOPQRSTUVWXYZABCDEFGHIJ';
--
function obf(clear_string varchar2) return varchar2 is
begin
  return translate(clear_string, fromstr, tostr);
end obf;
--
function unobf(obs_string varchar2) return varchar2 is
begin
  return translate(obs_string, tostr, fromstr);
end unobf;
end obfus;
/
```

Now, when you import the data into the database, you apply the obfuscation function to the LAST_NAME column of the CUSTOMERS table:

```
$ impdp darl/foo directory=dp dumpfile=cust.dmp tables=customers  \
remap_data=customers.last_name:obfus.obf
```

Selecting LAST_NAME from CUSTOMERS shows that it has been imported in an obfuscated manner:

```
SQL> select last_name from customers;
LAST_NAME
------------------
yYZEJ
tOXXSMU
xERX
```

You can manually apply the package's UNOBF function to see the real values of the column:

```
SQL> select obfus.unobf(last_name) from customers;
OBFUS.UNOBF(LAST_NAME)
-------------------------
Lopuz
Gennick
Kuhn
```

Cloning a User

Suppose you need to move a user's objects and data to a new database. As part of the migration, you want to rename the user. First, create an export file that contains the user you want to clone. In this example, the user name is INV:

```
$ expdp darl/foo directory=dp schemas=inv dumpfile=inv.dmp
```

Now you can use Data Pump import to clone the user. You can do this in the database from which the user was exported or in a different database. Use the REMAP_SCHEMA parameter to create a copy of a user. In this example, the INV user is cloned to the INV_DW user:

```
$ impdp darl/foo directory=dp remap_schema=inv:inv_dw dumpfile=inv.dmp
```

This command copies all structures and data in the INV user to the INV_DW user. The resulting INV_DW user is identical in terms of objects to the INV user. The duplicated schema also contains the same password as the schema from which it was copied.

If you just want to duplicate the metadata from one schema to another, use the CONTENT parameter with the METADATA_ONLY option:

```
$ impdp darl/foo remap_schema=inv:inv_dw content=metadata_only dumpfile=inv.dmp
```

The REMAP_SCHEMA parameter provides an efficient way to duplicate a schema with or without the data. During a schema duplication operation, if you want to change the tablespace in which the objects reside, also use the REMAP_TABLESPACE parameter. This allows you to duplicate a schema and also place the objects in a different tablespace than the source objects' tablespaces.

You can also duplicate a user from one database to another without first creating a dump file. To do this, use the NETWORK_LINK parameter. See the prior section in this chapter on Exporting and Importing Directly Across the Network for details on copying data directly from one database to another.

Suppressing a Log File

By default, Data Pump creates a log file when generating an export or an import. If you know that you don't want a log file generated, you can suppress it by specifying the NOLOGFILE parameter. Here's an example:

```
$ expdp heera/foo directory=dk tables=inv nologfile=y
```

If you choose to not create a log file, Data Pump still displays status messages on the output device. In general, I recommend that you create a log file with every Data Pump operation. This gives you an audit trail of your actions.

Using Parallelism

Use the PARALLEL parameter to parallelize a Data Pump job. For example, if you know you have four CPUs on a box, and you want to set the degree of parallelism to 4, use PARALLEL as follows:

```
$ expdp darl/foo parallel=4 dumpfile=exp.dmp directory=datapump full=y
```

To take full advantage of the parallel feature, ensure that you specify multiple files when exporting. The following example creates one file for each thread of parallelism:

```
$ expdp darl/foo parallel=4 dumpfile=exp1.dmp,exp2.dmp,exp3.dmp,exp4.dmp
```

You can also use the %U substitution variable to instruct Data Pump to automatically create dump files to match the degree of parallelism. The %U variable starts at the value 01 and increments as additional dump files are allocated. This example uses the %U variable:

```
$ expdp darl/foo parallel=4 dumpfile=exp%U.dmp
```

Now, say you need to import from the dump files created from an export. You can either individually specify the dump files or, if the dump files were created with the %U variable, use that on import:

```
$ impdp darl/foo parallel=4 dumpfile=exp%U.dmp
```

When using the % U substitution variable, in this example the import process starts by looking for a file with the name of exp01.dmp, then exp02.dmp, and so on.

■ **Tip** Oracle recommends that the degree of parallelism not be set to more than two times the number of CPUs available on the server.

You can also modify the degree of parallelism while the job is running. First, attach in the interactive command mode to the job for which you want to modify the degree of parallelism. Then, use the PARALLEL option. In this example, the job attached to is SYS_IMPORT_TABLE_01:

```
$ impdp darl/foo attach=sys_import_table_01
Import> parallel=6
```

You can check the degree of parallelism via the STATUS command:

```
Import> status
```

Here's some sample output:

```
Job: SYS_IMPORT_TABLE_01
  Operation: IMPORT
  Mode: TABLE
  State: EXECUTING
  Bytes Processed: 0
  Current Parallelism: 6
```

■ **Note** The PARALLEL feature is only available in the Enterprise Edition of the Oracle Database.

Specifying Additional Dump Files

If you run out of space in the primary dump-file location, then you can specify additional dump-file locations on the fly. Use the ADD_FILE command from the interactive command prompt. Here's the basic syntax for adding additional files:

```
ADD_FILE=[directory_object:]file_name [,...]
```

This example adds another output file to an already existing Data Pump export job:

```
Export> add_file=alt2.dmp
```

You can also specify a separate database-directory object:

```
Export> add_file=alt_dir:alt3.dmp
```

Reusing Output File Names

By default, Data Pump doesn't overwrite an existing dump file. For example, the first time you run this job, it will run fine because there is no dump file named inv.dmp in the directory being used:

```
$ expdp heera/foo directory=dk dumpfile=inv.dmp
```

If you attempt to run the previous command again with the same directory and the same dump-file name, this error is thrown:

```
ORA-39000: bad dump file specification
ORA-31641: unable to create dump file "/home/oracle/dp/inv.dmp"
ORA-27038: created file already exists
```

You can either specify a new dump-file name for the export job or use the REUSE_DUMPFILES parameter to direct Data Pump to overwrite an existing dump file. For example:

```
$ expdp heera/foo directory=dk dumpfile=inv.dmp reuse_dumpfiles=y
```

You should now be able to run the Data Pump export regardless of an existing dump file in the output directory with the same name. When you set REUSE_DUMPFILES to a value of y, if Data Pump finds a dump file with the same name, it overwrites the file.

■ **Note** The default value for REUSE_DUMPFILES is n. The REUSE_DUMPFILES parameter is available only in Oracle Database 11*g* or higher.

Creating a Daily DDL File

Sometimes, in database environments, changes occur to database objects in unexpected ways. You may have a developer who somehow obtains the production user passwords and decides to make a change on the fly without telling anybody. Or a DBA may decide not to follow the standard release process and make a change to an object while troubleshooting an issue. These scenarios can be frustrating for production-support DBAs. Whenever there's an issue, the first question raised is, "What changed?"

When you use Data Pump, it's fairly simple to create a file that contains all the DDL to re-create every object in your database. You can instruct Data Pump to export or import just the metadata via the CONTENT=METADATA_ONLY option.

For instance, in a production environment you can set up a daily job to capture this DDL. If there is ever a question about what changed and when, you can go back and compare the DDL in the daily dump files to see exactly what changed and when.

Listed next is a simple shell script that first exports the metadata content from the database and then uses Data Pump import to create a DDL file from that export:

```
#!/bin/bash
# source OS variables
. /var/opt/oracle/oraset DWREP
#
DAY=$(date +%Y_%m_%d)
SID=DWREP
#----------------------------------------------------
# First create export dump file with metadata only
expdp darl/foo dumpfile=${SID}.${DAY}.dmp content=metadata_only \
directory=dwrep_dp full=y logfile=${SID}.${DAY}.log
#----------------------------------------------------
# Now create DDL file from the export dump file.
impdp darl/foo directory=dwrep_dp dumpfile=${SID}.${DAY}.dmp \
SQLFILE=${SID}.${DAY}.sql logfile=${SID}.${DAY}.sql.log
#
exit 0
```

This code listing depends on a database-directory object being created that points to where you want the daily dump file to be written. You may also want to set up another job that periodically deletes any files older than a certain amount of time.

Compressing Output

When you use Data Pump to create large files, you should consider compressing the output. As of Oracle Database 11g, the COMPRESSION parameter can be one of the following values: ALL, DATA_ONLY, METADATA_ONLY, or NONE. If you specify ALL, then both data and metadata are compressed in the output. This example exports one table and compresses both the data and metadata in the output file:

```
$ expdp dbauser/foo tables=locations directory=datapump \
dumpfile=compress.dmp compression=all
```

If you're using Oracle Database 10g, then the COMPRESSION parameter only has the METADATA_ONLY and NONE values.

▨ Note The ALL and DATA_ONLY options of the COMPRESS parameter require a license for the Oracle Advanced Compression option.

Encrypting Data

One potential security issue with Data Pump dump files is that anybody with operating-system access to the output file can search for strings in the file. On Linux/Unix systems, you can do this with the strings command:

```
$ strings inv.dmp | grep -i secret
```

Here's the output for this particular dump file:

```
Secret Data<
top secret data<
corporate secret data<
```

This command allows you to view the contents of the dump file because the data is in regular text and not encrypted. If you require that the data be secured, you can use Data Pump's encryption features.

Data Pump lets you easily encrypt the output of a dump file. This example uses the ENCRYPTION parameter to secure all data and metadata in the output:

```
$ expdp darl/foo encryption=all directory=dp dumpfile=inv.dmp
```

For this command to work, your database must have an encryption wallet in place and open. See the *Oracle Advanced Security Guide* (available on OTN) for more details about how to create and open a wallet.

▨ Note The Data Pump ENCRYPTION parameter requires that you use the Enterprise Edition of Oracle Database 11*g* or higher and also requires a license for the Oracle Advanced Security option.

The ENCRYPTION parameter takes the following options:

- ALL
- DATA_ONLY
- ENCRYPTED_COLUMNS_ONLY
- METADATA_ONLY
- NONE

The ALL option enables encryption for both data and metadata. The DATA_ONLY option encrypts just the data. The ENCRYPTED_COLUMNS_ONLY option specifies that only columns encrypted in the database are written to the dump file in an encrypted format. The METADATA_ONLY option encrypts just metadata in the export file.

Monitoring Data Pump Jobs

When you have long-running Data Pump jobs, you should occasionally check the status of the job to make sure the job hasn't failed, or it's become suspended for some reason, and so on. There are several ways to monitor the status of Data Pump jobs:

- Screen output
- Data Pump log file
- Database alert log
- Querying the status table
- Querying data-dictionary views
- Interactive command-mode status
- Using operating-system utilities' process status ps

The most obvious way to monitor a job is to view the status that Data Pump displays on the screen as the job is running. If you've disconnected from the command mode, then the status is no longer displayed on your screen. In this situation, you must use another technique to monitor a Data Pump job.

Data Pump Log File

By default, Data Pump generates a log file for every job. When you start a Data Pump job, it's a good practice to name a log file that is specific for that job:

```
$ impdp darl/foo directory=dp dumpfile=archive.dmp logfile=archive.log
```

This job creates a file named archive.log that is placed in the directory referenced in the database object DP. If you don't explicitly name a log file, Data Pump import creates one named import.log, and Data Pump export creates one named export.log.

■ **Note** The log file contains the same information you see displayed interactively on your screen when running a Data Pump job.

Data-Dictionary Views

A quick way to determine whether a Data Pump job is running is to check the DBA_DATAPUMP_JOBS view for anything running with a STATE that has an EXECUTING status:

```
select
 job_name
,operation
,job_mode
,state
from dba_datapump_jobs;
```

Here's some sample output:

```
JOB_NAME                    OPERATION            JOB_MODE    STATE
-------------------------   -------------------  ----------  ---------------
SYS_IMPORT_TABLE_04         IMPORT               TABLE       EXECUTING
SYS_IMPORT_FULL_02          IMPORT               FULL        NOT RUNNING
```

You can also query the DBA_DATAPUMP_SESSIONS view for session information via the following query:

```
select
 sid
,serial#
,username
,process
,program
from v$session s,
    dba_datapump_sessions d
where s.saddr = d.saddr;
```

Here's some sample output showing that several Data Pump sessions are in use:

```
    SID    SERIAL# USERNAME               PROCESS          PROGRAM
---------- ---------- --------------------   ---------------  ----------------------
   1049       6451 STAGING                11306            oracle@xengdb (DM00)
   1058      33126 STAGING                11338            oracle@xengdb (DW01)
   1048      50508 STAGING                11396            oracle@xengdb (DW02)
```

Database Alert Log

If a job is taking much longer than you expected, look in the database alert log for any messages similar to this:

```
statement in resumable session 'SYS_IMPORT_SCHEMA_02.1' was suspended due to
ORA-01652: unable to extend temp segment by 64 in tablespace REG_TBSP_3
```

This indicates that a Data Pump import job is suspended and is waiting for space to be added to the REG_TBSP_3 tablespace. After you add space to the tablespace, the Data Pump job automatically resumes processing. By default, a Data Pump job waits two hours for space to be added.

■ Note In addition to writing to the alert log, for each Data Pump job, Oracle creates a trace file in the ADR_HOME/trace directory. This file contains information such as the session ID and when the job started. The trace file is named with the following format: <SID>_dm00_<process_ID>.trc.

Status Table

Every time you start a Data Pump job, a status table is automatically created in the account of the user running the Data Pump job. For export jobs, the table name depends on what type of export job you're running. The table is named with the format SYS_<OPERATION>_<JOB_MODE>_NN, where OPERATION is either EXPORT or IMPORT. JOB_MODE can be FULL, SCHEMA, TABLE, TABLESPACE, and so on.

Here's an example of querying the status table for particulars about a currently running job:

```
select
 name
,object_name
,total_bytes/1024/1024 t_m_bytes
,job_mode
,state
,to_char(last_update, 'dd-mon-yy hh24:mi')
from SYS_IMPORT_TABLE_04
where state='EXECUTING';
```

Interactive Command-Mode Status

A quick way to verify that Data Pump is running a job is to attach in interactive command mode and issue a STATUS command. For example:

```
$ impdp staging/staging_xst attach=SYS_IMPORT_TABLE_04
Import> status
```

Here's some sample output:

```
Job: SYS_IMPORT_TABLE_04
  Operation: IMPORT
  Mode: TABLE
  State: EXECUTING
  Bytes Processed: 0
  Current Parallelism: 4
```

You should see a state of EXECUTING, which indicates that the job is actively running. Other items to inspect in the output are the number of objects processed and bytes processed. Those numbers should increase as the job progresses.

Operating-System Utilities

You can use the process status (ps) operating-system utility to display jobs running on the server. For example, you can search for master and worker processes as follows:

```
$ ps -ef | egrep 'ora_dm|ora_dw' | grep -v egrep
```

Here's some sample output:

```
oracle 29871  717  5 08:26:39 ?       11:42 ora_dw01_STAGE
oracle 29848  717  0 08:26:33 ?        0:08 ora_dm00_STAGE
oracle 29979  717  0 08:27:09 ?        0:04 ora_dw02_STAGE
```

If you run this command multiple times, you should see the processing time (seventh column) increase for one or more of the jobs running. This is a good indicator that Data Pump is still executing and doing work.

Data Pump Legacy Mode

This feature is covered last in this chapter, but it's quite useful especially if you're an old-school DBA. As of Oracle Database 11g release 2, Data Pump allows you to use the old exp and imp utility parameters. This is known as *legacy mode*. You don't have to do anything special to use legacy mode Data Pump. As soon as Data Pump detects a legacy parameter, it attempts to process the parameter as if it were from the old exp/imp utilities. You can even mix and match old legacy parameters with newer parameters. For example:

```
$ expdp darl/foo consistent=y tables=inv directory=dk
```

In the output, Data Pump indicates that it has encountered legacy parameters and gives you the syntax for what it translated the legacy parameter to in Data Pump syntax. For the previous command, here's the output from the Data Pump session that shows what the consistent=y parameter was translated into:

```
Legacy Mode Active due to the following parameters:
Legacy Mode Parameter: "consistent=TRUE" Location: Command Line, Replaced with:
"flashback_time=TO_TIMESTAMP('2010-07-01 08:10:20', 'YYYY-MM-DD HH24:MI:SS')"
```

This feature can be *extremely* handy, especially if you're really familiar with the old legacy syntax and wonder how it's implemented in Data Pump.

I recommend that you try to use the newer Data Pump syntax whenever possible. However, you may run into situations where you have legacy exp/imp jobs and want to continue running the scripts as they are without any modifications.

■ **Note** When Data Pump runs in legacy mode, it doesn't create an old exp/imp formatted file. Data Pump always creates a Data Pump file and can only read Data Pump files.

Data Pump Mapping to the exp Utility

If you're used to the old exp/imp parameters, you may initially be confused by some of the syntax semantics. However, after you use Data Pump, you'll find the newer syntax fairly easy to remember and use. Table 13–3 describes how the legacy export parameters map to Data Pump export.

In many instances, there isn't a one-to-one mapping. Often, Data Pump automatically provides features that used to require a parameter in the legacy utilities. For example, whereas you used to have to specify DIRECT=Y to get a direct path export, Data Pump automatically uses direct path whenever possible.

Table 13–3. Mapping of Old Export Parameters to Data Pump

Original exp Parameter	Similar Data Pump expdp Parameter
BUFFER	N/A
COMPRESS	TRANSFORM
CONSISTENT	FLASHBACK_SCN or FLASHBACK_TIME
CONSTRAINTS	EXCLUDE=CONSTRAINTS
DIRECT	N/A; Data Pump automatically uses direct path when possible
FEEDBACK	STATUS in client output
FILE	Database-directory object and DUMPFILE
GRANTS	EXCLUDE=GRANT
INDEXES	INCLUDE=INDEXES, INCLUDE=INDEXES
LOG	Database-directory object and LOGFILE
OBJECT_CONSISTENT	N/A
OWNER	SCHEMAS
RECORDLENGTH	N/A
RESUMABLE	N/A; Data Pump automatically provides functionality
RESUMABLE_NAME	N/A
RESUMABLE_TIMEOUT	N/A
ROWS	CONTENT=ALL
STATISTICS	N/A; Data Pump export always exports statistics for tables
TABLESPACES	TRANSPORT_TABLESPACES
TRANSPORT_TABLESPACE	TRANSPORT_TABLESPACES
TRIGGERS	EXCLUDE=TRIGGER
TTS_FULL_CHECK	TRANSPORT_FULL_CHECK
VOLSIZE	N/A; Data Pump doesn't support tape devices

Data Pump Mapping to the imp Utility

As with Data Pump export, Data Pump import often doesn't have a one-to-one mapping of the legacy utility parameter. Data Pump import automatically provides many features of the old imp utility. For example, COMMIT=Y isn't required because Data Pump import automatically commits after each table is imported. Table 13–4 describes how legacy import parameters map to Data Pump import.

Table 13–4. *Mapping of Old Import Parameters to Data Pump*

Original imp Parameter	Similar Data Pump impdp Parameter
BUFFER	N/A
CHARSET	N/A
COMMIT	N/A; Data Pump import automatically commits after each table is exported
COMPILE	N/A; Data Pump import compiles procedures after they're created
CONSTRAINTS	EXCLUDE=CONSTRAINT
DATAFILES	TRANSPORT_DATAFILES
DESTROY	REUSE_DATAFILES=y
FEEDBACK	STATUS in client output
FILE	Database-directory object and DUMPFILE
FILESIZE	N/A
FROMUSER	REMAP_SCHEMA
GRANTS	EXCLUDE=OBJECT_GRANT
IGNORE	TABLE_EXISTS_ACTION with APPEND, REPLACE, SKIP, or TRUNCATE
INDEXES	EXCLUDE=INDEXES
INDEXFILE	SQLFILE
LOG	Database-directory object and LOGFILE
RECORDLENGTH	N/A
RESUMABLE	N/A; this functionality is automatically provided
RESUMABLE_NAME	N/A
RESUMABLE_TIMEOUT	N/A
ROWS=N	CONTENT, with METADATA_ONLY or ALL
SHOW	SQLFILE

Original imp Parameter	Similar Data Pump impdp Parameter
STATISTICS	N/A
STREAMS_CONFIGURATION	N/A
STREAMS_INSTANTIATION	N/A
TABLESPACES	TRANSPORT_TABLESPACES
TOID_NOVALIDATE	N/A
TOUSER	REMAP_SCHEMA
TRANSPORT_TABLESPACE	TRANSPORT_TABLESPACES
TTS_OWNERS	N/A
VOLSIZE	N/A; Data Pump doesn't support tape devices

Summary

Data Pump is an extremely powerful and feature-rich tool. If you haven't used Data Pump much, then I implore you to take some time to read this chapter and work through the examples. This tool greatly simplifies tasks like moving users and data from one environment to another. You can export and import subsets of users, filter and remap data via SQL and PL/SQL, rename users and tablespaces, compress, encrypt, and parallelize, all with one command. It really is that powerful.

DBAs sometimes stick with the old exp/imp utilities because that's what they're familiar with (I'm occasionally guilty of this). If you're running Oracle Database 11g release 2, you can directly use the old exp/imp parameters and options directly from the command line. Data Pump translates these parameters on the fly to Data Pump–specific syntax. This feature nicely facilitates the migration from the old to the new. For reference, I've also provided a mapping of the old exp/imp syntax and how it relates to Data Pump commands.

Although Data Pump is an excellent tool for moving database objects and data from one environment to another, sometimes you need to transfer large quantities of data to and from operating-system flat files. You use external tables to achieve this task. This is the topic of the next chapter in this book.

CHAPTER 14

■■■

External Tables

Sometimes DBAs and developers don't grasp the utility of external tables. The Oracle external-table feature enables you to perform two distinct operations:

- Directly select information from operating-system flat files via SQL, which allows you to do tasks such as loading operating-system comma-separated-value (CSV) files into the database.

- Create platform-independent dump files that can be used to transfer data. You can also create these files as compressed and encrypt them for efficient and secure data transportation.

One common use of an external table is that it allows you to use SQL*Plus to select data from an operating-system flat file. When using an external table in this mode, you must specify what type of data is in the file and how it's organized. You can select from an external table but aren't permitted to modify the data (no inserts, updates, or deletes).

You can also use an Oracle's external-table feature that lets you select data from the database and write that information to a binary dump file. The definition of the external table defines what tables and columns will be used to unload data. Using an external table in this mode provides a method for extracting large amounts of data to a platform-independent file that you can later load into a different database.

All that is required to enable external tables is to first create a database-directory object that specifies the location of the operating-system file. Then, you use the CREATE TABLE...ORGANIZATION EXTERNAL statement to make the database aware of operating-system files that can be used as sources or targets of data.

This chapter starts by comparing using SQL*Loader—Oracle's traditional data-loading utility—to external tables for the loading of data into the database. Several examples illustrate the flexibility and power of using external tables as a loading and data-transformation tool. The chapter finishes with an external-table example of how to unload data into a dump file.

SQL*Loader vs. External Tables

One general use of an external table lets you use SQL to load data from an operating-system file into a regular database table. This facilitates the loading of large amounts of data from flat files into the database. In older versions of Oracle, this type of loading was performed via SQL*Loader or through custom Pro*C programs.

Almost anything you can do with SQL*Loader, you can achieve with external tables. External tables are more flexible and intuitive to use than SQL*Loader. Additionally, you can obtain very good performance when loading data with external tables by using direct path and parallel features.

A quick comparison of using SQL*Loader and external tables highlights the differences. Listed next are the SQL*Loader steps that you use to load and transform of data:

1. Create a parameter file that SQL*Loader uses to interpret the format of the data in the operating-system file.

2. Create a regular database table into which SQL*Loader will insert records. The data will be staged here until it can be further processed.

3. Run the SQL*Loader sqlldr utility to load data from the operating-system file into the database table (created in step 2). When loading data, SQL*Loader has some features that allow you to transform data. This step is sometimes frustrating because it can take several trial-and-error runs to correctly map the parameter file to the table and corresponding columns.

4. Create another table that will contain the completely transformed data.

5. First run SQL statements to load the data from the staging table (created in step 2); then transform and insert the data into the production table (created in step 4).

Compare the previous SQL*Loader list to the following steps to load and transform data using external tables:

1. Execute a CREATE TABLE...ORGANIZATION EXTERNAL script that maps the structure of the operating-system file to table columns. After this script is run, you can directly use SQL to query the contents of the operating-system file.

2. Create a regular table to hold the completely transformed data.

3. Run SQL statements to load and fully transform the data from the external table into the table created in step 2.

For many shops, SQL*Loader underpins large data-loading operations. It continues to be a good tool to use for that task. However, you may want to investigate using external tables. External tables have the following advantages:

- Loading data with external tables is more straightforward and requires fewer steps.

- The interface for creating and loading from external tables is SQL*Plus. Many DBAs/developers find using SQL*Plus more intuitive and powerful than SQL*Loader's parameter-file interface.

- You can view data in an external table before it's loaded into a database table.

- You can load, transform, and aggregate the data without an intermediate staging table. For large amounts of data, this can be a huge space savings.

The next several sections contain examples of using external tables to read from operating-system files.

Loading CSV Files into the Database

You can load small or very large CSV flat files into the database using external tables and SQL. Figure 14–1 shows the architectural components involved with using an external table to view and load data from an operating-system file. A directory object is required that specifies the location of the operating-system file. The CREATE TABLE...ORGANIZATION EXTERNAL statement creates a database object that SQL*Plus can use to directly select from the operating-system file.

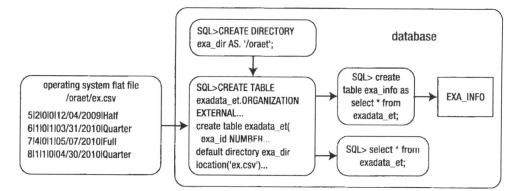

Figure 14–1. Architectural components of an external table used to read a flat file

Here are the steps for using an external table to access an operating-system flat file:

1. Create a database-directory object that points to the location of the CSV file.

2. Grant read and write privileges on the directory object to the user creating the external table. I usually use a DBA privileged account, so I don't need to perform this step.

3. Run the CREATE TABLE...ORGANIZATION EXTERNAL statement.

4. Use SQL*Plus to access the contents of the CSV file.

In this example, the flat file is named ex.csv and is located in the /oraet directory. It contains the following data:

```
5|2|0|0|12/04/2009|Half
6|1|0|1|03/31/2010|Quarter
7|4|0|1|05/07/2010|Full
8|1|1|0|04/30/2010|Quarter
```

⬛ **Note** Some of the CSV file examples used in this chapter are actually separated by characters other than a comma, such as a pipe | character. The character used depends on the data and the user who supplies the CSV file. CSV files are also often commonly referred to as *flat files*.

Creating a Directory Object and Granting Access

First, create a directory object that points to the location of the flat file on disk:

```
SQL> create directory exa_dir as '/oraet';
```

This example uses a database account that has the DBA role granted to it; therefore, you don't need to grant READ and WRITE to the directory object to the user (your account) that is accessing the directory object. If you're not using a DBA account to read from the directory object, then grant these privileges to the account using this object:

```
SQL> grant read, write on directory exa_dir to reg_user;
```

Creating an External Table

Next, fashion the script that creates the external table that will reference the flat file. The CREATE TABLE...ORGANIZATION EXTERNAL statement provides the database with the following information:

- How to interpret data in the flat file, and a mapping of data in file-to-column definitions in the database

- A DEFAULT DIRECTORY clause that identifies the directory object, which in turn specifies the directory of the flat file on disk

- The LOCATION clause, which identifies the name of the flat file

The next statement creates a database object that looks like a table yet is able to retrieve data directly from the flat file:

```
create table exadata_et(
  exa_id          NUMBER
 ,machine_count NUMBER
 ,hide_flag      NUMBER
 ,oracle         NUMBER
 ,ship_date      DATE
 ,rack_type      VARCHAR2(32)
)
organization external (
  type                oracle_loader
  default directory exa_dir
  access parameters
  (
    records delimited  by newline
    fields  terminated by '|'
    missing field values are null
    (exa_id
    ,machine_count
    ,hide_flag
    ,oracle
    ,ship_date char date_format date mask "mm/dd/yyyy"
    ,rack_type)
  )
  location ('ex.csv')
)
reject limit unlimited;
```

An external table named EXADATA_ET is created when you execute this script. Now, use SQL*Plus to view the contents of the flat file:

```
SQL> select * from exadata_et;

    EXA_ID MACHINE_COUNT  HIDE_FLAG     ORACLE SHIP_DATE RACK_TYPE
---------- -------------  ----------  --------- --------- ---------
         5             2           0          0 04-DEC-09 Half
         6             1           0          1 31-MAR-10 Quarter
         7             4           0          1 07-MAY-10 Full
         8             1           1          0 30-APR-10 Quarter
```

Viewing External-Table Metadata

At this point, you can also view metadata regarding the external table. Query the DBA_EXTERNAL_TABLES view for details:

```
select
 owner
,table_name
,default_directory_name
,access_parameters
from dba_external_tables;
```

Here's a partial listing of the output:

```
OWNER       TABLE_NAME        DEFAULT_DIRECTO   ACCESS_PARAMETERS
---------   ----------------- ----------------- --------------------------
BARTS       EXADATA_ET        EXA_DIR           records delimited  by newline
```

Additionally, you can select from the DBA_EXTERNAL_LOCATIONS table for information regarding any flat files referenced in an external table:

```
select
 owner
,table_name
,location
from dba_external_locations;
```

Here's some sample output:

```
OWNER           TABLE_NAME             LOCATION
--------------- ---------------------- ---------------
BARTS           EXADATA_ET             ex.csv
```

Loading a Regular Table from the External Table

Now you can load data contained in the external table into a regular database table. When you do this, you can take advantage of Oracle's direct-path loading and parallel features. This example creates a regular database table that will be loaded with data from the external table:

```
create table exa_info(
  exa_id         NUMBER
 ,machine_count  NUMBER
 ,hide_flag      NUMBER
```

```
,oracle       NUMBER
,ship_date    DATE
,rack_type    VARCHAR2(32)
) nologging parallel 2;
```

You can direct-path load this regular table (via the APPEND hint) from the contents of the external table as follows:

```
SQL> insert /*+ APPEND */ into exa_info select * from exadata_et;
```

You can verify that the table was direct-path loaded by attempting to select from it before you commit the data:

```
SQL> select * from exa_info;
```

Here's the expected error:

```
ORA-12838: cannot read/modify an object after modifying it in parallel
```

After you commit the data, you can select from the table:

```
SQL> commit;
SQL> select * from exa_info;
```

The other way to direct-path load a table is to use the CREATE TABLE AS SELECT (CTAS) statement. A CTAS statement automatically attempts to do a direct-path load. In this example, the EXA_INFO table is created and loaded in one statement:

```
SQL> create table exa_info nologging parallel 2 as select * from exadata_et;
```

By using direct-path loading and parallelism, you can achieve loading performance similar to that from using SQL*Loader. The advantage of using SQL to create a table from an external table is that you can now perform complex data transformations using standard SQL*Plus features when building your regular database table (EXA_INFO, in this example).

Any CTAS statements automatically process with the degree of parallelism that has been defined for the underlying table. However, when you use INSERT AS SELECT statements, you need to enable parallelism for the session:

```
SQL> alter session enable parallel dml;
```

As a last step, you should generate statistics for any table that has been loaded with a large amount of data. Here's an example:

```
exec dbms_stats.gather_table_stats(-
 ownname=>'BARTS',-
 tabname=>'EXA_INFO',-
 estimate_percent => 20, -
 cascade=>true);
```

Performing Advanced Transformations

Oracle provides sophisticated techniques for transforming data. This section details how to use a pipelined function to transform data in an external table. Listed next are the steps for doing this:

1. Create an external table.

2. Create a record type that maps to the columns in the external table.

3. Create a table based on the record type created in step 2

4. Create a piplelined function that is used to inspect each row as it's loaded and transform data based on business requirements.

5. Use an INSERT statement that selects from the external table and uses the pipelined function to transform data as it's loaded.

This example uses the same external table and CSV file created in the previous section on loading data from CSV files. Recall that the external table name is EXADATA_ET and the CSV file name is ex.csv. After you create the external table, next create a record type that maps to the column names in the external table:

```
create or replace type rec_exa_type is object
(
  exa_id        number
 ,machine_count number
 ,hide_flag     number
 ,oracle        number
 ,ship_date     date
 ,rack_type     varchar2(32)
);
/
```

Next, create a table based on the previous record type:

```
create or replace type table_exa_type is table of rec_exa_type;
/
```

Oracle PL/SQL allows you to use functions as a row source for SQL operations. This feature is known as *pipelining*. It lets you use complex transformation logic combined with the power of SQL*Plus. For this example, you create a pipelined function to transform selected column data as it's loaded. Specifically, this function adds 30 days to the SHIP_DATE when the ORACLE column has a 0 value:

```
create or replace function exa_trans
return table_exa_type pipelined is
begin
for r1 in
   (select rec_exa_type(
      exa_id, machine_count, hide_flag
     ,oracle, ship_date, rack_type
    ) exa_rec
    from exadata_et) loop
  if (r1.exa_rec.oracle = 0) then
    r1.exa_rec.ship_date := r1.exa_rec.ship_date + 30;
  end if;
 pipe row (r1.exa_rec);
end loop;
return;
end;
/
```

Now you can use this function to load data into a regular database table. For reference, here's the CREATE TABLE statement that instantiates the table to be loaded:

```
create table exa_info(
  exa_id          NUMBER
 ,machine_count NUMBER
 ,hide_flag       NUMBER
 ,oracle          NUMBER
 ,ship_date       DATE
 ,rack_type       VARCHAR2(32)
) nologging parallel 2;
```

Next, use the pipelined function to transform data selected from the external table and insert it into the regular database table in one step:

```
SQL> insert into exa_info select * from table(exa_trans);
```

Here's the data that was loaded into the EXA_INFO table for this example:

```
SQL> select * from exa_info;
    EXA_ID MACHINE_COUNT  HIDE_FLAG      ORACLE SHIP_DATE RACK_TYPE
---------- ------------- ---------- ---------- --------- ------------
         5             2          0          0 03-JAN-10 Half
         6             1          0          1 31-MAR-10 Quarter
         7             4          0          1 07-MAY-10 Full
         8             1          1          0 30-MAY-10 Quarter
```

Although the example in this section is simple, you can use the technique to apply any degree of sophisticated transformational logic. This technique allows you to embed the transformation requirements in a pipelined PL/SQL function that modifies data as each row is loaded.

Viewing Text Files from SQL

External tables allow you to use SQL SELECT statements to retrieve information from operating-system flat files. For example, say you want to report on the contents of the alert log file. First, create a directory object that points to the location of the alert log:

```
SQL> select value from v$parameter where name ='background_dump_dest';
```

Here's the output for this example:

```
/oracle/app/oracle/diag/rdbms/o11r2/O11R2/trace
```

Next, create a directory object that points at the location of the background dump destination:

```
SQL> create directory t_loc as '/oracle/app/oracle/diag/rdbms/o11r2/O11R2/trace';
```

Now, create an external table that maps to the database alert log operating-system file. In this example, the database name is O11R2, and thus the alert log file name is alert_O11R2.log:

```
create table alert_log_file(
  alert_text varchar2(4000))
organization external
( type              oracle_loader
  default directory t_loc
  access parameters (
    records delimited by newline
    nobadfile
    nologfile
```

```
    nodiscardfile
    fields terminated by '#$~=ui$X'
    missing field values are null
    (alert_text)
  )
  location ('alert_O11R2.log')
)
reject limit unlimited;
```

You can query the table via SQL queries. For example:

```
SQL> select * from alert_log_file where alert_text like 'ORA-%';
```

This allows you to use SQL to view and report on the contents of the alert log. You may find this a convenient way to provide SQL access to otherwise inaccessible operating-system files.

The ACCESS PARAMETERS clause of an external table's ORACLE_LOADER access driver may look familiar if you've previously worked with SQL*Loader. Table 14–1 describes some of the more commonly used access parameters. For a full list of access parameters, see Oracle's *Database Utilities* guide (available on OTN).

Table 14–1. Selected Access Parameters for the ORACLE_LOADER Driver

Access Parameter	Description
DELIMITED BY	Indicates which character delimits the fields
TERMINATED BY	Indicates how a field is terminated
FIXED	Specifies the size of records having a fixed length
BADFILE	Name of the file that stores records that can't be loaded due to an error
NOBADFILE	Specifies that a file shouldn't be created to hold records that can't be loaded due to errors
LOGFILE	Name of the file in which general messages are recorded when creating an external table
NOLOGFILE	Specifies that no log file should be created
DISCARDFILE	Names the file to which records are written that fail the LOAD WHEN clause
NODISCARDFILE	Specifies that no discard file should be created
SKIP	Skips the specified number of records in the file before loading
PREPROCESSOR	Specifies the user-named program that runs and modifies the contents of the file before Oracle loads the data
MISSING FIELD VALUES ARE NULL	Loads fields that have no data as NULL values

Unloading and Loading Data Using an External Table

Another use for external tables is to select data from a regular database table and create a binary dump file. This is referred to as *unloading* data. The advantage of this technique is that the dump file is platform independent and can be used to move large amounts of data between servers of different platforms.

You can also encrypt and/or compress data when creating the dump file. Doing so provides you with an efficient and secure way of transporting databases between database servers.

Figure 14–2 illustrates the components involved with using an external table to unload and load data. On the source database (referred to as Database A), you create a dump file using an external table that selects data from a table named INV. After it's created, you copy the dump file to a destination server (referenced as Database B) and subsequently load it into the database using an external table.

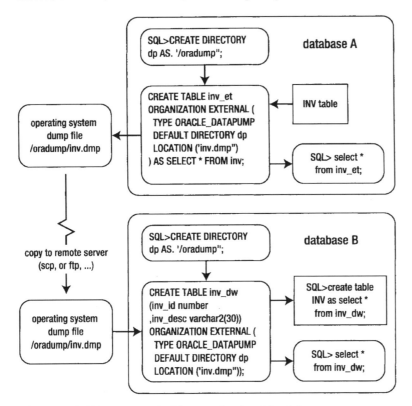

Figure 14–2. Using external tables to unload and load data

A small example illustrates the technique of using an external table to unload data. Here are the steps required:

1. Create a directory object that specifies where you want the dump file placed on disk. If you're not using a DBA account, then grant read and write access to the directory object to the database user that needs access.

2. Use the CREATE TABLE...ORGANIZATION EXTERNAL...AS SELECT statement to unload data from the database into the dump file.

First, create a directory object. The next bit of code creates a directory object named DP that points at the /oradump directory:

```
SQL> create directory dp as '/oradump';
```

If you're not using a user with DBA privileges, then explicitly grant access to the directory object to the required user:

```
SQL> grant read, write on directory dp to larry;
```

To create a dump file, use the ORACLE_DATAPUMP access driver of the CREATE TABLE...ORGANIZATION EXTERNAL statement. This example unloads the INV table's contents into the inv.dmp file:

```
CREATE TABLE inv_et
ORGANIZATION EXTERNAL (
  TYPE ORACLE_DATAPUMP
  DEFAULT DIRECTORY dp
  LOCATION ('inv.dmp')
)
AS SELECT * FROM inv;
```

The previous command does two things:

- Creates an external table named INV_ET based on the INV table

- Creates a platform-independent dump file named inv.dmp

Now you can copy the inv.dmp file to a separate database server and base an external table on this dump file. The remote server (to which you copy the dump file) can be a different platform than the server where you created the file. For example, you can create a dump file on a Windows box, copy to a Solaris server, and select from the dump file via an external table. In this example, the external table is named INV_DW:

```
CREATE TABLE inv_dw
(inv_id number
,inv_desc varchar2(30))
ORGANIZATION EXTERNAL (
  TYPE ORACLE_DATAPUMP
  DEFAULT DIRECTORY dp
  LOCATION ('inv.dmp')
);
```

After it's created, you can access the external table data from SQL*Plus:

```
SQL> select * from inv_dw;
```

You can also create and load data into regular tables using the dump file:

```
SQL> create table inv as select * from inv_dw;
```

This provides a simple and efficient mechanism for transporting data from one platform to another.

Using Parallelism to Reduce Elapsed Time

To maximize the unload performance when you create a dump file via an external table, use the PARALLEL clause. This example creates two dump files in parallel:

```
CREATE TABLE inv_et
ORGANIZATION EXTERNAL (
  TYPE ORACLE_DATAPUMP
  DEFAULT DIRECTORY dp
  LOCATION ('inv1.dmp','inv2.dmp')
)
PARALLEL 2
AS SELECT * FROM inv;
```

To access the data in the dump files, create a different external table that references the two dump files:

```
CREATE TABLE inv_dw
(inv_id number
,inv_desc varchar2(30))
ORGANIZATION EXTERNAL (
  TYPE ORACLE_DATAPUMP
  DEFAULT DIRECTORY dp
  LOCATION ('inv1.dmp','inv2.dmp')
);
```

You can now use this external table to select data from the dump files:

```
SQL> select * from inv_dw;
```

Compressing a Dump File

You can create a compressed dump file via an external table. For example, use the COMPRESS option of the ACCESS PARAMETERS clause:

```
CREATE TABLE inv_et
ORGANIZATION EXTERNAL (
  TYPE ORACLE_DATAPUMP
  DEFAULT DIRECTORY dp
  ACCESS PARAMETERS (COMPRESSION ENABLED)
  LOCATION ('inv1.dmp')
)
AS SELECT * FROM inv;
```

You should see quite good compression ratios when using this option. In my testing, the output dump file was 10 to 20 times smaller when compressed. Your mileage may vary, depending on the type data being compressed.

Encrypting a Dump File

You can also create an encrypted dump file using an external table. This example uses the ENCRYPTION option of the ACCESS PARAMETERS clause:

```
CREATE TABLE inv_et
ORGANIZATION EXTERNAL (
  TYPE ORACLE_DATAPUMP
  DEFAULT DIRECTORY dp
  ACCESS PARAMETERS
    (ENCRYPTION ENABLED)
  LOCATION ('inv1.dmp')
)
AS SELECT * FROM inv;
```

For this example to work, you need to have a security wallet in place and open for your database.

■ **Note** Using encryption requires an additional license from Oracle. Contact Oracle for details on using the Advanced Security Option.

You enable compression and encryption via the ACCESS PARAMETERS clause. Table 14–2 contains a listing of all access parameters available with the ORACLE_DATAPUMP access driver.

Table 14–2. Parameters of the ORACLE_DATAPUMP Access Driver

Access Parameter	Description
COMPRESSION	Compresses the dump file. DISABLED is the default value.
ENCRYPTION	Encrypts the dump file. DISABLED is the default value.
NOLOGFILE	Suppresses the generation of a log file.
LOGFILE=[directory_object:]logfile_name	Allows you to name a log file.
VERSION	Specifies the minimum version of Oracle that can read the dump file.

Preprocessing an External Table

Oracle added (in 10.2.0.5 and higher) the ability to preprocess the file on which an external table is based. For example, you can instruct the CREATE TABLE...ORGANIZATION EXTERNAL statement to uncompress a compressed operating-system file before it's processed.

Here's a simple example to illustrate this concept. First, create a directory object that contains the location of the compressed file:

```
SQL> create or replace directory data_dir as '/orahome/oracle/dk/et';
```

You also need to create a directory object that contains the location of the script that will perform the preprocessing on the data file. In this example, the directory is /bin:

```
SQL> create or replace directory exe_dir as '/bin';
```

This example compressed the operating-system flat file with the gzip utility. The compressed file is named exa.csv.gz. You instruct the CREATE TABLE...ORGANIZATION EXTERNAL statement to preprocess the compressed file by specifying the PREPROCESSOR clause. Because the CSV file was compressed by the gzip utility, it can be uncompressed by the corresponding uncompress utility, gunzip. Look carefully for the PREPROCESSOR clause in the following listing; it's nested under ACCESS PARAMETERS:

```
create table exadata_et(
  machine_count NUMBER
 ,hide_flag     NUMBER
 ,oracle        NUMBER
 ,ship_date     DATE
 ,rack_type     VARCHAR2(32)
)
organization external (
  type             oracle_loader
  default directory data_dir
  access parameters
  (
    records delimited  by newline
    preprocessor exe_dir: 'gunzip'
    fields  terminated by '|'
    missing field values are null
    (exa_id
    ,machine_count
    ,hide_flag
    ,oracle
    ,ship_date char date_format date mask "mm/dd/yyyy"
    ,rack_type)
  )
  location ('ex.csv.gz')
)
reject limit unlimited;
```

The advantage of preprocessing the dump file is that it saves you the step of having to first uncompress the file.

■ **Note** Oracle doesn't let you use the PREPROCESSOR clause in databases that have the Database Vault feature installed.

Summary

I used to use SQL*Loader for all types of data-loading tasks. In the past few years, I've become an external-table convert. Almost anything you can do with SQL*Loader, you can also do with an external table. The external-table approach is advantageous because there are fewer moving parts and the interface is SQL*Plus. Most DBAs and developers find SQL*Plus easier to use than a SQL*Loader control file.

You can easily use an external table to enable SQL*Plus access to operating-system flat files. You simply have to define the structure of the flat file in your CREATE TABLE...ORGANIZATION EXTERNAL statement. After the external table is created, you can select directly from the flat file as if it were a database table. You can select from an external table, but you can't insert, update, or delete.

When you create an external table, if required, you can then create regular database tables by using CREATE TABLE AS SELECT from the external table. Doing so provides a fast and effective way to load data stored in external operating-system files.

The external-table feature also allows you to select data from a table and write it to a binary dump file. The external table CREATE TABLE...ORGANIZATION EXTERNAL statement defines which tables and columns are used to unload the data. A dump file created in this manner is platform independent, meaning you can copy it to a server using a different operating system and seamlessly load the data. Additionally, the dump file can be encrypted and compressed for secure and efficient transportation. You can also use parallel features to reduce the amount of time it takes to create the dump file.

The next chapter deals with materialized views. These database objects provide you with a flexible, maintainable, and scalable mechanism for aggregating and replicating data.

CHAPTER 15

■■■

Materialized Views

Materialized view (MV) technology was introduced in Oracle Database version 7. This feature was originally called *snapshots*, and you can still see this nomenclature reflected in some data-dictionary structures. A materialized view allows you to execute a SQL query at a point in time and store the result set in a table (either locally or in a remote database). After the MV is initially populated, at some later point in time you can re-run the MV query and store the fresh results in the underlying table. There are two main uses for materialized views:

- Replicating of data to offload query workloads to separate reporting databases

- Improving performance of queries by periodically computing and storing the results of complex aggregations of data, which lets users query point-in-time results (of the complex queries)

The MV can be a query based on tables, views, and other materialized views. The base tables are often referred to as *master tables*. When you create an MV, Oracle internally creates a table (with the same name as the MV) and also create a materialized view object.

Understanding Materialized Views

A good way of describing MVs is by walking through how you'd manually perform a task if the MV feature wasn't available. Suppose you have a query that reports on historical daily sales:

```
select
 sum(sales_amt)
,sales_dtt
from sales
group by sales_dtt;
```

You observe from a database-performance report that this query is executed 1,000 times a day and is consuming a large amount of database resources. The business users use the report to display historical sales information and therefore don't need the query to be re-executed each time they run a report. To reduce the amount of resources the query is consuming, you decide to create a table and populate it as follows:

```
create table daily_sales as
select
 sum(sales_amt)
,sales_dtt
from sales
group by sales_dtt;
```

After the table is created, you put in a daily process to delete from it at 8:00 pm and completely refresh it:

```
-- Step 1 delete from daily aggregated sales data:
delete from daily_sales;
--
-- Step 2 repopulate table with a snapshot of aggregated sales table:
insert into daily_sales
select
 sum(sales_amt)
,sales_dtt
from sales
group by sales_dtt;
```

You inform the users that they can have subsecond query results by selecting from DAILY_SALES (instead of running the query that directly selects and aggregates from the master SALES table). This process roughly describes a complete refresh process.

Oracle's MV technology automates and greatly enhances this process. This chapter describes the procedure for implementing both basic and complex MV features. After reading this chapter and working through the examples, you should be able to create MVs to replicate and aggregate data in a wide variety of situations.

Before delving into the details of creating MVs, it's useful to cover basic terminology and helpful data-dictionary views related to MVs. The next two subsections briefly describe the various MV features and the many data-dictionary views that contain MV metadata.

▓ **Note** This chapter doesn't cover topics like multimaster replication and updateable MVs. See the *Oracle Advanced Replication Guide* (available on Oracle's OTN web site) for more details on those topics.

Materialized View Terminology

A great many terms relate to refreshing MVs. You should be familiar with these terms before delving into how to implement the features. Table 15-1 describes the various terms relevant to MVs.

Table 15-1. Descriptions of MV Terminology

Term	Meaning
Materialized view	Database object used for replicating data and improving performance.
Materialized view SQL statement	SQL query that defines what data is stored in the underlying MV base table.
Materialized view underlying table	Database table that has the same name as the MV that stores the result of the MV SQL query.
Master (or base) table	Table that an MV references in its FROM clause of the MV SQL statement.
Complete refresh	Process in which an MV is deleted from and completely refreshed with an MV SQL statement.
Fast refresh	Process during which only DML changes that have occurred since the last refresh are applied to an MV.
Materialized view log	Database object that tracks DML changes to the MV base table. An MV log is required for fast refreshes. It can be based on the primary key, ROWID, or object ID.
Simple MV	MV based on a simple query that can be fast-refreshed.
Complex MV	MV based on a complex query that isn't eligible for fast refresh.
Build mode	Mode that specifies whether the MV should be immediately populated or deferred.
Refresh mode	Mode that specifies whether the MV should be refreshed on demand, on commit, or never.
Refresh method	Option that specifies whether the MV refresh should be complete or fast.
Query rewrite	Feature that allows the optimizer to choose to use MVs (instead of base tables) to fulfill the requirements of a query (even though the query doesn't directly reference the MVs).
Local MV	MV that resides in the same database as the base table(s).
Remote MV	MV that resides in a separate database from the base table(s).
Refresh group	Set of MVs refreshed at the same consistent transactional point.

Refer back to Table 15–1 as you read the rest of this chapter. These terms and concepts are explained and expounded on in subsequent sections.

Referencing Useful Views

When you're working with MVs, sometimes it's hard to remember which data-dictionary view to query under what circumstance. A wide variety of data-dictionary views are available. Table 15–2 contains a description of the MV-related data-dictionary views. Examples of using these views are shown throughout this chapter where appropriate. These views are invaluable for troubleshooting, diagnosing issues, and understanding your MV environment.

Table 15–2. Materialized View Data-Dictionary View Definitions

Data-Dictionary View	Description
DBA/ALL/USER_MVIEWS	Information about MVs such as owner, base query, last refresh time, and so on.
DBA/ALL/USER_MVIEW_REFRESH_TIMES	MV last refresh times, MV names, master table, and master owner.
DBA/ALL/USER_REGISTERED_MVIEWS	All registered MVs. Helps identify which MVs are using which MV logs.
DBA/ALL/USER_MVIEW_LOGS	MV log information.
DBA/ALL/USER_BASE_TABLE_MVIEWS	Base-table names and last refresh dates for tables that have MV logs.
DBA/ALL/USER_MVIEW_AGGREGATES	Aggregate functions that appear in SELECT clauses for MVs.
DBA/ALL/USER_MVIEW_ANALYSIS	Information about MVs. Oracle recommends that you use DBA/ALL/USER_MVIEWS instead of these views.
DBA/ALL/USER_MVIEW_COMMENTS	Any comments associated with MVs.
DBA/ALL/USER_MVIEW_DETAIL_PARTITION	Partition and freshness information.
DBA/ALL/USER_MVIEW_DETAIL_SUBPARTITION	Subpartition and freshness information.
DBA/ALL/USER_MVIEW_DETAIL_RELATIONS	Local tables and MVs that an MV is dependent on.
DBA/ALL/USER_MVIEW_JOINS	Joins between two columns in the WHERE clause of an MV definition.
DBA/ALL/USER_MVIEW_KEYS	Columns or expressions in the SELECT clause of an MV definition.

Data-Dictionary View	Description
DBA/ALL/USER_TUNE_MVIEW	Result of executing the DBMS_ADVISOR.TUNE_MVIEW procedure.
V$MVREFRESH	Information about MVs currently being refreshed.
DBA/ALL/USER_REFRESH	Details about MV refresh groups.
DBA_RGROUP	Information about MV refresh groups.
DBA_RCHILD	Children in an MV refresh group.

Creating Basic Materialized Views

This section covers how to create an MV. The two most common configurations used are as follows:

- Creating complete-refresh MVs that are refreshed on demand
- Creating fast-refresh MVs that are refreshed on demand

It's important to understand these basic configurations. They lay the foundation for everything else you do with an MV. Therefore, this section starts with these basic configurations. Later, the section covers more advanced configurations. Make sure you understand the material in the following two sections before you move on to advanced MV topics.

Creating a Complete-Refreshable Materialized View

This section explains how to set up an MV that is periodically completely refreshed, which is about the simplest example possible. Complete refreshes are appropriate for MVs that have base tables in which significant portions of the rows change from one refresh interval to the next. Complete refreshes are also required in situations where a fast refresh isn't possible (due to restrictions imposed by Oracle—more on this later in the chapter).

■ Note To create an MV, you need both the CREATE MATERIALIZED VIEW system privilege and the CREATE TABLE system privilege.

The example in this section uses the following base table named SALES:

```
create table sales(
 sales_id   number
,sales_amt number
,region_id number
,sales_dtt timestamp
,constraint sales_pk primary key(sales_id)
);
```

Insert some sample data into the SALES table:

```
insert into sales values(1,101,100,sysdate-50);
insert into sales values(2,511,200,sysdate-20);
insert into sales values(3,11,100,sysdate);
commit;
```

The next step is to create the MV, using a CREATE MATERIALIZED VIEW...AS SELECT statement. This statement names the MV, specifies its attributes, and defines the SQL query on which the MV is based:

```
create materialized view sales_mv
segment creation immediate
refresh
  complete
  on demand
as
select
 sales_amt
,sales_dtt
from sales;
```

The SEGMENT CREATION IMMEDIATE clause is available with Oracle 11g release 2 and higher. It instructs Oracle to create the segment and allocate an extent when you create the MV. This was the behavior in previous versions of Oracle. If you don't want immediate segment creation, use the SEGMENT CREATION DEFERRED clause. If the newly created MV has any rows in it, then segments are created and extents are allocated regardless of whether you use SEGMENT CREATION DEFERRED.

Let's look at the USER_MVIEWS data dictionary to verify that the MV was created as expected. Here's the query to run:

```
select
 mview_name
,refresh_method
,refresh_mode
,build_mode
,fast_refreshable
from user_mviews
where mview_name = 'SALES_MV';
```

Here's the output for this MV:

```
MVIEW_NAME   REFRESH_ REFRESH_MODE BUILD_MOD FAST_REFRESHABLE
------------ -------- ------------ --------- --------------------
SALES_MV     COMPLETE DEMAND       IMMEDIATE NO
```

It's also informative to inspect the USER_OBJECTS and USER_SEGMENTS views to see what has been created. When you query USER_OBJECTS, notice that several objects have been created:

```
select
 object_name
,object_type
from user_objects
where object_name like 'SALES%'
order by object_name;
```

Here's the corresponding output:

```
OBJECT_NAME          OBJECT_TYPE
-------------------- --------------------
```

```
SALES               TABLE
SALES_MV            MATERIALIZED VIEW
SALES_MV            TABLE
SALES_PK            INDEX
```

The MV is a logical container that stores data in a regular database table. Querying the USER_SEGMENTS view shows the base table, its primary-key index, and the table that stores data returned by the MV query:

```
select
 segment_name
,segment_type
from user_segments
where segment_name like 'SALES%'
order by segment_name;
```

Here's the output for this example:

```
SEGMENT_NAME        SEGMENT_TYPE
------------------- --------------------
SALES               TABLE
SALES_PK            INDEX
SALES_MV            TABLE
```

■ **Note** Oracle sometimes automatically creates an index on the MV. In this scenario, no index for the MV was created.

Finally, let's look at how to refresh the SALES_MV MV. Here's the data contained in SALES_MV:

```
SQL> select sales_amt, to_char(sales_dtt,'dd-mon-yyyy') from sales_mv;
```

Here's the output:

```
SALES_AMT TO_CHAR(SALES_DTT
---------- -----------------
      101 17-jun-2010
      511 17-jul-2010
       11 06-aug-2010
```

Next, insert some additional data into the base SALES table:

```
SQL> insert into sales values(4,99,200,sysdate);
SQL> insert into sales values(5,127,300,sysdate);
```

Now you attempt to initiate a fast refresh of the MV using the REFRESH procedure of the DBMS_MVIEW package. This example passes two parameters to the REFRESH procedure: the name and the refresh method. The name is SALES_MV, and the parameter is F (for *fast*):

```
SQL> exec dbms_mview.refresh('SALES_MV','F');
```

Because this MV wasn't created in conjunction with an MV log, a fast refresh isn't possible. The following error is thrown:

```
ORA-12004: REFRESH FAST cannot be used for materialized view "MV"."SALES_MV"
```

Instead, a complete fresh is initiated. The parameter passed in is C (for *complete*):

```
SQL> exec dbms_mview.refresh('SALES_MV','C');
```

The output indicates success:

```
PL/SQL procedure successfully completed.
```

Now, when you select from the MV, it returns data showing that more information has been added:

```
SQL> select sales_amt, to_char(sales_dtt,'dd-mon-yyyy') from sales_mv;
```

Here's the output:

```
SALES_AMT TO_CHAR(SALES_DTT
---------- -----------------
      101 17-jun-2010
      511 17-jul-2010
       11 06-aug-2010
       99 06-aug-2010
      127 06-aug-2010
```

Figure 15–1 illustrates the architectural components involved with a complete refresh. If you're new to MVs, pause a few minutes here and make sure you understand all the components.

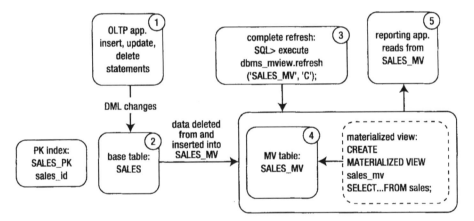

Figure 15–1. *Architectural components of a complete-refresh MV*

This diagram illustrates that a complete refresh isn't difficult to understand. The numbers show the flow of data in the complete refresh process:

1. Users/applications create transactions.

2. Data is committed in the base table.

3. A complete refresh is manually initiated with the DBMS_MVIEW package.

4. Data in the underlying MV is deleted and completely refreshed with the contents of the base table.

5.   Users can query data from the MV, which contains a point-in-time snapshot of the base table's data.

In the next section, a more complicated example shows you how to set up a fast-refreshable MV.

Creating a Fast-Refreshable Materialized View

When you create a fast-refreshable MV, it initially populates the MV table with the entire result set of the MV query. After the initial result set is in place, only data modified (in the base table) since the last refresh needs to be applied to the MV. In other words, any updates, inserts, or deletes from the master table that have occurred since the last refresh are copied over. This feature is appropriate when you have a small amount of changes to a base table over a period of time compared to the total number of rows in the table.

Here are the steps to implement a fast-refreshable MV:

1.   Create a base table (if it's not already created).

2.   Create an MV log on the base table.

3.   Create an MV as fast-refreshable.

This example first creates a base table. In most environments, you already have a base table in place. For illustrative purposes, here's the table-creation script and some sample data:

```
create table sales(
 sales_id   number
,sales_amt number
,region_id number
,sales_dtt timestamp
,constraint sales_pk primary key(sales_id)
);
--
insert into sales values(1,101,100,sysdate-50);
insert into sales values(2,511,200,sysdate-20);
insert into sales values(3,11,100,sysdate);
commit;
```

A fast-refreshable MV requires an MV log on the base table. When a fast refresh occurs, the MV log must have a unique way to identify which records have been modified and thus need to be refreshed. You can do this two different approaches. One method is to specify the PRIMARY KEY clause when you create the MV log, and the other is to specify the ROWID clause. If the underlying base table has a primary key, then use the primary key–based MV log. If the underlying base table has no primary key, then you have to create the MV log using ROWID. In most cases, you'll probably have a primary key defined for every base table. However, the reality is that some systems are poorly designed or have some rare reason for a table not to have a primary key.

In this example, a primary key is defined on the base table, so you create the MV log with the PRIMARY KEY clause:

```
SQL> create materialized view log on sales with primary key;
```

If there was no primary key defined on the base table, this error is thrown when attempting to create the MV log:

```
ORA-12014: table does not contain a primary key constraint
```

If the base table has no primary key, and you don't have the option to add one, you must specify ROWID when you create the MV log:

```
SQL> create materialized view log on sales with rowid;
```

Now that you've created the MV log, you can create the fast-refreshable MV. There are a couple of interesting architectural considerations to point out. If there is no MV log on the base table, then Oracle doesn't allow you to create a fast-refreshable MV. This error is thrown:

```
ORA-23413: table does not have a materialized view log.
```

Also, when you create the fast-refreshable MV, you must specify whether it's refreshed via the PRIMARY KEY (which is the default) or via the ROWID. This example uses a table with a primary key and an MV log created with a primary key. In this example, the MV is fast-refreshed via a primary key. When you use a primary key–based fast-refreshable MV, the primary-key column(s) of the base table must be part of the fast-refreshable MV SELECT statement:

```
create materialized view sales_mv
segment creation immediate
refresh
  with primary key
  fast
  on demand
as
select
 sales_id
,sales_amt
,sales_dtt
from sales;
```

At this point, it's useful to inspect the objects that are associated with the MV. The following query selects from USER_OBJECTS:

```
select
 object_name
,object_type
from user_objects
where object_name like '%SALES%'
order by object_name;
```

Here are the objects that have been created:

```
OBJECT_NAME          OBJECT_TYPE
-------------------- --------------------
MLOG$_SALES          TABLE
RUPD$_SALES          TABLE
SALES                TABLE
SALES_MV             MATERIALIZED VIEW
SALES_MV             TABLE
SALES_PK             INDEX
SALES_PK1            INDEX
```

Several objects in the previous output require some explanation:

- MLOG$_SALES
- RUPD$_SALES
- SALES_PK1

First, when an MV log is created, a corresponding table is also created that stores the rows in the base table that changed and how they changed (insert, update, or delete). The MV log table name is of the format MLOG$_<base table name>.

A table is also created with the format RUPD$_<base table name>. Oracle automatically creates this RUPD$ table when you create a fast-refreshable MV using a primary key. It's there to support the updateable MV feature. You don't have to worry about this table unless you're dealing with updatable MVs (see the *Oracle Advanced Replication Guide* for more details on updatable MVs). If you're not using the updatable MV feature, then you can ignore the RUPD$ table.

Oracle also creates an index with the format <base table name>_PK1. This index is automatically created for primary key–based MVs and is based on the primary-key column(s) of the base table. If this is a ROWID instead of a primary key, then the index name has the format I_SNAP$_<table name> and is based on the ROWID. If you don't explicitly name the primary-key index on the base table, then Oracle gives the MV table primary-key index a system-generated name such as SYS_C008780.

Now that you understand the underlying architectural components, let's look at the data in the MV:

```
SQL> select sales_amt, to_char(sales_dtt,'dd mon-yyyy') from sales_mv;
```

Here's the output:

```
SALES_AMT TO_CHAR(SALES_DTT
---------- -----------------
      101 12-jun-2010
      511 12-jul-2010
       11 01-aug-2010
```

Let's add two records to the base SALES table:

```
insert into sales values(4,99,200,sysdate);
insert into sales values(5,127,300,sysdate);
commit;
```

At this point, it's instructional to inspect the M$LOG table. You should see two records that identify how the data in the SALES table has changed:

```
SQL> select count(*) from mlog$_sales;
```

There are two records:

```
  COUNT(*)
----------
         2
```

Next, let's refresh the MV. This MV is fast-refreshable, so you call the REFRESH procedure of the DBMS_MVIEW package with the F (for *fast*) parameter:

```
SQL> exec dbms_mview.refresh('SALES_MV','F');
```

A quick inspection of the MV shows two new records:

```
SQL> select sales_amt, to_char(sales_dtt,'dd-mon-yyyy') from sales_mv;
```

Here's some sample output:

```
SALES_AMT TO_CHAR(SALES_DTT
---------- ------------------
       101 12-jun-2010
       511 12-jul-2010
        11 01-aug-2010
        99 01-aug-2010
       127 01-aug-2010
```

In addition, the count of the MLOG$ has dropped to zero. After the MV refresh is complete, those records are no longer required:

```
SQL> select count(*) from mlog$_sales;
```

Here's the output:

```
  COUNT(*)
----------
         0
```

You can verify the last method in which an MV was refreshed by querying the USER_MVIEWS view:

```
select
mview_name
,last_refresh_type
,last_refresh_date
from user_mviews
order by 1,3;
```

Here's some sample output:

```
MVIEW_NAME                      LAST_REF LAST_REFR
------------------------------- -------- ---------
SALES_MV                        FAST     01-AUG-10
```

Figure 15–2 illustrates the architectural components involved with a fast refresh. The numbers in the boxes represent the sequential flow of the fast-refresh process. If you're new to MVs, pause a few minutes here and make sure you understand all the components.

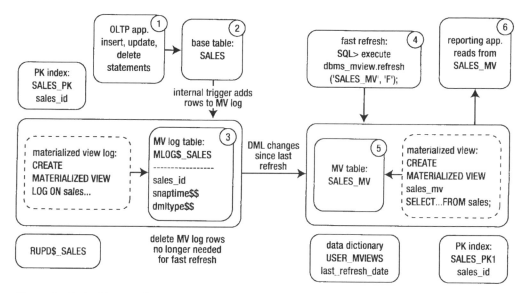

Figure 15–2. Architectural components of a fast-refreshable MV

The numbers in the diagram describe the flow of data for a fast-refreshable MV:

1. Users create transactions.

2. Data is committed in the base table.

3. An internal trigger on the base table populates the MV log table.

4. A fast refresh is initiated via the DBMS_MVIEW package.

5. DML changes that have been created since the last refresh are applied to the MV. Rows no longer needed by the MV are deleted from the MV log.

6. Users can query data from the MV, which contains a point-in-time snapshot of the base table's data.

When you have a good understanding of the architecture of a fast refresh, you won't have difficulty learning advanced MV concepts. If you're new to MVs, it's important to realize that an MV's data is stored in a regular database table. This will help you understand architecturally what is and is not possible. For the most part, because the MV and MV log are based on tables, most features available with a regular database table can also be applied to the MV table and MV log table. For example, the following Oracle features are readily applied to MVs:

*   Storage and tablespace placement

*   Indexing

*   Partitioning

*   Compression

*   Encryption

- Logging
- Parallelism

The next section in this chapter shows examples of how to create MVs with various features.

Going Beyond the Basics

Numerous MV features are available. Many of them are related to attributes that you can apply to any table, such as storage, indexing, compression, encryption, and so on. Other features are related to the type of MV created and how it's refreshed. These aspects are described in the next several subsections.

Creating MVs and Specifying Tablespace for MVs and Indexes

Every MV has an underlying tables associated with it. Additionally, depending on the type of MV, an index may be automatically created. When you create an MV, you can specify the tablespace and storage characteristics for both the underlying table and index. The next example shows how to specify the tablespace to be used for the MV table and a separate tablespace for the index:

```
create materialized view inv_mv
tablespace mv_data
using index tablespace mv_index
as
select
 inv_id
,inv_desc
from inv;
```

You can also specify storage characteristics. For example, if you know you're loading data into MVs that will rarely be updated, it's appropriate to set PCTUSED to a high value, such as 95. For example:

```
create materialized view inv_mv
pctused 95
pctfree 5
tablespace mv_data
using index tablespace mv_index
as
select
 inv_id
,inv_desc
from inv;
```

Creating Indexes on MVs

An MV stores its data in a regular database table. Therefore, you can create indexes on the underlying table (just as you can for any other table). In general, follow the same guidelines for creating an index on an MV table as you would a regular table. (See Chapter 8 for more details on creating indexes.) Keep in mind that although indexes can significantly improve query performance, overhead is associated with maintaining the index for any inserts, updates, and deletes. Indexes also consume disk space.

Listed next is an example of creating an index based on a column in an MV. The syntax is the same as for creating an index on a regular table:

```
SQL> create index inv_mv_idx1 on inv_mv(region_id) tablespace mv_index;
```

You can display the indexes created for an MV by querying the USER_INDEXES view:

```
select
 a.table_name
,a.index_name
from user_indexes a
    ,user_mviews  b
where a.table_name = b.mview_name;
```

■ **Note** If you create a simple MV with the WITH PRIMARY KEY clause that selects from a base table that has a primary key, Oracle automatically creates an index on the corresponding primary-key columns in the MV. If you create a simple MV using the WITH ROWID clause that selects from a base table that has a primary key, Oracle automatically creates an index on a hidden column named M_ROW$$.

Partitioning Materialized Views

You can partition an MV table like any other regular table in the database. If you work with large MVs, you may want to consider partitioning to better manage and maintain a large table. Use the PARTITION clause when you create the MV. This example builds an MV that is partitioned by range on the DATE_ID column:

```
create materialized view inv_mv
partition by range (date_id)
(partition p1
 values less than (20100101)
,partition p2
 values less than (20110101)
,partition p3
 values less than (20120101))
refresh on demand complete with rowid
as
select
 inv_id
,inv_desc
,date_id
from inv;
```

The result set from the query is stored in a partitioned table. You can view the partition details for this table in USER_TAB_PARTITIONS and USER_PART_TABLES (just like any other partitioned table in your database). See chapter 12 for more details on partitioning strategies and maintenance.

Compressing a Materialized View

As mentioned earlier, when you create an MV, an underlying table is created to store the data. Because this table is a regular database table, you can implement features such as compression. For example:

```
create materialized view inv_mv
compress
as
select
 inv_id
,inv_desc
from inv;
```

You can confirm the compression details with the following query:

```
select
  table_name
 ,compression
 ,compress_for
from user_tables where table_name='INV_MV';
```

Here's the output:

```
TABLE_NAME                      COMPRESS COMPRESS_FOR
------------------------------- -------- ------------
INV_MV                          ENABLED  BASIC
```

> ▦ **Note** Basic table compression doesn't require an extra license from Oracle. Online transaction processing (OLTP) compression requires the Advanced Compression option, which requires an extra license from Oracle. See the *Oracle Database Licensing Information* documentation (available on OTN) for details.

Encrypting Materialized View Columns

As mentioned earlier, when you create an MV, an underlying table is created to store the data. Because this table is a regular database table, you can implement features such as encryption of columns. For example:

```
create materialized view inv_mv
(inv_id   encrypt no salt
,inv_desc encrypt)
as
select
 inv_id   inv_id
,inv_desc inv_desc
from inv;
```

For the previous statement to work, you must create and open a security wallet for your database. This feature requires the Advanced Security option from Oracle (which requires an additional license).

You can verify that encryption is in place by describing the MV:

```
SQL> desc inv_mv
 Name                                      Null?    Type
 ----------------------------------------- -------- --------------------
 INV_ID                                    NOT NULL NUMBER ENCRYPT
 INV_DESC                                           VARCHAR2(30) ENCRYPT
```

Building a Materialized View on a Prebuilt Table

In data-warehouse environments, sometimes you need to create a table, populate it with large quantities of data, and then transform it into an MV. Or you may be replicating a large table and find that it's more efficient to initially populate the remote MV by prebuilding the table with data using Data Pump. Listed next are the steps for building an MV on a prebuilt table:

1. Create a table.

2. Populate it with data.

3. Create an MV on the table created in step 1.

Here's a simple example to illustrate the process. First, you create a table:

```
create table inv_mv
(inv_id number
,inv_desc varchar2(30)
);
```

Now, populate the table with data. For example, in a data-warehouse environment, this can be a table loaded using Data Pump, SQL*Loader, or external tables.

Finally, run the CREATE MATERIALIZED VIEW...ON PREBUILT TABLE statement to turn the table into an MV. The MV name and the table name must be identical. Additionally, each column in the query must correspond to a column in the table. For example:

```
create materialized view inv_mv
on prebuilt table
using index tablespace mv_index
as
select
 inv_id
,inv_desc
from inv;
```

Now the INV_MV object is an MV. If you attempt to drop the INV_MV table, the following error is thrown, indicating that INV_MV is now a materialized view:

```
SQL> drop table inv_mv;
ORA-12083: must use DROP MATERIALIZED VIEW to drop "MV"."INV_MV"
```

The prebuilt-table feature is useful in data-warehouse environments where typically there are long periods when a base table isn't being actively updated. This gives you time to load a prebuilt table and ensure that its contents are identical to the base table. After you create the MV on the prebuilt table, you can fast-refresh the MV and keep it in synch with the base table.

If your base table (specified in the SELECT clause of the MV) is continuously being updated, then creating an MV on a prebuilt table may not be a viable option. This is because there is no way to ensure that the prebuilt table stays in synch with the base table.

■ Note For MVs created on prebuilt tables, if you subsequently issue a DROP MATERIALIZED VIEW statement, the underlying table isn't dropped. This has some interesting implications when you need to modify a base table (like adding a column). For details, see the section later in this chapter on Modifying Base-Table DDL and Propagating to Materialized Views.

Creating an Unpopulated Materialized View

When you create an MV, you have the option of instructing Oracle whether or not to initially populate the MV with data. For example, if it takes several hours to initially build an MV, you may want to first define the MV and then populate it as a separate job.

This example uses the BUILD DEFERRED clause to instruct Oracle not to initially populate the MV with the results of the query:

```
create materialized view inv_mv
tablespace mv_data
build deferred
refresh complete on demand
as
select
 inv_id
,inv_desc
from inv;
```

At this point, querying the MV results in zero rows returned. At some later point, you can initiate a complete refresh to populate the MV with data.

Creating a Materialized View Refreshed on Commit

You may have a requirement when data is modified in the master table to have it immediately copied to an MV. In this scenario, use the ON COMMIT clause when you create the MV. The master table must have an MV log created on it for this technique to work. Here's a simple example that creates a table with a primary key, creates an MV log, and then creates an MV refreshed on commit:

```
create table inv(inv_id number primary key,
inv_desc varchar2(30));
--
create materialized view log on inv with primary key;
--
create materialized view inv_mv
refresh
on commit
as
select inv_id, inv_desc from inv;
```

As data is inserted and committed in the master table, any changes are also available in the MV that would be selected by the MV query.

The ON COMMIT refreshable MV has a few restrictions you need to be aware of:

- The master table and MV must be in the same database.

- You can't execute distributed transaction on the base table.

- This approach isn't supported with MVs that contain object types or Oracle-supplied types.

Also consider the overhead associated with committing data simultaneously in two places; this can impact the performance of a high-transaction OLTP system. Additionally, if there is any problem with updating the MV, then the base table can't commit a transaction. For example, if the tablespace in which the MV is created becomes full (and can't allocate another extent), you see an error such as this when trying to insert into the base table:

```
ORA-12008: error in materialized view refresh path
ORA-01653: unable to extend table MV.INV_MV by 16 in tablespace TBSP2
```

For these reasons, you should use this feature only when you're sure it won't affect performance or availability.

■ Note You can't specify an MV to be refreshed with both ON COMMIT and ON DEMAND. In addition, ON COMMIT isn't compatible with the START WITH and NEXT clauses of the CREATE MATERIALIZED VIEW statement.

Creating a Never-Refreshable Materialized View

You may never want an MV to be refreshed. For example, you may want to guarantee that you have a snapshot of table at a point in time for auditing purposes. Specify the NEVER REFRESH clause when you create the MV to achieve this:

```
create materialized view inv_mv
tablespace mv_data
using index tablespace mv_index
never refresh
as
select
 inv_id
,inv_desc
from inv;
```

If you attempt to refresh a nonrefreshable MV, you receive this error:

```
ORA-23538: cannot explicitly refresh a NEVER REFRESH materialized view
```

You can alter a never-refreshable view to being refreshable. Use the ALTER MATERIALIZED VIEW statement to do this:

```
SQL> alter materialized view inv_mv refresh on demand complete;
```

You can verify the refresh mode and method with the following query:

```
select
 mview_name
,refresh_mode
,refresh_method
from user_mviews;
```

Creating Materialized Views for Query-Rewrite

Query rewrite allows the optimizer to recognize that an MV can be used to fulfill the requirements of a query instead of using the underlying master (base) tables. If you have an environment where users frequently write their own queries and are unaware of the available MVs, this feature can help greatly with performance. There are three prerequisites for enabling query-rewrite:

- Oracle Enterprise Edition

- Database initialization parameter QUERY_REWRITE_ENABLED must be set to TRUE (which is the default in Oracle Database 10g or higher

- MV either created or altered with the ENABLE QUERY REWRITE clause

This example creates an MV with query-rewrite enabled:

```
create materialized view sales_mv
tablespace mv_data
using index tablespace mv_index
enable query rewrite
as
select
 sum(sales_amt)
,b.reg_desc
from sales   a
     ,region b
where a.region_id = b.region_id
group by b.reg_desc;
```

You can tell if query-rewrite is enabled for an MV by selecting the REWRITE_ENABLED column from USER_MVIEWS:

```
select
 mview_name
,rewrite_enabled
,rewrite_capability
from user_mviews
where mview_name = 'SALES_MV';
```

Here's the output:

```
MVIEW_NAME R REWRITE_C
---------- - ---------
SALES_MV   Y GENERAL
```

If for any reason a query isn't using the query-rewrite functionality, and you think it should be, use the EXPLAIN_REWRITE procedure of the DBMS_MVIEW package to diagnose issues.

Creating a Fast-Refreshable MV Based on a Complex Query

In many situations, when you base an MV on a query that joins multiple tables, it's deemed complex, and therefore is available only for a complete refresh. However, in some scenarios, you can create a fast-refreshable MV when you reference two tables that are joined together in the MV query.

This section describes how to use the EXPLAIN_MVIEW procedure of the DBMS_MVIEW to determine whether it's possible to fast-refresh a complex query. To help you completely understand the example, this section shows the SQL used to create the base tables. Say you have two base tables, REGION and INV, which are defined as follows:

```
create table region(
 region_id number
,reg_desc varchar2(30)
,constraint region_pk primary key(region_id));
--
create table inv(
 inv_id    number
,inv_desc  varchar2(30)
,region_id number
,constraint inv_pk primary key(inv_id)
,constraint dept_fk foreign key (region_id) references region(region_id));
```

Additionally, REGION and INV have MV logs created on them as follows:

```
SQL> create materialized view log on region with primary key;
SQL> create materialized view log on inv with primary key;
```

Also, for this example, the base tables have the following data inserted into them:

```
insert into region values(10,'East');
insert into region values(20,'West');
insert into region values(30,'South');
insert into region values(40,'North');
--
insert into inv values(1,'book',10);
insert into inv values(2,'table',20);
insert into inv values(3,'chair',30);
```

Suppose you want to create an MV that joins the REGION and INV base tables as follows:

```
create materialized view inv_mv
tablespace mv_data
using index tablespace mv_index
as
select
 a.inv_desc
,b.reg_desc
from inv    a
    ,region b
where a.region_id = b.region_id;
```

Next, let's attempt to fast-refresh the MV:

```
SQL> exec dbms_mview.refresh('INV_MV','F');
```

This error is thrown:

```
ORA-12032: cannot use rowid column from materialized view log on "MV"."REGION"
```

The error indicates that the MV has issues and can't be fast-refreshed. To determine whether this MV can become fast-refreshable, use the output of the EXPLAIN_MVIEW procedure of the DBMS_MVIEW package. This procedure requires that you first create MV_CAPABILITIES_TABLE first be created. Oracle provides a script to do this. Run this as the owner of the MV:

```
SQL> @?/rdbms/admin/utlxmv.sql
```

After you create the table, run the EXPLAIN_MVIEW procedure to populate it:

```
SQL> exec dbms_mview.explain_mview(mv=>'INV_MV',stmt_id=>'100');
```

Now, query MV_CAPABILITIES_TABLE to see what potential issues this MV may have:

```
select
 capability_name
,possible
,msgtxt
,related_text
from mv_capabilities_table
where capability_name like 'REFRESH_FAST_AFTER%'
and statement_id = '100'
order by 1;
```

Listed next is the output. The P (POSSIBLE) column contains an N (NO) for every fast-refresh possibility:

```
CAPABILITY_NAME                 P MSGTXT                          RELATED_TEXT
------------------------------- - ------------------------------- ----------------
REFRESH_FAST_AFTER_ANY_DML      N see the reason why REFRESH_FAS
                                  T_AFTER_ONETAB_DML is disabled
REFRESH_FAST_AFTER_INSERT       N mv log must have ROWID          MV.REGION
REFRESH_FAST_AFTER_INSERT       N the SELECT list does not have   B
                                  the rowids of all the detail t
                                  ables
REFRESH_FAST_AFTER_INSERT       N mv log must have ROWID          MV.INV
REFRESH_FAST_AFTER_ONETAB_DML   N see the reason why REFRESH_FAS
                                  T_AFTER_INSERT is disabled
```

MSGTXT indicates one issue: the MV logs need to be ROWID based. Let's drop and re-create the MV logs with ROWID (instead of a primary key):

```
drop materialized view log on region;
drop materialized view log on inv;
--
create materialized view log on region with rowid;
create materialized view log on inv with rowid;
```

Next, reset MV_CAPABILITIES_TABLE and repopulate it via the EXPLAIN_MVIEW procedure:

```
SQL> delete from mv_capabilities_table where statement_id=100;
SQL> exec dbms_mview.explain_mview(mv=>'INV_MV',stmt_id=>'100');
```

Re-running the previous query that selects from MV_CAPABILITIES_TABLE (not reproduced here) shows the output:

```
CAPABILITY_NAME                 P MSGTXT                          RELATED_TEXT
------------------------------- - ------------------------------- ----------------
REFRESH_FAST_AFTER_ANY_DML      N see the reason why REFRESH_FAS
```

```
                                 T_AFTER_ONETAB_DML is disabled
REFRESH_FAST_AFTER_INSERT        N mv log is newer than last full MV.REGION
                                   refresh
REFRESH_FAST_AFTER_INSERT        N the SELECT list does not have  B
                                   the rowids of all the detail t
                                   ables
REFRESH_FAST_AFTER_INSERT        N mv log is newer than last full MV.INV
                                   refresh
REFRESH_FAST_AFTER_ONETAB_DML    N see the reason why REFRESH_FAS
                                   T_AFTER_INSERT is disabled
```

From the previous output, the MV SELECT statement needs to contain the ROWIDs of the base tables. The next few lines of code drop the MV and re-create it with the SQL statement rewritten to contain the ROWIDs:

```
drop materialized view inv_mv;
--
create materialized view inv_mv
as
select
 a.rowid inv_rowid
,b.rowid region_rowid
,a.inv_desc
,b.reg_desc
from inv    a
    ,region b
where a.region_id = b.region_id;
```

Next, reset MV_CAPABILITIES_TABLE and repopulate it via the EXPLAIN_MVIEW procedure:

```
SQL> delete from mv_capabilities_table where statement_id=100;
SQL> exec dbms_mview.explain_mview(mv=>'INV_MV',stmt_id=>'100');
```

The output shows that it's now possible to fast-refresh the MV:

```
CAPABILITY_NAME                  P MSGTXT                            RELATED_TEXT
-------------------------------- - --------------------------------- ---------------
REFRESH_FAST_AFTER_ANY_DML       Y
REFRESH_FAST_AFTER_INSERT        Y
REFRESH_FAST_AFTER_ONETAB_DML    Y
```

Execute the following statement to see if the fast refresh works:

```
SQL> exec dbms_mview.refresh('INV_MV','F');
PL/SQL procedure successfully completed.
```

The EXPLAIN_MVIEW procedure is a powerful tool that allows you to determine whether a refresh capability is possible and, if it's not possible, why it isn't and how to potentially resolve the issue.

Viewing Materialized View DDL

To quickly view the SQL query on which an MV is based, select from the QUERY column of DBA/ALL/USER_MVIEWS. If you're using SQL*Plus, first set the LONG variable to a value large enough to display the entire contents of a LONG column:

```
SQL> set long 5000
SQL> select query from dba_mviews where mview_name=UPPER('&&mview_name');
```

To view the entire Data Definition Language ()DDL required to re-create an MV, use the
DBMS_METADATA package (you also need to set the LONG variable to a large value if using SQL*Plus):

```
SQL> select dbms_metadata.get_ddl('MATERIALIZED_VIEW','INV_MV') from dual;
```

Here's the output for this example:

```
CREATE MATERIALIZED VIEW "MV"."INV_MV" ("INV_ROWID", "REGION_ROWID", "INV_DESC",
"REG_DESC") ORGANIZATION HEAP PCTFREE 10 PCTUSED 40 INITRANS 1
MAXTRANS 255 NOCOMPRESS LOGGING
   STORAGE(INITIAL 65536 NEXT 1048576 MINEXTENTS 1 MAXEXTENTS 2147483645
   PCTINCREASE 0 FREELISTS 1 FREELIST GROUPS 1 BUFFER_POOL DEFAULT FLASH_CACHE
DEFAULT CELL_FLASH_CACHE DEFAULT)
   TABLESPACE "USERS"
   BUILD IMMEDIATE
   USING INDEX
   REFRESH FORCE ON DEMAND
   USING DEFAULT LOCAL ROLLBACK SEGMENT
   USING ENFORCED CONSTRAINTS DISABLE QUERY REWRITE
   AS select
 a.rowid inv_rowid
,b.rowid region_rowid
,a.inv_desc
,b.reg_desc
from inv     a
    ,region b
where a.region_id = b.region_id
```

This output shows the DDL that Oracle thinks is required to re-create the MV. This is usually the
most reliable way to generate the DDL associated with an MV.

Dropping a Materialized View

You may occasionally need to drop an MV. Perhaps a view is no longer being used, or you need to drop
and re-create an MV to change the underlying query on which the MV is based (such as adding a column
to it). Use the DROP MATERIALIZED VIEW command to drop an MV. This example drops a view named
ORDERS_MV:

```
SQL> drop materialized view orders_mv;
```

When you drop an MV, the MV object, the table object, and any corresponding indexes are also
dropped. Dropping an MV doesn't affect any MV logs—an MV log is dependent only on the master table.
You can also specify that the underlying table be preserved. You may want to do this if you're
troubleshooting and need to drop the MV definition but keep the MV table and data. For example:

```
SQL> drop materialized view inv_mv preserve table;
```

In this scenario, you can also use the underlying table later as the basis for an MV by building the
MV using the ON PREBUILT TABLE clause.

If the MV was originally built using the ON PREBUILT TABLE clause, then when you drop the MV, the underlying table isn't dropped. If you want the underlying table dropped, you must use a DROP TABLE statement:

```
SQL> drop materialized view inv_mv;
SQL> drop table inv_mv;
```

Modifying Materialized Views

This section describes common maintenance tasks associated with MVs. Topics covered include how to modify an MV to reflect column changes that have been applied to the base table some time after the MV was initially created, and modifying attributes such as logging and parallelism.

Modifying Base-Table DDL and Propagating to Materialized Views

A common task involves adding a column to or dropping a column from a base table (because business requirements have changed). After the column is added to or dropped from the base table, you want those DDL changes to be reflected in any dependent MVs. You have a few options for propagating base-table column changes to dependent MVs:

- Drop and re-create the MV with the new column definitions.

- Drop the MV, but preserve the underlying table, modify the MV table, and then re-create the MV (with the new column changes) using the ON PREBUILT TABLE clause.

- If the MV was originally created using the ON PREBUILT TABLE clause, drop the MV object, modify the MV table, and then re-create the MV (with the new column changes) using the ON PREBUILT TABLE clause.

With any of the previous options, you have to drop and re-create the MV so that it's aware of the column changes in the base table. These approaches are described next.

Re-creating a Materialized View to Reflect Base-Table Modifications

Suppose you make a modification to a base table, such as adding a column:

```
SQL> alter table inv add(inv_loc varchar2(30));
```

You also have a simple MV named INV_MV that is based on this table. You want the base-table modification to be reflected in the MV. How do you accomplish this task? You know that the MV contains an underlying table that stores the results. You decide to modify the underlying MV table directly:

```
SQL> alter table inv_mv add(inv_loc varchar2(30));
```

The alteration is successful. You next refresh the MV but realize that the additional column isn't being refreshed. To understand why, recall that an MV is a SQL query that stores its results in an underlying table. Therefore, to modify an MV, you have to change the SQL query that the MV is based on. Because there is no ALTER MATERIALIZED VIEW ADD/DROP/MODIFY <column> statement, you must do the following to add/delete columns in an MV:

1. Alter the base table.

2. Drop and re-create the MV to reflect the changes in the base table.

Here's an example. Say you need to add a column INV_LOC to the base INV table:

```
SQL> alter table inv add(inv_loc varchar2(30));
```

Drop and re-create the MV to include the column definition:

```
drop materialized view inv_mv;
--
create materialized view inv_mv
refresh fast on demand
as
select
 inv_id
,inv_desc
,inv_loc
from inv;
```

This approach may take a long time if large amounts of data are involved. You have downtime for any application that accesses the MV while it's being rebuilt. If you work in a large data-warehouse environment, then due to the amount of time it takes to completely refresh the MV, you may want to consider not dropping the underlying table. This option is discussed in the next section.

Altering a Materialized View but Preserving the Underlying Table

When you drop an MV, you have the option of preserving the underlying table and its data. You may find this approach advantageous when you're working with large MVs in data-warehouse environments. Here are the steps:

1. Alter the base table.

2. Drop the MV, but preserve the underlying table.

3. Modify the underlying table.

4. Re-create the MV using the ON PREBUILT TABLE clause.

Here's a simple example to illustrate this procedure:

```
SQL> alter table inv add(inv_loc varchar2(30));
```

Drop the MV, but specify that you want to preserve the underlying table:

```
SQL> drop materialized view inv_mv preserve table;
```

Now, modify the underlying table:

```
SQL> alter table inv_mv add(inv_loc varchar2(30));
```

Next, create the MV using the ON PREBUILT TABLE clause:

```
create materialized view inv_mv
on prebuilt table
using index tablespace mv_index
as
select
```

```
 inv_id
,inv_desc
,inv_loc
from inv;
```

This allows you to redefine the MV without dropping and completely refreshing the data. Be aware that if there is any Data Manipulation Language (DML) activity against the base table during the MV rebuild operation, those transactions aren't reflected in the MV when you attempt to refresh it. In data-warehouse environments, you typically have a known schedule for loading base tables and therefore should be able to schedule the MV alteration during a maintenance window when no transactions are occurring in the base table.

Altering a Materialized View Created on a Prebuilt Table

If you originally created an MV using the ON PREBUILT TABLE clause, then you can perform a procedure similar to that shown in the previous section when preserving the underlying table. Here are the steps for modifying an MV that was created using the ON PREBUILT TABLE clause:

1.   Alter the base table.

2.   Drop the MV. For MVs built on prebuilt tables, this doesn't drop the underlying table.

3.   Alter the prebuilt table.

4.   Re-create the MV on the prebuilt table.

Here's a simple example to illustrate this process. For clarity, the original definition of the table and MV are shown. Here's the base-table definition:

```
create table inv(
 inv_id number primary key
,inv_desc varchar2(30));
```

To create an MV on a prebuilt table, you must first create a table:

```
create table inv_mv (
 inv_id number
,inv_desc varchar2(30));
```

Here's the definition of a simple MV that is created using a prebuilt table and uses INV as a base table:

```
create materialized view inv_mv
on prebuilt table
using index tablespace mv_index
as
select
 inv_id
,inv_desc
from inv;
```

Suppose you alter the base table as follows:

```
SQL> alter table inv add (inv_loc varchar2(30));
```

Drop the MV:

```
SQL> drop materialized view inv_mv;
```

For MVs created on prebuilt tables, this doesn't drop the underlying table—only the MV object is dropped. Next, add a column to the prebuilt table:

```
SQL> alter table inv_mv add(inv_loc varchar2(30));
```

Now you can rebuild the MV using the prebuilt table with the new INV_LOC column added:

```
create materialized view inv_mv
on prebuilt table
using index tablespace mv_index
as
select
 inv_id
,inv_desc
,inv_loc
from inv;
```

This process has the advantage of allowing you to modify an MV definition without dropping the underlying table. You have to drop the MV, alter the underlying table, and then re-create the MV with the new definition. If the underlying table contains a large amount of data, this method can prevent unwanted downtime.

As mentioned in the previous section, you need to be aware that if there is any DML activity against the base table during the MV rebuild operation, those transactions aren't reflected in the MV when you attempt to refresh it.

Toggling Redo Logging on a Materialized View

Recall that an MV has an underlying database table. When you refresh an MV, this initiates transactions in the underlying table that result in the generation of redo (just as with a normal database table). In the event of a database failure, you can restore and recover all the transactions associated with an MV.

By default, redo logging is enabled when you create an MV. You have the option of specifying that redo not be logged when an MV is refreshed. To enable no logging, create the MV with the NOLOGGING option:

```
create materialized view inv_mv
nologging
tablespace mv_data
using index tablespace mv_index
as
select
 inv_id
,inv_desc
from inv;
```

You can also alter an existing MV into no-logging mode:

```
SQL> alter materialized view inv_mv nologging;
```

If you want to re-enable logging, then do as follows:

```
SQL> alter materialized view inv_mv logging;
```

To verify that the MV has been switched to NOLOGGING, query the USER_TABLES view:

```
select
 a.table_name
,a.logging
from user_tables a
     ,user_mviews b
where a.table_name = b.mview_name;
```

The advantage of enabling no logging is that refreshes take place more quickly, because the database doesn't have the overhead of logging redo information. The big downside is that if a media failure occurs soon after an MV has been refreshed, you can't recover the data in the MV. In this scenario, the first time you attempt to access the MV, you receive an error such as:

```
ORA-01578: ORACLE data block corrupted (file # 32, block # 131)
ORA-01110: data file 32: '/ora01/dbfile/O11R2/mvdata01.dbf'
ORA-26040: Data block was loaded using the NOLOGGING option
```

If you get the previous error, then you'll most likely have to completely refresh the MV to make the data accessible again. In many environments, this may be acceptable. You save on database resources by not generating redo for the MV, but the downside is a longer restore process (in the event of a failure) that requires you to completely refresh the MV.

Altering Parallelism

Sometimes an MV is created with a high degree of parallelism to improve the performance of the creation process. After you create the MV, you may not need the same degree of parallelism associated with the underlying table. You can alter an MV's parallelism as follows:

```
SQL> alter materialized view inv_mv parallel 1;
```

You can check on the degree of parallelism by querying USER_TABLES:

```
SQL> select table_name, degree from user_tables where table_name= upper('&mv_name');
TABLE_NAME                    DEGREE
----------------------------- ------
INV_MV                             1
```

Moving a Materialized View

As the operating environment's conditions change, you may need to move an MV from one tablespace to another. In these scenarios, use the ALTER MATERIALIZED VIEW...MOVE TABLESPACE statement. This example moves the table associated with an MV to a different tablespace:

```
SQL> alter materialized view inv_mv move tablespace tbsp2;
```

If any indexes are associated with the MV table, the move operation renders them unusable. You can check the status of the indexes as follows:

```
select
 a.table_name
,a.index_name
,a.status
from user_indexes a
     ,user_mviews  b
where a.table_name = b.mview_name;
```

You must rebuild any associated indexes after moving the table. For example:

```
SQL> alter index inv_mv_pk1 rebuild;
```

Managing Materialized View Logs

MV logs are required for fast-refreshable MVs. The MV log is a table that stores DML information for a master (base) table. It's created in the same database as the master table with the same user that owns the master table. You need the CREATE TABLE privilege to create an MV log.

The MV log is populated by an Oracle internal trigger (that you have no control over). This internal trigger inserts a row into the MV log after an INSERT, UPDATE, or DELETE on the master table. You can view the internal triggers in use by querying DBA/ALL/USER_INTERNAL_TRIGGERS.

An MV log is associated with only one table, and each master table can have only one MV log defined for it. You can create an MV log on a table or on another MV. Multiple fast-refreshable MVs can use one MV log.

After an MV performs a fast refresh, any records in the MV log that are no longer needed are deleted. In the event that multiple MVs are using one MV log, then records are purged from the MV log only after they aren't required by any of the fast-refreshable MVs.

Table 15–3 describes terms used with MV logs. These terms are referred to in the following sections in this chapter that relate to MV logs.

Table 15–3. Materialized View Log Terminology and Features

MV Log Term	Description
Materialized view log	Database object that tracks DML changes to MV base table. An MV log is required for fast refreshes.
Primary key MV log	MV log that uses the base-table primary key to track DML changes.
ROWID MV log	MV log that uses the base table ROWID to track DML changes.
Commit SCN MV log	MV log based on the commit system change number (SCN) instead of a timestamp. Available in Oracle Database 11g R2 or higher.
Object ID	Object identifier used to track DML changes.
Filter column	Non-primary-key column referenced by an MV subquery. Required by some fast-refresh scenarios.
Join column	Non-primary-key column that defines a join in the subquery WHERE clause. Required by some fast-refresh scenarios.
Sequence	Sequence value required for some fast-refresh scenarios.
New values	Specifies that old and new values be recorded in the MV log. Required for single-table aggregate views to be eligible for fast refresh.

Creating a Materialized View Log

Fast-refreshable views require an MV log to be created on the master (base) table. Use the CREATE MATERIALIZED VIEW LOG command to create an MV log. This example creates an MV log on the USERS table, specifying that the primary key should be used to identify rows in the MV log:

```
SQL> create materialized view log on users with primary key;
```

You can also specify storage information such as the tablespace name:

```
create materialized view log
on users
pctfree 5
tablespace mv_data
with primary key;
```

When you create an MV log on a table, Oracle creates a table to store the changes to a base table since the last refresh. The name of the MV log table follows this format: MLOG$_<master_table_name>. You can use the SQL*Plus DESCRIBE statement to view the columns of the MV log:

```
SQL> desc mlog$_users;
 Name                             Null?    Type
 ------------------------------- -------- -------------------------
 USER_ID                                  NUMBER
 SNAPTIME$$                                DATE
 DMLTYPE$$                                 VARCHAR2(1)
 OLD_NEW$$                                 VARCHAR2(1)
 CHANGE_VECTOR$$                           RAW(255)
 XID$$                                     NUMBER
```

You can query this underlying MLOG$ table to determine the number of transactions since the last refresh. After each refresh, the MV log table is purged. If multiple MVs use the MV log, the log table isn't purged until all dependent MVs are refreshed.

If you create the MV log on a table with a primary key, then a RUPD$_<master_table_name> table is also created. This table is used for updatable MVs. If you're not using the updatable MV feature, then this table is never used, and you can ignore it.

When you create an MV log, you can specify that it use PRIMARY KEY, ROWID, or OBJECT ID to uniquely identify rows in the MV log table. If the master table has a primary key, then use WITH PRIMARY KEY when you create the MV log. If the master table doesn't have a primary key, then you have to use WITH ROWID to specify that a ROWID value is used to uniquely identify MV log records. You can use WITH OBJECT ID when you create an MV log on an object table.

For database versions prior to Oracle Database 11g release 2, the MV log table will contains a SNAPTIME$$ time column. This column is used to determine which records need to be applied to any dependent MVs.

As of Oracle Database 11g release 2, you have the option of creating a COMMIT SCN–based MV log. This type of MV log uses the SCN of a transaction to determine which records need to be applied to any dependent MVs. COMMIT SCN–based MV logs are more efficient than timestamp-based MV logs. If you're using Oracle Database 11g release 2 or higher, then you should consider using COMMIT SCN–based MV logs. Use the WITH COMMIT SCN clause to create an SCN–based MV log:

```
SQL> create materialized view log on inv tablespace users with commit scn;
```

You can view whether an MV log is SCN based by querying USER_MVIEW_LOGS:

```
select
 log_table
,commit_scn_based
from user_mview_logs;
```

Indexing Materialized View Log Columns

Sometimes you may need better performance from your fast-refreshing MVs. One way to do this is through indexes on columns of the MV log table. In particular, consider indexing the primary-key column and the SNAPTIME$$ column. Oracle potentially uses two columns in WHERE clauses when refreshing an MV or purging the MV log. Here are examples of creating indexes on MV log columns:

```
SQL> create index mlog$_inv_idx1 on mlog$_inv(snaptime$$) tablespace mv_index;
SQL> create index mlog$_inv_idx2 on mlog$_inv(inv_id) tablespace mv_index;
```

You shouldn't add indexes just because you think it may be a good idea. Only add indexes on the MV log tables when you have known performance issues with fast refreshes. Keep in mind that adding indexes consumes resources in the database. Oracle has to maintain the index for DML operations on the table, and an index consumes disk space. Indexes aren't free silver bullets for performance issues; they come with some cost, so you should use them judiciously.

Viewing Space Used by a Materialized View Log

You should consider periodically checking the space consumed by an MV log. If the space consumed is growing (and never shrinking), you may have an issue with an MV not successfully refreshing (and hence causing the MV log never to be purged). Here's a query to check the space of MV logs:

```
select
 segment_name
,tablespace_name
,bytes/1024/1024 meg_bytes
,extents
from dba_segments
where segment_name like 'MLOG$%'
order by meg_bytes;
```

Here's some sample output:

SEGMENT_NAME	TABLESPACE_NAME	MEG_BYTES	EXTENTS
MLOG$_USER_ROLES_ASSOC	MV_DATA	24.00	48
MLOG$_ASSET_GEO_LOCATIONS	MV_DATA	60.50	121
MLOG$_USERS	MV_DATA	88.50	177
MLOG$_REGISTRATIONS	MV_DATA	465.00	930

This output indicates that several MV logs most likely have purging issues. The MLOG$_REGISTRATIONS segment is consuming nearly 500MB of space. In this situation, there are probably multiple MVs that are using the MV log, and one of the MVs isn't refreshing on a daily basis, thus preventing the log from being purged.

You may run into a situation where an MV log hasn't been purged for quite some time. This can happen because you have multiple MVs using the same MV log and one of those MVs isn't successfully refreshing anymore. This can happen when a DBA builds a development environment and connects development MVs to the production environment (it shouldn't happen, but it does). At some later point in time, the DBA drops the development database. The production environment still has information regarding the remote development MV and won't purge MV log records because it thinks a fast-refreshable MV needs the log data to refresh.

In these scenarios, you should determine which MVs are using the log (see the section on Determining How Many MVs Reference a Central MV Log) and resolve any issues. After the problem is solved, check the space being used by the log and see if it can be shrunk (see the next section).

Shrinking the Space in a Materialized View Log

If an MV log doesn't successfully delete records, this causes it to grow to a large size. After you resolve the issue and the records are deleted from the MV log, you can set the high-water mark for the MV log table to a high value. But doing so may cause performance issues and also unnecessarily consumes disk space. In this situations, consider shrinking the space used by the MV log.

In this example, MLOG$_REGISTRATIONS had a problem with not purging records because of an issue with an associated MV not successfully refreshing. This MV log subsequently grew to a large size. The issue was identified and resolved, and now the log's space needs to be reduced. To shrink the space in an MV log, first enable row movement on the appropriate MV log MLOG$ table:

```
SQL> alter table mlog$_registrations enable row movement;
```

Next, issue the ALTER MATERIALIZED VIEW LOG ON...SHRINK statement. Notice that the table after the ON keyword is the master table name (in this example, it's the REGISTRATIONS table):

```
SQL> alter materialized view log on registrations shrink space;
```

This statement may take a long time, depending on the amount of space it shrinks. After the statement finishes, you can disable row movement:

```
SQL> alter table mlog$_registrations disable row movement;
```

You can verify that the space has been reduced by querying DBA_SEGMENTS:

```
select
 segment_name
,tablespace_name
,bytes/1024/1024 meg_bytes
,extents
from dba_segments
where segment_name = 'MLOG$_REGISTRATIONS';
```

The space used by this segment is quite small:

SEGMENT_NAME	TABLESPACE_NAME	MEG_BYTES	EXTENTS
MLOG$_REGISTRATIONS	MV_DATA	.50	1

Checking the Row Count of a Materialized View Log

As mentioned earlier in this chapter, sometimes there are problems with an MV refreshing, and this results in large numbers of rows building up in the corresponding MV log table. This sometimes happens when multiple MVs are using one MV log, and one of the MVs can't perform a fast refresh. In this situation, the MV log continues to grow until the issue is resolved.

One way of detecting whether an MV log isn't being purged is to periodically check the row counts of the MV log tables. The following query uses SQL to generate SQL that creates a script that checks row counts for MV log tables owned by the currently connected user:

```
set head off pages 0 lines 132 trimspool on
spo mvcount_dyn.sql
select 'select count(*) || ' || '''' || ': ' || table_name || ''''
|| ' from ' || table_name || ';'
from user_tables
where table_name like 'MLOG%';
spo off;
```

This script generates a script named mvcount_dyn.sql that contains the SQL statements to select row counts from the MLOG$ tables. When you're inspecting row counts, you must be somewhat familiar with your application and have an idea what a normal row count is. Here's some sample code generated by the previous script:

```
select count(*) || ': MLOG$_PRODUCT_TAXONOMY' from MLOG$_PRODUCT_TAXONOMY;
select count(*) || ': MLOG$_REGISTRATIONS' from MLOG$_REGISTRATIONS;
select count(*) || ': MLOG$_ROLES' from MLOG$_ROLES;
```

Moving a Materialized View Log

You may need to move an MV log because the initial creation script didn't specify the correct tablespace. A common scenario is when the tablespace isn't specified, and the MV log is placed by default in a tablespace like USERS. You can verify the tablespace information with this query:

```
select
 table_name
,tablespace_name
from user_tables
where table_name like 'MLOG%';
```

If any MV log tables need to be relocated, use the ALTER MATERIALIZED VIEW LOG ON <table_name> MOVE statement. Notice that you specify the name of the master table (and not the underlying MLOG$ table) on which the MV is created:

```
SQL> alter materialized view log on inv move tablespace tbsp2;
```

Also keep in mind that when you move a table, any associated indexes are rendered unusable (because the ROWID of every record in the table has just changed). You can check the status of the indexes as shown:

```
select
 a.table_name
,a.index_name
,a.status
from user_indexes a
    ,user_mview_logs b
where a.table_name = b.log_table;
```

Any unusable indexes must be rebuilt. Here's an example of rebuilding an index:

```
SQL> alter index mlog$_inv_idx1 rebuild;
```

Dropping a Materialized View Log

There are a couple of reasons why you may want to drop an MV log:

- You initially created an MV log, but requirements have changed and you no longer need it.

- The MV log has grown large and is causing performance issues, and you want to drop it to reset the size.

Before you drop an MV log, you can verify the owner, master table, and MV log table with the following query:

```
select
 log_owner
,master      -- master table
,log_table
from user_mview_logs;
```

Use the DROP MATERIALIZED VIEW LOG ON statement to drop an MV log. You don't need to know the name of the MV log, but you do need to know the name of the master table on which the log was created. This example drops the MV log on the INV table:

```
SQL> drop materialized view log on inv;
```

You should see the following message (if successful):

```
Materialized view log dropped.
```

If you have permissions, and you don't own the table on which the MV log is created, you can specify the schema name when dropping the materialized view log:

```
SQL> drop materialized view log on <schema>.<table>;
```

If you're cleaning up an environment and want to drop all MV logs associated with a user, then use SQL to generate SQL to accomplish this. The following script creates the SQL required to drop all MV logs owned by the currently connected user:

```
set lines 132 pages 0 head off trimspool on
spo drop_dyn.sql
select 'drop materialized view log on ' || master || ';'
from user_mview_logs;
spo off;
```

The previous SQL*Plus code creates a script named drop_dyn.sql that contains the SQL statements that can be used to drop all MV logs for a user.

Refreshing Materialized Views

Typically, you refresh MVs at periodic intervals. You can either refresh the MVs manually or automate this task. The following sections cover these related topics:

- Manually refreshing MVs from SQL*Plus

- Automating refreshes using a shell script and scheduling utility

- Automating refreshes using the built-in Oracle job scheduler

> ■ **Note** If you require that a group of MV be refreshed as a set, see the section "Managing Materialized Views in Groups" later in this chapter.

Manually Refreshing Materialized Views from SQL*Plus

Sooner or later, you'll need to refresh an MV manually. Usually this is because you're testing a refresh or troubleshooting an issue. To do so, use SQL*Plus to call the REFRESH procedure of the DBMS_MVIEW package. The procedure takes two parameters: the MV name and the refresh method. This example uses the EXEC[UTE] statement to call the procedure. The MV being refreshed is INV_MV, and the refresh method is F (for *fast*):

```
SQL> exec dbms_mview.refresh('INV_MV','F');
```

You can also manually run a refresh from SQL*Plus using an anonymous block of PL/SQL. This example performs a fast refresh:

```
SQL> begin
  2  dbms_mview.refresh('INV_MV','F');
  3  end;
  4  /
```

In addition, you can use a question mark (?) to invoke the force-refresh method. This instructs Oracle to perform a fast refresh if possible. If a fast refresh isn't possible, then Oracle performs a complete refresh:

```
SQL> exec dbms_mview.refresh('INV_MV','?');
```

You can also use a C (for *complete*) to specifically execute the complete-refresh method:

```
SQL> exec dbms_mview.refresh('INV_MV','C');
```

MATERIALIZED VIEWS VS. ROW CACHE

Oracle Database 11*g* has a result-cache feature that stores the result of a query in memory and makes that result set available to any subsequent identical queries that are issued. If a subsequent identical query is issued, and none of the underlying table data has changed since the original query was issued, Oracle makes the result available to the subsequent query. For databases with relatively static data and many identical queries being issued, using the result cache can significantly improve performance.

How do MVs compare to the result cache? Recall that an MV stores the result of a query in a table and makes that result available to reporting applications. The two features sound similar but differ in a couple of significant ways:

1. The result cache stores results in memory. An MV stores results in a table.

2. The result cache needs to be refreshed any time the underlying data in the tables changes. MVs are refreshed on commit or at a periodic interval (such as on a daily basis).

The result cache can significantly improve performance if you have long-running queries that operate on relatively static data. MVs are better suited for replicating data and storing the results of complex queries that only require new results on a periodic basis (such as daily, weekly, or monthly).

Automating Refreshes Using a Shell Script and Scheduling Utility

Many MVs must be refreshed on a daily basis. To achieve this, you can use a Linux/Unix utility such as cron that calls a shell script to refresh the MVs. This approach

- Is easy to implement and maintain

- Makes it easy to create a daily log file for auditing

- Sends e-mail when the job has problems or when the database isn't available

Here's an example of a shell script that contains the logic to refresh an MV:

```
#!/bin/bash
if [ $# -ne 1 ]; then
  echo "Usage: $0 SID"
  exit 1
fi
#
HOSTNAME=`uname -a | awk '{print$2}'`
MAILX-'/bin/mailx'
MAIL_LIST='lellison@oracle.com'
ORACLE_SID=$1
jobname=CWP
# See Chapter 2 for details on using a utility
# like oraset to source OS variables
# Source oracle OS variables
. /var/opt/oracle/oraset $ORACLE_SID
date
#
sqlplus -s <<EOF
rep_mv2/foobar
WHENEVER SQLERROR EXIT FAILURE
exec dbms_mview.refresh('CWP_COUNTRY_INFO','C');
EOF
#
if [ $? -ne 0 ]; then
echo "not okay"
$MAILX -s "Problem with MV refresh on $HOSTNAME $jobname" $MAIL_LIST <<EOF
$HOSTNAME $jobname MVs not okay.
EOF
else
echo "okay"
$MAILX -s "MV refresh OK on $HOSTNAME $jobname" $MAIL_LIST <<EOF
$HOSTNAME $jobname MVs okay.
EOF
fi
#
date
```

```
exit 0
```

For this particular MV refresh job, here's the corresponding cron entry that invokes it:

```
25 16 * * * /orahome/oracle/bin/mvref_cwp.bsh DWREP \
1>/orahome/oracle/bin/log/mvref_cwp.log 2>&1
```

This job runs on a daily basis at 4:25 p.m. For details on using cron to schedule jobs, see Chapter 21.

Creating an MV with a Refresh Interval

When you initially create an MV, you have the option of specifying START WITH and NEXT clauses that instruct Oracle to set up an internal database job (via the DBMS_JOB package) to initiate the refresh of an MV on a periodic basis. If you omit START WITH and NEXT, then no job is set up, and you have to use another technique (such as a scheduling utility like cron).

I almost never specify START WITH and NEXT as a refresh mechanism. I strongly prefer to use another scheduling utility such as cron. When using cron, it's easy to create a log file that details how the job ran and whether there were any issues. Also, when using cron, it's easy to have the log file e-mailed to a distribution list so the support DBAs are aware of any issues.

Regardless, it's important to understand how START WITH and NEXT work, because sooner or later you'll find yourself in an environment where DBAs or developers prefer to use the DBMS_JOB package for refreshes. When you're troubleshooting refresh issues, you must understand how this refresh mechanism works.

The START WITH parameter specifies the date when you want the first refresh of an MV to occur. The NEXT parameter specifies a date expression that Oracle uses to calculate the interval between refreshes. For example, this MV initially refreshes one minute in the future (sysdate+1/1440) and subsequently refreshes on a daily basis (sysdate+1):

```
create materialized view inv_mv
refresh
start with sysdate+1/1440
next sysdate+1
as
select
 inv_id
,inv_desc
from inv;
```

You can view details of the scheduled job by querying USER_JOBS:

```
select
 job
,schema_user
,to_char(last_date,'dd-mon-yyyy hh24:mi:ss') last_date
,to_char(next_date,'dd-mon-yyyy hh24:mi:ss') next_date
,interval
,broken
from user_jobs;
```

Here's some sample output:

JOB	SCHEMA_USE	LAST_DATE	NEXT_DATE	INTERVAL	B
50	INV		21-oct-2010 15:30:28	sysdate+1	N

You can also view job information in the USER_REFRESH view:

```
select
 rowner
,rname
,job
,to_char(next_date,'dd-mon-yyyy hh24:mi:ss')
,interval
,broken
from user_refresh;
```

Here's some sample output:

```
ROWNER      RNAME           JOB TO_CHAR(NEXT_DATE,'DD-MON- INTERVAL          B
----------- ----------- ------ -------------------------- --------------- -
INV         INV_MV          50 22-oct-2010 15:30:29       sysdate+1       N
```

When you drop an MV, the associated job is also removed. If you want to manually remove a job, use the REMOVE procedure of DBMS_JOB. This example removes job number 32, which was identified from the previous queries:

```
SQL> exec dbms_job.remove(32);
```

■ **Note** You can't use START WITH or NEXT in conjunction with an MV that refreshes ON COMMIT.

Efficiently Performing a Complete Refresh

When an MV does a complete refresh, the default behavior is to use a DELETE statement to remove all records from the MV table. After the delete is finished, records are selected from the master table and inserted into the MV table. The delete and insert are done as one transaction; this means anybody selecting from the MV during the complete-refresh process sees the data as it existed before the DELETE statement. Anybody accessing the MV immediately after the INSERT commits sees a fresh view of the data.

In some scenarios, you may want to modify this behavior. If a large amount of data is being refreshed, the DELETE statement can take a long time. You have the option of instructing Oracle to perform the removal of data as efficiently as possible via the ATOMIC_REFRESH parameter. When this parameter is set to FALSE, it allows Oracle to use a TRUNCATE statement instead of a DELETE when performing a complete refresh:

```
SQL> exec dbms_mview.refresh('INV_MV',method=>'C',atomic_refresh=>false);
```

TRUNCATE works faster than DELETE for large data sets because TRUNCATE doesn't have the overhead of generating redo. The disadvantage of using the TRUNCATE statement is that a user selecting from the MV may see zero rows while the refresh is taking place.

Handling the ORA-12034 Error

When you attempt to perform a fast refresh of an MV, you may sometimes get the ORA-12034 error. For example:

```
SQL> exec dbms_mview.refresh('PRODUCTLINEITEM','F');
```

The statement subsequently throws this error message:

```
BEGIN dbms_mview.refresh('PRODUCTLINEITEM','F'); END;
*
ERROR at line 1:
ORA-12034: materialized view log on "CDS_PROD_ES2_LIVE"."PRODUCTLINEITEM"
younger than last refresh
```

To resolve this error, try to completely refresh the MV:

```
SQL> exec dbms_mview.refresh('PRODUCTLINEITEM','C');
```

After the complete refresh has finished, you should be able to perform a fast refresh without receiving an error:

```
SQL> exec dbms_mview.refresh('PRODUCTLINEITEM','F');
```

The ORA-12034 error is thrown when Oracle determines that the MV log was created after the last refresh took place in the associated MV. In other words, the MV log is younger than the last refresh of MV. There are several possible causes:

- The MV log was dropped and re-created.

- The MV log was purged.

- The master table was reorganized.

- The master table was truncated.

- The previous refresh failed.

In this situation, Oracle knows that transactions may have been created between the last refresh time of the MV and when the MV log was created. In this scenario, you have to first perform a complete refresh before you can start using the fast-refresh mechanism.

Monitoring Materialized View Refreshes

This section contains some very handy examples of how to monitor MV refresh jobs. Examples include how to view the last refresh time, determine whether a job is currently executing, determine the progress of a refresh job, and checks to see whether MVs haven't refreshed within the last day. Scripts like these are invaluable for troubleshooting and diagnosing refresh problems.

Viewing Materialized Views' Last Refresh Times

When you're troubleshooting issues with MVs, usually the first item to check is the LAST_REFRESH_DATE in DBA/ALL/USER_MVIEWS. Viewing this information allows you to determine whether the MVs are refreshing on schedule. Run this query as the owner of the MV to display the last refresh date:

```
select
 mview_name
,to_char(last_refresh_date,'dd-mon-yy hh24:mi:ss')
,refresh_mode
,refresh_method
from user_mviews
order by 2;
```

Here's some sample output:

```
MVIEW_NAME                       TO_CHAR(LAST_REFRESH_DAT REFRES REFRESH_
-------------------------------- ------------------------ ------ --------
GEM_COMPANY_MV                   29-jul-10 06:18:58       DEMAND COMPLETE
TOP_REG_DAILY                    29-jul-10 06:57:33       DEMAND FORCE
```

The LAST_REFRESH_DATE column of DBA/ALL/USER_MVIEWS shows the last date and time that an MV successfully finished refreshing. The LAST_REFRESH_DATE is NULL if the MV has never successfully refreshed.

Determining Whether a Refresh Is in Progress

If you need to know what MVs are running, then use this query:

```
select
 sid
,serial#
,currmvowner
,currmvname
from v$mvrefresh;
```

Here's some sample output:

```
      SID     SERIAL# CURRMVOWNER          CURRMVNAME
---------- ---------- -------------------- -------------------------------
     1034       47872 REP_MV               USERS_MV
```

Monitoring Real-Time Refresh Progress

If you deal with large MVs, the next query shows you the real-time progress of the refresh operation. When you're troubleshooting issues, this query can be very useful. Run the following as the user that has privileges on the internal SYS tables:

```
column "MVIEW BEING REFRESHED" format a25
column inserts format 9999999
column updates format 9999999
column deletes format 9999999
--
select
  currmvowner_knstmvr || '.' || currmvname_knstmvr "MVIEW BEING REFRESHED",
  decode(reftype_knstmvr, 1, 'FAST', 2, 'COMPLETE', 'UNKNOWN') reftype,
  decode(groupstate_knstmvr, 1, 'SETUP', 2, 'INSTANTIATE',
    3, 'WRAPUP', 'UNKNOWN' ) STATE,
  total_inserts_knstmvr inserts,
  total_updates_knstmvr updates,
  total_deletes_knstmvr deletes
from x$knstmvr x
where type_knst = 6
and exists (select 1
            from v$session s
            where s.sid=x.sid_knst
            and s.serial#=x.serial_knst);
```

When an MV first starts refreshing, you see this output:

```
MVIEW BEING REFRESHED       REFTYPE  STATE         INSERTS  UPDATES  DELETES
--------------------------- -------- ------------- -------- -------- --------
REP_MV.USERS_MV             UNKNOWN  SETUP               0        0        0
```

After a few seconds, the MV reaches the INSTANTIATE state:

```
REP_MV.USERS_MV             FAST     INSTANTIATE         0        0        0
```

As the MV refreshes, the INSERTS, UPDATES, and DELETES columns are updated appropriately:

```
REP_MV.USERS_MV             FAST     INSTANTIATE       860      274        0
```

When the MV is almost finished refreshing, it reaches the WRAPUP state:

```
REP_MV.USERS_MV             FAST     WRAPUP           5284     1518        0
```

After the MV has completed refreshing, the query returns no rows:

```
no rows selected
```

As you can imagine, this query can be quite useful for troubleshooting and diagnosing MV refresh issues.

Checking Whether MVs Are Refreshing Within a Time Period

When you're dealing with MVs, it's nice to have some sort of automated way of determining whether refreshes are occurring. Use the following shell script to detect which MVs haven't refreshed within the last day and then send an e-mail if any are detected:

```
#!/bin/bash
# See Chapter 2 for details on using a utility
# like oraset to source OS variables
# Source oracle OS variables
. /var/opt/oracle/oraset $1
#
crit_var=$(sqlplus -s <<EOF
rep_mv/jc00le
SET HEAD OFF FEED OFF
SELECT count(*) FROM user_mviews
WHERE sysdate-last_refresh_date > 1;
EOF)
#
if [ $crit_var -ne 0 ]; then
  echo $crit_var
  echo "mv_ref refresh problem with $1" | mailx -s "mv_ref problem" \
dkuhn@sun.com
else
  echo $crit_var
  echo "MVs ok"
fi
#
exit 0
```

This script takes the output of the SQL*Plus statement and returns it to the shell crit_var variable. If any MVs for the REP_MV user haven't refreshed within the last day, then the crit_var variable has a non-zero value. If crit_var isn't equal to zero, then an e-mail is sent indicating that there is an issue.

Creating Remote Materialized View Refreshes

You can create MVs that select from remote tables, MVs, and/or views. This allows you to quickly and efficiently replicate data. The setup for basing MVs on remote objects is as follows:

1. Ensure that Oracle Net connectivity exists from the replicated database environment to the database with the master tables. If you don't have this connectivity, you can't replicate using MVs.

2. Obtain access to a user account in the remote database that has access to the remote tables, MVs, or views that you want to replicate.

3. For fast refreshes, create an MV log on the master (base) table. You only need to do this if you intend to perform fast refreshes.

4. Create a database link in the replicated database environment that points to the master database.

5. Create MVs in a replicated database environment that access remote master objects via the database link created in step 4.

Here's a simple example. First, ensure that you can establish Oracle Net connectivity from the replicated environment to the master database. You can verify connectivity and ensure that you can log on to the master database by connecting via SQL*Plus from the replicated database environment to the remote master. From the command prompt on the database that will contain the MVs, attempt to connect to the user REP_MV in the master database named ENGDEV on the XENGDB server:

```
$ sqlplus rep_mv/foo@'xengdb:1522/engdev'
```

When you're connected to the remote master database, also be sure you have access to the tables that you base the MV on. In this example, the name of the remote master table is INV:

```
SQL> select count(*) from inv;
```

Next, create a database link in the database that will contain the MVs. The database link points to the user in the remote master database:

```
create database link engdev
connect to rep_mv identified by foo
using 'xengdb:1522/engdev';
```

Now, create an MV that accesses the master INV table:

```
create materialized view inv_mv
refresh complete on demand
as
select
 inv_id
,inv_desc
from inv@engdev;
```

You access the remote database by appending the @<database_link_name> to the table name. This instructs Oracle to select from the remote table. The remote table's location is defined in the CREATE DATABASE LINK statement.

Understanding Remote-Refresh Architectures

You can use numerous configurations with remotely refreshed MVs. This section details three common scenarios; you can build on them to meet most remote-replication needs.

Figure 15–3 shows a common configuration that uses MV logs on the master OLTP database. The remote database uses MV logs to enable fast refreshes. This configuration is commonly used when you can't report directly from an OLTP database because of concerns that the reporting activity will greatly hamper production performance. This architecture is also useful when you have users on the other side of the planet and you want to replicate data to a database that is physically closer to them, so they have acceptable reporting performance.

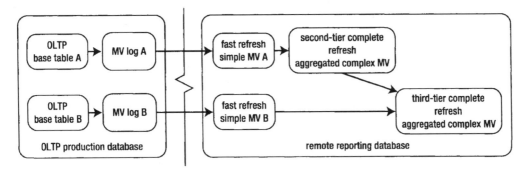

Figure 15–3. *Remote-refresh using MV logs at a master site*

Figure 15–4 shows a scenario in which you aren't allowed to create MV logs on the master base tables. This may happen in situations where another team or organization owns the master (base) database, and the owners are unwilling to let you create MV logs in the master environment. In this case, you have to use complete MV refreshes to the remote reporting database. This architecture is also appropriate when a large percentage of the base table records are modified each day. In this situation, a complete refresh may be more efficient than a fast refresh (because you're replicating most of the data, not just a small subset).

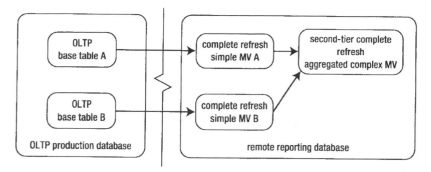

Figure 15–4. Remote-refresh using complete MV refreshes

Figure 15–5 shows a situation in which you replicate the base tables to a staging database and then replicate from the staging database to a reporting database. This scenario is common when the network architecture is configured so that the reporting database is placed on a network segment that can't be directly connected to a hardened production environment. In this case, you can build an intermediate database that resides in a network that can connect to both the OLTP database and the reporting database. Notice that MV logs built are on the MVs in the secure staging database. When refreshing in this configuration, you must coordinate the refresh times of the staging and reporting databases so there is no overlap during the refresh.

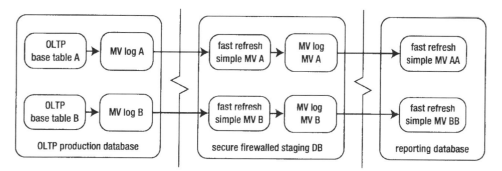

Figure 15–5. Two-hop remote fast MV refresh

■ Note Sometimes an MV built on another MV is called a *nested* MV.

Viewing Materialized View Base-Table Information

When you're diagnosing issues with MVs, it's useful to view the MV and its associated remote master table. Run the following query (on the database that contains the MV) to extract master owner and table information:

```
select
owner          mv_owner
,name          mv_name
,master_owner mast_name
,master        mast_table
from dba_mview_refresh_times
order by 1,2;
```

The previous query reports on every MV and the master table it's based on. The base table can be local or remote.

Determining How Many MVs Reference a Central MV Log

Suppose you have one master table with an MV log. Additionally, more than one remote MV uses the central master MV log. Figure 15–6 illustrates this configuration.

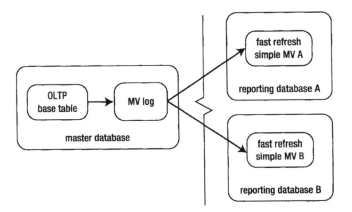

Figure 15–6. Multiple remote MVs using the same centralized MV log

In this situation, Oracle keeps records in the MV log until all MVs have refreshed. For example, suppose MV A has a LAST_REFRESH_DATE of 01-JUL-2010, and MV B has a LAST_REFRESH_DATE of 01-SEP-2010. MV A refreshes on 01-OCT-2010. The master log only purges records older than 01-SEP-2010 (because the more recent log records are still needed by MV B).

If an MV was dropped and unable to un-register itself from a master MV log table, then records grow indefinitely in the master MV log table. To resolve this issue, you need information regarding which MVs are tied to which MV logs. This query displays the master-table owner information and the SNAPID (MV ID) of all dependent MVs:

```
select
 mowner
,master base_table
,snapid
,snaptime
from sys.slog$;
```

Here's some sample output that shows two MVs connected to one MV log:

```
MOWNER               BASE_TABLE                    SNAPID SNAPTIME
-------------------- ------------------------- ---------- ---------
INV_MGMT             CMP_GRP_ASSOC                 651 05-AUG-10
INV_MGMT             CMP_GRP_ASSOC                 541 02-JAN-08
```

The next query displays information regarding all MVs that have been created that tie into an MV log. Run this query on the master site:

```
select
 a.log_table
,a.log_owner
,b.master mast_tab
,c.owner   mv_owner
,c.name    mview_name
,c.mview_site
,c.mview_id
from dba_mview_logs a
    ,dba_base_table_mviews b
    ,dba_registered_mviews c
where b.mview_id = c.mview_id
and    b.owner    = a.log_owner
and    b.master   = a.master
order by a.log_table;
```

Here's some sample output:

```
LOG_TABLE            LOG_OWNE MAST_TAB        MV_OWN MVIEW_NAME       MVIEW_S MVIEW_ID
-------------------- -------- ------------- ------ ---------------- ------- --------
MLOG$_CMP_GRP_ASSOC INV_MGMT CMP_GRP_ASSOC REP_MV CMP_GRP_ASSOC_MV DWREP       651
MLOG$_CMP_GRP_ASSOC INV_MGMT CMP_GRP_ASSOC TSTDEV CMP_GRP_ASSOC_MV ENGDEV      541
```

When you drop a remote MV, it should de-register from the master database. However, this doesn't always happen. A remote database may get wiped out (maybe a short-term development database), and the MV doesn't get a chance to un-register itself (via the DROP MATERIALIZED VIEW statement). In this situation, the MV log is unaware that a dependent MV is no longer available, and therefore it keeps records indefinitely.

To purge unwanted MV information from the database that contains the MV log, execute the PURGE_MVIEW_FROM_LOG procedure of DBMS_MVIEW. This example passes in the ID of the MV to be purged:

```
SQL> exec dbms_mview.purge_mview_from_log(541);
```

This statement should update the data dictionary and remove information from the internal table SLOG$ and DBA_REGISTERED_MVIEWS. If the MV being purged is the oldest MV associated with the MV log table, the associate old records are also deleted from the MV log.

If a remote MV is no longer available but still registered with the MV log table, you can manually un-register it at the master site. Use the UNREGISTER_MVIEW procedure of the DBMS_MVIEW package to un-register a remote MV. To do this, you need to know the remote MV owner, MV name, and MV site (available from the output of the previous query in this section):

```
SQL> exec dbms_mview.unregister_mview('TSTDEV','CMP_GRP_ASSOC_MV','ENGDEV');
```

If successful, the previous operation removes a record from DBA_REGISTERED_MVIEWS.

Managing Materialized Views in Groups

An MV group is a useful feature that enables you to refresh a set of MVs at a consistent transactional point in time. If you refresh MVs based on master tables that have parent/child relationships, then you should most likely use a refresh group. This method guarantees that you won't have any orphaned child records in your set of refreshed MVs. The following sections describe how to create and maintain MV refresh groups.

■ **Note** You use the DBMS_REFRESH package to accomplish most of the tasks in this section. This package is fully documented in the *Oracle Advanced Replication Management API Reference* guide (available on OTN).

Creating a Materialized View Group

You use the MAKE procedure of the DBMS_REFRESH package to create an MV group. When you create an MV group, you must specify a name, a comma-separated list of MVs in the group, the next date to refresh, and the interval used to calculate the next refresh time. Here's an example of a group that consists of two MVs:

```
begin
  dbms_refresh.make(
    name       => 'INV_GROUP'
    ,list      => 'INV_MV, REGION_MV'
    ,next_date => sysdate-100
    ,interval  => 'sysdate+1'
);
end;
/
```

When you create an MV group, Oracle automatically creates a database job to manage the refresh of the group. You can view the details of an MV group by querying from DBA/ALL/USER_REFRESH:

```
select
 rname
,job
,next_date
,interval
from user_refresh;
```

Here's some sample output:

```
RNAME             JOB NEXT_DATE INTERVAL
---------- ---------- --------- ---------------
INV_GROUP          34 26-APR-10 sysdate+1
```

I hardly ever use the internal database job as a refresh mechanism. Notice that the NEXT_DATE value specified in the previous SQL is sysdate-100. That means the only way the database job will kick off this job is if the date somehow gets set to 100 days in the past. This way, the job scheduler never initiates the refresh.

In most environments, the refresh needs to start at a specific time. In these scenarios, you use a cron job or some similar utility that has job-scheduling capabilities.

Altering a Materialized View Refresh Group

You can alter characteristics of a refresh group such as the refresh date and/or interval. If you rely on a database job for your refresh mechanism, then you may need to occasionally tweak your refresh characteristics. Use the CHANGE function of the DBMS_REFRESH package to achieve this. This example changes the INTERVAL calculation:

```
SQL> exec dbms_refresh.change(name=>'CCIM_GROUP',interval=>'SYSDATE+1');
```

Again, you need to change refresh intervals only if you're using the internal database job to initiate the materialized group refresh. You can verify the details of a refresh group's interval and job information with this query:

```
select
 a.job
,a.broken
,b.rowner
,b.rname
,b.interval
from dba_jobs    a
    ,dba_refresh b
where a.job = b.job
order by a.job;
```

Here's the output for this example:

```
    JOB  B ROWNER          RNAME           INTERVAL
---------- - --------------- --------------- ------------
    104 N REP_MV          CCIM_GROUP      SYSDATE+1
```

Refreshing a Materialized View Group

After you've created a group, you can manually refresh it using the REFRESH function of the DBMS_REFRESH package. This example refreshes the group that you previously created:

```
SQL> exec dbms_refresh.refresh('INV_GROUP');
```

If you inspect the LAST_REFRESH_DATE column of USER_MVIEWS, you'll notice that all MVs in the group have the same refresh time. This the expected behavior because the MVs in the group are all refreshed at a consistent transaction point in time.

DBMS_MVIEW vs. DBMS_REFRESH

You may have noticed that you can use the DBMS_MVIEW package to refresh a group of MVs. For example, you can refresh a set of MVs in a list as follows using DBMS_MVIEW:

```
SQL> exec dbms_mview.refresh(list=>'INV_MV,REGION_MV');
```

This refreshes each MV in the list as a single transaction. It's the equivalent of using an MV group. However, when you use DBMS_MVIEW, you have the option of setting the ATOMIC_REFRESH parameter to TRUE (default) or FALSE. For example, here the ATOMIC_REFRESH parameter is set to FALSE:

```
SQL> exec dbms_mview.refresh(list=>'INV_MV,REGION_MV',atomic_refresh=>false);
```

Setting ATOMIC_REFRESH to FALSE instructs DBMS_MVIEW to refresh each MV in the list as a separate transaction. It also instructs complete refreshes of MV to consider using the TRUNCATE statement. The previous line of code is equivalent to the following two lines:

```
SQL> exec dbms_mview.refresh(list=>'INV_MV', atomic_refresh=>false);
SQL> exec dbms_mview.refresh(list=>'REGION_MV', atomic_refresh=>false);
```

Compare that to the behavior of DBMS_REFRESH, which is the package you should use to set up and maintain an MV group. The DBMS_REFRESH package always refreshes a group of MVs as a consistent transaction.

If you always need a set of MVs to be refreshed as a transactionally consistent group, use DBMS_REFRESH. If you need some flexibility as so whether a list of MVs is refreshed as a consistent transaction (or not), use DBMS_MVIEW.

Determining Materialized Views in a Group

When you're investigating issues with an MV refresh group, a good starting point is to display which MVs the group contains. Query the data-dictionary views DBA_RGROUP and DBA_RCHILD to view the MVs in a refresh group:

```
select
  a.owner
 ,a.name mv_group
 ,b.name mv_name
from dba_rgroup a
    ,dba_rchild b
where a.refgroup = b.refgroup
and   a.owner    = b.owner
order by a.owner, a.name, b.name;
```

Here's a snippet of the output:

```
OWNER           MV_GROUP             MV_NAME
--------------- -------------------- --------------------
DARL            INV_GROUP            INV_MV
DARL            INV_GROUP            REGION_MV
```

In the DBA_RGROUP view, the NAME column represents the name of the refresh group. The DBA_RCHILD view contains the name of each MV in the refresh group.

Adding an MV to a Refresh Group

As your business requirements change, you occasionally need to add an MV to a group. Use the ADD procedure of the DBMS_REFRESH package to accomplish this task:

```
SQL> exec dbms_refresh.add(name=>'INV_GROUP',list=>'PRODUCTS_MV,USERS_MV');
```

You must specify a name and provide a comma-separated list of the MV names to add. The newly added MVs are refreshed the next time the group is refreshed.

The other way to add an MV to a group is to drop the group and re-create it with the new MV. However, it's usually preferable to add an MV.

Removing Materialized Views from a Refresh Group

Sometimes you need to remove an MV from a group. To do so, use the SUBTRACT function of the DBMS_REFRESH package. This example removes one MV from a group:

```
SQL> exec dbms_refresh.subtract(name=>'INV_GROUP',list=>'REGION_MV');
```

You have to specify the name of the MV group and provide a comma-separated list containing the names of the MVs you want to remove.

The other way to remove an MV from a group is to drop the group and re-create it without unwanted MV(s). However, it's usually preferable to remove an MV.

Dropping a Materialized View Refresh Group

If you need to drop an MV refresh group, use the DESTROY procedure of the DBMS_REFRESH package. This example drops the MV group named INV_GROUP:

```
SQL> exec dbms_refresh.destroy('INV_GROUP');
```

This only drops the MV refresh-group object—it doesn't drop any of the actual MVs. If you need to also drop the MVs, use the DROP MATERIALIZED VIEW statement.

Summary

Sometimes the term *materialized view* confuses people who are new to the technology. Perhaps Oracle should have named this feature "periodically purge and repopulate a table that contains the results of a query," but that's probably too long a phrase. Regardless, when you understand the power of this tool, you can use it to replicate and aggregate large amounts of data. You can greatly improve the performance of queries by periodically computing and storing the results of complex aggregations of data.

MVs can be *fast-refreshable*, which means they only copy over changes from the master table that have occurred since the last refresh. To use this type of MV, you must create an MV log on the master table. It's not always possible to create an MV log; in these scenarios, the MV must be completely refreshed.

If need be, you can also compress and encrypt the data with an MV. This allows for better space management and security. Additionally, you can partition the underlying table used by an MV, to allow for greater scalability, performance, and availability.

MVs provide an efficient method for replicating data. In some cases, you need to replicate entire databases or just certain database objects and portions of data. The next couple of chapters focus on Data Pump, which you can use to unload, transport, and load entire databases or subsets of objects and data.

CHAPTER 16

■■■

User-Managed Backup and Recovery

All DBAs should know how to back up databases. Even more critical, you must be able to restore and recover a database. When there is a media failure, everybody looks to the DBA to successfully perform a restore and recovery. You can use two very different Oracle approaches for backup and recovery (B&R):

- The user-managed approach

- The Oracle Recovery Manager (RMAN) approach

User-managed backups are called that because you manually perform all steps associated with the backup and/or recovery. There are two types of user-managed backups: cold backups and hot backups. *Cold backups* are sometimes called *offline backups* because the database is shut down during the backup process. *Hot backups* are also referred to as *online backups* because the database is available during the backup procedure.

RMAN is Oracle's flagship B&R tool. It automates and manages most aspects of B&R. For Oracle B&R, you should use RMAN. So, why have a chapter about user-managed backups when this approach has been gathering dust for over a decade? Consider the following reasons for understanding user-managed B&R:

- You still find shops using user-managed B&R techniques. Therefore, you're required to be knowledgeable about this technology.

- Manually executing a user-managed backup, restore, and recovery solidifies your knowledge of the Oracle B&R architecture. This helps immensely when you're troubleshooting issues with any B&R tool and lays the foundation of core knowledge for key Oracle tools such as RMAN and Data Guard.

- You'll more fully appreciate RMAN and the value of its features.

- Nightmarish database-recovery stories recounted by the old DBAs will now make sense.

For these reasons, you should be familiar with user-managed B&R techniques. Manually working through the scenarios in this chapter will greatly increase your understanding of which files are backed up and how they're used in a recovery. You'll be much better prepared to understand and use RMAN. RMAN makes much of B&R automated and push-button. However, knowledge of how to manually back up and recover a database helps you think through and troubleshoot any issues with any type of backup technology.

This chapter begins with cold backups. These types of backups are viewed as the simplest form of user-managed backups because even a system administrator can implement them. Next, the chapter discusses hot backups. You also investigate several common restore and recover scenarios. These examples build your base knowledge of Oracle B&R internals. Finally, this chapter covers Oracle's flashback technology and how that complements many user-managed recovery scenarios.

Implementing a Cold-Backup Strategy for a Noarchivelog-Mode Database

You perform a user-managed cold backup by copying files after the database has been shut down. This type of backup is also known as an offline backup. Your database can be in either noarchivelog mode or archivelog mode when you make a cold backup.

For some reason, DBAs tend to think of a cold backup as being synonymous with a backup of a database in noarchivelog mode. That isn't correct. You can make a cold backup of a database in archivelog mode, and that's a backup strategy that many shops employ. The differences between a cold backup with the database in noarchivelog and in archivelog mode are detailed in the following sections.

Making a Cold Backup of a Noarchivelog-Mode Database

One main reason to make a cold backup of a database in noarchivelog mode is to give you a way to restore a database back to a point in time in the past. You should use this type of backup only if you don't need to recover transactions that occurred after the backup. This type of B&R strategy is acceptable only if your business requirements allow for the loss of data and downtime. Rarely would you ever implement this type of B&R solution for a production business database.

Having said that, there are some good reasons to implement this type of backup. One common use is to make a cold backup of a development/test/training database and periodically reset the database back to the baseline. This gives you a way to restart a performance test or a training session with the same point-in-time snapshot of the database.

■ Tip Consider using the Flashback Database feature to set your database back to a point in time in the past. Flashback Database is discussed later in this chapter.

The example in this section shows you how to make a backup of every critical file in your database: all control files, datafiles, temporary datafiles, and online-redo log files. With this type of backup, you can easily restore your database back to the point in time when the backup was made. The main advantages of this approach are that it's conceptually simple and easy to implement. Here are the steps required for a cold backup of a database in noarchivelog mode:

1. Determine where to copy the backup files and how much space is required.

2. Determine the locations and names of the database files to copy.

3. Shut down the database with the IMMEDIATE, TRANSACTIONAL, or NORMAL clause.

4. Copy the files (identified in step 2) to the backup location (determined in step 1).

5. Restart your database.

The following sections elaborate on these steps.

Step 1: Determine Where to Copy the Backup Files and How Much Space Is Required

Ideally, the backup location should be on a separate set of disks from your live datafiles location. However, in many shops you may not have a choice and are told which mount points are to be used by the database. Often it's not up to you architect the underlying subdisk system.

For this example, the backup location is the directory /oradump/cbackup/O11R2. To get a rough idea of how much space you need to store one copy of the backups, you can run this query:

```
select sum(sum_bytes)/1024/1024 m_bytes
from(
select sum(bytes) sum_bytes from v$datafile
union
select sum(bytes) sum_bytes from v$tempfile
union
select (sum(bytes) * members) sum_bytes from v$log
group by members);
```

Step 2: Determine the Locations and Names of the Files to Copy

Run this query to list the names (and paths) of files that are included in a cold backup of a noarchivelog-mode database:

```
select name from v$datafile
union
select name from v$controlfile
union
select name from v$tempfile
union
select member from v$logfile;
```

Do you need to back up the online-redo logs? No; you never need to back up the online-redo logs as part of any type of backup. Then why do DBAs back up the online-redo logs as part of a cold backup? One reason is that it makes the restore process for the noarchivelog mode scenario slightly easier. The online-redo logs are required to normally open the database. If you back up all files (including the online-redo logs), then to get your database back to the state it was in at the time of the backup, you restore all files (including the online-redo logs) and start up your database.

■ Tip See the later sections in this chapter on scripting for examples of SQL-generating commands you can use to automate B&R steps.

Step 3: Shut Down the Database

Connect to your database as the SYS (or as a SYSDBA privileged user), and shut down your database using IMMEDIATE, TRANSACTIONAL, or NORMAL In almost every situation, using IMMEDIATE is the preferred method. This mode disconnects users, rolls back uncompleted transactions, and shuts down the database:

```
$ sqlplus / as sysdba
SQL> shutdown immediate;
```

Step 4: Create Backup Copies of the Files

For every file identified in step 2, use an OS utility to copy the files to a backup directory (identified in step 1). In this simple example, all the datafiles, control files, temporary database files, and online-redo logs are in the same directory. In production environments, you'll most likely have files spread out in several different directories. This example uses the Linux/Unix cp command to copy the database files from /ora01/dbfile/O11R2 to the /oradump/cbackup/O11R2 directory:

```
$ cp /ora01/dbfile/O11R2/*.*   /oradump/cbackup/O11R2
```

Step 5: Restart Your Database

After all the files are copied, you can start up your database:

```
$ sqlplus / as sysdba
SQL> startup;
```

Restoring a Cold Backup in Noarchivelog Mode with Online-Redo Logs

The next example explains how to restore from a cold backup of a database in noarchivelog mode. If you included the online-redo logs as part of the cold backup, you can include the online-redo logs when you restore the files. Here are the steps involved with this procedure:

1. Shut down the instance.

2. Copy the datafiles, online-redo logs, temporary files, and control files back from the backup.

3. Start up your database.

4. These steps are detailed in the following sections.

Step 1: Shut Down the Instance

Shut down the instance, if it's running. In this scenario, it doesn't matter how you shut down the database, because you're restoring back to a point in time. Any files in the live database directory locations are overwritten when the backup files are copied back. If your instance is running, you can abruptly abort it. As a SYSDBA privileged user, do the following:

```
$ sqlplus / as sysdba
SQL> shutdown abort;
```

Step 2: Copy the Files Back from the Backup

This step does the reverse of the backup: you're copying files from the backup location to the live database file locations. In this example, all the backup files are located in the /oradump/cbackup/O11R2 directory and all files are being copied to the /ora01/dbfile/O11R2 directory:

```
$ cp /oradump/cbackup/O11R2/*.*  /ora01/dbfile/O11R2
```

Step 3: Start Up the database

Connect to your database as SYS (or a user that has SYSDBA privileges), and start up your database:

```
$ sqlplus / as sysdba
SQL> startup;
```

After you finish these steps, you should have an exact copy of your database as it was when you made the cold backup. It's as if you set your database back to the point in time when you made the backup.

Restoring a Cold Backup in Noarchivelog Mode Without Online-Redo Logs

As mentioned earlier, you don't ever need the online-redo logs when restoring from a cold backup. If you made a cold backup of your database in noarchivelog mode and didn't include the online-redo logs as part of the backup, the steps to restore are nearly identical to the steps in the previous section. The main difference is that the last step requires you to open your database using the OPEN RESETLOGS clause. Here are the steps:

1. Shut down the instance.
2. Copy the control files and datafiles back from the backup.
3. Start up the database in mount mode.
4. Open the database with the OPEN RESETLOGS clause.

Step 1: Shut Down the Instance

Shut down the instance, if it's running. In this scenario, it doesn't matter how you shut down the database because you're restoring back to a point in time. Any files in the live database directory locations are overwritten when the backups are copied. In this scenario, if your instance is running, you can abruptly abort it. As a SYSDBA privileged user, do the following:

```
$ sqlplus / as sysdba
SQL> shutdown abort;
```

Step 2: Copy the Files Back from the Backup

Copy the control files and datafiles from the backup location to the live datafile locations:

```
$ cp <backup directory>/*.*  <live database file directory>
```

Step 3: Start Up the Database in Mount Mode

Connect to your database as SYS or a user with SYSDBA privileges, and start the database in mount mode:

```
$ sqlplus / as sysdba
SQL> startup mount
```

Step 4: Open the Database with the OPEN RESETLOGS Clause

Open your database for use with the OPEN RESETLOGS clause:

```
SQL> alter database open resetlogs;
```

If you see the "Database altered" message, the command was successful. However, you may see this error:

```
ORA-01139: RESETLOGS option only valid after an incomplete database recovery
```

In this case, issue the following:

```
SQL> recover database until cancel;
```

You should see this message:

```
Media recovery complete.
```

Now, attempt to open your database with the OPEN RESETLOGS clause:

```
SQL> alter database open resetlogs;
```

This statement instructs Oracle to re-create the online-redo logs. Oracle uses information in the control file for the placement, name, and size of the redo logs. If there are old online-redo log files in those locations, they're overwritten.

If you're monitoring your alert.log throughout this process, you may see ORA-00312 and ORA-00313. This means Oracle can't find the online-redo log files; this is okay because these files aren't physically available until they're re-created by the OPEN RESETLOGS command.

Scripting a Cold Backup and Restore

It's instructional to view how you script a cold backup. The basic idea is to dynamically query the data dictionary to determine the locations and names of the files to be backed up. This is preferable to hard-coding the directory locations and file names in a script. The dynamic generation of a script is less prone to errors and surprises (for example, when new datafiles are added to a database but not added to an old hard-coded backup script).

■ **Note** The scripts in this section aren't meant to be production-strength B&R scripts. Rather, they illustrate the basic concepts of scripting a cold backup and subsequent restore.

The first script in this section makes a cold backup of a database. Before you use the cold-backup script, you need to modify these variables contained in the script to match your database environment:

- ORACLE_SID

- ORACLE_HOME

- cbdir

The cbdir variable specifies the name of the backup-directory location. The script creates a file named coldback.sql, which is executed from SQL*Plus to initiate a cold backup of the database:

```
#!/bin/bash
ORACLE_SID=O11R2
ORACLE_HOME=/oracle/app/oracle/product/11.2.0/db_1
PATH=$PATH:$ORACLE_HOME/bin
#
sqlplus -s <<EOF
/ as sysdba
set head off pages0 lines 132 verify off feed off trimsp on
define cbdir=/oradump/cbackup/O11R2
spo coldback.sql
select 'shutdown immediate;' from dual;
select '!cp ' || name   || ' ' || '&&cbdir'  from v\$datafile;
select '!cp ' || name   || ' ' || '&&cbdir'  from v\$tempfile;
select '!cp ' || member || ' ' || '&&cbdir' from v\$logfile;
select '!cp ' || name   || ' ' || '&&cbdir'  from v\$controlfile;
select 'startup;' from dual;
spo off;
@@coldback.sql
EOF
exit 0
```

This file generates commands that are to be executed from a SQL*Plus script to make a cold backup of a database. You place an exclamation mark (!) in front of the Unix cp command to instruct SQL*Plus to host out to the OS to run the copy command. You also place a backward slash (\) in front of each dollar sign ($) when referencing v$ data-dictionary views; this is required in a Linux/Unix shell script. The \ escapes the $ and tells the shell script not to treat the $ character as a special character (the $ normally signifies a shell variable).

After you run this script, here's a sample of the copy commands written to the coldback.sql script:

```
shutdown immediate;
!cp /ora01/dbfile/O11R2/system01.dbf /oradump/cbackup/O11R2
!cp /ora01/dbfile/O11R2/sysaux01.dbf /oradump/cbackup/O11R2
!cp /ora02/dbfile/O11R2/undotbs01.dbf /oradump/cbackup/O11R2
!cp /ora02/dbfile/O11R2/users01.dbf /oradump/cbackup/O11R2
...
!cp /ora01/oraredo/O11R2/redo02a.rdo /oradump/cbackup/O11R2
!cp /ora02/oraredo/O11R2/redo02b.rdo /oradump/cbackup/O11R2
!cp /ora01/dbfile/O11R2/control01.ctl /oradump/cbackup/O11R2
startup;
```

At the same time you make a cold backup, you should also generate a script that provides the commands to copy datafiles, tempfiles, logfiles, and control files back to their original locations. You can use this file to restore from the cold backup (either on purpose or in the event of a media failure). The next script in this section dynamically creates a coldrest.sql script that copies files from the backup location to the original datafile locations. You need to modify this script in the same manner that you modified the cold-backup script (change the ORACLE_SID, ORACLE_HOME, and cbdir variables to match your environment):

```
#!/bin/bash
ORACLE_SID=O11R2
ORACLE_HOME=/oracle/app/oracle/product/11.2.0/db_1
PATH=$PATH:$ORACLE_HOME/bin
#
sqlplus -s <<EOF
/ as sysdba
set head off pages0 lines 132 verify off feed off trimsp on
define cbdir=/oradump/cbackup/O11R2
define dbname=$ORACLE_SID
spo coldrest.sql
select 'shutdown abort;' from dual;
select '!cp ' || '&&cbdir/' || substr(name, instr(name,'/',-1,1)+1) ||
       ' ' || name   from v\$datafile;
select '!cp ' || '&&cbdir/' || substr(name, instr(name,'/',-1,1)+1) ||
       ' ' || name   from v\$tempfile;
select '!cp ' || '&&cbdir/' || substr(member, instr(member,'/',-1,1)+1) ||
       ' ' || member from v\$logfile;
select '!cp ' || '&&cbdir/' || substr(name, instr(name,'/',-1,1)+1) ||
       ' ' || name   from v\$controlfile;
select 'startup;' from dual;
spo off;
EOF
exit 0
```

This script creates a script named coldrest.sql that generates the copy commands to restore your datafiles, tempfiles, logfiles, and control files back to their original locations. After you run this shell script, here's a partial snippet of the code in the coldrest.sql file:

```
shutdown abort;
!cp /oradump/cbackup/O11R2/system01.dbf /ora01/dbfile/O11R2/system01.dbf
!cp /oradump/cbackup/O11R2/sysaux01.dbf /ora01/dbfile/O11R2/sysaux01.dbf
!cp /oradump/cbackup/O11R2/undotbs01.dbf /ora02/dbfile/O11R2/undotbs01.dbf
!cp /oradump/cbackup/O11R2/users01.dbf /ora02/dbfile/O11R2/users01.dbf
...
!cp /oradump/cbackup/O11R2/redo02a.rdo /ora01/oraredo/O11R2/redo02a.rdo
!cp /oradump/cbackup/O11R2/redo02b.rdo /ora02/oraredo/O11R2/redo02b.rdo
!cp /oradump/cbackup/O11R2/control01.ctl /ora01/dbfile/O11R2/control01.ctl
startup;
```

If you need to restore from a cold backup using this script, log on to SQL*Plus as SYS and execute the script:

```
$ sqlplus / as sysdba
SQL> @coldrest.sql
```

Implementing Archivelog Mode

Recall from the discussion in Chapter 5 that archive redo logs are created only if your database is in archivelog mode. In this mode, as the online-redo logs fill up, a log switch is initiated. When a log switch occurs, the log-writer process stops writing to the most recently filled online-redo logs and starts writing to a new online-redo log group. The online-redo log groups are written to in a round-robin fashion.

Archivelog mode is a prerequisite for the following technologies: user-managed hot backups, the Flashback Database feature, and RMAN online backups. If you don't have archiving enabled, and you attempt to make a user-managed hot backup, you receive this error when altering a database or tablespace into backup mode:

```
ORA-01123: cannot start online backup; media recovery not enabled
```

At this point, you need to place your database in archivelog mode.

Making Architectural Decisions

When you implement archivelog mode, you also need a strategy for managing these files. The archive-redo logs consume disk space. If left unattended, these files will eventually consume all the space allocated for them. If this happens, the archiver can't write a new archive redo log file to disk, and your database will stop processing transactions. At this point you have a hung database. You need to manually intervene by creating space for the archiver to resume work. For these reasons, there are several architectural decisions you must carefully consider before you turn on archiving:

- Where to place the archive-redo logs, and whether to use the fast-recovery area (formerly known as the flash-recovery area) to store the archive-redo logs

- How to name the archive-redo logs

- How much space should be allocated to the archive-redo log location

- How often to back up the archive-redo logs

- When it's okay to permanently remove archive-redo logs from disk

- Whether multiple archive-redo log locations should be enabled

- If this is a production database, when to schedule the small amount of downtime that's required

Minimally, you should have enough space in your primary archive-redo location to hold at least a day's worth of archive-redo logs. This lets you back them up on a daily basis and then remove them from disk after they've been backed up.

If you decide to use a fast-recovery area (FRA) for your archive-redo log location, you must ensure that it contains sufficient space to hold the number of archive-redo logs generated between backups. Keep in mind that the FRA typically contains other types of files, such as RMAN backup files, flashback logs, and so on. If you use an FRA, be aware that the generation of other types of files can potentially impact the space required by the archive-redo log files.

You need a strategy to automate the backup and removal of archive-redo log files. For user-managed backups, this can be implemented with a shell script that periodically copies the archive-redo logs to a backup location and then removes them from the primary location. As you see in later chapters, RMAN automates the backup and removal of archive-redo log files.

If your business requirements are such that you must have a certain degree of high availability and redundancy, then you should consider writing your archive-redo logs to more than one location. Some shops set up jobs to copy the archive-redo logs periodically to a different location on disk or even copy them to a different server.

Setting the Archive-Redo File Location

Before you set your database mode to archiving, you should specifically instruct Oracle where you want the archive-redo logs to be placed. You can set the archive-redo log-file destination with the following techniques:

- Set the LOG_ARCHIVE_DEST_N database initialization parameter.

- Implement an FRA.

These two approaches are discussed in detail in the following sections.

■ **Tip** If you don't specifically set the archive-redo log location via an initialization parameter or by enabling the FRA, then the archive-redo logs are written to a default location. This location depends on the database version and operating system. For active production database systems, the default archive-redo log location is rarely appropriate.

Setting the Archive Location to a User-Defined Disk Location (non-FRA)

If you're using an init.ora file, modify the file with an OS utility (such as vi) and place in it the location where you want the archive-redo logs written. In this example, the archive-redo log location is set to /ora02/oraarch/O11R2:

```
log_archive_dest_1='location=/ora02/oraarch/O11R2'
log_archive_format='%t_%s_%r.arc'
```

If you're using an spfile, use ALTER SYSTEM to modify the appropriate initialization variables:

```
SQL> alter system set log_archive_dest_1='location=/ora02/oraarch/O11R2' scope=both;
SQL> alter system set log_archive_format='%t_%s_%r.arc' scope=spfile;
```

You can dynamically change the LOG_ARCHIVE_DEST_n parameters while your database is open. However, you have to stop and start your database for the LOG_ARCHIVE_FORMAT parameter to take effect. Take care not to set the LOG_ARCHIVE_FORMAT to an invalid value, because then you can't start your database:

```
SQL> startup nomount;
ORA-19905: log_archive_format must contain %s, %t and %r
```

In this situation, if you're using an spfile, you can't start your instance. You have to rename the spfile, create a pfile from the spfile (SQL> create pfile from spfile;), modify the parameter to a valid value, start the database with the pfile, and re-create the spfile from the pfile.

When you specify LOG_ARCHIVE_FORMAT, you must include %t (or %T), %s (or %S), and d% in the format string. Table 16–1 lists the valid variables you can use with the LOG_ARCHIVE_FORMAT initialization parameter.

Table 16–1. Valid Variables for the Log Archive Format String

Format String	Meaning
%s	Log-sequence number
%S	Log-sequence number padded to the left with zeros
%t	Thread number
%T	Thread number padded to the left with zeros
%a	Activation ID
%d	Database ID
%r	Resetlogs ID required to ensure uniqueness across multiple incarnations of the database

If you don't specify a value for LOG_ARCHIVE_FORMAT, Oracle uses a default such as %t_%s_%r.dbf. One aspect of the default format that I don't like is that it ends with the extension .dbf, which is widely used for datafiles. This can cause confusion about whether a particular file can be safely removed because it's an old archive-redo log file or whether the file shouldn't be touched because it's a live datafile. Most DBAs are reluctant to issue commands like this (for fear of accidentally removing a critical datafile):

```
$ rm *.dbf
```

You can view the value of the LOG_ARCHIVE_DEST_N parameter by running the following:

```
SQL> show parameter log_archive_dest
```

Here's a partial listing of the output:

```
NAME                                 TYPE         VALUE
------------------------------------ -----------  ------------------------------
log_archive_dest                     string
log_archive_dest_1                   string       location=/ora02/oraarch/O11R2
log_archive_dest_10                  string
log_archive_dest_11                  string
```

For Oracle Database 11g, you can enable up to 31 different locations for the archive-redo log file destination. For most production systems, you can enable just one archive-redo log destination location. If you need a higher degree of protection, you can enable multiple destinations. Keep in mind that when you use multiple destinations, the archiver must be able to write to at least one location successfully. If you enable multiple mandatory locations and set LOG_ARCHIVE_MIN_SUCCEED_DEST to be higher than 1, then your database may hang if the archiver can't write to all mandatory locations.

You can check the details regarding the status of archive-redo log locations via this query:

```
select
 dest_name
,destination
,status
,binding
from v$archive_dest;
```

Here's a small sample of the output:

```
DEST_NAME              DESTINATION                      STATUS     BINDING
-------------------    ------------------------------   --------   ---------
LOG_ARCHIVE_DEST_1     /ora02/oraarch/O11R2             VALID      OPTIONAL
LOG_ARCHIVE_DEST_2                                      INACTIVE   OPTIONAL
```

Using the FRA for Archive Log Files

The FRA is an area on disk—specified via database-initialization parameters—that instructs Oracle to place specific files like archive-redo logs, RMAN backup files, flashback logs, and multiplexed control files and online-redo logs. To enable the use of an FRA, you must set two initialization parameters:

- DB_RECOVERY_FILE_DEST_SIZE specifies the maximum space to be used for all files that are stored the FRA.

- DB_RECOVERY_FILE_DEST specifies the base directory for the FRA.

When you create an FRA, you're not really creating anything—you're telling Oracle which directory to use when storing files that go in the FRA. For example, say 200GB of space are reserved on a mount point, and you want the base directory for the FRA to be /ora02/fra. To enable the FRA, first set DB_RECOVERY_FILE_DEST_SIZE:

```
SQL> alter system set db_recovery_file_dest_size=200g;
```

Next, set the DB_RECOVERY_FILE_DEST parameter:

```
SQL> alter system set db_recovery_file_dest='/ora02/fra';
```

If you're using an init.ora file, be sure you modify it with an OS utility (such as vi) so the changes persist across database restarts.

After you enable an FRA, by default, Oracle writes archive-redo logs to subdirectories in the FRA.

■ **Note** If you've set the LOG_ARCHIVE_DEST_N parameter to be a location on disk, archive-redo logs aren't written to the FRA.

You can verify that the archive location is using an FRA:

```
SQL> archive log list;
```

If archive files are being written to the FRA, you should see output like this:

```
Database log mode          Archive Mode
Automatic archival         Enabled
Archive destination        USE_DB_RECOVERY_FILE_DEST
```

You can display the directory associated with the FRA like this:

```
SQL> show parameter db_recovery_file_dest
```

When you first implement an FRA, there are no subdirectories beneath the base FRA directory (specified with DB_RECOVERY_FILE_DEST). The first time Oracle needs to write a file to the FRA, it creates any required directories beneath the base directory. For example, after you implement an FRA, if archiving for your database is enabled, then the first time a online-redo log switch occurs, Oracle creates the following directories beneath the base FRA directory:

```
<SID>/archivelog/<YYYY_MM_DD>
```

For this database example, the archive logs are written to the following directory:

```
/ora02/fra/O11R2/archivelog/2010_08_25
```

Each day that archive-redo logs are generated results in a new directory being created in the FRA using the directory name format of YYYY_MM_DD.

If you want archive-redo logs written to both an FRA and a non-FRA location, you can enable that as follows:

```
SQL> alter system set log_archive_dest_1='location=/ora02/oraarch/O11R2';
SQL> alter system set log_archive_dest_2='location=USE_DB_RECOVERY_FILE_DEST';
```

Thinking Unoraclethodox FRA Thoughts

Oracle recommends that you use an FRA for archive-redo logs and RMAN backups. However, I usually don't implement an FRA in production environments—not for the archive-redo logs, not for the RMAN backup files, not for any types of files. Why is that?

When you enable an FRA, if you don't set the initialization parameter LOG_ARCHIVE_DEST_N, then by default, the archive-redo logs are written to the FRA. It's the same with RMAN backups: if you don't specifically configure an RMAN channel disk location, then by default, the RMAN backup files are written to the FRA.

When you use an FRA (as described earlier), the disk space consumed by the archive-redo logs and RMAN backups must fit in the disk space assigned to the FRA. What happens if you have an unexpected spike in the amount of redo generated for a database, or if an unforeseen issue arises with the RMAN backups that results in unanticipated amounts of disk space being consumed?

With regard to the RMAN backups, if the FRA fills up, the RMAN backups abort. An RMAN backup failure isn't catastrophic, because usually you can quickly resolve space issues and manually run another backup. In most situations, this doesn't compromise your database availability; in the event of a backup failure, you still have a previous RMAN backup that you can use to restore and recover your database.

However, in the event that the archive-redo log destination fills up, and the archiver can't write to the file system, your database will hang. In many 24x7 mission-critical environments, this type of downtime is unacceptable and will jeopardize your ability to keep your job.

I find it easier to control the space allocated to the archive-redo logs by using a dedicated mount point for these critical files. If possible, don't share the disk space allocated to the archive-redo logs with the RMAN backups. A problem with the RMAN backups can cause disk-space issues for the archive-redo logs, and you want the space consumed by the archive-redo logs to be as stable and predictable as possible.

For production environments, set the LOG_ARCHIVE_DEST_1 parameter to be a specific location that is separate from any other types of database files. This isn't always possible: you may have a server for which you have no choice but to share mount points for the various file types. But whenever possible, try to isolate your archive-redo logs from other types of database files. The archive-redo log files are the mechanism for recovering your database.

You should be able to estimate how much space is consumed and allow for some wiggle room. But the reality is that sometimes very unpredictable events happen, such as an application process erroneously getting stuck in a loop and generating enormous amounts of redo. This can quickly consume more disk space than anticipated. It shouldn't happen, but it does happen; and when you're the DBA who's called at 2:30 a.m., you design defensively.

I'm not saying, "Don't use a fast recovery area." Rather, you should think carefully about any database feature that you enable and what impact it may have on database availability.

ANOTHER PERSPECTIVE ON THE FRA

The technical editor for this book provided a different perspective on using the FRA. I think it's worth hearing what he has to say. He prefers the archivelog files in the FRA, because it's easier to maintain. One feature he likes is that archivelog files that are already beyond the retention policy (set via RMAN) are automatically deleted when space is needed in the FRA. The technical editor has raised a valid concern here, and you should be aware of it.

However, the FRA can be a single point of failure and a potential performance bottleneck if the archivelog files, RMAN backups/copies, control files and redo-log files are all stored in the FRA. What to do isn't always an easy decision. The technical editor and I agree that the storage location of the archivelog files, whether inside or outside the FRA, is the DBA's preference.

Enabling Archivelog Mode

After you've set the location for your archive-redo log files, you can enable archiving. To enable archiving, you need to connect to the database as SYS (or a user with the SYSDBA privilege) and do the following:

```
$ sqlplus / as sysdba
SQL> shutdown immediate;
SQL> startup mount;
SQL> alter database archivelog;
SQL> alter database open;
```

You can confirm archivelog mode with the following:

```
SQL> archive log list;
```

You can also confirm it as follows:

```
SQL> select log_mode from v$database;

LOG_MODE
------------
ARCHIVELOG
```

Disabling Archivelog Mode

Usually, you don't disable archivelog mode for a production database. However, you may be doing a big data load and want to reduce any overhead associated with the archiving process, so you want to turn off archivelog mode before the load begins and then re-enable it after the load. If you do this, be sure you make a backup as soon as possible after you re-enable archiving.

To disable archiving, do the following as SYS (or a user with the SYSDBA privilege):

```
$ sqlplus / as sysdba
SQL> shutdown immediate;
SQL> startup mount;
SQL> alter database noarchivelog;
SQL> alter database open;
```

You can confirm archivelog mode with the following:

```
SQL> archive log list;
```

You can also confirm the log mode as follows:

```
SQL> select log_mode from v$database;
```

```
LOG_MODE
------------
NOARCHIVELOG
```

Reacting to a Lack of Disk Space in Your Archive Log Destination

The archiver background process writes archive-redo logs to a location that you specify. If for any reason the archiver process can't write to the archive location, your database hangs. Any users attempting to connect receive this error:

```
ORA-00257: archiver error. Connect internal only, until freed.
```

As a production-support DBA, you never want to let your database get into that state. Sometimes unpredictable events happen, and you have to deal with issues that weren't ever supposed to happen.

■ **Note** DBAs who support production databases have a completely different mindset that architect DBAs who get new ideas from flashy presentations or regurgitated documentation.

In this situation, your database is as good as down and completely unavailable. To fix the issue, you have to do something quickly:

- Move files to a different location.

- Compress old files in the archive-redo log location.

- Permanently remove old files.

- Switch the archive-redo log destination to a different location.

Moving files is usually the quickest and safest way to resolve the archiver error. You can use an OS utility such as mv to move old archive-redo logs to a different location. If they're needed for a subsequent restore and recovery, you can let the recovery process know about the new location. Be careful not to move an archive-redo log that is currently being written to. If an archived redo log file appears in V$ARCHIVED_LOG, that means it has been completely archived.

You can use an OS utility such as gzip to compress archive-redo log files in the current archive destination. If you do this, you have to remember to uncompress any files that may be later needed for a restore and recovery. Be careful not to compress an archive-redo log that is currently being written to.

Another option is to use an OS utility such as rm to permanently remove archive-redo logs from disk. This approach is dangerous because you may need those archive-redo logs for a subsequent recovery. If you do remove archive-redo log files, and you don't have a backup of them, you should make a full backup of your database as soon as possible.

If another location on your server has plenty of space, you can consider changing the location to which the archive-redo logs are being written. For example:

```
SQL> alter system set log_archive_dest_1='location=/oraarch02';
```

After you've resolve the issue with the primary location, you can switch back the original location. You can perform this operation while the database is up and running.

When the archive-redo log-file destination is full, you have to scramble to resolve it. This is why a good deal of thought should precede enabling archiving for production 24x7 databases.

For most databases, writing the archive-redo logs to one location is sufficient. However, if you have any type of disaster-recovery or high-availability requirement, then you should write to multiple locations. Sometimes DBAs set up a job to back up the archive-redo logs every hour and copy them to an alternate location or even an alternate server.

Backing Up Archive-Redo Log Files

Depending on your business requirements, you may need a strategy for backing up archive-redo log files. Minimally, you should back up any archive-redo logs generated during a backup of a database in archivelog mode. Additional strategies may include

- Periodically copying archive-redo logs to an alternate location and then removing them from the primary destination
- Copying the archive-redo logs to tape and then deleting them from disk
- Using two archive-redo log locations
- Using Data Guard for a robust disaster-recovery solution

Keep in mind that you need all archive-redo logs generated since the begin time of the last good backup to ensure that you can completely recover your database. Only after you're sure you have a good backup of your database should you consider removing archive-redo logs that were generated prior to the backup.

Making a Cold Backup of an Archivelog-Mode Database

You can use a backup of a database in archivelog mode to restore and recover up to the last committed transaction prior to a failure. Therefore, unlike a backup of a noarchivelog-mode database, this type of backup is never intended to be used to reset the database back to a point in time in the past from which no recovery can be applied. The purpose of a backup of an archivelog-mode database is to restore the database and roll forward and apply transactions to fully recover the database.

This has significant implications for the backups. Recall that for a noarchivelog-mode database, DBAs sometimes include the online-redo logs as part of the backup. For a backup of an archivelog-mode database, you should never include the online-redo logs in the backup. The online-redo logs contain the most currently generated redo transaction information for the database. Any redos in the current online-redo logs that hasn't been archived are required for a complete recovery. In the event of a failure, you don't want to overwrite the online-redo logs with copies of online-redo logs taken from a point in time in the past; this would result in the inability to perform a complete recovery.

The high-level steps for a cold backup of a database in archivelog mode are identical for the noarchivelog-mode database:

1. Determine where to copy the backup files and how much space is required.

2. Determine the locations and names of the database files to copy.

3. Shut down the database with IMMEDIATE, TRANSACTIONAL, or NORMAL.

4. Copy the files (identified in step 2) to the backup location (determined in step 1).

5. Restart your database.

The main difference between the cold-backup archivelog-mode backup and the noarchivelog-mode backup is that in step 2, you run a query like this to identify the files to be backed up:

```
select name from v$datafile
union
select name from v$controlfile;
```

Also, you don't need to back up the datafiles associated with the TEMP tablespace. As of Oracle Database 10g, Oracle automatically attempts to create missing datafiles associated with the TEMP tablespace (for locally managed temp tablespaces) when the database is started.

Restoring and recovering with a cold backup of a database in archivelog mode is nearly identical to the restore and recovery from a hot backup. See the later sections in this chapter on how to restore and recover from a database in archivelog mode.

UNDERSTANDING THE MECHANICS DOES MATTER

Knowing how a hot backup works also helps in untangling and surviving difficult RMAN scenarios. RMAN is a sophisticated and highly automated tool. With just a few commands, you can back up, restore, and recover your database. However, if there is a failure with any RMAN command or step, it pays huge dividends to understand Oracle's underlying internal restore and recovery architecture. A detailed knowledge of how to restore and recover from a hot backup helps you logically think your way through any RMAN scenario.

Similarly, when you ride a bike, understanding how the derailleurs and gears and shifting works helps a great deal. You can usually tell when a rider knows only to push one button to go slower and to push another button to go faster. Riders who understand in more detail how the chain moves between gears will always be smoother at shifting gears. My editor, Jonathan Gennick, recounted the following anecdote while reading an early draft of this chapter:

"I loaned my bike to a guy the other week and went on a ride with him. You should have heard the horrible noises he conjured out of my derailleurs and drivetrain. I thought he was going to damage the bike. After a few minutes, he rode up to me and told me that my front derailleur wasn't working right.

The derailleur was fine. He was just one of those guys who knows only to push the button, without any understanding of what goes on underneath that action."

Efforts you put in to understanding how B&R is implemented pay off in the long run. You actually have less to remember—because your understanding of the underlying implementation enables you to think through problems and solve them in ways that checklists don't.

Implementing a Hot-Backup Strategy

As mentioned earlier in this chapter, RMAN should be your tool of choice for any type of Oracle database backup (either online or offline). RMAN is more efficient than user-managed backups and automates almost all of the tasks. Having said that, one of the best ways to gain an understanding of Oracle B&R internals is to make a hot backup and then use that backup to restore and recover your database. Manually issuing the commands involved in a hot backup, and then a restore and recovery, helps you understand the role of each type of file (control files, datafiles, archive-redo logs, and online-redo logs) in a restore-and-recovery scenario.

This section begins by showing you how to implement a hot backup. It also provides basic scripts that you can use to automate the hot-backup process. Later sections explain some of the internal mechanics of a hot backup and clarify why you must put tablespaces in backup mode before the hot backup takes place.

Making a Hot Backup

Here are the steps required for a hot backup:

1. Ensure that the database is in archivelog mode.

2. Determine where to copy the backup files.

3. Determine which files need to be backed up.

4. Note the maximum sequence number of the online-redo logs.

5. Alter the database/tablespace into backup mode.

6. Copy the datafiles with an OS utility.

7. Alter the database/tablespace out of backup mode.

8. Archive the current online-redo log, and note the maximum sequence number of the online-redo logs.

9. Back up the control file.

10. Back up any archive-redo logs generated during the backup.

These steps are covered in detail in the following sections.

Step 1: Ensure That the Database Is in Archivelog Mode

Run the following command to check the archivelog-mode status of your database:

```
SQL> archive log list;
```

The output shows that this database is in archivelog mode:

```
Database log mode          Archive Mode
Automatic archival         Enabled
Archive destination        /ora02/oraarch/O11R2
```

If you're not sure how to enable archiving, see the earlier section in this chapter on Enabling Archivelog Mode that details how to implement archiving.

Step 2: Determine Where to Copy the Backup Files

Now, determine the backup location. For this example, the backup location is the directory /oradump/hbackup/O11R2. To get a rough idea of how much space you need, you can run this query:

```
SQL> select sum(bytes) from dba_data_files;
```

Ideally, the backup location should be on a separate set of disks from your live datafiles. But in practice, many times you're given a slice of space on a storage area network (SAN) and have no idea about the underlying disk layout. In these situations, you rely on redundancy being built into the SAN hardware (RAID disks, multiple controllers, and so on) to ensure high availability and recoverability.

Step 3: Determine Which Files Need to Be Backed Up

For this step, you only need to know the locations of the datafiles:

```
SQL> select name from v$datafile;
```

When you get to step 5, you may want to consider altering tablespaces one at a time into backup mode. If you take that approach, you need to know which datafiles are associated with which tablespace:

```
select
 tablespace_name
,file_name
from dba_data_files
order by 1,2;
```

Step 4: Note the Maximum Sequence Number of the Online-Redo Logs

To recover successfully using a hot backup, you require at minimum all the archive-redo logs that were generated during the backup. For this reason, you need to note the archivelog sequence before starting the hot backup:

```
select
 thread#
,max(sequence#)
from v$log
group by thread#
order by thread#;
```

Step 5: Alter the Database/Tablespaces into Backup Mode

You can put all your tablespaces into backup mode at the same time using the ALTER DATABASE BEGIN BACKUP statement:

```
SQL> alter database begin backup;
```

If it's an active OLTP database, doing this can greatly degrade performance. This is because when a tablespace is in backup mode, Oracle copies a full image of any block (when it's first modified) to the redo stream. This is discussed in detail later in the chapter.

The alternative is to alter only one tablespace at a time into backup mode. After the tablespace has been altered into backup mode, you can copy the associated datafiles (step 6) and then alter the tablespace out of backup mode (step 7). You have to do this for each tablespace:

```
SQL> alter tablespace <tablespace_name> begin backup;
```

Step 6: Copy the Datafiles with an OS Utility

Use an OS utility (Linux/Unix cp command) to copy the datafiles to the backup location. In this example, all the datafiles are in one directory, and they're all copied to the same backup directory:

```
$ cp /ora01/dbfile/O11R2/*.dbf   /oradump/hbackup/O11R2
```

Step 7: Alter the Database/Tablespaces Out of Backup Mode

After you're finished copying all your datafiles to the backup directory, you need to alter the tablespaces out of backup mode. This example alters all tablespaces out of backup mode at the same time:

```
SQL> alter database end backup;
```

If you're altering your tablespaces into backup mode one at a time, you need to alter each tablespace out of backup mode after its datafiles have been copied:

```
SQL> alter tablespace <tablespace_name> end backup;
```

If you don't take the tablespaces out of backup mode, you can seriously degrade performance and compromise the ability to recover your database.

Step 8: Archive the Current Online-Redo Log and Note the Maximum Sequence Number of the Online-Redo Logs

The following statement instructs Oracle to archive any unarchived online-redo logs and also to initiate a log switch. This ensures that an end-of-backup marker is written to the archive-redo logs:

```
SQL> alter system archive log current;
```

Also note the maximum online-redo log sequence number. If a failure occurs immediately after the hot backup, you need any archive-redo logs generated during the hot backup to fully recover your database:

```
select
 thread#
,max(sequence#)
from v$log
group by thread#
order by thread#;
```

Step 9: Back Up the Control File

For a hot backup, you can't use an OS copy command to make a backup of control file. Oracle's hot-backup procedure specifies that you must use the ALTER DATABASE BACKUP CONTROLFILE statement. This example makes a backup of the control file and places it in the same location as the database backup files:

```
SQL> alter database backup controlfile
     to '/oradump/hbackup/O11R2/controlbk.ctl' reuse;
```

The REUSE clause instructs Oracle to overwrite the file if it already exists in the backup location.

Step 10: Back Up Any Archive-Redo Logs Generated During the Backup

Back up the archive-redo logs that were generated during the hot backup. You can back up the archive-redo logs with an OS copy command:

```
$ cp <archive redo logs generated during backup>  <backup directory>
```

This guarantees that you have the logs in the event of a failure that occurs soon after the hot backup finishes. Be sure you don't back up an archive-redo log that is currently being written to by the archiver process—doing so results in an incomplete copy of that file. Sometimes, DBAs script this process by checking the maximum SEQUENCE# with the maximum RESETLOGS_ID in the V$ARCHIVED_LOG view. Oracle updates that view when it's finished copying the archive-redo log to disk. Therefore, any archive-redo log file that appears in the V$ARCHIVED_LOG view should be safe to copy.

The script in this section covers the minimal tasks associated with a hot backup. For a production environment, a hot backup script can be quite complex. The script listed here provides you with a baseline of what you should include in a hot-backup script.

You need to modify these variables in the script for it to work in your environment:

- hbdir

- dbname

The SQL*Plus variable hbdir points to the base directory for the hot backups. The script also needs the dbname to be set to the Oracle system identifier (SID) of your database. The script copies files to a directory that is the concatenated string of the hbdir and dbname variables. For example, if you set hbdir to /oradump/hbackup and set dbname to O11R2, the backup files are copied to the /oradump/hbackup/O11R2 directory:

```
#!/bin/bash
# Either hardcode or source the OS variables via a script,
# see chapter 2 for more details on the oraset script.
. /var/opt/oracle/oraset $1
#
sqlplus -s <<EOF
/ as sysdba
set head off pages0 lines 132 verify off feed off trimsp on
define hbdir=/oradump/hbackup
define dbname=O11R2
spo hotback.sql
select 'spo &&hbdir/&&dbname/hotlog.txt' from dual;
select 'select max(sequence#) from v\$log;' from dual;
select 'alter database begin backup;' from dual;
select '!cp ' || name || ' ' || '&&hbdir/&&dbname' from v\$datafile;
select 'alter database end backup;' from dual;
select 'alter database backup controlfile to ' || '''' || '&&hbdir' || '/'
     || '&&dbname' || '/controlbk.ctl' || '''' || ' reuse;' from dual;
select 'alter system archive log current;' from dual;
select 'select max(sequence#) from v\$log;' from dual;
select 'select member from v\$logfile;' from dual;
select 'spo off;' from dual;
spo off;
@@hotback.sql
EOF
exit 0
```

The script generates a hotback.sql script. This script contains the commands to perform the hot backup. Here's a listing of the hotback.sql script for a test database:

```
spo /oradump/hbackup/O11R2/hotlog.txt
select max(sequence#) from v$log;
alter database begin backup;
!cp /ora01/dbfile/O11R2/system01.dbf /oradump/hbackup/O11R2
!cp /ora01/dbfile/O11R2/sysaux01.dbf /oradump/hbackup/O11R2
!cp /ora02/dbfile/O11R2/undotbs01.dbf /oradump/hbackup/O11R2
```

```
!cp /ora02/dbfile/O11R2/users01.dbf /oradump/hbackup/O11R2
!cp /ora01/dbfile/O11R2/appdata.dbf /oradump/hbackup/O11R2
!cp /ora01/dbfile/O11R2/inv_mgmt_data01.dbf /oradump/hbackup/O11R2
!cp /ora01/dbfile/O11R2/inv_mgmt_index01.dbf /oradump/hbackup/O11R2
!cp /ora01/dbfile/O11R2/mvdata01.dbf /oradump/hbackup/O11R2
!cp /ora01/dbfile/O11R2/mvindex01.dbf /oradump/hbackup/O11R2
alter database end backup;
alter database backup controlfile to '/oradump/hbackup/O11R2/controlbk.ctl' reuse;
alter system archive log current;
select max(sequence#) from v$log;
select member from v$logfile;
spo off;
```

You can run this script manually from SQL*Plus like this:

```
SQL> @hotback.sql
```

■ **Caution** If the previous script fails on a statement before ALTER DATABASE END BACKUP is executed, you must take your database (tablespaces) out of backup mode by manuallly running ALTER DATABASE END BACKUP as SYS from SQL*Plus.

At the same time that you generate the hot-backup script, it's prudent to generate a script that you can use to copy the datafiles from a backup directory. You have to modify the hbdir and dbname variables in this script to match your environment. Here's a script that generates the copy commands:

```
#!/bin/bash
# source oracle OS variables
. /var/opt/oracle/oraset $1
#
sqlplus -s <<EOF
/ as sysdba
set head off pages0 lines 132 verify off feed off trimsp on
define hbdir=/oradump/hbackup
define dbname=O11R2
spo hotrest.sql
select '!cp ' || '&&hbdir' || substr(name,instr(name,'&&dbname')-1)
       || ' ' || name from v\$datafile;
spo off;
#
exit 0
```

Here's a listing of the code you can execute from SQL*Plus to copy the datafiles back from the backup directory in the event of a failure:

```
!cp /oradump/hbackup/O11R2/system01.dbf /ora01/dbfile/O11R2/system01.dbf
!cp /oradump/hbackup/O11R2/sysaux01.dbf /ora01/dbfile/O11R2/sysaux01.dbf
!cp /oradump/hbackup/O11R2/undotbs01.dbf /ora02/dbfile/O11R2/undotbs01.dbf
!cp /oradump/hbackup/O11R2/users01.dbf /ora02/dbfile/O11R2/users01.dbf
!cp /oradump/hbackup/O11R2/appdata.dbf /ora01/dbfile/O11R2/appdata.dbf
!cp /oradump/hbackup/O11R2/inv_mgmt_data01.dbf \
```

```
 /ora01/dbfile/011R2/inv_mgmt_data01.dbf
!cp /oradump/hbackup/011R2/inv_mgmt_index01.dbf \
 /ora01/dbfile/011R2/inv_mgmt_index01.dbf
!cp /oradump/hbackup/011R2/mvdata01.dbf /ora01/dbfile/011R2/mvdata01.dbf
!cp /oradump/hbackup/011R2/mvindex01.dbf /ora01/dbfile/011R2/mvindex01.dbf
```

In this output, you can remove the ! character from each line if you prefer to run the commands from the OS prompt. The main idea is that these commands are available in the event of a failure so you know what files have been backed up to what location and how to copy them back. In the prior code listing, also notice that two lines have been wrapped with the \ character. This is to fit the output within the page width constraints of this book.

■ **Tip** Don't use user-managed hot-backup technology for online backups. Use RMAN for backups. RMAN doesn't need to place tablespaces in backup mode and automates nearly everything related to B&R.

Understanding the Split-Block Issue

To perform a hot backup, one critical step is to alter a tablespace into backup mode before you copy any of the datafiles associated with the tablespace using an OS utility. To understand why you have to alter a tablespace into backup mode, you must be familiar with what is sometimes called the *split* (or *fractured*) *block issue*.

Recall that a database block is often a different size than the OS block. For example, a database block may be sized at 8KB, whereas the OS block size is 4KB. As part of the hot backup, you use an OS utility to copy the live datafiles. While the OS utility is copying the datafile, the possibility exists that database writers are writing to a block at the same time the OS utility is copying the block. Because the Oracle block and the OS block are different sizes, the following may happen:

1. The OS utility copies part of the Oracle block.

2. A moment later, a database writer updates the entire block.

3. A split second later, the OS utility copies the latter half of the Oracle block.

This can result in the OS copy of the block being inconsistent with what Oracle wrote to the OS. Figure 16–1 illustrates this concept.

Looking at Figure 16–1, the block copied to disk at time 3 is corrupt as far as Oracle is concerned. The first half of the block is from time 1, and the latter half of the block is copied at time 3. This is why you can't copy datafiles in an open Oracle database to make a backup. When you make a hot backup, you're guaranteeing block-level corruption in the backups of the datafiles.

To understand how Oracle resolves the split-block issue, first consider a database operating in its normal mode (not in backup mode). The redo information that is written to the online-redo logs is only what Oracle needs to reapply transactions. The redo stream doesn't contain entire blocks of data. Oracle only records a change vector in the redo stream that specifies which block changed and how it was changed. Figure 16–2 shows Oracle under normal operations.

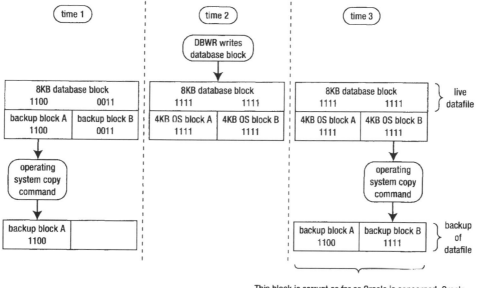

Figure 16–1. Hot-backup split (or fractured) block issue

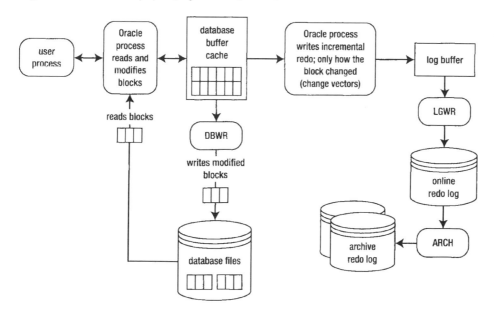

Figure 16–2. Oracle normally only writes change vectors to the redo stream.

Now, consider what happens during a hot backup. For a hot backup, before you copy the datafiles associated with a tablespace, you must first alter the tablespace into backup mode. While in this mode, before Oracle modifies a block, the entire block is copied to the redo stream. Any subsequent changes to the block only require that the normal redo-change vectors be written to the redo stream. This is illustrated in Figure 16–3.

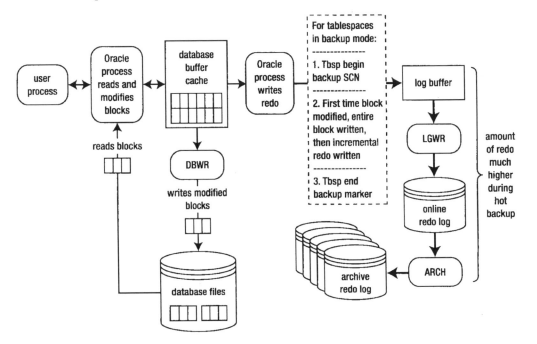

Figure 16–3. Entire blocks are written to the redo stream.

To understand why Oracle logs the entire block to the redo stream, consider what happens in the event of a restore and recovery. First, the backup files from the hot backup are restored. As explained, these backup files contain corrupt blocks due to the split-block issue. But it doesn't matter, because when Oracle recovers the datafiles, for any block that was modified during the hot backup, Oracle has an image copy of the block as it was before it was modified. Oracle uses the copy of the block it has in the redo stream as a starting point for the recovery. This process is illustrated in Figure 16–4.

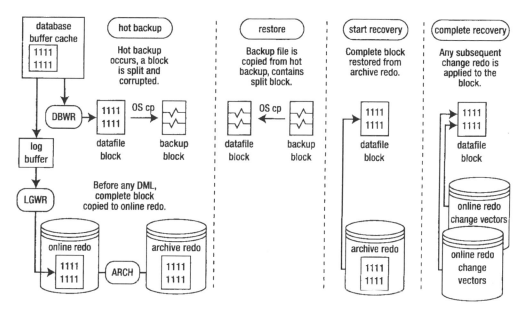

Figure 16–4. Restore and recovery of a split block

In this way, it doesn't matter if there are corrupt blocks in the hot-backup files. Oracle always starts the recovery process for a block from a copy in the redo stream.

Understanding the Need for Redo Generated During Backup

What happens if you experience a failure soon after you make a hot backup? Oracle knows when a tablespace was put in backup mode (begin-backup system change number [SCN] written to the redo stream), and Oracle knows when the tablespace was taken out of backup mode (end-of-backup marker written to the redo stream). Oracle requires every archive-redo log generated during that timeframe to successfully recover the datafiles.

Figure 16–5 shows that at minimum, the archive-redo logs from sequence number 100 to 102 are required to recover the tablespace. These archive-redo logs were generated during the hot backup.

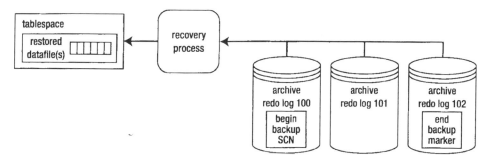

Figure 16–5. Recovery applied

439

If you attempt to stop the recovery process before all redo between the begin and end markers has been applied to the datafile, Oracle throws this error:

```
ORA-01195: online backup of file 1 needs more recovery to be consistent
```

All redo generated during the hot backup of a tablespace must be applied to the datafiles before they can be opened. Oracle at minimum needs to apply everything between the begin-backup SCN marker and the end-backup marker, to account for every block modified while the tablespace was in backup mode. This redo is in archive-redo log files; or, if the failure happened right after the backup ended, some of the redo may not have been archived and is in the online-redo logs. Therefore, you have to instruct Oracle to apply what's in the online-redo logs.

Understanding that Datafiles *Are* Updated

Notice in Figure 16–2 and Figure 16–3 that the behavior of the database writer is for the most part unchanged throughout the backup procedure. The database writer continues to write blocks to datafiles regardless of the backup mode of the database. It doesn't care if a hot backup is taking place; its job is to write blocks from the buffer cache to the datafiles.

Every once in a while, you run into a DBA who states that the database writer doesn't write to datafiles during user-managed hot backups. This is a widespread misconception. Use some common sense: if the database writer isn't writing to the datafiles during a hot backup, then where are the changes being written? If the transactions are being written to somewhere other than the datafiles, how would those datafiles be resynchronized after the backup? It doesn't make any sense.

Some DBAs say, "The datafile header is frozen, which means no changes to the datafile." Oracle does freeze the SCN to indicate the start of the hot backup in the datafile header and doesn't update that SCN until the tablespace is taken out of backup mode. This "frozen SCN" doesn't mean blocks aren't being written to datafiles during the backup. You can easily demonstrate that a datafile is written to during backup mode by doing this:

1. Put a tablespace in backup mode:

```
SQL> alter tablespace users begin backup;
```

2. Create a table that has a character field:

```
SQL> create table cc(cc varchar2(20)) tablespace users;
```

3. Insert a string into that table:

```
SQL> insert into cc values('DBWR does write');
```

4. Switch the online-redo log files to force a checkpoint:

```
SQL> alter system switch logfile;
```

5. From the OS, use the strings and grep commands to search for the string in the datafile:

```
$ strings /ora02/dbfile/O11R2/users01.dbf | grep "DBWR does write"
```

6. Here's the output proving that the database writer did write the data to disk:

```
DBWR does write
```

7. Don't forget to take the tablespace out of backup mode:

```
SQL> alter tablespace users end backup;
```

Performing a Complete Recovery of an Archivelog-Mode Database

Complete recovery means you can recover all transactions that were committed before a failure occurred. Complete recovery doesn't mean you completely restore and recover the entire database. For example, if only one datafile has experienced media failure, you only need to restore and recover the damaged datafile to perform a complete recovery.

■ Tip If you have access to a test or development database, take the time to walk through each step in each example in this section. Going through these steps can teach you more about B&R than any documentation.

The steps in this section apply to any database backed up while in archivelog mode. It doesn't matter if you made a cold backup or hot backup. The steps to restore and recover datafiles are the same, as long as the database was in archivelog mode during the backup. For a complete recovery, you need

- To be able to restore the datafiles that have experienced media failure

- Access to all archive-redo logs generated since the last backup was started

- Have intact online-redo logs.

Here's the basic procedure for a complete recovery:

1. Any datafiles being restored need to be offline before the restoration can take place; the easiest way to achieve this is to place your database in mount mode.

2. Restore the damaged datafiles with an OS copy utility.

3. Issue the appropriate SQL*Plus RECOVER command to apply any information required in the archive-redo logs and online-redo logs.

4. Alter the database open.

The next several sections demonstrate some common complete restore and recovery scenarios. You should be able to apply these basic scenarios to diagnose and recover from any complex situation you find yourself in.

Restoring and Recovering with the Database Offline

This section details a simple restore-and-recovery scenario. Described next are the steps to simulate a failure and then perform a complete restore and recovery. Try this scenario in a development database. Ensure that you have a good backup and that you aren't trying this experiment in a database that contains critical business data.

Before you start this example, create a table and insert some data. This table and data are selected from at the end of the complete recovery process to demonstrate a successful recovery:

```
SQL> create table foo(foo number) tablespace users;
SQL> insert into foo values(1);
SQL> commit;
```

Now, switch the online logs several times. Doing so ensures that you have to apply archive-redo logs as part of the recovery:

```
SQL> alter system switch logfile;
```

The forward slash (/) reruns the most recently executed SQL statement:

```
SQL> /
SQL> /
SQL> /
```

Next, simulate a media failure by renaming the datafile associated with the USERS tablespace. You can identify the name of the datafile associated with the USERS tablespace with this query:

```
SQL> select file_name from dba_data_files where tablespace_name='USERS';

FILE_NAME
----------------------------------
/ora02/dbfile/O11R2/users01.dbf
```

From the OS, rename the file:

```
$ mv /ora02/dbfile/O11R2/users01.dbf /ora02/dbfile/O11R2/users01.dbf.old
```

And attempt to stop your database:

```
$ sqlplus / as sysdba
SQL> shutdown immediate;
```

You should see an error similar to the following:

```
ORA-01110: data file 4: '/ora02/dbfile/O11R2/users01.dbf'
ORA-27041: unable to open file
```

If this were a real disaster, it would be prudent to navigate to the datafile directory, list the files, and see if the file in question was in its correct location. You should also inspect the alert.log file to see if any relevant information is logged there by Oracle.

Now that you've simulated a media failure, the next several steps walk you through a restore and complete recovery.

Step 1: Place Your Database in Mount Mode

Before you place your database in mount mode, you may need to first shut it down using ABORT:

```
$ sqlplus / as sysdba
SQL> shutdown abort;
SQL> startup mount;
```

Step 2: Restore the Datafile from the Backup

The next step is to copy from the backup the datafile that corresponds to the one that has had a failure:

```
$ cp /oradump/hbackup/O11R2/users01.dbf /ora02/dbfile/O11R2/users01.dbf
```

At this point, it's instructional to ponder what Oracle would do if you attempted to start your database. When you issue the ALTER DATABASE OPEN statement, Oracle inspects the SCN in the control file for each datafile. You can inspect this SCN by querying V$DATAFILE:

```
SQL> select checkpoint_change# from v$datafile where file#=4;

CHECKPOINT_CHANGE#
------------------
          17788196
```

Oracle compares the SCN in the control file with the SCN in the datafile header. You can inspect the SCN in the datafile header by querying V$DATAFILE_HEADER. For example:

```
SQL> select file#, checkpoint_change# from v$datafile_header where file#=4;

     FILE# CHECKPOINT_CHANGE#
---------- ------------------
         4           17779631
```

Notice that the SCN recorded in V$DATAFILE_HEADER is less than the SCN in V$DATAFILE for the same datafile. If you attempt to open your database, Oracle throws an error stating that media recovery is required (meaning you need to apply redo) to synchronize the SCN in the datafile with the SCN in the control file. Here's what happens when you attempt to open the database at this point:

```
SQL> alter database open;

alter database open;
alter database open
*
ERROR at line 1:
ORA-01113: file 4 needs media recovery
ORA-01110: data file 4: '/ora02/dbfile/O11R2/users01.dbf'
```

Oracle doesn't let you open the database until the SCN in all datafile headers matches the corresponding SCN in the control file.

Step 3: Issue the Appropriate RESTORE Statement

The archive-redo logs and online-redo logs have the information required to catch the datafile SCN up to the control-file SCN. You can apply redo to the datafile that needs media recovery by issuing one of the following SQL*Plus statements:

- RECOVER DATAFILE
- RECOVER TABLESPACE
- RECOVER DATABASE

Because only one datafile in this example needs to be recovered, the RECOVER DATAFILE statement is appropriate. However, keep in mind that you can run any of the previously listed RECOVER statements, and Oracle will figure out what needs to be recovered. In this particular scenario, you may find it easier to remember the name of the tablespace that contains the restored datafile(s) than to remember the datafile name(s). Next, any datafiles that need recovery in the USERS tablespace are recovered:

```
SQL> recover tablespace users;
```

At this point, Oracle uses the SCN in the datafile header to determine which archive-redo log or online-redo log to use to begin applying redo. If all of the redo required is in the online-redo logs, Oracle applies that redo and displays this message:

```
Media recovery complete.
```

If Oracle needs to apply redo that is only contained in archived redo logs (meaning that the online-redo log that contained the appropriate redo has already been overwritten), you're prompted with a recommendation from Oracle as to which archive-redo log to apply first:

```
ORA-00279: change 17779631 generated at 08/21/2010 04:51:22 needed for thread 1
ORA-00289: suggestion : /ora02/oraarch/O11R2/1_33_726314508.arc
ORA-00280: change 17779631 for thread 1 is in sequence #33

Specify log: {<RET>=suggested | filename | AUTO | CANCEL}
```

You can press Enter or Return (<RET>) to have Oracle apply the suggested archive-redo log file, or specify a filename, or specify AUTO to instruct Oracle to automatically apply any suggested files, or type CANCEL to cancel out of the recovery operation.

In this example, specify AUTO. Oracle applies all redo in all archive-redo log files and online-redo log files to perform a complete recovery:

```
AUTO
```

The last message displayed after all required archive redo and online redo has been applied is this:

```
Log applied.
Media recovery complete.
```

Step 4: Alter Your Database Open

After the media recovery is successful, you can open your database:

```
SQL> alter database open;
```

You can now verify that the transaction you committed just prior to the media failure was restored and recovered:

```
SQL> select * from foo;

       FOO
----------
         1
```

Restoring and Recovering with a Database Online

If you lose a datafile associated with a tablespace other than with SYSTEM and UNDO, you can restore and recover the damaged datafile while leaving the database online. For this to work, any datafiles being restored and recovered must be taken offline first. You may be alerted to an issue with one datafile when a user is attempting to update a table and sees an error such as this:

```
SQL> insert into foo values(2);

ORA-01116: error in opening database file 4
ORA-01110: data file 4: '/ora02/dbfile/O11R2/users01.dbf'
ORA-27041: unable to open file
```

You navigate to the OS directory that contains the datafile, and determine that the datafile has been erroneously removed by a system administrator.

In this example, the datafile associated with the USERS tablespace is taken offline and subsequently restored and recovered while the rest of the database remains online. First, place take the datafile offline:

```
SQL> alter database datafile '/ora02/dbfile/O11R2/users01.dbf' offline;
```

Now, restore the appropriate datafile from the backup location:

```
$ cp /oradump/hbackup/O11R2/users01.dbf /ora02/dbfile/O11R2/users01.dbf
```

In this situation, you can't use RECOVER DATABASE. The RECOVER DATABASE statement attempts to recover all datafiles in the database, of which the SYSTEM tablespace is part. The SYSTEM tablespace can't be recovered while the database is online. If you use the RECOVER TABLESPACE, all datafiles associated with the tablespace must be offline. In this case, it's more appropriate to recover at the datafile level of granularity:

```
SQL> recover datafile '/ora02/dbfile/O11R2/users01.dbf';
```

Oracle inspects the SCN in the datafile header and determines which archive-redo log or online-redo log to use to start applying redo. If all redo required is in the online-redo logs, you see this message:

```
Media recovery complete.
```

If the starting point for redo is contained only in an archive-redo log file, Oracle suggests which file to start with:

```
ORA-00279: change 17809451 generated at 08/21/2010 10:10:56 needed for thread 1
ORA-00289: suggestion : /ora02/oraarch/O11R2/1_45_726314508.arc
ORA-00280: change 17809451 for thread 1 is in sequence #45

Specify log: {<RET>=suggested | filename | AUTO | CANCEL}
```

You can type AUTO to have Oracle apply all required redo in archive-redo log files and online-redo log files:
```
AUTO
```
You should see this message if successful:

```
Log applied.
Media recovery complete.
```

You can now bring the datafile back online:

```
SQL> alter database datafile '/ora02/dbfile/O11R2/users01.dbf' online;
```

Restoring Control Files

When you're dealing with user-managed backups, you usually restore the control file in one of these situations:

- One control file is damaged, and the control file is multiplexed.

- All control files are damaged.

These two situations are covered in this section.

Restoring One Damaged Control File When Multiplexed

If you configure your database with more than one control file, you can shut down the database and use an OS command to copy an existing control file to the location of the missing control file. For example, from the initialization file, you know that two control files are used for this database:

```
SQL> show parameter control_files
```

NAME	TYPE	VALUE
control_files	string	/ora01/dbfile/O11R2/control01.ctl, /ora01/dbfile/O11R2/control02.ctl

Suppose the control02.ctl file has become damaged. Oracle throws this error when querying the data dictionary:

```
ORA-00210: cannot open the specified control file
ORA-00202: control file: '/ora01/dbfile/O11R2/control02.ctl'
```

When a good control file is available, you can shut down the database, and copy the existing good control file to the name and location of the bad control file:

```
SQL> shutdown abort;
```

```
$ cp /ora01/dbfile/O11R2/control01.ctl /ora01/dbfile/O11R2/control02.ctl
```

Now, restart the database:

```
SQL> startup;
```

In this manner, you can restore a control file from an existing control file.

Restoring When All Control Files Are Damaged

If you lose all of your control files, you can restore one from a backup or you can re-create the control file. As long as you have all your datafiles and any required redo (archive redo and online redo), you should be able to completely recover your database. The steps for this scenario are as follows:

1. Shut down the database.

2. Restore a control file from the backup.

3. Restore all datafiles from the backup.

4. Start the database in mount mode, and initiate database recovery using the RECOVER DATABASE USING BACKUP CONTROLFILE clause.

5. For a complete recovery, manually apply the redo contained in the online-redo logs.

6. Open the database with the RESETLOGS clause.

In this example, all control files for the database were accidentally deleted, and Oracle subsequently reports this error:

```
ORA-00202: control file: '/ora01/dbfile/O11R2/control01.ctl'
ORA-27041: unable to open file
```

Step 1: Shut Down the Database

In this case, you have to shut down your database and restore all datafiles and the control file from the backup location to the live database locations. First, shut down the database:

```
SQL> shutdown abort;
```

Step 2: Restore the Control File from the Backup

This database was configured with just one control file, which you copy back from the backup location as shown:

```
$ cp /oradump/hbackup/O11R2/controlbk.ctl /ora01/dbfile/O11R2/control01.ctl
```

If more than one control file is being used, you have to copy the backup control file to each control file and location name listed in the CONTROL_FILES initialization parameter.

Step 3: Restore All Datafiles from the Backup

As part of this recovery procedure, all datafiles must be restored from the backup. In this example, all the backup files are in the /oradump/hbackup/O11R2 directory:

```
$ cp /oradump/hbackup/O11R2/*.dbf  /ora01/dbfile/O11R2
```

In this type of recovery scenario, you need to copy all the datafiles back from the last hot backup. If you didn't, the SCN information in the datafile headers would be more current than the SCN in the control file. There is no way for Oracle to apply redo to a control file to catch it up to a datafile (it works just the opposite: redo must be applied to the datafiles).

Step 4: Start the Database in Mount Mode, and Initiate Database Recovery

Next, start the database in mount mode:

```
SQL> startup mount;
```

After the control file(s) and datafiles have been copied back, you can perform a recovery. Oracle knows that the control file was from a backup (because it was created with the ALTER DATABASE BACKUP CONTROLFILE statement), so the recovery must be performed with the USING BACKUP CONTROLFILE clause:

```
SQL> recover database using backup controlfile;
```

At this point, you're prompted for the application of archive-redo log files:

```
ORA-00279: change 17779631 generated at 08/21/2010 04:51:22 needed for thread 1
ORA-00289: suggestion : /ora02/oraarch/O11R2/1_33_726314508.arc
ORA-00280: change 17779631 for thread 1 is in sequence #33

Specify log: {<RET>=suggested | filename | AUTO | CANCEL}
```

Type AUTO to instruct the recovery process to automatically apply all archive-redo logs:

```
AUTO
```

After all archive-redo logs have been applied, it's instructional to think about what would happen if you tried to open your database at this point:

```
SQL> alter database open;
```

Oracle throws the following error in this situation:

```
ORA-01589: must use RESETLOGS or NORESETLOGS option for database open
```

In this scenario, the online-redo logs are still intact, so a complete recovery is possible by applying the redo that exists in the online-redo logs (and doesn't exist in the archive-redo logs). To apply what's in the online-redo logs, first determine the locations and names of the online-redo log files:

```
select
 a.first_change#
,b.member
from v$log a
     ,v$logfile b
where a.group# = b.group#;
```

Here's the partial output for this example:

```
FIRST_CHANGE# MEMBER
------------- -----------------------------------
     17779560 /ora01/oraredo/011R2/redo01a.rdo
     17779678 /ora02/oraredo/011R2/redo02a.rdo
```

Now, re-initiate the recover process:

```
SQL> recover database using backup controlfile;
```

The last archive-redo log generated for this database was sequence 51. The recovery process prompts for an archive-redo log that doesn't exist:

```
ORA-00279: change 17815760 generated at 08/21/2010 13:21:58 needed for thread 1
ORA-00289: suggestion : /ora02/oraarch/011R2/1_52_726314508.arc
ORA-00280: change 17815760 for thread 1 is in sequence #52
```

Instead of supplying the recovery process with an archive-redo log file, you type in the name of an online-redo log file. This instructs the recovery process to apply any redo in the online-redo log:

```
/ora01/oraredo/011R2/redo02a.rdo
```

You should see this message when the correct online-redo log is applied:

```
Log applied.
Media recovery complete.
```

The database is completely recovered at this point. However, because a backup control file was used for the recovery process, the database must be opened with the RESETLOGS clause:

```
SQL> alter database open resetlogs;
```

Upon success, you should see this:

```
Database altered.
```

Performing an Incomplete Recovery of an Archivelog-Mode Database

Incomplete recovery means you don't restore all transactions that were committed before the failure. With this type of recovery, you're recovering to a point in time in the past, and transactions are lost. This is why incomplete recovery is also referred to as *database point-in-time recovery* (DBPITR).

Incomplete recovery doesn't mean you're restoring and recovering only a subset of datafiles. In fact, with most incomplete scenarios, you have to restore all datafiles from the backup as part of the procedure. If you don't restore all datafiles, you first need to take offline any datafiles you don't intend to participate in the incomplete-recovery process. Any datafiles taken offline can't be later restored and recovered.

You may want to perform an incomplete recovery for many different reasons:

- You attempt to perform a complete recovery but are missing the required archive-redo logs or unarchived online-redo log information.

- You want to restore the database back to a point in time in the past just prior to an erroneous user error (such as deleted data, dropped table, and so on).

- You have a testing environment in which you have a baseline copy of the database. After the testing is finished, you want to reset the database back to baseline for another round of new testing.

If you're using user-managed incomplete recovery for any of these reasons, you should consider using the Flashback Table or Flashback Database feature. These features are discussed in detail later in the chapter.

You can perform user-managed incomplete recovery three ways:

- Cancel based

- SCN based

- Time based

Cancel based allows you to apply archive redo and halt the process at the boundary based on an archive-redo log file. For example, say you're attempting to restore and recover your database, and you realize that you're missing an archive-redo log. You have to stop the recover process at the point of your last good archive-redo log. You initiate cancel-based incomplete recovery with the CANCEL clause of the RECOVER DATABASE statement:

```
SQL> recover database until cancel;
```

If you want to recover up to and including a certain SCN number, use *SCN-based* incomplete recovery. You may know from the alert log or from the output of LogMiner the point to which you want to restore to a certain SCN. Use the UNTIL CHANGE clause to perform this type of incomplete recovery:

```
SQL> recover database until change 12345;
```

If you know the time at which you want to stop the recovery process, use *time-based* incomplete recovery. For example, you may know that a table was dropped at a certain time and want to restore and recover the database up to the specified time. The format for a time-based recovery is always as follows: 'YYYY-MM-DD:HH24:MI:SS'. Here's an example:

```
SQL> recover database until time '2010-10-21:02:00:00';
```

When you perform an incomplete recovery, you have to restore all datafiles that you plan to have online when the incomplete restoration is finished. Here are the steps for an incomplete recovery:

1. Shut down the database.

2. Restore all the datafiles from the backup.

3. Start the database in mount mode.

4. Apply redo (roll forward) to the desired point, and halt the recovery process (use cancel-, SCN-, or time-based recovery).

5. Open the database with the RESETLOGS clause.

The following example performs a cancel-based incomplete recovery. If the database is open, shut it down:

```
$ sqlplus / as sysdba
SQL> shutdown abort;
```

Next, copy *all* datafiles from the backup (either a cold or hot backup). This example restores all datafiles from a hot backup. For this example, the current control file is intact and doesn't need to be restored. Here's a partial snippet of the OS copy commands for the database being restored:

```
$ cp /oradump/cbackup/O11R2/system01.dbf /ora01/dbfile/O11R2/system01.dbf
$ cp /oradump/cbackup/O11R2/sysaux01.dbf /ora01/dbfile/O11R2/sysaux01.dbf
$ cp /oradump/cbackup/O11R2/undotbs01.dbf /ora02/dbfile/O11R2/undotbs01.dbf
$ cp /oradump/cbackup/O11R2/users01.dbf /ora02/dbfile/O11R2/users01.dbf
$ cp /oradump/cbackup/O11R2/appdata.dbf /ora01/dbfile/O11R2/appdata.dbf
```

After the datafiles have been copied back, you can initiate the recovery process. This example performs a cancel-based incomplete recovery:

```
$ sqlplus / as sysdba
SQL> startup mount;
SQL> recover database until cancel;
```

At this point, the Oracle recovery process suggests an archive-redo log to apply:

```
ORA-00279: change 17851736 generated at 08/22/2010 07:33:42 needed for thread 1
ORA-00289: suggestion : /ora02/oraarch/O11R2/1_3_727625398.arc
ORA-00280: change 17851736 for thread 1 is in sequence #3
Specify log: {<RET>=suggested | filename | AUTO | CANCEL}
```

In this example, you know that the last good archive-redo log that you have is sequence 7, so you apply redo to that point and then type CANCEL:

```
CANCEL
```

This stops the recovery process. Now you can open the database with the RESETLOGS clause:

```
SQL> alter database open resetlogs;
```

The database has been opened to a point in time in the past. The recovery is deemed incomplete because not all redo was applied.

Flashing Back a Table

In older versions of the database, if a table was accidentally dropped, you had to do the following to restore the table:

1. Restore a backup of the database to a test database.

2. Perform an incomplete recovery up to the point in time when the table was dropped.

3. Export the table.

4. Import the table into the production database.

This process can be time-consuming and resource-intensive. It requires extra server resources as well as time and effort from a DBA.

Oracle introduced the Flashback feature in recent versions; it lets you quickly restore from an accidentally dropped table. Oracle applies the term *flashback* to several different database features, which can be confusing. In regard to flashing back tables, Oracle provides two distinctly different types of flashback operations:

*   FLASHBACK TABLE TO BEFORE DROP quickly undrops a previously dropped table. This feature uses the recycle bin.

*   FLASHBACK TABLE flashes back to a recent point in time to revert the effects of undesired Data Manipulation Language (DML) statements. You can flash back to an SCN, timestamp, or restore point.

Oracle introduced FLASHBACK TABLE TO BEFORE DROP to allow you to quickly recover a dropped table. As of Oracle Database 10g, when you drop a table, if you don't specify the PURGE clause, Oracle doesn't drop the table—instead, the table is renamed. Any tables you drop (that Oracle actually renames) are placed into a logical container named the *recycle bin*. The recycle bin provides you with an efficient way to view and manage dropped objects.

■ **Note** To use the Flashback Table feature, you don't need to implement an FRA. Nor do you need Flashback Database enabled.

The FLASHBACK TABLE TO BEFORE DROP operation only works if your database has the recycle bin feature enabled (which it is by default). You can check the status of the recycle bin as follows:

```
SQL> show parameter recyclebin

NAME                                 TYPE        VALUE
------------------------------------ ----------- ------------------------------
recyclebin                           string      on
```

FLASHBACK TABLE TO BEFORE DROP

When you drop a table, if you don't specify the PURGE clause, Oracle renames the table with a system-generated name. Because the table isn't really dropped, you can use FLASHBACK TABLE TO BEFORE DROP to instruct Oracle to rename the table with its original name. Here's an example. Suppose the INV table is accidentally dropped:

```
SQL> drop table inv;
```

Verify that the table has been renamed by viewing the contents of the recycle bin:

```
SQL> show recyclebin;
```

```
ORIGINAL NAME    RECYCLEBIN NAME                      OBJECT TYPE  DROP TIME
---------------- ----------------------------------- ------------ -------------------
INV              BIN$jmx7BIkFlYrgQAB/AQBIgg==$0 TABLE            2010-08-22:10:36:11
```

The SHOW RECYCLEBIN statement only shows tables that have been dropped. To get a more complete picture of renamed objects, query the RECYCLEBIN view:

```
select
 object_name
,original_name
,type
from recyclebin;
```

Here's the output:

```
OBJECT_NAME                     ORIGINAL_NAME         TYPE
------------------------------- --------------------- -------------------------
BIN$jmx7BIkFlYrgQAB/AQBIgg==$0 INV                   TABLE
BIN$jmx7BIkElYrgQAB/AQBIgg==$0 INV_TRIG              TRIGGER
BIN$jmx7BIkDlYrgQAB/AQBIgg==$0 INV_PK                INDEX
```

In this output, the table also has a primary key that was renamed when the object was dropped. To undrop the table, do the following:

```
SQL> flashback table inv to before drop;
```

This restores the table to its original name. This statement doesn't restore the index to its original name, though:

```
SQL> select index_name from user_indexes where table_name='INV';
```

```
INDEX_NAME
-------------------------------
BIN$jmx7BIkDlYrgQAB/AQBIgg==$0
```

In this scenario, you have to rename the index:

```
SQL> alter index "BIN$jmx7BIkDlYrgQAB/AQBIgg==$0" rename to inv_pk;
```

You have to rename any trigger objects in the same manner. If referential constraints were in place before the table was dropped, you must manually re-create them.

If for some reason you need to flash back a table to a different name than the original name, you can do so as follows:

```
SQL> flashback table inv to before drop rename to inv_bef;
```

Flashing Back a Table to a Previous Point in Time

The Flashback Table feature that flashes back to a previous point in time is completely different from FLASHBACK TABLE TO BEFORE DROP. Flashing back a table to a previous point in time uses information in the undo tablespace. The point in time in the past depends on your undo tablespace retention period, which specifies the minimum time that undo information is kept.

If the required flashback information isn't in the undo tablespace, you receive an error such as this:

```
ORA-01555: snapshot too old
```

In other words, to be able to flash back to a point in time in the past, the required information in the undo tablespace must not have been overwritten.

FLASHBACK TABLE TO SCN

Suppose you're testing an application feature, and you want to quickly restore a table back to a specific SCN. As part of the application testing, you record the SCN before testing begins:

```
SQL> select current_scn from v$database;

CURRENT_SCN
-----------
   17879789
```

You perform some testing and then want to flash back the table to the SCN previously recorded. First, ensure that row movement is enabled for the table:

```
SQL> alter table inv enable row movement;
SQL> flashback table inv to scn 17879789;
```

The table should now reflect transactions that were committed as of the historical SCN value specified in the FLASHBACK statement.

FLASHBACK TABLE TO TIMESTAMP

You can also flash back a table to a prior point in time. For example, to flash back a table to 15 minutes in the past, first enable row movement, and then use FLASHBACK TABLE:

```
SQL> alter table inv enable row movement;
SQL> flashback table inv to timestamp(sysdate-1/96) ;
```

The timestamp you provide must evaluate to a valid format for an Oracle timestamp. You can also explicitly specify a time as follows:

```
SQL> flashback table inv to timestamp
    to_timestamp('22-aug-10 12:07:33','dd-mon-yy hh:mi:ss');
```

FLASHBACK TABLE TO RESTORE POINT

A *restore point* is a name associated with a timestamp or SCN in the database. You can create a restore point that contains the current SCN of the database as follows:

```
SQL> create restore point point_a;
```

Later, if you decide to flash back a table to that restore point, first enable row movement:

```
SQL> alter table inv enable row movement;
SQL> flashback table inv to restore point point_a;
```

The table should now contain transactions as they were at the SCN associated with the specified restore point.

Flashing Back a Database

The Flashback Database feature allows you to perform an incomplete recovery to a point in time in the past. Flashback Database uses information stored in flashback logs; it doesn't rely on restoring database files (like a cold backup, hot backup, or RMAN). In some situations, Flashback Database can restore your database to a point in time in the past much more quickly than performing a user-managed incomplete recovery (which requires you to copy datafiles from the backup).

■ **Tip** Flashback Database isn't a substitute for a backup of your database. If you experience a media failure with a datafile, you can't use Flashback Database to flash back to before the failure. If a datafile is damaged, you have to restore and recover using a physical backup (hot, cold, or RMAN).

The Flashback Database feature may be desirable in situations where you want to consistently reset your database to a point in time in the past. For example, you may want to periodically set a test or training database back to a known baseline. Or you may be upgrading an application and, before making large-scale changes to the application database objects, mark the starting point. After the upgrade, if things don't go well, you want the ability to quickly reset the database back to the point in time before the upgrade took place.

There are several prerequisites for Flashback Database:

- The database must be in archivelog mode.

- You must be using an FRA.

- The Flashback Database feature must be enabled.

See the earlier sections in this chapter about enabling archivelog mode and using the FRA. You can verify the status of these features using the following SQL*Plus statements:

```
SQL> archive log list;
SQL> show parameter db_recovery_file_dest;
```

To enable the Flashback Database feature, alter your database into flashback mode as shown:

```
SQL> alter database flashback on;
```

■ **Note** In Oracle Database 10g, the database must be in mount mode to enable Flashback Database.

You can verify the flashback status as follows:

```
SQL> select flashback_on from v$database;
```

```
FLASHBACK_ON
------------------
YES
```

After you enable Flashback Database, you can view the flashback logs in your FRA with this query:

```
select
 name
,log#
,thread#
,sequence#
,bytes
from v$flashback_database_logfile;
```

The range of time you can flash back is determined by the DB_FLASHBACK_RETENTION_TARGET parameter. This specifies the upper limit in minutes of how far your database can be flashed back.

You can view the oldest SCN and time you can flash back your database by running the following SQL:

```
select
 oldest_flashback_scn
,to_char(oldest_flashback_time,'dd-mon-yy hh24:mi:ss')
from v$flashback_database_log;
```

If you need to disable Flashback Database for any reason, you can turn it off as follows:

```
SQL> alter database flashback off;
```

You can use either RMAN or SQL*Plus to flash back a database. You can specify a point in time in the past using one of the following:

- SCN

- Timestamp

- Restore point

- Last RESETLOGS operation (works from RMAN only)

This example creates a restore point:

```
SQL> create restore point flash_1;
```

Next, the application performs some testing, after which the database is flashed back to the restore point so that a new round of testing can begin:

```
SQL> shutdown immediate;
SQL> startup mount;
SQL> flashback database to restore point flash_1;
SQL> alter database open resetlogs;
```

At this point, your database should be transactionally consistent as it was at the SCN associated with the restore point.

Summary

This chapter covers B&R techniques that aren't taught or used much anymore. Most DBAs are (and should be) using RMAN for their Oracle B&R requirements. However, it's critical for you to understand how cold backups and hot backups work. You may find yourself consulting in a shop where they've implemented old technology and now need you to restore and recover their database or assist them in migrating to RMAN. In these scenarios, you must fully understand the older backup technologies.

This chapter also discussed restore and recovery techniques using cold and hot backups. Understanding what happens at each step and why the step is required is vital for complete knowledge of the Oracle B&R architecture. This awareness translates into key troubleshooting skills when you're using Oracle tools such as RMAN (B&R) and Data Guard (disaster recovery, high availability, and replication).

Now that you have an in-depth understanding of Oracle B&R mechanics, you're ready to investigate RMAN. The next several chapters in this book examine how to configure and use RMAN for production-strength B&R.

CHAPTER 17

■ ■ ■

Configuring RMAN

Oracle Recovery Manager (RMAN) is Oracle's flagship backup and recovery (B&R) tool. It has been available since Oracle Database 8. This tool is provided by default when you install the Oracle software (for both the Standard Edition and Enterprise Edition). RMAN provides a robust and flexible set of B&R features. The following list highlights some of the most salient qualities:

- Easy-to-use commands for backup, restore, and recovery.

- Ability to track which files have been backed up and to where. Manages the deletion of obsolete backups and archive-redo logs.

- Parallelization: can use multiple processes for backup, restore, and recovery.

- Incremental backups that only back up changes since the previous backup.

- Block-level recovery, which allows you to recover individual blocks in a datafile.

- Compression and encryption features.

- Integration with media managers for tape backups.

- Backup validation and testing.

- Cross-platform data conversion.

- Data Recovery Advisor, which assists with diagnosing failures and providing solutions.

- Ability to detect corrupt blocks in datafiles.

- Advanced reporting capabilities from the RMAN command line.

The goal of this chapter is to provide enough information about RMAN that you can make reasonable decisions about how to implement a solid backup strategy. The basic RMAN components are described first, after which you walk through many of the decisions points involved with implementing RMAN.

■ Note The RMAN-related chapters in this book aren't intended to be a complete reference on all aspects of B&R. That would take an entire book. These chapters provide the basic information you need to successfully use RMAN for B&R. If you require advanced RMAN information regarding backup, restore, and recovery, see *RMAN Recipes for Oracle Database 11g*, available from Apress.

Understanding RMAN

RMAN consists of many different components. Figure 17–1 shows the interactions of the main RMAN pieces. Refer back to this diagram when reading through this section.

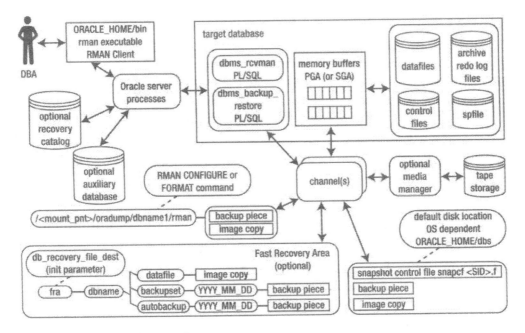

Figure 17–1. RMAN architectural components

The following list describes the RMAN architectural components:

> *DBA:* Appears somewhat short and bald in the diagram, which isn't far from the truth (in my case).

> *Target database:* The database being backed up by RMAN. You connect to the target database with the RMAN command-line TARGET parameter (more on this in the next section of this chapter).

> *RMAN client:* The rman utility from which you issue BACKUP, RESTORE, and RECOVER commands. On most database servers, the rman utility is located in the ORACLE_HOME/bin directory (along with all the other Oracle utilities, such as sqlplus, expdp, and so on).

> *Oracle server processes (channels):* When you execute the rman client and connect to the target database, two Oracle server background processes are started. One process interacts with the PL/SQL packages to coordinate the backup activities. The secondary process occasionally updates Oracle data-dictionary structures. You can query the RMAN metadata information via views such as V$SESSION_LONGOPS.

PL/SQL packages: RMAN uses two internal PL/SQL packages (owned by SYS) to perform B&R tasks: DBMS_RCVMAN and DBMS_BACKUP_RESTORE. DBMS_RCVMAN accesses information in the control file and passes that to the RMAN server processes. The DBMS_BACKUP_RESTORE package performs most of RMAN's work. For example, this package creates the system calls that direct the channel processes to perform B&R operations.

Memory buffers (PGA or SGA): RMAN uses a memory area in the program global area (and sometimes in the system global area) as a buffer when reading from datafiles and copying subsequent blocks to back up files.

Auxiliary database: A database to which RMAN restores target database datafiles for the purpose of duplicating a database, creating a Data Guard standby database, or performing a database point-in-time recovery.

Channel(s): Oracle server processes for handling I/O between files being backed up and the backup device (disk or tape).

Backups and backup sets: When you run an RMAN BACKUP command, it creates one or more backup sets. A *backup set* is an internal RMAN construct that logically groups backup piece files. You can think of the relationship of a backup set to a backup piece as similar to the relationship between a tablespace and a datafile. One is a logical construct, and the other is a physical file.

Backup piece file: RMAN binary backup files. Each logical backup set consists of one or more backup piece files. These are the physical files that RMAN creates on disk or tape. They're binary, proprietary format files that only RMAN can read or write to. A backup piece can contain blocks from many different datafiles. Backup piece files are typically smaller than datafiles because backup pieces only contain blocks that have been used in the datafiles.

Image copy: A type of backup in which RMAN creates identical copies of a datafile, archive-redo log file, or control file. Image copies can be operated on by OS utilities such as the Linux cp and mv commands. Image copies are used as part of incrementally updated image backups. Sometimes it's preferable to use image copies over backup sets if you need to be able to restore quickly.

Recovery catalog: An optional database schema that contains tables used to store metadata information regarding RMAN backup operations. Oracle strongly recommends using a recovery catalog, because it provides more options for B&R.

Media manager: Third-party software that allows RMAN to back up files directly to tape. Backing up to tape is desirable when you don't have enough room to back up directly to disk or when disaster-recovery requirements necessitate a backup to storage that can be easily moved offsite.

Fast-recovery area: An optional disk area that RMAN can use for backups (formerly known as the flash recovery area). You can also use the FRA to multiplex control files and online-redo logs. You instantiate a fast recovery with the database initialization parameters DB_RECOVERY_FILE_DEST_SIZE and DB_RECOVERY_FILE_DEST.

Snapshot control file: RMAN requires a read-consistent view of the control file when either backing up the control file or synchronizing with the recovery catalog (if it's being used). In these situations, RMAN first creates a temporary copy (snapshot) of the control file. This allows RMAN to use a version of the control file that is guaranteed not to change while backing up the control file or synchronizing with the recovery catalog.

You can make several types of backups with RMAN:

Full backup: All modified blocks associated with the datafile are backed up. A full backup doesn't refer to backing up the entire database. For example, you can make a full backup of one datafile.

Incremental level 0 backup: Backs up the same blocks as a full backup. The only difference is that you can use a level 0 backup with other incremental backups, whereas you can use a full backup that way.

Incremental level 1 backup: Backs up only blocks that have been modified since the previous backup. Level 1 incremental backups can be either differential or cumulative. A *differential* level 1 backup backs up all blocks that have been modified since the last level 0 or level 1 backup. A *cumulative* level 1 backup backs up all blocks that have changed since the last level 0 backup.

Incrementally updated backup: First creates an image copy of the datafiles, after which subsequent backups are incremental backups that are merged with the image copy. This is an efficient way to use image copies for backups. Media recoveries using incrementally updated backups are fast because the image copy of the datafile is used during the restore.

Block-change tracking: Database feature that keeps track of blocks that have changed in the database. A record of the changed blocks is kept in a binary file. RMAN can use the contents of the binary file to improve the performance of incremental backups: instead of having to scan all modified blocks in a datafile, RMAN can determine which blocks have changed from the binary block-change tracking.

Now that you understand the RMAN architectural components and the types of backups you can make, you're ready to start up RMAN and configure it for your environment.

Starting RMAN

To connect to RMAN, you need to establish the following:

- OS environment variables

- Access to a privileged operating-system account or a database user with SYSDBA privileges

The easiest way to connect to RMAN is to log on to the server where the target database resides and log in as the owner of the Oracle software (usually named oracle on Linux/Unix boxes). When you log in as oracle, you need to establish several OS variables before you can use utilities such as rman, sqlplus, and so on. Setting these required OS variables is covered in detail in Chapter 2.

At minimum, you need to set ORACLE_HOME and ORACLE_SID. Additionally, it's convenient if the PATH variable includes the directory ORACLE_HOME/bin. This is the directory that contains the Oracle utilities.

After you've established your OS variables, you can invoke RMAN from the OS as shown:

```
$ rman target /
```

When connecting to RMAN, you don't have to specify the AS SYSDBA clause (as you do when connecting to a database as a privileged user in SQL*Plus). This is because RMAN always requires that you connect as a database user with SYSDBA privileges.

The previous example of logging in to RMAN uses OS authentication. This type of authentication means if you can log on to an authorized OS account (such as the owner of the Oracle software, usually oracle), then you're allowed to connect to the database without having to provide a username and password. You administer OS authentication by assigning special groups to OS accounts. When you install the Oracle binaries in a Linux/Unix environment, you're required to specify at installation time the names of the OS groups that are assigned the database privileges of SYSDBA and SYSOPER (typically the dba group).

CALLING RMAN FROM SQL*PLUS, NOT

I teach Oracle B&R classes at a local institute of higher learning. Nearly every term, one of the students asks why the following RMAN command doesn't work:

```
SQL> rman
SP2-0042: unknown command "rman" - rest of line ignored.
```

The answer is short: the rman client is an OS utility. It's not a SQL*Plus function. You must invoke the rman client from the OS prompt.

If you don't have access to log in directly to a server as the Oracle software owner, you need a privileged database user account to connect to RMAN. Granting SYSDBA privileges to database users requires that you first implement a password file. To create a password file on Linux/Unix servers, first navigate to the ORACLE_HOME/dbs directory, and then use the orapwd utility to create a password file:

```
$ cd $ORACLE_HOME/dbs
$ orapwd file=orapw<ORACLE_SID> password=<sys password>
```

Before you grant SYSDBA to a database user, ensure that the initialization parameter REMOTE_LOGIN_PASSWORDFILE is set to EXCLUSIVE (the default):

```
SQL> show parameter remote_login_passwordfile

NAME                            TYPE         VALUE
------------------------------- ------------ ------------------------------
remote_login_passwordfile       string       EXCLUSIVE
```

You can now grant the SYSDBA privilege to a database user:

```
SQL> grant sysdba to lellison;
```

You can view the users who have SYSDBA privileges via the following query:

```
SQL> select * from v$pwfile_users;

USERNAME                        SYSDB SYSOP SYSAS
------------------------------- ----- ----- -----
SYS                             TRUE  TRUE  FALSE
LELLISON                        TRUE  FALSE FALSE
```

■ Note If you want to connect remotely to RMAN via Oracle Net, you need to first implement a password file.

RMAN Architectural Decisions

If archiving is enabled for your database, you can use RMAN out of the box to run commands such as this to back up your entire target database:

```
$ rman target /
RMAN> backup database;
```

If you experience a media failure, you can restore all datafiles as follows:

```
RMAN> shutdown immediate;
RMAN> startup mount;
RMAN> restore database;
```

After your database is restored, you can fully recover it:

```
RMAN> recover database;
RMAN> alter database open;
```

You're good to go, right? No, not quite. RMAN's default attributes are reasonably set for simple backup requirements. The RMAN out-of-the-box settings may be appropriate for small development or test databases. But for any type of business-critical database, you need to carefully consider items such as where the backups are stored, how long to store backups on disk or tape, which RMAN features are appropriate for the database, and so on. The following sections in this chapter walk you through many of the B&R architectural decisions that you need to consider when implementing RMAN in a production environment. RMAN has a vast and robust variety of options for customizing B&R; and typically, you don't need to implement many of its features. However, each time you implement RMAN to back up a production database, you should think through each decision point and decide whether you require an attribute.

Table 17–1 summarizes the RMAN implementation decisions and recommendations. Each of the decision points in the table is elaborated on in subsequent sections in this chapter. Many DBAs will disagree with some of these recommendations; that's fine. The point is that you need to consider each architectural aspect and determine what makes sense for your business requirements.

Table 17–1. Overview of Architectural Decisions and Recommendations

Decision Point	Recommendation
1. Running the RMAN client remotely or locally	Run the client locally on the target database server.
2. Specifying the backup user	Use SYS unless you have a security requirement that dictates otherwise.
3. Using online or offline backups	Depends on your business requirements. Most production databases require online backups, which means you must enable archiving.

Decision Point	Recommendation
4. Setting the archive-redo log destination and file format	If you're using an FRA, archive logs are written there with a default format. I prefer to use the `LOG_ARCHIVE_DEST_N` initialization parameter to specifically set the location outside of the FRA.
5. Configuring the RMAN backup location and file format	Depends on your business requirements. Some shops require tape backups. If you're using disk, place the backup in the FRA or specify a location via channel settings. I prefer not to use an FRA and to explicitly specify the location and file format via a `CONFIGURE` command.
6. Setting autobackup of the control file	Always enable autobackup of the control file.
7. Specifying the location of the autobackup of the control file	Either place it in the FRA or configure a location. I prefer to write the autobackup of the control file to the same location as the database backups (usually outside of the FRA).
8. Backing up archive-redo logs	Depends on your business requirements. For many environments, I back up the archive-redo logs on a daily basis with the same command I use to back up the database.
9. Determining the location for the snapshot control file	Use the default location.
10. Using a recovery catalog	Depends on your business requirements. For many environments, I don't use a recovery catalog. Oracle recommends that you do use a recovery catalog. If the RMAN retention policy is greater than `CONTROL_FILE_RECORD_KEEP_TIME`, then I recommend that you use a recovery catalog.
11. Using a media manager	Required for backing up directly to tape.
12. Setting the `CONTROL_FILE_RECORD_KEEP_TIME` Initialization Parameter	Usually, the default of seven days is sufficient.
13. Configuring RMAN's backup-retention policy	Depends on your database and business requirements. For many environments, I use a backup-retention redundancy of 1 or 2.
14. Configuring the archive-redo logs' deletion policy	Depends on your database and business requirements. In many scenarios, applying the backup-retention policy to the archive-redo logs is sufficient (this is the default behavior).

Decision Point	Recommendation
15. Setting the degree of parallelism	Depends on the available hardware resources and business requirements. For most production servers, where there are multiple CPUs, I configure a degree of parallelism of 2 or more.
16. Using backup sets or image copies	I prefer backup sets. Backup sets are usually smaller and easier to manage.
17. Using incremental backups	Use incremental backups for large databases where a small percentage of the database changes between backups and where you want to conserve on disk space.
18. Using incrementally updated backups	Use this approach if you require image copies of datafiles.
19. Using block-change tracking	Use this to improve the performance of incremental backups.
20. Configuring binary compression	Depends on your business requirements. Compressed backups consume less space but require more CPU resources (and time) for backup and restore operations.
21. Configuring encryption	Depends on your business requirements.
22. Configuring miscellaneous settings	You can set many channel-related properties, such as the backup-set size and the backup-piece size. Configure as needed.

1. Running the RMAN Client Remotely or Locally

It's possible to run the rman utility from a remote server and connect to a target database via Oracle Net:

```
$ rman target sys/foo@remote_db
```

This allows you to run RMAN backups on disparate remote servers from one central location. When you run RMAN remotely, the backup files are always created on the target database server.

Whenever possible, I run the rman client locally on the target server and connect like this:

```
$ rman target /
```

This approach is simple and adequate for most requirements. You don't have to worry about network issues or password files, and there are never compatibility issues with the rman client and the target database. If you run RMAN remotely, you need to be sure the remote rman executable is compatible with the target database. For example, is the remote rman executable you're running an Oracle Database 10g version of the RMAN client, and is it possible to connect that client to a remote Oracle Database 8i target database? If you run the rman client locally on the target server, there never is a compatibility issue because the rman client is always the same version as the target database.

2. Specifying the Backup User

As described in the previous section, RMAN requires that you use a database user with SYSDBA privileges. Whether I'm running RMAN from the command line or invoking RMAN in a script, in most scenarios, I connect directly as SYS to the target database. For example, here's how I connect to RMAN from the command line:

```
$ rman target /
```

Some DBAs don't use that approach; they prefer to set up a separate user from SYS and cite security concerns as a reason for doing this.

I prefer to use the SYS account directly because when connecting to RMAN locally on the server, there is no need to specify a username and password. This means you never have to hard-code usernames and passwords into any backup scripts or specify a username and password on the command line that can be viewed by rogue developers or managers looking over your shoulder.

3. Using Online or Offline Backups

Most production databases have 24x7 availability requirements. Therefore, your only option is online RMAN backups. Your database must be in archivelog mode for online backups. You need to carefully consider where to place archive-redo logs, how to format them, how often to back them up, and how long to retain them before deletion. These topics are discussed in subsequent sections.

▓ **Note** If you make offline backups, you must shut down your database with IMMEDIATE, NORMAL, or TRANSACTIONAL and then place it in mount mode. RMAN needs the database in mount mode so it can read from and write to the control file.

---

4. Setting the Archive-Redo Log Destination and File Format

Enabling archive-redo log mode is a prerequisite for making online backups. See Chapter 16 for a full discussion of architectural decisions regarding the archive-redo log destination and format and how to enable/disable archivelog mode.

When archivelog mode is enabled, Oracle writes the archive-redo logs to one or more of the following locations (you can configure archive-redo logs to be written both to the FRA and several other locations that you manually set via initialization parameters):

- Default location

- FRA

- Location specified via LOG_ARCHIVE_DEST_N initialization parameter(s)

If you don't use an FRA and if you don't explicitly set the archive-redo log destination via a LOG_ARCHIVE_DEST_N initialization parameter, then by default the archive-redo logs are written to an OS-dependent location. On many Linux/Unix boxes, the default location is the ORACLE_HOME/dbs/arch directory. The default filename format for archive-redo logs is %t_%s_%r.dbf.

If you enable an FRA, then by default the archive-redo logs are written to a directory in the FRA. The default format of the name of archive-redo log files created in the FRA is an Oracle Managed File format. For example:

```
/<fra>/<db_name>/archivelog/<YYYY_MM_DD>/o1_mf_1_1078_68dx5dyj_.arc
```

Oracle recommends using an FRA. I prefer not to use an FRA because I don't like to be surprised with a hung database when there are issues with the FRA filling up and not being purged of old files quickly enough. Instead, I prefer to use the LOG_ARCHIVE_DEST_N parameter to set the location of the archive-redo log files. Here's an example:

```
log_archive_dest_1='LOCATION=/oraarch1/CHNPRD'
```

I also prefer to use this for the default archivelog file name format:

```
log_archive_format='%t_%s_%r.arc'
```

Sometimes DBAs use .dbf as an extension for both datafiles and archive-redo log files. This format avoids potential confusion with identifying a file as an archive-redo log file or a live database datafile.

5. Configuring the RMAN Backup Location and File Format

When you run a BACKUP command for disk-based backups, RMAN creates backup pieces in one of the following locations:

- Default location
- FRA
- Location specified via the BACKUP or FORMAT command

If you don't configure any RMAN variables and don't set up an FRA, by default RMAN allocates one disk-based channel and writes the backup files to a default location. For example, you can run the following command without configuring any RMAN parameters:

```
RMAN> backup database;
```

If nothing has been configured, RMAN allocates a disk-based channel and writes the backups to the default disk location. This location varies by OS. In many Linux/Unix environments, the default location is ORACLE_HOME/dbs. The default format of the name of the backup files created is an Oracle Managed File format. For example:

```
<ORACLE_HOME>/dbs/01ln9g7e_1_1
```

When backing up to disk, if you don't explicitly instruct RMAN to write the backups to a specific location (via the FORMAT or CONFIGURE command), and if you're using an FRA, RMAN automatically writes the backup files to directories in the FRA. The default format of the name of the backup files created in the FRA is an Oracle Managed File format. For example:

```
/<fra>/<db_name>/backupset/<YYYY_MM_DD>/o1_mf_nnndf_TAG20100907T025402_68czfbdf_.bkp
```

I usually don't use an FRA for the placement of RMAN backups. In many of the environments I work in, there isn't enough disk space on a single mount point to accommodate the entire size of the database backups. In such situations, you need to allocate two or more channels that point to different mount points. Using an FRA in these environments is somewhat unwieldy.

Also, for performance reasons, you may want to instruct RMAN to write to multiple disk locations. If you can ensure that different mount points are based on different physical disks and are written to by separate controllers, you can reduce I/O contention by allocating multiple channels pointing to separate mount points.

When you're using an FRA, RMAN automatically creates separate directories when backing up a database for the first time on a given date. I prefer to have the backups written to one directory and not separate the directories and backups by date. I find it easier to manage, maintain, and troubleshoot the backups if I use one standard directory for each database on each server.

If you don't want to place RMAN backup files in the FRA, there are a couple of methods for directly specifying a backup location:

- BACKUP...FORMAT

- CONFIGURE CHANNEL...FORMAT

You can directly specify where you want backups to be placed when you issue the BACKUP command. For example:

```
RMAN> backup database format '/ora01/011R2/rman/rman_%U.bkp';
```

Here's a corresponding file generated by RMAN:

```
/ora01/011R2/rman/rman_05ln9hk6_1_1.bkp
```

The %U instructs RMAN to dynamically construct a unique string for the backup file name. A unique name is required in most situations, because RMAN won't write over the top of a file that already exists. This is important because if you instruct RMAN to write in parallel, it needs to create unique file names for each channel. For example:

```
RMAN> configure device type disk parallelism 2;
```

Now, when you run this command, RMAN allocates multiple channels and write in parallel to two different backup files. The U% in the format string guarantees that unique file names are created.

I usually don't use the BACKUP...FORMAT syntax to specify the location for RMAN backups. I prefer to use the CONFIGURE CHANNEL...FORMAT command. This is because I'm usually writing to multiple disk locations and need the flexibility to specify directories located on different mount points. Here's a typical configuration specifying CONFIGURE CHANNEL...FORMAT:

```
RMAN> configure device type disk parallelism 3;
RMAN> configure channel 1 device type disk format '/ora01/011R2/rman/rman1_%U.bk';
RMAN> configure channel 2 device type disk format '/ora02/011R2/rman/rman2_%U.bk';
RMAN> configure channel 3 device type disk format '/ora03/011R2/rman/rman3_%U.bk';
```

In these lines of code, you should configure the device-type parallelism degree to match the number of channels that you allocated. RMAN only allocates the number of channels as specified by the degree of parallelism; other configured channels are ignored. For example, if you specify a degree of parallelism of 2, RMAN allocates only two channels regardless of the number of channels you configured via the CONFIGURE CHANNEL command.

In this example of configuring channels, suppose the BACKUP command is issued like this:

```
RMAN> backup database;
```

RMAN allocates three channels, all on separate mount points (/ora01, /ora02, /ora03), and writes in parallel to the specified locations. RMAN creates as many backup pieces in the three locations as it deems necessary to create a backup of the database.

6. Setting Autobackup of the Control File

You should always configure RMAN to automatically back up the control file after running any RMAN BACKUP or COPY command or after you make physical changes to the database that result in updates to the control file (such as adding/removing a datafile). Use the SHOW command to display the current setting of the control file autobackup:

```
RMAN> show controlfile autobackup;
```

Here's some sample output:

```
RMAN configuration parameters for database with db_unique_name O11R2 are:
CONFIGURE CONTROLFILE AUTOBACKUP OFF;
```

The following line of code shows how to enable automatic backup of the control-file feature:

```
RMAN> configure controlfile autobackup on;
```

The automatic control-file backup always goes into its own backup set. When autobackup of the control file is enabled, if you're using an spfile, it's automatically backed up along with the control file.

If for any reason you want to disable automatic backup of the control file, you can do so as follows:

```
RMAN> configure controlfile autobackup off;
```

■ **Note** If autobackup of the control file is off, then any time you back up datafile 1 (SYSTEM tablespace datafile), RMAN automatically backs up the control file.

---

7. Specifying the Location of the Autobackup of the Control File

When you enable autobackup of the control file, RMAN creates the backup of the control file in one of the following locations:

- Default location
- FRA
- Location specified via the BACKUP or FORMAT command

If you aren't using an FRA or if you haven't specified a location for the control-file autobackups, the control-file autobackup is written to an OS-dependent default location. In many Linux/Unix environments, the default location is ORACLE_HOME/dbs. For example:

```
/oracle/app/oracle/product/11.2.0/db_1/dbs/c-3453199553-20100907-04
```

If you've enabled an FRA, then RMAN automatically writes the control-file autobackup files to directories in the FRA using an Oracle Managed File format for the name. For example:

```
/<fra>/<db_name>/autobackup/<YYYY_MM_DD>/o1_mf_s_729103049_68fho9z2_.bkp
```

I usually don't use the default location or the FRA for control-file autobackups. I prefer these backups to be placed in the same directory the database backups are in. Here's an example:

```
RMAN> configure controlfile autobackup format for device type disk to
'/ora01/O11R2/rman/rman_ctl_%F.bk';
```

8. Backing Up Archive-Redo Logs

You should back up your archive-redo logs on a regular basis. The archivelog files shouldn't be removed from disk until you've backed them up at least once. I usually like to keep on disk any archive-redo logs that have been generated after the last good RMAN backup.

Usually, I instruct RMAN to back up the archive-redo logs at the same time the datafiles are backed up. This is a sufficient strategy in most situations. Here is the command to back up the archive-redo logs along with the datafiles:

```
RMAN> backup database plus archivelog;
```

Sometimes, if your database generates a great deal of redo, you may need to back up your archive-redo logs at a different frequency than the datafiles. Sometimes DBAs back up the archive-redo logs two or three times a day; after the logs are backed up, the DBAs delete them to make room for more current archivelog files.

In most situations, you don't need any archive-redo logs that were generated before your last good backup. For example, a datafile has experienced media failure, you need to restore the datafile from a backup and then apply any archive-redo logs that were generated during and after the backup of the datafile.

On some occasions, you may need archive-redo logs that were generated before the last backup. For example, you may experience a media failure, attempt to restore your database from the last good backup, find corruption in that backup, and therefore need to restore from an older backup. At that point, you need a copy of all archive-redo logs that have been generated since that older backup was made.

9. Determining the Location for the Snapshot Control File

RMAN requires a read-consistent view of the control file for the following tasks:

- Synchronizing with the recovery catalog

- Backing up the current control file

In these situations, RMAN creates a snapshot copy of the current control file that it uses as a read-consistent copy while it's performing these tasks. This ensures that RMAN is working from a copy of the control file that isn't being modified.

The default location of the snapshot control file is OS-specific. On Linux platforms, the default location is ORACLE_HOME/dbs/snapcf_@.f. Notice that the default location isn't in the FRA (even if you've implemented an FRA).

You can display the current snapshot control file details using the SHOW command:

```
RMAN> show snapshot controlfile name;
```

Here's some sample output:

```
CONFIGURE SNAPSHOT CONTROLFILE NAME TO
'/oracle/app/oracle/product/11.2.0/db_1/dbs/snapcf_011R2.f'; # default
```

For most situations, the default location and format of the snapshot control file are sufficient. This file doesn't use much space or have any intensive I/O requirements. I recommend that you use the default setting.

If you have a good reason to configure the snapshot control file to a nondefault location, you can configure it as follows:

```
RMAN> configure snapshot controlfile name to '/oradump/011R2/snapcf.ctl';
```

You can set the snapshot control file back to the default like this:

```
RMAN> configure snapshot controlfile name clear;
```

10. Using a Recovery Catalog

RMAN always stores its latest backup operations in the target database control file. You can set up an optional recovery catalog to store metadata regarding RMAN backups. The recovery catalog is a separate schema (usually in a different database than the target database) that contains database objects (tables, indexes, and so on) that store the RMAN backup information. The recovery catalog doesn't store RMAN backup pieces—only backup metadata.

The main advantages of using a recovery catalog are as follows:

- Provides a secondary repository for RMAN metadata. If you lose all your control files and backups of your control files, you can still retrieve RMAN metadata from the recovery catalog.

- Stores RMAN metadata for a much longer period than is possible when you just use a control file for the repository.

- Provides access to all RMAN features. Some restore and recovery features are simpler when using a recovery catalog.

The disadvantages of using a recovery catalog are that this is another database you have to set up, maintain, and back up. When you start a backup and attempt to connect to the recovery catalog, if the recovery catalog isn't available for any reason (server down, network issues, and so on), you must decide whether you want to continue with the backup without a recovery catalog.

You must also be aware of versioning aspects when using a recovery catalog. You need to make sure the version of the database you use to store the recovery catalog is compatible with the version of the target database. When you upgrade a target database, be sure the recovery catalog is upgraded (if necessary).

■ **Note** See the last section in this chapter for details on how to implement a recovery catalog.

RMAN works fine with or without a recovery catalog. For most of the databases I maintain, I don't use a recovery catalog; this eliminates having to set it up and maintain it. For me, simplicity takes precedence over the features available with the recovery catalog.

However, if you have good business reasons to use a recovery catalog, then implement and use one. The recovery catalog isn't that difficult to set up and maintain, and Oracle recommends that you use it.

11. Using a Media Manager

A media manager is required for RMAN to back up directly to tape. Several vendors provide this feature (for a cost). Media managers are used in large database environments like data warehouses where you may not have enough room to back up a database to disk. You may also have a disaster-recovery requirement to back up directly to tape.

If you have such requirements, then you should purchase a media-management package and implement it. If you don't need to back up directly to tape, there's no need to implement a media manager. RMAN works fine backing up directly to disk.

Keep in mind that many shops use RMAN to back up directly to disk and then have the system administrator back up the RMAN backups to tape after the RMAN backups to disk have finished. If you do this, you have to be sure your RMAN backups aren't running the same time the tape backups are running (because you may get partial files backed up to tape).

12. Setting the CONTROL_FILE_RECORD_KEEP_TIME Initialization Parameter

The `CONTROL_FILE_RECORD_KEEP_TIME` initialization parameter specifies the minimum number of days a reusable record in the control file is retained before the record can be overwritten. The RMAN metadata is stored in the reusable section of the control file and therefore is eventually overwritten.

If you're using a recovery catalog, then you don't need to worry about this parameter because RMAN metadata is stored in the recovery catalog indefinitely. Therefore, when you use a recovery catalog, you can access any historical RMAN metadata.

If you're only using the control file as the RMAN metadata repository, then the information stored there will eventually be overwritten. The default value for `CONTROL_FILE_RECORD_KEEP_TIME` is seven days:

```
SQL> show parameter control_file_record_keep_time

NAME                                 TYPE        VALUE
------------------------------------ ----------- ------------------------------
control_file_record_keep_time        integer     7
```

You can set the value to anything from 0 to 365 days. Setting the value to 0 means the RMAN metadata information can be overwritten at any time.

The `CONTROL_FILE_RECORD_KEEP_TIME` parameter was more critical in older versions of Oracle where it wasn't easy to repopulate the control file with RMAN information in the event that metadata was overwritten. Starting with Oracle Database 10g, you can use the `CATALOG` command to quickly make the control file aware of RMAN backup files.

I recommend that you leave this parameter at seven days. If for some reason you have a retention policy greater than seven days, and you're not using a recovery catalog, then you may want to consider increasing the value. The downside to increasing this parameter is that if you have a significant amount of RMAN backup activity, this can increase the size of your control file.

13. Configuring RMAN's Backup-Retention Policy

RMAN retention policies allow you to specify how long you want to retain backups. RMAN has two mutually exclusive methods of specifying a retention policy:

- Recovery window
- Number of backups (redundancy)

With a recovery window, you specify a number of days in the past for which you want to be able recover to any point in that window. For example, if you specify a retention policy window of five days, then RMAN doesn't mark as obsolete backups of datafiles and archive-redo logs that are required to be able to restore to any point in that five-day window:

```
RMAN> configure retention  policy to recovery window of 5 days;
```

For the specified recovery, RMAN may need backups older than the five-day window because it may need an older backup to start with to be able to recover to the recovery point specified. For example, suppose your last good backup was made six days ago, and now you want to recover to four days in the past. For this recovery window, RMAN needs the backup from six days ago to restore and recover to the point specified.

You can also specify that RMAN keep a minimum number of backups. For example, if redundancy is set to 2, then RMAN doesn't mark as obsolete the latest two backups of datafiles and archive-redo log files:

```
RMAN> configure retention policy to redundancy 2;
```

I find that a retention policy based on redundancy is easier to work with and more predictable with regard to how long backups are retained. If I set redundancy to 2, I know RMAN won't mark as obsolete the latest two backups. The recovery-window retention policy depends on the frequency of the backups and the window length to determine whether a backup is obsolete.

You can report on backups that RMAN has determined to be obsolete per the retention policy as follows:

```
RMAN> report obsolete;
```

To delete obsolete backups, run the DELETE OBSOLETE command:

```
RMAN> delete obsolete;
```

You're prompted with:

```
Do you really want to delete the above objects (enter YES or NO)?
```

If you're scripting this, you can specify the delete not to prompt for input:

```
RMAN> delete noprompt obsolete;
```

I usually have the DELETE NOPROMPT OBSOLETE command coded into the same shell script that backs up the database. This instructs RMAN to delete any obsolete backups and any obsolete archive-redo logs as specified by the retention policy. See the shell script later in this chapter for an example of how to automate the deleting of obsolete backups.

The default retention policy is redundancy of 1. You can completely disable the RMAN retention policy via the TO NONE command:

```
RMAN> configure retention policy to none;
```

To set the retention policy back to the default, use the CLEAR command:

```
RMAN> configure retention policy clear;
```

14. Configuring the Archive-Redo Logs' Deletion Policy

In most scenarios, I have RMAN delete the archive-redo logs based on the retention policy of the database backups. This is the default behavior. You can view the database retention policy using the SHOW command:

```
RMAN> show retention policy;
```

```
CONFIGURE RETENTION POLICY TO REDUNDANCY 1; # default
```

To remove archive-redo logs (and backup pieces) based on the database retention policy, run the following:

```
RMAN> delete obsolete;
```

As of Oracle Database 11g, you can specify an archive-redo log deletion policy that is separate from the database backups. This deletion policy applies to both archive-redo logs outside of the FRA and in the FRA.

■ Note Prior to Oracle Database 11g, the archive-deletion policy only applied to archive-redo logs associated with a standby database.

To configure an archive-redo log deletion policy, use the CONFIGURE ARCHIVELOG DELETION command. The following command configures the archive-redo deletion policy so that archive-redo logs aren't deleted until they have been backed up twice to disk:

```
RMAN> configure archivelog deletion policy to backed up 2 times to device type disk;
```

To have RMAN delete obsolete archive-redo logs as defined by the archivelog-deletion policy, issue the following:

```
RMAN> delete archivelog all;
```

To see whether a retention policy has been set specifically for the archive-redo log files, use this command:

```
RMAN> show archivelog deletion policy;
```

To clear the archive deletion policy, do this:

```
RMAN> configure archivelog deletion policy clear;
```

■ Tip Run the CROSSCHECK command before running the DELETE command. Doing so ensures that RMAN is aware of whether a file is on disk.

---

15. Setting the Degree of Parallelism

You can significantly increase the performance of RMAN backup and restore operations if your database server is equipped with the hardware to support multiple channels. If your server has multiple CPUs and multiple storage devices (disks or tape devices), then you can improve performance by enabling multiple backup channels.

If you require better performance from backup and restore operations and have hardware that facilitates parallel operations, you should enable parallelism and perform tests to determine the optimal degree. If you have hardware that can take advantage of parallel RMAN channels, there is little downside to enabling parallelism.

If you have multiple CPUs but just one storage-device location, you can enable multiple channels to write to and read from one location. For example, if you're backing up to an FRA, you can still take advantage of multiple channels by enabling parallelism. Suppose you have four CPUs on a server and want to enable a corresponding degree of parallelism:

```
RMAN> configure device type disk parallelism 4;
```

You can also write to separate locations in parallel by configuring multiple channels associated with different mount points. For example:

```
RMAN> configure device type disk parallelism 4;
RMAN> configure channel 1 device type disk format '/ora01/O11R2/rman/rman1_%U.bk';
RMAN> configure channel 2 device type disk format '/ora02/O11R2/rman/rman2_%U.bk';
RMAN> configure channel 3 device type disk format '/ora03/O11R2/rman/rman3_%U.bk';
RMAN> configure channel 3 device type disk format '/ora04/O11R2/rman/rman4_%U.bk';
```

This code configures four channels that write to separate locations on disk. When you configure separate channels for different locations, make sure you enable the degree of parallelism to match the number of configured device channels. If you allocate more channels than the specified degree of parallelism, RMAN only writes to the number of channels specified by the degree of parallelism and ignores the other channels.

If you need to clear the degree of parallelism, you can do so as follows:

```
RMAN> configure device type disk clear;
```

Similarly, to clear the channel device types, use the CLEAR command. This example clears channel 3:

```
RMAN> configure channel 3 device type disk clear;
```

16. Using Backup Sets or Image Copies

When you issue an RMAN BACKUP command, you can specify the backup to be one of the following:

- Backup set
- Image copy

A backup set is the default type of backup that RMAN creates. A backup set contains backup pieces, which are binary files that only RMAN can write to or read from. Backup sets are desirable because they're usually smaller than the datafiles being backed up. If you're using Oracle Database 10g release 2 or higher, RMAN automatically attempts to create backup pieces with *unused block compression*. In this mode, RMAN reads a bitmap to determine which blocks are allocated and only reads from those blocks in the datafiles. This feature is supported only for disk-based backup sets and Oracle Secure Backup tape backups.

If you're using a database version prior to Oracle Database 10g release 2, by default backup sets are created using *null block compression* (sometimes referred to more aptly as *block skipping*). In this mode, RMAN checks blocks in the datafile; if the blocks haven't been used, they aren't backed up.

■ **Note** RMAN can also create backup sets using true binary compression. This is the type of compression you get from an OS compression utility (such as zip). Oracle supports several levels of binary compression. The BASIC compression algorithm is available without an additional license. Oracle provides further compression features with the Oracle Advanced Compression option (see the later section in this chapter for details on how to enable binary compression).

When you create a backup as a backup set, the binary backup piece files can only be manipulated by RMAN processes. Some DBAs view this as a disadvantage because they must use RMAN to back up and restore these files (you have no direct access to or control over the backup pieces). But these perceptions aren't warranted. Unless you hit a rare bug, RMAN is dependable and works reliably in all backup and restore situations.

Contrast the backup set to an image copy. An image copy creates a byte-for-byte identical copy of each datafile. The advantages of creating an image copy are that (if necessary) you can manipulate the image copy without using RMAN (as with an OS copy utility). Additionally, in the event of a media failure, an image copy is a fast method of restoring datafiles, because RMAN has to copy the file back from the backup location (there is no reconstructing of the datafile, because it's an exact copy).

I almost always use backup sets for database backups, rather than image copies. Usually, I require some form of RMAN compression (block skipping). The size of the backup to disk is almost always a concern. Backup sets are more efficient regarding disk-space consumption. Because backup sets can take advantage of RMAN compression, there is also less I/O involved with a backup set compared to an image copy. In many environments, reducing the I/O so as not to impact other applications is a concern.

But if you feel that you need direct control over the backup files that RMAN creates, or you're in an environment in which the speed of the restore process is paramount, consider using image copies.

17. Using Incremental Backups

For most of the databases I'm responsible for, I run a daily level 0 backup. I usually don't implement any type of incremental backup strategy.

Incremental backup strategies are appropriate for large databases where only a small portion of the database blocks change from one backup to the next. If you're in a data-warehouse environment, you may want to consider an incremental backup strategy, because it can greatly reduce the size of your backups. For example, you may want to run a weekly level 0 backup and then run a daily level 1 incremental backup.

■ **Note** See Chapter 18 for details on how to back up a database using incremental backups.

18. Using Incrementally Updated Backups

Incrementally updated backups are an efficient way to implement an image-copy backup strategy. This technique instructs RMAN to first create image copies of datafiles; then, the next time the backup runs, instead of creating a fresh set of image copies, RMAN makes an incremental backup (changes to blocks since the image copy was created) and applies that incremental backup to the image copies.

If you have the disk space available for full image copies of your database, and you want the flexibility to be able to directly use the image copies in the event of a media failure, consider this backup strategy.

One potential disadvantage of this approach is that if you're required to restore and recover to some point in the past, you can only restore and recover to the point where the image copies were last updated with the incremental backup.

■ **Note** See Chapter 18 for details on how to back up a database using incrementally updated backups.

19. Using Block-Change Tracking

This feature keeps track of when a database block changes. The idea is that if you're using an incremental backup strategy, you can enhance performance by implementing this feature so that RMAN doesn't have to scan each block (under the high-water mark) in the datafiles to determine whether a block needs to be backed up. Rather, RMAN only has to access the block-change tracking file to determine which blocks have changed since the last backup and directly access blocks that have been identified as changed. If you work in a large data-warehouse environment and are using an incremental backup strategy, consider enabling block-change tracking to enhance performance.

■ **Note** See Chapter 18 for details on how to implement block-change tracking.

---

20. Configuring Binary Compression

You can configure RMAN to use true binary compression when generating backup sets. You can enable compression in one of two ways:

- Specify AS COMPRESSED BACKUPSET with the BACKUP command.

- Use a one-time CONFIGURE command.

Here's an example of backing up with compression when issuing the BACKUP command:

```
RMAN> backup as compressed backupset database;
```

Here's an example of configuring compression for the disk device:

```
RMAN> configure device type disk backup type to compressed backupset;
```

If you need to clear the device-type compression, issue this command:

```
RMAN> configure device type disk clear;
```

I've found the default compression algorithm to be quite efficient. For a typical database, the backups are usually about four to five times smaller than the regular backups. Of course, your compression results may vary depending on your data.

Why not compress all backups? Compressed backups consume more CPU resources and take a longer time to create and restore from, but they result in less I/O spread out over a longer time. If you have multiple CPUs and the speed of making a backup isn't an issue, then you should consider compressing your backups.

You can view the type of compression enabled using the SHOW command:

```
RMAN> show compression algorithm;
```

Here's some sample output:

```
CONFIGURE COMPRESSION ALGORITHM 'BASIC' AS OF RELEASE 'DEFAULT'
OPTIMIZE FOR LOAD TRUE ; # default
```

The basic compression algorithm doesn't require an extra license from Oracle. If you're using Oracle Database 11g release 2 or higher, and if you have a license for the Advanced Compression Option, then you have available three additional configurable levels of binary compression. For example:

```
RMAN> configure compression algorithm 'HIGH';
```

```
RMAN> configure compression algorithm 'MEDIUM';
RMAN> configure compression algorithm 'LOW';
```

You can query V$RMAN_COMPRESSION_ALGORITHM to view details regarding the compression algorithms available for your release of the database. To reset the current compression algorithm to the default of BASIC, use the CLEAR command:

```
RMAN> configure compression algorithm clear;
```

21. Configuring Encryption

You may be required to encrypt backups. Some shops especially require this for backups that contain sensitive data and that are stored offsite. To use encryption when backing up, you must use the Oracle Enterprise Edition, possess a license for the Advanced Security Option, and use Oracle Database 10g release 2 or higher.

If you've configured a security wallet (see the *Oracle Advanced Security Administrator's Guide* for details, available on Oracle's OTN website), you can configure transparent encryption for backups as shown:

```
RMAN> configure encryption for database on;
```

Any backups you make will now be encrypted. If you need to restore from a backup, it's automatically unencrypted (assuming the same security wallet is in place as when you encrypted the backup). To disable encryption, use the CONFIGURE command:

```
RMAN> configure encryption for database off;
```

You can also clear the encryption setting with CLEAR:

```
RMAN> configure encryption for database clear;
```

You can query V$RMAN_ENCRYPTION_ALGORITHMS to view details regarding the encryption algorithms available for your release of the database.

22. Configuring Miscellaneous Settings

RMAN provides a flexible number of channel-configuration commands. You occasionally need to use them depending on special circumstances and requirements for your database. Here are some of the options:

- Maximum backup-set size

- Maximum backup-piece size

- Maximum rate

- Maximum open files

By default, the maximum backup-set size is unlimited. You can use the MAXSETSIZE parameter with the CONFIGURE or BACKUP command to specify the overall maximum backup-set size. Make sure the value of this parameter is at least as large as the largest datafile being backed up by RMAN. Here's an example:

```
RMAN> configure maxsetsize to 2g;
```

Sometimes you may want limit the overall size of a backup piece due to physical limitations of storage devices. Use the MAXPIECESIZE parameter of the CONFIGURE CHANNEL or ALLOCATE CHANNEL command do this. For example:

```
RMAN> configure channel device type disk maxpiecesize = 2g;
```

If you need to set the maximum number of bytes that RMAN reads each second on a channel, you can do so using the RATE parameter. This configures the maximum read rate for channel 1 to 200MB per second:

```
configure channel 1 device type disk rate 200M;
```

If you have a limit on the number of files you can have open simultaneously, you can specify a maximum open files number via the MAXOPENFILES parameter:

```
RMAN> configure channel 1 device type disk maxopenfiles 32;
```

You may need to configure any of these settings when you need to make RMAN aware of some OS or hardware limitation. You'll rarely need to use these parameters but should be aware of them.

Segueing from Decisions to Action

Now that you have a good understanding of what types of decisions you should make before implementing RMAN, it's instructional to view a script that implements some of these components. I mainly work with Linux/Unix servers. In these environments, I use shell scripts to automate the RMAN backups. These shell scripts are automated through a scheduling utility such as cron.

This section contains a typical shell script for RMAN backups. The shell script has line numbers in the output for reference in the discussion of the architectural decisions I made when writing the script. (If you copy the script, take out the line numbers before running it.)

Following is the script. Table 17-2 details every RMAN architectural decision point covered in this chapter, how it's implemented (or not) in the shell script, and the corresponding line number in the shell script. The script doesn't cover every aspect of how to use RMAN. If you use the script, be sure to modify it to meet the requirements and RMAN standards for your own environment:

```
1   #!/bin/bash
2   HOLDSID=${1}  # SID name
3   PRG=`basename $0`
4   USAGE="Usage: ${PRG} <database name> "
5   if [ -z "${HOLDSID}" ]; then
6       echo "${USAGE}"
7       exit 1
8   fi
9   #-----------------------------------------------
10  # source environment variables (see Chapter 2 for details on oraset)
11  . /var/opt/oracle/oraset $HOLDSID
12  BOX=`uname -a | awk '{print$2}'`
13  MAILX='/bin/mailx'
14  MAIL_LIST='larry@oracle.com'
15  NLS_DATE_FORMAT='dd-mon-yy hh24:mi:ss'
16  date
17  #-----------------------------------------------
18  LOCKFILE=/tmp/$PRG.lock
19  if [ -f $LOCKFILE ]; then
20      echo "lock file exists, exiting..."
21      exit 1
```

```
22  else
23    echo "DO NOT REMOVE, $LOCKFILE" > $LOCKFILE
24  fi
25  #----------------------------------------------
26  rman nocatalog <<EOF
27  connect target /
28  set echo on;
29  show all;
30  # Synchronize RMAN with files on OS
31  crosscheck backup;
32  crosscheck copy;
33  crosscheck archivelog all;
34  # Configure environment, redundant to run each time, but ensures set correctly.
35  configure controlfile autobackup on;
36  configure controlfile autobackup format for device type disk to
    '/oradump01/DWREP/rman/rman_ctl_%F.bk';
37  configure retention policy to redundancy 1;
38  configure          device type disk parallelism 5;
39  configure channel 1 device type disk format '/ora08/DWREP/rman/rman1_%U.bk';
40  configure channel 2 device type disk format '/ora08/DWREP/rman/rman2_%U.bk';
41  configure channel 3 device type disk format '/ora08/DWREP/rman/rman3_%U.bk';
42  configure channel 4 device type disk format '/ora09/DWREP/rman/rman4_%U.bk';
43  configure channel 5 device type disk format '/ora09/DWREP/rman/rman5_%U.bk';
44  # Backup datafiles, archive redo logs, and control file
45  backup as compressed backupset incremental level=0 database plus archivelog;
46  # Delete obsolete backups and archive logs as defined by retention policy.
47  delete noprompt obsolete;
48  EOF
49  #----------------------------------------------
50  if [ $? -ne 0 ]; then
51    echo "RMAN problem..."
52    echo "Check RMAN backups" | $MAILX -s
    "RMAN issue: $ORACLE_SID on $BOX" $MAIL_LIST
53  else
54    echo "RMAN ran okay..."
55  fi
56  #----------------------------------------------
57  sqlplus -s /nolog <<EOF
58  connect / as sysdba;
59  alter database backup controlfile to trace;
60  COL dbid NEW_VALUE hold_dbid
61  SELECT dbid FROM v\$database;
62  exec dbms_system.ksdwrt(2,'DBID: '||TO_CHAR(&hold_dbid));
63  EXIT
64  EOF
65  #----------------------------------------------
66  if [ -f $LOCKFILE ]; then
67    rm $LOCKFILE
68  fi
69  #----------------------------------------------
70  date
71  exit 0
```

Table 17–2. Implementation of Architectural Decisions

Decision Point	Implementation in Script	Line Number in Script
1. Running the RMAN client remotely or locally	Running script locally on the database server.	Line 26, connecting locally (not a network connection).
2. Specifying the backup user	Using SYS to connect.	Line 27, starting rman connecting with /.
3. Using online or offline backups	Online backup.	N/A. The database is assumed to be up during the backup.
4. Setting the archive-redo log destination and file format	LOG_ARCHIVE_DEST_N and LOG_ARCHIVE_FORMAT initialization parameters set outside of the script in a database-initialization file.	N/A. Set outside of the script.
5. Configuring the RMAN backup location and file format	Using the CONFIGURE command directly in the script.	Lines 38 through 43.
6. Setting autobackup of the control file	Enabled in the script.	Line 35.
7. Specifying the location of the autobackup of the control file	Placed in the same directory as the backups.	Line 36.
8. Backing up archive-redo logs	Backing up with the rest of the database. Specifically, using the PLUS ARCHIVELOG clause.	Line 45.
9. Determining the location for the snapshot control file	Using the default location.	N/A
10. Using a recovery catalog	Not using.	Line 26, connecting as nocatalog.
11. Using a media manager	Not using.	Lines 38 through 43, device type disk.
12. Setting the CONTROL_FILE_RECORD_KEEP_TIME initialization parameter	Using the default.	N/A

Decision Point	Implementation in Script	Line Number in Script
13. Configuring RMAN's backup-retention policy	Configuring to a redundancy of 1, crosschecking, and deleting obsolete backups and archive redo log files.	Line 37, configuring. Line 47, using RMAN to delete old files.
14. Configuring the archive-redo logs' deletion policy	Using the same retention policy as applied to the backups.	N/A
15. Setting the degree of parallelism	Setting a degree of 5.	Lines 38 through 43.
16. Using backup sets or image copies	Using backup sets.	Line 45.
17. Using incremental backups	Incremental level 0, the same as a full backup.	Line 45.
18. Using incrementally updated backups	Not using.	N/A
19. Using block-change tracking	Not using.	N/A
20. Configuring compression	Using basic compression.	Line 45.
21. Configuring encryption	Not using.	N/A
22. Configuring miscellaneous settings	Not using.	N/A

A few aspects about this script need further discussion (in addition to what's included in the table). Line 11 sets the required OS variables by running a script named oraset. See Chapter 2 for details on running oraset and sourcing OS variables. Many DBAs choose to hard-code OS variables such as ORACLE_HOME and ORACLE_SID into the script. However, you should avoid hard-coding variables and instead use a script to source the required variables. Running a script is much more flexible, especially when you have many databases on a box with different versions of Oracle installed.

Line 15 sets the NLS_DATE_FORMAT OS variable to a value that includes hours, minutes, and seconds. This ensures that when RMAN runs commands that are appropriate, it displays the date output with a time component. This can be invaluable when you're debugging and diagnosing issues. By default, RMAN displays only the date component. Knowing just the date when a command ran is rarely enough information to determine the timing of the commands as they were executed. At minimum, you need to see hours and minutes (along with the date).

Lines 18 through 24 check for the existence of a lock file. You don't want to run this script if it's already running. The script checks for the lock file, and if it exists, the script exits. After the backup has finished, the lock file is removed (lines 66 through 68).

Line 28 sets the ECHO parameter to on. This instructs RMAN to display in the output the command before it runs it. This can be invaluable for debugging issues. Line 29 displays all the configurable variables. This also comes in handy for troubleshooting issues because you can see what the RMAN variables were set to before any commands are executed.

Lines 35 through 43 use the CONFIGURE command. These commands run each time the script is executed. Why do that? You only need to run a CONFIGURE command once, and it's stored in the control file—you don't have to run it again, right? That is correct. However, I've occasionally been burned when a DBA with poor habits configured a setting for a database and didn't tell anybody, and I didn't discover the misconfiguration until I attempted to make another backup. I strongly prefer to place the CONFIGURE commands in the script so the behavior is the same regardless of what another DBA may have done outside of the script. The CONFIGURE settings in the script also act as a form of documentation: I can readily look at the script and determine how settings have been configured.

Lines 31 through 33 run CROSSCHECK commands. Why do that? Sometimes files go missing, or a rogue DBA may remove archive-redo log files from disk with an OS command outside of RMAN. When RMAN runs, if it can't find files that it thinks should be in place, it throws an error and stops the backup. I prefer to run the CROSSCHECK command and let RMAN reconcile what files it thinks should be on disk with those that are actually on disk. This keeps RMAN running smoothly.

You run DELETE NOPROMPT OBSOLETE on line 47. This removes all backup files and archive-redo log files that have been marked as OBSOLETE by RMAN as defined by the retention policy. This lets RMAN manage which files should be kept on disk. I prefer to run the DELETE command after the backup has finished (as opposed to running it before the backup). The retention policy is defined to be 1, so if you run DELETE after the backup, it leaves one backup copy on disk. If you run DELETE before the backup, it leaves one copy of the backup on disk. After the backup runs, there are be two copies of the backup on disk, which I don't have room for on this server.

Line 59 creates a trace file that contains the CREATE CONTROLFILE SQL statement that would be required for this database in the event you had to re-create the control file. Line 62 writes the database identifier (DBID) to the alert log file. This may come in handy for some types of control-file restores when you need the database ID to perform the restore.

You can execute the shell script from the Linux/Unix scheduling utility cron as follows:

```
0 16 * * * $HOME/bin/rmanback.bsh INVPRD >$HOME/bin/log/INVPRDRMAN.log 2>&1
```

The script runs daily at 1600 hours military time on the database server. A log file is created (INVPRDRMAN.log) to capture any output and any errors associated with the RMAN job. See Chapter 21 for details on automating jobs through cron.

Again, the script in this section is basic; you'll no doubt want to enhance and modify it to meet your requirements. This script gives you a starting point with tangible RMAN recommendations and how to implement them.

Using a Recovery Catalog

When you use a recovery catalog, it's possible to create the recovery-catalog user in the same database on the same server as your target database. However, that approach isn't recommended because you don't want the availability of your target database or the availability of the server on which the target database resides to affect the recovery catalog. Therefore, you should create the recovery-catalog database on a different server than your target database.

Creating a Recovery Catalog

When I use a recovery catalog, I prefer to have a dedicated database that is used only for the recovery catalog. This ensures that the recovery catalog isn't affected by any maintenance or downtime required by another application (and vise versa).

Listed next are the steps for creating a recovery catalog:

1. Create a database on a different server than your target database, to be used for a recovery catalog. Make sure the database is adequately sized. I've found that Oracle's recommended sizes are usually much too small. Here are some adequate recommendations:

- SYSTEM tablespace: 500MB

- SYSAUX tablespace: 500MB

- TEMP tablespace: 500MB

- UNDO tablespace: 500MB

- Online-redo logs: 25MB each, 3 groups, multiplexed with 2 members per group

- RECCAT tablespace 500MB

2. Create a tablespace to be used by the recovery-catalog user. I recommend naming the tablespace something like RECCAT so it's readily identifiable as the tablespace that contains the recovery-catalog metadata:

```
CREATE TABLESPACE reccat
  DATAFILE '/ora01/dbfile/O11R2/reccat01.dbf'
  SIZE 500M
  EXTENT MANAGEMENT LOCAL
  UNIFORM SIZE 128k
  SEGMENT SPACE MANAGEMENT AUTO;
```

3. Create a user that will own the tables and other objects used to store the target database metadata. I recommend that you name the recovery-catalog user something like RCAT so you can readily identify it as the user that owns the recovery-catalog objects. Also grant the RECOVERY_CATALOG_OWNER role to the RCAT user as well as CREATE SESSION:

```
CREATE USER rcat IDENTIFIED BY foo
TEMPORARY TABLESPACE temp
DEFAULT TABLESPACE reccat
QUOTA UNLIMITED ON reccat;
--
GRANT RECOVERY_CATALOG_OWNER TO rcat;
GRANT CREATE SESSION TO rcat;
```

4. Connect through RMAN as RCAT, and create the recovery-catalog objects:

```
$ rman catalog rcat/foo
```

5. Now, run the CREATE CATALOG command:

```
RMAN> create catalog;
RMAN> exit;
```

6. This command may take a few minutes to run. When it's finished, you can verify that the tables were created with the following query:

```
$ sqlplus rcat/foo
SQL> select table_name from user_tables;
```

7. Here's some sample output:

```
TABLE_NAME
-----------------------------
DB
NODE
CONF
DBINC
BRDSTN
CKP
TS
```

Registering a Target Database

Now you can register a target database with the recovery catalog. Log on to the target database server. Ensure that you can establish Oracle Net connectivity to the recovery-catalog database. For example, one approach is to populate the TNS_ADMIN/tnsnames.ora file with an entry that points to the remote database. On the target database server, register the recovery catalog as follows:

```
$ rman target / catalog rcat/foo@rcat
```

When you connect, you should see verification that you're connecting to both the target and the recovery catalog:

```
connected to target database: 011R2 (DBID=3457609395)
connected to recovery catalog database
```

Next, run the REGISTER DATABASE command:

```
RMAN> register database;
```

Now, you can run backup operations and have the metadata about the backup tasks written to both the control file and the recovery catalog. Make sure you connect to the recovery catalog along with the target database each time you run RMAN commands:

```
$ rman target / catalog rcat/foo@rcat
```

Backing Up the Recovery Catalog

Make sure you include a strategy for backing up and recovering the recovery-catalog database. For the most protection, be sure the recovery-catalog database is in archivelog mode, and use RMAN to back up the database.

You can also use a tool like Data Pump to take a snapshot of the database. The downside to using Data Pump is that you can potentially lose some information in the recovery catalog that was created after the Data Pump export.

Keep in mind that if you experience a complete failure on your recovery-catalog database server, that you can still use RMAN to back up your target databases. You just can't connect to the recovery catalog. So, any scripts that instruct RMAN to connect to the target and the recovery catalog must be modified.

Also, if you completely lose a recovery catalog and don't have a backup, one option is to re-create it from scratch. As soon as you re-create it, you re-register the target databases with the recovery catalog. You lose any long-term historical recovery-catalog metadata.

Synchronizing the Recovery Catalog

You may have an issue with the network that renders the recovery catalog inaccessible. In the meantime, you connect to your target database and perform backup operations. Some time later, the network issues are resolved, and you can again connect to the recovery catalog.

In this situation, you need to resynchronize the recovery catalog with the target database so that the recovery catalog is aware of any backup operations that aren't stored in the recovery catalog. Run the following command to ensure that the recovery catalog has the most recent backup information:

```
$ rman target / catalog rcat/foo@rcat
RMAN> resync catalog;
```

Keep in mind that you have to resynchronize the catalog only if for some reason you're performing backup operations without connecting to the catalog. Under normal conditions, you don't have to run the RESYNC command.

Recovery Catalog Versions

I recommend that you create a recovery catalog for each version of target databases that you're backing up. Doing so will save you some headaches with compatibility issues and upgrades. I've found it easier to use a recovery catalog when the database version of the rman client is the same version of the database used when creating the catalog.

Yes, having multiple versions of the recovery catalog can cause some confusion. However, if you're in an environment where you have several different versions of the Oracle database, then multiple recovery catalogs may be more convenient.

Dropping a Recovery Catalog

If you determine that you're not using a recovery catalog and you no longer need the data, you can drop it. To do so, connect to the catalog database as the catalog owner, and issue the DROP CATALOG command:

```
$ rman catalog rcat/foo
RMAN> drop catalog;
```

You're prompted as follows:

```
recovery catalog owner is RCAT
enter DROP CATALOG command again to confirm catalog removal
```

If you enter the DROP CATALOG command again, all the objects in the recovery catalog are removed from the catalog database.

The other way to drop a catalog is to drop the owner. To do so, connect to the recovery catalog as a user with DBA privileges, and issue the DROP USER statement:

```
$ sqlplus system/manager
SQL> drop user rcat cascade;
```

SQL*Plus doesn't prompt you twice. It does as you instructed and drops the user and its objects. Again, the only reason to do this is when you're certain you don't need the recovery catalog or its data any longer. Use caution when dropping a user or the recovery catalog: I recommend that you take a Data Pump export of the recovery-catalog owner before dropping it.

Summary

RMAN is Oracle's flagship B&R tool. If you're still using the older user-managed backup technologies, then I strongly recommend that you switch to RMAN. RMAN contains a powerful set of features that are unmatched by any other backup tool available. It's easy to use and configure. RMAN will save you time and effort and give you peace of mind when you're implementing a rock-solid B&R strategy.

If you're new to RMAN, it may not be obvious which features should always be enabled and implemented and likewise which aspects you'll rarely need. This chapter contains a checklist for you to follow that walks you through each architectural decision point. You may disagree with some of my conclusions, or some recommendations may not meet your business requirements—that's fine. The point is that you should carefully consider each component and how to implement the features that make sense.

The chapter ended with a real-world example of a script used to implement RMAN in a production environment. Now that you have a good idea of RMAN's features and how to use them, you're ready to start making backups. The next chapter deals with RMAN backup scenarios.

■ ■ ■

RMAN Backups and Reporting

Chapter 17 provided the details on configuring RMAN and using specialized features to control the behavior of RMAN. After you consider which features you require, you're ready to create backups. RMAN can back up the following types of files:

- Datafiles
- Control files
- Archived redo log files
- Spfile
- Backup pieces

For most scenarios, you will use RMAN to back up datafiles, control files, and archive redo log files. If you have the autobackup of the control file feature enabled, then RMAN will automatically back up the control file and the spfile (if you're using one) when a BACKUP or COPY command is issued. You can also back up the backup piece files that RMAN has created.

RMAN does not back up Oracle Net files, password files, block change tracking files, or the Oracle binary files (files created when you installed Oracle). You should put in place operating system backups that include those files.

Also note that RMAN does not back up online redo log files. If you did back up the online redo log files, it would be pointless to restore them. The online redo log files contain the latest redo generated by the database. You would not want to overwrite them from a backup with old redo information. When your database is in archivelog mode, the online redo log files contain the most recently generated transactions required to perform complete recovery.

This chapter details many of the features related to running the RMAN BACKUP command. Also covered in this chapter are techniques for logging output and reporting on RMAN backup operations. This chapter begins by covering a few common practices to enhance what is displayed in the RMAN output when running commands.

Preparing to Run RMAN Backup Commands

Before I run RMAN backups, I usually set a few things so as to enhance what is shown in the output. You don't need to set these variables every time you login and run an RMAN command. However, when troubleshooting or debugging issues, it's almost always a good idea to enable the following:

- Set NLS_DATE_FORMAT operating system variable
- Set ECHO
- Show RMAN variables

The bulleted items are discussed in the following sections.

Setting NLS_DATE_FORMAT

Before running any RMAN job, I set the operating system variable NLS_DATE_FORMAT to include a time (hours, minutes, and seconds) component. For example:

```
$ export NLS_DATE_FORMAT='dd-mon-yyyy hh24:mi:ss'
```

Additionally, if I have a shell script that calls RMAN, I put the prior line directly in the shell script (see the shell script at the end of Chapter 17 for an example):

```
NLS_DATE_FORMAT='dd-mon-yyyy hh24:mi:ss'
```

This ensures that when RMAN displays a date, it always includes the hours, minutes, and seconds as part of the output. By default, RMAN only includes the date component (DD-MON-YYYY) in the output. For example, when starting a backup, here is what RMAN displays:

```
Starting backup at 15-sep-2010
```

When you set the NLS_DATE_FORMAT OS variable to include a time component, the output will look like this instead:

```
Starting backup at 15-sep-2010 03:20:17
```

When troubleshooting, it's essential to have a time component so that you can determine how long a command took to run, or how long a command was running before a failure occurred. Oracle Support will almost always ask you to set this variable to include the time component before capturing output and sending it to them.

The only downside to setting the NLS_DATE_FORMAT is if you set it to a value unknown to RMAN, it can cause connectivity issues. For example, here the NLS_DATE_FORMAT is set to an invalid value:

```
$ export NLS_DATE_FORMAT='dd-mon-yyyy hh24:mi:sd'
$ rman target /
```

When set to an invalid value, you get this error when logging into RMAN:

```
RMAN-03999: Oracle error occurred while converting a date: ORA-01821:
```

To unset the NLS_DATE_FORMAT variable, set it to a blank value, like so:

```
$ export NLS_DATE_FORMAT=''
```

Setting ECHO Setting ECHO

Another value that I always set in any RMAN scripts is the ECHO command, seen here:

```
RMAN> set echo on;
```

This instructs RMAN to display the command that it's running in the output, so you can see what RMAN command is running along with any relevant error or output messages associated with the command. This is especially important when you're running RMAN commands within scripts, because you're not directly typing in a command (and may not know what command was issued within the shell script). For example, without SET ECHO ON, here's what is displayed in the output for a command:

```
Starting backup at 15-sep-2010 03:49:55
using target database control file instead of recovery catalog
```

With SET ECHO ON, this output shows the actual command that was run:

```
backup datafile 4;
Starting backup at 15-sep-2010 03:49:55
using target database control file instead of recovery catalog
```

From the prior output you can see which command is running, when it started, and so on.

Showing Variables

Another good practice is to run the SHOW ALL command within any script, like so:

```
RMAN> show all;
```

This displays all of the RMAN configurable variables. When troubleshooting, you may not be aware of something that another DBA has configured. This gives you a snapshot of the settings as they were when the RMAN session executed.

Running Backups

Before you run an RMAN backup, make sure you read Chapter 17 for details on how to configure RMAN with settings for a production environment. For production databases, I mainly run RMAN from a shell script similar to the script shown at the end of Chapter 17. Within the shell script, I configure every aspect of RMAN that I want to use for a particular database. If you run RMAN out-of-the-box with its default settings, you will be able to back up your database. However, these settings will not be adequate for most production database applications.

Backing up the Entire Database

If you're not sure where RMAN will be backing up your database files, you need to read Chapter 17 because it describes how to configure RMAN to create the backup files in the location of your choice. Here is how I usually configure RMAN to write to specific locations on disk (note that the CONFIGURE command must be executed before you run the BACKUP command):

```
RMAN> configure channel 1 device type disk format '/ora01/O11R2/rman/rman1_%U.bk';
```

After a backup location is configured, I almost always use a command similar to the one shown next to back up the entire database:

```
RMAN> backup incremental level=0 database plus archivelog;
```

This command ensures that RMAN will back up all datafiles in the database, all archive redo logs generated prior to the backup, and all archive redo logs generated during the backup. This command also ensures that you have all of the datafiles and archive redo logs that would be required to restore and recover your database.

If you have the autobackup of the control file feature enabled (see Chapter 17 for details), the last task RMAN does as part of the backup is generate a backup set that contains a backup of the control file. This control file will contain all information regarding the backup that took place and any archive redo logs that were generated during the backup.

■ Tip Always enable the autobackup of the control file feature.

There are many nuances to the RMAN BACKUP command. For production databases, I usually back up the database with the BACKUP INCREMENTAL LEVEL=0 DATABASE PLUS ARCHIVELOG command. That's usually sufficient. However, you will encounter many situations where you need to run a backup that uses a specific RMAN feature or you might troubleshoot an issue where you need to be aware of the other ways to invoke an RMAN backup. These aspects are discussed in the next several sections of this chapter.

Full Backup versus Incremental Level=0

The term "RMAN full backup" sometimes causes confusion. A more apt way of phrasing what a full backup is doing would be "RMAN is backing up all modified blocks within one or more datafiles." The term "full" does not mean that all blocks are backed up or that all datafiles are backed up. It simply refers to the fact that all blocks that would be required to rebuild a datafile (in the event of a failure) are being backed up. You can take a full backup of a single datafile and the contents of that backup piece may be quite a bit smaller than the datafile itself.

The term "RMAN level 0 incremental backup" doesn't exactly describe itself very well, either. A level 0 incremental backup is backing up the exact same blocks as a full backup. In other words, the following two commands back up the exact same blocks in a database:

```
RMAN> backup as backupset full database;
RMAN> backup as backupset incremental level=0 database;
```

The only difference between the prior two commands is that an incremental level 0 backup can be used in conjunction with other incremental backups whereas a full backup can not participate in an incremental backup strategy.

Therefore, I almost always prefer to use the INCREMENTAL LEVEL=0 syntax (as opposed to a full backup). This is because it gives me the flexibility to use the level 0 incremental backup with different incremental level backups.

Backup Sets versus Image Copies

The default backup mode of RMAN instructs it to only back up blocks that have been used in a datafile; these are known as backup sets. RMAN can also make byte-for-byte copies of the datafiles; these are known as image copies. Creating a backup set is the default type of backup that RMAN creates. The next command creates a backup set backup of the database:

```
RMAN> backup database;
```

If you prefer, you can explicitly place the AS BACKUPSET command when creating backups:

```
RMAN> backup as backupset database;
```

You can instruct RMAN to create image copies by using the AS COPY command. The following creates image copies of every datafile in the database:

```
RMAN> backup as copy database;
```

Since image copies are identical copies of the datafiles, they can be directly accessed by the DBA with operating system commands. For example, say you had a media failure and you didn't want to use

RMAN to restore an image copy. You could use an operating system command to copy the image copy of a datafile to a location where it can be used by the database, whereas a backup set consists of binary files that only the RMAN utility can write to or read from.

I prefer to use backup sets when working with RMAN. The backup sets tend to be smaller than the datafiles and can have true binary compression applied to them. Also, I don't find it inconvenient to use RMAN as the mechanism for creating backup files that only RMAN can restore. Using RMAN with backup sets is efficient and very reliable.

Backing up Tablespaces

RMAN has the ability to back up at the entire database level (as shown in prior examples), the tablespace level, or even more granularly at the datafile level. When you back up a tablespace, RMAN backs up any datafiles associated with the tablespaces(s) that you specify. For example, the following command will back up all of the datafiles associated with the SYSTEM and SYSAUX tablespaces:

```
RMAN> backup tablespace system, sysaux;
```

One scenario where I back up at the tablespace level is if I've recently created a new tablespace and want to take a backup of just the datafiles (associated with the newly added tablespace). Note that when troubleshooting backup and recovery issues, it's often more efficient to work with one tablespace (because it's usually much faster to back up one tablespace than the entire database).

Backing up Datafiles

You may occasionally need to back up individual datafiles. For example, when troubleshooting issues with backups, it's often helpful to attempt to successfully backup one datafile. You can specify datafiles by filename or by file number like so:

```
RMAN> backup datafile '/ora01/dbfile/O11R2/system01.dbf';
```

Here's an example where file numbers are specified:

```
RMAN> backup datafile 1,3;
```

Here are some other examples of backing up datafiles using various features:

```
RMAN> backup as copy datafile 3;
RMAN> backup incremental level 1 datafile 4;
```

■ Tip Use the RMAN REPORT SCHEMA command to list tablespace, datafile name, and datafile number information.

Backing up the Control File

The most reliable way to back up the control file is to configure the autobackup feature:

```
RMAN> configure controlfile autobackup on;
```

This command ensures that the control file is automatically backed up when a BACKUP or COPY command is issued. I usually enable the autobackup of the control file feature and then never worry about explicitly issuing a separate command to back up the control file. When in this mode, the control file is always created in its own backup set and backup piece after the datafile backup pieces have been created.

If you need to manually back up the control file, you can do so like this:

```
RMAN> backup current controlfile;
```

The location of the backup is either a default operating system location, the FRA (if using), or a manually configured location. As shown in Chapter 17, I prefer to set the location of the control file backup piece to the same location as the datafile backups:

```
RMAN> configure controlfile autobackup format for device type disk to
'/ora01/O11R2/rman/rman_ctl_%F.bk';
```

Backing up the Spfile

If you have enabled the autobackup of the control file feature, the spfile will be backed up automatically (along with the control file) anytime a BACKUP or COPY command is issued. If you need to manually back up the spfile, use the following command:

```
RMAN> backup spfile;
```

The location of the file that contains the backup of the spfile is dependent on what you have configured. By default, if you don't use a FRA and you haven't explicitly configured a location via a channel, then for Linux/Unix servers the backup goes to the ORACLE_HOME/dbs directory.

▓ **Note** RMAN can only back up the spfile if the instance was started using a spfile.

Backing up Archive Redo Logs

I don't usually back up the archive redo logs separately from the database backups. As mentioned earlier, I normally back up the database files and the archive redo log files by using the following command:

```
RMAN> backup incremental level=0 database plus archivelog;
```

However, you will occasionally find yourself in a situation where you need to take a special one off backup of the archive redo logs. You can issue the following command to back up the archive redo logs files:

```
RMAN> backup archivelog all;
```

If you have a mount point that is nearly full and you determine that you want to back up the archive redo logs (so that they exist in a backup file) but then you want to immediately delete the archive redo log files (that were just backed up) from disk, you can use the following syntax to back up the archive redo logs and then have RMAN delete them from the storage media:

```
RMAN> backup archivelog all delete input;
```

Listed next are some other ways in which you can back up the archive redo log files:

```
RMAN> backup archivelog sequence 300;
```

```
RMAN> backup archivelog sequence between 300 and 400 thread 1;
RMAN> backup archivelog from time "sysdate-7" until time "sysdate-1";
```

If an archive redo log has been removed from disk manually via an operating system delete command, RMAN will throw the following error when attempting to back up the non-existent archive redo log file:

```
RMAN-06059: expected archived log not found, loss of archived log compromises recoverability
```

In this situation, first run a CROSSCHECK command to let RMAN know which files are physically available on disk:

```
RMAN> crosscheck archivelog all;
```

Backing up Fast Recovery Area

If you use a fast recovery area, one nice RMAN feature is that you can back up all of the files in that location with one command. If you're using a media manager and have a tape backup channel enabled, you can back up everything in the fast recovery area to tape like this:

```
RMAN> configure channel device type sbt_tape parms 'ENV=(OB_MEDIA_FAMILY=RMAN-DB11R2)';
RMAN> backup device type sbt_tape recovery area;
```

You can also back up the fast recovery area to a location on disk. Use the TO DESTINATION command to accomplish this:

```
RMAN> backup recovery area to destination '/ora01/O11R1/fra_back';
```

RMAN will automatically create directories as required beneath the directory specified by the TO DESTINATION command.

■ Note The format of the subdirectory under the directory <TO_DESTINATION> is

<SID>/backupset_<YYYY_MM_DD>.

RMAN will back up full backups, incremental backups, control file autobackups, and archive redo log files. Keep in mind that flashback logs, online redo log files, and the current control file are not backed up.

Excluding Tablespaces from Backups

Suppose you have a tablespace that contains non-critical data and you don't ever want to back it up. RMAN can be configured to exclude such tablespaces from the backup. To determine if RMAN is currently configured to exclude any tablespaces, run this command:

```
RMAN> show exclude;
RMAN configuration parameters for database with db_unique_name O11R2 are:
RMAN configuration has no stored or default parameters
```

Use the EXCLUDE command to instruct RMAN which tablespaces to not back up:

```
RMAN> configure exclude for tablespace users;
```

Now for any database level backups, RMAN will exclude the datafiles associated with the USERS tablespace. You can instruct RMAN to back up any excluded tablespaces with this command:

```
RMAN> backup database noexclude;
```

You can clear the exclude setting via the following command:

```
RMAN> configure exclude for tablespace users clear;
```

Backing up Datafiles Not Backed Up

Suppose you have just added several datafiles to your database and you want to ensure that you have a backup of them. You can issue the following command to instruct Oracle to back up datafiles that have not been backed up yet:

```
RMAN> backup database not backed up;
```

You can also specify a time range for files that haven't been backed up yet. Suppose you discover that your backups haven't been running for the last several days and you want to back up everything that hasn't been backed up within the last 24 hours. The following command backs up all datafiles that have not been backed up within the last day:

```
RMAN> backup database not backed up since time='sysdate-1';
```

This command is also useful if your backups aborted for some reason, such as a power failure in the data center or your backup directory became full during backups. After you have resolved the issue that caused your backup job to fail, you can issue the previous command and RMAN will only back up the datafiles that haven't been backed up in the specified time period.

Skipping Read-Only Tablespaces

Since data in read-only tablespaces can't change while in read-only mode, you may only want to back up read-only tablespaces once and then skip them in subsequent backups. Use the SKIP READONLY command to achieve this:

```
RMAN> backup database skip readonly;
```

Keep in mind that when you skip read-only tablespaces, you'll need to keep available a backup that contains these tablespaces. You don't want to find yourself in the situation where you haven't backed up a read-only tablespace for six months and then have a media failure.

Skipping Offline or Inaccessible Files

Sometimes datafiles become corrupt. You know that you don't need this datafile for anything so you take it offline, like so:

```
SQL> alter database datafile '/ora01/INVDEV/sysaux01.dbf' offline for drop;
```

Now, suppose you attempt to run an RMAN backup:

```
RMAN> backup database;
```

The following error is thrown when RMAN encounters a datafile that it can't back up:

```
RMAN-03002: failure of backup command at 09/14/2010 13:24:04
```

```
RMAN-06056: could not access datafile 3
```

In this situation, you'll have to instruct RMAN to exclude the offline datafile from the backup. The SKIP OFFLINE command instructs RMAN to ignore datafiles with an offline status:

```
RMAN> backup database skip offline;
```

If a file has gone completely missing, use SKIP INACCESSIBLE to instruct RMAN to ignore files that are not available on disk. This might happen if the datafile was deleted using an operating system command. Here's an example of excluding inaccessible datafiles from the RMAN backup:

```
RMAN> backup database skip inaccessible;
```

You can skip read-only, offline, and inaccessible datafiles with one command:

```
RMAN> backup database skip readonly skip offline skip inaccessible;
```

When dealing with offline and inaccessible files, you should figure out why the files are offline or inaccessible and try to resolve any issues.

Backing Up Large Files in Parallel

Normally, RMAN will only use one channel to back up a single datafile. When you enable parallelism, it allows RMAN to spawn multiple processes to back up multiple files. However, even when parallelism is enabled, RMAN will not use parallel channels simultaneously to back up one datafile, but starting with Oracle Database 11g, you can instruct RMAN to use multiple channels to back up one datafile in parallel. This is known as a *multisection backup*. This feature can speed up the backups of very large datafiles.

Use the SECTION SIZE parameter to make a multisection backup. The following example configures two parallel channels to back up one file:

```
RMAN> configure device type disk parallelism 2;
RMAN> configure channel 1 device type disk format '/ora01/O11R2/rman/r1%U.bk';
RMAN> configure channel 2 device type disk format '/ora02/O11R2/rman/r2%U.bk';
RMAN> backup section size 2500M datafile 10;
```

When this code runs, RMAN will allocate two channels to back up datafile 10 in parallel.

■ **Note** If you specify a section size greater than the size of the datafile, RMAN will not back up the file in parallel.

Adding RMAN Backup Information to the Repository

Another scenario is when you need to populate the control file with information regarding RMAN backups. For example, say you had to recreate your control file, and now the control file no longer contains any information regarding RMAN. In this situation, use the CATALOG command to populate the control file with RMAN metadata. For example, if all of the RMAN backup files are kept in the /ora01/O11R2/rman directory, you can make the control file aware of these backups files in this directory like this:

```
RMAN> catalog start with '/ora01/O11R2/rman';
```

This causes RMAN to look for any backup pieces, image copies, control file copies, or archive redo logs in the specified directory, and if found, populate the control file with the appropriate metadata. For this example, two backup piece files are found in the given directory:

```
searching for all files that match the pattern /ora01/O11R2/rman

List of Files Unknown to the Database
========================================
File Name: /ora01/O11R2/rman/r1otlns90o_1_1.bk
File Name: /ora01/O11R2/rman/r1xyklnrveg_1_1.bk

Do you really want to catalog the above files (enter YES or NO)?
```

If you enter YES, then metadata regarding the backup files will be added to the control file. In this way, the CATALOG command allows you to make the RMAN repository (control file and recovery catalog) aware of files that RMAN can work with for backup and recovery.

You can also instruct RMAN to catalog any files in the recovery area that the control file isn't currently aware of like this:

```
RMAN> catalog recovery area;
```

You can also catalog specific files. This example instructs RMAN to add metadata to the control file for a specific backup piece file:

```
RMAN> catalog backuppiece '/ora01/O11R2/rman/r1xyklnrveg_1_1.bk';
```

Creating Incremental Backups

RMAN has three separate and distinct incremental backup features:

- Incremental level backups

- Incrementally updating backups

- Block change tracking

With incremental level backups, RMAN only backs up the blocks that have been modified since a previous backup. Incremental backups can be applied to the entire database, tablespaces, or datafiles. This is the most commonly used incremental feature with RMAN.

Incrementally updating backups is an entirely different feature from incremental level backups. These backups take image copies of the datafiles and then use incremental backups to update the image copies. This gives you an efficient way to implement and maintain image copies as part of your backup strategy. You only take the image copy backup once, and then use incremental backups to keep the image copies updated with the most recent transactions.

Block change tracking is another feature designed to speed up the performance of incremental backups. The idea here is that an operating system file is used to record which blocks have changed since the last backup. RMAN can use the block change tracking file to quickly identify which blocks need to be backed up when performing incremental backups. This feature can greatly improve the performance of incremental backups.

Taking Incremental Level Backups

RMAN implements incremental backups through levels. Starting with Oracle Database 10*g*, there are only two documented levels of incremental backups: level 0 and level 1. Prior versions of Oracle offer five levels, 0 through 4. These levels (0 through 4) are still available in Oracle Database 10g and 11g, but are not specified in the Oracle documentation. You must first take an incremental level 0 backup to establish a baseline, after which you can take a level 1 incremental backup.

■ **Note** A full backup backs up the exact same blocks as a level 0 backup. However, you can't use a full backup with incremental backups. You have to start an incremental backup with a level 0 backup. If you attempt to take a level 1 backup and no level 0 exists, RMAN will automatically take a level 0 backup.

Here's an example of taking an incremental level 0 backup:

```
RMAN> backup incremental level=0 database;
```

Suppose for the next several backups you only want to back up the blocks that have changed since the last level 0 baseline backup. This line of code takes a level 1 backup:

```
RMAN> backup incremental level=1 database;
```

There are two different types of incremental backups: differential and cumulative. Which type of incremental (differential or cumulative) you use depends on your requirements. Differential backups (the default) are smaller but take more time to recover from. Cumulative backups are larger than differential backups but take less time to recover from.

A differential incremental level 1 backup instructs RMAN to back up blocks that have changed since the last level 1 or level 0 backups, whereas a cumulative incremental level 1 backup instructs RMAN to back up blocks that have changed since the last level 0 backup. Cumulative incremental backups, in effect, ignore any level 1 incremental backups.

■ **Note** The RMAN incremental level 0 backups are used to restore the datafiles, while the RMAN incremental level 1 backups are used to recover the datafiles.

When using incremental backups, I almost always use the default of differential. Usually I don't worry about the differences between incremental and cumulative backups. If you require cumulative backups, you must specify the key word CUMULATIVE. Here's an example of taking a cumulative level 1 backup:

```
RMAN> backup incremental level=1 cumulative database;
```

Here are some other examples of taking incremental backups at more granular level than the database:

```
RMAN> backup incremental level=0 tablespace sysaux;
RMAN> backup incremental level=1 tablespace sysaux plus archivelog;
RMAN> backup incremental level=1 datafile 3;
```

Making Incrementally Updating Backups

The basic idea behind an incrementally updating backup is to create image copies of datafiles and then use incremental backups to update the image copies. In this manner, you have image copies of your database that are kept somewhat current by applying an incremental backup to them. This can be an efficient way to combine image copy backups with incremental backups.

To understand how this backup technique works, you'll need to inspect the commands that perform an incrementally updating backup. You need two lines of RMAN code to enable this feature:

```
RMAN> recover copy of database with tag 'incupdate';
RMAN> backup incremental level 1 for recover of copy with tag 'incupdate' database;
```

In the first line, a tag is specified (this example uses incupdate). You can use whatever you want for the tag name; the tag name lets RMAN associate the backup files being used each time the commands are run. Then, this code will do the following the first time you run the script:

- RECOVER COPY generates a message saying there's nothing for it to do.

- If no image copies exist, the BACKUP INCREMENTAL creates an image copy of the database datafiles.

You should see messages like this in the output when the RECOVER COPY command runs the first time:

```
no parent backup or copy of datafile ... found
```

In the output for the BACKUP INCREMENTAL, you should see text like this indicating that image copies are being created:

```
channel ORA_DISK_1: datafile copy complete, elapsed time: 00:00:25
```

The second time you run the incrementally updating backup, it does as follows:

- RECOVER COPY still has nothing to do.

- BACKUP INCREMENTAL makes an incremental level 1 backup and assigns it the tag name specified; this backup will subsequently be used by the RECOVER COPY command.

The third time you run the incrementally updating backup, it does this:

- Now that an incremental backup has been created, the RECOVER COPY applies the incremental backup to the image copies.

- BACKUP INCREMENTAL makes an incremental level 1 backup and assigns it the tag name specified; this backup will subsequently be used by the RECOVER COPY command.

Going forward, each time that you run the two lines of code you will have a regularly repeating backup pattern. If you use image copies for backups, you might consider using an incrementally updating backup strategy because you avoid creating entire image copies each time the backup runs.

The image copies are updated each time the backup runs with the incremental changes from the previous backup.

Using Block Change Tracking

Block change tracking is where a binary file is used to record changes to database datafile blocks. The idea is that incremental backup performance can be improved because RMAN can use the block change tracking file to pinpoint which blocks have changed since the last backup. This saves a great deal of time because otherwise RMAN would have to scan all blocks that have been backed up to determine if they've changed since the last backup. You can enable block change tracking by doing the following:

   1. If not already enabled, set the *DB_CREATE_FILE_DEST* parameter to a location. For example:

```
SQL> alter system set db_create_file_dest='/ora01/O11R2/bct' scope=both;
```

   2. Enable block change tracking via the ALTER DATABASE command:

```
SQL> alter database enable block change tracking;
```

This example creates a file with an OMF name in the directory specified by DB_CREATE_FILE_DEST. In this example, the file created is named as:

```
/ora01/O11R2/bct/O11R2/changetracking/o1_mf_68wxc16g_.chg
```

You can also enable block change tracking by directly specifying a file name, which does not require DB_CREATE_FILE_DEST to be set. For example:

```
SQL> alter database enable block change tracking using file '/ora01/O11R2/bct/btc.bt';
```

You can verify the details of block change tracking by running the following query:

```
SQL> select * from v$block_change_tracking;
```

For space planning purposes, the size of the block change tracking file is approximately 1/30,000 the size of the total size of the blocks being tracked in the database. Therefore, the size of the block change tracking file is proportional to the size of the database and not the amount of redo generated.

To disable block change tracking, run the following command:

```
SQL> alter database disable block change tracking;
```

■ **Note** When you disable block change tracking, Oracle will automatically delete the block change tracking file.

Checking for Corruption in Datafiles and Backups

You can use RMAN to check for corruption in datafiles, archive redo logs, and control files. You can also verify whether a backup set is restorable. The RMAN VALIDATE command is used to perform these types of integrity checks. There are three ways you can run the VALIDATE command:

   • VALIDATE
   • BACKUP...VALIDATE

- RESTORE...VALIDATE

■ **Note** The standalone VALIDATE command is available in Oracle Database 11*g* or higher. The
BACKUP...VALIDATE and RESTORE...VALIDATE commands are available in Oracle Database 10*g* or higher.

Using VALIDATE

The VALIDATE command can be used alone (without BACKUP or RESTORE) to check for missing files or
physical corruption in database datafiles, archive redo log files, control files, spfile, and backup set
pieces. For example, this command will validate all datafiles and the control files:

RMAN> validate database;

You can also validate just the control file as follows:

RMAN> validate current controlfile;

You can validate the archive redo log files like so:

RMAN> validate archivelog all;

You can combine all of the prior three integrity checks into one command, as shown:

RMAN> validate database include current controlfile plus archivelog;

Under normal operations the VALIDATE command only checks for physical corruption. You can
specify that you want to also check for logical corruption by using the CHECK LOGICAL clause like so:

RMAN> validate check logical database include current controlfile plus archivelog;

You can use VALIDATE in a variety of ways. Here are a few more examples:

RMAN> validate database skip offline;
RMAN> validate copy of database;
RMAN> validate tablespace system;
RMAN> validate datafile 3 block 20 to 30;
RMAN> validate spfile;
RMAN> validate backupset <primary_key_value>;
RMAN> validate recovery area;

If RMAN detects any corrupt blocks, the V$DATABASE_BLOCK_CORRUPTION is populated. This view
contains information on the file number, block number, and the number of blocks affected. You can use
this information to perform a block level recovery. See Chapter 19 for details on block level recovery.

■ **Note** Physical corruption is when the block contents don't match the physical format that Oracle expects. By
default, RMAN checks for physical corruption when backing up, restoring, or validating datafiles. Logical corruption
is when the block is in the correct format but the contents aren't consistent with what Oracle expects. Logical
corruption would be issues such as corruption in a row piece or an index entry.

Using BACKUP...VALIDATE

The `BACKUP VALIDATE` command is very similar to the `VALIDATE` command in that it can check to see if datafiles are available and if the datafiles contain any corrupt blocks. For example:

```
RMAN> backup validate database;
```

This command doesn't actually perform any type of backup or create any files. It only scans the datafiles and checks for corruption. Like the `VALIDATE` command, `BACKUP VALIDATE` by default only checks for physical corruption. You can instruct it to also check for logical corruption as shown:

```
RMAN> backup validate check logical database;
```

Here are some other variations of the `BACKUP...VALIDATE` command:

```
RMAN> backup validate database current controlfile;
RMAN> backup validate check logical database current controlfile plus archivelog;
```

Like the `VALIDATE` command, `BACKUP...VALIDATE` will populate `V$DATABASE_BLOCK_CORRUPTION` if it detects any corrupt blocks. The information in this view can be used to determine which blocks can potentially be restored by block level recovery. See Chapter 19 for more details on block level recovery.

Using RESTORE...VALIDATE

The `RESTORE...VALIDATE` command is used to verify backup files that would be used to restore. This command validates backup sets, datafile copies, and archive redo log files:

```
RMAN> restore validate database;
```

No actual files are restored when using `RESTORE...VALIDATE`. This means you can run the command while the database is online and available.

Logging RMAN Output

When troubleshooting RMAN output or checking on the status of a backup job, it's essential to have a record of what RMAN ran and the status of each command. There are several methods for logging RMAN output. Some of them are built-in aspects of the Linux/Unix operating system and others are RMAN-specific features:

- Linux/Unix redirect output to file
- Linux/Unix logging commands
- RMAN `LOG` command
- `V$RMAN_OUTPUT` view

These logging features are discussed in the next sections.

Redirecting Output to a File

I run almost all RMAN backup jobs from shell scripts. The shell scripts are usually run automatically from a scheduling tool such as cron. When running RMAN commands in this fashion, I always capture the output by instructing the shell command to redirect standard output messaging and standard error messaging to a log file. This is done with the redirection > character. This example runs a shell script (rmanback.bsh) and redirects both standard output and standard error output to a log fie named rmanback.log:

```
$ rmanback.bsh 1>/home/oracle/bin/log/rmanback.log 2>&1
```

Here, 1> instructs standard output to be redirected to the specified file. The 2>&1 instructs the shell script to send standard error output to the same location as standard output.

▪ **Tip** For full details on how DBAs use shell scripts and Linux features see *Linux Recipes for Oracle DBAs* (Apress, 2008).

Capturing Output with Unix/Linux Logging Commands

You can instruct Unix/Linux to create a log file to capture any output that is also being displayed on your screen. This can be done in one of two ways:

- tee
- script

Capturing Output with tee

When you start RMAN, you can send the output you see on your screen to an operating system text file using the tee command:

```
$ rman | tee /tmp/rman.log
```

Now you can connect to the target database and run commands. All of the output seen on your screen will be logged to the /tmp/rman.log file:

```
RMAN> connect target /
RMAN> backup database;
RMAN> exit;
```

The tee party session stops writing to the log file when you exit from RMAN.

Capturing Output with the script Command

The script command is useful because it instructs the operating system to log any output that appears on the terminal to a log file. To capture all output, run the script command before connecting to RMAN:

```
$ script /tmp/rman.log
Script started, file is /tmp/rman.log
$ rman target /
RMAN> backup database;
RMAN> exit;
```

To end a script session, type in Ctrl+D or type in exit. The /tmp/rman.log file will contain all output that was displayed on your screen. The script command is useful when you need to capture all output from one point in time to another point in time. For example, you may be running RMAN commands, exiting from RMAN, running SQL*Plus commands, and so on. The script session lasts from the point you start script to where you type in Ctrl+D.

Logging Output to a File

An easy way to capture RMAN output is to use the SPOOL LOG command to send the output to a file. This example spools a log file from within RMAN:

```
RMAN> spool log to '/tmp/rmanout.log'
RMAN> set echo on;
RMAN> <run RMAN commands>
RMAN> spool log off;
```

By default, the SPOOL LOG command will overwrite an existing file. If you want to append to the log file, use the keyword APPEND:

```
RMAN> spool log to '/tmp/rmanout.log' append
```

You can also direct output to a log file when starting RMAN on the command line, which will overwrite an existing file:

```
$ rman target / log /tmp/rmanout.log
```

You can also append to the log file as shown:

```
$ rman target / log /tmp/rmanout.log append
```

When you use SPOOL LOG as shown in the previous examples, the output goes to a file and not to your terminal. Therefore, I hardly ever use SPOOL LOG when running RMAN interactively. It's mainly a tool for capturing output when running RMAN from scripts.

Querying for Output in the Data Dictionary

If you don't capture any RMAN output, you can still view the most recent RMAN output by querying the data dictionary. The V$RMAN_OUTPUT view contains messages recently reported by RMAN:

```
select
 sid
,recid
,output
from v$rman_output
order by recid;
```

Here is some sample output:

```
173      1108 Starting backup at 13-SEP-10
173      1109 using channel ORA_DISK_1
173      1110 using channel ORA_DISK_2
```

The V$RMAN_OUTPUT view is an in-memory object that holds up to 32,768 rows. Information in this view is cleared out when you stop and restart your database. This view is handy when you're using the RMAN SPOOL LOG command to spool output to a file and cannot view what is happening on your terminal.

RMAN Reporting

There are several different methods for reporting on the RMAN environment:

- LIST command
- REPORT command
- Query metadata via data dictionary views

When first learning RMAN, the difference between the LIST and REPORT commands may seem confusing because the distinction between the two commands is not clear cut. In general, I use the LIST command to view information about existing backups, whereas the REPORT command is used to determine what files need to be backed or to display information on obsolete or expired backups.

I use SQL queries for specialized reports (not available via the LIST or REPORT) or for automating reports. For example, I'll generally implement an automated check via a shell script and SQL that reports whether the RMAN backups have run within the last day.

Using LIST

When investigating issues with RMAN backups, one of the first tasks I usually do is connect to the target database and run the LIST BACKUP command. This command shows backup sets, backup pieces, and the files included in the backup:

```
RMAN> list backup;
```

It shows all RMAN backups recorded in the repository. You may want to spool that to an output file so that you can save the output and then use an operating system editor to search through and look for specific strings in the output.

To get a summarized view of backup information, use the LIST BACKUP SUMARY command:

```
RMAN> list backup summary;
```

You can also use the LIST command to report just image copy information:

```
RMAN> list copy;
```

The next command reports on archive redo log backups:

```
RMAN> list archivelog all;
```

There are a great number of ways in which you can run the LIST command (and likewise the REPORT command, covered in the next section). The prior methods listed are the ones you'll run most of the time. For a complete list of options available see the Oracle Database *Backup and Recovery Reference* guide (available on Oracle's OTN website).

Using REPORT

The RMAN REPORT command is useful for reporting on a variety of details. You can quickly view all of the datafiles associated with a database via the following:

```
RMAN> report schema;
```

The REPORT command provides detailed information about backups marked as obsolete via the RMAN retention policy. For example:

```
RMAN> report obsolete;
```

You can report on datafiles that need to be backed up as defined by the retention policy like so:

```
RMAN> report need backup;
```

There are several ways to report on datafiles that need to be backed up. Here are some other varieties:

```
RMAN> report need backup redundancy 2;
RMAN> report need backup redundancy 2 datafile 2;
```

Another way to use the REPORT command is for datafiles that have never been backed up or may contain data created from a NOLOGGING operation. For example, say you have direct path loaded data into a table, and the datafile in which the table resides has not been backed up. The following command will detect these situations:

```
RMAN> report unrecoverable;
```

Using SQL

There are a number of data dictionary views available for querying about backup information. Table 18–1 describes RMAN-related data dictionary views. These views are available regardless of your use of a recovery catalog (the information in these views is derived from the control file).

Table 18–1. Description of RMAN Backup Data Dictionary Views

View Name	Information Regarding
V$RMAN_BACKUP_JOB_DETAILS	RMAN backup jobs.
V$BACKUP	Backup status of online datafiles.
V$BACKUP_ARCHIVELOG_DETAILS	Archive logs backed up.
V$BACKUP_CONTROLFILE_DETAILS	Control files backed up.
V$BACKUP_COPY_DETAILS	Control file and datafile copies.
V$BACKUP_DATAFILE	Control files and datafiles backups.
V$BACKUP_DATAFILE_DETAILS	Datafiles backed up in backup sets, image copies, and proxy copies.
V$BACKUP_FILES	Datafiles, control files, spfiles, and archive redo logs backed up.
V$BACKUP_PIECE	Backup piece files.
V$BACKUP_PIECE_DETAILS	Backup piece detailed information.
V$BACKUP_SET	Backup sets.
V$BACKUP_SET_DETAILS	Backup set detailed information.

Sometimes DBAs new to RMAN have a hard time grasping the concept of backups, backup sets, backup pieces, datafiles, and how those concepts relate. I find the following query useful when discussing RMAN backup components. This query will display backup sets, the backup pieces with the set, and the datafiles that are backed up within the backup piece:

```
SET LINES 132 PAGESIZE 100
BREAK ON REPORT ON bs_key ON completion_time ON bp_name ON file_name
COL bs_key    FORM 99999 HEAD "BS Key"
COL bp_name   FORM a40   HEAD "BP Name"
COL file_name FORM a40   HEAD "Datafile"
--
SELECT
 s.recid                   bs_key
,TRUNC(s.completion_time) completion_time
,p.handle                  bp_name
,f.name                    file_name
FROM v$backup_set      s
    ,v$backup_piece    p
    ,v$backup_datafile d
    ,v$datafile        f
WHERE p.set_stamp = s.set_stamp
AND    p.set_count = s.set_count
AND    d.set_stamp = s.set_stamp
AND    d.set_count = s.set_count
AND    d.file#     = f.file#
ORDER BY
 s.recid
,p.handle
,f.name;
```

The output here has been shortened to fit on the page:

```
BS Key COMPLET  BP Name                      Datafile
------ -------- ---------------------------- --------------------------------
414    14-SEP-10 /ora01/O11R2/rman/r1j_1_1.bk /ora01/dbfile/O11R2/mvindex01.dbf
                                               /ora01/dbfile/O11R2/sysaux01.dbf
                                               /ora01/dbfile/O11R2/system01.dbf
                                               /ora02/dbfile/O11R2/users01.dbf
```

Sometimes it's useful to report on the performance of RMAN backups. The following query reports on the time taken for an RMAN backup per session.

```
COL hours             FORM 9999.99
COL time_taken_display FORM a20
SET LINESIZE 132
--
SELECT
 session_recid
,compression_ratio
,time_taken_display
,(end_time - start_time) * 24 as hours
,TO_CHAR(end_time,'dd-mon-yy hh24:mi') as end_time
FROM v$rman_backup_job_details
ORDER BY end_time;
```

Here is some sample output:

```
SESSION_RECID COMPRESSION_RATIO TIME_TAKEN_DISPLAY   HOURS END_TIME,
------------- ----------------- ------------------   ------ ----------------
         7509        4.55050595 03:20:48              3.35 04-sep-10 19:23
         7515        4.51185084 03:23:04              3.38 05-sep-10 19:25
         7521        4.43947443 03:31:48              3.53 06-sep-10 19:34
         7527        4.35619748 03:45:03              3.75 07-sep-10 19:47
         7533         4.2773889 04:20:04              4.33 08-sep-10 20:23
         7547          4.51488 03:22:21               3.37 09-sep-10 19:24
         7554        4.49303627 03:28:06              3.47 10-sep-10 19:31
         7561        4.51925905 03:17:00              3.28 11-sep-10 19:19
         7568        4.54671383 03:14:03              3.23 12-sep-10 19:16
         7575        4.52995677 03:17:07              3.29 13-sep-10 19:19
```

The contents of V$RMAN_BACKUP_JOB_DETAILS are summarized by a session connection to RMAN. Therefore, the report output is more accurate if you connect to RMAN (establishing a session) and then exit out of RMAN after the backup job is complete. If you remain connected to RMAN while running multiple backup jobs, the query output reports on all backup activity while connected (for that session).

You should have an automated method of detecting whether or not RMAN backups are running and if datafiles are being backed up. One reliable method of automating such a task is to embed SQL into a shell script and then run the script on a periodic basis from a scheduling utility such as cron.

I typically run two basic types of checks regarding the RMAN backups:

- Have the RMAN backups run recently?

- Are there any datafiles that have not been backed up recently?

The following shell script checks for the conditions listed above. You'll need to modify the script and provide it with a username and password for a user that can query the data dictionary objects referenced in the script (in this script the username/password is darl/foobar). When running the script, you'll need to pass in two variables: the Oracle SID and the threshold number of days that you want to check in the past for the last time the backups ran or when a datafile was backed up.

```
#!/bin/bash
#
if [ $# -ne 2 ]; then
  echo "Usage: $0 SID threshold"
  exit 1
fi
# source oracle OS variables
. /var/opt/oracle/oraset $1
crit_var=$(sqlplus -s <<EOF
darl/foobar
SET HEAD OFF FEEDBACK OFF
SELECT COUNT(*) FROM
(SELECT (sysdate - MAX(end_time)) delta
 FROM v\$rman_backup_job_details) a
WHERE a.delta > $2;
EOF)
#
if [ $crit_var -ne 0 ]; then
  echo "rman backups not running on $1" | mailx -s "rman problem" dkuhn@oracle.com
else
  echo "rman backups ran ok"
```

```
fi
#-------------------------------------------
crit_var2=$(sqlplus -s <<EOF
darl/foobar
SET HEAD OFF FEEDBACK OFF
SELECT COUNT(*)
FROM
(
SELECT name
FROM v\$datafile
MINUS
SELECT DISTINCT
 f.name
FROM v\$backup_datafile d
     ,v\$datafile        f
WHERE d.file#      = f.file#
AND   d.completion_time > sysdate - $2);
EOF)
#
if [ $crit_var2 -ne 0 ]; then
  echo "datafile not backed up on $1" | mailx -s "rman problem" dkuhn@oracle.com
else
  echo "datafiles are backed up..."
fi
#
exit 0
```

For example, to check if backups have been running successfully within the past two days, run the script (named rman_chk.bsh) like this:

```
$ rman_chk.bsh INVPRD 2
```

The prior script is basic but effective. You can enhance and add to it as required for your RMAN environment.

Summary

RMAN provides many flexible and feature rich options for backups. By default, RMAN only takes backups of blocks that have been modified in the database. The incremental features allow you to also backup only blocks that have been modified since the last backup. These incremental features are particularly useful in reducing the size of backups in large database environments where you only have a small percentage of data in the database that changes from one backup to the next.

You can instruct RMAN to back up every block in each datafile via an image copy. An image copy is a block-for-block identical copy of the datafile. Image copies have the advantage of being able to restore the backup files directly from the backup (without using RMAN). You can use the incrementally updated backup feature to implement an efficient hybrid of image copy backups and incremental backups.

RMAN contains built-in commands for reporting on many aspects of backups. The LIST command reports on backup activity. The REPORT command is useful for determining which files need to be backed up as dictated by the retention policy.

After you've successfully configured RMAN and created backups, you are in a position to be able to restore and recover your database in the event of a media failure. Restore and recovery topics are detailed in the next chapter.

■ ■ ■

RMAN Restore and Recovery

I was out on a long Saturday morning bike ride last year. About half way through the ride, my cell phone rang. It was one of the data center operational support technicians. He told me that a mission critical database server was acting strange and that I should logon as soon as possible and make sure things were okay. I told him that I was about 15 minutes from being able to logon. So I scurried home as fast as I could to check out the production box. When I got home and logged onto the database servers, I tried to start SQL*Plus and immediate got an error indicating that the SQL*Plus binary file had corruption. Great. I couldn't even log into SQL*Plus. This was not good.

■ **Mental Note** Ensure that all bicycle rides are taken outside of cell phone coverage. – Ed.

I had the SA restore the Oracle binaries from an operating system backup. I started SQL*Plus. The database had crashed so I attempted to start the database. The output indicated that there was a media failure with all of the datafiles. After some analysis, it was discovered that there had been some file system issues and that all of these files on disk were corrupt:

- Data files
- Control files
- Archive redo logs
- Online redo log files
- RMAN backup pieces on disk

This was almost a total disaster. My director asked about our options. I responded, "All we have to do is restore the database from our last tape backup and we'll lose whatever data is in archive redo logs that hadn't been backed up to tape yet."

The storage administrators were called in and instructed to restore the last set of RMAN backups that had been written to tape. About 15 minutes later, we could hear the tape guys talking to each other in hushed voices. One of them said, "We are sooooo hosed. We don't have any tape backups of RMAN for any databases on this box."

That was a dark moment. The worst case scenario was to rebuild the database from DDL scripts and lose three years of production data. Not a very palatable option.

After looking around the production box, I discovered that the prior production support DBA (ironically, this DBA had just been let go a few days prior due to budget cuts) had implemented a job to copy the RMAN backups to another server in the production environment. The RMAN backups on this other server were intact. I was able to restore and recover the production database from these backups. We lost about a days worth of data (between corrupt archive logs and downtime when no incoming transactions were allowed), but we were able to get the database restored and recovered about 20 hours after the initial phone call. That was a long day.

Most situations in which you need to restore and recovery will not be as bad as the one just described. However, the previous scenario does highlight the need for:

- A Backup strategy.

- A DBA with backup & recovery skills.

- A restore and recovery strategy, including a requirement to periodically test the restore and recovery.

This chapter walks you through restore and recovery using RMAN. It covers many of the common tasks you will have to perform when dealing with media failures.

Determining Media Recovery Required

The term "media recovery" refers to the need to restore files that have been lost or damaged due to failure of the underlying storage media (usually a disk of some sort). Usually, you know that media recovery is required by some sort of an error like the following:

```
ORA-01157: cannot identify/lock data file 1 - see DBWR trace file
ORA-01110: data file 1: '/u02/oracle/oradata/E64208/system01.dbf'
```

The error may be displayed on your screen when performing DBA tasks such as stopping and starting the database. Or you might see such an error in a trace file or the alert.log file. If you don't notice the issue right away, with a severe media failure, the database will stop processing transactions and users will start calling you.

To understand how Oracle is determining that media recovery is required, you must understand how Oracle determines that everything is okay. When Oracle shuts down normally (IMMEDIATE, TRANSACTIONAL, NORMAL), part of the shutdown process is to flush all modified blocks to disk and mark the header of each datafile with the current SCN and to update the control file with the current SCN information.

Upon startup, Oracle checks to see if the SCN in the control file matches the SCN in the header of the datafile. If there is a match, then Oracle attempts to open the datafiles and online redo log files. If all files are available and can be opened, Oracle starts normally. The following query compares the SCN in the control file (for each datafile) with the SCN in the datafile header:

```
SET LINES 132
COL name              FORM a40
COL status            FORM A8
COL file#             FORM 9999
COL control_file_SCN  FORM 999999999999999
COL datafile_SCN      FORM 999999999999999
--
SELECT
 a.name
,a.status
,a.file#
,a.checkpoint_change# control_file_SCN
,b.checkpoint_change# datafile_SCN
,CASE
```

```
    WHEN ((a.checkpoint_change# - b.checkpoint_change#) = 0) THEN 'Startup Normal'
    WHEN ((b.checkpoint_change#) = 0)                        THEN 'File Missing?'
    WHEN ((a.checkpoint_change# - b.checkpoint_change#) > 0) THEN 'Media Rec. Req.'
    WHEN ((a.checkpoint_change# - b.checkpoint_change#) < 0) THEN 'Old Control File'
    ELSE 'what the ?'
  END datafile_status
FROM v$datafile        a -- control file SCN for datafile
    ,v$datafile_header b -- datafile header SCN
WHERE a.file# = b.file#
ORDER BY a.file#;
```

If the control file SCN values are greater than the datafile SCN values, then media recovery is most likely required.

Determining What to Restore

Media recovery requires that you perform manual tasks to get your database back in one piece. These tasks usually involve a combination of RESTORE and RECOVER commands. You will have to issue an RMAN RESTORE command if your datafiles have experienced media failure. This could be because of somebody accidentally deleting files or a disk failure.

How the Process Works

When you issue the RESTORE command, RMAN will automatically determine how to extract the datafiles from any of the following available backups:

- Full database backup

- Incremental level 0 backup

- Image copy backup generated by BACKUP AS COPY command

After the files are restored from a backup, you are required to apply redo to them via the RECOVER command. When you issue the RECOVER command, Oracle will examine the SCNs in the affected datafiles and determine whether any of them need to be recovered. If the SCN in the datafile is less than the corresponding SCN in the control file, then media recovery will be required.

Oracle will retrieve the datafile SCN and then look for the corresponding SCN in the redo stream to determine where to start the recovery process. If the starting recovery SCN is in the online redo log files, the archived redo log files are not required for recovery.

During a recovery, RMAN will automatically determine how to apply redo. First, RMAN will apply any incremental backups available that are greater than zero, such as the incremental level 1. Next, any archived redo log files on disk will be applied. If the archived redo log files do not exist on disk, RMAN will attempt to retrieve them from a backup set.

To be able to perform a complete recovery, all of the following conditions need to be true:

- Your database is in archivelog mode.

- You have a good baseline backup of your database.

- You have any required redo that has been generated since the backup (archived redo log files, online redo log files, or incremental backups that RMAN can use for recovery instead of applying redo).

There are a wide variety of restore and recovery scenarios. How you restore and recover depends directly on your backup strategy and what files have been damaged. Listed next are the general steps to follow when facing a media failure:

1. Determine what files need to be restored.

2. Depending on the damage, set your database mode to nomount, mount, or open.

3. Use the RESTORE command to retrieve files from RMAN backups.

4. Use the RECOVER command for datafiles requiring recovery.

5. Open your database.

Your particular restore and recovery scenario may not require that all of the previous steps be performed. For example, you may just want to restore your spfile, which doesn't require a recovery step.

The first step in a restore and recovery process is to determine what files have experienced media failure. You can usually determine what files need to be restored from the following sources:

- Error messages displayed on your screen, either from RMAN or SQL*Plus

- Alert.log file and corresponding trace files

- Data dictionary views

If you're using Oracle Database 11g or higher, then in addition to the previously listed methods you should consider the Data Recovery Advisor for obtaining information about the extent of a failure and corresponding corrective action.

Using Data Recovery Advisor

The Data Recovery Advisor tool was introduced in Oracle Database 11g. In the event of a media failure, this tool will display the details of the failure, recommend corrective actions, and it will perform the recommended actions if you specify it to do so. It's like having another set of eyes to provide feedback when in a restore and recovery situation. There are three modes to Data Recovery Advisor:

- Listing failures.

- Suggesting corrective action.

- Running commands to repair failures.

The Data Recovery Advisor is invoked from RMAN. You can think of the Data Recovery Advisor as a set of RMAN commands that can assist you when dealing with media failures.

Listing Failures

When using the Data Recovery Advisor, the LIST FAILURE command is used to display any issues with the datafiles, control files, or online redo logs:

```
RMAN> list failure;
```

If there are no detected failures, you'll see a message indicating that there are no failures. Here is some sample output indicating that there may be an issue with a datafile:

```
List of Database Failures
=========================

Failure ID Priority Status    Time Detected Summary
---------- -------- --------- ------------- -------
662        HIGH     OPEN      16-SEP-10     One or more non-system datafiles are missing
```

The prior message doesn't indicate which specific file may be experiencing a failure. To dig a little deeper, use the DETAIL clause:

```
RMAN> list failure 662 detail;

List of Database Failures
=========================

Failure ID Priority Status    Time Detected Summary
---------- -------- --------- ------------- -------
662        HIGH     OPEN      16-SEP-10
One or more non-system datafiles are missing
  Impact: See impact for individual child failures
  List of child failures for parent failure ID 662
  Failure ID Priority Status    Time Detected Summary
  ---------- -------- --------- ------------- -------
  665        HIGH     OPEN      16-SEP-10     Datafile 7:
'/ora01/dbfile/O11R2/users02.dbf' is missing
    Impact: Some objects in tablespace USERS might be unavailable
```

This output details which file has experienced a failure and the nature of the problem (file missing).

Suggesting Corrective Action

The ADVISE FAILURE command gives advice about how to recover from potential problems detected by the Data Recovery Advisor. If you have multiple failures with your database, you can directly specify the failure ID to get advice on a given failure like so:

```
RMAN> advise failure 665;
```

Here is some sample output for this particular issue:

```
========================
1. If file /ora01/dbfile/O11R2/users02.dbf was unintentionally renamed or moved, restore it

Automated Repair Options
========================
Option Repair Description
------ ------------------
1      Restore and recover datafile 7
  Strategy: The repair includes complete media recovery with no data loss
  Repair script: /ora01/app/oracle/diag/rdbms/o11r2/O11R2/hm/reco_1184243250.hm
```

In this case, the Data Recovery Advisor created a script that can be used to potentially fix the problem. The contents of the repair script can be viewed with an operating system editor. For example:

```
$ vi /ora01/app/oracle/diag/rdbms/o11r2/O11R2/hm/reco_1184243250.hm
```

Here are the contents of the script (for this particular example):

```
# restore and recover datafile
 sql 'alter database datafile 7 offline';
 restore datafile 7;
 recover datafile 7;
 sql 'alter database datafile 7 online';
```

After reviewing the script, you can decide to manually run the suggested commands, or you can have the Data Recovery Advisor run the script via the REPAIR command (see the next section for details).

Repairing Failures

If you have identified a failure and viewed the recommended advice, you can proceed to actually repairing a failure. If you want to inspect what the REPAIR FAILURE command will do without actually running the commands, use the PREVIEW clause. Before you run the command, make sure you first run the LIST FAILURE and ADVISE FAILURE commands from the same connected session. In other words, the RMAN session that you're in must run the LIST and ADVISE commands within the same session before running the REPAIR command.

```
RMAN> repair failure preview;
```

If you're satisfied with the repair suggestions, then run the REPAIR FAILURE command.

```
RMAN> repair failure;
```

You'll be prompted at this point for confirmation.

```
Do you really want to execute the above repair (enter YES or NO)?
```

Type in YES to proceed.

```
YES
```

If all goes well, you should see a final message like this:

```
media recovery complete, elapsed time: 00:00:02
Finished recover at 16-SEP-10
sql statement: alter database datafile 7 online
repair failure complete
```

■ **Note** You can run the Data Recovery Advisor commands from the RMAN command prompt or from Enterprise Manager.

In this way, you can use the RMAN commands of LIST FAILURE, ADVISE FAILURE, and REPAIR FAILURE to resolve media failures. The Data Recovery Advisor can assist with most issues that you'll run into. I did have a couple scenarios where the following recommendation was provided:

```
Mandatory Manual Actions
========================
1. Please contact Oracle Support Services to resolve failure 149165...
Optional Manual Actions
=======================
no manual actions available
Automated Repair Options
========================
no automatic repair options available
```

This output indicates that you (the DBA) aren't quite out of a job yet. ;)

Using RMAN to Stop/Start Oracle

You can use RMAN to stop and start your database with methods that are almost identical to those available through SQL*Plus. When performing restore and recovery operations, it's often more convenient to stop and start your database from within RMAN. The following RMAN commands can be used to stop and start your database:

- SHUTDOWN
- STARTUP
- ALTER DATABASE

Shutting Down

The SHUTDOWN command works the same from RMAN as it does from SQL*Plus. There are four types of shutdown: ABORT, IMMEDIATE, NORMAL, and TRANSACTIONAL. I usually first attempt to use SHUTDOWN IMMEDIATE to stop a database. If that doesn't work, don't hesitate to use SHUTDOWN ABORT. Here are some examples:

```
RMAN> shutdown immediate;
RMAN> shutdown abort;
```

If you don't specify a shutdown option, NORMAL is the default. Shutting a database down with NORMAL is rarely viable as this mode waits for currently connected users to disconnect at their leisure. I never use NORMAL when shutting down a database.

Starting Up

As with SQL*Plus, you can use a combination of STARTUP and ALTER DATABASE commands to step the database through startup phases using RMAN, like so:

```
RMAN> startup nomount;
RMAN> alter database mount;
RMAN> alter database open;
```

Here's another example:

```
RMAN> startup mount;
RMAN> alter database open;
```

If you want to start the database with restricted access, use the DBA option:

```
RMAN> startup dba;
```

Complete Recovery

Complete recovery means that you can restore all transactions that were committed before the failure occurred. Complete recovery does not mean that you are restoring and recovering all datafiles in your database. For example, you can perform a complete recovery if you have a media failure with one datafile, and you restore and recover the one datafile. For complete recovery, the following conditions must be true:

- Your database is in archivelog mode.

- You have a good baseline backup of your database.

- You have any required redo that has been generated since the last backup.

- All archive redo logs start from the point that the last online backup began.

- If using, any incremental backups that RMAN can use for recovery must be available

- Online redo logs that contain transactions that have not yet been archived must be available.

If you've experienced a media failure and you have the required files to perform a complete recovery, then you can restore and recover your database.

Testing Restore and Recovery

You can determine which files RMAN will use for restore and recovery before you actually perform the restore and recovery. You can also instruct RMAN to verify the integrity of the backup files that will be used for restore and recovery.

Previewing Backups Used for Recovery

Use the RESTORE...PREVIEW command to list the backups and archive redo log files that RMAN will use to restore and recover database datafiles. The RESTORE...PREVIEW does not actually restore any files; rather, it lists out the backup files that will be used for a restore operation. This example previews in detail the backups required for restore and recovery for the entire database:

```
RMAN> restore database preview;
```

You can also preview require backup files at a summarized level of detail:

```
RMAN> restore database preview summary;
```

Here is a snippet of the output:

```
List of Backups
===============
Key     TY LV S Device Type Completion Time #Pieces #Copies Com Tag
------- -- -- - ----------- --------------- ------- ------- --- ---
571     B  F  A DISK        22-SEP-10       1       1       YES TAG20100922T141215
570     B  F  A DISK        22-SEP-10       1       1       YES TAG20100922T141215
List of Archived Log Copies for database with db_unique_name O11R2
=====================================================================
Key     Thrd Seq    S Low Time
------- ---- ------- - ---------
878     1    1       A 22-SEP-10
Media recovery start SCN is 19993679
Recovery must be done beyond SCN 19993680 to clear datafile fuzziness
```

Here are some more examples of how to preview backups required for restore and recovery:

```
RMAN> restore tablespace system preview;
RMAN> restore archivelog from time 'sysdate -1' preview;
RMAN> restore datafile 1, 2, 3 preview;
```

Validating Backup Files Before Restoring

There are several levels of verification that you can perform on backup files without actually restoring anything. If you just want RMAN to verify that the files exist and check the file headers, the use the RESTORE...VALIDATE HEADER command like so:

```
RMAN> restore database validate header;
```

This command only validates the existence of files and the file headers. You can further instruct RMAN to verify the integrity of blocks within backup files required to restore the database datafiles via the RESTORE...VALIDATE command (sans the HEADER clause). Again, RMAN will not restore any datafiles in this mode:

```
RMAN> restore database validate;
```

This command only checks for physical corruption within the backup files. You can also check for logical corruption (along with physical corruption) as follows:

```
RMAN> restore database validate check logical;
```

Here are some other examples of using RESTORE...VALIDATE:

```
RMAN> restore datafile 1,2,3 validate;
RMAN> restore archivelog all validate;
RMAN> restore controlfile validate;
RMAN> restore tablespace system validate;
```

Testing Media Recovery

The prior sections covered reporting and verifying the restore operations. You can also instruct RMAN to verify the recovery process via the RECOVER...TEST command. Before performing a test recovery, you need to ensure that the datafiles being recovered are offline. Oracle will throw an error for any online datafiles being recovered in test mode.

In this example, the tablespace USERS is restored first, and then a trial recovery is performed:

```
RMAN> connect target /
RMAN> startup mount;
RMAN> restore tablespace users;
RMAN> recover tablespace users test;
```

If there are any missing archive redo logs that are required for recovery, the following error is thrown:

```
RMAN-06053: unable to perform media recovery because of missing log
RMAN-06025: no backup of archived log for thread 1 with sequence 10 and starting SCN...
```

If the testing of the recovery succeeded, you will messages like the following, indicating the application of redo was tested but not applied:

```
ORA-10574: Test recovery did not corrupt any data block
ORA-10573: Test recovery tested redo from change 19993679 to 19993861
ORA-10572: Test recovery canceled due to errors
ORA-10585: Test recovery can not apply redo that may modify control file
```

Here are some other examples of testing the recovery process:

```
RMAN> recover database test;
RMAN> recover tablespace users, tools test;
RMAN> recover datafile 1,2,3 test;
```

Restoring Entire Database

The RESTORE DATABASE command will restore every datafile in your database. The exception to this is when RMAN detects that datafiles have already been restored; in that case, it will not restore them again. If you want to override that behavior, use the FORCE command.

When you issue the RECOVER DATABASE command, RMAN will automatically apply redo to any datafiles that need recovery. The recovery process includes applying changes found in the following:

- Incremental backup pieces (applicable only if using incremental backups)

- Archived redo log files (generated since the last backup or last incremental backup that is applied)

- Online redo log files (current and unarchived)

You can open your database after the restore and recovery process is complete. Complete database recovery works only if you have good backups of your database and have access to all redo generated after the backup was taken. You need all the redo required to recover the database datafiles. If you don't have all the required redo, then you'll most likely have to perform an incomplete recovery (covered later in this chapter).

■ **Note** Your database has to be at least mounted to restore datafiles using RMAN. This is because RMAN reads information from the control file during the restore and recovery process.

You can perform a complete database-level recovery with either the current control file or a backup control file.

Using Current Control File

You must first put your database in mount mode to perform a database-wide restore and recovery. This is because the SYSTEM tablespace datafile(s) must be offline when being restored and recovered. Oracle won't allow you to operate your database in open mode with datafiles associated with the SYSTEM tablespace offline. In this situation, start up the database in mount mode, issue the RESTORE and RECOVER commands, and then open the database like so:

```
RMAN> connect target /
RMAN> startup mount;
RMAN> restore database;
RMAN> recover database;
RMAN> alter database open;
```

If everything went as expected, the last message you should see is this:

```
database opened
```

Using Backup Control File

This solution uses a backup of the control file retrieved from the fast recovery area. For more examples of how to restore your control file, see the "Restoring Control Files" section of this chapter. In this scenario, the control file is first retrieved from a backup before restoring and recovering the database:

```
RMAN> connect target /
RMAN> startup nomount;
RMAN> restore controlfile from autobackup;
RMAN> alter database mount;
RMAN> restore database;
RMAN> recover database;
RMAN> alter database open resetlogs;
```

If everything went as expected, the last message you should see is this:

```
database opened
```

■ **Note** You are required to open your database with the OPEN RESETLOGS command anytime you use a backup control file during a recovery operation.

Restoring Tablespaces

Sometimes you'll have media failures that are localized to a particular tablespace or set of tablespaces. In these circumstances, it's appropriate to restore and recover at the tablespace level of granularity. The RMAN RESTORE TABLESPACE and RECOVER TABLESPACE commands will restore and recover all datafiles associated with the specified tablespace(s).

Restoring Tablespace While Database is Open

If your database is open, then you must take offline the tablespace you want to restore and recover. You can do this for any tablespaces except for SYSTEM and UNDO. This example restores and recovers the USERS tablespace while database is open:

```
RMAN> connect target /
RMAN> sql 'alter tablespace users offline immediate';
RMAN> restore tablespace users;
RMAN> recover tablespace users;
RMAN> sql 'alter tablespace users online';
```

After the tablespace is brought online, you should see a message similar to this:

```
sql statement: alter tablespace users online
```

Restoring Tablespace While Database in Mount Mode

Usually when performing a restore and recovery, DBAs will shut down the database re-start the database in mount mode in preparation to perform the recovery. While a database is mount mode this ensures that no users are connecting to the database and also ensures that no transactions are transpiring. This next example restores the SYSTEM tablespace while the database is in mount mode:

```
RMAN> connect target /
RMAN> shutdown immediate;
RMAN> startup mount;
RMAN> restore tablespace system;
RMAN> recover tablespace system;
RMAN> alter database open;
```

If everything was successful, the last message you should see is this:

```
database opened
```

Restoring Read-Only Tablespaces

RMAN will restore read-only tablespaces along with the rest of the database when you issue a RESTORE DATDABASE command. For example, the following command will restore all datafiles (including those in read-only mode):

```
RMAN> restore database;
```

Prior to Oracle Database 11g, you were required to issue RESTORE DATABASE CHECK READONLY to instruct RMAN to restore read-only tablespaces along with tablespaces in read-write mode. This is no longer a requirement in Oracle Database 11g or higher.

■ **Note** If you are using a backup that was created after the read-only tablespace was placed into read-only mode, then no recovery is necessary for the read-only datafiles. In this situation, there is no redo that has been generated for the read-only tablespace since it was backed up.

Restoring Temporary Tablespaces

Starting with Oracle Database 10*g*, you don't have to restore or re-create missing locally managed temporary tablespace tempfiles. When you open your database for use, Oracle automatically detects and re-creates locally managed temporary tablespace tempfiles.

When Oracle automatically re-creates a temporary tablespace, it will log a message to your target database alert.log similar to the following:

```
Re-creating tempfile <your temporary tablespace filename>
```

If for any reason your temporary tablespace becomes unavailable, you can also re-create it yourself. Since there are never any permanent objects in temporary tablespaces, you can simply re-create them as needed. Here is an example of how to create a locally managed temporary tablespace:

```
CREATE TEMPORARY TABLESPACE temp TEMPFILE
'/ora03/oradata/BRDSTN/temp01.dbf' SIZE 5000M REUSE
EXTENT MANAGEMENT LOCAL UNIFORM SIZE 512K;
```

If your temporary tablespace exists but the temporary datafiles are missing, you can simply add the temporary datafile(s) as shown here:

```
alter tablespace temp
add tempfile '/ora03/oradata/BRDSTN/temp01.dbf' SIZE 5000M REUSE;
```

Restoring Datafiles

A datafile-level restore and recovery works well when a media failure is isolated to a small set of datafiles. With datafile-level recoveries, you can instruct RMAN to restore and recover either with datafile number or the datafile name. For datafiles not associated with the SYSTEM or UNDO tablespaces, you have the option of restoring and recovering while the database remains open. While the database is open, you have to first take offline any datafiles being restored and recovered.

Restoring Datafile While Database Is Open

Use the RESTORE DATAFILE and RECOVER DATAFILE commands to restore and recover at the datafile level. When your database is open, you're required to take offline any datafiles you're attempting to restore and recover. This example restores and recovers datafiles 32 and 33 while the database is open:

```
RMAN> sql 'alter database datafile 32, 33 offline';
RMAN> restore datafile 32, 33;
RMAN> recover datafile 32, 33;
RMAN> sql 'alter database datafile 32, 33 online';
```

⬛ **Tip** Use the RMAN REPORT SCHEMA command to list datafile names and file numbers. You can also query the NAME and FILE# columns of V$DATAFILE to take names and numbers.

You can also specify the name of the datafile that you want to restore and recover. In this example, the mvdata01.dbf datafile is restored and recovered:

```
RMAN> sql "alter database datafile ''/ora01/dbfile/O11R2/mvdata01.dbf'' offline";
RMAN> restore datafile '/ora01/dbfile/O11R2/mvdata01.dbf';
RMAN> recover datafile '/ora01/dbfile/O11R2/mvdata01.dbf';
RMAN> sql "alter database datafile ''/ora01/dbfile/O11R2/mvdata01.dbf'' online";
```

■ **Note** When using the RMAN SQL command, if there are single quote marks within the SQL statement, then you are required to use double quotes to enclose the entire SQL statement and to use two single quote marks where you would ordinarily just use one quote mark.

Restoring Datafile While Database Is Not Open

In this scenario, the database is first shut down and then started in mount mode. You can restore and recover any datafile in your database while the database is not open. This example shows restoring the datafile 1, which is associated to the SYSTEM tablespace:

```
RMAN> connect target /
RMAN> shutdown abort;
RMAN> startup mount;
RMAN> restore datafile 1;
RMAN> recover datafile 1;
RMAN> alter database open;
```

You can also specify the filename when performing a datafile recovery:

```
RMAN> connect target /
RMAN> shutdown abort;
RMAN> startup mount;
RMAN> restore datafile '/ora01/dbfile/O11R2/system01.dbf';
RMAN> recover datafile '/ora01/dbfile/O11R2/system01.dbf';
RMAN> alter database open;
```

Restoring Datafiles to Non-Default Locations

Sometimes a failure will occur that renders the disks associated with a mount point inoperable. In situations like this, you will need to restore and recover the datafiles to a different location from where they originally resided. Another typical need for restoring datafiles to non-default locations is that you're restoring to a different database server where the mount points are completely different from the server where the backup originated.

Use the SET NEWNAME and SWITCH commands to restore datafiles to non-default locations. Both of these commands must be run from within an RMAN run{} block. You can think of using SET NEWNAME and SWITCH as a way to rename datafiles (similar to the SQL*Plus ALTER DATABASE RENAME FILE statement).

This example changes the location of datafiles 32 and 33:

```
RMAN> connect target /
RMAN> startup mount;
RMAN> run{
2> set newname for datafile 32 to '/ora02/dbfile/O11R2/mvdata01.dbf';
```

```
3> set newname for datafile 33 to '/ora02/dbfile/O11R2/mvindex01.dbf';
4> restore datafile 32, 33;
5> switch datafile all; # Updates repository with new datafile location.
6> recover datafile 32, 33;
7> alter database open;
8> }
```

This is a partial listing of the output:

```
channel ORA_DISK_2: restore complete, elapsed time: 00:00:01
Finished restore at 22-SEP-10
...
datafile 32 switched to datafile copy
input datafile copy RECID=92 STAMP=730375692 file name=/ora02/dbfile/O11R2/mvdata01.dbf
datafile 33 switched to datafile copy
input datafile copy RECID=93 STAMP=730375692 file name=/ora02/dbfile/O11R2/mvindex01.dbf
...
Starting recover at 22-SEP-10
media recovery complete, elapsed time: 00:00:05
Finished recover at 22-SEP-10
database opened
```

If the database is open, you can place the datafiles offline and then set their new names for restore and recovery like so:

```
RMAN> run{
2> sql 'alter database datafile 32, 33 offline';
3> set newname for datafile 32 to '/ora02/dbfile/O11R2/mvdata01.dbf';
4> set newname for datafile 33 to '/ora02/dbfile/O11R2/mvindex01.dbf';
5> restore datafile 32, 33;
6> switch datafile all; # Updates repository with new datafile location.
7> recover datafile 32, 33;
8> sql 'alter database datafile 32, 33 online';
9> }
```

You should now see a message similar to the following:

```
starting media recovery
Finished recover at 22-SEP-10
sql statement: alter database datafile 32, 33 online
```

Performing Block Level Recovery

Block-level corruption is rare and is usually caused by some sort of I/O error. However, if you do have an isolated corrupt block within a large datafile, it's nice to have the option of performing a block-level recovery. Block-level recovery is useful when a small number of blocks are corrupt within a datafile. Block recovery is not appropriate if the entire datafile needs media recovery.

RMAN will automatically detect corrupt blocks whenever a BACKUP, VALIDATE, or BACKUP VALIDATE command is run. Details on corrupt blocks can be viewed in the V$DATABASE_BLOCK_CORRUPTION view. In the following example, the regular backup job has reported a corrupt block in the output:

```
ORA-19566: exceeded limit of 0 corrupt blocks for file...
```

Querying the V$DATABASE_BLOCK_CORRUPTION view indicates which file contains corruption:

```
SQL> select * from v$database_block_corruption;
```

```
    FILE#     BLOCK#    BLOCKS CORRUPTION_CHANGE# CORRUPTIO
---------- ---------- ---------- ------------------- ---------
         5         20          1                   0 ALL ZERO
```

Your database can be either mounted or open when performing block level recovery. You do not have to take the datafile being recovered offline. You can instruct RMAN to recover all blocks reported in V$DATABASE_BLOCK_CORRUPTION as shown:

```
RMAN> recover corruption list;
```

If successful, the following message is displayed:

```
media recovery complete...
```

Another way to recover the block is to specify the datafile and block number like so:

```
RMAN> recover datafile 5 block 20;
```

It's preferable to use the RECOVER CORRUPTION LIST syntax because it will clear out any blocks recovered from the V$DATABASE_BLOCK_CORRUPTION view.

Note RMAN cannot perform block-level recovery on block 1 (datafile header) of the datafile.

Block-level media recovery allows you to keep your database available and also reduces the mean time to recovery since only the corrupt blocks are offline during the recovery. Your database must be in archivelog mode for performing block-level recoveries. In Oracle Database 11g, RMAN can restore the block from the flashback logs (if available). If the flashback logs are not available, then RMAN will attempt to restore the block from a full backup, a level 0 backup, or an image copy backup generated by BACKUP AS COPY command. After the block has been restored, any required archived redo logs must be available to recover the block. RMAN can't perform block media recovery using incremental level 1 (or higher) backups.

Note If you're using Oracle Database 10g or Oracle9i Database, use the BLOCKRECOVER command to perform block media recovery. Block level recovery is not available in Oracle version 8.

Restoring Archive Redo Log Files

RMAN will automatically restore any archived redo log files that it needs during a recovery process. You normally don't need to manually restore archived redo log files. However, you may want to manually restore the archived redo log files if any of the following situations apply:

- You need to restore archived redo log files in anticipation of later performing a recovery; the idea is that if the archived redo log files are already restored, it will speed up the recovery operation.

- You're required to restore the archived redo log files to a non-default location, either because of media failure or because of storage space issues.

- You need to restore specific archived redo log files because you want to inspect them via LogMiner.

If you've enabled a flash recovery area, then RMAN will by default restore archived redo log files to the destination defined by the initialization parameter DB_RECOVERY_FILE_DEST. Otherwise, RMAN uses the LOG_ARCHIVE_DEST_1 initialization parameter to determine where to restore the archived redo log files.

If you restore archived redo log files to a non-default location, RMAN knows the location they were restored to and automatically finds these files when you issue any subsequent RECOVER commands. RMAN will not restore archived redo log files that it determines are already on disk. Even if you specify a non-default location, RMAN will not restore an archived redo log file to disk if the file already exists. In this situation, RMAN will simply return a message stating that the archived redo log file has already been restored. Use the FORCE option to override this behavior.

If you are uncertain of the sequence numbers to use during a restore of log files, you can query the V$LOG_HISTORY view or issue an RMAN LIST BACKUP command for more information.

■ **Note** When restoring archived redo log files, your database can be either mounted or open.

Restoring to the Default Location

The following command will restore all archived redo log files that RMAN has backed up:

```
RMAN> restore archivelog all;
```

If you want to restore from a specified sequence, use the FROM SEQUENCE clause. You may want to run this query first to determine the most recent log files and sequence numbers that have been generated:

```
SQL> select sequence#, first_time from v$log_history order by 2;
```

This example restores all archived redo log files from sequence 68:

```
RMAN> restore archivelog from sequence 68;
```

If you want to restore a range of archived redo log files, use the FROM SEQUENCE and UNTIL SEQUENCE clauses or the SEQUENCE BETWEEN clause, as shown here. The following commands restore archived redo log files from sequence 68 through (and including) sequence 78 using thread 1:

```
RMAN> restore archivelog from sequence 68 until sequence 78 thread 1;
RMAN> restore archivelog sequence between 68 and 78 thread 1;
```

By default, RMAN won't restore an archived redo log file if it is already on disk. You can override this behavior if you use the FORCE like so:

```
RMAN> restore archivelog from sequence 1 force;
```

Restoring to a Nondefault Location

Use the SET ARCHIVELOG DESTINATION clause if you want to restore archived redo log files to a different location than the default. The following example restores to the non-default location of /ora01/archtemp. This option of the SET command must be executed from within an RMAN run RMAN run{} block.

```
RMAN> run{
2> set archivelog destination to '/ora01/archtemp';
3> restore archivelog from sequence 68 force;
4> }
```

Restoring the Spfile

You might want to restore a spfile for several different reasons:

- You accidentally set a value in the spfile that keeps your instance from starting.

- You accidentally deleted the spfile.

- You are required to see what it looked like at some time in the past.

One scenario (this has happened to me more than once) is that you're using a spfile and one of the DBAs on your team does something inexplicable like this:

```
SQL> alter system set processes=1000000 scope=spfile;
```

The parameter is changed in the pfile on disk but not in memory. Several months later, the database is stopped for some maintenance. When attempting to start the database, you can't even get the instance to start in a NOMOUNT state. This is because a parameter has been set to a ridiculous value that will consume all memory on the box. In this scenario, the instance may hang or you might see this message:

```
ORA-01078: failure in processing system parameters
LRM-00109: could not open parameter file
```

If you are using a recovery catalog, it's a fairly simple procedure to restore the spfile:

```
RMAN> connect target /
RMAN> connect catalog rmancat/foo@rcat
RMAN> startup nomount;
RMAN> restore spfile;
```

If you're not using a recovery catalog, there are a number of ways to restore your spfile. The approach you take depends on several variables such as:

- If you're using a FRA

- If you've configured a channel backup location for the autobackup

- If you're using the default location for autobackups

I'm not going to show every detail of all of these scenarios. Usually I determine the location of the backup piece that contains the backup of the spfile and do the restore like this:

```
RMAN> startup nomount force;
RMAN> restore spfile from
'/ora01/fra/O11R2/autobackup/2010_09_18/o1_mf_s_730048900_69bcc8h2_.bkp';
```

You should see a message similar to this:

```
channel ORA_DISK_1: SPFILE restore from AUTOBACKUP complete
```

In this example, I knew that a FRA was in use and located the latest backup file in the autobackup directory and used it.

■ **Note** For a complete description of all possible spfile and control file restore scenarios, refer to *RMAN Recipes for Oracle Database 11g* (Apress, 2007).

Restoring a Control File

If you are missing one control file and you have multiple copies, then you can shutdown your database, and simply restore the missing or damaged control file by copying a good control file to the correct location and name of the missing control file (see Chapter 5 for details).

The following sections cover these specific scenarios when restoring a control file:

- Using a Recovery Catalog.

- Using an autobackup.

- Specifying a backup file name.

Using a Recovery Catalog

When you're connected to the recovery catalog, you can view backup information about your control files even while your target database is in NOMOUNT mode. To list backups of your control files, use the LIST command as shown here:

```
RMAN> connect target /
RMAN> connect catalog rcat/rcat@recov
RMAN> startup nomount;
RMAN> list backup of controlfile;
```

If you are missing all of your control files and you are using a recovery catalog, then issue STARTUP NOMOUNT and issue the RESTORE CONTROLFILE command. In this example, the recovery catalog owner and password are both *rcat* and the name of the recovery catalog is *recov*. You'll have to change those values to match the username/password@service in your environment.

```
RMAN> connect target /
RMAN> connect catalog rcat/rcat@recov
RMAN> startup nomount;
RMAN> restore controlfile;
```

RMAN restores the control files to the location defined by your CONTROL_FILES initialization parameter. You should see a message indicating that your control files have been successfully copied back from an RMAN backup piece. Here's a partial listing of RMAN's message stack after a successful control file restore:

```
allocated channel: ORA_DISK_1
channel ORA_DISK_1: sid=156 devtype=DISK
channel ORA_DISK_1: restoring control file
channel ORA_DISK_1: reading from backup piece
channel ORA_DISK_1: restore complete, elapsed time: 00:00:05
```

You can now alter your database into mount mode and perform any additional restore and recovery commands required for your database.

▪ **Note** When you restore a control file from a backup, you are required to perform media recovery on your entire database and open your database with the OPEN RESETLOGS command, even if you didn't restore any datafiles. You can determine whether your control file is a backup by querying the CONTROLFILE_TYPE column of the V$DATABASE view.

Using an Autobackup to Restore

When you enable the autobackup of your control file and are using a fast recovery area, restoring your control file is fairly simple. First, connect to your target database, then issue a STARTUP NOMOUNT command, and lastly issue the RESTORE CONTROLFILE FROM AUTOBACKUP command like so:

```
RMAN> connect target /
RMAN> startup nomount;
RMAN> restore controlfile from autobackup;
```

RMAN restores the control files to the location defined by your CONTROL_FILES initialization parameter. You should see a message indicating that your control files have been successfully copied back from an RMAN backup piece. Here is a partial snippet of the output:

```
allocated channel: ORA_DISK_1
channel ORA_DISK_1: sid=156 devtype=DISK
database name (or database unique name) used for search: ORCL
channel ORA_DISK_1: autobackup found in the recovery area
```

You can now alter your database into mount mode and perform any additional restore and recovery commands required for your database.

Specifying a Filename

When restoring a database to a different server, the first few steps in the process usually are: take a backup of the target database, copy to the remote server, and then restore the control file from the RMAN backup. In these scenarios, I usually know the name of the backup piece that contains the control file. Here is an example where you instruct RMAN to restore a control file from a specific backup piece file:

```
RMAN> startup nomount;
RMAN> restore controlfile from '/ora01/O11R2/rman/c-3453199553-20100923-07.bk';
```

The control file will be restored to the location defined by the CONTROL_FILES initialization parameter.

Incomplete Recovery

Incomplete database recovery means that you cannot recover all committed transactions. Incomplete means that you do not apply all redo to restore to the point of the last committed transaction that occurred in your database. In other words, you are restoring and recovering to a point in time in the past. For this reason, incomplete database recovery is also called *database point-in-time recovery* (DBPITR). Usually you perform incomplete database recovery because of one of the following reasons:

- You don't have all the redo required to perform a complete recovery. You're missing either the archived redo log files or online redo log files that are required for complete recovery. This situation could arise because the required redo files are damaged or missing.

- You purposely want to roll the database back to a point in time. For example, you would do this if somebody accidentally truncated a table and you intentionally wanted to roll the database back to just before the truncate table command was issued.

■ Tip To minimize the chance of failure with your online redo log files, I recommend you multiplex them with at least two members in each group and have each member on separate physical devices governed by separate controllers.

Incomplete database recovery consists of two steps: restore and recovery. The restore step will re-create datafiles, and the recover step will apply redo up to the specified point in time. The restore process can be initiated from RMAN in several ways:

- `RESTORE DATABASE UNTIL`
- `RESTORE TABLESPACE UNTIL`
- `FLASHBACK DATABASE`

For the majority of incomplete database recovery circumstances, you use the `RESTORE DATABASE UNTIL` command to instruct RMAN to retrieve datafiles from the RMAN backup files. This type of incomplete database recovery is the main focus of this chapter. The `UNTIL` portion of the `RESTORE DATABASE` command instructs RMAN to retrieve datafiles from a point in the past based on one of the following methods:

- Time
- Change (sometimes called *system change number* or SCN)
- Log sequence number
- Restore point

The `RMAN RESTORE DATABASE UNTIL` command will retrieve all datafiles from the most recent backup set or image copy. RMAN will automatically determine from the UNTIL clause which backup set contains the required datafiles. If you omit the UNTIL clause of the `RESTORE DATABASE` command, RMAN will retrieve datafiles from latest available backup set or image copy. In some situations, this may be the behavior you desire. I recommend you use the UNTIL clause to ensure that RMAN restores from the correct backup set. When you issue the RESTORE DATABASE UNTIL command, RMAN will determine how to extract the datafiles from any of the following:

- Full database backup

- Incremental level 0 backup

- Image copy backup generated by the BACKUP AS COPY command

You cannot perform an incomplete database recovery on a subset of your database's online datafiles. When performing incomplete database recovery, all of the checkpoint SCNs for all online datafiles must be synchronized before you can open your database with the alter database open resetlogs command. You can view the datafile header SCNs and the status of each datafile via this SQL query:

```
select
 file#
,status
,fuzzy
,error
,checkpoint_change#,
to_char(checkpoint_time,'dd-mon-rrrr hh24:mi:ss') as checkpoint_time
from v$datafile_header;
```

■ **Note** The FUZZY column of V$DATAFILE_HEADER refers to a datafile that contains one or more blocks that have an SCN value greater than or equal to the checkpoint SCN in the datafile header. If datafile is restored and has a FUZZY value of YES, then media recovery is required.

The only exception to this rule of not performing an incomplete recovery on a subset of online database files is a tablespace point-in-time recovery (TSPITR), which uses the RECOVER TABLESPACE UNTIL command. TSPITR is used in rare situations; it restores and recovers only the tablespace(s) you specify.

The recovery portion of an incomplete database recovery is always initiated with the RECOVER DATABASE UNTIL command. RMAN will automatically recover your database to the point specified with the UNTIL clause. Just like the RESTORE command, you can recover until time, change/SCN, log sequence number, or restore point. When RMAN reaches the specified point, it will automatically terminate the recovery process.

■ **Note** Regardless of what you specify in the UNTIL clause, RMAN will convert that into a corresponding UNTIL SCN clause and assign the appropriate SCN. This is to avoid any timing issues, particularly those caused by daylight saving time.

During a recovery, RMAN will automatically determine how to apply redo. First, RMAN will apply any incremental backups available. Next, any archived redo log files on disk will be applied. If the archived redo log files do not exist on disk, then RMAN will attempt to retrieve them from a backup set. If you want to apply redo as part of an incomplete database recovery, the following conditions must be true:

- Your database must be in archivelog mode.

- You must have a good backup of all datafiles.

- You must have all redo required to restore up to the specified point.

▪ **Tip** Starting with Oracle Database 10*g*, you can perform parallel media recovery by using the RECOVER DATABASE PARALLEL command.

When performing an incomplete database recovery with RMAN, you must have your database in mount mode. RMAN needs the database in mount mode to be able to read and write to the control file. Also, with an incomplete database recovery, the system datafile is always one of the datafiles being recovered. The SYSTEM tablespace's datafile(s) must be offline while it is being recovered. Oracle will not allow your database to be open while this is happening.

▪ **Note** After incomplete database recovery is performed, you are required to open your database with the ALTER DATABASE OPEN RESETLOGS command.

Depending on your scenario, you can use RMAN to perform a variety of incomplete recovery methods. The next section discusses how to determine what type of incomplete recovery to perform.

Determining the Type of Incomplete Recovery

Time-based restore and recovery is commonly used when you know the approximate date and time to which you want to recover your database. For example, you may know approximately the time you want to stop the recovery process but not a particular SCN.

Log sequence–based and cancel-based recovery work well in situations where you have missing or damaged log files. In such scenarios, you can recover only up to your last good archived redo log file.

SCN-based recovery works well if you can pinpoint the SCN at which you want to stop the recovery process. You can retrieve SCN information from views such as V$LOG and V$LOG_HISTORY. You can also use tools such as LogMiner to retrieve the SCN of a particular SQL statement.

Restore point recoveries work only if you have established restore points. In these situations, you restore and recover up to the SCN associated with the specified restore point.

Tablespace point-in-time recovery is used in situations where you can restore and recover just a few tablespaces. You can use RMAN to automate many of the tasks associated with this type of incomplete recovery.

■ **Note** Flashing back your database works only if you have enabled the flashback database feature (see Chapter 16 for details).

Performing Time-Based Recovery

To restore and recover your database back to a point in time, you can use either the UNTIL TIME clause of the RESTORE and RECOVER commands or the SET UNTIL TIME clause within a run{} block. RMAN will restore and recover the database up to, but not including, the specified time. In other words, RMAN will restore any transactions committed prior to the time specified. RMAN automatically stops the recovery process when it reaches the time you specified.

The default date format that RMAN expects is YYYY-MM-DD:HH24:MI:SS. However, I recommend using the TO_DATE function and specifying a format mask. This eliminates ambiguities with different national date formats and having to set the operating system NLS_DATE_FORMAT variable. The following example specifies a time when issuing the restore and recover commands:

```
RMAN> connect target /
RMAN> startup mount;
RMAN> restore database until time
2> "to_date('04-sep-2010 14:00:00', 'dd-mon-rrrr hh24:mi:ss')";
RMAN> recover database until time
2> "to_date('04-sep-2010 14:00:00', 'dd-mon-rrrr hh24:mi:ss')";
RMAN> alter database open resetlogs;
```

If everything went well, you should now see output similar to this:

```
Database altered
```

Performing Log Sequenced-Based Recovery

Usually this type of incomplete database recovery is initiated because you have a missing or damaged archived redo log file. If that's the case, you can recover only up to your last good archived redo log file, because you cannot skip a missing archived redo log.

How you determine which archived redo log file to restore up to (but not including) will vary by situation. For example, if you are physically missing an archived redo log file and if RMAN can't find it in a backup set, then you'll receive the following message when trying to apply the missing file:

```
RMAN-06053: unable to perform media recovery because of missing log
RMAN-06025: no backup of log thread 1 seq 45 lowscn 2149069 found to restore
```

Based on the previous error message, you would restore up to (but not including) log sequence 45.

```
RMAN> connect target /
RMAN> startup mount;
RMAN> restore database until sequence 45;
RMAN> recover database until sequence 45;
RMAN> alter database open resetlogs;
```

If everything went well, you should now see output similar to this:

```
Database altered
```

■ Note Log sequenced-based recovery is similar to user-managed cancel based recovery. See Chapter 16 for details on a user-managed cancel based recovery.

Performing Change/SCN-Based Recovery

SCN-based incomplete database recovery works in situations where you know the SCN value up to where you want to end the restore and recovery session. RMAN will recover up to, but not including, the specified SCN. RMAN automatically terminates the restore process when it reaches the specified SCN.

You can view your database SCN information in several ways:

- By using LogMiner to determine an SCN associated with a DDL or DML statement.

- By looking in the alert.log file.

- By looking in your trace files.

- By querying the FIRST_CHANGE# column of VLOG, VLOG_HISTORY, and V$ARCHIVED_LOG.

After establishing the SCN to which you want to restore, use the UNTIL SCN clause to restore up to, but not including, the SCN specified. The following example restores all transactions that have an SCN that is less than 950:

```
RMAN> connect target /
RMAN> startup mount;
RMAN> restore database until scn 95019865425;
RMAN> recover database until scn 95019865425;
RMAN> alter database open resetlogs;
```

If everything went well, you should now see output similar to this:

```
Database altered
```

Restoring to a Restore Point

There are two types of restore points: normal and guaranteed. Guaranteed restore points require that you have the flashback database feature enabled. You can create a normal restore point using SQL*Plus as follows:

```
SQL> create restore point MY_RP;
```

This command creates a restore point named MY_RP that is associated with the SCN of the database at the time the command was issued. You can view the current SCN of your database as shown here:

```
SQL> select current_scn from v$database;
```

You can view restore point information in the V$RESTORE_POINT view like so:

```
SQL> select name, scn from v$restore_point;
```

The restore point acts like a synonym for the particular SCN. It allows you to restore and recover to an SCN without having to specify a number. RMAN will restore and recover up to, but not including, the SCN associated with the restore point.

This example restores and recovers to the MY_RP restore point:

```
RMAN> connect target /
RMAN> startup mount;
RMAN> restore database until restore point MY_RP;
RMAN> recover database until restore point MY_RP;
RMAN> alter database open resetlogs;
```

Restoring and Recovering to Different Server

When you think about backups, you must as the same time think about restore and recovery. Your backups are only as good as the last time you tested a restore and recovery. A backup strategy can be rendered worthless without a good restore and recovery strategy. The last thing you want to happen is to have a media failure, go to restore your database, and then find out you're missing critical pieces, don't have enough space to restore, learn that something is corrupt, and so on.

One of the best ways to test an RMAN backup is to restore and recover it to a different database server. This will exercise all of your backup, restore, and recovery DBA skills. If you can restore and recover an RMAN backup on a different server, it will give you confidence when a real disaster hits. You can think of all of the prior material in this book as the building blocks for performing technically challenging tasks. Moving a database from one server to another using an RMAN backup requires an expert level understanding of the Oracle architecture and how backup and recovery works.

■ **Note** RMAN does have a DUPLICATE DATABASE command which works well for copying a database from one server to another. If you're going to be performing this type of task often, I would recommend that you use RMAN's duplicate database functionality. However, you may still have to manually copy a backup of a database from one server to another, especially when the security is such that you can't directly connect a production server to a development environment. I work with many production databases where there is no direct access to a production server, so the only way to duplicate a database is by manually copying the RMAN backups from production to a test environment.

In this example, the originating server and destination server have completely different mount points and disk layouts. Listed next are the high-level steps required to take an RMAN backup and use it to recreate a database on a separate server:

1. Create an RMAN backup on the originating database.

2. Copy RMAN backup to the destination server. All steps after this step are performed on the destination database server.

3. Ensure that Oracle is installed.

4. Source the required OS variables.

5. Create an init.ora file for the database to be restored.

6. Create any required directories for datafiles, control files, and dump/trace files.

7. Startup the database in NOMOUNT mode.

8. Restore a control file from the RMAN backup.

9. Startup the database in MOUNT mode.

10. Make the control file aware of the location of the RMAN backups.

11. Rename and restore the datafiles to reflect new directory locations.

12. Recover the database.

13. Set the new location for the online redo logs.

14. Open the database.

15. Add tempfile.

16. Rename the database.

Each of the prior steps is covered in detail in the next several sections. Steps 1 and 2 occur on the source database server. All other steps are performed on the destination server. For this example, the source database is named E64202, and the destination database will be named O11DEV.

On the source database, the location of the datafiles, control files, and online redo logs are all in this directory:

```
/u02/oracle/oradata/E64202
```

The source database archive redo log file location is here:

```
/u02/oracle/product/11.2.0/dbhome_1/dbs/arch
```

The RMAN backup location is determined by the following configurations:

```
CONFIGURE CONTROLFILE AUTOBACKUP ON;
CONFIGURE CONTROLFILE AUTOBACKUP FORMAT FOR DEVICE TYPE DISK TO '/u02/rman/%F.bk';
CONFIGURE CHANNEL 1 DEVICE TYPE DISK FORMAT    '/u02/rman/rman1_%U.bk';
```

On the destination database, the datafiles and control files will be renamed and restored to this directory:

```
/ora02/dbfile/O11DEV
```

The destination database online redo logs will be recreated in this directory:

```
/ora02/oraredo/O11DEV
```

The destination database archive redo log file location will be set as follows:

```
/ora02/oraarch/O11DEV
```

Step 1: Create an RMAN Backup on the Originating Database

When backing up a database, make sure you have the autobackup control file feature turned on. Also include the archive redo logs as part of the backup, like so:

```
RMAN> backup database plus archivelog;
```

I usually configure a channel and have both the backup pieces and the control file autobackup go to the same directory. For example, this is what the backup pieces look like for the source database:

```
rman1_03lol0i0_1_1.bk
rman1_04lol0i1_1_1.bk
rman1_05lol0j5_1_1.bk
c-1984315547-20100923-00.bk
```

Step 2: Copy RMAN Backup to Destination Server

For this step, I usually use a utility such as rsync or scp to copy the backup pieces from one server to another. This example uses the scp command:

```
$ scp *.bk oracle@ora03:/ora02/rman/O11DEV
```

In this example, the /ora02/rman/O11DEV directory must be created on the destination server before copying the backup files.

▪ **Note** If the RMAN backups are on tape instead on disk, then the same media manager software must be installed/configured on the destination server. Also, that server must have direct access to the RMAN backups on tape.

Step 3: Ensure that Oracle is Installed

Make sure you have the same version of Oracle binaries installed on the destination as you do on the originating database. In this example, Oracle Database 11g release 2 is used for both the source and destination databases.

Step 4: Source the Required OS Variables

You need to establish the operating system variables such as ORACLE_SID, ORACLE_HOME, and PATH. I usually set the ORACLE_SID variable to match what it was on the original database. The database name will be changed as part of the last step in this section. Here are the settings for ORACLE_SID and ORACLE_HOME on the destination server:

```
$ echo $ORACLE_SID
E64202

$ echo $ORACLE_HOME
/oracle/app/oracle/product/11.2.0/db_1
```

Step 5: Create an init.ora File for the Database to be Restored

Copy the init.ora file from the original server to the destination server and modify it so that it matches the destination box in terms of any directory paths. For example, make sure you modify the

CONTROL_FILES parameter so that the path names are reflective of where the control files will be placed on the new server.

For now, the name of the init.ora file is ORACLE_HOME/dbs/initE64202.ora. This file will be renamed when the database is renamed to O11DEV in a later step. For now, the name of the database is E64202; this will be renamed in a later step.

Here are the contents of the init.ora file:

```
db_name='E64202'
control_files='/ora02/dbfile/O11DEV/control01.ctl'
            ,'/ora02/dbfile/O11DEV/control02.ctl'
diagnostic_dest='/oracle/app/oracle'
log_archive_dest_1='location=/ora02/oraarch/O11DEV'
log_archive_format='%t_%s_%r.arc'
db_block_size=8192
memory_target=408944640
open_cursors=300
processes=100
remote_login_passwordfile='EXCLUSIVE'
sessions=115
undo_tablespace='UNDOTBS1'
```

Notice that the CONTROL_FILES, DIAGNOSTIC_DEST, and LOG_ARCHIVE_DEST_1 reflect the new path directories on the destination server.

■ **Note** If this was an Oracle Database 10g example, you would need to set the parameters of:
BACKGROUND_DUMP_DEST, USER_DUMP_DEST, CORE_DUMP_DEST.

Step 6: Create any Required Directories for Datafiles, Control Files, and Dump/Trace Files

For this example, the directories of /ora02/dbfile/O11DEV, /oracle/app/oracle, and /ora02/oraarch/O11DEV are created:

```
$ mkdir -p /ora02/dbfile/O11DEV
$ mkdir -p /oracle/app/oracle
$ mkdir -p /ora02/oraarch/O11DEV
```

Step 7: Startup the Database in NOMOUNT Mode

You should now be able to startup the database in NOMOUNT mode:

```
$ rman target /
RMAN> startup nomount;
```

Step 8: Restore a Control File from the RMAN Backup

Now restore the control file from the backup that was previously copied. In this example, the backup piece that contains the control file backup is c-1984315547-20100923-00.bk:

```
RMAN> restore controlfile from '/ora02/rman/011DEV/c-1984315547-20100923-00.bk';
```

The control file will be restored to all locations specified by the CONTROL_FILES initialization parameter. Here is some sample output:

```
channel ORA_DISK_1: restoring control file
channel ORA_DISK_1: restore complete, elapsed time: 00:00:01
output file name=/ora02/dbfile/011DEV/control01.ctl
output file name=/ora02/dbfile/011DEV/control02.ctl
```

Step 9: Startup Database in Mount Mode

You should be able to startup your database in mount mode now:

```
RMAN> alter database mount;
```

Step 10: Make the Control File Aware of the Location of the RMAN Backups

First, use the CROSSCHECK command to let the control file know that none of the backups or archive redo logs are in the same location that they were on the original server:

```
RMAN> crosscheck backup;
RMAN> crosscheck copy;
RMAN> crosscheck archivelog all;
```

Now use the CATALOG command to make the control file aware of the location and names of the backup pieces that were copied to the destination server. In this example, any RMAN files that are in the /ora02/rman/011DEV directory will be cataloged in the control file:

```
RMAN> catalog start with '/ora02/rman/011DEV';
```

Here is some sample output:

```
searching for all files that match the pattern /ora02/rman/011DEV
List of Files Unknown to the Database
=====================================
File Name: /ora02/rman/011DEV/rman1_05lol0j5_1_1.bk
File Name: /ora02/rman/011DEV/c-1984315547-20100923-00.bk
File Name: /ora02/rman/011DEV/rman1_04lol0i1_1_1.bk
File Name: /ora02/rman/011DEV/rman1_03lol0i0_1_1.bk
Do you really want to catalog the above files (enter YES or NO)?
```

Now, type in YES (if everything looks okay). You should be able to use the RMAN LIST BACKUP command now to view the newly cataloged backup pieces:

```
RMAN> list backup;
```

Step 11: Rename and restore the datafiles to Reflect New Directory Locations

If your destination server has the exact same directory structure as the original server directories, you can issue the RESTORE command directly:

```
RMAN> restore database;
```

However, when restoring datafiles to locations are different from the original directories, you'll have to use the SET NEWNAME command. Create a file that uses an RMAN run{} block that contains the appropriate SET NEWNAME and RESTORE commands. I like to use a SQL script that generates SQL to give me a starting point. Here is a sample script:

```
set head off feed off verify off pages 0 trimspool on
set lines 132 pagesize 0
spo newname.sql
--
select 'run{' from dual;
--
select
'set newname for datafile ' || file# || ' to ' || '''' || name || '''' || ';'
from v$datafile;
--
select
'restore database;' || chr(10) ||
'switch datafile all;' || chr(10) ||
'}'
from dual;
--
spo off;
```

After running the script, here are the contents of the newname.sql script that was generated:

```
run{
set newname for datafile 1 to '/u02/oracle/oradata/E64202/system01.dbf';
set newname for datafile 2 to '/u02/oracle/oradata/E64202/sysaux01.dbf';
set newname for datafile 3 to '/u02/oracle/oradata/E64202/undotbs01.dbf';
set newname for datafile 4 to '/u02/oracle/oradata/E64202/users01.dbf';
restore database;
switch datafile all;
}
```

Now, modify the contents of the newname.sql script to reflect the directories on the destination database server. Here is what the final newname.sql script looks like for this example:

```
run{
set newname for datafile 1 to '/ora02/dbfile/O11DEV/system01.dbf';
set newname for datafile 2 to '/ora02/dbfile/O11DEV/sysaux01.dbf';
set newname for datafile 3 to '/ora02/dbfile/O11DEV/undotbs01.dbf';
set newname for datafile 4 to '/ora02/dbfile/O11DEV/users01.dbf';
restore database;
switch datafile all;
}
```

Now, connect to RMAN and run the prior script to restore the datafiles to the new locations:

```
$ rman target /
RMAN> @newname.sql
```

Here is a snippet of the output for this example:

```
channel ORA_DISK_1: restore complete, elapsed time: 00:01:05
Finished restore at 24-SEP-10
datafile 1 switched to datafile copy
input datafile copy RECID=5 STAMP=730527824 file name=/ora02/dbfile/O11DEV/system01.dbf
datafile 2 switched to datafile copy
input datafile copy RECID=6 STAMP=730527824 file name=/ora02/dbfile/O11DEV/sysaux01.dbf
datafile 3 switched to datafile copy
input datafile copy RECID=7 STAMP=730527824 file name=/ora02/dbfile/O11DEV/undotbs01.dbf
datafile 4 switched to datafile copy
input datafile copy RECID=8 STAMP=730527824 file name=/ora02/dbfile/O11DEV/users01.dbf
RMAN> **end-of-file**
```

All of the datafiles have been restored to the new database server. You can use the RMAN REPORT SCHEMA command to verify that the files have been restored and are in the correct locations:

```
RMAN> report schema;
```

Here is some sample output:

```
RMAN-06139: WARNING: control file is not current for REPORT SCHEMA
Report of database schema for database with db_unique_name E64202
List of Permanent Datafiles
===========================
File Size(MB) Tablespace          RB segs Datafile Name
---- -------- ------------------- ------- ------------------------
1    670      SYSTEM              ***     /ora02/dbfile/O11DEV/system01.dbf
2    470      SYSAUX              ***     /ora02/dbfile/O11DEV/sysaux01.dbf
3    30       UNDOTBS1            ***     /ora02/dbfile/O11DEV/undotbs01.dbf
4    5        USERS               ***     /ora02/dbfile/O11DEV/users01.dbf
List of Temporary Files
=======================
File Size(MB) Tablespace          Maxsize(MB) Tempfile Name
---- -------- ------------------- ----------- --------------------
1    0        TEMP                32767       /u02/oracle/oradata/E64202/temp01.dbf
```

From the prior output, the database name and temporary tablespace datafile still don't reflect the destination database. Those will be modified in subsequent steps.

Step 12: Recover the Database

Next, you need to apply any archive redo files that were generated during the backup. These should be included in the backup because the ARCHIVELOG ALL clause was used to take the backup. Initiate the application of redo via the RECOVER DATABASE command:

```
RMAN> recover database;
```

RMAN will restore and apply as many archive redo logs as it has in the backup pieces and then will throw an error when it reaches an archive redo log which doesn't exist:

```
channel ORA_DISK_1: starting archived log restore to default destination
channel ORA_DISK_1: restoring archived log
```

```
archived log thread=1 sequence=4
channel ORA_DISK_1: reading from backup piece /ora02/rman/O11DEV/rman1_05lol0j5_1_1.bk
channel ORA_DISK_1: piece handle=/ora02/rman/O11DEV/rman1_05lol0j5_1_1.bk
tag=TAG20100923T200037
channel ORA_DISK_1: restored backup piece 1
channel ORA_DISK_1: restore complete, elapsed time: 00:00:01
archived log file name=/ora02/oraarch/O11DEV/1_4_729167134.arc thread=1 sequence=4
unable to find archived log
archived log thread=1 sequence=5
RMAN-00571: ===========================================================
RMAN-00569: =============== ERROR MESSAGE STACK FOLLOWS ===============
RMAN-00571: ===========================================================
RMAN-03002: failure of recover command at 09/24/2010 04:35:09
RMAN-06054: media recovery requesting unknown archived log
for thread 1 with sequence 5 and starting SCN of 977214
```

Now is a good time to verify that your datafiles are online and not in a fuzzy state. Run the following query:

```
select
 file#
,status
,fuzzy
,error
,checkpoint_change#,
to_char(checkpoint_time,'dd-mon-rrrr hh24:mi:ss') as checkpoint_time
from v$datafile_header;
```

Step 13: Set the New Location for the Online Redo Logs

Set the names for the online redo logs to reflect the new directory structures on the destination database server. I sometimes use a SQL script that generates SQL to assist with this step:

```
set head off lines 132 pages 0 trimspoo on
spo renlog.sql
select
 'alter database rename file ' || chr(10)
 || '''' || member || '''' || ' to ' || chr(10) || '''' || member || '''' ||';'
from v$logfile;
spo off;
```

For this example, here are the contents of the renlog.sql file that was generated:

```
alter database rename file
'/u02/oracle/oradata/E64202/redo03.log' to
'/u02/oracle/oradata/E64202/redo03.log';

alter database rename file
'/u02/oracle/oradata/E64202/redo02.log' to
'/u02/oracle/oradata/E64202/redo02.log';

alter database rename file
'/u02/oracle/oradata/E64202/redo01.log' to
'/u02/oracle/oradata/E64202/redo01.log';
```

The contents of renlog.sql need to be modified to reflect the directory structure on the destination server. Here is what renlog.sql looks like after being edited for this example:

```
alter database rename file
'/u02/oracle/oradata/E64202/redo03.log' to
'/ora02/oraredo/O11DEV/redo03.log';

alter database rename file
'/u02/oracle/oradata/E64202/redo02.log' to
'/ora02/oraredo/O11DEV/redo02.log';

alter database rename file
'/u02/oracle/oradata/E64202/redo01.log' to
'/ora02/oraredo/O11DEV/redo01.log';
```

Update the control file by running the prior script:

```
SQL> @renlog.sql
```

You can select from V$LOGFILE to verify that the online redo log names are correct:

```
SQL> select member from v$logfile;
```

Here is the output for this example:

```
/ora02/oraredo/O11DEV/redo03.log
/ora02/oraredo/O11DEV/redo02.log
/ora02/oraredo/O11DEV/redo01.log
```

Make sure the directories exist on the new server that will contain the online redo logs. For this example, here's the mkdir command:

```
$ mkdir -p /ora02/oraredo/O11DEV
```

Step 14: Open the Database

You must open the database with the OPEN RESETLOGS command (because there are no redo logs and they must be recreated at this point):

```
SQL> alter database open resetlogs;
```

If successful, you should see this message:

```
Database altered.
```

Step 15: Add tempfile

When you start your database, Oracle will automatically try to add any missing tempfiles to the database. Oracle won't be able to do this if the directory structure on the destination server is different from the source server. In this scenario you will have to manually add any missing tempfile(s). To do this, first take offline the temporary tablespace tempfile. The file definition from the originating database is taken offline like so:

```
SQL> alter database tempfile '/u02/oracle/oradata/E64202/temp01.dbf' offline;
```

Next, add a temporary tablespace file to the TEMP tablespace that matches the directory structure of the destination database server:

```
SQL> alter tablespace temp add tempfile '/ora02/dbfile/O11DEV/temp01.dbf' size 100m;
```

Step 16: Rename the Database

If you need to rename the database to reflect the name for a development or test database, create a trace file that contains the CREATE CONTROLFILE statement and use it to rename your database. These steps are covered in detail in Chapter 4. The basic steps involved are:

    1.   Generate a trace file.

```
SQL> oradebug setmypid
SQL> alter database backup controlfile to trace resetlogs;
SQL> oradebug tracefile_name
```

    2.   Modify the trace file to include the SET DATABASE.

```
CREATE CONTROLFILE SET DATABASE "O11DEV" RESETLOGS...
```

    3.   Create an init.ora file that matches the new name.

    4.   ORACLE_HOME/dbs/init<newSID>.ora.

    5.   Modify the DB_NAME variable within the new init.ora file (in this example, it's set to O11DEV).

    6.   Set ORACLE_SID to reflect the new SID name (in this example, it's set to O11DEV),

    7.   SQL> startup nomount;

    8.   Run the trace file to recreate the control file (trace file from Step 2).

    9.   SQL> alter database open resetlogs;

If successful, you should have a database that is a copy of the original database. All of the datafiles, control files, archive redo logs, and online redo logs are in the new locations, and the database has a new name.

> ▪ Tip You can also use the NID utility to change the database name and DBID. For additional information, see My Oracle Support note 863800.1 for more details.

Summary

RMAN is an acronym short for Recovery Manager. It's worth noting that Oracle did not name this tool Backup Manager. The Oracle team recognized that while backups are important, the real value of a B&R tool is its ability to restore and recover the database. Being able to managing the recovery process is the critical skill. When a database is damaged and needs to be restored, everybody looks to the DBA to perform a smooth and speedy recovery of the database. Oracle DBAs should use RMAN to protect, secure, and ensure the availability of the company's data assets.

Restore and recovery are analogous to the healing process when you break a bone. Restoring is similar to the process of setting the bone back to its original position. This is like restoring datafiles from a backup and placing them in their original directories. Recovering a datafile is similar to the healing process of a broken bone—returning the bone back to its state before it was broken. When you recover datafiles, you apply transactions (obtained from archive redo and online redo) to transform the restored datafiles back to the state they were in before the media failure occurred.

RMAN can be used for any type of restore and recovery scenario. Depending on the situation, RMAN can be used to restore the entire database, specific datafiles, control files, server parameter files, archive redo logs, or just specific data blocks. You can instruct RMAN to perform a complete recovery or incomplete.

The last section in this chapter details how to use RMAN to restore and recover a database to a remote server. I recommend that you periodically attempt to test this type of recover. This will fully exercise your backup and recovery strategy. You will gain much confidence and fully understand backup and recovery internals once you can successfully restore a database to a different server from the original.

CHAPTER 20

∎∎∎

Oracle Secure Backup

Protecting and securing data is a core responsibility of a database administrator. DBAs must be proficient with backup and recovery skills. As shown in Chapters 17 through 19, you can use RMAN to manage and automate the backup of Oracle databases. RMAN is easily configured to back up and restore database files to and from disk.

Most production database environments will have an additional requirement to store database backups on tape. If your database server experiences a complete failure, you can use tape backups to restore and recover. Furthermore, tape backups are easily transported outside of the data center to provide additional protection in the event an entire data center experiences a complete failure (like a tornado or flood), the idea being that the tapes are safely stored offsite and can be brought back when disaster strikes.

To this end, Oracle provides a centralized tape backup solution, Oracle Secure Backup (OSB). This tool is a full-feature enterprise backup management system that automates the tape backup and restore of operating system files. More importantly to you as the DBA, OSB can also be configured as a media management layer with RMAN. This means you can implement RMAN and OSB together for the backup and restore of database files directly to and from tape.

There are myriad tape management solutions available. Why consider OSB? OSB is particularly compelling if one of your main goals is database backups to tape. Since OSB is an Oracle product, it is tightly integrated with RMAN. OSB is aware of the Oracle database file format and can take advantage of block level validation, encrypting backups as they are written to tape, integration with Oracle's Enterprise Manager, and so on.

OSB Editions and Features

There are two different editions of Oracle Secure Backup:

- Oracle Secure Backup Express
- Oracle Secure Backup

The Oracle Secure Backup Express edition is free (well, "free" when you purchase a license for the Oracle database). It provides core features such as backup and restore of operating system files and RMAN integration, but is limited to use on a single host with one directly attached tape device.

The Oracle Secure Backup edition requires an extra license and is well suited for tape backup and restore in a distributed server environment with heterogeneous file systems (Linux, Unix, Windows, and Network Attached Storage). The Oracle Secure Backup edition contains the following additional features not available with the Express edition:

- Backup and restore of database files in a Real Application Clusters (RAC) environments

545

- Integrated with Oracle Enterprise Manager Grid Control (with Oracle Database 10g Release 2 or higher)

- Supports multiple tape drives

- Encrypted tape backups

- Fibre-attached device support

- Fast backup compression (with Oracle Database 11g Release 1 or higher)

- RMAN medium level compression (with Oracle Database 11g Release 2 or higher)

- Networked backup of distributed hosts and tape devices

- Automated cartridge system library software (ACSLS) and automated rotation of tapes between multiple locations (vaulting)

If you are a small shop with just one production database server, then Oracle Secure Backup Express may satisfy your business requirements, whereas the full fledged Oracle Secure Backup edition is more suitable for environments with multiple distributed hosts that require advanced data protection requirements.

■ **Note** OSB is available on most Linux and Unix platforms as well as Windows. See My Oracle Support's certification matrix for a current list (https://support.oracle.com).

OSB Terminology

Take some time to familiarize yourself with the architectural terms used with OSB. This section gives a brief description of the major OSB parts, starting with an administrative domain.

OSB Administrative Domain and Servers

An administrative domain is collection of servers (hosts) that you manage as a single group for backup and restore operations. Within an OSB administrative domain, each server can be assigned one or more of the following roles:

- Administrative (admin) server

- Media server

- Client server (or client host)

For each administrative domain, as shown in Figure 20–1, there is only one administrative server that controls the backup, restore, and scheduling operations. An administrative server manages one or more media servers and one or more clients.

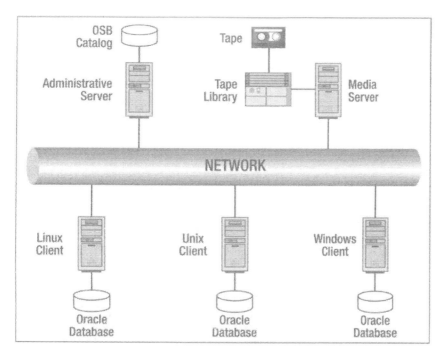

Figure 20–1. *Oracle Secure Backup Administrative Domain*

A media server is a host that has at least one physical tape device connected to it. Media servers are responsible for transferring data to and from the attached tape devices.

The client host is the server where the Oracle databases and file-system data reside that you want to back up (and potentially restore). For a single-host environment, a server can be the admin server, media server, and client host in the OSB administrative domain.

OSB Interfaces

There are four tools you can use to run and manage OSB backup and restore tasks:

- Enterprise Manager database control and grid control

- Oracle Secure Backup Web tool

- Oracle Secure Backup command line tool (obtool)

- Recover Manager command line tool (rman)

While the graphical interfaces are somewhat intuitive and easy to use, I'm a strong believer in learning how to run a tool from the command line. There's something about running a tool from the command line gives you a better understanding of the underlying architecture. This knowledge is invaluable when troubleshooting and diagnosing problems. In that vein, this chapter focuses on using obtool and rman to configure and run OSB backup and restore tasks operations.

Tip For complete details on all of the OSB interfaces, see the *Oracle Secure Backup Administrator's Guide* and *Oracle Secure Backup Reference* available at www.oracle.com/technetwork/database/secure-backup/documentation/.

OSB Users and Classes

An Oracle Secure Backup user is an account defined within an OSB administrative domain. These users are separate from operating system users. OSB user information is stored in the OSB administrative domain server. You are required to enter a username and password when accessing OSB through its interfaces such as obtool or OSB Web tool.

An OSB class is a set of privileges and rights granted to a user. Each user can be assigned to only one OSB class. OSB classes help maintain a consistent user experience across all servers in an administrative domain.

OSB Daemons

Oracle Secure Backup uses seven different background processes (daemons) to manage the configuration, backup, and restore operations. The executables that start the daemons are in the OSB_HOME/etc directory on each of the servers. These processes are described in this list:

> **Schedule daemon** runs only on the administrative server and manages the scheduled backups.

> **Index daemon** runs only on the administrative server and manages the backup catalog for each client.

> **Apache web server daemon** runs only on the administrative server and services the OSB web tool.

> **Service Daemon** runs on the administrative, media, and client servers. On the administrative server, it runs jobs as requested by the schedule daemon. When running on the media or client server, it allows for remote administration of the host.

> **Network data management protocol (NDMP) daemon** runs on the administrative, media, and client servers; it provides data communication between servers in the administrative domain.

> **Robot Daemon** runs only on the media server and helps manage communication to tape devices.

> **Proxy Daemon** runs only on the client server and verifies user access for SBT backup and restore operations.

Now that you have a basic understanding of the OSB architecture, you are ready to download and install the OSB software.

Download and Installation

You can download the OSB software from Oracle's Technology Network (OTN) site at www.oracle.com/technetwork/database/secure-backup/downloads/.

For the examples in this chapter, I downloaded OSB version 10.3.0.3.0, and saved the zip file osb-10.3.0.3.0_linux32.zip under a staging directory /stage/osb of my admin server in the OSB administrative domain. You can stage this binary file in a choice of your location on your server.

Oracle recommends installing the OSB software under the directory /usr/local/oracle/backup for Unix and Linux platforms and C:\Program Files\Oracle\Backup for the Windows platform. Once you have downloaded the OSB zip file and copied it to the appropriate directory, then you may proceed to the installation steps, as shown here:

1. To perform the OSB installation, you must logon as root.

```
$ su - root
```

2. If the uncompress utility is not available, create a link.

```
# ln -s /bin/gunzip /bin/uncompress
```

3. Go to the staging directory, and unzip the zip file that you downloaded from OTN.

```
# cd /stage/osb
# unzip osb-10.3.0.3.0_linux32.zip
```

4. If the OSB home directory does not exist, create the directory.

```
# mkdir -p /usr/local/oracle/backup
```

5. Go to the OSB home directory and run the setup script.

```
# cd /usr/local/oracle/backup
# /stage/osb/osb-10.3.0.3.0_linux32/setup
```

The following output is displayed:

```
Welcome to Oracle's setup program for Oracle Secure Backup.  This
program loads Oracle Secure Backup software from the CD-ROM to a
filesystem directory of your choosing.
This CD-ROM contains Oracle Secure Backup version 10.3.0.3.0_LINUX32.
Please wait a moment while I learn about this host... done.
- - - - - - - - - - - - - - - - - - - - - - - - - - - - - - - -
    1. linux32
       administrative server, media server, client
- - - - - - - - - - - - - - - - - - - - - - - - - - - - - - - -
Loading Oracle Secure Backup installation tools... done.
Loading linux32 administrative server, media server, client... done.
- - - - - - - - - - - - - - - - - - - - - - - - - - - - - - - -
Oracle Secure Backup has installed a new obparameters file.
Your previous version has been saved as install/obparameters.savedbysetup.
Any changes you have made to the previous version must be
made to the new obparameters file.
Would you like the opportunity to edit the obparameters file
Please answer 'yes' or 'no' [no]:
```

6. Since you are not modifying the obparameters file, accept the default parameters by pressing the Enter key. The following output is displayed:

```
Loading of Oracle Secure Backup software from CD-ROM is complete.
You may unmount and remove the CD-ROM.
Would you like to continue Oracle Secure Backup installation with
'installob' now?  (The Oracle Secure Backup Installation Guide
contains complete information about installob.)
Please answer 'yes' or 'no' [yes]:
```

7. Press the Enter key to proceed with running the installob. The following output is displayed:

```
Welcome to installob, Oracle Secure Backup's installation program.
For most questions, a default answer appears enclosed in square brackets.
Press Enter to select this answer.
Please wait a few seconds while I learn about this machine... done.

Have you already reviewed and customized install/obparameters for your
Oracle Secure Backup installation [yes]?
```

8. Press Enter to proceed with the OSB installation. The following output is displayed:

```
Oracle Secure Backup is already installed on this machine (BLLNX4).
Would you like to re-install it preserving current configuration data[no]?
```

9. If OSB is already installed and you are performing an OSB upgrade, enter yes to retain the previous configuration. The following output is displayed:

```
Oracle Secure Backup's Web server has been loaded, but is not yet configured.
Choose from one of the following options. The option you choose defines
the software components to be installed.
Configuration of this host is required after installation completes.
You can install the software on this host in one of the following ways:
   (a) administrative server, media server and client
   (b) media server and client
   (c) client
If you are not sure which option to choose, please refer to the Oracle
Secure Backup Installation Guide. (a,b or c) [a]? a
```

10. Press Enter to accept the default value a, which is to configure the server as the administrative server, media server, and client. The following output is displayed:

```
Beginning the installation.  This will take just a minute and will produce
several lines of informational output.

Installing Oracle Secure Backup on BLLNX4 (Linux version 2.6.9-67.EL)

You must now enter a password for the Oracle Secure Backup admin user.
Oracle suggests you choose a password of at least eight characters in length,
containing a mixture of alphabetic and numeric characters.

Please enter the admin password:
Re-type password for verification:
```

11. Enter the password twice for the admin user. The following output is displayed:

```
You should now enter an email address for the Oracle Secure Backup 'admin'
```

user. Oracle Secure Backup uses this email address to send job summary
reports and to notify the user when a job requires input. If you leave this
blank, you can set it later using the obtool's 'chuser' command.

Please enter the admin email address: juan.cruz@oracle.com

12. Enter the email address for the admin user. The following output is displayed:

```
generating links for admin installation with Web server
checking Oracle Secure Backup's configuration file (/etc/obconfig)
protecting the Oracle Secure Backup directory
creating /etc/rc.d/init.d/observiced
activating observiced via chkconfig
upgrading the administrative domain (where required)
***************************** N O T E *****************************
On Linux systems Oracle recommends that you answer no to the next two
questions. The preferred mode of operation on Linux systems is to use
the /dev/sg devices for attach points as described in the 'ReadMe'
and in the 'Installation and Configuration Guide'.
Is BLLNX4 connected to any tape libraries that you'd like to use with
Oracle Secure Backup [no]? no
Is BLLNX4 connected to any tape drives that you'd like to use with
Oracle Secure Backup [no]? no
```

13. Since I am installing OSB on a Linux server, then I accept the default and type
no for both prompts. The following final output is displayed showing the
installation summary.

```
Installation summary:
    Installation  Host         OS       Driver      OS Move    Reboot
         Mode     Name         Name     Installed?  Required?  Required?
    admin         BLLNX4       Linux    no          no         no
Oracle Secure Backup is now ready for your use.
```

■ **Note** To remove the Oracle Secure Backup, as root run the uninstallob shell script located in the
OSB_HOME/install directory. The operating system variable OSB_HOME is commonly set to the
/usr/local/oracle/backup directory.

Command-line Access to OSB

All the examples in this chapter use either obtool or RMAN to access OSB and perform tasks such as
creating backups and restoring files. This section focuses on connecting to the obtool utility. The first
time you run the obtool utility, you will be prompted for the password of the admin user, which is the
default OSB user created when you installed OSB. When prompted, use the password you specified
when you installed the OSB software:

```
$ obtool
Oracle Secure Backup 10.3
login:
```

To launch obtool utility and logon to a specific user, use the -u option, as shown here. You will learn on how to maintain OSB users in the next section.

```
$ obtool -u apress_oracle
```

To verify the OSB user that you are logged in as, issue the id command:

```
ob> id
apress_oracle
```

To view a list of obtool help topics, enter the following command:

```
ob> help topics
```

Here is a small snippet of the output:
```
Help is available on the following topics:
        advanced        .. advanced and seldom-used commands
        backups         .. data backup operations
        backupwindow    .. backup window definition
        browser         .. file system browser
        checkpoint      .. checkpoint management
        class           .. user class rights
```
To exit the obtool utility, issue either exit or quit commands, as shown here:

```
ob> exit
```

OSB Configuration

Once OSB is installed, you can run a simple backup command. However, for an environment where security is one of the top priorities, you may want to change the OSB default settings first. Imagine that tight security is strictly enforced on your production database, and a single OSB user account is used to backup both production and test databases. You are in a vulnerable situation because a DBA on your testing team can restore the backup of your production database to another server and access the data from there. To increase security and better manage your tape backups, I recommend creating new user accounts and assigning specific roles, as well as creating media families and database backup storage selectors. These topics are discussed in the next several subsections.

Configuring Users and Classes

When OSB is installed, the default user account created is named admin, which has all of the privileges relating to OSB. For security reasons, create separate OSB user accounts to access the different environments, such as production, test, and development. Also, assign specific classes (or roles) to these users, such as admin, operator, oracle, user, and reader. Monitor them to limit their rights to modify OSB administrative domain configurations and perform backup and restore operations. Limiting rights ensures that a particular OSB user can back up the test database, but has no rights to, say, restore the production database.

To determine the rights of class admin, issue the lsclass command, as shown here:

```
ob> lsclass -l admin
```

Here is some sample output:

```
admin:
```

```
browse backup catalogs with this access:          privileged
access Oracle database backups:                    all
access file system backups:                        all
display administrative domain's configuration:     yes
modify own name and password:                      yes
modify administrative domain's configuration:      yes
modify catalog:                                    yes
perform file system backups as self:               yes
perform file system backups as privileged user:    yes
list any jobs owned by user:                        yes
modify any jobs owned by user:                      yes
perform file system restores as self:              yes
perform file system restores as privileged user:   yes
receive email requesting operator assistance:      yes
receive email describing internal errors:          yes
receive email regarding expired passphrase keys:   yes
query and display information about devices:       yes
manage devices and change device state:            yes
list any job, regardless of its owner:             yes
modify any job, regardless of its owner:           yes
perform Oracle database backups and restores:      yes
```

■ Note To display the complete syntax of an OSB command, issue the help command followed by the OSB command.

To create an OSB user, issue the mkuser command. In the following example, OSB user apress_oracle is created and assigned with oracle rights:

```
ob> mkuser --class oracle apress_oracle --preauth BLLNX3:oracle+cmdline+rman
```

The +cmdline attribute in the --preauth option grants the oracle OS user preauthorized access to obtool utility, while the +rman attribute grants Oracle Database SBT backups via RMAN. If no +rman preauthorization is defined for the server hosting the target database that you want to backup, then the RMAN backup fails with ORA-19511 error, as shown here:

```
ORA-19511: Error received from media manager layer, error text:
    sbt__rpc_cat_query: Query for piece u8lr5bs6_1_1 failed.
(Oracle Secure Backup error: 'no preauth config found for OS user (OB tools) oracle').
```

If you want to view all OSB users, issue the lsuser command:

```
ob> lsuser
```

Table 20–1 describes the various OSB commands used to maintain the OSB user accounts.

Table 20–1. OSB Commands to Maintain OSB User

Command	Meaning
mkuser	To create an OSB user.
lsuser	To display information about OSB users.
renuser	To rename an OSB user.
chuser	To modify the attributes of an OSB user.
rmuser	To delete an OSB user.

Configuring Media Families

The media family classifies and defines the characteristics of the tape volume, such as the volume ID, volume expiration, and write window. The volume ID, which is used by OSB to uniquely identify the tape volume, consists of the name of the media family affixed with a six-digit sequence number generated by OSB. For example, if the name of the media family is APRESS_BACKUP, then the first volume ID is APRESS_BACKUP-000001, the second is APRESS_BACKUP-000002, and so on.

There are two types of volume expiration policies: time-managed and content-managed. The tape volumes in a time-managed media family can expire after surpassing the expiration time; in a content-managed media family, they expire when all of the backup pieces on the volume are marked as deleted. For file-system backups, you must use a time-managed media family to let OSB manage the volume expiration. For RMAN backups, you must use content-managed media family to let RMAN manage the expiration of the backup pieces on the tape volume instead of OSB. This avoids inconsistency between the RMAN metadata and contents of the tapes.

To create a time-managed media family, issue the mkmf command. In the following example, media family APRESS_OS has 7 days of write-period and 14 days of retention period. This means the volumes of media family APRESS_OS will expire and are ready for recycling after 21 days since the first backup piece is created on the tape volume:

```
ob> mkmf --writewindow 7days --retain 14days APRESS_OS
```

To create a content-managed media family, issue the mkmf, as shown here. Since the default volume expiration policy is content-managed, you can omit the --contentmanaged option.

```
ob> mkmf --contentmanaged APRESS_RMAN
```

Table 20–2 describes OSB commands used to maintain the media families.

Table 20–2. OSB Commands to Maintain Media Family

Command	Meaning
mkmf	To create a media family.
lsmf	To display information about media families.
renmf	To rename a media family.
chmf	To modify the attributes of a media family.
rmmf	To delete a media family.

To increase security and better manage your tape backups, you may create separate media families for different environments, such as production, test, and development. In this way, the backup of the production database and test database are not sharing the same tape volumes.

Configuring Database Backup Storage Selector

The default media family for RMAN backup is RMAN-DEFAULT. To use a different media family when running RMAN backup, create a database backup storage selector using the mkssel command. In the following example, the database backup storage selector name is BLLNX3-DB11R2.ssel, which assigns the media family APRESS_RMAN for RMAN backups on Oracle database DB11R2 hosted on client server BLLNX3:

```
ob> mkssel --host BLLNX3 --dbname DB11R2 --family APRESS_RMAN BLLNX3-DB11R2.ssel
```

■ **Note** If an RMAN backup matches the Oracle database and/or client host defined on a database backup storage selector, then you don't have to pass the OS environment variable OB_MEDIA_FAMILY parameter when allocating the RMAN channel for SBT_TAPE.

Refer to Table 20–3 for descriptions of OSB commands related to maintaining the database backup storage selector.

Table 20-3. OSB Commands to Maintain Database Backup Storage Selector

Command	Meaning
mkssel	To create a database backup storage selector.
lsssel	To display information about database backup storage selectors.
renssel	To rename a database backup storage selector.
chssel	To modify the attributes of a database backup storage selector.
rmssel	To delete a database backup storage selector.

Database Backup

In Chapter 18, you learned how to use RMAN to back up database files to disk. In this section, you will use OSB and RMAN to create backups on tape. There are two ways to configure RMAN for a backup to tape:

- Allocating a channel

- Configuring a channel

The first option is to allocate an RMAN channel for SBT_TAPE inside the run{} block. In the following example, the media family APRESS_RMAN is passed as a parameter to the environment variable OB_MEDIA_FAMILY. The tape volumes will have a volume ID of APRESS_RMAN affixed with a six-digit sequence number generated by OSB.

```
RMAN> run {
  allocate channel t1 type sbt_tape parms 'ENV=(OB_MEDIA_FAMILY=APRESS_RMAN)';
  backup database;
}
```

You can configure multiple channels for SBT_TAPE equivalent to the number of available physical tape devices. However, if you allocate two channels and only have one physical tape device, the other channel will just wait for the tape resource to become available. You can also use the CONFIGURE command to set the RMAN channel for SBT_TAPE, as shown here:

```
RMAN> configure channel device type sbt_tape
        parms 'ENV=(OB_MEDIA_FAMILY=APRESS_RMAN)';
RMAN> backup device type sbt_tape database;
```

To monitor the backup jobs you have submitted, refer to the "OSB Job Monitoring" section in this chapter. For descriptions of other OSB media management parameters, refer to Table 20-4.

▪ **Note** If no media family is explicitly passed when allocating/configuring RMAN channel for SBT_TAPE or no Database Backup Storage Selector defined for the specific host and/or database, OSB will use the default media family RMAN-DEFAULT, which is created when OSB is installed.

Table 20–4. OSB Media Management Parameters

Parameter	Meaning
OB_MEDIA_FAMILY	To specify the media family that defines the characteristics of the tape volumes.
OB_DEVICE	To specify the tape drives to use during backup.
OB_RESOURCE_WAIT_TIME	To specify the wait time for resources to become available.
OB_ENCRYPTION	To specify the OSB encryption. If this is set, then OSB does not perform further encryption.
OB_RESTORE_DEVICE	To specify the tape drives to use during restore.

Database Restore

For RMAN restore and recover, you have to allocate an RMAN channel for SBT_TAPE. In the following example, the RMAN channel for SBT_TAPE is allocated inside the run{} block:

```
RMAN> run {
  allocate channel t1 type sbt_tape;
  restore database;
  recover database;
}
```

Another option is to run the CONFIGURE command. Unlike the previous example, you must include the PARMS clause in the CONFIGURE command (if you don't use the PARMS clause, a syntax error is returned):

```
RMAN> configure channel device type sbt_tape
        parms 'ENV=(OB_MEDIA_FAMILY=APRESS_RMAN)';
RMAN> restore device type sbt_tape database;
RMAN> recover device type sbt_tape database;
```

Suppose you have a scenario where the production server is completely gone due to a catastrophic event, but luckily you have an offsite tape backup of the database. In addition, you are not using an RMAN recovery catalog, and control file autobackup is disabled. You discover that the latest backup of the control file is corrupted, but you are able to restore the control file from a backup taken two days ago. After mounting the database, you realize that the latest RMAN backups taken yesterday are not in the list when you issue the RMAN LIST BACKUP command (because the control file restored was from two days ago and has no knowledge of yesterday's RMAN backup).

In this situation, the control file restored from a backup taken two days ago has no information about the backup pieces created on tape yesterday. To make the RMAN repository (control file in this scenario) aware of backup pieces on tape, do the following:

1. Configure a channel for tape.

2. Make the RMAN repository aware of the backup piece via the CATALOG command.

Next, issue the CATALOG DEVICE TYPE SBT_TAPE BACKUPPIECE command, followed by the name of the backup piece. In this example, one backup piece is cataloged:

```
RMAN> catalog device type sbt_tape backuppiece 'silr06fk_1_1';
```

If you have multiple backup pieces that you want to catalog, you must issue the CATALOG DEVICE TYPE SBT_TAPE BACKUPPIECE command for each individual backup piece. The key in cataloging the RMAN backup pieces on tape is you must know the exact names of the backup pieces.

■ **Note** As mentioned in Chapter 19, for disk-based backups, you can easily make the RMAN repository aware of multiple backup pieces via the CATALOG START WITH <directory> command. However, this technique only works for disk-based backups and not tape backups.

What if you don't know the names of the back pieces? One way to figure out their names is to check the RMAN log file generated during the RMAN backup. In the snippet of the RMAN log file shown here, the RMAN backup piece is silr06fk_1_1:

```
channel ORA_SBT_TAPE_1: finished piece 1 at 21-OCT-2010 08:29:35
piece handle=silr06fk_1_1 tag=TAG20101021T082105 comment=API Version 2.0,MMS Version 10.3.0.2
channel ORA_SBT_TAPE_1: backup set complete, elapsed time: 00:08:26
```

But what if the RMAN log file is not available? You can issue the lspiece command using the obtool utility. In the following example, the output is filtered to display only the backup pieces for the hostname BLLNX3 that hosts the database DB11R2:

The following is the snippet of the output of the LSPIECE command:

```
POID Database    Content      Copy Created      Host         Piece name
8830 DB11R2      incremental   0 10/21.08:23  BLLNX3        silr06fk_1_1
```

This listing shows information such as the creation date and backup piece name. In this example, the missing RMAN backup piece is silr06fk_1_1. After you catalog the missing RMAN backup pieces, you can proceed with the RMAN restore and recovery.

File System Backup

Like any backup job, you need to define the three Ws and one H. What data to backup? When to run the backup? Where to store the backup? How the backup runs? To accomplish these 3 Ws and 1 H using OSB, you need to create a dataset file, as well configure a backup window, a schedule, and a trigger.

Creating Dataset Files

Dataset files define the directories and files on the client hosts that you want to backup. In the following example, this dataset file specifies to include all files under the directory /home/oracle on the client hosts BLLNX1 except for files under the directory /home/oracle/temp and Oracle database-related files:

```
include host BLLNX1
include path /home/oracle {
    exclude path /home/oracle/temp
    exclude oracle database files
}
```

To create a dataset file named bllnx1_home-oracle.ds, perform the following steps using the obtool utility, as shown here:

1. Issue the mkds command and followed by the name of the dataset file.

```
ob> mkds bllnx1_home-oracle.ds
```

2. The vi editor is invoked, and a dataset template is displayed.

3. Comment out or remove all existing lines, and add the following lines:

```
include host BLLNX1
include path /home/oracle {
    exclude oracle database files
    exclude path /home/oracle/temp
}
```

4. Save the file by typing Esc key, : and wq!

5. The following prompt is displayed. Press the Enter key to confirm the changes.

```
Apply your changes, if any [yes]?
```

You just created a dataset file. For descriptions of other dataset commands, refer to Table 20–5.

Table 20–5. Dataset Commands

Command	Meaning
catds	To display the contents of a dataset file.
cdds	To change the dataset directory.
chkds	To check the syntax in a dataset file.
edds	To modify a dataset file.
lsds	To list the dataset file and dataset directory names.
mkds	To create a dataset file or dataset directory.
pwdds	To show the current directory in the dataset directory tree.
rends	To rename a dataset file or dataset directory.
rmds	To delete a dataset file or dataset directory.

Configuring Backup Windows

The backup window defines the range of time the scheduled backups are allowed to run. The default backup window is daily 00:00 to 24:00. If there is no backup window defined, the scheduled backups are not going to run at all.

For production servers, you may want the backups to run daily only between 1 a.m. and 5 a.m. when there is minimal database traffic. To define a range of time for your backup window, perform the following steps:

1. Remove the existing daily 00:00-24:00 backup window, since it overlaps the backup window you want to create by issuing the rmbw command, as shown here:

```
ob> rmbw daily
```

2. Issue the lsbw command.

```
ob> lsbw
```

There are no backup windows.
This result indicates that the daily backup window is already removed.

3. To create the backup window, issue the addbw command. The following example defines the backup window daily from 01:00 to 0500:

```
ob> addbw --times '01:00-05:00' ,mon,tue,wed,thu,fri,sat,sun
```

For other backup window commands, refer to Table 20–6.

Table 20–6. Backup Window Commands

Command	Meaning
addbw	To add a backup window.
chkbw	To check whether there is a backup window defined.
lsbw	To list the backup windows.
rmbw	To remove a backup window.
setbw	To modify a backup window.

Configuring Backup Schedules and Triggers

The backup schedule defines what data to backup, where to store the backup, and how the backup runs, while the triggers define when a backup is scheduled to run. For what data to backup, set the specific datasets. For where to store the backup, set the specific tape drives. If no specific tape drive is selected, then any available tape drive will be used. For how the backup runs, set the job priority and backup encryption options. The lower the value of the job priority number, the greater preference is assigned to the job by the scheduler. The default value of the job priority is 100 and no for the encryption option.

The following example uses the MKSCHED command to create a backup schedule named bllnx1_home-oracle.sched for dataset bllnx1_home-oracle.ds:

```
ob> mksched --dataset bllnx1_home-oracle.ds bllnx1_home-oracle.sched
```

After creating the backup schedule, create a trigger to define when to run the scheduled backup. The following example uses the CHSCHED command to define a trigger for schedule bllnx1_home-oracle.sched to run daily at 02:00 (2 a.m.). The -a option means the addtrigger, the –d option means day, the –t option means time, and the –f means media family.

```
ob> chsched -a -d daily -t 02:00 -f APRESS_OS bllnx1_home-oracle.sched
```

To display the information about the backup schedules, issue the lssched command, like so:

```
ob> lssched -l bllnx1_home-oracle.sched
bllnx1_home-oracle.sched:
    Type:               backup
    State:              enabled
    Dataset:            bllnx1_home-oracle.ds
    Encryption:         no
    UUID:               1ea82008-bfdd-102d-a743-0002a530c867
    Trigger 1:
        Day/date:       daily
        At:             02:00
        Backup level:   full
        Media family:   APRESS_OS
```

You just scheduled a backup named bllnx1_home-oracle.sched that is going to run daily at 2 a.m. To monitor the jobs, refer to the "OSB Job Monitoring" section in this chapter.

To remove a backup schedule, issue the rmsched command, as shown here:

```
ob> rmsched bllnx1_home-oracle.sched
```

Performing On-Demand File-System Backups

To run a one-time backup on a specific client host use the backup command. In the following example, the dataset file is bllnx1_home-oracle.ds, which was created earlier:

```
ob> backup --dataset bllnx1_home-oracle.ds --go
```

If you omit the --go option, the backup request is still in the queue. You can issue the lsbackup command to display the backup requests that are queued, as shown here:

```
ob> lsbackup
Item #    Save data
1         dataset bllnx1_home-oracle.ds
```

To forward the backup request to the OSB scheduler, issue the following backup command with the GO option, as shown here:

```
ob> backup --go
```

To manually back up the OSB catalog of the admin server, issue the following backup command:

```
ob> backup --level 0 --dataset OSB-CATALOG-DS --go
```

To monitor the backup jobs you have submitted, refer to the "OSB Job Monitoring" section of this chapter.

■ **Note** By default, OSB-CATALOG-SCHED is scheduled to run daily at 1 a.m. to backup the OSB catalog using the dataset file OSB-CATALOG-DS.

File System Restore

There are three options on how you can restore from a file-system backup:

- catalog-based restore
- raw restore
- obtar command

In a catalog-based restore, you provide the directory and file, which you can browse from the OSB catalog. In both the raw restore and the obtar command, you provide the volume ID and file number. The volume ID is the unique name (that contains the media family) assigned to a tape volume, and the file number is the number of the backup image on the tape volume. Both the catalog-based restore and raw restore are performed using the obtool utility, while the obtar commands are issued at the operating system prompt.

Performing Catalog-Based Restore

For a catalog-based restore, you can browse the OSB catalog to determine and verify the files you want to restore. In the following example, you want to restore the file /home/oracle/scripts/rmanbkup.sh of the client host BLLNX1. To restore the files using the OSB catalog, perform the following steps:

1. Set the host variable to BLLNX1, which is the source host.

```
ob> set host BLLNX1
```

2. Issue the cd command to navigate to the directory.

```
ob> cd /home/oracle/scripts
```

3. Issue the ls command to verify the files in the directory.

```
ob> ls -l rmanbkup.sh
-rwxr-xr-x   oracle.oinstall  782     2010/01/13.18:14 rmanbkup.sh         (0)
```

4. Issue the restore command.

```
ob> restore '/home/oracle/scripts/rmanbkup.sh' --go
```

To monitor the restore job, refer to the OSB Job Monitoring section (covered a bit later in this chapter).

Performing a Raw Restore

To restore a data using the raw restore, you must know the volume ID and file number where to extract the data from. However, you know that the backups are using a particular media family, which can make the search a bit easier.

In the following example, you are going to restore the file /home/oracle/scripts/rmanbkup.sh from a tape volume that has media family APRESS_OS.

1. Issue the lsvol command with --contents option to display the contents of the volumes associated to media family APRESS_OS:

```
ob> lsvol --contents --family APRESS_OS --nobarcode
VOID   OOID Seq Volume ID         Family    Created      Attributes
2845   2845 1 APRESS_OS-000001   APRESS_OS 10/21.04:41 open; closes 10/28.04:41
       BSOID File Sect Level Host        Size Created    Attributes
       31250   1 1      0 BLLNX1      208.6 MB 10/21.04:41
       31258   2 1      0 BLLNX1      208.8 MB 10/21.06:04
       31260   3 1      0 BLLNX1      210.1 MB 10/21.12:23
       31261   4 1      0 BLLNX1      210.1 MB 10/21.12:34
```

2. According to the output shown above, you want to restore from a backup taken on 10/21.06:04 (i.e. October 21 at 6:04am). The corresponding file number is 2, and the volume ID is APRESS_OS-000001. Issue the following restore command, as shown here. The -R option indicates a raw restore operation and does not use an OSB catalog, while the –F option means the filenumber, and the –v option means the volume ID.

```
ob> restore -R -F 2 -v APRESS_OS-000001 /home/oracle/scripts/rmanbkup.sh --go
```

To monitor the restore job, refer to the "OSB Job Monitoring section" of this chapter.

Performing an obtar Restore

When you run the OSB restores, they are actually translated to obtar commands in the background. The obtar commands are issued at the operating system level. The obtar command is seldom used to perform restore operations, since you need to provide the volume ID and file number, which is not readily available especially if you have no access to the OSB catalog.

In the following example, you are going to restore the file /home/oracle/scripts/rmanbkup.sh from the tape that has volume ID APRESS_OS-000001 at file number 2.

1. Issue the loadvol command to manually load the tape that has volume ID APRESS_OS-000001 to an available tape drive. Here I used tape drive vdrive8.

```
ob> loadvol -D vdrive8 --volume APRESS_OS-000001
```

2. To check the contents of the tape, issue the obtar command with -t option.

```
$ obtar -t -f vdrive8
```

3. To perform the restore operation using the obtar command, issue the following command with the -x option. The -F option means the file number, and the -k option avoids overwriting the existing file.

```
$ obtar -F 2 -x -f vdrive8 -k /home/oracle/scripts/rmanbkup.sh
```

4. Since you restore using the obtar command, which is executed at the operating system level, you can't monitor the restore job using the obtool utility. However, one way to verify whether the file is restored is to issue the ls OS command.

```
$ ls -l /home/oracle/scripts/rmanbkup.sh
```

OSB Job Monitoring

You submitted a backup or restore operation for an Oracle database using RMAN or file-system data using Oracle Enterprise Manager (OEM), OSB Web tool, or obtool utility, and you want to check whether the job is active, pending, or completed. To check the status of an OSB job, issue the lsjob command and catxcr command to show the details about the operation of a job.

Listing Jobs

To display the jobs that are still running, issue lsjob command with the --active or -a option. For other job states, use --complete or -c option for completed jobs, --pending or -p for pending jobs, --inputrequest or -i for jobs currently requesting input, and --all or -A to display all jobs regardless of the job state. For example, to list active jobs:

```
ob> lsjob --active
```

For RMAN jobs, use the --dbname or -d option to limit the output for a specific Oracle database. If you know the database ID, you can use the --dbid or -I option instead. This example uses the dbname parameter:

```
ob> lsjob --active --dbname DB11R2
```

In the following output, the State column indicates that the job is still running. Once the job is done without errors, the State column displays "completed successfully."

```
Job ID            Sched time Contents          State
----------------- ---------- ----------------- ----------------------------
apress_oracle/83.1 none      incremental backup running since 2010/10/22.22:13
```

For file-system jobs, use the --host or -h option to limit the output for a specific client host, as shown here:

```
ob> lsjob --active --host BLLNX1
Job ID            Sched time Contents      State
----------------- ---------- ------------- ----------------------------
apress_admin/36.1 none       backup BLLNX1 running since 2010/10/22.22:11
```

To monitor active jobs, use the lsjob command. If there are several active jobs running, you can filter the output by providing the job ID. However, if the job is already completed, you can use the same command, but you need to remove the -a option and provide the corresponding job ID. I usually run the lsjob command with the following options:

```
ob> lsjob -a -l -j -o -R -L -C
```

The prior command displays detailed information about the status of the job. Here is some sample output:

```
apress_oracle/83:
    Type:               database DB11R2 (dbid=4187425583)
    Scheduled time:     none
    Introduction time:  2010/10/22.22:12
    Earliest exec time: 10/22.22:12
    Last update time:   2010/10/22.22:12
    Expire time:        never
    State:              processed; Oracle job(s) scheduled
    Priority:           100
```

```
        Run on host:           (administrative server)
        Attempts:              0
        Log:
apress_oracle/83.1:
        Type:                  incremental backup
        Backup piece:          tclr1n5v_1_1
        Family:                APRESS_RMAN
        Encryption:            awaiting job completion
        Scheduled time:        none
        Introduction time:     2010/10/21.22:12
        Earliest exec time:    10/21.22:12
        Last update time:      2010/10/22.22:15
        Expire time:           never
        State:                 running since 2010/10/22.22:15
        Priority:              100
        Run on host:           BLLNX3
        Requires:              family APRESS_RMAN and any device
        Attempts:              4
        Processed:             744.7 MB
        Log:
    2010/10/22.22:12:35 Dispatching job to run on BLLNX3.
    2010/10/22.22:12:46 Drive or volume on which mount attempted is unusable.
    2010/10/22.22:13:52 Dispatching job to run on BLLNX3.
    2010/10/22.22:14:05 Drive or volume on which mount attempted is unusable.
    2010/10/22.22:14:52 Dispatching job to run on BLLNX3.
    2010/10/22.22:15:11 Drive or volume on which mount attempted is unusable.
    2010/10/22.22:15:52 Dispatching job to run on BLLNX3.
```

In the output shown above, the lsjob command displays all active jobs using the -a option. Aside from showing the information about the job ID, scheduled time, contents and job state, the -l option shows more information, such as the RMAN backup piece, media family, encryption status, priority number, the host where the job runs, and number of times OSB attempted to run the job. The --subjobs or -j shows the subordinate job (subjob), which is apress_oracle/83.1. The --progress or -o option shows the progress of the active job, which is 744.7 MB processed so far. The --requires or -R option show resources required to run each job, which is media family APRESS_RMAN and any device. The --log or -L option shows the log associated for the job, which is the log information shown at the bottom of the output. The --times or -C option shows all relevant times for each job, such as introduction time, earliest exec time, last update time, and expire time.

Showing Job Transcripts

Aside from the lsjob command to help monitor the OSB job, you can issue the catxcr command to gather detailed information about the operation of the job. The --folow or -f option shows the transcript as the file grows, which is useful when monitoring active jobs. The --msgno or -m shows the number for each line in the transcript. The --level or -l option indicates the message level, which is useful to generate additional messages for debugging or troubleshooting. For example:

```
ob> catxcr -f -m -l 0 apress_oracle/88
```

If you run an RMAN backup and allocated two RMAN channels for SBT_TAPE, then two sub-jobs are created. The lsjob command with the --subjobs option displays details for each sub-job. For example:

```
ob> lsjob --active --subjobs
Job ID          Sched time  Contents              State
--------------- ----------- --------------------- -----------------------------
apress_oracle/88 none       database DB11R2 (dbid=4187425583) processed;
Oracle job(s) scheduled
apress_oracle/88.1 none       incremental backup  running since 2010/10/22.23:34
apress_oracle/88.2 none       incremental backup  running since 2010/10/22.23:34
```

The prior output shows two sub-job IDs, namely apress_oracle/88.1 and apress_oracle/88.2, which is one for each of the two RMAN channels. To show the transcript of a particular sub-job, provide the sub-job ID apress_oracle/88.2, as shown here:

```
ob> catxcr -f -m -l 0 apress_oracle/88.2
```

Virtual Test Devices

You may relate to the expression "experience is the best teacher." You have read this chapter, and you want to try the OSB commands and examples yourself. However, you don't have a physical tape device connected to any test servers in your environment. In this situation, where you are going to install and experiment with OSB? Well, you can configure a virtual test device solely for testing purposes.

■ **Caution** You should not implement virtual test devices in a production environment. Oracle Support does not provide support for virtual test devices.

To configure a virtual test device, perform the following steps. In this example, the hostname of the media server is BLLNX3.

1. Logon as the oracle OS user at your designated media server of the OSB administrative domain.

```
$ su - oracle
```

2. At the OSB media server, create a directory that hosts the virtual storage elements and virtual tape devices. Make sure you have enough disk space on the mount point where you are going to create the directory.

```
$ mkdir /osb_vdevices
```

3. Logon as admin user to the obtool utility, and provide the corresponding password.

```
$ obtool -u admin
 Password:
```

4. Configure the virtual tape library by running the following mkdev command using the -t option to specify the device as a tape library and the -v option to specify as a virtual tape library. The -S option specifies the number of storage elements. The -I option specifies the number of export and import elements. The -o option specifies that the tape device is logically available to OSB. The -B option with the yes value specifies that the barcode reader is present. The -a option attaches the virtual library vlib1 to directory /osb_vdevices/vlib1 of host BLLNX3.

```
ob> mkdev -t library -v -S20 -I2 -o -B yes -a BLLNX3:/osb_vdevices/vlib1  vlib1
```

5. Configure the virtual tape devices by running the following mkdev command using the -t option to specify the device as a tape device and the -v option to specify as a virtual tape device. The -o option specifies that the tape device is logically available to OSB. The -l option specifies the name of the associated tape library. The -d option specifies the data transfer element (DTE). The -a option attaches the virtual tape vdrive1 to directory /osb_vdevices/vdrive1 of host BLLNX3. To configure additional virtual tape devices, run the same mkdev command. However, for the second virtual tape device, change the name vdrive1 and directory /osb_vdevices/vdrive1 to vdrive2 and directory /osb_vdevices/vdrive2, respectively, and so on.

```
ob> mkdev -t tape -v -o -l vlib1 -d1 -a BLLNX3:/osb_vdevices/vdrive1  vdrive1
```

6. Run the insertvol command to manually insert a volume to the tape library. The -L option specifies the library name, which is vlib1. Since there are 20 storage elements defined when the virtual library is created, then issue unlabeled 1-20 to insert 20 new volumes.

```
ob> insertvol -L vlib1 unlabeled 1-20
```

7. Issue the lsvol command to display the volumes in the tape library vlib1.

```
ob> lsvol -l -L vlib1
```

OSB Software Upgrades

You have an older version of the OSB installed and you want to upgrade to the current release. To perform an OSB upgrade, perform steps similar to installing OSB. However, before performing the OSB upgrade, make sure to backup the OSB catalog in the admin server and stop the OSB daemons and services at all hosts in the administrative domain. Also, upgrade the admin server first, then the media servers and client hosts.

For OS-specific commands to start and stop OSB services, refer to Table 20-7. You must have root privilege on Linux/Unix or be a member of the Administrators group for Windows to run these commands.

Table 20–7. OSB Service Shutdown and Startup Commands

Operating System	Shutdown Command	Startup Command
Linux	`/etc/init.d/observiced stop`	`/etc/init.d/observiced start`
Solaris	`/etc/init.d/OracleBackup stop`	`/etc/init.d/OracleBackup start`
AIX	`/etc/rc.d/init.d/OracleBackup stop`	`/etc/rc.d/init.d/OracleBackup start`
HP-UX	`/sbin/init.d/OracleBackup stop`	`/sbin/init.d/OracleBackup start`
Windows	`net stop observiced`	`net start observiced`

■ **Note** Oracle Secure Backup release 10.3 is not backward compatible with previous releases, such 10.1 and 10.2.

Summary

OSB is a tool you can use to back up and restore operating system files to and from tape. OSB is a full-featured tape management utility. OSB can be integrated with RMAN to facilitate the backup of database files directly to tape. This provides you with extra data protection in the event that the entire server or data center experiences a failure.

OSB is available in two editions: Oracle Secure Backup Express and Oracle Secure Backup. The Express version is available for use without extra licensing costs and is suitable for small shops with one server and one physical tape device. The full-fledged Oracle Secure Backup edition is suitable for distributed servers across multiple platforms (Linux, Unix, Windows).

You can access OSB through graphical tools like Enterprise Manager and OSB Web tool or through command line tools such as obtool. This chapter focused on demonstrating how to use the command line obtool for backup and restore operations.

This chapter concludes the section covering backup and recovery. The next chapter focuses on automating jobs and database troubleshooting.

■■■

Automating Jobs

In almost any type of database environment—from development to testing to production—database administrators rely heavily on automating tasks. Typical jobs that DBAs automate include the following:

- Shutdown and startup of databases and listeners
- Backups
- Validating the integrity of backups
- Checking for errors
- Removing old trace or log files
- Checking for errant processes
- Checking for abnormal conditions

Automating routine tasks allows DBAs to be much more effective and productive. Automated environments inherently run smoother and more efficiently than manually administered systems. DBA jobs that run automatically from scripts consistently execute the same set of commands each time and therefore are less prone to human error and mistakes. There are two scheduling utilities described in this chapter:

- Oracle Scheduler
- The Linux/Unix cron utility

This chapter begins with a section detailing the basic aspects of the Oracle Scheduler utility. This scheduler is available if you have an Oracle database installed. Oracle Scheduler can be used to schedule jobs in a wide variety of configurations.

Also contained in this chapter is a section detailing how to use the Linux/Unix cron scheduling tool. In Linux/Unix environments, DBAs often use the cron scheduling utility to automatically run jobs. The cron utility is ubiquitous and easy to implement and use. If you're an Oracle DBA, you must be familiar with cron because sooner or later, you'll find yourself in an environment that relies heavily on this tool to automate database jobs.

The last several sections in this chapter show you how to implement several real-world DBA jobs such as performance reporting, monitoring, and operating system file maintenance. You should be able to extend these scripts to meet the automation requirements of your environment.

Automating Jobs with Oracle Scheduler

Oracle Scheduler is a tool that provides you a way of automating the scheduling of jobs. Oracle Scheduler is implemented via the DBMS_SCHEDULER internal PL/SQL package. Oracle Scheduler provides you with a sophisticated set of features for scheduling jobs. The following sections of this chapter only cover the basics of using Oracle Scheduler to automate jobs with simple requirements.

■ Tip There are currently nearly 70 procedures and functions available within the DBMS_SCHEDULER package. See the Oracle Database *PL/SQL Packages and Types Reference* guide (available on OTN) for complete details.

Creating and Scheduling a Job

In Listing 21–1, a shell script is created that contains an RMAN backup command. This shell script is named rmanback.bsh and is located in the /orahome/oracle/bin directory. The shell script also assumes that there is a /orahome/oracle/bin/log directory available.

Listing 21–1. A Shell Script Containing an RMAN Backup Command

```
#!/bin/bash
# source oracle OS variables; see chapter 2 for an example of oraset script
. /var/opt/oracle/oraset  RMDB1
rman target / <<EOF
spool log to '/orahome/oracle/bin/log/rmanback.log'
backup database;
spool log off;
EOF
exit 0
```

In Listing 21–2, you use the CREATE_JOB procedure of the DBMS_SCHEDULER package to create a job. Run it as SYS (from the SQL*Plus).

Listing 21–2. Using the CREATE_JOB Procedure

```
BEGIN
DBMS_SCHEDULER.CREATE_JOB(
job_name => 'RMAN_BACKUP',
job_type => 'EXECUTABLE',
job_action => '/orahome/oracle/bin/rmanback.bsh',
repeat_interval => 'FREQ=DAILY;BYHOUR=14;BYMINUTE=11',
start_date => to_date('21-OCT-10'),
job_class => '"DEFAULT_JOB_CLASS"',
auto_drop => FALSE,
comments => 'RMAN backup job',
enabled => TRUE);
END;
/
```

In Listing 21-2, some of the parameters warrant additional explanation. The JOB_TYPE parameter can be one of the following types: STORED PROCEDURE, PLSQL BLOCK, or EXTERNAL. In this example, an external shell script is executed so the job is of type EXTERNAL. If you have a PL/SQL stored procedure that you want to run, you use the STORED PROCEDURE type. The PLSQL BLOCK type allows you to directly run an anonymous block of PL/SQL.

The REPEAT_INTERVAL parameter is set to FREQ=DAILY;BYHOUR=14;BYMINUTE=11. This instructs the job to run daily, at 1400 hours (military time) at 11 minutes after the hour (in other words, to run daily at 2:11 p.m.). The REPEAT_INTERVAL parameter of the CREATE_JOB is capable of implementing sophisticated calendaring frequencies. For example, it supports a variety of yearly, monthly, weekly, daily, hourly, minutely, and secondly schedules. The Oracle Database *PL/SQL Packages and Types Reference* guide contains several pages of syntax details for just the REPEAT_INTERVAL parameter.

The JOB_CLASS parameter specifies which job class to assign the job to. Typically, you would create a job class to provide a method for a job to automatically inherit attributes by virtue of being assigned to a particular class. For example, you might want all jobs in a particular class to have the same logging level or purge log files in the same manner. There's a default job class that can be used if you haven't created any job classes. This example uses the default job class.

The AUTO_DROP parameter is set to FALSE in this example. This instructs the Oracle Scheduler to not automatically drop the job after it runs. I want this job to persist and run at the scheduled frequency.

Viewing Job Details

To view details about how a job is configured, query the DBA_SCHEDULER_JOBS view. Listing 21-3 selects information for the RMAN_BACKUP job:

Listing 21-3. *Information for the RMAN_BACKUP Job*

```
SELECT
  job_name
 ,last_start_date
 ,last_run_duration
 ,next_run_date
 ,repeat_interval
FROM dba_scheduler_jobs
WHERE job_name='RMAN_BACKUP';
```

Here is a snippet of the output (the output has been wrapped to fit on the page):

```
JOB_NAME     LAST_START_DATE LAST_RUN_DURATION NEXT_RUN_DATE     REPEAT_INTERVAL
-----------  --------------- ----------------- -----------------  ----------------
RMAN_BACKUP 21-OCT-10 02.12 +000000000 00:00: 22-OCT-10 02.11.0 FREQ=DAILY;BYHOUR
            .59.257151 PM - 41.933585         0.300000 PM -06:0 =14;BYMINUTE=11
            06:00                             0
```

Each time a job runs, a record of the job execution is logged in the data dictionary. To check on the each statuses of job executions, query DBA_SCHEDULER_JOB_LOG. There should be one entry for every time a job has run, like so:

```
SELECT
 job_name
,log_date
,operation
,status
FROM dba_scheduler_job_log
WHERE job_name='RMAN_BACKUP';
```

Here is some sample output:

```
OB_NAME     LOG_DATE                                OPERATION STATUS
----------- --------------------------------------- --------- ---------
RMAN_BACKUP 21-OCT-10 02.13.41.196695 PM -06:00     RUN       SUCCEEDED
```

Modifying Job Logging History

By default, Oracle Scheduler keeps 30 days worth of log history. You can modify the default retention period via the SET_SCHEDULER_ATTRIBUTE procedure. For example, this changes the default number of days to 15:

```
SQL> exec dbms_scheduler.set_scheduler_attribute('log_history',15);
```

To completely remove the contents of the log history, use the PURGE_LOG procedure:

```
SQL> exec dbms_scheduler.purge_log();
```

Modifying a Job

You can modify various attributes of a job via the SET_ATTRIBUTE procedure. This example modifies the RMAN_BACKUP job to run weekly on Monday:

```
BEGIN
  dbms_scheduler.set_attribute(
    name=>'RMAN_BACKUP'
    ,attribute=>'repeat_interval'
    ,value=>'freq=weekly; byday=mon');
END;
/
```

For this particular example, you can verify the change by selecting the REPEAT_INTERVAL column from DBA_SCHEDULER_JOBS. The following is the output from running query from the prior section of Viewing Job Details:

```
JOB_NAME    LAST_START_DATE LAST_RUN_DURATION NEXT_RUN_DATE     REPEAT_INTERVAL
----------- --------------- ----------------- ----------------- -----------------
RMAN_BACKUP 21-OCT-10 02.12 +000000000 00:00: 25-OCT-10 12.00.0 freq=weekly; byda
            .59.257151 PM - 41.933585         0.500000 AM -06:0 y=mon
            06:00                             0
```

From the prior output, the job will run on the next Monday, and since there was no BYHOUR and BYMINUTE options specified (when modifying the job), it is now scheduled to run at the default time of 12:00 a.m.

Stopping a Job

If you have a job that has been running for an abnormally long time, you may want to abort it. Use the STOP_JOB procedure to stop a currently running job. This example stops the RMAN_BACKUP job while it is running:

```
SQL> exec dbms_scheduler.stop_job(job_name=>'RMAN_BACKUP');
```

The STATUS column of DBA_SCHEDULER_JOB_LOG will show STOPPED for jobs stopped using the STOP_JOB procedure.

Disabling a Job

You may want to temporarily disable a job because it's not running correctly. You want to ensure that the job does not run while you're troubleshooting the issue. Use the DISABLE procedure to disable a job:

```
SQL> exec dbms_scheduler.disable('RMAN_BACKUP');
```

If the job is currently running, consider stopping the job first or using the FORCE option of the DISABLE procedure:

```
SQL> exec dbms_scheduler.disable(name=>'RMAN_BACKUP',force=>true);
```

Enabling a Job

You can enable a previously disabled job via the ENABLE procedure of the DBMS_SCHEDULER package. This example re-enables the RMAN_BACKUP job:

```
SQL> exec dbms_scheduler.enable(name=>'RMAN_BACKUP');
```

■ Tip You can check to see if a job has been disabled or enabled by selecting the ENABLED column from DBA_SCHEDULER_JOBS.

Copying a Job

If you have a current job that you want to clone, you can use the COPY_JOB procedure to accomplish this. This procedure takes two arguments: the old job name and the new job name. Here's an example of copying a job where RMAN_BACKUP is a previously created job and RMAN_NEW_BACK is the new job that will be created:

```
begin
  dbms_scheduler.copy_job('RMAN_BACKUP','RMAN_NEW_BACK');
end;
/
```

The copied job will be created but not enabled. You must enable the job first (see the prior section in this chapter) before it will run.

Running a Job Manually

You can manually run a job outside of its regular schedule. You might want to do this to test the job to ensure that it's working correctly. Use the RUN_JOB procedure to manually initiate a job. This example manually runs the previously created RMAN_BACKUP job:

```
BEGIN
  DBMS_SCHEDULER.RUN_JOB(
  JOB_NAME => 'RMAN_BACKUP',
  USE_CURRENT_SESSION => FALSE);
END;
/
```

The USE_CURRENT_SESSION parameter instructs Oracle Scheduler to run the job as the current user (or not). A value of FALSE means run the job as the user it would run as when regularly scheduled (asynchronously).

Deleting a Job

If you no longer require a job, you should delete it from the scheduler. Use the DROP_JOB procedure to permanently remove a job. This example removes the RMAN_BACKUP job:

```
BEGIN
  dbms_scheduler.drop_job(job_name=>'RMAN_BACKUP');
END;
/
```

The code will drop the job and remove any information regarding the dropped job from the DBA_SCHEDULER_JOBS view.

Oracle Scheduler versus cron

DBAs often debate whether they should use Oracle Scheduler or the Linux/Unix cron utility for scheduling and automating tasks. The benefits that Oracle Scheduler has over cron include the following:

- Can make the execution of a job dependent on the completion of another job

- Robust resource balancing and flexible scheduling features

- Can run jobs based on a database event

- The Oracle Scheduler DBMS_SCHEDULER PL/SQL package syntax works the same regardless of the OS

- Can run status reports using the data dictionary

- If working in clustered environment, no need to worry about synchronizing multiple cron tables for each node in the cluster

- Can be maintained and monitored via Enterprise Manager

The Oracle Scheduler is implemented via the DBMS_SCHEDULER PL/SQL package. It's fairly easy to create and maintain jobs using this utility (as shown previously in this chapter). While Oracle Scheduler has many benefits, many DBAs prefer to use a scheduling utility such as cron. The advantages of using cron include the following:

- Easy to use; simple, tried and true; only takes seconds to create and/or modify jobs

- Almost universally available on all Linux/Unix boxes; for the most part, runs nearly identically regardless of the Linux/Unix platform (yes, there are minor differences)

- Database agnostic; operates independently of the database and works the same regardless of the database vendor or database version

- Works whether the database is available or not

The prior lists aren't comprehensive, but should give you a flavor of the uses of each scheduling tool. I prefer to use cron, but if you require a more sophisticated scheduler, then consider using Oracle Scheduler. The following sections in this chapter provide information on how to implement and schedule automated jobs via cron.

Automating Jobs via cron

The cron program is a job-scheduling utility that is ubiquitous in Linux/Unix environments. This tool derives its name from *chronos* (the Greek word for time). The cron (the geek word for scheduler) tool allows you to schedule scripts or commands to run at a specified time and repeat at a designated frequency.

How cron Works

When your Linux server boots up, a cron background process is automatically started to manages all cron jobs on the system. The cron background process is also known as the cron daemon. This process is started on system startup by the /etc/init.d/crond script. You can check to see whether the cron daemon process is running with the ps command:

```
$ ps -ef | grep crond | grep -v grep
root      3049     1  0 Aug02 ?        00:00:00 crond
```

You can also check to see whether the cron daemon is running using the service command:

```
$ /sbin/service crond status
crond (pid 3049) is running...
```

The root user uses several files and directories when executing system cron jobs. The /etc/crontab file contains commands to run system cron jobs. Here is a typical listing of the contents of the /etc/crontab file:

```
SHELL=/bin/bash
PATH=/sbin:/bin:/usr/sbin:/usr/bin
MAILTO=root
HOME=/
# run-parts
01 * * * * root run-parts /etc/cron.hourly
02 4 * * * root run-parts /etc/cron.daily
22 4 * * 0 root run-parts /etc/cron.weekly
42 4 1 * * root run-parts /etc/cron.monthly
```

This /etc/crontab file uses the run-parts utility to run scripts located in the following directories: /etc/cron.hourly, /etc/cron.daily, /etc/cron.weekly, and /etc/cron.monthly. If there is a system utility that needs to run other than on an hourly, daily, weekly, or monthly basis, then it can be placed in the /etc/cron.d directory.

Each user can create a crontab (also known as a cron table) file. This file contains the list of programs that you want to run at a specific time and interval. This file is usually located in the /var/spool/cron directory. For every user who creates a cron table, there will be a file in the /var/spool/cron directory named after the user. As root, you can list the files in that directory:

```
# ls /var/spool/cron
oracle   root
```

The cron background process is mostly idle. It wakes up once every minute and checks /etc/crontab, /etc/cron.d, and the user cron table files and determines whether there are any jobs that need to be executed.

Table 21–1 summarizes the purpose of the various files and directories used by cron. Knowledge of these files and directories will help you troubleshoot any issues as well as understand cron in more detail.

Table 21–1. Descriptions of Files and Directories Used by the cron Utility

File	Purpose
/etc/init.d/crond	Starts the cron daemon in system boot.
/var/log/cron	System messages related to the cron process. Useful for troubleshooting problems.
/var/spool/cron/<username>	User crontab files are stored in the /var/spool/cron directory.
/etc/cron.allow	Specifies users who can create a cron table.
/etc/cron.deny	Specifies users who are not allowed to create a cron table.
/etc/crontab	The system cron table that has commands to run scripts located in the following directories: /etc/cron.hourly, /etc/cron.daily, /etc/cron.weekly, and /etc/cron.monthly.
/etc/cron.d	A directory that contains cron tables for jobs that need to run on a schedule other than hourly, daily, weekly, or monthly.
/etc/cron.hourly	A directory that contains system scripts to run on an hourly basis.
/etc/cron.daily	A directory that contains system scripts to run on a daily basis.
/etc/cron.weekly	A directory that contains system scripts to run on a weekly basis.
/etc/cron.monthly	A directory that contains system scripts to run on a monthly basis.

Enabling Access to cron

Sometimes when system administrators set up a new box, they don't (by default) enable the use of cron for all users on the system. To verify whether you have access to access cron, type in the following:

```
$ crontab -e
```

If you receive the following error message, then you do not have access:

```
You (oracle) are not allowed to use this program (crontab)
```

To enable cron access as the root user, add oracle to the /etc/cron.allow file with the echo command:

```
# echo oracle >> /etc/cron.allow
```

Once the oracle entry is added to the /etc/cron.allow file, you can use the crontab utility to schedule a job.

■ **Note** You can also use an editing utility (such as vi) to add an entry to the cron.allow file.

The root user can always schedule jobs with the crontab utility. Other users must be listed in the /etc/cron.allow file. If the /etc/cron.allow file does not exist, then the operating system user must not appear in the /etc/cron.deny file. If neither the /etc/cron.allow nor the /etc/cron.deny file exists, then only the root user can access the crontab utility.

■ **Note** On some Unix operating systems (such as Solaris), the cron.allow and cron.deny files are located in the /etc/cron.d directory.

Understanding cron Table Entries

Your cron table is a list of numbers and commands that the cron background process (cron daemon) will run at a specified time and schedule. The crontab utility expects entries to follow a well-defined format. It's a good idea to add a comment line at the beginning of your crontab file that documents the required format:

```
# min(0-59) hr(0-23) dayMonth(1-31) monthYear(1-12) dayWeek(0/7-6) commandOrScript
```

In the previous line, the number (#) sign in a cron file represents the start of a comment. Any text entered after # is ignored by cron.

Each entry in the crontab is a single line comprised of six fields. The first five fields specify the execution time and frequency. These entries can be separated by commas or hyphens. A comma indicates multiple values for an entry, whereas a hyphen indicates a range of values. An entry can also be an asterisk (*), which indicates that all possible values are in effect. Here's an example to help clarify. The following entry sends an e-mail saying "wake up" every half hour from 8 a.m. to 4:30 p.m. Monday through Friday:

```
0,30 8-16 * * 1-5 echo "wake up" | mailx -s "wake up" larry@oracle.com
```

On some Linux systems, you can skip a value within a range by following the entry with /<integer>. For example, if you wanted to run a job every other minute, use 0-59/2 in the minute column. You can also use a slash (/) with an asterisk to skip values. For example, to run a job every fourth minute, you would use */4 in the minute column.

The sixth field in the crontab can be one or more Linux commands or a shell script. Or put it another way, the sixth column can be any combination of commands or a script that you can run on one line from the Linux command line.

The cron utility has a few quirks that need further explanation. The fifth column is the day of the week. Sunday is designated by either a 0 or a 7, Monday by a 1, Tuesday by a 2, and so forth, to Saturday, which is indicated with a 6.

The hour numbers in the second column are in military time format ranging from 0 to 23. The fourth column (month of year) and fifth column (day of week) can be represented with numeric values or by three-letter character abbreviations. For example, the following entry in the crontab uses three-letter character abbreviations for months and days:

```
0,30 8-16 * Jan-Dec Mon-Fri echo "wake up" | mailx -s "get up" larry@oracle.com
```

There also appear to be overlapping columns such as the third column (day of the month) and the fifth column (day of the week). These columns allow you to create flexible schedules for jobs that need to run on schedules such as the 1st and 15th day of the month or on every Tuesday. Put an asterisk in the column that you're not using. If you need to run a job on the 1st and 15th and every Tuesday, then fill in both columns.

If you're running a shell script from cron that contains a call to an Oracle utility such as sqlplus or rman, ensure that you instantiate (source) any required OS variables such as ORACLE_SID and ORACLE_HOME. If you don't source these variables, you'll see errors such as the following when your shell script runs from cron:

```
sqlplus: command not found
```

When cron runs a script as a user, it doesn't run the user's startup or login files (like .bashrc). Therefore, any script (being run from cron) needs to explicitly set any required variables. You can directly set the variables within the script or call another script (such as Oracle's oraenv script) that exports these variables.

■ **Tip** Don't schedule every job that you enter in cron to run all at the same time. Rather, spread them out so as not to bog down cron or the system at any particular point in time.

Scheduling a Job to Run Automatically

To schedule a job, you must add a line in your cron table specifying the time you want the job to execute. There are two methods for adding entries in your cron table:

- Editing the cron table file directly
- Loading the cron table from a file

These two techniques are described in the following sections.

Editing the cron Table Directly

You can edit your cron table directly with the -e (editor) option of the crontab command:

```
$ crontab -e
```

When issuing the previous command, you will be presented with a file to edit. This file is known as your cron table (or crontab). To schedule a script named backup.bsh to run daily at 11:05 p.m., enter the following line into your cron table:

```
5 23 * * * /home/oracle/bin/backup.bsh
```

Here the 5 specifies that the job will run at 5 minutes after the top of the hour. The 23 is military time specifying that the job should run in the 2300 hour window (in this example, 5 minutes after the hour). The next three stars * * * signify that the job should run every day of the month, every month of the year, and every day of the week.

Exit the cron table file. If your default editor is vi, then type :wq to exit. When you exit crontab, your cron table is saved for you. To view your cron entries, use the -l (list) option of the crontab command:

```
$ crontab -l
```

To completely remove your cron table, use the -r option:

```
$ crontab -r
```

Before running the previous command, you should save your cron table in a text file:

```
$ crontab -l > saved.cron
```

so you can refer to the saved file in the event that you didn't really mean to delete your cron table.

SETTING DEFAULT EDITOR

The default editor invoked to modify the cron table is dependent on the value of your VISUAL operating system variable. In this environment, the VISUAL variable is set to vi:

```
$ echo $VISUAL
vi
```

If the VISUAL operating system variable isn't set, then the value of EDITOR is used to define the default editor. Make sure that either VISUAL or EDITOR is set to your editor of choice. If neither VISUAL nor EDITOR is set, your system will default to the ed editor. In this scenario, you'll be presented with the following prompt:

```
26
<blank prompt>
```

Press the Q key to exit from ed. You can have the VISUAL or EDITOR variable automatically set for you when you log on to the system. You can also manually set the editor with the export command. The following sets the default editor to vi:

```
$ export EDITOR=vi
```

Consider putting the prior line of code in a startup file (such as .bashrc) so that your editor is always set consistently.

Loading the cron Table from a File

The other way to modify your cron table is to load it directly with a file name using the following syntax:

```
$ crontab <filename>
```

Here the crontab utility will load the contents of the specified file into your cron table. The recommended steps to modify your cron table with this method are as follows:

1. First create a file with the contents of your existing cron table, like so:

```
$ crontab -l > mycron.txt
```

Listed below is a sample entry from a cron table on a database server:

```
#------------------------------------------------------------------------
# min(0-59) hr(0-23) dayMonth(1-31) monthYear(1-12) dayWeek(0/7-6) commandOrScript
#------------------------------------------------------------------------
# RMAN backups, dk: 01-may-10, updated.
1 16 * * * /u01/oracle/bin/rmanback.bsh INV >/u01/oracle/bin/log/bck.log 2>&1
#------------------------------------------------------------------
# Tablespace check, sp: 17-jul-09, created.
5 * * * * /u01/oracle/bin/tbsp_chk.bsh INV 10 1>/u01/oracle/bin/log/tbsp.log 2>&1
#------------------------------------------------------------------
```

Take note of a few aspects in the above cron table entry. I always place a line at the top of every cron table (on every database server) that briefly describes the meanings of the date scheduling features:

```
# min(0-59) hr(0-23) dayMonth(1-31) monthYear(1-12) dayWeek(0/7-6) commandOrScript
```

I also separate each entry with a comment line. This makes the cron table entry much more readable:

```
#------------------------------------------------------------------
```

I also put a brief note (with my initials) describing what the cron job and the last time that I edited the cron entry:

```
# RMAN backups, dk: 01-may-10, updated.
```

If you manage dozens of database servers (each with its own cron job) with multiple DBAs, you'll need some mechanism (and it doesn't have to be sophisticated) for tracking who made changes and when.

2. Next, make a copy of your cron table before you edit it. This allows you to revert to the original in the event you introduce errors and can't readily figure out what's incorrect. This also provides you with an audit trail of changes to your cron table:

```
$ cp mycron.txt mycron.jul29.txt
```

3. You can now edit the mycron.txt file with your favorite text editor:

```
$ vi mycron.txt
```

For example, to schedule a script named backup.bsh to run daily at 11:05 p.m., enter the following into the file:

```
#------------------------------------------------------------------------------
# File backup, dk: 20-oct-10, inserted.
5 23 * * * /home/oracle/bin/backup.bsh
#------------------------------------------------------------------------------
```

    4.   When you are finished making edits, load the crontab back, as shown here:

```
$ crontab mycron.txt
```

If your file doesn't conform to the cron syntax, you'll receive an error such as the following:

```
"mycron.txt":6: bad day-of-week
errors in crontab file, can't install.
```

In this situation, either correct the syntax error or reload the original copy of the cron table.

Redirecting cron Output

Whenever you run a Linux shell command, by default the standard output (of the command) will be displayed on your screen. Also, if any error messages are generated, they will by default be displayed on your terminal. You can use either > or 1> (they are synonymous) to redirect any standard output to an operating system file. Additionally, you can use 2> redirect any error messages to a file. The notation of 2>&1 instructs the shell to send any error messages to the same location as standard output.

When you create a cron job, you can use these redirection features to send the output of a shell script to a log file. For example, in the following cron table entry, any standard output and error messages generated by the backup.bsh shell script are captured in a file named bck.log:

```
11 12 * * * /home/oracle/bin/backup.bsh 1>/home/oracle/bin/log/bck.log 2>&1
```

If you don't redirect the cron job output, then any output will be e-mailed to the user who owns the cron job. You can override this behavior by specifying the MAILTO variable directly within the cron table. In this next example, you want to aggravate the system administrator and send cron output to the root user:

```
MAILTO=root
11 12 * * * /home/oracle/bin/backup.bsh
```

If you don't want the output to go anywhere, then redirect it to the proverbial bit bucket. The following entry sends the standard output and standard error to the /dev/null device:

```
11 12 * * * /home/oracle/bin/backup.bsh 1>/dev/null 2>&1
```

Troubleshooting cron

If you have a cron job that isn't running correctly, follow these steps to troubleshoot the issue:

    1.   Copy your *cron* entry, paste it to the operating system command line, and manually run the command. Often a slight typo in a directory or file name can be the source of the problem. Manually running the command will highlight errors like this.

2.   If the script runs Oracle utilities, ensure that you *source* (set) the required operating system variables within the script such as `ORACLE_HOME` and `ORACLE_SID`. Oftentimes these variables are set by startup scripts (like `HOME/.bashrc`) when you log on. Since `cron` doesn't run a user's startup scripts, any required variables must be set explicitly within the script.

3.   Ensure that the first line of any shell scripts invoked from `cron` specifies the name of the program that will be used to interpret the commands within the script. For example, `#!/bin/bash` should be the first entry in a Bash shell script. Since `cron` doesn't run a user's startup scripts (like `HOME/.bashrc`), you can't assume that your operating system user's default shell will be used to run a command or script evoked from `cron`.

4.   Ensure that the `cron` background process is running. Issue the following from the operating system to verify:

```
$ ps -ef | grep cron
```

5.   If the `cron` daemon (background process) is running, you should see something similar to this:

```
root       2969      1   0 Mar23 ?        00:00:00 crond
```

6.   Check your e-mail on the server. The `cron` utility will usually send an e-mail to the operating system account when there are issues with a misbehaving `cron` job.

7.   Inspect the contents of the `/var/log/cron` file for any errors. Sometimes this file has relevant information regarding a `cron` job that has failed to run.

Examples of Automated DBA Jobs

In today's often chaotic business environment, it's almost mandatory to automate jobs. If you don't automate, you might forget to do a task or you may introduce error into the procedure if performing a job manually. If you don't automate, you may find yourself replaced or outsourced by a more efficient or cheaper set of DBAs.

When I automate jobs, usually the script will only send an e-mail in the event of a failure. Generating an e-mail upon success often leads to a full mailbox. Some DBAs like to see success messages. I usually don't.

DBAs automate a wide variety of tasks and jobs. Almost any type of environment requires that you create some sort of operating system script that encapsulates a combination of OS commands, SQL statements, and PL/SQL blocks.

The following scripts in this chapter are a sample of the wide variety of different types of tasks that DBAs will automate. This set of scripts is by no means complete. Many of these scripts you may not need in your environment. The point is to give you a good sampling of the types of jobs automated and the techniques used to accomplish a given task.

■ **Note** Chapter 3 contains basic examples of some core scripts that DBAs require. This section provides advanced examples of tasks and scripts that DBAs commonly automate.

Starting and Stopping Database and Listener

In many environments, it's desirable to have the Oracle database and listener automatically shutdown and startup when the server reboots. If you have that requirement, then follow the next several steps to automate your database and listener shutdown and startup:

1. Edit the */etc/oratab* file, and place a *Y* at the end of the entry for the databases you want to automatically restart when the system reboots. You might need *root* privileges to edit the file:

   # vi /etc/oratab

2. Place within the file a line similar to this for your environment:

   O11R2:/oracle/app/oracle/product/11.2.0/db_1:Y

3. In the previous line, O11R2 is the database name, and /oracle/app/oracle/product/11.2.0/db_1 specifies the directory ORACLE_HOME. The Y on the end of the string signifies that the database can be started and stopped by the ORACLE_HOME/bin/dbstart and ORACLE_HOME/bin/dbshut scripts. You can replace the Y with an N if you do not want the database automatically stopped and restarted.

■ Note With some Unix systems (such as Solaris), the oratab file is usually located in the /var/opt/oracle directory.

---

4. As *root*, navigate to the */etc/init.d* directory, and create a file named *dbora*:

```
# cd /etc/init.d
# vi dbora
```

5. Place the following lines in the *dbora* file. Make sure you change the values of variables *ORA_HOME* and *ORA_OWNER* to match your environment. This is a bare bones script of what you minimally would need to stop and start a database and listener:

```
#!/bin/bash
# chkconfig: 35 99 10
# description: Starts and stops Oracle processes
ORA_HOME=/oracle/app/oracle/product/11.2.0/db_1
ORA_OWNER=oracle
case "$1" in
  'start')
    su - $ORA_OWNER -c "$ORA_HOME/bin/lsnrctl start"
    su - $ORA_OWNER -c $ORA_HOME/bin/dbstart
  ;;
  'stop')
    su - $ORA_OWNER -c "$ORA_HOME/bin/lsnrctl stop"
    su - $ORA_OWNER -c $ORA_HOME/bin/dbshut
  ;;
esac
```

These lines look like comments in the dbora file, but are actually mandatory lines:

```
# chkconfig: 35 99 10
# description: Starts and stops Oracle processes
```

These lines describe the service characteristics of the script. The 35 means the service will be started in runlevels 3 and 5. The 99 indicates that the service will be started near the end of the init processing. The 10 signifies that the service will be stopped near the beginning of the init processing. A description is also required that provides textual information about the service.

▦ **Note** A Linux *runlevel* is a logical container for specifying which services will run when the system is started.

---

1. Change the group of the *dbora* file to match the group assigned to the operating system owner of the Oracle software (usually *oinstall* or *dba*):

```
# chgrp dba dbora
```

2. Change the permissions on the *dbora* file to 750:

```
# chmod 750 dbora
```

3. Run the following *chkconfig* command:

```
# /sbin/chkconfig --add dbora
```

Here, the chkconfig command registers the service script. This also creates the appropriate symbolic links to files beneath the /etc/rc.d directory. Use the --list option to display whether a service is on or off for each runlevel:

```
# chkconfig --list | grep dbora
dbora           0:off   1:off   2:off   3:on    4:off   5:on    6:off
```

This output indicates the dbora service is on for runlevels 3 and 5. If you need to delete a service, use the --del option of chkconfig.

▦ **Tip** If you want to automatically stop and start (on system reboots) other processes such as the Intelligent Agent, Management Server, and the HTTP Server, see My Oracle Support Note 222813.1 for details.

Automating the shutdown and startup of your Oracle database will vary depending on whether you're using tools like cluster software or ASM. The solution in this section demonstrates the typical steps to implement the shutdown and startup of your database in the scenarios where you don't have other software that manages this task.

■ **Note** If you are attempting to implement this shutdown/startup script on a non-Linux system (that is, Solaris, AIX, and so on), see Oracle's installation documentation specific to that operating system for the details on required symbolic links.

To test whether the dbora script is working, as root run the following to stop your database and listener:

```
# /etc/init.d/dbora stop
```

To test the startup of your database and listener, as root issue the following command:

```
# /etc/init.d/dbora start
```

As of the writing of this book, there is slight modification that you may need to make to the Oracle supplied ORACLE_HOME/bin/dbstart and ORACLE_HOME/bin/dbshut scripts. If you inspect these scripts with an OS editor (such as vi) you'll notice the following line:

```
ORACLE_HOME_LISTNER=$1
```

I would recommend that you change it to this:

```
ORACLE_HOME_LISTNER=${1:-$ORACLE_HOME}
```

This line instructs the scripts to accept a parameter if one is passed in. If a parameter is not passed in, then set ORACLE_HOME_LISTNER to the value contained in the variable of $ORACLE_HOME. This preserves the functionality of dbstart and dbshut and additionally makes these scripts work when called from dbora.

If you have the opportunity to reboot your system, I recommend you do that to ensure that the database stops and restarts correctly. There are log files created in your ORACLE_HOME directory named startup.log and shutdown.log. You can inspect the contents of these to verify that the shutdown and startup are working as expected.

LINUX SYSTEM V INIT RUNLEVELS

A Linux *service* is an application that typically runs in the background (conceptually similar to a Windows service). A *runlevel* is used to configure which services are running on a box. Typically, there are seven runlevels (0–6). The chkconfig command manages which services you want running in which runlevel(s).

When Linux starts up, the /sbin/init program reads the /etc/inittab file to determine the runlevel to which it should run at. The following is a snippet from /etc/inittab that shows the runlevels used by Red Hat (these are similar to runlevels in other Linux distributions):

```
#   0 - halt (Do NOT set initdefault to this)
#   1 - Single user mode
#   2 - Multiuser, without NFS (The same as 3, if you do not have networking)
#   3 - Full multiuser mode
#   4 - unused
#   5 - X11
#   6 - reboot (Do NOT set initdefault to this)
```

To set the default runlevel, specify N in the id:<N>:initdefault line in the /etc/inittab file. The following example sets the default runlevel to 5:

```
id:5:initdefault:
```

The runlevel of 1 is used by system administrators (SAs) when performing maintenance and repairs. The runlevel of 5 will start the Linux server with a graphical login screen at the console plus networking capabilities. However, if you have a problem running the display manager at the console—due to a video driver issue, for example—then you can start in runlevel 3 instead, which is command-line-based but still has networking services.

Most SAs who are security conscious operate their servers on runlevel 3. With the wide acceptance of VNC, SAs oftentimes do not see the benefit of running on runlevel 5. If an SA wants to take advantage of graphical utilities, they'll just use VNC (or a similar tool). Do not, by the way, attempt to set initdefault to either 0 or 6, because your Linux server will never start.

To determine the current runlevel, you can run who -r or runlevel as follows:

```
# runlevel
N 5
# who -r
run-level 5   Jun 17 00:29                    last=S
```

A given runlevel governs which scripts Linux will run when starting. These scripts are located in the directory /etc/rc.d/rc<N>.d, where <N> corresponds to the runlevel. For runlevel 5, the scripts are in the /etc/rc.d/rc5.d directory. For example, when Linux starts up in runlevel 5, one of the scripts it will run is /etc/rc.d/rc5.d/S55sshd, which is actually a softlink to /etc/rc.d/init.d/sshd.

Checking for Archive Redo Destination Fullness

Sometimes DBAs and system administrators don't adequately plan and implement a location to be used on disk to store archive redo log files. In these scenarios it's sometimes convenient to have a script that checks for space in the primary location and send out warnings before the archive redo destination becomes full. In addition, you may want to implement within the script to automatically switch the archive redo log location to an alternate location that has adequate disk space.

I've only used scripts like this in chaotic environments that have issues with the archive redo log destination filling up at unpredictable frequencies. If the archive redo log destination fills up, the database will hang. In some environments, this is highly unacceptable. You could argue that a DBA should plan and never let herself get into this type of situation. However, if you're brought in to maintain an unpredictable environment and you're the one getting the phone calls at 2:00 a.m., you may want to consider implementing a script such as the one listed in the section.

Before using the script in Listing 21–4, change the variables within the script to match your environment. For example, SWITCH_DIR should point to an alternate location on disk where you can safely switch the archive redo log destination in the event the primary destination becomes full. The script will send warning e-mails when the threshold gets below the amount of space specified by the THRESH_GET_WORRIED variable. If the archive redo log space falls below the value contained in the THRESH_SPACE_CRIT variable, then the destination will automatically be switched to the directory contained in the SWITCH_DIR variable.

Listing 21–4. Archive Redo Destination Space Survey Script

```
#!/bin/bash
PRG=`basename $0`
DB=$1
USAGE="Usage: ${PRG} <sid>"
if [ -z "$DB" ]; then
  echo "${USAGE}"
  exit 1
fi
# source OS variables
. /var/opt/oracle/oraset ${DB}
# Set an alternative location, make sure it exists and has space.
SWITCH_DIR=/oradump01/${DB}/archivelog
# Set thresholds for getting concerned and switching.
THRESH_GET_WORRIED=2000000 # 2Gig from df -k
THRESH_SPACE_CRIT=1000000  # 1Gig from df -k
MAILX="/bin/mailx"
MAIL_LIST="dkuhn@sun.com "
BOX=`uname -a | awk '{print$2}'`
#
loc=`sqlplus -s <<EOF
CONNECT / AS sysdba
SET HEAD OFF FEEDBACK OFF
SELECT SUBSTR(destination,1,INSTR(destination,'/',1,2)-1)
FROM v\\$archive_dest WHERE dest_name='LOG_ARCHIVE_DEST_1';
EOF`
#
free_space=`df -k | grep ${loc} | awk '{print $4}'`
echo box = ${BOX}, sid = ${DB}, Arch Log Mnt Pnt = ${loc}
echo "free_space        = ${free_space} K"
echo "THRESH_GET_WORRIED= ${THRESH_GET_WORRIED} K"
echo "THRESH_SPACE_CRIT = ${THRESH_SPACE_CRIT} K"
#
if [ $free_space -le $THRESH_GET_WORRIED ]; then
$MAILX -s "Arch Redo Space Low ${DB} on $BOX" $MAIL_LIST <<EOF
Archive log dest space low, box: $BOX, sid: ${DB}, free space: $free_space
EOF
fi
#
if [ $free_space -le $THRESH_SPACE_CRIT ]; then
sqlplus -s << EOF
CONNECT / AS sysdba
ALTER SYSTEM SET log_archive_dest_1='location=${SWITCH_DIR}';
ALTER SYSTEM SWITCH LOGFILE;
EOF
$MAILX -s "Archive Switch ${DB} on $BOX" $MAIL_LIST <<EOF
Archive log dest, box: $BOX, sid: ${DB} has switched.
Then ALTER SYSTEM SET LOG_ARCHIVE_DEST_1='location=<Normal Location>';
EOF
else
  echo no need to switch, ${free_space} KB free on ${loc}
fi
```

```
#
exit 0
```

The prior script assumes that you've set your `LOG_ARCHIVE_DEST_1` initialization parameter to set your archive redo location. If you're using a FRA for the location of your archive redo log files, you can derive the archive location from the `V$ARCHIVED_LOG` view, for example:

```
select
  substr(name,1,instr(name,'/',1,2)-1)
from v$archived_log
where first_time =
 (select max(first_time) from v$archived_log);
```

Typically I'll run a script to check the archive redo log destination once an hour. Here's a typical cron entry:

```
#----------------------------------------------------
# Archive directory check for fullness.
38 * * * * /u01/oracle/bin/arch_check.bsh DWREP
  1>/u01/oracle/bin/log/arch_check.log 2>&1
#----------------------------------------------------
```

(Note that the code should be on one line. It's placed on two lines in this book so that it fits on the page.)

Truncating Large Log Files

Sometimes log files can grow to very large sizes and cause issues by filling up critical mount points. The `listener.log` will record information about incoming connections to the database. For active systems, this file can quickly grow to several gigabytes. For most of my environments, the information in the `listener.log` file does not need to be retained for any reason. If there are Oracle Net connectivity issues, then the file can be inspected to help troubleshoot issues.

The `listener.log` file is actively written to, so you shouldn't just delete it. If you remove the file, the listener process won't recreate the file and start writing to it again. You have to stop and restart the listener to reinstatiate its writing to the `listener.log` file. You can, however, null out the `listener.log` file or truncate it. In Linux/Unix environments this is done via the following technique:

```
$ cat /dev/null >listener.log
```

The previous command replaces the contents of the `listener.log` file with the contents of `/dev/null` (a default file on Linux/Unix systems that contains nothing). The result of the prior line of code is that the `listener.log` file is truncated and the listener can continue to actively write to it.

Listing 21–5 is a shell script that truncates the default `listener.log` file and a named listener `appinvprd.log` file. This script is dependent on setting on the operating system variable `TNS_ADMIN`. If you don't set that variable in your environment, you'll have to hard code the directory path within this script:

Listing 21–5. Script to Truncate the Default `listener.log`

```
#!/bin/bash
#
if [ $# -ne 1 ]; then
  echo "Usage: $0 SID"
  exit 1
fi
# See chapter 2 for details on setting OS variables
# Source oracle OS variables with oraset script
. /var/opt/oracle/oraset $1
#
MAILX='/bin/mailx'
MAIL_LIST='dkuhn@sun.com'
#
if [ -f $TNS_ADMIN/../log/listener.log ]; then
  cat /dev/null > $TNS_ADMIN/../log/listener.log
fi
if [ $? -ne 0 ]; then
  echo "trunc list. problem" | $MAILX -s "trunc list. problem $1" $MAIL_LIST
else
  echo "no problem..."
fi
# A named listener log file
if [ -f $TNS_ADMIN/../log/appinvprd.log ]; then
  cat /dev/null > $TNS_ADMIN/../log/appinvprd.log
fi
if [ $? -ne 0 ]; then
  echo "trunc list. problem" | $MAILX -s "trunc list. problem $1" $MAIL_LIST
else
  echo "no problem..."
fi
#
exit 0
```

The following cron entry runs the prior script on a monthly basis:

```
#---------------------------------------------------
# Trunc log files once a month.
30 6 1 * * /orahome/oracle/bin/trunc_log.bsh DWREP
  1>/orahome/oracle/bin/log/trunc_log.log 2>&1
#---------------------------------------------------
```

(Note that this cron table entry is broken into two lines to fit on the page. In the cron table, it needs to be all on one line.)

Checking for Locked Production Accounts

Usually I have a database profile in place that specifies that a database account become locked after a specified number of failed login attempts. For example, I'll set the DEFAULT profile FAILED_LOGIN_ATTEMPTS to 5. What sometimes happens is that a rogue user or developer will attempt to guess the production account password, and after 5 attempts, this locks the production account. When this happens, I need to know about it as soon as possible so that I can investigate the issue and then unlock the account.

Listing 21–6 is a shell script that checks the LOCK_DATE value in DBA_USERS for a list of production database accounts:

Listing 21–6. A shell script to check the LOCK_DATE value in DBA_USERS

```
#!/bin/bash
if [ $# -ne 1 ]; then
  echo "Usage: $0 SID"
  exit 1
fi
# source oracle OS variables
. /var/opt/oracle/oraset $1
#
crit_var=$(sqlplus -s <<EOF
/ as sysdba
SET HEAD OFF FEED OFF
SELECT count(*)
FROM dba_users
WHERE lock_date IS NOT NULL
AND username in ('CIAP','REPV','CIAL','STARPROD');
EOF)
#
if [ $crit_var -ne 0 ]; then
  echo $crit_var
  echo "locked acct. issue with $1" | mailx -s "locked acct. issue" dkuhn@sun.com
else
  echo $crit_var
  echo "no locked accounts"
fi
exit 0
```

This shell script is called from a scheduling tool such as cron. For example, this cron entry instructs the job to run every ten minutes:

```
#-----------------------------------------------------
# Job to detect locked database accounts
0,10,20,30,40,50 * * * * /home/oracle/bin/lock.bsh DWREP
    1>/home/oracle/bin/log/lock.log 2>&1
#-----------------------------------------------------
```

In this way, I am notified when one of the production database accounts becomes locked. In this cron entry, the code should be on one line. It's placed on two lines in this book so that it fits on the page.

Checking for Files over a Certain Age

For some jobs that I run from shell scripts (like backups) I'll first check to see if another backup job is already running. The check involves looking for a lock file. If the lock file exists then the shell script exits. If the lock file doesn't exist, then one is created. At the end of the job the lock file is removed.

What happens sometimes is that there's a problem with the job and it aborts abnormally before the lock file can be removed. In these situations, I want to know if a lock file exists on a server that is older than one day old. The existence of an old lock file indicates there has been an issue, so I need to investigate. Listing 21–7 checks for any lock files in the /tmp directory older than one day.

***Listing 21–7.** A Script that checks for any lock files in the /tmp directory older than one day*

```
#!/bin/bash
BOX=$(uname -a | awk '{print $2}')
# find all lock files gt 1 day old.
# Find all lock files in /tmp, if found, find any older than one day
ls /tmp/*.lock 2>/dev/null && \
filevar=$(find /tmp/*lock -type f -mtime +1 | wc -l) || filevar=0
if [ $filevar -gt 0 ]; then
  echo "$BOX, lockfile issue: $filevar" | \
  mailx -s "$BOX lockfile problem" dkuhn@sun.com
else
  echo "Lock file ok: $filevar"
fi
exit 0
```

I usually check for the existence of a lock file on a daily basis. Here is a typical cron entry to run the prior script named lock_chk.bsh:

```
#---------------------------------------------------
# lock file count check
33 5 * * * /orahome/oracle/bin/lock_chk.bsh
   1>/orahome/oracle/bin/log/lock_chk.log 2>&1
#---------------------------------------------------
```

(Again, the code for this cron entry should be on one line. It's placed on two lines in this book so that it fits on the page.)

Checking for Too Many Processes

On some database servers you may have many background SQL*Plus jobs. These batch jobs might perform tasks such as copying data from remote databases, large daily update jobs, and so on. In these environments it's useful to know if at any given time there are an abnormal number of shell scripts running or an unusually large number of SQL*Plus processes running on the database server. An abnormal amount of job could be an indication that something is broken or hung.

The shell script in Listing 21–8 has two checks in it, one check for the number of shell scripts that are named with the extension of bsh, and another check for the number of processes that contain the string of sqlplus:

***Listing 21–8.** A Script That Runs Two Checks*

```
#!/bin/bash
#
if [ $# -ne 0 ]; then
  echo "Usage: $0"
  exit 1
fi
#
crit_var=$(ps -ef | grep -v grep | grep bsh | wc -l)
if [ $crit_var -lt 20 ]; then
```

```
  echo $crit_var
  echo "processes running normal"
else
  echo "too many processes"
  echo $crit_var | mailx -s "too many bsh procs: $1" dkuhn@sun.com
fi
#
crit_var=$(ps -ef | grep -v grep | grep sqlplus | wc -l)
if [ $crit_var -lt 30 ]; then
  echo $crit_var
  echo "processes running normal"
else
  echo "too many processes"
  echo $crit_var | mailx -s "too many sqlplus procs: $1" dkuhn@sun.com
fi
#
exit 0
```

The prior shell script is named proc_count.bsh and is run once an hour from a cron job:

```
#----------------------------------------------------
# Process count check, sqlplus process count check.
33 * * * * /home/oracle/bin/proc_count.bsh
  1>/home/oracle/bin/log/proc_count.log 2>&1
#----------------------------------------------------
```

(Again, the code for this cron entry should be on one line. It's placed on two lines in this book so that it fits on the page.)

Verifying Integrity of RMAN Backups

As part of your backup and recovery strategy you should periodically validate the integrity of the backup files. RMAN provides a RESTORE...VALIDATE command that checks for physical corruption within the backup files. Listing 21–9 is a script starts RMAN and spools a log file. The log file is subsequently searched for the keyword "error". If there are any errors in the log file, an email is sent.

Listing 21–9. A Script that Starts RMAN and Spools a Log File

```
#!/bin/bash
#
if [ $# -ne 1 ]; then
  echo "Usage: $0 SID"
  exit 1
fi
# source oracle OS variables
. /var/opt/oracle/oraset $1
#
date
BOX=`uname -a | awk '{print$2}'`
rman nocatalog <<EOF
connect target /
spool log to $HOME/bin/log/rman_val.log
set echo on;
restore database validate;
```

```
EOF
grep -i error $HOME/bin/log/rman_val.log
if [ $? -eq 0 ]; then
  echo "RMAN verify issue $BOX, $1" | \
  mailx -s "RMAN verify issue $BOX, $1" dkuhn@sun.com
else
  echo "no problem..."
fi
#
date
exit 0
```

The RESTORE...VALIDATE doesn't actually restore any files; it only validates that the required files to restore the database are available and checks for physical corruption.

If you need to also check for logical corruption, specify the CHECK LOGICAL clause. For example, to check for logical corruption, Listing 21–6 would have this line in it:

```
restore database validate check logical;
```

For large databases, the validation process can take a great deal of time (because it checks each block in the backup file for corruption). If you only want to check that the backup files exist, specify the VALIDATE HEADER clause, like so:

```
restore database validate header;
```

This command only checks for valid information in the header of each file that would be required for a restore and recovery.

Summary

Automating routine database jobs is a key attribute of the successful DBA. Automated jobs ensure that tasks are repeatable, verifiable, and that you are immediately notified when there are any problems. Your job as a DBA depends on successfully running backups and ensuring the database is highly available. This chapter includes several scripts and examples that detail how to run routine jobs at defined frequencies.

If you are a DBA who works in a Linux/Unix shop, you should familiarize yourself with the cron utility. This scheduler is simple to use and is almost universally available. Even if you don't use cron in your current work assignment, you're sure to encounter its use in future work environments.

Oracle provides Oracle Scheduler utility (implemented via the DBMS_SCHEDULER PL/SQL package) for scheduling jobs. This tool can be used to automate any type of database task. You can also initiate jobs based on system events or based on the success/failure of other scheduled jobs. I prefer to use cron for scheduling database jobs. However, you might have sophisticated scheduling requirements that dictate the use of a tool such as the Oracle Scheduler.

At this point in the book, you've learned how to implement and perform many tasks required of a DBA. Even if you manage just one database, no doubt you've also been embroiled in a vast number of troubleshooting activities. The next chapter of the book focuses on diagnosing and resolving many of the issues that a DBA encounters.

Database Troubleshooting

Database troubleshooting is a vague and general term that is applied to a wide variety of topics. It can mean anything from investigating database connectivity issues to detailed performance tuning. In this chapter, I will discuss the following troubleshooting activities:

- Assessing database availability issues quickly.
- Identifying system performance issues with operating system utilities.
- Querying data dictionary views to display resource intensive SQL statements.
- Using Oracle performance tools to identify resource consuming SQL statements.
- Identifying and resolving locking issues.
- Troubleshooting open cursor issues.
- Investigating issues with the undo and temporary tablespaces.
- Auditing database activities.

The above list doesn't encompass all types of database troubleshooting and performance issues that you'll encounter. Rather, I'll cover the most common types of database troubleshooting techniques that DBAs use and methods for diagnosing and resolving common problems.

Quickly Triaging

When I get a call reporting some vague performance issues with a database, I perform a few quick standard checks to establish whether there are really problems or not. Probably 70% of the time, it turns out to be something other than the database. Regardless, when somebody (developer, user, boss, and so on) reports an issue, the DBA must respond and verify that if there is an issue or if the problem is with a non-database component of the system.

■ **Tip** Keep in mind that you should have automated jobs that perform tasks such as verifying the database availability (see Chapter 21 for examples of automating DBA tasks). Automated jobs help you proactively handle issues before they turn into database downtime.

Checking Database Availability

The first few checks that I perform don't require the DBA to logon to the database server. Rather, they can be performed remotely via SQL*Plus and operating system commands. In fact, I perform all of the initial checks remotely over the network; this establishes whether all of the system components are working.

One quick check to establish whether the remote server is available, the database is up, the network is working, and the listener is accepting incoming connections is to connect via a SQL*Plus client to the remote database over the network. I usually have a standard database account and password that I create in all databases for use in such scenarios. Here's an example of connecting over the network to a remote database as the barts user with a password of l1sa; the network connect information is embedded directly into the connect string (where dwdb1 is the server, 1521 is the port, and dwrep1 is the database service name):

```
$ sqlplus barts/l1sa@'dwdb1:1521/dwrep1'
```

If a connection can be established, then the remote server is available and the database and listener are up and working. At this point, I contact whomever reported an issue and see if the connectivity issue has something to do with the application or something other than the database.

If the prior SQL*Plus command doesn't work, try to establish whether the remote server is available. This example uses the ping command to the remote server named dwdb1:

```
$ ping dwdb1
```

If ping works, you should see output similar to this:

```
64 bytes from dwdb1 (192.168.254.215): icmp_seq=1 ttl=64 time=0.044 ms
```

If ping doesn't work, there is probably an issue with either the network or the remote server. If the remote server isn't available, I usually try to contact a system administrator or network administrator.

If ping does work, I check to see if the remote server is reachable via the port that the listener is listening on. I use the telnet command to accomplish this:

```
$ telnet IP <port>
```

In this example, a network connection is attempted to the server's IP address on the 1521 port:

```
$ telnet 192.168.254.215 1521
```

If the IP address is reachable on the specified port, you should see "Connected to ..." in the output, like so:

```
Trying 192.168.254.216...
Connected to ora04.
Escape character is '^]'.
```

If the telnet command doesn't work, I contact the system administrator or the network administrator.

If the telnet command works, there is network connectivity to the server on the specified port. Next, I use tnsping command to test network connectivity using Oracle Net to the remote server and database. This example attempts to reach the DWREP1 remote service:

```
$ tnsping DWREP1
```

If successful, the output should contain the string "OK", like so:

```
Attempting to contact (DESCRIPTION = (ADDRESS = (PROTOCOL = TCP)(HOST = DWDB1)
(PORT = 1521)) (CONNECT_DATA = (SERVICE_NAME = DWREP1)))
OK (20 msec)
```

If tnsping works, it means the remote listener is up and working. It doesn't necessarily mean that the database is up, so you may need to log onto the database server to further investigate. If tnsping doesn't work, then the listener or the database is down or hung. At this point, I logon directly to the server to perform additional checks such as a mount point filling up.

Investigating Disk Fullness

To further diagnose issues, you need to logon directly to the remote server. Typically, you will need to logon as the owner of the Oracle software (usually the oracle operating system account). When first logging onto a box, one issue that will cause a database to hang or have problems is a full mount point. The df command with the human readable -h switch assists with verifying disk fullness:

```
$ df -h
```

Any mount point that is full needs to be investigated. If the mount point that contains ORACLE_HOME becomes full, then you'll receive errors like this when connecting to the database:

```
Linux Error: 28: No space left on device
```

To fix issues with a full mount point, first identify files that can either be moved or removed. Usually, I first look for old trace files; often, there's a gigabyte of old files that can safely be removed.

Locating the Alert Log and Trace Files

If you've set up all of the databases using consistent standards, there should never be issues with locating the alert.log and/or associated trace files. As seen in Chapter 3, I define an operating system function that will derive the location of the alert.log from the ORACLE_BASE and ORACLE_SID variables. For example, the following shell function works in either an 11g or 10g environment (assuming that standard Oracle OFA standards are in place for directory names):

```
#-------------------------------------------------------------#
# cd to bdump
  function bdump {
    echo $ORACLE_HOME | grep 11 >/dev/null
    if [ $? -eq 0 ]; then
      lower_sid=$(echo $ORACLE_SID | tr '[:upper:]' '[:lower:]')
      cd $ORACLE_BASE/diag/rdbms/$lower_sid/$ORACLE_SID/trace
    else
      cd $ORACLE_BASE/admin/$ORACLE_SID/bdump
    fi
  } # bdump
#-------------------------------------------------------------#
```

When the prior function is placed within a startup file (like .bashrc), you'll be able to immediately navigate to the directory that contains the alert.log and trace files, like so:

```
$ bdump
$ pwd
/ora01/app/oracle/diag/rdbms/o11r2/O11R2/trace
```

If you inherit environments that were setup by other DBAs, then you've probably noticed that the alert.log and trace files are sometimes located in non-standard locations. When looking for old trace files, I start by attempting to find the alert.log. Usually, there are associated trace files in the same directory as the `alert.log` file. Since the `alert.log` file has a specific and well-known name (alert_<SID>.log), it's usually easier to first find the it and then look for associated trace files.

For Oracle Database 11g and higher, there's a text version of the `alert.log` in the following standard directory and name:

```
<ADR base>/diag/rdbms/<DB_UNIQUE_NAME>/<SID>/trace/alert_<SID>.log
```

The ADR base location is defined by `DIAGNOSTIC_DEST` database initialization parameter. If you haven't set `DIAGNOSTIC_DEST`, then Oracle derives the value from the `ORACLE_BASE` operating system environment variable. If the operating system `ORACLE_BASE` variable is not set, then `DIAGNOSTIC_DEST` is set to the value of `ORACLE_HOME/log` (where `ORACLE_HOME` is an operating system variable that is almost universally set).

For Oracle Database 10g, the standard location for the `alert.log` is defined to be:

```
<ORACLE_BASE>/admin/<SID>/bdump
```

For Oracle Database 10g, the prior path is usually the same value as what the `BACKGROUND_DUMP_DEST` database initialization parameter is customarily set to. Typical values for the `ORACLE_BASE` operating system variable are `/ora01/app/oracle` or `/u01/app/oracle`. For example, here's an entry in the `init.ora` for the `DEVDB` database for the `BACKGROUND_DUMP_DEST` initialization variable:

```
background_dump_dest=/ora01/app/oracle/admin/DEVDB/bdump
```

However, nothing prevents an inexperienced DBA from setting parameters like `BACKGROUND_DUMP_DEST` to completely non-standard locations. For example, here's a setting from a database I was recently asked to maintain:

```
background_dump_dest=/oralogs08/dba/admin/bdump
```

Why would a DBA set a parameter like that to such a non-standard location? It really doesn't matter. You just have to be aware that DBAs sometimes enable features in ways that make maintenance much more difficult.

Regardless, if you can connect to your database through SQL*Plus, it's trivial to determine the location of even the most non-standard locations for the `alert.log`. This will correctly show the location of the `alert.log` for any version of the Oracle database:

```
SQL> show parameter background_dump_dest
```

How do you determine the location of the `alert.log` and trace files when the database won't start and the file has been placed in a non-standard (and not obvious) directory? In these situations, use the `find` command to locate the `alert.log` file. First, change directories to `ORACLE_BASE`:

```
$ cd $ORACLE_BASE
```

Next, use the `find` command to attempt to locate the file:

```
$ find . -name "alert*.log"
```

If you don't have `ORACLE_BASE` defined or the `alert.log` isn't in a somewhat standard location, then the prior command may not find any files. In this situation, perform a more system-wide global search. Navigate to the root directory of the box and then issue the `find` command:

```
$ cd /
$ find . -name "alert*.log" 2>/dev/null
```

In the prior command, you're inspecting all files on the operating system in an attempt to locate a file named with "alert" in the first part of the string and ".log" in the last section of the string. When performing a global search, an error will be thrown when the `find` command attempts to access files that it has no permissions to read. The `2>/dev/null` is useful because it redirects all error messages to the

/dev/null (bit bucket) file. The result is that you don't see volumes of error messages, and you only see output when find successfully locates a file that matches the string pattern.

When attempting to find the alert.log, you may find more than one file. This happens when inexperienced DBAs move the alert.log from a standard location to a non-standard location and leaves old files scattered throughout the operating system.

When you think you've located the correct alert.log file, check the date on it to ensure that it has been recently updated. Sometimes you find an alert.log, but it turns out not to be the current file. You can check the last update time with the ls command long listing:

```
$ ls -altr alert_<SID>.log
```

Once you have found the correct alert.log, inspect the most recent entries in it for errors and or look for trace files in the same directory as the alert.log file:

```
$ ls -altr *.trc
```

If any of these trace files are over several days old, consider moving or removing them.

Removing Files

Needless to say, be very careful when removing files. When trying to resolve issues, the last thing you want to do is make things worse. Accidentally removing one critical file can be catastrophic. For any files you identify as candidates for deletion, consider moving the files (instead of deleting) them. If you have a mount point that has free space, move the files there and leave them for a couple of days and then remove them.

If you have identified files that can be removed, first list out the files that you will be removed before you actually delete them. Minimally, I do this before removing any file:

```
$ ls -altr <file_name>
```

After viewing the results returned by the ls command, remove the file(s). This example uses the Linux/Unix rm command to permanently delete the file:

```
$ rm <file_name>
```

You can also remove files based on the age of the file. For example, say you determine that any trace files over two days old can be safely deleted. Typically, the find command is used in conjunction with the rm command to accomplish this task. Before removing files, first list out the result of the find command:

```
$ find . -type f -mtime +2 -name "*.trc"
```

If you are satisfied with the list of files, then add the rm command to remove them:

```
$ find . -type f -mtime +2 -name "*.trc" | xargs rm
```

In the prior line of code, the results of the find command are piped to xargs command, which executes the rm command for every file found by the find command. This is an efficient method for deleting files based on age. However, make very sure that you know which files will be deleted.

Another file that sometimes consumes large amounts of space is the listener.log file. Since this file is actively written to by the listener process, you can't simply remove it. If you need to preserve the contents of this file, then first copy it to a backup location (that contains free disk space) and then truncate the file. In this example, the listener.log file is first copied to /ora01/backups and then the file is truncated by:

```
$ cp listener.log /ora01/backups
```

Next, use the cat command to replace the contents of the listener.log with the /dev/null file (which contains zero bytes):

```
$ cat /dev/null > listener.log
```

Inspecting the Alert Log

When dealing with database issues, the alert.log should be one of the first files you check for relevant error messages. You can use either operating system tools or the ADRCI utility to view the alert.log file and corresponding trace files.

Viewing the Alert Log via OS Tools

After navigating to the directory that contains the alert.log, you can view the most current messages by viewing the end (furthest down) in the file (in other words, the most current messages are written to the end of the file). To view the last 50 lines, use the tail command:

```
$ tail -50 alert_<SID>.log
```

You can continuously view the most current entries by using the -f switch:

```
$ tail -f alert_<SID>.log
```

You can also directly open the alert.log with an operating system editor (such as vi):

```
$ vi alert_<SID>.log
```

Sometimes it's handy to define a function that will allow you to open the alert.log regardless of your current working directory. The next few lines of code define a function that locates and opens the alert.log with the view command in either an 11g or 10g environment:

```
#------------------------------------------------------------#
# view alert log
  function valert {
  echo $ORACLE_HOME | grep 11 >/dev/null
  if [ $? -eq 0 ]; then
    lower_sid=$(echo $ORACLE_SID | tr '[:upper:]' '[:lower:]')
    view $ORACLE_BASE/diag/rdbms/$lower_sid/$ORACLE_SID/trace/alert_$ORACLE_SID.log
  else
    view $ORACLE_BASE/admin/$ORACLE_SID/bdump/alert_$ORACLE_SID.log
  fi
  } # valert
#------------------------------------------------------------#
```

Usually the prior lines of code are placed in a startup file so that the function is automatically defined when you logon to a server. Once defined, you can view the alert.log by typing in:

```
$ valert
```

When inspecting the bottom of the alert.log, look for errors that indicate issues with:

- Archiver process hung due to inadequate disk space.
- File system out of space.
- Tablespace out of space.

- Running out of memory in the buffer cache or shared pool.

- Media error indicating a datafile is missing or damaged.

- For example, here's an error indicating there is an issue writing an archive redo log:

```
ORA-19502: write error on file "/ora01/fra/O11R2/archivelog/...
```

For a serious error message listed in the alert.log file there is almost always a corresponding trace file. For example, here is the accompanying message to the prior error message:

```
Errors in file
/oracle/app/oracle/diag/rdbms/o11r2/O11R2/trace/O11R2_arc0_4485.trc
```

Inspecting the trace file will often (but not always) provide additional insight into the issue.

Viewing the alert.log Using the ADRCI Utility

If you're using Oracle Database 11g or higher, you can use the ADRCI utility to view the contents of the alert.log file. Run the following command from the operating system to start the ADRCI utility:

```
$ adrci
```

You should be presented with a prompt:

```
adrci>
```

Use the SHOW ALERT command to view the alert.log file:

```
adrci> show alert
```

If there are multiple Oracle homes on the server, then you will be prompted to choose which alert.log you want to view. The SHOW ALERT command will open up the alert.log with the utility that has been set as the default editor for your operating system. On Linux/Unix systems, the default editor is derived from the operating system EDITOR variable (which is usually set to an utility such as vi).

■ **Tip** When presented with the alert.log, if you are unfamiliar with vi, and want to exit, first hit the escape key, then press and hold down the shift key while also pressing the : key. Then type in a q!. That should exit you out of the vi editor and back to the ADRCI prompt.

You can override the default editor within ADRCI using the SET EDITOR command. This example sets the default editor to emacs:

```
adrci> set editor emacs
```

You can view the last N number of lines in the alert.log with the TAIL option. The following command displays the last 50 lines of the alert.log:

```
adrci> show alert -tail 50
```

If you have multiple Oracle homes, you may see a message like this:

DIA-48449: Tail alert can only apply to single ADR home

The ADRCI utility doesn't assume that you want to work with one Oracle home over another on a server. To specifically set the Oracle home (for the ADRCI utility), first use the SHOW HOMES command to display all available Oracle homes:

adrci> show homes

Here is some sample output for this server:

diag/rdbms/e64208/E64208
diag/rdbms/e64211/E64211
diag/rdbms/e64214/E64214

Now to specifically set the Oracle home, use the SET HOMEPATH command. This sets the HOMEPATH to diag/rdbms/e64208/E64208:

adrci> set homepath diag/rdbms/e64208/E64208

To continuously display the end of the file, use the following command:

adrci> show alert -tail -f

Press Ctrl+C to break out of continuously viewing the alert.log file. To display lines from the alert.log that contains specific strings, use the MESSAGE_TEXT LIKE command. This example shows messages that contain the ORA-27037 string:

adrci> show alert -p "MESSAGE_TEXT LIKE '%ORA-27037%'"

You will be presented with a file that contains all lines in the alert.log that match the specified string.

▪ **Tip** See the *Oracle Database Utilities* guide for full details on how to use the ADRCI utility.

Identifying Bottlenecks via Operating System Utilities

In the Oracle world, there is sometimes a tendency to assume that you have a dedicated machine for one Oracle database. Furthermore, this database is the latest version of Oracle, fully patched, and monitored by a sophisticated graphical tool. This database environment is completely automated and kept trouble free through the use of visual tools that quickly pinpoint problems and efficiently isolate and resolve issues. If you live in this ideal world, then you probably don't need any of the material in this chapter.

Let me paint a slightly different picture. I have an environment where one machine has a dozen databases running on it. There's a MySQL database, a PostgreSQL database, and a mix of Oracle version 9i, version 10g, and version 11g databases. Furthermore, many of these old databases are on non-terminal releases of Oracle and are therefore technically not supported by Oracle Support. There are no plans to upgrade any of these unsupported databases because the business can't take the risk of potentially breaking the applications that depend on these databases.

So what does one do in this type of environment when somebody reports that a database application is performing poorly? In this scenario, it's often something else in a different database that is causing other applications on the box to behave poorly. It may not be an Oracle process or an Oracle databases that is causing problems.

In this situation, it's almost always more effective to start investigating issues by using an operating system tool. The OS tools are database agnostic. OS performance utilities help pinpoint where the most resources are consumed regardless of database vendor or version.

In Linux/Unix environments, there are several tools available for monitoring resource usage. Table 22-1 summarizes the most commonly used OS utilities for diagnosing performance issues. Being familiar with how these operating system commands work and how to interpret the output will allow you to better diagnose server performance issues, especially when it's a non-Oracle or even a non-database process that is tanking performance for every other application on the box.

Table 22-1. Performance and Monitoring Utilities

Tool	Purpose
vmstat	Monitors processes, CPU, memory, or disk I/O bottlenecks.
top	Identifies sessions consuming the most resources.
watch	Periodically runs another command.
ps	Identifies highest CPU- and memory-consuming sessions. Used to identify Oracle sessions consuming the most system resources.
mpstat	Reports CPU statistics.
sar	Displays CPU, memory, disk I/O, and network usage, both current and historical.
free	Displays free and used memory.
df	Reports on free disk space.
du	Displays disk usage.
iostat	Displays disk I/O statistics.
netstat	Reports on network statistics.

When diagnosing performance issues, it's useful to determine where the operating system is constrained. For example, try to identify whether the issue is related to CPU, memory, I/O, or a combination of these resources.

Identifying System Bottlenecks

Whenever there are application performance issues or availability problems, seemingly (from the DBA's perspective) the first question asked is, what's wrong with the database? Regardless of the source of the problem, the onus is often on the DBA to either prove or disprove whether the database is behaving well. I usually approach this issue by determining what system-wide resources are being consumed. There are two Linux/Unix operating system tools that are particularly useful for displaying system wide resource usage:

603

- vmstat

- top

The vmstat (virtual memory statistics) tool is intended to help you quickly identify bottlenecks on your server. The top utility provides a dynamic real-time view of system resource usage. These two utility are discussed in the next two subsections.

Using vmstat

The vmstat utility displays real-time performance information about processes, memory, paging, disk I/O, and CPU usage. This example shows using vmstat to display the default output with no options specified:

```
$ vmstat
procs -----------memory---------- ---swap-- -----io---- --system-- ----cpu----
 r  b   swpd   free   buff  cache   si   so    bi    bo   in   cs us sy id wa
14  0  52340  25272   3068 1662704    0    0    63    76    9   31 15  1 84  0
```

Here are some general heuristics you can use when interpreting the output of vmstat:

- If the wa (time waiting for I/O) column is high, this is usually an indication that the storage subsystem is overloaded.

- If b (processes sleeping) is consistently greater than 0, then you may not have enough CPU processing power.

- If so (memory swapped out to disk) and si (memory swapped in from disk) are consistently greater than 0, you may have a memory bottleneck.

By default, only one line of server statistics is displayed when running vmstat (without supplying any options). This one line of output displays average statistics calculated from the last time the system was rebooted. This is fine for a quick snapshot. However, if you want to gather metrics over a period of time, use vmstat with this syntax:

```
$ vmstat <interval in seconds> <number of intervals>
```

While in this mode, vmstat reports statistics sampling from one interval to the next. For example, if you wanted to report system statistics every two seconds for ten intervals, you'd issue this command:

```
$ vmstat 2 10
```

You can also send the vmstat output to a file. This is useful for analyzing historical performance over a period of time. This example samples statistics every 5 seconds for a total of 60 reports and records the output in a file:

```
$ vmstat 5 60 > vmout.perf
```

Another useful way to use vmstat is with the watch tool. The watch command is used to execute another program on a periodic basis. This example uses watch to run the vmstat command every five seconds and to highlight on the screen any differences between each snapshot:

```
$ watch -n 5 -d vmstat
Every 5.0s: vmstat                              Thu Aug  9 13:27:57 2007
procs -----------memory---------- ---swap-- -----io---- --system-- ----cpu----
 r  b   swpd   free   buff  cache  si   so    bi    bo   in   cs us sy id wa
 0  0    144  15900  64620 1655100   0    0     1     7   16    4  0  0 99  0
```

When running vmstat in watch -d (differences) mode, you'll visually see changes on your screen as they alter from snapshot to snapshot. To exit from watch, press Ctrl+C.

Note that the default unit of measure for the memory columns of vmstat is in kilobytes. If you want to view memory statistics in megabytes, then use the -S m (statistics in megabytes) option:

```
$ vmstat -S m
```

For reference, Table 22-2 details the meanings of the columns displayed in the default output of vmstat.

Table 22-2. Column Descriptions of vmstat Output

Column	Description
r	Number of processes waiting for runtime
b	Number of processes in uninterruptible sleep
swpd	Total virtual memory (swap) in use (KB)
free	Total idle memory (KB)
buff	Total memory used as buffers (KB)
cache	Total memory used as cache (KB)
si	Memory swapped in from disk (KB/s)
so	Memory swapped out to disk (KB/s)
bi	Blocks read in (blocks/s) from block device
bo	Blocks written out (blocks/s) per second to block device
in	Interrupts per second
cs	Context switches per second
us	User-level code time as a percentage of total CPU time
sy	System level code time as a percentage of total CPU time
id	Idle time as a percentage of total CPU time
wa	Time waiting for I/O completion

Using top

Another tool for identifying resource-intensive processes is the top command. Use this utility to quickly identify which processes are the highest consumers of resources on the server. By default, top will repetitively refresh (every three seconds) information regarding the most CPU-intensive processes. Here's the simplest way to run top:

```
$ top
```

Here's a fragment of the output:

```
top - 21:05:39 up 43 days, 23:45,  8 users,  load average: 1.10, 0.87, 0.72
Tasks: 576 total,   2 running, 574 sleeping,   0 stopped,   0 zombie
Cpu(s):  0.1%us,  0.2%sy,  0.0%ni, 98.8%id,  0.8%wa,  0.0%hi,  0.0%si,  0.0%st
Mem:  16100352k total, 12480204k used,  3620148k free,    38016k buffers
Swap: 18481144k total,   380072k used, 18101072k free,  8902940k cached

  PID USER      PR  NI  VIRT  RES  SHR S %CPU %MEM    TIME+  COMMAND
 9236 mscd642   15   0 13000 1468  812 R  0.7  0.0  0:00.03 top
 3179 oracle    16   0 2122m 1.9g 1.9g S  0.3 12.3 97:54.00 oracle
 4116 oracle    16   0  618m 133m 124m S  0.3  0.8  0:08.62 oracle
20763 mscd642   15   0  609m  91m  88m S  0.3  0.6  0:00.26 oracle
    1 root      15   0 10344  684  572 S  0.0  0.0  0:25.98 init
    2 root      RT  -5     0    0    0 S  0.0  0.0  0:16.01 migration/0
    3 root      34  19     0    0    0 S  0.0  0.0  0:03.16 ksoftirqd/0
```

The process IDs of the top-consuming sessions are listed in the first column (PID). You can use this process ID to see if it maps to a database process (see the section in this chapter on mapping a PID to a database process).

While top is running, you can interactively change its output. For example, if you type >, this will move the column that top is sorting one position to the right. Table 22–3 lists some key features that you can use to alter the top display to the desired format.

Table 22–3. Commands to Interactively Change the top Output

Command	Function
Spacebar	Immediately refreshes the output.
< or >	Moves the sort column one to the left or to the right. By default, top sorts on the CPU column.
D	Changes the refresh time.
R	Reverses the sort order.
Z	Toggles the color output.
H	Displays help menu.
F or O	Chooses a sort column.

Type q or press Ctrl+C to exit top. Table 22–4 describes several of the columns displayed in the default output of top.

Table 22–4. Column Descriptions of the top Output

Column	Description
PID	Unique process identifier.
USER	OS username running the process.
PR	Priority of the process.
NI	Nice value or process. Negative value means high priority. Positive value means low priority.
VIRT	Total virtual memory used by process.
RES	Nonswapped physical memory used.
SHR	Shared memory used by process.
S	Process status.
%CPU	Processes percent of CPU consumption since last screen refresh.
%MEM	Percent of physical memory the process is consuming.
TIME	Total CPU time used by process.
TIME+	Total CPU time, showing hundredths of seconds.
COMMAND	Command line used to start a process.

You can also run top using the -b (batch mode) option and send the output to a file for later analysis:

```
$ top -b > tophat.out
```

While running in batch mode, the top command will run until you kill it (with a Ctrl+C) or until it reaches a specified number of iterations. You could run the previous top command in batch mode with a combination of nohup and & to keep it running regardless if you were logged onto the system. The danger there is that you might forget about it and eventually create a very large output file (and an angry system administrator).

If you have a particular process that you're interesting in monitoring, use the -p option to monitor a process ID or the -U option to monitor a specific username. You can also specify a delay and number of iterations by using the -d and -n options. The following example monitors the oracle user with a delay of 5 seconds for 25 iterations:

```
$ top -u oracle -d 5 -n 25
```

■ **Tip** Use the man top or top --help commands to list all the options available in your operating system version.

Mapping an Operating System Process to a SQL Statement

When identifying operating system processes, it's useful to view which processes are consuming the most amount of CPU. If the resource hog is a database process, it's also useful to map the operating system process to a database job or query. To determine the ID of the processes consuming the most CPU resources, use a command like ps, like so:

```
$ ps -e -o pcpu,pid,user,tty,args | sort -n -k 1 -r | head
```

Here is some sample output:

```
72.4 25922 mscd642    ?    oracleE64215 (DESCRIPTION=(LOCAL=YES)(ADDRESS=(PROTOCOL=beq)))
 1.5 28215 oracle     ?    oracleemrep (LOCAL=NO)
 0.2 24764 oracle     ?    /u01/oracle/product/11.0.0/grid/agent10g/bin/emagent
 0.1  3179 oracle     ?    ora_j000_emrep
```

From the output, the operating system session of 25922 is consuming the most CPU resources at 72.4 percent. In this example, the 25922 process is associated with the E64215 database. Next, log onto the appropriate database and use the following SQL statement to determine what type of program is associated with the operating system process of 25922:

```
select
  'USERNAME : ' || s.username|| chr(10) ||
  'OSUSER   : ' || s.osuser  || chr(10) ||
  'PROGRAM  : ' || s.program || chr(10) ||
  'SPID     : ' || p.spid    || chr(10) ||
  'SID      : ' || s.sid     || chr(10) ||
  'SERIAL#  : ' || s.serial# || chr(10) ||
  'MACHINE  : ' || s.machine || chr(10) ||
  'TERMINAL : ' || s.terminal
from v$session s,
     v$process p
where s.paddr = p.addr
and   p.spid = '&PID_FROM_OS';
```

When you run the example, SQL*Plus will prompt you for the value to use in place of &PID_FROM_OS. In this example, you'll enter 25922. Here is the output:

```
'USERNAME:'||S.USERNAME||CHR(10)||'OSUSER:'||S.OSUSER||CHR(10)||'PROGRAM:'||S.PR
--------------------------------------------------------------------------------
USERNAME : SYS
OSUSER   : mscd642
PROGRAM  : sqlplus@ora04.regis.local (TNS V1-V3)
SPID     : 25922
SID      : 139
SERIAL#  : 90
MACHINE  : ora04.regis.local
TERMINAL : pts/9
```

In this output, the PROGRAM value is sqlplus@ora04.regis.local. This indicates that a SQL*Plus session is the program consuming the inordinate amount of resources on the server. Next, run the following query to display the SQL statement associated with the operating system process ID (in this example, the SPID is 25922):

```
select
   'USERNAME :  '  ||  s.username  ||  chr(10)  ||
   'OSUSER   :  '  ||  s.osuser    ||  chr(10)  ||
   'PROGRAM  :  '  ||  s.program   ||  chr(10)  ||
   'SPID     :  '  ||  p.spid      ||  chr(10)  ||
   'SID      :  '  ||  s.sid       ||  chr(10)  ||
   'SERIAL#  :  '  ||  s.serial#   ||  chr(10)  ||
   'MACHINE  :  '  ||  s.machine   ||  chr(10)  ||
   'TERMINAL :  '  ||  s.terminal  ||  chr(10)  ||
   'SQL TEXT :  '  ||  q.sql_text
from v$session s
    ,v$process p
    ,v$sql     q
where  s.paddr  = p.addr
and    p.spid   = '&PID_FROM_OS'
and    s.sql_id = q.sql_id;
```

The result shows the resource-consuming SQL as part of the output in the SQL TEXT column:

```
'USERNAME:'||S.USERNAME||CHR(10)||'OSUSER:'||S.OSUSER||CHR(10)||'PROGRAM:'||S.PR
--------------- ---------------------------------------------------------------
USERNAME : SYS
OSUSER   : mscd642
PROGRAM  : sqlplus@ora04.regis.local (TNS V1-V3)
SPID     : 25922
SID      : 139
SERIAL#  : 90
MACHINE  : ora04.regis.local
TERMINAL : pts/9
SQL TEXT : select a.table_name from dba_tables a,dba_indexes,dba_constraints uni
```

When you run multiple databases on one server and are experiencing server performance issues, it can sometimes be difficult to pinpoint which database and associated process are causing the problems. In these situations, you have to use an operating system tool to identify the top-consuming sessions on the system.

In a Linux or Unix environment, you can use utilities such as ps, top, or vmstat to identify top-consuming operating system processes. The ps utility is handy because it lets you identify processes consuming the most CPU or memory. The previous ps command identified the top consuming CPU processes. Here, it's used it to identify the top Oracle memory-using processes:

```
$ ps -e -o pmem,pid,user,tty,args | grep -i oracle | sort -n -k 1 -r | head
```

Once you have identified a top-consuming process associated with a database, you can query the data dictionary views based on the server process ID to identify what the database process is executing.

OS WATCHER

Oracle provides a collection of scripts that gather and store metrics for CPU, memory, disk, and network usage. On Linux/Unix systems, the OS Watcher tool suite automates the gathering of statistics using tools such as `top`, `vmstat`, `iostat`, `mpstat`, `netstat`, and `traceroute`. This utility also has an optional graphical component for visually displaying performance metrics.

You can obtain OS Watcher from Oracle's My Oracle Support (MetaLink) website. For the Linux/Unix version, search for document ID 301137.1 or for the document titled "OS Watcher User Guide." For details on the Windows version of OS Watcher, search for document ID 433472.1.

Finding Resource Intensive SQL Statements

One of the best ways to isolate a poorly performing query is to have a user or developer complain about a specific SQL statement. In this situation, there is no detective work involved. You can directly pinpoint the SQL query that is in need of tuning.

However, you don't often have the luxury of a human letting you know specifically where to look when investigating performance issues. There are several methods for determining which SQL statements are consuming the most resources in a database:

- Real-time execution statistics (11g)

- Near real-time statistics

- Oracle performance reports

These techniques are described in the following several sections.

Monitoring Real-Time SQL Execution Statistics

If you're using Oracle Database 11g, you can use the following query to select from the V$SQL_MONITOR to monitor the near real-time resource consumption of SQL queries:

```
select * from (
select
 a.sid session_id
,a.sql_id
,a.status
,a.cpu_time/1000000 cpu_sec
,a.buffer_gets
,a.disk_reads
,b.sql_text sql_text
from v$sql_monitor a
    ,v$sql b
where a.sql_id = b.sql_id
order by a.cpu_time desc)
where rownum <=20;
```

The output of this query doesn't fit easily onto a page. Here is a subset of the output:

```
SESSION_ID SQL_ID        STATUS      CPU_SEC BUFFER_GETS  DISK_READS SQL_TEXT
```

```
----------  --------------  ---------  ----------  -----------  ----------  ---------------
       139 d07nngmx93rq7 DONE        331.88         5708       3490 select count(*)
       130 9dtu8zn9yy4uc EXECUTING    11.55         5710        248 select task_name
```

In the query, an inline view is utilized to first retrieve all records and organize them by CPU_TIME in descending order. The outer query then limits the result set to the top twenty rows using the ROWNUM pseudocolumn. You can modify the previous query to order by the statistic of your choice or modify it to display only the queries that are currently executing. For example, the next SQL statement monitors currently executing queries ordered by the number of disk reads:

```
select * from (
select
 a.sid session_id
,a.sql_id
,a.status
,a.cpu_time/1000000 cpu_sec
,a.buffer_gets
,a.disk_reads
,substr(b.sql_text,1,15) sql_text
from v$sql_monitor a
    ,v$sql b
where a.sql_id = b.sql_id
and   a.status='EXECUTING'
order by a.disk_reads desc)
where rownum <=20;
```

The statistics in V$SQL_MONITOR are updated every second so you can view resource consumption as it changes. These statistics are gathered by default if a SQL statement runs in parallel or consumes more than 5 seconds of CPU or I/O time.

The V$SQL_MONITOR view includes a subset of statistics contained in the VSQL, VSQLAREA, and V$SQLSTATS views. The V$SQL_MONITOR view displays real-time statistics for each execution of a resource-intensive SQL statement, whereas VSQL, VSQLAREA, and V$SQLSTATATS contain cumulative sets of statistics over several executions of a SQL statement.

Once the SQL statement execution ends, the run time statistics are not immediately flushed from V$SQL_MONITOR. Depending on activity in your database, the statistics can be available for some period of time. If you have a very active database, the statistics could potentially be flushed soon after the query finishes.

■ **Tip** You can uniquely identify an execution of a SQL statement in V$SQL_MONITOR from a combination of the following columns: SQL_ID, SQL_EXEC_START, SQL_EXEC_ID.

Displaying Resource Intensive SQL

As mentioned in the prior section, the V$SQL_MONITOR view is available with Oracle Database 11g or higher. If you're using an older version of Oracle, you can query views like V$SQLSTATS to determine which SQL statements are consuming inordinate amounts of resources. For example, use the following query to identify the ten most resource-intensive queries based on CPU time:

```
select * from(
select
  sql_text
 ,buffer_gets
 ,disk_reads
 ,sorts
 ,cpu_time/1000000 cpu_sec
 ,executions
 ,rows_processed
from v$sqlstats
order by cpu_time DESC)
where rownum < 11;
```

In the prior query, an inline view is utilized to first retrieve all records and sorts the output by CPU_TIME in descending order. The outer query then limits the result set to the top ten rows using the ROWNUM pseudocolumn. The query can be easily modified to sort by a column other than CPU_TIME. For example, if you want to report resource usage by BUFFER_GETS, simply change the ORDER BY clause to use BUFFER_GETS instead of CPU_TIME. The CPU_TIME column is calculated in microseconds; to convert it to seconds, divided it by 1000000.

The V$SQLSTATS view displays performance statistics for SQL statements that have recently executed. You can also use V$SQL and V$SQLAREA to report on SQL resource usage. V$SQLSTATS is faster and retains information for a longer period of time, but contains only a subset of the columns in V$SQL and V$SQLAREA. Thus, there are scenarios where you may want to query from V$SQL or V$SQLAREA. For example, if you want to display information such as the user who first parsed the query, use the PARSING_USER_ID column of V$SQLAREA:

```
select * from(
select
  b.sql_text
 ,a.username
 ,b.buffer_gets
 ,b.disk_reads
 ,b.sorts
 ,b.cpu_time/1000000 cpu_sec
from v$sqlarea b
    ,dba_users a
where b.parsing_user_id = a.user_id
order by b.cpu_time DESC)
where rownum < 11;
```

Running Oracle Diagnostic Utilities

Oracle provides several utilities for diagnosing database performance issues:

- Automatic Workload Repository (AWR)

- Automatic Database Diagnostic Monitor (ADDM)

- Active Session History (ASH)

- Statspack

AWR, ADDM, and ASH were introduced in Oracle Database 10g. These tools provide advanced reporting capabilities that allow you to troubleshoot and resolve performance issues. These new utilities require an extra license from Oracle. The older Statspack utility is free and requires no license.

All of these tools rely heavily on the underlying V$ dynamic performance views. Oracle maintains a vast collection of these views that track and accumulate metrics of database performance. For example, if you run the following query, you'll notice that for Oracle Database 11g release 2, there are 600 or so V$ views:

```
SQL> select count(*) from dictionary where table_name like 'V$%';

  COUNT(*)
----------
       600
```

The Oracle performance utilities rely on periodic snapshots gathered from these internal performance views. Two of the most useful views with regard to performance statistics are the V$SYSSTAT and V$SESSTAT views. The V$SYSSTAT view contains over 400 types of database statistics. This V$SYSSTAT view contains information about the entire database, whereas the V$SESSTAT view contains statistics for individual sessions. A few of the values in the V$SYSSTAT and V$SESSTAT views contain the current usage of the resource. These values are:

- opened cursors current
- logons current
- session cursor cache current
- work area memory allocated

The rest of the values are cumulative. The values in V$SYSSTAT are cumulative for the entire database from the time the instance was started. The values in V$SESSTAT are cumulative per session from the time the session was started. Some of the more important performance-related cumulative values are:

- CPU used
- consistent gets
- physical reads
- physical writes

For the cumulative statistics, the way to measure periodic usage is to note the value of a statistic at a starting point, then note the value at a later point in time, and capture the delta. This is the approach used by the Oracle performance utilities such as AWR and Statspack. Periodically, Oracle will take a snapshot of the dynamic wait interface views and store them in a repository.

The following sections in this chapter detail how access AWR, ADDM, ASH, and Statspack from SQL*Plus.

▪ **Tip** You can access AWR, ADDM, and ASH from Enterprise Manager. You may find the Enterprise Manager screens more intuitive and efficient than using SQL*Plus.

Using AWR

An AWR report is good for viewing the entire system performance and identifying the top resource-consuming SQL queries. Run the following script to generate an AWR report:

```
SQL> @?/rdbms/admin/awrrpt
```

From the AWR output, identify top resource-consuming statements in the "SQL ordered by Elapsed Time" or the "SQL ordered by CPU Time" sections of the report. Here is some sample output:

```
SQL ordered by CPU Time          DB/Inst: DWREP/DWREP  Snaps: 11384-11407
-> Resources reported for PL/SQL code includes the resources used by all SQL
   statements called by the code.
-> % Total DB Time is the Elapsed Time of the SQL statement divided
   into the Total Database Time multiplied by 100

    CPU     Elapsed                CPU per  % Total
  Time (s)  Time (s)  Executions  Exec (s) DB Time   SQL Id
 --------- --------- ------------ ---------- ------- -------------
    4,809    13,731           10 .  480.86     6.2 8wx77jyhdr31c
Module: JDBC Thin Client
SELECT D.DERIVED_COMPANY ,CB.CLUSTER_BUCKET_ID ,CB.CB_NAME ,CB.SOA_ID ,COUNT(*)
TOTAL ,NVL(SUM(CASE WHEN F.D_DATE_ID > TO_NUMBER(TO_CHAR(SYSDATE-30,'YYYYMMDD'))
THEN 1 END), 0) RECENT ,NVL(D.BLACKLIST_FLG,0) BLACKLIST_FLG FROM F_DOWNLOADS F
,D_DOMAINS D ,D_PRODUCTS P ,PID_DF_ASSOC PDA ,( SELECT * FROM ( SELECT CLUSTER_
```

As of Oracle Database 10g, Oracle will automatically take a snapshot of your database once an hour and populate the underlying AWR tables that store the statistics. By default, seven days of statistics are retained.

You can also generate an AWR report for a specific SQL statement by running the awrsqrpt.sql report. When you run the following script, you will be prompted for the SQL_ID of the query of interest:

```
SQL> @?/rdbms/admin/awrsqrpt.sql
```

Using ADDM

The ADDM report provides useful suggestions on which SQL statements are candidates for tuning. Use the following SQL script to generate an ADDM report:

```
SQL> @?/rdbms/admin/addmrpt
```

Look for the section of the report labeled "SQL statements consuming significant database time." Here is some sample output:

```
FINDING 2: 29% impact (65043 seconds)

-------------------------------------

SQL statements consuming significant database time were found.

   RECOMMENDATION 1: SQL Tuning, 6.7% benefit (14843 seconds)
      ACTION: Investigate the SQL statement with SQL_ID "46cc3t7ym5sx0" for
         possible performance improvements.
         RELEVANT OBJECT: SQL statement with SQL_ID 46cc3t7ym5sx0 and
         PLAN_HASH 1234997150
   MERGE INTO d_files a
```

```
USING
( SELECT
```

The ADDM report analyzes data in the AWR tables to identify potential bottlenecks and high resource-consuming SQL queries.

Using ASH

The ASH report allows you to focus on short-lived SQL statements that have been recently run and may have only executed for a brief amount of time. Use the following script to generate an ASH report:

```
SQL> @?/rdbms/admin/ashrpt
```

Search the output for the section labeled "Top SQL." Here is some sample output:

```
                                          Sampled #
            SQL ID          Planhash      of Executions    % Activity
------------------- ------------------- ----------------- --------------
Event                  % Event Top Row Source              % RwSrc
------------------- ------- --------------------------------- -------
      4k8runghhh31d        3219321046             12           51.61
CPU + Wait for CPU         51.61 HASH JOIN                      12.26
select countryimp0_.COUNTRY_ID as COUNTRY_ID, countryimp0_.COUNTRY_NAME
```

The previous output indicates that the query is waiting for CPU resources. In this scenario, it may actually be another query that is consuming the CPU resources that is the problem.

When is the ASH report more useful than the AWR or ADDM reports? The AWR and ADDM output shows top-consuming SQL in terms of total database time. If the SQL performance problem is transient and short-lived, it may not appear on the AWR and ADDM reports. In these situations, an ASH report is more useful.

Using Statspack

If you don't have a license to use the AWR, ADDM, and ASH reports, the free Statspack utility can help you identify poorly performing SQL statements. Run the following script as SYS to install Statspack:

```
SQL> @?/rdbms/admin/spcreate.sql
```

This script creates a PERFSTAT user that owns the Statspack repository. To enable the automatic gathering of Statspack statistics, run this script:

```
SQL> @?/rdbms/admin/spauto.sql
```

After some snapshots have been gathered, you can run the following script as the PERFSTAT user to create a Statspack report:

```
SQL> @?/rdbms/admin/spreport.sql
```

Once the report is created, search for the section labeled "SQL ordered by CPU." Here is some sample output:

```
SQL ordered by CPU  DB/Inst: DW11/DW11  Snaps: 11-14
-> Total DB CPU (s):          107
-> Captured SQL accounts for  246.0% of Total DB CPU
-> SQL reported below exceeded  1.0% of Total DB CPU
```

CPU Time (s)	Executions	CPU per Exec (s)	%Total	Elapsd Time (s)	Buffer Gets	Old Hash Value
254.95	4	63.74	238.1	249.74	12,811	2873951798

Module: SQL*Plus
select count(*) from dba_indexes, dba_tables

■ **Tip** View the ORACLE_HOME/rdbms/admin/spdoc.txt file for Statspack documentation.

Detecting and Resolving Locking Issues

Sometimes a developer or application user will report that a process that normally takes seconds to run is now taking several minutes and doesn't appear to be doing anything. In these situations, the problem is usually one of the following:

- Space related issue (for example, archive redo destination is full and has suspended all transactions).

- One process has a lock on a row in a table and is not committing or rolling back, thus preventing another session from modifying the same row.

In this scenario, I first check the alert.log to see if there are any obvious issues that have occurred recently (like a tablespace not being able to allocate another extent). If there is nothing obvious in the alert.log file, I run a SQL query to check for locking issues. The query listed here is a more sophisticated version of the lock detecting script introduced in Chapter 3. This query shows information such as the locking session SQL statement and the waiting SQL statement:

```
set lines 80
col blkg_user form a10
col blkg_machine form a10
col blkg_sid form 99999999
col wait_user form a10
col wait_machine form a10
col wait_sid form 9999999
col obj_own form a10
col obj_name form a10
col blkg_sql form a50
col wait_sql form a50
--
select
 s1.username    blkg_user
,s1.machine     blkg_machine
,s1.sid         blkg_sid
,s1.serial#     blkg_serialnum
,s1.process     blkg_OS_PID
,substr(b1.sql_text,1,50) blkg_sql
,chr(10)
,s2.username    wait_user
,s2.machine     wait_machine
,s2.sid         wait_sid
```

```
,s2.serial#      wait_serialnum
,s2.process      wait_OS_PID
,substr(w1.sql_text,1,50) wait_sql
,lo.object_id    blkd_obj_id
,do.owner        obj_own
,do.object_name obj_name
from v$lock       l1
    ,v$session    s1
    ,v$lock       l2
    ,v$session    s2
    ,v$locked_object lo
    ,v$sqlarea    b1
    ,v$sqlarea    w1
    ,dba_objects  do
where s1.sid = l1.sid
and s2.sid = l2.sid
and l1.id1 = l2.id1
and s1.sid = lo.session_id
and lo.object_id = do.object_id
and l1.block = 1
and s1.prev_sql_addr = b1.address
and s2.sql_address = w1.address
and l2.request > 0;
```

The output from this query does not fit well on one page. When running this query, you will have to format it so that it fits within the size of your terminal. Here is some sample output indicating that the INV table is locked by the STAR2 user and that the CIA_SEL user is waiting for the lock to be released:

```
BLKG_USER  BLKG_MACHI  BLKG_SID BLKG_SERIALNUM BLKG_OS_PID
---------- ---------- --------- -------------- -----------
BLKG_SQL                                           C WAIT_USER  WAIT_MACHI
-------------------------------------------------- - ---------- ----------

STAR2      dwdb          1084         265 3153
update inv set inv_id=5 where inv_id = 7         CIA_SEL     xengdb
    1086            222 21436

WAIT_SID WAIT_SERIALNUM WAIT_OS_PID
-------- -------------- -----------
WAIT_SQL                                           BLKD_OBJ_ID OBJ_OWN
-------------------------------------------------- ----------- ----------
OBJ_NAME
----------
update  star2.inv set inv_id=3 where inv_id=7        150553 STAR2
INV
```

This situation is typical when applications don't explicitly issue a COMMIT or ROLLBACK at appropriate times in the code. This leaves a lock on a row and prevents one transaction from continuing until the lock is released. In this scenario, you can try to locate the user who is blocking the transaction and see if they need to push a button on the screen that says something like "commit your changes." If that's not possible, you can manually kill one of the sessions. Keep in mind that terminating a session may have unforeseen side effects (like rolling back data that a user thought was committed).

If you decide to kill one of the sessions, you need to identify the SID and serial number of the session you want to terminate. Once identified, use the ALTER SYSTEM KILL SESSION statement to terminate a user session. In this example, I decide to kill the lock held by the STAR2 user with the SID of 1072 and a serial number of 29, so from a DBA privileged account I run the following statement:

```
SQL> alter system kill session '1084,265';
```

Again, be careful when killing sessions. Ensure that you know the impact of killing a session and thereby rolling back any active transactions currently open in that session.

The other way to kill a session is to use an operating system command such as kill. From the prior output, you can identify the operating system processes from the BLKG_OS_PID column and WAIT_OS_PID column. Before you terminate a process from the operating system, ensure that it isn't a critical process. For this example, to terminate the blocking OS process, first check the blocking process ID:

```
$ ps -ef | grep 3153
```

Here is some sample output:

```
oracle 3153  1690  0  10:40:30  pts/1  0:00  sqlplus star2....
```

Next use the kill command as shown:

```
$ kill -9  3153
```

The kill command will unceremoniously terminate a process. Any open transactions associated with the process will be rolled back by the Oracle process monitor.

Resolving Open Cursor Issues

The OPEN_CURSORS initialization parameter determines the maximum number of cursors a session can have open. This setting is per each session. The default value of 50 is usually too low for any application. When an application exceeds the number of open cursors allowed, the following error is thrown:

```
ORA-01000: maximum open cursors exceeded
```

Usually the prior error is encountered when:

- OPEN_CURSORS initialization parameter is set too low.

- Developers write code that doesn't close cursors properly.

To investigate this issue, first determine the current setting of the parameter:

```
SQL> show parameter open_cursors;
```

If the value is less than 300, consider setting it higher. I typically set this value to 1000 for busy OLTP systems. You can dynamically modify this value while your database is open as shown:

```
SQL> alter system set open_cursors=1000;
```

If you're using an spfile, consider making the change both in memory and in the spfile at the same time:

```
SQL> alter system set open_cursors=1000 scope=both;
```

After setting OPEN_CURSORS to a higher value, if the application still continues to exceed the maximum value, you probably have an issue with code that is not properly closing cursors. Run a query such as the following to determine the number of open cursors each session has opened:

```
select
  a.value
 ,c.username
 ,c.machine
 ,c.sid
 ,c.serial#
from v$sesstat  a
    ,v$statname b
    ,v$session  c
where a.statistic# = b.statistic#
and   c.sid        = a.sid
and   b.name       = 'opened cursors current'
and   a.value      != 0
and   c.username IS NOT NULL
order by 1,2;
```

■ Tip I recommend that you query V$SESSION instead of V$OPEN_CURSOR to determine the number of open cursors. V$SESSION provides a more accurate number of the cursors currently open.

If you work in an environment that has thousands of connections to the database, you may want to view only the top cursor-consuming sessions. The following query uses an inline view and the pseudo-column ROWNUM to display the top twenty values:

```
select * from (
select
  a.value
 ,c.username
 ,c.machine
 ,c.sid
 ,c.serial#
from v$sesstat  a
    ,v$statname b
    ,v$session  c
where a.statistic# = b.statistic#
and   c.sid        = a.sid
and   b.name       = 'opened cursors current'
and   a.value      != 0
and   c.username IS NOT NULL
order by 1 desc,2)
where rownum < 21;
```

If a single session has over 1000 open cursors, there is probably something in the code that is not closing a cursor. When this limit is reached, somebody should inspect the application code to determine if a cursor is not being closed.

Troubleshooting Undo Tablespace Issues

Problems with the undo tablespace are usually of the following nature:

- ORA-01555: snapshot too old
- ORA-30036: unable to extend segment by ... in undo tablespace 'UNDOTBS1'

The prior listed errors can be caused by many different issues such as the undo tablespace not being sized correctly or poorly written SQL or PL/SQL code.

Determining if Undo is Correctly Sized

Suppose that you have a long-running SQL statement that is throwing an ORA-01555 "snapshot too old" error and you want to determine if adding space to the undo tablespace might help alleviate the issue. Run this next query to identify potential issues with your undo tablespace. The query checks for issues with the undo tablespace that have occurred within the last day:

```
select
 to_char(begin_time,'MM-DD-YYYY HH24:MI') begin_time
,ssolderrcnt    ORA_01555_cnt
,nospaceerrcnt  no_space_cnt
,txncount       max_num_txns
,maxquerylen    max_query_len
,expiredblks    blck_in_expired
from v$undostat
where begin_time > sysdate - 1
order by begin_time;
```

Here is some sample output. Part of the output has been omitted to fit this on the page:

```
BEGIN_TIME        ORA_01555_CNT NO_SPACE_CNT MAX_NUM_TXNS MAX_QUERY_LEN
----------------- ------------- ------------ ------------ -------------
07-20-2009 18:10              0            0          249             0
07-20-2009 18:20              0            0          290             0
07-20-2009 18:30              0            0          244             0
07-20-2009 18:40              0            0          179             0
```

The ORA_01555_CNT column indicates the number of times your database has encountered the ORA-01555 "snapshot too old" error. If this column reports a non-zero value, you need to do one or more of the following:

- Ensure that code does not contain COMMIT statements within cursor loops.
- Tune the SQL statement throwing the error so that it runs faster.
- Ensure that you have good statistics (so your SQL runs efficiently).
- Increase the UNDO_RETENTION initialization parameter.

The NO_SPACE_CNT column displays the number of times space was requested in the undo tablespace but none was to be found. If the NO_SPACE_CNT is reporting a non-zero value, you may need to add more space to your undo tablespace.

There is a maximum of four days' worth of information stored in the V$UNDOSTAT view. The statistics are gathered every ten minutes for a maximum of 576 rows in the table. If you've stopped and started your database within the last four days, this view will only have information in it from the time you last started your database.

Another way to get advice on the undo tablespace sizing is to use the Oracle Undo Advisor, which you can invoke by querying the PL/SQL DBMS_UNDO_ADV package from a SELECT statement. The following query displays the current undo size and the recommended size for an undo retention setting of 900 seconds:

```
select
  sum(bytes)/1024/1024                 cur_mb_size
  ,dbms_undo_adv.required_undo_size(900) req_mb_size
from dba_data_files
where tablespace_name =
  (select
    value
   from v$parameter
   where name = 'undo tablespace');
```

Here is some sample output:

```
CUR_MB_SIZE REQ_MB_SIZE
----------- -----------
      36864       20897
```

The output shows that the undo tablespace currently has 36.8 gigabytes allocated to it. In the prior query, you used 900 seconds as the amount of time to retain information in the undo tablespace. To retain undo information for 900 seconds, the Oracle Undo Advisor estimates that the undo tablespace should be 20.8 gigabytes. For this example, the undo tablespace is sized adequately. If it were not sized adequately, you would either have to add space to an existing datafile or add a datafile to the undo tablespace.

Here's a slightly more complex example of using the Oracle Undo Advisor to find the required size of the undo tablespace. This example uses PL/SQL to display information about potential issues and recommendations to fix the problem:

```
SET SERVEROUT ON SIZE 1000000
DECLARE
  pro    VARCHAR2(200);
  rec    VARCHAR2(200);
  rtn    VARCHAR2(200);
  ret    NUMBER;
  utb    NUMBER;
  retval NUMBER;
BEGIN
  DBMS_OUTPUT.PUT_LINE(DBMS_UNDO_ADV.UNDO_ADVISOR(1));
  DBMS_OUTPUT.PUT_LINE('Required Undo Size (megabytes): ' || DBMS_UNDO_ADV.REQUIRED_UNDO_SIZE
(900));
  retval := DBMS_UNDO_ADV.UNDO_HEALTH(pro, rec, rtn, ret, utb);
  DBMS_OUTPUT.PUT_LINE('Problem:  ' || pro);
  DBMS_OUTPUT.PUT_LINE('Advice:   ' || rec);
  DBMS_OUTPUT.PUT_LINE('Rational: ' || rtn);
  DBMS_OUTPUT.PUT_LINE('Retention: ' || TO_CHAR(ret));
  DBMS_OUTPUT.PUT_LINE('UTBSize:  ' || TO_CHAR(utb));
END;
/
```

If no issues are found, a 0 will be returned for the retention size. Here is some sample output:

```
Finding 1:The undo tablespace is OK.
Required Undo Size (megabytes): 20897
Problem:   No problem found
Advice:
Rational:
Retention: 0
UTBSize:   0
```

Viewing SQL that is Consuming Undo Space

Sometimes a piece of code does not commit properly, which results in large amounts of space being allocated in the undo tablespace and never being released. Sooner or later you'll get the ORA-30036 error indicating that the tablespace can't extend. Usually the first time a space related error is thrown, I simply increase the size of one of the datafiles associated with the undo tablespace.

However, if a SQL statement continues to run and fills up the newly added space, then the issue is probably with a poorly written application. For example, a developer might not have appropriate commit statements in the code.

In these situations it's helpful to identify which users are consuming space in the undo tablespace. Run this query to report on basic information regarding space allocated on a per user basis:

```
select
 s.sid
,s.serial#
,s.osuser
,s.logon_time
,s.status
,s.machine
,t.used_ublk
,t.used_ublk*16384/1024/1024 undo_usage_mb
from v$session     s
    ,v$transaction t
where t.addr = s.taddr;
```

If you want to view the SQL statement associated with the user consuming undo space, then join to V$SQL as shown:

```
select
 s.sid
,s.serial#
,s.osuser
,s.logon_time
,s.status
,s.machine
,t.used_ublk
,t.used_ublk*16384/1024/1024 undo_usage_mb
,q.sql_text
from v$session     s
    ,v$transaction t
    ,v$sql         q
where t.addr = s.taddr
and s.sql_id = q.sql_id;
```

If you need more information, such as the name and status of the rollback segment, run a query that joins to the V$ROLLNAME and V$ROLLSTAT views, like so:

```
select
 s.sid
,s.serial#
,s.username
,s.program
,r.name undo_name
,rs.status
,rs.rssize/1024/1024 redo_size_mb
,rs.extents
from v$session     s
    ,v$transaction t
    ,v$rollname    r
    ,v$rollstat    rs
where s.taddr = t.addr
and t.xidusn  = r.usn
and r.usn     = rs.usn;
```

The prior queries allow you to pinpoint which users are responsible for space allocated within the undo tablespace. This can be especially useful when there is code that is not committing at appropriate times and is excessively consuming undo space.

Handling Temporary Tablespace Issues

Issues with temporary tablespaces are somewhat easy to spot. For example, when the temporary tablespace runs out of space, the following error will be thrown:

`ORA-01652: unable to extend temp segment by 128 in tablespace TEMP`

When you see this error, you need to determine if there's enough space in the temporary tablespace or if it's a rare runaway SQL query that has temporarily consumed an inordinate amount of temp space. Both of these issues are discussed in the following sections.

Determining if Temporary Tablespace is Sized Correctly

The temporary tablespace is used as a sorting area on disk when a process has consumed the available memory and needs more space. Operations that require a sorting area include:

- Index creation
- SQL sorting operations
- Temporary tables and temporary indexes
- Temporary LOBs
- Temporary B-trees

There is no exact formula for determining if your temporary tablespace is sized correctly. It depends on the number and types of queries, index build operations, parallel operations, and size of your memory sort space (program global area). You'll have to monitor your temporary tablespace while there is a load on your database to determine its usage patterns. If you are using Oracle Database 11g or higher, run the following query to show both the allocated and free space within the temporary tablespace:

```
select
 tablespace_name
,tablespace_size/1024/1024 mb_size
,allocated_space/1024/1024 mb_alloc
,free_space/1024/1024      mb_free
from dba_temp_free_space;
```

Here is some sample output:

```
TABLESPACE_NAME    MB_SIZE    MB_ALLOC    MB_FREE
---------------  ----------  ----------  ----------
TEMP                   200         200         170
```

If the FREE_SPACE (MB_FREE) value drops to near zero, there are SQL operations in your database consuming most of the available space. The FREE_SPACE (MB_FREE) column is the total free space available, including space currently allocated and available for reuse.

If you are using an Oracle Database 10g database, run this query to view space being used in your temporary tablespace:

```
select
 tablespace_name
,sum(bytes_used)/1024/1024 mb_used
from v$temp_extent_pool
group by tablespace_name;
```

Here is some sample output:

```
TABLESPACE_NAME    MB_USED
---------------  ----------
TEMP                   120
```

If the used amount is getting near your current allocated amount, you may need to allocate more space to the temporary tablespace datafiles. Run the following query to view the temporary datafile names and allocated sizes:

```
SQL> select name, bytes/1024/1024 mb_alloc from v$tempfile;
```

Here is some typical output:

```
NAME                               MB_ALLOC
--------------------------------  ----------
/ora02/DWREP/temp01.dbf              12000
/ora03/DWREP/temp03.dbf              10240
/ora01/DWREP/temp02.dbf               2048
```

When first creating a database, if I have no idea as to "correct" size of the temporary tablespace, I'll usually size this tablespace at something like 2GB. If I'm building a data warehouse type database, I might size the temporary tablespace at something like 20GB. You'll have to monitor your temporary tablespace with the appropriate SQL and adjust the size as necessary.

Viewing SQL that is Consuming Temporary Space

When Oracle throws the ORA-01652 "unable to extend temp" error, it's one indicator that your temporary tablespace is too small. However, Oracle may throw that error if it runs out of space because of a one-time event, like a large index build. You'll have to decide whether a one-time index build or a query that consumes large amounts of sort space in the temporary tablespace warrants adding space.

To view the space a session is using in the temporary tablespace, run this query:

```
SELECT
 s.sid
,s.serial#
,s.username
,p.spid
,s.module
,p.program
,SUM(su.blocks) * tbsp.block_size/1024/1024 mb_used
,su.tablespace
FROM v$sort_usage    su
    ,v$session       s
    ,dba_tablespaces tbsp
    ,v$process       p
WHERE su.session_addr = s.saddr
AND    su.tablespace   = tbsp.tablespace_name
AND    s.paddr         = p.addr
GROUP BY
 s.sid, s.serial#, s.username, s.osuser, p.spid, s.module,
 p.program, tbsp.block_size, su.tablespace
ORDER BY s.sid;
```

If you determine that you need to add space, you can either resize an existing datafile or add a new datafile. To resize a temporary tablespace datafile, use the ALTER DATABASE TEMPFILE...RESIZE statement. The following resizes a temporary datafile to 12GB:

```
SQL> alter database tempfile '/ora03/DWREP/temp03.dbf' resize 12g;
```

You can add a datafile to a temporary tablespace as follows:

```
SQL> alter tablespace temp add tempfile '/ora04/DWREP/temp04.dbf' size 2g;
```

Auditing

Auditing usually means creating a record whenever a certain event happens. Activities that are typically audited include:

- When a table is inserted into, selected from, updated, or deleted from.
- User logon/logoff times.
- What SQL was used to update a table.
- When was an index last used.

Auditing is especially helpful when troubleshooting security issues with the database. Auditing gives you information to diagnose what objects are accessed by which users and when. This gives you a mechanism to detect and report on unauthorized actions or security breaches. For this reason, many databases are required to enable some degree of auditing to comply with regulatory agencies or internal company security requirements.

Auditing can also help with diagnosing some performance issues. For example, knowing what SQL ran and when or how many users are connected to the database at a specific time will help with diagnosing and resolving some issues.

There are several different ways to enable auditing:

- Setting database initialization parameters.

- Oracle Standard Auditing enabled via the AUDIT SQL statement.

- Enabling fine-grained auditing.

- Using data dictionary views.

- Custom DBA developed triggers that populate columns or tables based on certain events.

I'm not going to cover every aspect of auditing in the prior list (that would be a large amount of documentation). Rather, I'll show the basic techniques that DBAs use to audit databases. If you need more details, see the Oracle *Database Security Guide* (available on Oracle's OTN website).

Enabling Oracle Standard Auditing

Oracle Standard Auditing allows you to audit nearly any type of SQL activity in the database. You can audit any type of insert, update, delete, or select on a tables. You can also audit any system privilege activity such as CREATE TABLE, DROP INDEX, and so on.

You can enable auditing BY ACCESS or BY SESSION. Prior to Oracle Database 11g release 2, the BY SESSION would record just one record per session for an auditing action. With the current version of Oracle, the BY SESSION will record multiple records for the same auditing action.

You can also enable auditing by WHENEVER SUCCESSFUL or WHENEVER NOT SUCCESSFUL. This allows you to audit specifically for the success or failure of a particular statement.

Oracle's Standard Auditing feature is enabled through setting the AUDIT_TRAIL initialization parameter. I usually set the AUDIT_TRAIL parameter to DB, which specifies that Oracle will write audit records to an internal database table named AUD$. For example, when using an spfile, here's how to set the AUDIT_TRAIL parameter:

```
SQL> alter system set audit_trail=db scope=spfile;
```

If you are using an init.ora file, open it with a text editor and set the AUDIT_TRAIL value to DB. See Table 22–5 for a description of valid values for the AUDIT_TRAIL parameter.

■ Tip I typically set the AUDIT_TRAIL parameter to DB even if I'm not doing any auditing. This way when I want to enable auditing for a specific action, I can do so without having to stop and re-start the database.

Table 22-5. Valid `AUDIT_TRAIL` *Settings*

Setting	Meaning
DB	Enables auditing and sets the `SYS.AUD$` table as the audit repository.
DB_EXTENDED	Enables auditing and sets the `SYS.AUD$` table as the audit repository and includes the `SQLTEXT` and `SQLBIND` columns. This is useful for viewing the actual SQL statement that was issued. Be careful when using this option as it will consume much more space. In prior releases of Oracle, the parameter was specified as `'DB, EXTENDED'`.
OS	Enables auditing and specifies that an operating system file will store auditing information.
XML	Enables auditing and writes audit records in XML format to an OS file.
NONE	Disables database auditing.

You must stop and start your database for the `AUDIT_TRAIL` parameter to take effect:

```
SQL> shutdown immediate;
SQL> startup;
SQL> show parameter audit_trail;
NAME                                 TYPE        VALUE
------------------------------------ ----------- ------------------------------
audit_trail                          string      DB
```

After you've set the `AUDIT_TRAIL` parameter, no actual auditing events are enabled. You have to use the `AUDIT` statement to control auditing for specific database events. Examples of enabling auditing are shown in the next few sections.

▓ Tip Set the database initialization parameter `AUDIT_SYS_OPERATIONS` to `TRUE`. This ensures that all `SYS` activities are logged to files in the directory specified by `AUDIT_FILE_DEST` (regardless of the setting of `AUDIT_TRAIL`). This provides you with a simple and effective method for auditing the `SYS` user.

Auditing DML Usage

Sometimes it's handy when troubleshooting disk space or performance issues to know which tables in the database are actually being used by the application. If you've inherited a database that contains hundreds of tables, it may not be obvious which objects are being accessed. The idea is that if you can identify tables that are not being used, then you can rename and eventually drop them so that you can free up space and have less objects cluttering up your database.

Auditing allows you to capture the types of SQL statements being used to access a table. For example, the following statement enables auditing on all DML access to the EMP table owned by INV_MGMT:

```
SQL> audit select, insert, update, delete on inv_mgmt.emp;
```

From this point on, any DML access to the INV_MGMT.EMP table will be recorded in the SYS.AUD$ table. You can use a query such as this to report on DML access to a table:

```
select
  username
 ,obj_name
 ,timestamp
 ,substr(ses_actions,4,1)  del
 ,substr(ses_actions,7,1)  ins
 ,substr(ses_actions,10,1) sel
 ,substr(ses_actions,11,1) upd
from dba_audit_object;
```

In the prior SQL statement, notice the use of the SUBSTR function to reference the SES_ACTIONS column of the DBA_AUDIT_OBJECT view. That column contains a 16-character string in which each character means that a certain operation has occurred. The 16 characters represent the following operations in this order: ALTER, AUDIT, COMMENT, DELETE, GRANT, INDEX, INSERT, LOCK, RENAME, SELECT, UPDATE, REFERENCES, and EXECUTE. Positions 14, 15, and 16 are reserved by Oracle for future use. The character of S represents success, F represents failure, and B represents both success and failure.

Once you have identified tables that are not being used, you can simply rename the tables and see if this breaks the application or if any users complain. If there are no complaints, then after some time you can consider dropping the tables. Make sure you take a good backup of your database with both RMAN and Data Pump before you drop any tables you might have to later recover.

To turn off auditing on an object, use the NOAUDIT statement:

```
SQL> noaudit select, insert, update, delete on inv_mgmt.inv;
```

■ **Tip** If you simply need to know whether a table is being inserted, updated, or deleted from, you can use the USER_TAB_MODIFICATIONS view to report on that type of activity. This view has columns such as INSERTS, UPDATES, DELETES, and TRUNCATED that will provide information as to how data in the table is being modified.

Auditing Logon/Logoff Events

One basic security auditing technique is to record all user logon and logoff activity in the database. This allows the auditor to determine who was using the database and when. This information is critical when diagnosing security breaches and unauthorized actions.

Use the BY ACCESS clause of AUDIT to enable auditing of logon and logoff activities, like so:

```
SQL> audit create session by access;
```

Now every user that logs on and logs off the database will result in a record being inserted into the AUD$ table. You can report on logon and logoff activity with a query such as this:

```
select
 username
,action_name
,to_char(timestamp,'dd-mon-yyyy hh24:mi:ss') event_time
,to_char(logoff_time,'dd-mon-yyyy hh24:mi:ss') logoff_time
from dba_audit_trail;
```

Here is some sample output:

```
USERNAME   ACTION_NAME   EVENT_TIME            LOGOFF_TIME
---------- ------------- --------------------- -----------------------
LARRY      LOGON         08-oct-2010 16:18:45
LARRY      LOGOFF        08-oct-2010 16:18:49 08-oct-2010 16:18:49
DW_MAINT   LOGON         08-oct-2010 16:19:33
```

You can enable logon and logoff access for a specific user by specifying the username:

```
SQL> audit session by larry by access;
```

You can disable logon/logoff auditing as shown:

```
SQL> noaudit create session;
```

To disable logon/logoff for individual sessions, specify the username:

```
SQL> noaudit session by larry;
```

Another way to audit connections is via the CONNECT option of AUDIT, like so:

```
SQL> audit connect;
```

To disable this option, run this SQL:

```
SQL> noaudit connect;
```

The prior techniques provide a way to quickly enable the auditing of connections to the database. This can be useful when troubleshooting security violations or application issues.

NOTE: Some DBAs enable auditing of logon and logoff through an AFTER LOGON ON DATABASE trigger and BEFORE LOGOFF ON DATDABASE trigger that inserts into a custom table. I'm not a fan of this approach because it requires custom objects and custom code. Why write code to achieve something that Oracle already has a simple and effective solution? Furthermore, if there is an issue with the trigger or custom table, you may find that you can't logon to Oracle anymore. Not good.

Viewing Enabled Audit Actions

There are several data dictionary views that allow you to view what auditing actions have been enabled. Use the following query to enabled auditing at the privilege level:

```
select
 user_name
,privilege
,success
,failure
from dba_priv_audit_opts;
```

Here is some sample output:

```
USER_NAME       PRIVILEGE                        SUCCESS    FAILURE
--------------- -------------------------------- ---------- ----------
                CREATE ANY PROCEDURE             BY ACCESS  BY ACCESS
                CREATE PROCEDURE                 BY ACCESS  BY ACCESS
                DELETE ANY TABLE                 BY SESSION BY SESSION
```

Run the following query to view statement level auditing actions:

```
select
 user_name
,audit_option
,success
,failure
from dba_stmt_audit_opts;
```

The next query audits object level auditing actions. For this example, only a small subset of the columns available is selected (to keep the output on one page):

```
select
 owner
,object_name
,object_type
,alt
,del
,upd
from dba_obj_audit_opts;
```

Here is some sample output:

```
OWNER           OBJECT_NAME     OBJECT_TYPE     ALT        DEL        UPD
--------------- --------------- --------------- ---------- ---------- -------
SYS             AUD$            TABLE           -/-        S/S        -/-
```

In the prior output, a dash (-) means the audit option is not enabled, an S indicates that the audit option by session is enabled, and an A indicates that the audit action is enabled by access. For each option, there are two possible settings: WHENEVER SUCCESSFUL and WHENEVER NOT SUCCESSFUL. These are separated by a forward slash. So in the prior output, auditing by delete from the AUD$ table is enabled by session for both successful and unsuccessful statements.

Turning Auditing Off

To permanently disable auditing, set the AUDIT_TRAIL initialization parameter to none:

```
SQL> alter system set audit_trail='none' scope=spfile;
```

Now stop and restart your database to turn off Oracle's Standard Auditing feature.

> ■ **Note** Some database events are always audited (regardless of the setting of AUDIT_TRAIL) such as connections as SYSDBA or SYSOPER and database startup and shutdown events.

If you only want to disable features that you have previously enabled with AUDIT, then use the NOAUDIT statement to turn off specific auditing events. For example, the following statement turns off all statement auditing that was enabled via an AUDIT ALL statement:

```
SQL> noaudit all;
```

This next example turns off the auditing of privileges:

```
SQL> noaudit all privileges;
```

You can turn off specific auditing actions. For example, say you had previously enabled auditing on a table like this:

```
SQL> audit delete any table;
```

You can turn off the prior auditing like this:

```
SQL> noaudit delete any table;
```

You can also use SQL to generate SQL to turn off auditing. The following script generates a script that can be used to turn off all statement auditing:

```
set head off pages 0
spo turn_off_audit.sql
select 'noaudit ' || audit_option || ';'
from dba_stmt_audit_opts;
spo off;
```

Purging the Audit Table and Files

You should periodically purge the AUD$ table so that it doesn't consume inordinate amounts of space in your SYSTEM tablespace. (To move the AUD$ table out of the SYSTEM tablespace, see the next section.) The easiest way to purge audit records is to delete from or truncate the audit table. This example truncates the AUD$ table:

```
SQL> truncate table aud$;
```

If you need to save the AUD$ data, you can first export the table and then use the TRUNCATE command to remove records. If you want to preserve newer records in the AUD$ table, then use a DELETE statement. For example, this deletes records over 21 days old:

```
SQL> delete from aud$ where timestamp# > sysdate + 21;
```

If you need to remove audit records from the operating system, use the Linux/Unix find command to identify files over a certain age and then remove them. First, determine the directory location of the audit files:

```
SQL> select value from v$parameter where name='audit_file_dest';
VALUE
-------------------------------------------- --------------------------------------
/oracle/app/oracle/product/11.2.0/db_1/rdbms/audit
```

Now from the operating system, navigate to the audit file directory and identify and remove audit files over a certain age:

```
$ cd /oracle/app/oracle/product/11.2.0/db_1/rdbms/audit
```

Use the find and rm command to remove any files over a certain age. The following command removes any files with the extension of .aud from the current working directory that are over seven days old:

```
$ find . -maxdepth 1 -type f -mtime +7 -name "*.aud" | xargs rm
```

The prior technique permanently removes files from the operating system. Ensure that you're in the correct location and that the audit files are no longer needed.

Keep in mind that you can use the DBMS_AUDIT_MGMT package to purge audit trail records and audit trail files. I personally prefer to truncate and remove files manually as shown in this section because it's simple and efficient. If you want to use the DBMS_AUDIT_MGMT package to manage your audit space, see the *Oracle Database Security* guide (available on Oracle's OTN site) for more details.

Moving the Audit Table to a Non-System Tablespace

If you're going to do an extensive amount of auditing, I recommend moving the AUD$ table to a non-SYSETM tablespace. You may want to do this so that auditing actions doesn't impact the space used in the SYSTEM tablespace or affect the performance of the SYSTEM tablespace.

Use the DBMS_AUDIT_MGMT package to move the AUD$ table to a separate tablespace. This example moves the AUD$ table to a tablespace named AUD_TBSP:

```
BEGIN
  DBMS_AUDIT_MGMT.SET_AUDIT_TRAIL_LOCATION(
  AUDIT_TRAIL_TYPE => DBMS_AUDIT_MGMT.AUDIT_TRAIL_AUD_STD,
  AUDIT_TRAIL_LOCATION_VALUE => 'AUD_TBSP');
END;
/
```

In the prior PL/SQL code, the AUDIT_TRAIL_TYPE parameter can have the following values:

- DBMS_AUDIT_MGMT.AUDIT_TRAIL_AUD_STD moves just the standard audit trail AUD$ table.

- DBMS_AUDIT_MGMT.AUDIT_TRAIL_FGA_STD moves just the fine-grained audit trail FGA_LOG$ table.

- DBMS_AUDIT_MGMT.AUDIT_TRAIL_DB_STD moves both standard and fine-grained audit trail tables.

Be aware that the previous PL/SQL can take a long time if there are numerous records in the AUD$ table. You can verify that the table was moved correctly via this query:

```
SQL> select table_name, tablespace_name from dba_tables where table_name='AUD$';
```

■ Tip If you want to manually move the AUD$ table to a non-SYSTEM tablespace, refer to My Oracle Support note 72460.1 for instructions. Be aware that manually moving the AUD$ table is not supported by Oracle Support and may cause issues when upgrading your database. I only mention it because I know many DBAs who manually move the AUD$ table. If you're maintaining a database that you inherited from other DBAs, you need to be aware of this type of activity.

Auditing at a Granular Level

Fine-grained auditing (FGA auditing) is a separate feature from regular database auditing. Fine-grained auditing allows you to audit SQL at a more granular level than simple INSERT, UPDATE, DELETE, and SELECT operations. FGA auditing allows you to audit for SQL activities that occur at the column level. FGA auditing also allows you to perform a Boolean check on an operation, such as "if the value selected is in a range then audit the activity."

You manage fine-grained auditing through the use of FGA policies. The DBMS_FGA package allows you to add, disable, enable, and drop FGA policies. You need execute privilege on the DBMS_FGA package to administer audit policies.

■ Note The fine-grained auditing feature requires the Enterprise Edition of Oracle.

The follow are the steps to implement FGA:

1. Create a policy using the DBMS_FGA package. This example creates a policy for the INV table and specifies that any INSERT, UPDATE, DELETE, or SELECT statement against the SALARY column of the EMP table will be recorded in the audit trail:

```
begin
dbms_fga.add_policy (
object_schema => 'INV',
object_name => 'EMP',
audit_column=> 'SALARY',
policy_name => 'S1_AUDIT',
statement_types => 'INSERT, UPDATE, DELETE, SELECT',
audit_trail => DBMS_FGA.DB_EXTENDED
);
end;
/
```

2. Verify that the policy exists by querying the DBA_AUDIT_POLICIES view:

```
select object_schema
 ,object_name
 ,policy_name
 ,sel, ins, upd, del, policy_column
from dba_audit_policies;
```

Here's the output for this example:

```
OBJECT_SCHEMA  OBJECT_NAME    POLICY_NAME     SEL   INS   UPD   DEL   POLICY_COL
-------------- -------------- --------------- ----- ----- ----- ----- ----------
INV            EMP            S1_AUDIT        YES   YES   YES   YES   SALARY
```

   3. To view the recorded SQL statements in the FGA audit trail, select from the
DBA_FGA_AUDIT_TRAIL view:

```
select
  db_user
 ,to_char(timestamp,'dd-mon-yy hh24:mi:ss') ts
 ,sql_text
from dba_fga_audit_trail
order by timestamp;
```

■ **Note** The DBA_FGA_AUDIT_TRAIL view is based on the FGA_LOG$ table.

Here's some sample output:

```
DB_USER          TS                       SQL_TEXT
---------------- ------------------------ --------------------------
INV              21-jul-09 21:47:07       select * from emp
SYSTEM           21-jul-09 21:58:36       select salary from inv.emp
```

If you need to disable a policy, use the DISABLE_POLICY procedure:

```
SQL> exec dbms_fga.disable_policy('INV','EMP','S1_AUDIT');
```

To drop a policy, use the DROP_POLICY procedure:

```
SQL> exec dbms_fga.drop_policy('INV','EMP','S1_AUDIT');
```

As the SYS schema you can purge records from the fine-grained auditing audit table as follows:

```
SQL> truncate table fga_log$;
```

■ **Tip** For more details on fine-grained auditing, see Oracle's *Security Guide* available on Oracle's OTN website.

Summary

A senior database administrator must be adept at efficiently determining the source of database unavailability and performance problems. Identifying and resolving problems defines a professional level DBA. Anyone can Google a topic (there's nothing worse than being on a trouble call with a manager who is Googling and recommending random solutions). Determining the appropriate solution and confidently applying it in a production database environment is where you add tremendous value.

Diagnosing issues sometimes requires some system and network administrator skills. An effective DBA must also know how to leverage the Oracle data dictionary to identify problems. As part of your strategy, you should also proactively monitor for the common sources of database unavailability. Ideally, you'll be aware of the problem before anybody else and will proactively solve the issue.

No book can cover every troubleshooting activity. This chapter includes some of the most common techniques for identifying problems and dealing with them. Often, basic operating system utilities will help you identify the source of a hung database. In almost every scenario, the alert.log and corresponding trace files should be inspected. Finding the actual root cause of a problem is often the hardest task. Use a consistent and methodical approach and you'll be much more successful in diagnosing and resolving issues.

This is the end of the book. I have tried to convey techniques and methods that will help you survive even the most chaotic database environments. To summarize these thoughts, a DBA's manifesto of sorts:

- Automate and monitor through scripts and schedulers. Be the first to know when something is broken.

- Strive for repeatability and efficiency in processes and scripts. Be consistent.

- Keep it simple. If a module is over a page long, it's too long. Don't implement a script or feature that another DBA won't be able to understand or maintain. Sometimes the simple solution *is* the correct solution.

- Remain calm regardless of the disaster. Be respectful.

- Don't be afraid to seek or take advice. Welcome feedback and criticism. Listen to others. Entertain the thought that you might be wrong.

- Take advantage of graphical tools, but always know how to manually implement a feature.

- Expect failure, predict failure, prepare for failure. You don't know what will go wrong but you do know something will go wrong. Be happy that you prepared for failure. The best lessons are painful.

- Test and document your operating procedures. This will help you stay calm(er) and focused when in stressful database-down situations.

- Don't write code to implement a feature that the database vendor has already provided a solution for (replication, disaster recovery, backup and recovery, and so on).

- Become proficient with SQL, procedural SQL, and OS commands. These skills separate the weak from the strong. The best DBAs posses both SA and developer expertise.

- Continually investigate new features and technology. Learning is a never-ending process. Question everything, re-evaluate, and look for a better way. Verify your solutions with repeatable peer-reviewed tests. Document and freely share your knowledge.

- Do what it takes to get the job done. You compete with the world now. Work harder and smarter.

The job of a database administrator can be quite rewarding. It can also be very painful and stressful. Hopefully, the techniques documented in this book will get you from being mostly stressed to an occasionally happy state. Good luck.

Index

■ ■ ■

■ E

■ S

▨ V

■ W

■ X, Y

■ Z

You Need the Companion eBook

Your purchase of this book entitles you to buy the companion PDF-version eBook for only $10. Take the weightless companion with you anywhere.

We believe this Apress title will prove so indispensable that you'll want to carry it with you everywhere, which is why we are offering the companion eBook (in PDF format) for $10 to customers who purchase this book now. Convenient and fully searchable, the PDF version of any content-rich, page-heavy Apress book makes a valuable addition to your programming library. You can easily find and copy code—or perform examples by quickly toggling between instructions and the application. Even simultaneously tackling a donut, diet soda, and complex code becomes simplified with hands-free eBooks!

Once you purchase your book, getting the $10 companion eBook is simple:

❶ Visit **www.apress.com/promo/tendollars/**.

❷ Complete a basic registration form to receive a randomly generated question about this title.

❸ Answer the question correctly in 60 seconds, and you will receive a promotional code to redeem for the $10.00 eBook.

THE EXPERT'S VOICE™

233 Spring Street, New York, NY 10013

Offer valid through 6/11.

Made in the USA
Lexington, KY
25 July 2012